Martin R. Delany

Major Martin R. Delany, ca. 1865.
Courtesy of the Moorland-Spingarn Research Center,
Howard University.

Martin R. Delany

A DOCUMENTARY READER

Edited by Robert S. Levine

THE UNIVERSITY OF NORTH CAROLINA PRESS

CHAPEL HILL AND LONDON

© 2003 The University of North Carolina Press
All rights reserved
Manufactured in the United States of America
Designed by April Leidig-Higgins
Set in Minion by Copperline Book Services, Inc.

The paper in this book meets the guidelines for permanence
and durability of the Committee on Production Guidelines
for Book Longevity of the Council on Library Resources.

Library of Congress Cataloging-in-Publication Data
Delany, Martin Robison, 1812–1885.
Martin R. Delany: a documentary reader /
edited by Robert S. Levine.
p. cm. Includes bibliographical references (p.) and index.
ISBN 0-8078-2763-0 (cloth: alk. paper)
ISBN 0-8078-5431-x (pbk.: alk. paper)

1. Delany, Martin Robison, 1812–1885 — Archives. 2. African
Americans — Archives. 3. African American political
activists — Archives. 4. African American social reformers —
Archives. 5. African American abolitionists — Archives.
6. Black nationalism — History — 19th century — Sources.
7. African Americans — Politics and government — 19th
century — Sources. 8. African Americans — Civil rights —
History — 19th century — Sources. 9. United States —
Race relations — Sources. I. Levine, Robert S.
(Robert Steven), 1953– II. Title.
E185.97.D33 A3 2003   973.7′092 — dc21   2002012606

cloth   06 05 04 03 02   5 4 3 2 1
paper   06 05 04 03 02   5 4 3 2 1

Martin Robison Delany's 14 May 1852 letter to William Lloyd
Garrison is reprinted by permission of the Boston Public
Library/Rare Books Department, courtesy of the Trustees. His
17 June 1858 letter to Henry Ward Beecher is reprinted by per-
mission of the American Missionary Association Archives,
Amistad Research Center at Tulane University.

Contents

Part Six
The Republic of Liberia 459

Acknowledgments

I BEGAN THIS PROJECT in the early 1990s and am pleased at long last to be able to acknowledge the assistance and generosity of a number of individuals and institutions. I did the bulk of my research and document collecting at the Library of Congress, and I am grateful for the assistance of its expert staff. I am also grateful for the assistance of librarians at the Carnegie Library, Boston Public Library, New York Public Library, Amistad Research Center at Tulane University, Moorland-Spingarn Research Center at Howard University, and McKeldin Library at the University of Maryland. I am particularly indebted to the energetic and skillful librarians of McKeldin's Interlibrary Loan Office, who were able to secure rare microfilm from across the country and from Canada. For travel support to visit out-of-state archives, I am grateful to the University of Maryland's Committee on Africa and the Americas.

My thanks to Delany scholar Allan Austin for sharing a photocopy of Delany's *Homes for the Freedmen* and for helping with the transcriptions of Delany's 1858 letter to Henry Ward Beecher; to Vincent Carretta, indefatigable archivist, who brought back from one of his own British lecture tours a sheaf of newspaper accounts of Delany's British tour of 1860; and to John McKivigan and Rachel Drenovsky of the Frederick Douglass Papers at Indiana University for supplying me with a copy of the Douglass essay that inspired Delany's "What Does It Mean?" For their wise counsel and support, I am grateful as well to Jonathan Auerbach, Leonard Cassuto, Russ Castronovo, John Ernest, Neil Fraistat, Dana Nelson, Carla Peterson, and Mary Helen Washington.

I got to know Delany's writings particularly well because I photocopied and typed up materials on my own. A number of graduate students subsequently helped me with the laborious editorial work of reading the typed copies against the originals. For their attention to detail, good humor, and patience, my thanks to Carol Breakstone, Anne Carroll, Jeana DelRosso, Mike Duvall, Lisa Koch, and Marcus Singer. And my thanks to the Department of English at the University of Maryland for providing funding for these graduate assistants. I am also grateful to Manju Suri for her last-minute help with manuscript preparation.

Anyone working on Delany is indebted to the pioneering biographies by Victor Ullman and Dorothy Sterling. Ullman's extraordinarily detailed biography was particularly helpful to my research, though, like Sterling's, it is a biography without footnotes, alas.

This project had its official beginnings when Barbara Hanrahan, former humanities editor at the University of North Carolina Press, offered me an advance contract for a Delany reader on the basis of my transcriptions of Delany's writings in the *North Star*. Her belief that Delany merited a book of his own, and that I could provide a good one, helped to inspire my 1997 book on Douglass and Delany and also this documentary reader. I remain especially grateful for (and even puzzled by!) her faith in the abilities of a scholar who at the time had done very little work in African American studies, and I can only hope that this volume comes close to fulfilling her expectations. Sian Hunter, my wonderfully supportive, enthusiastic, and knowledgeable editor at the University of North Carolina Press, continues to be everything I could hope for in an editor, and in numerous ways has helped to make this into a better book. I have also been greatly assisted by the Press's two readers, John Ernest and Roy Finkenbine, whose suggestions had a significant impact on my final revisions. For her expert editorial help (and good spirits) at the final stages of production, I would also like to thank Mary Caviness, and for her skillful work on the index, my thanks to Cynthia Landeen.

Finally, I am happy to thank my wife, Ivy Goodman, and son, Aaron Goodman Levine, for their sustaining love and sundry contributions to the manuscript. For me, one of the highlights of working on this project occurred when Aaron at age ten proclaimed with utter incredulity (after overhearing a conversation with one of my colleagues): "I can't believe he's never heard of Martin Delany!"

Martin R. Delany

Introduction

MARTIN ROBISON DELANY (1812–85) lived an extraordinarily complex life as a social activist and reformer, black nationalist, abolitionist, physician, reporter and editor, explorer, jurist, realtor, politician, publisher, educator, army officer, ethnographer, novelist, and political and legal theorist. A sketch of his career can only hint at the range of his interests, activities, and accomplishments. Born free in Charles Town, Virginia (now West Virginia), the son of a free seamstress and a plantation slave, Delany in the early 1820s was taken by his mother to western Pennsylvania after Virginia authorities threatened to imprison her for teaching her children to read and write. In 1831 he moved to Pittsburgh, where he studied with Lewis Woodson and other black leaders, and began his lifelong commitment to projects of black elevation. He organized and attended black conventions during the 1830s and 1840s and during this same period apprenticed as a doctor and began his own medical practice. In 1843 he founded one of the earliest African American newspapers, the *Mystery*, which he edited until 1847. In late 1847 he left the *Mystery* and teamed up with Frederick Douglass to coedit the *North Star*, the most influential African American newspaper of the period. After an approximately eighteen-month stint with Douglass, Delany attended Harvard Medical School for several months but was dismissed because of his color. Outraged by Harvard's racism and the Compromise of 1850, in 1852 he published *The Condition, Elevation, Emigration and Destiny of the Colored People of the United States*, a book-length critique of the failure of the nation to extend the rights of citizenship to African Americans, and a book that concludes by arguing for black emigration to Central and South America or the Caribbean. Delany's emigrationism conflicted sharply with Douglass's integrationist vision of black elevation in the United States. In response to Douglass's national black convention of 1853, Delany in 1854 organized and chaired a national black emigrationist convention, where he delivered "The Political Destiny of the Colored Race on the American Continent," the most important statement on black emigration published before the Civil War.

In 1856 Delany moved to Canada, where he set up a medical practice, wrote regularly for Mary Ann Shadd Cary's *Provincial Freeman*, and met with the radical abolitionist John Brown to discuss the possibility of fomenting a slave in-

surrection in the United States. During the late 1850s his views on emigration
underwent a significant change. Instead of advocating black emigration to the
southern Americas, he now argued for African American emigration to Africa.
By 1859 he had obtained the funds that allowed him to tour the Niger Valley, and
in December of that year he signed a treaty with the Alake (king) of Abeokuta
that gave him the land necessary to establish an African American settlement in
West Africa. In search of financial support for the project, he toured Great Britain and garnered international attention for his participation at the 1860 International Statistical Congress in London. Around this same time he published a
serialized novel, *Blake* (1859, 1861–62) in an African American journal. He also
published a book-length account of his travels and negotiations in Africa, *Official Report of the Niger Valley Exploring Party* (1861). Delany's African project
collapsed in the early 1860s when the Alake renounced the treaty, and by 1863 he
was recruiting black troops for the Union army.

From 1863 to 1877, Delany recommitted himself to the integrationist U.S. nationalistic vision that had been central to his work with Douglass at the *North
Star*. He achieved national fame for meeting with Abraham Lincoln in 1865 and
shortly thereafter receiving a commission as the first black major in the Union
army. Following the war, Delany served for three years as an officer at the Freedmen's Bureau in South Carolina, and he remained in South Carolina through
the late 1870s as he attempted to make Reconstruction work in a stronghold of
the former Confederacy. He published two major pamphlets for newly enfranchised African Americans, *University Pamphlets* (1870) and *Homes for the Freedmen* (1871), and in 1874 ran for lieutenant governor of South Carolina on the Independent Republican slate, losing by only 14,000 votes. Disillusioned by the
Republicans' half-hearted commitment to Reconstruction, Delany in 1876 endorsed Wade Hampton, the Democratic candidate for governor of South Carolina, and was nearly killed by shots from a black militia at a Hampton rally.
Hampton won the election, but Reconstruction came to an end in 1877, and a disillusioned Delany turned his attention to helping southern blacks who wished
to emigrate to Liberia. In 1879, as he was seeking a federal appointment that
would allow him to finance his own emigration to Africa, he published *Principia
of Ethnology: The Origin of Races and Color* (1879), an ethnographic study that,
like his earlier *Origin and Objects of Ancient Freemasonry* (1853), expressed a Pan-
African pride in blacks' historical, cultural, and racial ties to Africa.

Surveying Delany's dynamic and creative career a year after his death in 1885,
the African Methodist Episcopal priest James T. Holly proclaimed that Delany
was "one of the great men of this age," a person whose life was "filled with noble
purposes, high resolves, and ceaseless activities for the welfare of the race with
which he was identified," and who "has given us the standard of measurement
of all the men of our race, past, present, and to come, in the work of negro ele-

vation in the United States of America." Holly was not alone in regarding Delany as one of the great African American leaders of the nineteenth century. But a number of Delany's contemporaries, even while celebrating his intelligence and greatness, had problems with what Holly in the same tribute refers to as Delany's "strongly-marked individuality."[1] Like many strong individuals, Delany refused to shy away from conflict. One of Delany's closest friends, the African Methodist Episcopal bishop Daniel Alexander Payne, also extolled Delany for his "fine talents and more than ordinary attainments" but then turned his attention to what he portrayed as the political problems that could sometimes arise from Delany's bold combativeness:

> His oratory was powerful, at times magnetic. If he had studied law, made it his profession, kept an even course, and settled down in South Carolina, he would have reached the Senate-chamber of the proud state. But he was too intensely African to be popular, and therefore multiplied enemies where he could have multiplied friends by the thousands. Had his love for humanity been as great as his love for his race, he might have rendered his personal influence co-extensive with that of . . . Frederick Douglass at the present time.[2]

Payne's image here of Delany as a vitriolic, race-conscious black man was shared by a number of other notable African American leaders of the time. In 1861 the novelist, historian, and black abolitionist William Wells Brown commented on Delany's propensity to elevate race over humanity after hearing him attempt to recruit black emigrants in Chatham, Canada West, for his African emigration project:

> Considered in respect to hatred to the Anglo-Saxon, a stentorian voice, a violence of gestures, and a display of physical energies when speaking, Dr. Delany may be regarded as the ablest man in Chatham, if not in America. Like the Quaker, who when going to fight pulled off his coat, and laying it down, said, "There lie thee, Quaker, till I whip this fellow," so the Doctor, when going to address an audience, lays aside every classic idea of elocution and rhetoric, and says, "Remain there till I frighten these people."[3]

According to Frances Rollin, who published the first biography of Delany in 1868, Frederick Douglass similarly remarked, "I thank God for making me a man simply; but Delany always thanks him for making him a *black man.*" Douglass may not have said precisely those words (and in fact Rollin presents that alleged remark as a compliment), but in 1862 he complained that Delany "has gone about the same length in favor of black, as the whites have in favor of the doctrine of white superiority."[4]

Brown's and Douglass's assessments of Delany have contributed to the creation of an unfair but still widely held image of Delany as a leader and writer who was both empowered and limited by his racial pride. But as readers of this volume will see, Delany in fact shared in the inclusive integrationism of Douglass and Brown, particularly during the 1840s and the period of Reconstruction, and he consistently worked with blacks and whites alike in the pursuit of social justice. For a person who could make enemies, Delany had quite a lot of friends and associates, and there are good reasons to be particularly suspicious of Brown's and Douglass's assessments. Not surprisingly, there were telling contexts for their condescending remarks on Delany. Douglass was in conflict with Delany from the late 1840s through the 1870s, and his acerbic comments on Delany's race consciousness came at a time when Douglass was still angry at Delany for having championed black emigrationism during the 1850s and for having attacked him as overly accommodating to whites. Brown's remarks on Delany also have to be considered in the context of their political disputes. Ironically, Brown presented his caricatured picture of Delany recruiting black Canadians for African emigration at a time when *he* was recruiting black Canadians from the same towns to emigrate to Haiti, using precisely the same racialized argument that Delany used when promoting black emigration to the southern Americas during the mid-1850s.

An even larger context for the racial thinking that Brown and Douglass attacked in Delany must be considered here and is on display throughout this volume. When Delany asserted his black pride, and even racial superiority, he did so against the grain of a culture that regarded blackness as a mark of evil and inferiority. Whereas Brown and Douglass declared that they would be happy to see race simply vanish from the United States through intermarriage, Delany from the 1830s until his death in 1885 fought white racists' denigration of blackness by embracing it. And he did so, again and again, rhetorically: by insisting that within white culture his blackness in effect made an argument about racial identity and character that mulatto leaders, such as Brown and Douglass, simply could not make. The African American educator Anna Julia Cooper underscored this point in her remarks on Delany in 1892: "The late Martin R. Delany, who was an unadulterated black man, used to say when honors of state fell upon him, that when he entered the council of kings the black race entered with him; meaning, I suppose, that there was no discounting his race identity and attributing his achievements to some admixture of Saxon blood."[5] In this respect, Delany's race consciousness and pride, his very sense of himself as a representative black man, can be understood as his defiant response to the white racist gaze upon his black body.

Delany's rhetorical insistence on his status as representative and exemplary black man had a crucial role in his revival in the 1960s and 1970s. As historian

Nell Irvin Painter has remarked, Delany remained "forgotten until his resurrection as the father of black nationalism and the epitome of proud blackness."[6] During the 1960s and 1970s, as a result of the Black Arts movement and the upsurge of interest in black studies, Delany was suddenly being celebrated for precisely what Payne, Brown, and Douglass had professed not to like about him: his prideful race consciousness and Pan-African identity. Indeed, by the 1970s Delany had been virtually reified as the Father of Black Nationalism, a radical separatist who ultimately sought to lead blacks back to their "native" Africa.[7] But this image of Delany, which is a partial one, has hurt his reputation in the larger culture, for (white) Americans tend to value what is proclaimed to be the more humane, inclusive integrationism of leaders on the order of Frederick Douglass and Martin Luther King. Even though Delany often aligned himself with those very values, he has been defined in relation to a relatively small part of his career, and thus has suffered the typical fate of the black separatist in traditional fields of study: he has been marginalized and for the most part ignored, invoked primarily as the dark binary opposite of Douglass.[8] Although Delany was a prolific writer who was unable to conceive of political action apart from writing and who wrote in a range of genres, most anthologies of American literature fail to reprint any of his multifarious and engaging writings, and, perhaps most astonishing of all, he is not included in the *Norton Anthology of African American Literature*, the most widely used anthology in African American literary and cultural studies.[9] This neglect would have left his contemporaries, African American leaders such as Holly and Payne, and even, I would surmise, Douglass and Brown, truly mystified.

Much of the problem of assessing and evaluating Delany lies in the tricky term "black nationalist." To be sure, it makes relatively good sense to identify Delany as a black nationalist. But does the label have a single, comprehensible meaning? A scholar of nineteenth-century African American literature recently termed Delany "the tinderbox black nationalist."[10] Is "tinderbox" somehow naturally linked to "black nationalist"? Does a pride in blackness necessitate a hatred for whiteness and a separatist disdain for the United States that can only express itself in an inflamed violence? Another historian of African American culture has recently remarked that it would be "an egregious error to leave the talk of racial solidarity to persons who espouse black nationalism as their political project and predicate such actions on a rejection of America,"[11] with the implication being that black nationalism enforces a bad kind of racial solidarity and is ultimately un-American. Patriotic black Americans, according to this formulation, would never reject "their" country, no matter how often that country rejected them. It is worth keeping in mind that Delany's "rejection" of the United States during the 1850s came at a time when the Supreme Court's 1857

Dred Scott decision affirmed that black Americans were forever denied the
rights of citizenship.

Delany's rejection of the United States, which was never a full rejection and
was always couched in terms of sorrow (and anger), occurred at particular historical moments when particular formations of American nationality (such as
the antebellum formation that regarded blacks as little more than property)
made rejection seem the most politically useful way to strengthen African American community and force dramatic changes in U.S. culture (Delany thought
that whites would come to realize their dependence on black labor once blacks
began to leave the country). Delany sometimes talked of emigration as a form
of providentialism, what God required of blacks to bring about the regeneration
of the race. But at other times he presented emigration as a short-term, small-
scale effort that could ultimately improve blacks' condition in the United States.
It is worth underscoring that Delany's emigration projects and commitments
tended not to last for very long. For Delany, emigrationism was a way to sustain
black community when that community was being degraded and splintered by
white racist culture. In many respects, his form of black nationalism resembled
the black nationalism of Brown, Douglass, Payne, and Holly. The historian Sterling Stuckey has argued that what links various expressions of black nationalism
in the United States is a consciousness among African Americans "of a shared
experience at the hands of white people" and of "the need for black people to
rely primarily on themselves in vital areas of life."[12] Rather than representing a
single position—a race consciousness that is always aggressively separatist—
black nationalism can embrace a range of sometimes competing and conflicting
options—uplift, separatism, emigrationism, patriotism, racial anger, integrationism, and so on—and has to be constructed and reconstructed in response
to different exigencies and contexts. Delany's special genius lay in his ceaseless
and imaginative work at such construction and reconstruction.

In an influential revisionary overview of Delany's career, Paul Gilroy observes,
"Delany is a figure of extraordinary complexity whose political trajectory through
abolitionisms and emigrationisms, from Republicans to Democrats, dissolves
any simple attempts to fix him as consistently either conservative or radical."[13]
In fact, Delany can be refreshingly inconsistent in his beliefs and actions, arguing at one moment for a black nationalism linked to U.S. nationalism, at other
moments for a Pan-Africanism that dissolves the importance of the bounded
nation. Like Douglass, Delany advocates a politics of racial integrationism when
that politics seems possible and useful; at other moments, when that politics
seems an impossibility (or destined to keep blacks in a subordinate position), he
advocates creative modes of resistance, including separatism. Delany can be
somber, dogged, angry; he can also be lighthearted, comical, convivial. What-

ever label one wants to put on him, it will not stick for very long, though "black nationalist" will do once it is agreed that Delany was capable of changing the meaning of that term with his every action.

Delany was committed to action. "We must make an issue, create an event, and establish for ourselves a position," Delany declared at the 1854 National Emigration Convention.[14] Throughout his career, Delany sought to "make an issue, create an event" and to do so in solidarity with black people of the United States. The extraordinary persistence and creativity of his efforts to bring about social change make him one of the most fascinating African American leaders and writers of the nineteenth century and arguably one of the three or four most influential. That he would make different issues and different events at different historical moments speaks to the improvisatory, pragmatic nature of his career; and it is precisely that sometimes conflict-ridden and "inconsistent" career that is on display in *Martin R. Delany: A Documentary Reader*.

This volume invites readers to discover, or rediscover, Delany. It prints nearly 100 Delany documents, approximately three-fourths of which have not been reprinted since their initial nineteenth-century publications. Most readers familiar with Delany know him through his emigrationist writings of the 1850s. Selections from those writings are included in this edition, but Delany's Central and South American emigrationism is presented not as the "essential" Delany but rather as one of six discrete career moments that are highlighted in this volume, somewhat arbitrary divisions made in an effort to provide readers with a relatively clear picture of Delany's moves through various abolitionisms, emigrationisms, and other antiracist and antislavery activities. As to be expected, the emigrationist Delany sometimes overlapped with the integrationist Delany, and vice versa. But the fact is that Delany did make impassioned commitments at particular historical moments, and those commitments changed as the historical circumstances changed. In order to help the reader take the full measure of those commitments and changes, and to assess their sometimes contingent, improvisatory nature, I have provided, in addition to the major documents one would expect to find in a Delany reader, relatively minor works (such as letters and newspaper accounts) that provide clues, or guideposts, to Delany's evolving thought. I have also provided full introductions for each section and contextual headnotes for most of the selections. This documentary reader thus aspires to be both a Delany reader and a documentary life.

As a documentary life, this edition includes a number of texts that were not actually written by Delany, such as newspaper accounts of his speeches. Some selections are included in clusters of documents that show Delany in debate with others, particularly Douglass, and some reveal as much about the cultural contexts in which Delany worked as about Delany himself (note, for example, the racist tone of such pieces as "The Moral and Social Aspect of Africa," "The Colored Citizens of Xenia," and "Politics on Edisto Island"). Like many black activists of the nineteenth century, Delany worked in various genres (letters, essays, speeches, fiction) and published in a wide range of forums (newspapers, books, pamphlets) for a wide range of audiences (northern, southern, international; black, white, interracial). Many of the selections in this documentary reader thus call attention to the mediating cultural filters through which much of the available information about Delany's career is known, making us acutely aware of the performative nature of his career, the ways in which he skillfully shaped discourses and personae for different rhetorical occasions. Given the importance of performance and cultural filters to the documents in this collection, it is a challenge simply to try to piece together a coherent portrait of a writer whose improvisatory and *strategic* politics and rhetoric can suggest both great shifts and overarching continuities. The six-part structure of this book, as noted above, should be taken as a provisional and somewhat arbitrary effort to develop one sort of coherent narrative of Delany's complex public career.

Part 1 profiles the beginnings of Delany's career, which to a significant extent was defined and shaped by his experiences in Pittsburgh during the 1830s and 1840s. We do not know much about Delany's life with his mother and siblings in Chambersburg once they arrived there in 1822 (his father would join them in 1823 after he purchased his freedom). What we do know is that Delany came to regard the small town of Chambersburg as limiting and that in 1831, at the age of nineteen, he left his family and journeyed to Pittsburgh, which he hoped would offer better educational and vocational opportunities. He found what he was looking for: a strong black community with great leaders and teachers, and even supportive whites who helped him to begin a medical education. As the eight documents in Part 1 show, Pittsburgh was crucial to the development of Delany's sense of black pride and community, and his sense of purpose. Inspired by Pittsburgh's black leaders, Delany sought to become a leader himself. Among his most notable achievements was the founding and editing of the African American newspaper the *Mystery* (six of the eight documents in Part 1 are related to Delany's newspaper work of 1843–47). At this early phase in his career, Delany focused most of his attention on city and state politics, and on the black educational and fraternal groups that were emerging in Pittsburgh. Of particular importance to Delany was his association with the St. Cyprian Freemasons, a black Freemasonry lodge that he helped to establish in 1847. As his 1847 *Eulogy on the Life and Character of the Rev. Fayette Davis* and his *Origin and Objects of Ancient Freemasonry* make clear, Masonry legitimated Delany's conviction of blacks' equality (and even superiority) to whites. In its celebration of hierarchy and transnational community, black Freemasonry also provided him with a near-mystical sense of his potential as a black leader beyond the confines of Pittsburgh.

Delany assumed a more national stage when he relinquished control of the *Mystery* in late 1847 and joined Frederick Douglass as coeditor of the *North Star*. Delany's eighteen months as coeditor of this new African American newspaper are the focus of Part 2. The eleven selections in this section actually consist of thirty-five documents, the bulk of which make up the major text of Part 2, "Western Tour for the *North Star*"—twenty-three letters that Delany wrote Douglass while working as subscription agent, lecturer, and coeditor. Delany's letters to Douglass from his "Western Tour" of the free black communities of the Midwest constitute one of the great (and hitherto little known) African American travel narratives of the nineteenth century. The letters also point to significant changes in Delany's politics of black elevation. While editing the *Mystery*, Delany focused on local black groups and, as was consistent with his Masonry, asserted his black pride in terms of African genealogies and histories. These genealogies and histories, as emblematized in the black Masonic lodge, had separatist implications, even if Delany at the time was not arguing specifically for black emigration. While working with Douglass, however, Delany was much more the Garrisonian and U.S. black nationalist, asserting the importance of moral suasion and cross-racial abolitionist work and regularly praising blacks who worked within capitalist culture to gain wealth and station in the United States.

Delany elaborated the importance of black elevation in some of his essays for the *North Star*, eight of which are published in this section. For example, he states in his "Domestic Economy" essay of 1849: "We must have farmers, mechanics, and shopkeepers generally among us. By these occupations we make money—these are the true sources of wealth. Give us wealth, and we can obtain all the rest." But even as Delany took positions similar to Douglass's, he remained less optimistic about the possibilities of a sudden millennial flowering of amicable relations between whites and blacks. Readers of "Western Tour" and his essays in the *North Star* will also note that Delany never fully adopted a moral-suasionist position. Unlike Douglass, he regularly advocated black violence as a legitimate response to white violence. Delany became increasingly frustrated with Douglass's equanimity (and claims to black leadership), and his hostility toward Douglass, implied in his act of leaving the coeditorship in June 1849, became apparent in their 1850 letter exchange on Samuel R. Ward, though a full break between these two great leaders did not occur until 1853, when they debated the merits of Harriet Beecher Stowe's *Uncle Tom's Cabin*.

Central to that debate on Stowe was Delany's shift in thinking about antislavery, for by the early 1850s he turned against the politics of moral suasion and black elevation in the United States that had been central to his coeditorship of the *North Star* and was advocating black emigration to Central and South America or the Caribbean. Part 3 presents some of Delany's best-known writings on the topic, including selections from his 1852 *Condition, Elevation, Emigration and Destiny of the Colored People of the United States* and the complete text of his 1854 "Political Destiny of the Colored Race on the American Continent." There are approximately fifteen additional documents in this section, which show how Delany's emigrationism emerged, in part, as a response to Frederick Douglass and his allies. The selections follow Delany from his initial hesitations about black emigration, to his epistolary debate with Douglass on *Uncle Tom's Cabin*, to his efforts to argue for and organize the Cleveland emigration convention of 1854. Delany saw Douglass's promotion of *Uncle Tom's Cabin* as primae facie evidence that blacks were failing to think and act for themselves. He was particularly disturbed that Douglass would celebrate a novel by a white woman that seemed to advocate the colonization of free blacks to Africa, even as he ignored the black-authored *Condition*, which argued that blacks should take the initiative in developing their own emigration movements. Delany organized and ran an 1854 emigration convention that was specifically directed against the more integrationist (and patient) mandate of Douglass's 1853 Colored National Convention. The selections in Part 3 also follow Delany through the aftermath of the Cleveland convention, as Delany moved to Chatham, Canada West, in 1856 and there continued his emigrationist efforts (and attacks on Douglass).

A central text of Part 3 is "Political Destiny of the Colored Race on the American Continent," Delany's bold call for African Americans to emigrate to Central and South America or the Caribbean. Somewhat in the mode of David Walker's *Appeal* (1829), he sets forth the history of antiblack racism in U.S. law and custom, arguing that unless the free blacks are part of "the *ruling element* of the body politic," they are lacking in the full participatory rights of citizenship. He maintains that African Americans would have the best chance of achieving those rights by emigrating to a place where people of color are in the majority both in terms of population and political power. Elaborating his own version of Manifest Destiny to argue for the importance of African Americans remaining in the Americas, as opposed, say, to emigrating to Africa, he proclaims that the "finger of God" beneficently directed the forcible taking of Africans to the Americas, where blacks have a providential destiny to emerge as the ruling element. This belief informs his novel *Blake*, selections of which are included in Part 3.

In 1857 or early 1858, however, Delany abruptly shifted in his emigrationist thinking, deciding that Africa, and not Central and South America, or the Caribbean, was the best site for African American emigration. This shift, which was inspired by a sense of his genealogical connection to Africa, inaugurated a new phase in his career. The twelve documents in Part 4 focus on Delany's efforts from 1858 to the early 1860s to develop what he termed a black nationality in Africa. For Delany, this nationality would emerge under the leadership of talented African Americans; his was an elitist project that meant to contest the racial paternalism that informed the agenda of the American Colonization Society (ACS), a white reformist organization that sought to ship the free blacks to Liberia. In his writings on Liberia in the *North Star* (see Part 2), Delany complained that the ACS kept a paternalistic control over the black emigrants and their putative leaders. Delany aspired to send to Africa African American leaders who would operate independently of the ACS to "regenerate" the black Africans that he regarded as lacking in the progressive knowledge afforded by Western civilization. "*Africa for the African race, and black men to rule them*," Delany proclaimed in *Official Report of the Niger Valley Exploring Party*. To that end, he hoped to establish a cotton-producing settlement overseen by African Americans on land purchased from the ruler of Abeokuta. Such a settlement, he believed, would help to make Africa into an economic power by inspiring cotton production throughout the continent. And if that were to happen, he maintained, the South's cotton monopoly would be broken and slavery would soon come to an end.

The documents in Part 4 chart Delany's abrupt move from contempt for Liberia to a willingness to work with Liberia, his efforts at fund-raising, and his apparent success in achieving his goals when he signed a treaty in late 1859 that granted him the land that he needed to begin his settlement. The documents also situate his African plans in the larger context of his varied activities and interests at the time. Prior to committing himself to his African project, he met with John Brown and gave serious consideration to working with him to bring about a slave revolution in the United States. Once he determined to travel to Africa, Delany communicated with Henry Ward Beecher and other white leaders in an effort to gain financial support for his project. Most spectacularly, he made a British lecturing and fund-raising tour during 1860 that brought him celebrity when he participated at the International Statistical Congress at London and acquitted himself as a black scientist. He also interacted with a number of black leaders, many of whom resisted the idea that Africa was the best locale for black emigration. Taking a position similar to Delany's in "Political Destiny" on the importance of blacks remaining in the Americas, James T. Holly and William Wells Brown claimed that Haiti made better sense for African American emigration. Delany contested those leaders, in letters included in this section, but following the collapse of his treaty with the Alake in 1861 and the outbreak of the Civil War, Delany, like most African Americans of the time, embraced the Civil War as a war of emancipation and abandoned his emigrationism.

Part 5 presents twenty documents from the 1863 to 1877 period that display

Delany's efforts on behalf of the Union army and the nation's subsequent project of Reconstruction. Delany held off committing to the war until early 1863, when he became convinced that a Union victory would lead to fundamental constitutional changes that would guarantee blacks citizenship and equal rights—the changes brought about by the adoption of the Thirteenth, Fourteenth, and Fifteenth Amendments. Several of the documents in this section show Delany making the case for black rights and equality (see, for example, his letter to President Andrew Johnson of 25 July 1866). But he did most of his Reconstruction work on the local level. An official at South Carolina's Freedmen's Bureau and active from the late 1860s through the late 1870s in South Carolina state politics, Delany attempted to blend his vociferous calls for black pride and self-determination with pragmatic efforts to improve relations between blacks and whites of South Carolina. At times he could sound more cautious, more accommodationist, than his rival Frederick Douglass, whom he chastised, in a letter of 22 February 1866, for asking too much for the freedmen, too quickly, and too aggressively. He also chastised those blacks who called on the Republican Party to nominate a black vice presidential candidate in 1867. He believed that without the cooperation and encouragement of southern whites, the freed black people of the South would find it impossible to rise in the culture. Thus, shortly after the war's end, he proposed an alliance among white southern landholders, white northern capitalists, and black southern laborers. As he expounded in "Triple Alliance" (1865): "Capital, land, and labor require a copartnership. The capital can be obtained in the North; the land is in the South, owned by the old planters; and the blacks have the labor. Let, then, the North supply the capital (which no doubt it will do on demand, when known to be desired on this basis), the South the land (which is ready and waiting), and the blacks will readily bring the labor."

Delany's notion of a "triple alliance," which necessitated that blacks work with, and not alienate, whites, undergirded his politics of Reconstruction. Thus in 1875 he attempted to explain to northern whites why blacks needed to work with the former slaveowners (see "The South and Its Foes") and in 1876 he supported a former slaveholder for the governorship of South Carolina. But even as Delany was willing to make concessions to northern and southern whites, he regularly asserted an uncompromising pride in blackness, and he made rather aggressive demands on the culture, particularly when speaking to black audiences. In an 1865 speech at Charleston's Zion Church, he invoked the black conspirator Denmark Vesey as a model for black South Carolinians,[15] and in a letter debate with Frederick Douglass in 1871, he demanded full representation for African Americans in the Republican Party. The main issue for Delany during this period was black citizenship, which he fought to make into something more than nominal rights. Echoing language he had used in *Condition* and "Political Destiny," he proclaimed in *University Pamphlets*: "It must be understood that no people can be free who do not themselves constitute an essential part of the *ruling element* of the country in which they live."

With the failure of Reconstruction, marked by the withdrawal of federal troops from the southern states in 1877, Delany once again concluded that the white majority was never going to allow blacks to become an essential part of the ruling element. In a career characterized by an improvisatory politics of black nationalism and uplift, Delany in the late 1870s reconsidered the possibility of African emigration, but with a difference. Whereas his Niger project of 1858–62, the focus of Part 4, was first and foremost an African American–led venture that Delany hoped would regenerate the continent, Delany's interest in Africa circa 1877–80 far more modestly worked with existing structures in an effort to bring some African Americans to Liberia during a time of black "exodus" from the South. The final section of the reader, Part 6, brings together four late Delany documents on Africa and race. Despite his former hostility to Liberia and the American Colonization Society, beginning in 1877 he chose to link himself with the Liberian Exodus Joint Stock Steam Ship Company, which, with the help of Liberian government officials and the American Colonization Society, sought to take African Americans emigrants from southern cities to Liberia. Delany's work with the Liberian Exodus Company had a good deal to do with his changing views on race, for he came to see the failure of Reconstruction as a divine sign that blacks and whites were perhaps not intended to live together. In his last major publication, *Principia of Ethnology*, Delany elaborated theories of racial difference, based on his reading of ethnographic "science" and the Bible, in which the separation of the races fulfilled the will of God. And yet even as he argued in *Principia* that racial separatism upheld God's "designs and purposes," he initiated a friendly correspondence with William Coppinger, the white secretary of the American Colonization Society. He shared with Coppinger his frustrations and his African aspirations and in the concluding document in this volume, requested his help in obtaining a civil service job that would help to finance his own emigration to Africa. Delany's goal of seeking a civil service job in Washington, D.C., however, also suggests his continued desire to remain part of a nation that would see fit to honor him.

To a certain extent the six sections in this volume work as discrete units. But there are, of course, a number of overarching interests, themes, and concerns in Delany's politics and writings that brought coherence to his career. Though he could be inconsistent, or subject to dramatic shifts, he was always focused on strategies for achieving social justice for African Americans. And he regularly meditated on such large issues as the role of religion in the lives of blacks and whites, the value of work, the meaning of citizenship, and the nature of a good education. It would be useful to conclude this introduction with brief discussions of three particularly important (and volatile) issues in Delany's writings from 1840 to 1880: race, nation, and leadership.

In *Principia*, Delany theorizes that there are three principle races in the world (white, yellow, and black), that God intended the races to remain apart, and that blacks are the superior race, having "a prophetic destiny . . . in a higher scale of morals and religion than has yet been attained." For many, *Principia* is the essential Delany text on race and a text that shows the limitations of his racialist thinking, placing him in a camp, as Frederick Douglass suggests, similar to that of the white supremacist. But as readers of this volume will see, there is no essential statement on race by Delany, or at least no text that need be given absolute precedence over any other. True, in 1879 he argues for racial separatism, but in his 1875 "South and Its Foes," he states that the "two races must dwell together," and in his 1876 endorsement of the Democrat Wade Hampton, he states that his great hope is "to bring about *a union of the two races, white and black,* (by black I mean all colored people,) *in one common interest in the State.*" What had Delany discovered between the mid-1870s and 1879 that had suddenly convinced him that God intended for the races to be apart? Perhaps nothing more than the end of Reconstruction in 1877, which Delany regarded in 1879 as a sign that God may have *intended* the end of Reconstruction for the reasons elaborated in *Principia*. Delany's statement of 1879 is his "final" statement only because he became too ill, and died, before he could write about race in yet another context.

Indeed, Delany wrote about race throughout his career, beginning in the early 1840s, when we have his first extant publications, to the moment in 1879 when he published *Principia*. In his various, extensive writings one discerns a wavering, or shifting, between calls for interracial harmony, on the one hand, and racial separatism, on the other; a prideful sense of black superiority, on the one hand, and a racial egalitarianism, on the other. In his 1845 "Prospectus" to the *Mystery*, written two years after he had married the daughter of a white woman and a black man, he states that he advocates "no distinctive principles of race"; and in his columns for the *Mystery*, and Masonic writings, he principally emphasizes ideals of racial egalitarianism. This is true even for *Origin and Objects of Ancient Freemasonry*, which chides white Masons for refusing to deal with black Masons on equal terms. In his "Western Tour for the *North Star*," he extols interracial harmony, celebrating how in one Ohio town "[i]t is no unfrequent occurrence for the colored residents to receive the civilities of their white neighbors to attend parties and weddings, and *vice versa.*" Even when he adopts his emigrationist politics of the 1850s and early 1860s, he talks of how the elevation of the "pure" black can help to establish "beyond contradiction, the general equality of men" (*Condition*). That said, he makes claims during this period about black superiority, and his emigrationism conveys his belief at that time in the value of black separatism (especially given the evils of white racist practices). He states, for example, in his 1854 "Political Destiny": "We have then inherent traits, attributes—so to speak—and native characteristics, peculiar to our race—whether pure or mixed blood—and all that is required of us is to cultivate these and develop them in their purity, to make them desirable and emulated by the rest of the world." Only ten years later, however, Delany is once again proclaiming that blacks and whites should live together in a climate of egalitarianism.

And yet amidst the wavering there is a consistency in his thinking: a conviction that in white racist culture, blackness will always be demeaned or belittled by whites and that it is therefore incumbent upon African Americans, for political and psychological reasons, to make claims for the equality of blackness by asserting nothing less than that equality, and sometimes more. As mentioned above, Delany believed that the "pure" black could make the best argument about the equality (or superiority) of blackness, simply because white racists could not say about that person, as they could, for example, about Douglass or William Wells Brown, that the achievements could be "explained" by the "white" blood in that person's body. Again and again Delany advances a rhetoric of superiority to increase the possibility of achieving equality. Delany is very clear about the uses of such rhetoric in his 1865 speech in Xenia, Ohio, which he delivered to the black citizenry shortly after becoming the first black major of the Union army. He tells his auditors that they "must declare themselves to be the equals of white men, if not their superiors. In no other way could they attain to their proper position in the body politic." Even in the race-conscious "Political Destiny," Delany implies a belief that racial identity is more a matter of politics than biology, for when he declares that in a world consisting of whites and peoples of color, "every individual will be called upon for his identity with one or the other," he is basically saying that race is more a matter of political choice than of essence, a willingness to side with the oppressed rather than the oppressor.[16]

Readers of this volume will no doubt come to various conclusions about Delany's views on race and interracial relations. It would be a mistake, however, to make quick judgments about his beliefs based on one or two texts. Although Delany can seem conflicted (and sometimes even confused) about his views, it should be emphasized that he is never conflicted or apologetic about his unabashed embrace of his blackness.

Delany's views on nation are also subject to shifts and changes. Some of his writings challenge the value of the nation-state and make the case for an African diasporan politics. And yet Delany, like Douglass, was attracted to the United States and its ideologies of equality and freedom. For example, when he secretly met with John Brown and Canadian blacks in 1858 to plot a slave insurrection in the United States, he thought about that insurrection in terms of a U.S. nationalism. According to the transcript of that meeting, Delany was the main proponent of Article 46, which was adopted by the group: "The foregoing articles shall not be construed so as in any way to encourage the overthrow of any State Government or of the General Government of the United States, and look to no dissolution of the Union, but simply to amend and repeal. And our Flag shall be the same that our Fathers fought under in the Revolution."[17] Like Douglass in his great speech "What to the Slave is the Fourth of July?" (1852), Delany conceived of even his most radical politics as an effort to complete what he regarded as the unfinished American Revolution. Delany's commitment to the egalitarian ideology of the American Revolution, and to the United States itself, informed his work during the Civil War and Reconstruction, when it would be hard to find a more determined U.S. nationalist. But there are traces of this nationalism even in his emigrationist writings, such as *Condition*, when he proclaims in the midst of his call for black emigration: "We love our country, dearly love her, but she don't love us—she despises us, and bids us begone, driving us from her embraces."

When he began to champion black emigrationism in the early 1850s, Delany claimed to have jettisoned his commitments to the U.S. nation. But he stopped short of adopting what could be termed a politics of postnationalism. In his great (and neglected) essay "True Patriotism" (1848), Delany suggests the possibility of adopting such a politics when he declares, "Patriotism consists not in a mere professed love of country . . . but a pure and unsophisticated interest felt and manifested for man." During the 1850s and early 1860s, however, he thought in terms of an alternative nationhood, calling for the development of a black nationality in a large geographic area that could support a rapidly increasing population and provide the necessary resources for economic growth. Crucial to his vision of an emergent black nationality, whether in Central and South America or in Africa, was his hope that educated and talented African American leaders would bring it into being. In this light it could be argued that Delany never really disentangled himself from U.S. nationalism, for there was something imperialistic about his ventures, at least in the way he articulated them (his Central and South America projects were never put into practice). In *Condition* he states that Central and South America could be regarded as a single nation of peoples of color, who "are precisely the same people as ourselves," and in "Political Destiny" he similarly states that the different countries of Central and South America, and the Caribbean, "are in fact but one country—relatively considered—a part of this, the Western Continent." Delany can seem deliberately unconcerned about the fact that different countries have different histories and cultural practices that may make them resistant to the development of a single black nationality overseen by African Americans. He had similar hopes and blind spots about the different countries of Africa coming together as a unified black nationality. As with his Central and South American projects, he believed that a regenerated black nationality in Africa was most likely to occur if talented African Americans were in charge. He states his goals in *Official Report of the Niger Valley Exploring Party*: "I have but one object in view—the Moral, Social, and Political Elevation of Ourselves, and the Regeneration of Africa."[18] Ironically, what makes African American leaders ("ourselves") so suitable as leaders was precisely their Americanness—their connection to a nation that Delany conceives of (ideally) as progressive, Christian, civilized, egalitarian. When in 1863 he thought those ideals had a chance of being realized in the United States, he relinquished emigrationism, at least for a while.

Delany may have shifted in his views on race and nation, but he remained fairly consistent in arguing for the importance of black male leadership to black elevation, and thus in many respects anticipated W. E. B. Du Bois's notion of the "Talented Tenth."[19] In his writings on the topic, Delany sometimes emphasizes his own special qualities of leadership and at other times presents himself in relation to his generational cohort of leaders. In his 1848 "Western Tour for the *North Star*" he expresses his delight in joining hands with Henry Highland Garnet, Charles L. Remond, and Frederick Douglass as leaders engaged in a group effort to bring about social reform. Twenty years later, in a letter to the young black leader R. L. Perry, he similarly refers to himself in relation to the cohort of "Pennington, Garnet, Purvis, Vashon, and others."[20] And yet there are numerous moments in his career, and in his writings, when Delany can seem a cohort of one, energized by a conception of himself as the heroic black leader who alone can regenerate the race. His romantic conception (or fantasy) of heroic black leadership is expressed most powerfully in his novel, *Blake*, which focuses on the efforts of a single black leader to bring about a hemispheric slave revolution in the Americas. Although Blake does work with others, including the Cuban poet Placido, the novel suggests that nothing much can happen without the efforts of Blake. If there is a clue, or key, to Delany's conception of black leadership, it may well be contained in that self-mythologizing novel, particularly in the chapters excerpted in this volume in which Blake attempts to teach the plantation slaves a new way of thinking about slavery and religion.

In *Condition* Delany writes about blacks' religiosity: "[T]hey carry it too far. Their hope is largely developed, and consequently, they usually stand still— hope in God, and really expect Him to do that for them, which it is necessary they should themselves."[21] One of the slaves in an early chapter of *Blake* exemplifies this tendency when he urges Blake to renounce his rebelliousness and "stan still an' see de salbation."[22] Ironically, the phrase "stand still," regularly adduced by proslavery preachers to encourage slave obedience, has its sources in the emancipatory moment in Exodus when Moses convinces the fleeing Israelites at the Red Sea not to return to slavery but rather "to stand still, and see the salvation of the Lord" (Exodus 14:13). When Blake responds to the Uncle Tom–like slave that he will "'stand still' no longer,"[23] he appears suddenly to envision how those scriptural words speak to the possibility of black insurrectionary action under his Moses-like leadership, and how the very meaning of those words has hitherto been perverted by the white enslavers to serve their instrumentalist ends: "They use the Scriptures to make you submit, by preaching to you the texts of 'obedience to your masters' and 'standing still to see the salvation,' and we must now begin to understand the Bible so as to make it of interest to us."

Recuperating the revolutionary implications of the slaveholders' "Stand still and see the salvation" to serve his own instrumentalist ends, Blake organizes a slave conspiracy by word of mouth, with the intelligent slaves of the various southern slave plantations entrusted to spread the word. In effect, he takes it upon himself to create a sort of black Masonic network in the slave South with himself as grand master. Delany's *Origin and Objects of Ancient Freemasonry* is relevant here, for in that text Delany describes Moses as an African and a fugitive slave who recognized that wisdom must be "handed down only through the priesthood to the recipients of their favors." As Delany goes on to explain, it is the leader's job to inculcate among the enslaved "a manly determination to be free." It would not be much of an exaggeration to suggest that what guides Delany's sense of himself as a leader in nineteenth-century culture (and informs his conception of Blake) is a conviction that he is a Moses-like leader on a mission to free "his" people. This may seem megalomaniacal, or delusional, or simply typical (Douglass had similar fantasies of Mosaic leadership). Whatever it was, it worked: Delany's conception of himself as a nineteenth-century black Moses compelled him onward. As a leader, he talked back to white culture, in much the same way that Blake appropriated and parodied the slave preachers' "Stand still and see the salvation."

A few words on Delany's gendered language of leadership.[24] It is tempting to want to chide Delany for his patriarchal politics, for the way he seems to have exploited his wife (who took on the child-rearing and domestic responsibilities while Delany remained on the road or in South Carolina) and emphasized connections between manhood and freedom ("manly determination to be free"). Unsurprisingly, Delany operated within the conventional gender discourses of the time in which fully enfranchised citizenship was defined in relation to manhood. What is surprising, and worthy of emphasis, is the extent to which he challenged patriarchal ideology.[25] He regularly wrote of the importance of education to women, urging women to take their places as political and economic leaders. His early essay "Young Women" (1844) cautioned black women against aspiring simply to be the servants of whites, and in *Condition* he offers a mandate: "Let our young women have an education; let their minds be well informed; well stored with useful information and practical proficiency, rather than the light superficial acquirements, popularly and fashionably called accomplishments." The result of such an education, he maintains, would be this: "In a word, instead of our young women, transcribing in their blank books, recipes for *Cooking*, we desire to see them making the transfer of *Invoices to Merchandise*." Though the formal title of his 1854 convention, the National Emigration of Colored Men, sounds gender exclusive, Delany encouraged his wife and other women to attend the convention, and as a result more than 25 percent of the voting delegates were women. After that convention he worked with Mary Ann Shadd Cary both in Canada and in the United States, and he portrayed women as having a central role in the hemispheric black revolution that he imagined in his novel *Blake*. When he traveled to Africa and saw women at council meetings offering advice to the chiefs, he "thought the hint might be taken in countries a long way from Africa" ("The Moral and Social Aspect of Africa"). Although he believed that women had a central role in regenerating the race as mothers, the mothers he imagined were to be educated, worldly, and political.

As this brief discussion of Delany and gender might suggest, Delany's writings are of interest not simply in and of themselves but also for the ways they engaged key debates and discourses of the nineteenth century, in this instance, the debate on women's rights and education. As readers of this volume will see, Delany engaged numerous other issues of the time, particularly those centering on race and nation. This documentary reader should therefore prove useful for readers interested in thinking about minority discourses in relation to the dominant discourses of nineteenth-century U.S. culture. Delany's writings participated in broad questionings by minority writers about the location of the nation, the function of borders and territory, the question of difference and otherness, the tension between integrative and resistant narratives, the problematics of racial and national identity, the matter of U.S. imperialism and empire, and numerous other issues. Like many minority writers of the period, Delany both contested and attempted to appropriate (or lay claim to) the dominant culture. His writings have an unusually broad sweep, for Delany responded to a number of the most significant national debates and conflicts of the nineteenth century. In this respect, one could regard this book less as a monument to a single individual than as a contribution to the ongoing project of accenting neglected minority voices and perspectives on nineteenth-century U.S. culture.

That said, there remains something quite magnificent about Delany's unceasing efforts, as a writer and activist, to challenge the culture, address the big issues, and demand equality for African Americans. Delany's friends and enemies alike agreed that he was an uncommonly intelligent and proud person who was devoted to improving the situation of black people in the United States. Though he was known for what we might today term a strong ego, he was actually rather selfless in his devotion to the cause of black elevation. He certainly did not reap any material rewards from his years of service and political action. As James T. Holly noted, "Dr. Delany could never descend to the artifices of the selfish trickster, of the mere money-getter or fortune hunter," and thus he "struggled heroically with honest poverty all his life long!"[26] In the final years of his life, when he attempted to find a civil service job that would recognize his work during the Civil War and Reconstruction, he experienced what he had predicted in 1848 would be the fate of the person espousing "True Patriotism": "contempt and neglect are the certain and most bitter fruits of his reward." But in that same essay of 1848, Delany also offered a glimmer of hope for that patriot:

[T]he American colored patriot lives but to be despised, feared and hated, accordingly as his talents may place him in the community—moving amidst the masses, he passes unobserved, and at last goes down to the grave in obscurity, without a tear to condole his loss, or a breast to have in sympathy. But the time shall yet come, when the name of the despised, neglected American patriot, in spite of American prejudice, shall rise superior to the spirit that would degrade it, and take its place on the records of merit and fame.

It is my hope that this documentary reader will speed along the process of resurrecting and honoring—and honoring by engaging and interrogating—Martin Robison Delany.

Notes

1. James Theodore Holly, "In Memoriam," *African Methodist Episcopal Church Review* 3 (1886): 117, 124.

2. Bishop Daniel Alexander Payne, *Recollections of Seventy Years* (1888; reprint, New York: Arno Press, 1968), p. 160.

3. William Wells Brown, "The Colored People of Canada" (1861), in *The Black Abolitionist Papers*, vol. 2, ed. C. Peter Ripley et al. (Chapel Hill: University of North Carolina Press, 1986), pp. 472–73.

4. Frank [Frances] A. Rollin, *Life and Public Services of Martin R. Delany* (Boston: Lee and Shepard, 1868), p. 19; Frederick Douglass, "Dr. M. R. Delany," *Douglass' Monthly*, August 1862, p. 595.

5. Anna Julia Cooper, "Womanhood a Vital Element in the Regeneration and Progress of a Race," in *A Voice from the South*, ed. Mary Helen Washington (1892; reprint, New York: Oxford University Press, 1988), p. 30.

6. Nell Irvin Painter, "Martin R. Delany: Elitism and Black Nationalism," in *Black Leaders of the Nineteenth Century*, ed. Leon Litwack and August Meier (Urbana: University of Illinois Press, 1988), p. 149.

7. See Victor Ullman, *Martin R. Delany: The Beginnings of Black Nationalism* (Boston: Beacon Press, 1971); Dorothy Sterling, *The Making of an Afro-American: Martin R. Delany, 1812–1885* (Garden City, New York: Doubleday, 1971); and especially Cyril E. Griffith, *The African Dream: Martin R. Delany and the Emergence of Pan-African Thought* (University Park: Pennsylvania State University Press, 1975).

8. See Robert S. Levine, *Martin Delany, Frederick Douglass, and the Politics of Representative Identity* (Chapel Hill: University of North Carolina Press, 1997), ch. 1.

9. At this writing, Delany is not represented in the Harper, Heath, Norton, Prentice-Hall, or Macmillan anthologies of American literature. Selections from his 1852 *Condition, Elevation, Emigration and Destiny of the Colored People of the United States* appear in Melvin Donalson, ed., *Cornerstones: An Anthology of African American Literature* (New York: St. Martin's Press, 1996), and Patricia Liggins Hill et al., eds., *Call and Response: The Riverside Anthology of African American Literary Tradition* (Boston: Houghton Mifflin Company, 1998).

10. Barbara McCaskill, introduction to *Running a Thousand Miles for Freedom*, by William Craft and Ellen Craft (Athens: University of Georgia Press, 1999), p. viii.

11. Eddie S. Glaude Jr., *Exodus!: Religion, Race, and Nation in Early Nineteenth-Century Black America* (Chicago: University of Chicago Press, 2000), p. 163.

12. Sterling Stuckey, *The Ideological Origins of Black Nationalism* (Boston: Beacon Press, 1972), pp. 6, 1.

13. Paul Gilroy, *The Black Atlantic: Modernity and Double Consciousness* (Cambridge: Harvard University Press, 1993), p. 20. See also Tunde Adeleke's provocative "Black Biography in the Service of a Revolution: Martin R. Delany in Afro-American Historiography," *Biography* 17 (1994): 248–67.

14. Martin R. Delany, "Political Destiny of the Colored Race on the American Continent," in this book.

15. See "Large Meeting at Zion Church," *Charleston Courier*, 13 May 1865, p. 2.

16. Delany anticipates the "political" embrace of blackness by the light-complected Emily Garie in Frank J. Webb's novel, *The Garies and Their Friends*, ed. Robert Reid-Pharr (1857; reprint, Baltimore: Johns Hopkins University Press, 1997). She declares to her brother, who had decided to "pass" as white: "You walk on the side of the oppressor—I, thank God, am with the oppressed" (p. 336).

17. See the "Journal of the Provisional Constitution Held on Saturday, May 8th, 1858," in "The John Brown Insurrection: The Brown Papers: Copied from the Originals at Charlestown by Order of the Executive Department of the State of Virginia" (November 16th, 1859), reprint, in *Calendar of Virginia State Papers*, 11 (1893): 288.

18. M. R. Delany, *Official Report of the Niger Valley Exploring Party* (New York: Thomas Hamilton, 1861), p. 11.

19. See W. E. B. Du Bois, "On the Training of Black Men," in *The Souls of Black Folk* (1903).

20. Martin R. Delany, "Letter to Reverend R. L. Perry," *Christian Recorder*, 12 October 1867, p. 1.

21. Martin R. Delany, *The Condition, Elevation, Emigration and Destiny of the Colored People of the United States* (Philadelphia: published by the author, 1852), pp. 37–38.

22. Martin R. Delany, *Blake; or, The Huts of America*, ed. Floyd J. Miller (Boston: Beacon Press, 1970), p. 21.

23. Ibid.

24. For a critique of the masculinist and elitist biases inherent in models of black male leadership, see Hazel V. Carby, *Race Men* (Cambridge: Harvard University Press, 1998). See also Robyn Wiegman, *American Anatomies: Theorizing Race and Gender* (Durham: Duke University Press, 1995), ch. 2; Carla L. Peterson, *"Doers of the Word": African-American Women Speakers and Writers in the North (1830–1880)* (New York: Oxford University Press, 1995); and Frances Smith Foster, *Written by Herself: Literary Production by African American Women, 1746–1892* (Bloomington: Indiana University Press, 1993).

25. See Tolagbe Ogunleye, "Dr. Martin Robison Delany, 19th-Century Africana Womanist: Reflections on His Avant-Garde Politics Concerning Gender, Colorism, and Nation Building," *Journal of Black Studies* 28 (1998): 628–49. Ogunleye argues that Delany "distanced himself from European patriarchal attitudes" (p. 630).

26. Holly, "In Memoriam," p. 124.

A Note on the Texts

THIS DOCUMENTARY READER reprints over ninety Delany and Delany-related documents from the nineteenth century. I am indebted to C. Peter Ripley et al., eds., *The Black Abolitionist Papers*, 5 vols. (Chapel Hill: University of North Carolina Press, 1985–92), for one of those texts; otherwise I have worked with the original printings or, in a few instances, Frances A. Rollin's reprintings in her *Life and Public Services of Martin R. Delany* (Boston: Lee and Shepard, 1868). Obvious printers' errors have been silently corrected; otherwise, this edition preserves nineteenth-century spellings and usages, such as Delany's predilection for the semicolon and dash. Delany wrote voluminously, and in order to provide a one-volume documentary reader that covers his entire career, I have had to choose selections from book-length texts and cut material from some of the other documents. The letters that constitute "Western Tour for the *North Star*," for example, are about twice the length of what appears in this volume. I cut some of the local detail and repetition and, as is my practice throughout the volume, indicate the location of cut material by the use of ellipses. For those interested in looking at full original texts, bibliographical citations have been provided for all selections. The majority of the texts in this edition, however, appear in their entirety. The footnotes throughout are mine unless otherwise indicated as Delany's.

Part One.
Pittsburgh, the *Mystery*, Freemasonry

ON 29 JULY 1831, Martin Delany, in search of education and economic opportunities, left his family in Chambersburg, Pennsylvania, and walked the winding
150-mile route through the Alleghenies to Pittsburgh. He arrived in a city that
included among its burgeoning population approximately 450 African Americans. Though small in number, Pittsburgh's African American community, led
by Lewis Woodson, John B. Vashon, and John C. Peck, had made significant progress in organizing mutual aid societies, churches, and schools and would continue those efforts, with Delany's help, during the 1830s and 1840s. Shortly after
arriving in Pittsburgh, Delany began studying with Lewis Woodson at the
Bethel African Methodist Episcopal Church and meeting with John Vashon and
others for literary and political discussions. From those discussions emerged the
African Education Society, which proclaimed in its constitution "that ignorance
is the sole cause of the present degradation and bondage of the people of color
in these United States; that the intellectual capacity of the black man is equal to
that of the white, and that he is equally susceptible of improvement."[1]

The commitment to black pride, racial egalitarianism, education, and uplift
central to the African Education Society informed Delany's other activities of
the period as well. In 1832 he and his roommate Molliston M. Clark founded the
Theban Literary Society (modeled on Benjamin Franklin's Junto), and two years
later Delany helped to found a temperance society. He also participated in the
formation of the Pittsburgh Anti-Slavery Society and a philanthropic society
that aided fugitive slaves. The *Colored American*, the most influential African
American newspaper of the time, printed a number of notices of Delany's activities in Pittsburgh. The issue of 2 September 1837 listed Delany as one of eleven
cofounders (and the librarian) of the Young Men's Literary and Moral Reform
Society of the City of Pittsburgh and Vicinity; the issue of 12 April 1838 listed
Delany as having attending a meeting of Pittsburgh's African Americans protesting Pennsylvania's recent disenfranchisement of its black citizens; and the
issue of 3 July 1841 listed Delany as among those calling for a black state convention in Pennsylvania (noting that Delany was the secretary of the committee

organizing the convention).[2] Meanwhile, even as he was involved with numerous literary and political initiatives in the black community, Delany managed to begin a medical education, apprenticing with local physicians Andrew M. McDowell, William Elder, and several others, all of whom would continue to support him through the 1840s. In 1836 Delany set up his own office as a cupper and leecher, and it was through this medical work that he was able to earn the money that would sustain his career as an abolitionist and civil rights leader. He was also sustained, from 1843 to his death in 1885, by the seamstress work of his wife, Catherine A. Richards, the daughter of a wealthy black butcher and a white Irish immigrant, whom he married in Pittsburgh in 1843.

As this overview of Delany's first decade or so in Pittsburgh should suggest, the move to Pittsburgh was absolutely central to Delany's career. The documents in this section reveal a young black man of Pittsburgh in the process of emerging as a national leader and reveal as well how that emergence was indebted to his work and associations in Pittsburgh. During the 1830s Delany was nurtured by black and white leaders alike; during the 1840s he himself emerged as a leader, founding and editing an African American newspaper, the *Mystery*. In addition to his significant editorial career, Delany had a major role in establishing and promoting Pittsburgh's first black Freemasonry organization, which he conceived of as an organization that further contributed to black pride, black (male) community, and racial justice. This section prints six documents related to Delany's work on the *Mystery* and two documents related to his connections with black Freemasonry.

Delany no doubt wrote a great deal during the 1830s, but his first extant publications come from the *Mystery*, the African American newspaper that he founded in 1843 and edited (and basically wrote) through 1847. The newspaper had its origins in the State Convention of the Colored Freemen of Pennsylvania, held in Pittsburgh, 23–25 August 1841, which Delany had helped to organize. At the convention, the delegates resoundingly approved Resolution 11: "That in the opinion of this Convention, a newspaper conducted by the colored people, and adapted to their wants, is much needed in this state; and that we request their general co-operation, especially in the east, in establishing such a paper."[3] Two years later, with Pennsylvania still lacking an African American newspaper, Delany decided himself to establish such a newspaper without the help of the "east" and began publishing the *Mystery* in September 1843. Hoping for a wide readership, he recruited subscription agents to circulate the paper throughout Pennsylvania, as well as in Ohio, Iowa, and New York, and he reported to his biographer Frances Rollin (in what was probably an overstatement) that the typical run was 1,000 copies.[4] Though he encountered economic problems along the way, which necessitated the formation of a publishing committee in 1844, Delany managed to keep the paper in print until late 1847. During this time he was sued for libel by Thomas "Fiddler" Johnson, an African American whom Delany had accused of collaborating with fugitive slave catchers (a white jury found Delany guilty in 1846, but Governor Francis R. Shunk remitted the fine and the *Mystery* publishing committee paid his court costs). He also inspired the white philanthropist Charles Avery of Allegheny, Pennsylvania, who donated funds to establish a school for black men and women, the Allegheny Institute and Mission Church.

Delany's *Mystery* was a four-page paper committed to abolition and the development of black pride. Only the issues of 16 April 1845 and 16 December 1845 remain extant, and even those issues are heavily damaged. Nevertheless, it is clear from the surviving issues that the *Mystery* printed antislavery news, letters and editorials, and various announcements of events and meetings, along with advertisements of Pittsburgh's black laborers and professionals, including Delany, who regularly ran an ad for his medical services on page one: "LEECHING, CUPPING AND BLEEDING." Indicative of Delany's activist perspective on abolition and black self-help, beginning in 1845 he used as the epigraph to the paper the same passage from Lord Byron's *Childe Harold's Pilgrimage* (1818) that had inspired Henry Highland Garnet's militant "Address to the Slaves of the United States" (1843): "HEREDITARY BONDSMEN! KNOW YE NOT WHO WOULD BE FREE, THEMSELVES MUST STRIKE THE FIRST BLOW!" He printed the epigraph in the upper left corner of page one, and he printed his statement of principles in the upper left corner of page two: "I have determined never to be governed by the frivolous rules of *formality* but by PRINCIPLE, suggested by *conscience*, and guided by the light of REASON. I love ADVICE, I'll seek COUNSEL, but detest *dictation*."[5] The "Prospectus of THE MYSTERY" appeared on page four, and it is included in this section, along with four of Delany's editorial columns. Only one of those columns is from a surviving copy of the *Mystery*; the other three come from the *Liberator* and *Palladium of Liberty*, which reprinted Delany's columns. The fact that there was some reprinting of Delany's columns suggests that the *Mystery* had an influence beyond Pittsburgh's African American community. But it would be a mistake to overemphasize the influence of this local journal,[6] and presumably it was precisely because Delany sought a more national and diverse audience that he chose to leave the *Mystery* in late 1847 to assume the coeditorship of the *North Star* with Frederick Douglass (see Part 2). Delany's rationale for the move, his "Farewell to Readers of the *Mystery*," is also included in this section.

The epigraph of the *Mystery* during its first two years of publication, before Delany adopted the quote from Byron, was "AND MOSES WAS LEARNED IN ALL THE WISDOM OF THE EGYPTIANS."[7] For Delany, Egypt was a crucial marker of the African origins of Western civilization and thus of blacks' potentially regenerative role in the culture in terms of the Ethiopianism of Psalms 68:31: "Ethiopia shall soon stretch out her hands unto God." Celebrating black Africa at a time when many white racial "scientists" were arguing for the non-African sources of Western civilization, and for the "whiteness" of Egypt itself, Delany sought to challenge the new notions of polygenesis (separate creations of the races) that, according to many whites, legitimated blacks' lower place in the social hierarchy. Crucial to his efforts to contest the racist ethnology and practices of the time was his advocacy of black Freemasonry in the tradition of Prince Hall, who had established the first black Masonic lodges in Boston, Philadelphia, and other northern cities in the late eighteenth century.

Like Prince Hall, Delany regarded Freemasonry as a progressive and properly elitist organization that had crucial origins in African knowledge, rituals, religions, and practices. In 1847 Delany helped to form a black Freemason lodge in Pittsburgh, the St. Cyprian Lodge, and over the next six years delivered at least two major addresses to the St. Cyprians, both of which were printed as pamphlets and are reprinted in this section. The first, a eulogy for a fellow Freemason, the Reverend Fayette Davis, celebrates the model life of a black religious leader; the second, *The Origin and Objects of Ancient Freemasonry*, explores the black origins of the craft. Delany was attracted to Masonry's secrecy, hierarchy, and ritual, and he was inspired by the ways in which black Masonry in particular offered its members a shared sense of sacred history and holy bond. Masonry made Delany feel that he was one of the elect at a time in which the dominant culture taught that he was one of the damned; its fraternalism and hierarchy nurtured Delany's conception of a black masculine ideal of leadership. Pittsburgh, the *Mystery*, and black Freemasonry launched Delany onto the national scene, providing him with a sense of mission and community that would empower his work over the coming decades.

Notes

1. Dorothy Sterling, *The Making of an Afro-American: Martin Robison Delany, 1812–1885* (Garden City, New York: Doubleday, 1971), pp. 41–42.

2. See "Communication for the Colored American," *Colored American*, 2 September 1837, p. 2; "Public Meetings in Pittsburgh," ibid., 12 April 1838, p. 2; "A Call for a State Convention in Pennsylvania," ibid., 3 July 1841, p. 2.

3. *Proceedings of the Black State Conventions, 1840–1865*, ed. Philip S. Foner and George E. Walker (Philadelphia: Temple University Press, 1979), p. 110.

4. Frank [Frances] A. Rollin, *Life and Public Services of Martin R. Delany* (Boston: Lee and Shepard, 1868), p. 48.

5. The quotations are from the issue of 16 December 1845, the extant issue in the best condition. My thanks to the Carnegie Library for providing me with access to the *Mys-*

tery. For a good discussion of Delany's newspaper, see Mike Sajna, "*The Mystery* of Martin Delany," *Carnegie Magazine,* July/August 1990, pp. 36–40.

6. In their respective biographies of Delany, both Victor Ullman and Dorothy Sterling assert that Delany's columns in the *Mystery* were widely reprinted in abolitionist journals and local newspapers. But the only evidence they offer for their claims are the two well-known editorials that were reprinted in the 20 October 1843 issue of the *Liberator.* After reading the over 100 issues of Pittsburgh newspapers circa 1843–47 in the Library of Congress's collection, and after examining the *Liberator* and other abolitionist newspapers of the same period, I discovered only two columns in the *Palladium of Liberty,* the most interesting of which is included in this section. (See also "Kidnapping in Virginia," *Palladium of Liberty,* 21 February 1844, p. 1, which is for the most part a redaction of a fugitive slave case as reported in a Winchester, Virginia, newspaper.) There were no doubt other reprintings of Delany's editorials that I missed, but I think it is a mistake to make excessive claims for the national (eastern) influence of Delany's paper. It does seem to have been read widely among Pittsburgh's black community and no doubt had readers in other cities in Pennsylvania, New York, and Ohio. But the *North Star* offered Delany a considerably larger, and more racially and geographically diverse, readership.

7. Victor Ullman, *Martin R. Delany: The Beginnings of Black Nationalism* (Boston: Beacon Press, 1971), p. 60.

Prospectus of the *Mystery*

DELANY MARRIED Catherine A. Richards on 15 March 1843 and around the same time begin editing and publishing the *Mystery*, an abolitionist newspaper committed to black elevation, even as he kept on with his medical practice and apprenticing. A prospectus for Delany's Pittsburgh-based newspaper no doubt appeared in the inaugural issue, which is no longer extant. The "Prospectus," printed below, appeared in the issue of 16 December 1846. Affirming the large goals of the newspaper in language that was probably drawn from the inaugural issue, the "Prospectus" also points to some of the problems Delany had been facing with submissions and distribution during his first three years as editor.

The paper shall be free, independent and untrammeled, and while it shall aim at the Moral Elevation of the *Africo-American* and African race, civilly, politically and religiously, yet, it shall support no distinctive principles of race—no sectional distinctions, otherwise than such as may be necessary, for the establishment of true and correct principles pertaining to the universal benefit of man, since whatever is essentially necessary for the promotion and elevation of one class of society to a respectable and honorable standing, is necessary for the promotion and elevation of all classes; therefore our interests are and should be, one and inseparable.

We shall also aim at the different branches of Literary Sciences, the Mechanical Arts, Agriculture and the elevation of Labor.

We shall ever combat error, and repel every species of usurpation and tyranny, and never be found compromising with oppression of any kind, however mild its character.

Communications conveying intelligence of events, incidents, and circumstances of facts, may be received and noticed, when coming from any reliable creditable source, provided the same be *post paid*. But as our object is the *mental*, by literary *acquirement*, as well as the moral improvement of a certain class of our readers; and in consideration of having given full two years' opportunity to all such, to test their ability, henceforth no *literary contribution* will be admitted into our columns excepting they are *really* the *production* of the person's head and hand who send them. This provision is made to put a stop to the continual custom of getting *others* to write poetry and other literary articles for them, and sending them on as their own—even those whom it is known *cannot* READ! As you have a mind and talents, we wish you to improve them, and thereby *do your own work.*

Literary contributions must be correctly written, with a strict regard to the grammatical construction; particular attention being paid to punctuation. In all cases the fitness of such articles for publication will be at the option of the editor; and positively, no articles will be admitted under the head of "Literary Contributions," except the merits of the article entitle it to a notice—this restriction, however, does not interfere with the "Youth's Department."

TERMS—*One dollar and Fifty cents,* invariably in advance, and no subscription received for a shorter period than six months. Agents receiving subscriptions without the money, *must* be responsible for the same, or no paper will be forwarded.

☞ The inconvenience of sending one dollar and a half by mail, is entirely avoided by the new Post Office regulations, which enable a subscriber or agent to hand any sum of money under ten dollars, to the Post Master of their place, taking a receipt for the same, which Post Master will immediately notify the Post Master in Pittsburgh (or wherever the paper is printed) who will pay the money over to us.

All active Agents who do any thing for us in the way of money and subscriptions *get their paper free*—those who do nothing will be held as subscribers.

(*Mystery,* 16 December 1846, p. 4)

Not Fair

ON THE EVIDENCE OF the 16 December 1846 issue of the *Mystery*, Delany's four-page newspaper had speeches and news events on page one, editorials and letters on pages two and three, and advertisements and announcements on page four. As is true for many antislavery newspapers of the period, the "personality" of the *Mystery* was most fully on display in its editorial columns, just about all of which were written by Delany. Four of the five columns from the *Mystery* that follow, beginning with "Not Fair," first appeared in the *Mystery* and were subsequently reprinted in contemporaneous antislavery newspapers. The fifth, "Self-Elevation Tract-Society," survives from the sole fully extant issue of 16 December 1846.

The question is often asked, why it is that the colored people claim an equality with the whites, and so few of them have manifested even a propensity for that equality; that we never have produced authors, writers, professors, nor geniuses of any kind, notwithstanding some of us have been free from the formation of this government, up till the present day.

To say nothing about the disadvantage that would naturally arise to the *few*, while the many continued in slavery and degradation; yet, when Mr. Jefferson, the 'apostle of democracy,' was asked by a British statesman, 'Why it was that America, with all her boasted greatness, had produced so few great men, and learned authors,' the American statesman quickly replied, that, when the United States had been an independent government as long as Greece was before she produced her Homer, Socrates, and Demosthenese, and Rome, before she produced her Virgil, Horace, and her Cicero; or when this country had been free as long as England was, before she produced her Pope and Dryden, then he would be ready to answer that question.[1]

According to the above sensible position of the American statesman, so char-

---

1. See Jefferson, *Notes on the State of Virginia* (1785), "Query VI." Actually, Jefferson was responding to the French historian and philosopher Abbé Raynal (1713–96).

acteristic of himself, *we* answer, that more is asked of us, than ever was asked of any other people, and if it is expected that with all the disadvantages with which we are surrounded, that we should still equal the other citizens, it is giving us more than we claim; it is a tacit acknowledgement, that we are naturally superior to the rest of mankind, and, therefore, are much more susceptible than they.

With this cursory view of the subject, then, all that we have in conclusion to say is, that if we produce any equals at all, while we are in the present state, to say the least of it, we have done as much as Greece, Rome, England or America.

(from the *Mystery*; reprinted in the *Liberator*, 20 October 1843, p. 1)

Liberty or Death

The following anecdote was related to us on last Monday, by a gentleman recently from Georgia, now in this city:

George, a slave, belonged to the family of _____ in the State of Georgia, near the Ochmulgee river whom he served faithfully. He was an excellent *mechanic* (*!*) and during the life of his owners or claimants, (for he never had an *owner,*) they would take no money for him, and, in consequence of his faithfulness to them, at their death, George was will[ed] a *freeman!*

Poor George then looked upon himself as one of the lords, even of the accursed soil of Georgia. But George was doomed to disappointment. The unjust heirs broke the will, seized his person, and thrust him into the dark caverns of slavery again! Bound for a new residence, they started down the Ochmulgee. George was on board the steamboat, bound for his destination, but the vicious robbers of his liberty knew not where. George looked sad, and talked but little.

The steamer glided along, with a crowd of guests, unconscious of their weary fellow-passenger. In the night, a splash was heard which awakened the attention of boatmen and passengers; all looked with anxiety, but seeing all appeared to be safe, it was a just conclusion, that this must have been the noise occasioned by the falling in of the bank of the river. Morning came, the *grindstone* of the boat was missed, information was given, and search being made, George was gone, they knew not where.

The river was ordered to be scoured by the eager master, thirsting after the blood of the *mechanic!* it was scoured, and George was found with the *grindstone tied to his neck!* reposing in the depth of the Ochmulgee, preferring as a *man, Death* before slavery! George has *tasted* liberty!!!

(from the *Mystery*; reprinted in the *Liberator*, 20 October 1843, p. 1)

Young Women

Several persons have spoken to us, and lastly, an esteemed friend who writes to us, says, "that a good many of our people think that you should not fault our women for living out at service, that we are a poor people, and they must do something for an honest living." This induces us to make the explanation, especially for the satisfaction of our industrious young females. Certain, we say, it is no disgrace, to live out, or to do any honest work for a living when necessity so compels us.

As the generality of our people are unacquainted with the logical meaning of the word necessity, we will explain it here, for their express satisfaction. Necessity simply means something that cannot be done without, this is the sole meaning of the word. When we say that we admit that our people [are] doing this of necessity, we simply mean that we admit of them doing it, when they can't do without it. A man eats, and also dies of necessity, that is he eats to keep him from dying, and dies because he can't help it; he would not go to the trouble of either eating or dying, provided, it was left to his own choice. This is necessity; a thing done without your choice, a thing done that you can't do without doing.

But to make this plain, suppose that you knew of a young lady and gentleman, the son and daughter of a family in which you live, with all the comforts of life around them, leave their parents' house and their acquaintances, and throw themselves about in people's houses among their domestics, though such hired girls were white, would you not at once revolt at the idea, though you were at service yourselves, and strongly reprove them for thus traducing themselves?

Certainly you would. There's not a colored girl, but would feel indignant at the idea, and wish that she had the opportunities of such a young lady, that she might appreciate them. This is all we ask of the people; when you can do better, it is your duty to do so, if you can not, it is no shame to do the best you can. Yours is necessity, the young white lady's is choice. She's to blame, you are not.

(from the *Mystery*, reprinted in *Palladium of Liberty*, 21 February 1844, p. 2)

Self-Elevation Tract Society

The necessity for the effective establishment of such an institution as the Self Elevation Tract Society,[1] is plain to every mind, and none perhaps should more closely observe these facts than the females.

The condition of our race, yes, our poor unfortunate race, we say poor unfortunate, because, unless we can be brought to see well and be made really sensible of our *true* condition, all that we may attempt towards the amelioration of our condition must fall as "pearl cast among swine."[2] The condition then of our poor unfortunate race is such, that it implants degradation at once in the minds and bosoms of our youth—detracts from the graces and virtues of our tender maidens, and lamentable to reflect upon it, blights the fairest prospects of womanhood, disheartening and carrying desolation with it, almost totally plucking out and destroying the last remnant of those ennobling qualities so essential to a wife and mother, the first and true guardians of the rising generation, those indispensable propensities and qualities, which distinguish woman and make her the evident superior of her race.

Situated as we are, as mere nonentities in the midst of others—the most deserving, respectable and praiseworthy among us, in the eye of the law and its consequent enactments, being placed far beneath the most vile vagabond while being denied privileges granted to the pauper and vagrant—those by the laws, declared to be nuisance—while privileges are being enjoyed by other men, privileges which from their nature necessarily elevate the female, the wife, mother, sister and daughter, and stimulate the tender youth; we colored male citizens, are made the degraded vassals of the most insufferable servility, more intolerable than death itself.

Spurned the right of election as representatives, and peerage as jurors, denied and robbed of the elective franchise and consequently the right of representa-

---

1. Founded in 1825 by Protestant evangelicals, the American Tract Society (ATS) printed and distributed hundreds of thousands of tracts on spiritual and social reform. Delany's plan for a black self-elevation tract society was modeled on the ATS.
2. Matthew 7:6.

tion;[3] (in many of the states,) deprived of the right of testimony even against a vagabond; though our hoary headed father or mother may be maltreated, abused or murdered, our wives or sisters ravished before our eyes! Prohibited the right of bearing arms as patriots and soldiers in defence of our Country, thereby precluding us from those *claims* upon our country in common with other inhabitants or citizens; denied the right of *citizenship* in toto, in order thereby to exclude us from the protection of the laws, which of course we are prevented from having any part in making, thereby, disdaining to make us the subjects of legislation except it be for the object of stamping us with still deeper degradation.

This scheme of oppression being complete, as a matter of course it follows that the forfeiture of every claim to civil and decent respect, is fully implied in the base surrender of our manhood, crouching in servility at the feet of insolence and usurpation.

We shall continue this subject in our next.

(*Mystery*, 16 December 1846, p. 2)

---

3. In 1838 the Pennsylvania state legislature, on the recommendation of the Pennsylvania Reform Convention of 1837–38, approved a new state constitution that disenfranchised African Americans.

Farewell to Readers of the *Mystery*

DELANY MET FREDERICK DOUGLASS in August 1847 and shortly thereafter decided to relinquish his editorship of the *Mystery* to become coeditor of the *North Star*, which began publication in December 1847. Delany's "Farewell" appeared in the *Mystery* and was reprinted in the 21 January 1848 issue of the *North Star*, along with a prefatory note from Douglass.

☞ The following parting words, of our faithful friend and brother DELANY, to the readers of the *Mystery*, will be read by the Patrons of the NORTH STAR, with emotions of pleasure. We hope, soon, to lay before our readers, editorial correspondence from our absent coadjutor.[1]

This number ends the Fourth Volume, and with it, our connexion as Editor of the *Mystery*. For upwards of four years the paper has been afloat upon the breeze, during which time, excepting three months, (when it was edited by the Committee) we have stood at the helm of our steady little barque, steering right onward for the continent of Liberty and Equality. If ever we have touched successfully any of her ports, we leave those who have been the constant observers of our movements to decide.

We commenced the enterprise alone, on the 30th of August, 1843, and as many know, after nine months, transferred over to a Committee, the proprietorship. The position that we assumed, was to claim for our oppressed fellow countrymen both bond and free, every right and privilege belonging to man, holding as an indispensable prerequisite, that whatever is necessary for the elevation of the whites, is necessary for the colored. In order the more fully to illustrate the truthfulness of this position, we had frequently to touch subjects

1. At the time that Frederick Douglass wrote these prefatory words to Delany's letter, Delany was in Pittsburgh, preparing to begin his western tour for the *North Star*. (See Part 2 below.)

that at once affected the pride and interests of our brethren, who often in consequence, looked upon us more as an injurer than a friend.

But our determination being perseverance, and our course onward, we had not long been toiling with the popular tide and current of our people's errors, until the young people particularly of the West, were aroused to a quickening sense of their condition, and in many cases inexcusable positions in society, and we at one time, had the astonishment, as well as the pleasure of seeing ELEVEN papers spring up in different parts of the country, all of which joined issue with us, advocating the very same doctrines, or commending our course. Among the number were, the Disfranchised American, Colored Citizen, Palladium of Liberty, Clarksonian, Herald, (Harrisburg, Pa.) Advocate, (N.Y. city,) Elevator, &c.

In addition to which in every direction, they launched forth upon the mental ocean naturally enough concluding, that if we, an inexperienced adventurer, were capable of taking the helm and striking with certainty many of the ports of importance to us as a people, the same results might as probably follow like efforts on their own part. And we can safely say, in no period of our modern existence, was the talents of the colored people, male and female, developed to such an extent as since the existence of our paper; and now, those who before, had not the confidence in themselves, and would scarce venture a thought, look upon such efforts, as a matter of course.

There were quite too many papers according to our number and circumstances, but it only served to show what an interest from the course pursued, was excited in our present condition.

We have ever since, gone on steadily and stealthily, until the present date, fulfilling to the letter our promise as editor, and assisting the Publishers in the fulfillment of theirs; though as we have frequently noticed, gave our services gratuitously to the cause, as well as a portion of our private means, earned by our daily business; but all our above referred to cotemporaries have long since ceased to exist, with some others of a later period.

We admit, that we have fallen far short of what might have been effected in the same time; the paper frequently appearing quite cold and spiritless, but this could not be avoided, as we had our daily labor to perform to earn our bread.

The MYSTERY is still afloat, with the solemn promise of the Publishers, to keep her tiding on the broad waters of destiny, doing battle in the great struggle for liberty and right, elevation and equality, God and humanity, as in days bygone.[2]

2. Appearing irregularly after Delany departed, the *Mystery* was purchased in 1848 by the African Methodist Episcopal Church and moved to Philadelphia, where it was renamed the *Christian Recorder*. It quickly became the church's main newspaper.

The *Publishing Committee* with and for whom we have labored for years, faithful to their trust, and prompt to a man have done much, for which we feel proud to have it in our power to say, are well worthy of their task, and can still do more, and from our very heart, as our successors in the editorial career, we commend them to the readers of the Mystery.

As to the efficacy and merit of our own efforts, we leave the public to determine, as we have no other endorser.

It becomes necessary that we should retire from our present position—not that we are a traitor to the cause of Humanity, but from this to what we hope, a more useful and productive part of the moral vineyard. We leave the Mystery for a union with the far famed and world renowned FREDERICK DOUGLASS, as a co-laborer in the cause of our oppressed brethren, by the publication of a large and capacious paper, the NORTH STAR, in Rochester, N.Y., in which our whole time, energy and services will be given; which cannot fail to be productive of signal benefit to the slave and our nominally free brethren, when the head and heart of Douglass enters into the combination. We feel loath to leave our Mystery, but duty calls, and we must obey.

To all our friends and acquaintances, we return thanks for the kindness and many favors shown us, while occupying the editorial chair of the Mystery, and in whatever we may have erred, consider it of the head and not the heart.

We could not conclude and do justice to our own feelings, if we omitted to notice the Editorial corps in particular. We have ever received from them, especially at home, that degree of courtesy and respect common to the rank, and have been received and commended in our position beyond all expectation, and even perhaps beyond merit. We have received the fullest possible share of their welcome to the profession. If we meet with half the welcome in our new place of residence, it will far exceed our expectation.

To our brethren and oppressed fellow men everywhere, we give this assurance, that let our lot be cast wherever it will, and our circumstances be what they may; so long as reason serves as the dictator of our will, we shall never cease to war against slavery and oppression of every kind, and defend the cause of the oppressed. Readers and Patrons, as Editor of the Mystery, we bid you Farewell.

M. R. DELANY

(from the *Mystery*; reprinted in the *North Star*, 21 January 1848, p. 2)

Eulogy on the Life and Character of the Rev. Fayette Davis

IN 1847 A BELOVED African Methodist Episcopal preacher of Pittsburgh, the Reverend Fayette Davis, died at the age of thirty-nine. Davis was a friend of Delany's, and he was also, like Delany and many other black male leaders of Pittsburgh's African American community, a member of the St. Cyprian Lodge, No. 13, of Free and Accepted Ancient York Masons. Delany delivered his eulogy on Davis to the assembled members of the St. Cyprian Masons. Subsequently, a committee of the lodge, consisting of Richard H. Gleaves, George B. Vashon, and James L. Williams, requested that Delany publish his eulogy as a pamphlet. The pamphlet, which is reprinted in its entirety below, presents Delany's vision of Davis as an exemplary black leader.

To faithfully record the life and history of a good and virtuous man, requires more than the fleeting reflections of a moment—more time than has fallen to my lot; and is a task, for which more than ordinary talents should be employed. Had I have had the time necessary for the undertaking, the data and memoranda before me, when considering the person of the subject now under consideration, I feel myself inadequate to do it justice; but how much more so, when, without the proper source of references, and in possession of but an impartial account, upon which to lay the foundation of our subject.

BRETHREN OF ST. CYPRIAN:—We have met to day to commemorate the life, labors and death, of our well beloved and much esteemed brother, REV. FAYETTE DAVIS.

In this, you cannot expect to hear the elaborate history of one, born to the enjoyment of the largest liberty, the most abundant wealth, affluent circumstances, greatest advantages, and the highest station among men. No, in this, you may not deceive yourselves.

When considering the class with which the Rev. Fayette Davis was identified, and the condition of that class in this country, the United States of America, though our native land, nothing beyond the most ordinary and simple narrative need be expected, if indeed, there be any thing to interest, beyond your personal acquaintance with his excellent character.

FAYETTE DAVIS, was born in the State of Virginia, in the year 1808, the county, month and day, at present unknown to us.

When at the age of 15 months, he was taken to the State of Kentucky by his parents, George and Sarah Davis, who, at that early period, removed thence, entering in with the spirit of the earliest emigrants, who then considered it an endless journey, to commence a travel "out back," as a removal to the West was quaintly termed.

Mr. George Davis was a native African, and became a respectable farmer, though a colored man, even in the slaveholding territory of Kentucky. The parents being both free, Fayette, of course, according to the laws of slavery, was also free.

Here in consequence of the obscurity to which a colored family is consigned, in this Republic, especially in the slaveholding States, we know nothing of little Fayette, excepting that he was an active, industrious, and biddable youth, holding, as we may suppose, from his temperament and disposition, his parents in the highest reverence and esteem.

His mother was a strict Methodist of the old honest puritan stamp, and his father, from the excellent influence and examples set by a wife whom he dearly loved and could confide in, was consequently inclined to piety. Fayette was the fifth of eight or nine children, sons and daughters, and appeared to be the pride and most anxious care of his beloved parents. It has been remarked, that "the very heart of the old man, was set on his son Fayette."

Being a colored youth in a slave State; without school, without an opportunity of learning a trade, without any other incentive than that instilled by his fond and excellent parents, who, unlike the slaveholders with whom they were surrounded, having slaves to till their soil, but cultivated it with their own hands; this, instead of proving a stimulus to the then interesting boy Fayette, was rather looked upon by him, who, ambitious to equal his white comrades, as degrading, because, in a slaveholding region, labor is considered as degrading by them the *whites*, at least the slaveholding portion of them. Thus, losing all hopes of equaling those whom he desired to rival in the avocations common to man, Fayette yielding to the mandates of the oppressors' notion of his propensity, threw himself on the broad ocean of chance, and engaged to travel as a page to a monied Kentuckian. In this excursion he traversed perhaps the whole Southern country, where he was afforded ample opportunity of seeing the cruelties and horrors of American Slavery. Such scenes, as might naturally be expected, aroused his youthful soul to a sense of a loftier calling, and much higher duty. After an elapse of time, the wandering youth returned to the home of his fond and devoted parents in Kentucky, fully satisfied, that the life he had been leading, was incompatible with his desires and determination for self-elevation.

When about the age of eighteen or nineteen, the year 1825 or 1826, Fayette became aroused to a sense of his condition by the awakening influence of the Holy Spirit. He became hopefully converted, and at once, attached himself to the Methodist Episcopal Church, (the whites). He was almost immediately, after the then manner of the Methodists, promoted to the standing of a preacher. In this capacity, he traveled and preached throughout Kentucky, as well as in many of the more distant slaveholding States. And here we are compelled to regret, that it is not in our possession at present, to give the name of the place and particular Church with which he first connected himself, as also the clergymen under whom he [began] the ministry among the whites.

By self exertion, he taught himself sufficiently to read the Scriptures and hymns, which according to his advisers' idea of the capacity of a *colored* man, was all that was necessary for him. Such was the talent manifested by him, that among the whites of Kentucky he was known by the appellation of the "talented black."

He continued in this Connexion, probably without the knowledge of the existence of any other body of Methodists, save that to which he was united, until the fall of 1830 or 1831, approaching the border of Ohio, he heard of the existence of the African Methodist Episcopal Church, as an independent body in this country. The Rev. Fayette Davis resolved to visit them; when during the same season, he visited a Camp Meeting held near Hillsborough, Highland Co., who becoming in consequence, so deeply interested in the welfare of his race, determined without the least hesitancy, on joining the Connexion. His colored brethren in Ohio became highly pleased with him, and designated him by the title of the "little Kentuckian," as a mark of fondness towards one whom they respected.

Returning home to Kentucky, he hesitated not to make known to his brethren in the Church, his full determination. They at once dissented from him, and used all their endeavors and influence to prevent what they conceived to be an unfavorable policy, if not a dangerous precedent—dangerous, because with him, he would carry at least the reflections of his enslaved brethren, before whom he had often proclaimed the "everlasting gospel of eternal Truths,"[1] who if nothing more, might perchance to hear a whisper concerning the freedom of their brethren in this his new field of labor. Stern and decided as was the opposition made against his newly determined project, Mr. Davis paid no other at-

1. Revelation 14:6.

tention to it than such as might be expected from a professed brother, united to a people by all the ties of Christian friendship. His determination was fixed— the voice of his people called, and he obeyed.

During that season, he withdrew from the connexion of our white brethren in Kentucky, leaving his former field of labors, and united himself to the African Methodist Episcopal Church Connexion, by joining the Ohio Annual Conference.

Here was a new field of labor opened to his view; here new enterprizes presented themselves fresh before the vision; here he perceived that in truth it might be said, "the harvest is ready, but the laborers are few."[2] The Rev. Fayette Davis determined to qualify himself for the arduous duties that lay spread out before him. He immediately with a vigor, which can be realized only by those conversant with his energetic character, his high and lofty intellect, applied himself closely to study. He spared no pains to improve every opportunity, when not actually engaged in the duties of his high calling.

Mr. Davis received different appointments from the annual Conferences, two of which were held at Pittsburgh, he being present to fill his seat. He once visited this city in company with the highly respected and now afflicted Right Rev. Father, Morris Brown, who was then on his return from the annual Conference, endeavoring to obtain a Pastor for the Zanesville Circuit; when, being successful, he returned again to Ohio.

On the ____ day of ____, 1838, he united his destiny in the sacred ties of matrimony, to *Elizabeth Tinson*, an amiable young woman, his present relict *now before* us; five children being the fruits of their union. This duty was performed at Zanesville, Ohio, by the Rev. Samuel Enty. Elder Davis in the year 1841, was appointed to the charge of Pittsburgh Station. Here he had not long been, before there was a manifestation of the outpouring of the Spirit—a "season of refreshing,"[3] to use the Christian language. He continued his labors during this Conference year, with an increased acknowledgment on the part of many, that they had made their peace with God. As they professed to grow in grace, their Pastor evidently grew in their favor; none perhaps having previously borne so universal an esteem of the people as Elder Davis.

He was petitioned for, and reappointed to the Pittsburgh Charge. In the winter of 1843, a Revival under the pastoral charge of Mr. Davis, again commenced, and continued successively, day and night, for nearly three months. So great was this Revival, that it was called by many the "Day of Pentecost." Several hundred under the religious guidance of Pastor Davis, professed to be hopefully converted. Elder Davis still continued to grow in the favor of the people; not only of

2. Matthew 9:37.
3. Acts 3:19.

his own congregation, but those of other religious denominations. He was a third time appointed to the Pastoral Charge of what was then the Front St. Church. With unerring fidelity and Christian rectitude, as firm as what his course was marked with meekness, this good and pious man served out his pastorage, preserving to the last, the love, esteem, and affection of his acquaintances.

He was removed from the Pittsburgh Charge to the Washington Circuit, and that, because according to the Church Discipline, he could no longer be continued in the same station. On this Circuit, with two successive appointments, he served the people of his itinerancy wih the same perseverance and Christian fortitude, which guided and directed his pathway while traveling amidst the obstacles and difficulties that beset him, while in our midst. He only left the people of his last charge, because they could not longer keep him.

At the last Annual Conference held at Cincinnati in the fall of 1846, Elder Davis was again returned to the embraces of his much beloved Pittsburgh congregation, his pastoral charge being the Church in which we are at present assembled.

Who did not hail him with a brother's salutation, and greet him with the greetings of a brother? All who so much delighted to sit under the sound of his sonorous voice, which so often greeted our ears with those tender and endearing offerings, *Behold, how good and how pleasant it is for brethren to dwell together in unity!*[4]

In this, the last year of his charge among men, he manifested more than usual determination—as though conscious of his approaching end and anxious for the issue, it appeared as if every word he uttered, emanated from the Throne itself borne by a messenger from on high. Who cannot recollect, while standing in the sacred desk, the lively expressions of his lighted countenance? It may truly be said of him, during the period of his last appointment, that he *served his Master, with freedom, fervency and zeal.*

It was during this period, that he first became introduced into this great brotherhood among men, by attaching himself to *St. Cyprian*; not however, without the determination of withdrawing from it so soon as he discovered anything contrary to the spirit of true Christianity. Finding nothing to operate against his conscience, he continued an exemplary and truly pious member to the last—frequently smiling at the idea that some persons form of the institution, taking the position that were there good in it, he desired to know it for the benefits of that good—if there was harm in it, he also desired to know it, in order to take advantage of that wrong. Paul, was able to declare to the gentiles, "whatsoever you are, that am I also," and had the Apostle never studied Greek,

4. Psalms 133:1.

he never could have read while passing through Athens, the inscription upon the Heathen altar, "To the unknown God," by which he condemned them, by "words out of their own mouths."[5] But he found it a benevolent society, and he was satisfied, little regarding the name by which it was distinguished.[6]

Elder Davis, during his last year in Pittsburgh, bore with him an expression, which plainly told of a physical disability, a constitutional declension, as well as an unusual mental exertion. Many of his friends felt considerable anxiety for his welfare, advising him to labor less and indulge himself more. At every meeting of the Church where duty called him, the Rev. Fayette Davis was found in his place.

Elder Davis encouraged improvement, both by example and precept; he was the main spring of every effort at moral improvement among our people, emanating from the Church to which he belonged. With propriety it might have been said of him, "Behold! an Israelite indeed, in whom there is no guile."[7]

On Tuesday, the 23d of March of the present year, 1847, when attempting to rise from a chair where he then was sitting in his own house, brother Davis swooned and fell prostrate at the feet of his affectionate wife, who screamed and clasped him in her arms; when he partially recovered, and by the assistance of friends, was laid upon his bed, never to rise again!

When able to speak audibly, he observed to his weeping wife—"wife, I won't be here long—I believe I should have gone then, but your lamentations aroused me; God knows what is best," or words to that effect. I called to see him on Friday afternoon, and in company with two clergymen, had my last pleasant conversation with him.

He suffered on under the kind and attentive treatment of a skillful Physician, until Sabbath the 28, at 8 o'clock in the morning, when his happy spirit left its earthly tabernacle, and took its flight to the realms of unspeakable bliss, there to dwell forever in *that house not made with hands, eternal in the Heavens.*[8] His spirit has gone to God who gave it—may it rest in endless peace!

Here sits his widowed consort and orphan children, left to us as a refuge in the time of need. By the endearing ties of *Humanity, Friendship, and Brotherly Love,* I conjure you brethren, never to let the widow nor the orphan want; while

5. Acts 17:23.

6. When informed that the late great and good WILBERFORCE, was, up to the time of his death a member of the order, he smiled and said, it could not contain him if no good men were found in it. [Delany's note.] The great British antislavery advocate William Wilberforce (1759–1833) introduced the first bill calling for the abolition of slavery in the West Indies.

7. John 1:47.

8. 2 Corinthians 5:1.

you have a cent to divide with her, divide it, leaving the event to God; not only the widow and orphan, or those whom you are mutually bound to render assistance, but wherever you find a single *human being*, of whatever creed, origin, or color, *they applying to you as such*, or you knowing them to be in need, you are in duty bound to *contribute to their necessities, as far as in your power lies, without material injury to yourself and family*; remember the golden rule, "Do unto others as ye would they should do unto you." "He that giveth to the poor, lendeth to the Lord."[9]

I would here introduce the name of the family physician of Elder Davis, who attended his family from his first appointment to Pittsburgh until the day of his death, *Dr. E. Edrington*; who, from that time until now, a period of nearly six years, has continued to give his services *without the hope of favor or reward*. Such disinterested kindness in Dr. *Edrington*, should not be permitted to pass without deserved commendation.

It may be said that Elder Davis was not without his failings. This may be true, as no human being is without them. But whatever these may have been, we have yet got to learn them; indeed, the greatest complaints we ever heard against him were, that he was too sociable, that is, he treated everybody alike—or held himself superior to none.

It is true, that the relentless hand of calumny, once made an assassin stab at him, but his undefiled character, like gold seven times tried in the fire, only came forth the purer and shone with greater brilliancy.[10] He was a devoted and dutiful child, assigning the only property which he had but partially secured in Ohio, to the use of his aged parents, who still reside on it during their natural life; a kind and affectionate husband, and tender and indulgent parent.

The wide field of usefulness which he beheld before him when he looked upon his brethren both nominally free and bond, induced him with all his might to hasten the accomplishment of his qualification. To this end, he endeavored to embrace within the scope of his studies, all the sciences both ancient and modern, and to this great uncommon exertion, do we mainly lay the untimely decline of his body and eventful end of his existence.

If Elder Davis were not learned, it were not his fault, but misfortune—the want of an opportunity. If he were not wise, it were for the want of age and not intellect, as his mind was above the common order. But withal, he was *virtuous* and *good*, without which, he could not be, however learned, great and wise. Elder Fayette Davis, fell a self-martyr to the cause of his oppressed and downtrodden countrymen and brethren. He has yielded to the summons of grim

9. Matthew 7:12; Proverbs 19:17.
10. This incident remains obscure.

monster Death—this mighty edifice *erected to God and the Holy Order*, has lost a column broken in the centre—a branch has been stripped from the olive tree; a sprig acacia, has been plucked from its new made soil. He died to answer the demands of impartial Justice; with a lively hope of immortality beyond the grave.

Brethren, let each and every one of us endeavor so to conduct ourselves, that when we come to leave the chequered pathway of this life; when we too like him, shall be summoned by the Grand Architect of the Universe, to retire from labor to deserved reward after a long, difficult, and tedious *sojourn*, being *led captive* by the enemy, may we be able to take our stand in counsel with the *High Priest* and the *King*, there to sit and sing with all those faithful *travelers* who have gone before us, the sweet and harmonious anthems of never ending happiness, in unison with all the just made perfect, mingling our voices with *Moses, Aaron,* and *Zerubbabel*,[11] in honor to JEHOVAH.

(*Eulogy on the Life and Character of the Rev. Fayette Davis* [Pittsburgh: Benj. Franklin Peterson, Mystery Office, 1847])

---

11. Aaron, the brother of Moses, was the first high priest of the Hebrews (Exodus 4, 7, 28–32); Zerubbabel was a prince of Judah of the house of David who helped to rebuild the Hebrews' first Temple (Zechariah 4, 9, 10).

The Origin and Objects of Ancient Freemasonry: Its Introduction into the United States, and Legitimacy among Colored Men. A Treatise Delivered Before St. Cyprian Lodge, No. 13, June 24th, A.D. 1853—A.L. 5853

ON 24 JUNE 1853, Delany addressed St. Cyprian Lodge, No. 13, of Free and Accepted Ancient York Masons, on the history of "the colored Masons in the United States." Within a week, he received letters from two different St. Cyprian committees requesting that he publish his lecture in pamphlet form, and he complied by month's end. *Origin and Objects* is one of Delany's most significant publications, and in many respects it can be taken as a key to his political and literary career. He wrote his pamphlet on black Freemasonry at a time when racial ethnographic science was on the ascendency. That "science" would culminate with the publication of Josiah C. Nott and George R. Gliddon's *Types of Mankind* (1854), which argued, on the basis of comparative analyses of human skulls, that blacks were inferior to, and essentially different from, whites. Drawing on Samuel Morton's *Crania Ægyptiaca* (1844), Nott and Gliddon also argued that the ancient Egyptians were white and accordingly that the sources of Western civilization were white. In *Origin and Objects*, Delany pridefully limns the black African origins of Masonry in Egypt and Ethiopia and by extension locates the origins of Western civilization and progress in Africa. He depicts white Masons as the perverse enforcers of an inhumane and unjust color line that would separate black Masons from white Masons. Crucially, he depicts as well how Masonry can provide a model for black leadership and community. Through its hierarchy, myths, and rituals, Delany suggests, Masonry honors its black leaders and works to sustain black community. Delany, who helped to form the St. Cyprian Lodge in 1847, was himself sustained by Masonry, remaining a lifelong member. The selection that follows is the complete text of Delany's address to the lodge. The prefatory letters from the St. Cyprian committees and some of Delany's more arcane footnotes have been cut.

THIS LITTLE TREATISE

IS MOST RESPECTFULLY DEDICATED

TO THE

MASONIC FRATERNITY

THROUGHOUT THE WORLD.

BY THE AUTHOR.

———

PITTSBURGH, June 30, A.D. 1853, A.L.[1] 5853.

Gentlemen, Brethren, Companions, and Sir Knights:

I have received a note jointly from a Committee appointed by St. Cyprian Lodge, No. 13, and a Communication held by the District Deputy Grand Master, desiring that the Treatise delivered by me before the public, on the 24th day of June inst. (the Annual Festival of our Patron, St. John the Baptist,)[2] be published in pamphlet form. With this request I readily and cheerfully comply.

Permit me to say, in this connection, that whatever undue and unwarrantable obstructions may be thrown in our way by *American* Masons, and they are many—though there are *some* honorable exceptions—it is within the power of the Grand Lodge of England to decide in the matter, and at once establish our *validity*. For this purpose, I now suggest, through you, that all of our Subordinate Lodges throughout the United States, at once petition their respective Grand Lodges, and the Grand Lodges respectively agree, and together with the National Grand Lodge, meet by delegated representatives of *Past Masters*—not to exceed three from each Grand Lodge, and the same number from each District over which there may be a District Deputy Grand Master, the National Grand Lodge sending *one* for each *State Grand Lodge*—in a National Grand Masonic Convention, for the single purpose of petitioning the Grand Lodge of England for a *settlement* of the question of the *legality of Colored Masons in the United States*, claiming to have originated from the warrant granted to Prince Hall,[3] of Boston. This should at once be done, to settle the controversy, as it

1. A. L., from the Latin "anno lucis," refers to Year of Light, the moment of creation, which, according to Masonic lore, occurred in the year 4,000 B.C.

2. The Masonic festival honoring Christ's disciple John the Baptist also celebrates the summer solstice.

3. The black artisan Prince Hall (1735?–1807), who was a slave or indentured servant in Boston, was freed in 1770 and in 1775 established African Lodge No. 459, the first black

would to us be a great point gained, because it would be the acknowledgment and establishment of a *right* among us as a people, which is now *disputed*, but which *legitimately* belongs to us.

We have for years been fraternally outraged, simply for the want of a proper and judicious course being pursued on the part of *our* Masonic authorities, and the present loudly calls upon us for action in this matter. We are either Masons or not Masons, legitimate or illegitimate; if the affirmative, then we *must* be so *acknowledged* and *accepted*—if the negative, we *should* be *rejected*. We never will relinquish a claim to an everlasting inheritance, but by the force of stern necessity; and there is not that Masonic power in existence, with the exception of the Grand Lodge of England, to which we will yield in a decision on this point. Our rights are equal to those of other American Masons, if not better than some; and it comes not with the best grace for *them* to *deny* us.

The suggested Convention should be held in some central place, during the ensuing three years of the National Grand Lodge administration, and in not less than one year from this date, so that full time may be given, for reflection and action, on the part of the various Subordinate and Grand Lodges.

Let not the hopes of our brethren languish, though calumny and slander may have done their work.

> O, Slander! foulest imp of hell!
>   Thy tongue is like the scorpion's sting!
> Nor peace nor hope can near thee dwell;
>   Thy breath can blast the fairest thing!
> O, could I grasp the thunderbolt!
>   I'd crush thee, limping fiend of hell!
> From earth, I'd chase thy serpent soul,
>   And chain thee where the furies dwell!
> BISHOP PAYNE.[4]

Masonic lodge, with himself as Grand Master. Finding that white Masons refused to authorize the lodge, Hall, after fighting for the Revolutionary army, applied to the Grand Lodge of England for an official charter, which he received in 1784. Hall went on to found lodges in Philadelphia, Providence, and elsewhere, the legitimacy of which continued to be contested by white Masons.

4. From Daniel Alexander Payne (1811–93), "The Lament for the Slandered Loved One," in Payne's poetic volume *The Pleasures* (1850). Named a bishop of the African Methodist Episcopal denomination in 1852, Payne emerged as the church's most significant leader of the nineteenth century.

Fraternally Yours,

In the bonds of Union and Fellowship,

M. R. DELANY.

TO ELIAS EDMONDS, WM. B. AUSTIN, &c. *Committees.*[5]

A TREATISE

"Great is Truth and must prevail."[6]

To introduce the subject of Ancient Freemasonry at this period, with a design to adduce anything new, at least to the enlightened, would be a work of super-erogation, having the semblance of assumption, more than an effort to impart information.

Summoned by your invitation to deliver a Treatise, I have chosen for my subject, THE ORIGIN, OBJECTS, AND INTRODUCTION OF FREEMASONRY INTO THE UNITED STATES—and also its introduction among colored men in this country. I shall, therefore, proceed at once to the discharge of my duty, doing the best I can according to the opportunity and means at hand for the accomplishment of this end.

Masonry was originally intended for the better government of man—for the purpose of restraining him from a breach of the established ordinances. The first law given to man was by God himself—that given in the Garden of Eden, forbidding the eating of the reserved fruit. (Gen. 2:17.) The first institution was that of marriage. (Gen. 2:21, 24.) The first breach of the law was committed by eating the forbidden fruit. (Gen. 3:6.) The first punishment inflicted on man was by God himself, for a breach of the law. (Gen. 3:16–19.) The first city was built by Cain, and named after his first-born son, Enoch.

Man from Adam to Noah.

During the period from Adam to Noah, the life of man was of long duration, each individual living through several hundred years of time. His habits, cus-

---

5. Two committees were formed by the St. Cyprian lodge to request Delany's thoughts on Freemasonry; Elias Edmonds chaired one of the committees and William B. Austin, Grand Master, chaired the other.

6. Thomas Brooks (1608–80), *The Crown and Glory of Christianity* (1662). The author of over a dozen devotional books, Brooks was a Congregationalist preacher in England.

toms and manner of living were simple; residing in thinly peopled localities, for there were then no densely populated cities, and relying mainly on husbandry as a means of support.

Man from Noah to Solomon.

From Noah to Solomon, the character of man underwent an entire and important change. Noah's three sons, scattering abroad over the earth, built great cities, and established many and various policies, habits, manners and customs, for the government of their people. At this period, it will be remembered, a general separation in interests and sympathies took place among these brethren, (the children of one household parentage,) which continued to manifest itself in hostile array until the building of the temple by Solomon, king of Israel.[7] I do not intend to assert that hostilities then entirely ceased, but that mankind were better governed after that period, will not be denied.

In the earliest period of the Egyptian and Ethiopian dynasties, the institution of Masonry was first established. Discovering a defect in the government of man, first suggested an inquiry into his true state and condition. Being a people of a high order of intellect, and subject to erudite and profound thought, the Egyptians and Ethiopians were the first who came to the conclusion that man was created in the similitude of God. This, it will be remembered, was anterior to the Bible record, because Moses was the recorder of the Bible, subsequent to his exodus from Egypt, all his wisdom and ability having been acquired there; as a proof of which, the greatest recommendation to his fitness for so high and holy an office, and the best encomium which that book can possibly bestow upon him in testimony of his qualifications as its scriptor, the Bible itself tells us that "Moses was learned in all the *wisdom* of the Egyptians."[8]

The Ethiopians early adduced the doctrine and believed in a trinity of Godhead. Though heathens their mythology was of a high and pure order, agreeing in regard to the attributes of the Deity with the doctrine of Christians in after ages, as is beautifully illustrated in the person of Jupiter Ammon,[9] the great god of Egypt and Ethiopia, who was assigned a power over heaven, earth and hell, as well as over all the other gods, thereby acknowledging his omnipotence—all

---

7. A king of the ancient Hebrews renowned for his great wisdom, Solomon (c.972–c.932 B.C.) presided over the building of the first Hebrew temple at Jerusalem; see 1 Kings 8. Apocryphal events surrounding the building of that temple are at the foundational center of Masonic ritual and ceremony.

8. Acts 7:22.

9. The classical name of the Egyptian god Amen, identified by the Greeks as Zeus and the Romans as Jupiter.

other gods possessing but one divine attribute or function, which could only be exercised in his particular department of divinity.

Man the Likeness of God.

What is God that man should be his image, and what knowledge should man obtain in order to be like God? This wisdom was possessed in the remotest period by the wise men of Egypt and Ethiopia, and handed down only through the priesthood to the recipients of their favors, the mass of mankind being ignorant of their own nature, and consequently prone to rebel against their greatest and best interests.

God is a being possessing various attributes: and all Masons, whether Unitarian, Trinitarian, Greek, Jew or Mohammedan, agree upon this point, at least without controversy. Where there are various functions, there must be an organ for the exercise of each function,—and this conclusion most naturally led man to inquire into his own nature, to discover the similitude between himself and his Creator.

The three great attributes of Deity—omniscience, omnipotence, and omnipresence—were recognized by the ancients, and represented in the character given to their ruling god—as above mentioned—as presiding over the universe of eternal space—of *celum, terra,* and *tartarus*[10]—answering to the Christian doctrine of three persons in one—Father, Son and Holy Ghost.

Man, then, to assimilate God must, in his nature, be a trinity of systems—morally, intellectually and physically. This great truth appears to have been known to King David, who with emotion, exclaims, "We are wonderfully and fearfully made."[11]

To convince man of the importance of his own being and impress him with a proper sense of his duty to his Creator were what was desired, and to effect this would also impress him with a sense of his duty and obligations to society and the laws intended for his government. For this purpose was the beautiful fabric of Masonry established, and illustrated in the structure of man's person.

Man, scientifically developed, is a moral, intellectual, and physical being—composed of an osseous, muscular, and vital structure; of solid, flexible and liquid parts. With an intellect—a mind, the constituent principles of which he is incapable of analyzing or comprehending, which rises superior to its earthy tenement, with the velocity of lightning, soars to the summit of altitude, descends to the depth of profundity, and flies to the wide-spread expanse of eternal space.

10. The heavens, the earth, and the underworld.
11. Psalms 139:14.

What can be more God-like than this, to understand which is to give man a proper sense of his own importance, and consequently his duty to his fellows, by which alone, he fulfills the high mission for which he is sent on his temporary pilgrimage.

While the Africans, who were the authors of this mysterious and beautiful Order, did much to bring it to perfection by the establishment of the great principles of man's likeness to Jehovah in a tri-une existence, yet, until the time of King Solomon, there was a great deficiency in his government, in consequence of the policy being monopolized by the priesthood and certain privileged classes or families.

From Solomon Down.

For the purpose of remedying what was now conceived to be a great evil in the policy of the world, and for their better government to place wisdom within the acquirement of all men, King Solomon summoned together the united wisdom of the world,—men of all nations and races—to consider the great project of reducing the mystic ties to a more practical and systematic principle, and stereotyping it with physical science, by rearing the stupendous and magnificent temple at Jerusalem.[12] For the accomplishment of this masterpiece of all human projects, there were laborers or attendants, mechanics or workmen, and overseers or master-builders. Added to these, there was a designer or originator of all the schemes, an architect or draughtsman, and a furnisher of all the materials for the building—all and every thing of which was classified and arranged after the order of trinity, the building itself, when finished, being composed of an outer, an inner, and a central court.

After the completion of this great work, the implements of labor having been laid aside, there were scattered to the utmost parts of the earth, seventy thousand laborers, eighty thousand workmen, and three thousand and three hun-

---

12. Previous to the building of the temple, Masonry was only allegorical, consisting of a scientific system of theories, taught through the medium of Egyptian, Ethiopian, Assyrian, and other oriental hieroglyphics understood only by the priesthood and a chosen few. All the sovereigns and members of the royal families were Masons, because each member of the royal household had of necessity to be educated in the rituals of the priesthood. And it was not until after Masonry was introduced into Asia by the Jews— it being strictly forbidden by the Jewish laws for women to be priests—that females were prohibited from being Masons. Among other nations of the ancients, priestesses were common, as is known to the erudite in history; and Candace, queen of Sheba, was a high-priestess in her realm—hence her ability to meet King Solomon in the temple, having passed the guards, by the words of wisdom, from the outer to the inner court, where she met the king in all his wisdom, power and glory. [Delany's note]

dred master builders, making one hundred and fifty-three thousand and three hundred artizans,[13] each of whom having been instructed in all the mysteries of the temple, was fully competent to teach all the arts and sciences acquired at Jerusalem in as many different cities, provinces, states or tribes. At this period, the mysteries assumed the name of Masonry, induced from the building of the temple: and at this time, also, commenced the universality of the Order, arising from the going forth of the builders into all parts of the world. This then, was the *establishment of Masonry*, which has been handed down through all succeeding ages.

For a period of years after the destruction of the temple and the sacred or mystic records, there was some slight derangement in the Craft; men were becoming ungovernable both in church and state, owing to the want of proper instruction, and their consequent ignorance of the relation they bore to their Creator and society. For the purpose of again bringing back the "prodigal son" to the household of his father, the "stray sheep" to the rich pastures of the fold of Israel, and repairing the somewhat defaced, honored monument of time, Prince Edwin of England, in 930 of the Christian era, being nine hundred and twenty-two years ago, summoned together at York, all the wise men of the order, where the rites were again scientifically systematized, and preserved for coming time. At this point, the Order, in honor to Prince Edwin, assigned to itself the title of *York Masonry*.[14]

The Stages of Man's History.

We have here the history of man's existence from Adam to Solomon, showing three distinct periods, fraught with more mystery than all things else, save the ushering in the Christian era by the birth of the adorable Son of God: his origin in Adam's creation, his preservation in Noah's ark, and his prospects of redemption from the curse of God's broken laws by the promises held out in that mysteriously incomprehensible work of building the temple by Solomon. Adam, Noah, and Solomon, then, are the three great types of the condition of man—his sojourn here on earth, and his prospects of a future bliss.

Founded upon the similitude and consequent responsibility to his Creator, the ancients taught the doctrine of a rectitude of conduct and purpose of heart,

13. Here the Trinity is again typified: *three times* fifty thousand, *three times* one thousand, and *three times* one hundred. [Delany's note]

14. Delany follows traditional Masonic histories in linking the founding of York Masonry to the little known Prince Edwin, though many of these histories give the date as 926.

as the only surety for the successful government of man, and the regulations of society around him. Whether Gentiles, Greeks or Jews, all taught the same as necessary to his government on earth—his responsibility to a Supreme Being, the author and Creator of himself. But the mythology of those days, not unlike the scientific theology of the days in which we live, consisted of a sea of such metaphysical depth, that the mass of mankind was unable to fathom it. Instead, then, of accomplishing the object for which this wise policy was established, the design was thwarted by the manner in which it was propagated. Man adhered but little, and cared less, for that in which he could never be fully instructed, nor be made to understand, in consequence of his deficiency in a thorough literary education—this being the exclusive privilege of those in affluent circumstances. All these imperfections have been remedied, in the practical workings of the comprehensive system of Free and Accepted Masonry, as handed down to us from the archives at Jerusalem. All men, of every country, clime, color and condition, (when morally worthy,) are acceptable to the portals of Masonic jurisprudence.

In many parts of the world, the people of various nations were subject to lose their liberty in several ways. A forfeiture by crime, as in our country; by voluntary servitude for a stipulated sum or reward, as among the Hindoos; and by capture in battle and being sold into slavery, as in Algiers. Against these Masonry found it necessary to provide, and accordingly the first two classes were positively proscribed as utterly unworthy of its benefits, as they were equally unworthy of the respectful consideration of the good among mankind. In this, however, was never contemplated the third class of bondees; for none but him who *voluntarily* compromised his liberty was recognized as a slave by Masons. As there must be a criminal intention in the commission of a crime, so must the act of the criminal be voluntary; hence the criminal and the voluntary bondsman have both forfeited their Masonic rights by willing degradation. In the case of the captive, an entirely different person is presented before us, who has greater claims upon our sympathies than the untrammeled freeman. Instead of the degraded vassal and voluntary slave, whose prostrate position only facilitates the aspect of his horrible deformity, you have the bold, the brave, the high-minded, the independent-spirited, and manly form of a kindred brother in humanity, whose heart is burning, whose breast is heaving, and whose soul is wrung with panting aspirations for liberty—a commander, a chieftain, a knight, or a prince, it may be—still he is a captive and by the laws of captivity, a slave. Does Masonry, then, contemplate the withholding of its privileges from such applicants as these? Certainly not; since Moses, (to whom our great Grand Master Solomon, the founder of the temple, is indebted for his Masonic wisdom,) was born and lived in captivity eighty years, and by the laws of his captors a slave. It matters not whether captured in actual conflict, sleeping by the wayside, or in a cradle of bulrushes, after birth; so that there be a longing aspiration for liberty, and a manly determination to be free. Policy alone will not permit of the order to confer Masonic privileges on one while yet in captivity; but the fact of his *former* condition as such, or that of his parents, can have no bearing whatever on him. The *mind* and *desires* of the recipient must be *free*; and at the *time* of his endowment with these privileges, his *person* and mind must be unencumbered with all earthly trammels or fetters. This is what is meant by Free and Accepted Masonry, to distinguish it from the order when formerly conferred upon the few, like the order of nobility, taking precedence by rank and birth, whether the inheritor was worthy or not of so high and precious privileges.

In the three great periods as presented to view, you have the three great stages of man's existence—Adam, with childlike innocence in the Garden of Eden, turned out for disobedience, as a youth upon the world, without the protecting hand of his Omnipotent Parent—Noah, as in adventurous manhood, in constructing and launching his great vessel (the Ark) "upon the face of the great deep;"[15] and Solomon, as in old age, in devising, planning and counseling, and heaping up treasures in building the temple of Jerusalem; all of which are impressively typified, in the cardinal Degrees of Masonry. The Entered Apprentice as a child, and as in youth the Fellow Craft; the Master Mason, as in mature and thinking manhood; and as an old and reflective man of years and wisdom, the Royal Arch[16] completes the history of his journey of life.

Its Introduction into the United States.

Masonry was introduced into the United States by grant of a warrant to Henry Price, Esq. of Boston, on the 30th of July, 1733, as Right Worshipful Grand Master of North America, "with full power and authority to appoint his Deputy," by the Right Honorable and Most Worshipful Anthony Lord Viscount Montague "Grand Master of Masons in England." *Cole's Lib*, p. 332.[17] I do not conceive it necessary to prosecute the history of Masonry farther in this coun-

15. Genesis 7:18.
16. Drawing on Egyptian notions of deity, Royal Arch Masonry celebrates the mythical arch made in the heavens by the course of King Osiris, the Sun.
17. Delany draws on Samuel Coles, *The Freemasons' Library* (Baltimore: Cushing and Jewett, 1826). According to this and other Masonic histories, the appointment of Henry Price (1697–1780) as Provincial Grand Master of the Craft in New England, and the concurrent establishment of the St. John's Lodge in Boston as a Grand Lodge, marked the beginnings of Freemasonry in the American colonies. Montague, who made the appointment and designation, had become a Grand Master in 1721.

try; but let it suffice to say, that hostilities which commenced between Great Britain and America in 1775, absolved all Masonic ties between the two countries, and left American Masons free to act according to the suggestions of the peculiar circumstances in which they were then placed. With the independence of the country, commenced the independence of Masonic jurisdiction in the United States.

The Grand Lodge of Massachusetts was formed in 1769; Maine, New Hampshire, 1789; Rhode Island, 1791; Vermont, 1794; New York, 1787; (another being established in 1826, which has recently been denounced by England and all other legal Masonic jurisdictions throughout the world;) New Jersey, 1786; Pennsylvania, 1734, under England, to which she remained attached until September, 1786, when the connection was absolved; Delaware, 1806; Virginia, 1778; N. Carolina, 1787; S. Carolina, 1787; Georgia, 1786; Ohio, 1808; Kentucky, 1800; Louisiana, Mississippi and Tennessee, the data not being given. *Cole's Lib.* 363 *to* 375. This gives a fair history of the introduction of Masonry into the United States of America.

Among Colored Men in the United States.

In the year 178—, a number of colored men in Boston, Massachusetts, applied to the proper source for a grant of Masonic privileges, and this being denied them, by force of necessity they went to England, which at that time not recognizing the Masonic fraternity of America, the then acting Grand Master, (recorded on the warrant as the Right Honorable, Henry Frederick, Duke of Cumberland) granted a warrant to the colored men to make Masons and establish Lodges, subject, of course, to the Grand Lodge of England.[18] In course of time, their ties became absolved; not before it was preceded by the establishment of an independent Grand Lodge in Philadelphia, Pa., by colored men, and subsequently, a general Grand Lodge, known as the First Independent African Grand Lodge of North America.[19]

In the year 1832, another Grand Lodge was established by a party of dissatisfied colored Masons in the city of Philadelphia, known as the "Hiram Grand Lodge of the State of Pennsylvania." There was, also, for many years, a small faction who rather opposed the F. I. A. G. L., still adhering to what they conceived

18. Prince Hall and his fellow black Masons of the Boston African Lodge No. 459 received their warrant from Grand Master Henry Frederick, Duke of Cumberland (1745–90), in 1784.

19. After helping to establish the black Masonic lodge in Massachusetts, Prince Hall organized a black Masonic lodge in Philadelphia in 1797, which numbered among its original members thirteen African Americans who had been made Masons in England.

to be the most legitimate source—the old African Lodge of Boston, among whom was the colored Lodge of Boston, and a very respectable body in New York city, known as the "Boyer Lodge." In December, 1847, by a grand communication of a representative body of all the colored Lodges in the United States, held in the city of New York, the differences and wounds which long existed were all settled and healed, a complete union formed, and a National Grand Lodge, established, by the choice and election, in due Masonic form, of Past Master, John T. Hilton,[20] of Boston, Mass. Most Worshipful Grand Master of the National Grand Lodge, and William E. Ambush, M. W. N. G. Secretary. This, perhaps, was the most important period in the history of colored Masons in the United States; and had I the power to do so, I would raise my voice in tones of thunder, but with the pathetic affections of a brother, and thrill the cord of every true Masonic heart throughout the country and the world, especially of colored men, in exhortations to stability and to Union. Without it, satisfied am I that all our efforts, whether as Men or Masons, must fail—utterly fail. "A house divided against itself, cannot stand"[21]—the weak divided among themselves in the midst of the mighty, are thrice vanquished—conquered without a blow from the strong; the sturdy hand of the ruthless may shatter in pieces our column guidance, and leave the Virgin of Sympathy[22] to weep through all coming time.

I have thus, as cursorily as possible, given you a faint history of the origin and objects of ancient Free Masonry; its introduction into this country among white and colored men; and he who rejects Masonry as an absurd and irreligious institution, must object to the Scriptures of eternal truth, and spurn the Bible as a book of mummeries.

But there have been serious objections urged against the legitimacy of Ancient Freemasonry among *colored* men of African descent or affinity in the United States, emanating at various times from different directions, of high Masonic authority in the Republic, and, consequently, received and adopted with a readiness as surprising as it was unkind and unjust by almost all of the Subordinate, and many of the Grand Lodges throughout the country, especially in the non-slaveholding States.[23]

Among the earliest and, peradventure, the first of these intended fratricidal

20. John T. Hilton was Grand Master of the Prince Hall Grand Lodge in Boston during the 1820s; for an example of his oratory, see William H. Grimshaw, *Official History of Freemasonry among the Colored People in North America* (1903; reprint, Freeport, New York: Books for Libraries Press, 1971), pp. 99–102.

21. Mark 12:25. Abraham Lincoln's famous "House Divided" speech was delivered in Springfield, Illinois, in 1858.

22. Mary, the mother of Jesus.

23. A fact worthy of remark, is that there is no comparison between the feelings man-

assaults, was that of the Grand Lodge of Pennsylvania in the year 18—; a distinguished and talented ex-editor and present member of Congress, and Col. P. an
ex-Post Master, if I mistake not, being at the time among the Grand Officers, if
not the Committee who visited and reported concerning the African Grand
Lodge in Eleventh Street, Philadelphia.[24] And I should not at this late day refer
to the doings of those distinguished personages in this connection, but for the
purpose of—as it never as yet has publicly been done—vindicating the above
named First Independent African Grand Lodge of North America, against the
aspersions of those multifarious outward forces which have so long been leveled
against her Masonic ramparts. Lambparts would be a term far more appropriate; because our Masonic fathers have submitted really with the most lamb-like
passiveness to the terrible and disparaging ordeal.

In this wise, the circumstance referred to happened. The question had long
been mooted among the white members of the fraternity, as to the legitimacy
and *reality* of colored Masons; and, consequently, a Committee from the Grand
Lodge of Pennsylvania (white) was appointed to visit the colored Grand Lodge
then situated in Eleventh Street, (Phila) to apply the Masonic *test*, and *prove* or
disprove their capacity as recipients of the ancient and honorable rituals of the
mystic order.

A Grand Communication being congregated for the purpose, at the appointed time, the Committee went. A Committee of Examination being sent
out, who—instead of, as they should have done, had there been in waiting St.
John the Baptist, St. John the Evangelist, or St. Paul in his daring *attitude* as the
chief Christian on the Isle of Malta;[25] *examining* them—on seeing the gentlemen, all men of the first standing in the city of Philadelphia, who had often

---

ifested toward colored, by Northern and Southern Masons. Northern Masons, notwithstanding Masonry knows no man by descent, origin, or color, seldom visit colored Masonic Lodges; and when they do, it is frequently done by *stealth!* While, to the contrary,
Southern Masons recognize and fellowship [*sic*] colored men, as such, whenever they
meet them as Masons. The writer has more than once sat in Lodge in the city of C——,
with some of the first gentlemen of Kentucky, where there have been present Col. A., a
distinguished lawyer, Esquire L., one of the first Aldermen of the place, and Judge M.,
President of the Judges' Bench. This is a matter of no unfrequent occurrence, and many
of our members have done the same. [Delany's note]

24. Delany refers to the First African Independent Grand Lodge of Free and Accepted
Masons, which was formed in 1815 by the Reverend Absalom Jones (1746–1818) and
other black Philadelphia Masonic leaders, who merged four separate Masonic organizations into one, with Jones as the Right Worshipful Grand Master. Black lodges were regularly interrogated and found lacking by white Masonic organizations. This visit by notable (unnamed) white Masons probably occurred sometime between 1815 and 1830.

25. See Acts 28.

been seen in Masonic processions, and so far, *known*—as they thought—to be Masons—an unwise conclusion to-be-sure—reported them to the Chair, when without a question—and entirely through deference—the Chair replied: "Admit them," &c. They entered, inspected, oversighted, and examined the work of the colored Masons, applying the scrutiny of a suspicious eye, and the tests of plumb, level and square: all of this they pronounced to be good work, square, and just such work as was required to be done; but for this act of *courtesy*, and undue *deference* on their part, they were denounced by the Grand Lodge of Pennsylvania, as being unworthy of the high privileges they possessed.

Had these gentlemen been half so generous as they were determined on being just, they could and would readily have excused the blunder made by the colored Masons, when considering the relative position in the community of the two parties who then met as Committees; the one subservient to the other in all the relations of life. In all the social relations in which they had formerly met, the one was domestic and the other superior—the one ignorant and the other intelligent; in a word, the one master and the other servant.

But, I come not to plead in extenuation for the blunders—the palpable and reprehensible blunders of our colored Masonic brethren and fathers; may I not say that it served them right, and has done them good, since their too great deference for persons in certain relations of life in this country, has done as much injury in other respects than this. But that time is not *now*, neither are *we* those brethren; and they who now stand at the head of our Masonic jurisdiction, are competent and adequate to the task for which they have been selected; so that the same excuse no longer exists for the Grand Lodge of Pennsylvania. Neither would I vindictively censure our fathers, as they did very well for their day and generation; and all that they did was done for the best; they *meant* well, and that is all, at least, that I require at their hands. And now, in presence of this vast assemblage, before all the world, in the name of the Holy St. John—calling God to witness, I this day acquit them of all blame in the matter of that which they did, in admitting the Grand Lodge Visiting Committee, promising it will *never be done again!*

The second, and probably most formidable objection raised to colored Masons was, that they emanated from Grand Lodges, existing contrary to the general regulations of Masonry, in States where there were previously existing Grand Lodges.

This objection will easily be refuted, when it is considered that under the government of England, whence the general regulations of Masonry take their modern rise, for the sake of the craft, prompted by necessity, the establishment of a Grand Lodge was permitted in Scotland and Ireland; and at one time, for a short period, probably Wales; although the Grand Lodge of England extended her jurisdiction over all of these provinces.

At the time, the Scotch, Irish, and Welsh, all had certain domestic, social, and political relations which seriously forbade their identity with the Grand Lodge of England; consequently, they severally established their own jurisdictions, all of which were cordially acknowledged and sanctioned by the Grand Lodge of the British Empire. I may be mistaken about the Welsh, but as to the others, I am certain.

And can there be a greater demand for an independent jurisdiction of Masonry among the Scotch and Irish than among the colored men of the United States? Certainly not. Nothing like so great; as among them, it was a matter of *choice*, not wishing, for reasons better known to themselves, to be Subordinate to the Grand Lodge of England; while with us it was forced upon our fathers by *necessity*, they having applied to different Grand Lodges, at different times, in different States—as in Massachusetts and Pennsylvania—for warrants to work *under* them, and were as often spurned and rejected. What could, what should, or what would they do but establish an independent jurisdiction? If they desired to be Masons, they must do this; indeed, not to have done it, would have been to relinquish their rights as men, and certainly be less than Masons.

But we profess to be both men and Masons; and challenge the world to try us, prove us, and disprove us, if they can.[26]

As the *ultimum et unicum remedium*—the last and only remedy—a resort has been made to prove that colored men in the United States are *ineligible* to Masonic privileges. And among the many who have made this attack, none

---

26. The late Chief Justice, John Gibson,—as Col. J. S. of this city, a high Mason, will bear witness—when Grand Master of Pennsylvania, was known to acknowledge that the colored Masons of Pennsylvania were as legal as the whites, but intimated that it would be "bad policy" so to decide publicly. Bad policy! *Policy* in *Masonry!* and *wrong* to do *right!* Cherubim shrink back from the portals of Mercy, drooping their golden pinions in sorrow; and Justice casts down her balance, and cases her sword in despair!

In 1847, after the establishment of Star Lodge No. 18, in Carlisle, Pa., a Committee of white Masons from the white Lodge in Carlisle—working under the Grand Lodge of Pennsylvania—with the Worshipful Master at its head, visited a Committee from the colored Lodge and, after a satisfactory conference, decided that they were *legal* and worthy ancient York Masons, but never as they *promised*, made a report. The writer has met with white Masons, who have been frank enough to tell him that they had been *obligated* not to recognize nor fellowship a *colored Mason!* These were *Pennsylvania* Masons. But he is frank to say that while they are timid about *visiting*, there are hundreds who readily recognize a colored Mason wherever they *find* him, and consider it contrary to Masonry to act otherwise. [Delany's note]

stand forth with a bolder front than the honorable *Jacob Brinkerhoof* [*sic*],[27] of Ohio, ex-member of Congress, who, in an elaborate oration delivered before the Masonic Fraternity of that State in 1850 or '51, on an occasion of a Communication of the Grand Lodge, declared that no man who ever had been, or the descendant of any who had been a *slave*, could ever be a *Mason*. This coming from such authority, on such occasion, was eagerly seized hold of, and published in the news journals from Baffin's Bay to Behring Straits.[28] It may have been sport to him, but certainly was intended as death to us; and the honorable ex-member of Congress, may yet learn that he is much more of an adept in legal than Masonic jurisprudence — much better adapted to State than Lodge government. How will this bear the test of intelligent inquiry? Let us examine.

Moses, as before mentioned, of whom the highest encomium is given, is said to have been *learned* in *all* the *wisdom* of the Egyptians, and was not only the descendent of those who had been slaves, but of *slave parents*, and *himself, at the time* that he was so *taught* and *instructed* in this WISDOM, *was a slave!* Will it be denied that the man who appeared before Pharaoh, and was able to perform *mystically* all that the wisest among the wise men of that mysteriously wise nation were capable of doing, was a Mason? Was not the man who became the *Prime Minister* and *High Priest* of *Ceremonies* among the wise men of Africa, a *Mason?* If so, will it be disputed that he was *legitimately* such? Are not we as Masons, and the world of mankind, to *him* the Egyptian *slave*—may I not add, the *fugitive* slave—indebted for a transmission to us of the Masonic Records—the Holy Bible, the Word of God? What says the honorable Jacob Brinkerhoof to this? Let a silent tongue answer the inquiry, and a listening ear give sanction to his condemnation.

But if this doctrine held good, according to the acceptation of the term *slave*, any one who has been deprived of his liberty and thereby rendered politically and socially impotent *is* a slave; and, consequently, Louis Kossuth, ex-Governor of Hungary, bound by the chains of Austria, in the city of Pateya, was, to all intents and purposes, according to this definition, a slave.[29] And when he effected his escape to the United States, was (like Moses from Egypt) a fugitive slave

27. Jacob Brinkerhoff (1810–80) served in Congress as a representative from Ohio from 1843 to 1847. During the 1850s he affiliated himself with the Republican Party.

28. Reference to the body of water between Greenland and Canada and the straits between Alaska and Russia linking the Bering Sea and the Arctic Ocean.

29. The leader of the unsuccessful 1848 Hungarian revolution against Hapsburg rule, Louis Kossuth (1802–94) made a triumphal U.S. tour from December 1851 to July 1852. Antislavery groups attempted to link Kossuth's cause to the fight against slavery, but Kossuth resolutely refused to acknowledge the connection between the plight of the Hungarian and the plight of the slave.

from his masters in Austria and, therefore, by the decree of the honorable ex-member of Congress, *incapable* of ever becoming a Mason.

But Governor Kossuth was made a Mason in Cincinnati, Ohio, the resident State of Mr. Brinkerhoof, and therefore, according to him, the Governor is *not* a Mason at all. He *has been a slave!* Is the Order prepared for this? Is Mr. Brinkerhoof prepared for it? No, he is not. Then what becomes of his vaunting against colored men? for toward such he intended his declarations to have a bearing. Let the deserved rebuke of silence answer.

But was the requisition that men should be *free born,* or *free at the time* of making them Masons, intended, morally and logically, to apply to those who lost their liberty by any force of invasion and unjust superior power?

No such thing. In the days of King Solomon, as mentioned elsewhere, there were two classes of men denied Masonic privileges: he who lost his liberty by crime, and he who like Esau, "sold his birthright for a mess of pottage"[30]—a class who bartered away their liberty for a term of years, in consideration of a trifling pecuniary gain. These persons were the same in condition as the Coolies (so called) in China, and the Peons of Mexico,[31] both of whom voluntarily surrendered their rights, at discretion, to another. These persons, and these alone, were provided against, in the wise regulations concerning freemen, as Masons.

Did they apply to any others, the patriot, sage, warrior, chieftain, and hero— indeed, the only true, *brave* and chivalric, the most worthy and best specimens of mankind—would be denied a privilege, of which, it would seem, they should be the most legitimate heirs.

The North American Indians, too, have been enslaved; and yet there has not, to my knowledge, been a syllable spoken or written against their legitimacy; and they, too, are Masons, or have Masonry among them, the facts of which are frequently referred to by white Masonic orators, with pleasurable approbation and pride.[32]

But to deny to black men the privileges of Masonry, is to deny to a child the lineage of its own parentage. From whence sprung Masonry but from Ethiopia, Egypt, and Assyria—all settled and peopled by the children of Ham?[33]

---

30. Genesis 25:33–34.

31. "Coolie" and "peon" are relatively derogatory terms for unskilled laborers.

32. Many nineteenth-century Freemasons regarded the North American Indians' mythologies and arts as consistent with mystical Masonic conceptions of the Godhead. The explorer Albert Pike (1809–91) was celebrated by white Masons for having introduced Masonic practices to southwestern Indians.

33. In Genesis 9:20–27, Noah cursed his son Ham for viewing him when he lay naked in a drunken stupor. Oral traditions collected in the Talmud claim that the curse resulted in Ham having black descendants.

Does any one doubt the wisdom of Ethiopia? I have but to reply that in the days of King Solomon's renown and splendor she was capable of sending her *daughters* to prove him with hard questions. If this be true, what must have been her *sons!* A striking and important historical fact will be brought to bear, touching the truthfulness of this matter; and discarding all profane and general, I shall take sacred history as our guide.

Moses was quite a young man—and, consequently, could not have been endowed with *wisdom*—when, seeing the maltreatment of an Israelite by the Egyptian, he slew him, burying his body in the sand; when, immediately after, the circumstances having become known to Pharaoh, he fled into Midian, a kingdom of Ethiopia.[34]

He here sought the family of *Jethro*, the Ethiopian prince and Priest of Midian, in whose sight, after a short residence, he found favor, and married his daughter Zipporah.[35] Zipporah, being a princess, was a shepherdess and priestess, as all priests were shepherds; and Moses, consequently, became a shepherd, keeping the flocks of Jethro his father-in-law, watching them by day and by night, on hill and in valley. Here Moses continued to dwell, until called by the message of the Lord, to sue before Pharaoh for the deliverance of Israel.

From whence could Moses—he leaving Egypt when young—have derived his wisdom, if not from the Ethiopians? Is it not a reasonable, nay, the only just conclusion to infer that his deep seated knowledge was received from them and that his learned wife Zipporah, who accompanied him by day, and by night through hills and vales, contributed not a little to his acquirements? Certainly this must have been so; for the Egyptians were a colony from Ethiopia, and derived their first training from them; the former, as the country filled up, moving and spreading farther down the Nile, until at length, becoming very numerous, they separated the kingdom, establishing an independent nation, occupying the delta at the mouths of the river.

Where could there a place so appropriate be found for the study of those mysteries as upon the *highest hills* and in the *deepest valleys?* Is it not thus that the mysteries originated, the habits of the shepherds with their flocks, leading them to the hills and valleys?

It was also in Ethiopia where God appeared to Moses in a *burning bush*; and here where he told him, "Put off thy shoes from off thy feet; for the place whereon thou standeth is *holy ground.*"[36] And this "holy ground" was in Ethiopia or Midian, the true ancient Africa. Truly, if the African race have no legitimate claims to Masonry, then is it illegitimate to all the rest of mankind.

34. See Exodus 2:11–15.
35. Exodus 2:16–22.
36. Acts 7:33.

Upon this topic I shall not further descant, as I believe it is a settled and ac-knowledged fact, conceded by all *intelligent* writers and speakers, that to Africa is the world indebted for its knowledge of the mysteries of Ancient Freema-sonry. Had Moses or the Israelites never lived in Africa, the mysteries of the wise men of the East never would have been handed down to us.

Was it not Africa that gave birth to Euclid, the master geometrician of the world? and was it not in consequence of a twenty-five years' residence in Africa that the great Pythagoras was enabled to discover that key problem in geome-try—the forty-seventh problem of Euclid—without which Masonry would be incomplete? Must I hesitate to tell the world that, as applied to Masonry, the word—*Eureka*—was first exclaimed in Africa?[37] But—there! I have revealed the Masonic *secret*, and *must stop!*

Masons, Brethren, Companions and Sir Knights, hoping that for this disclo-sure, by a slip of the tongue, you will forgive me—as I may have made the world much wiser—I now commit you and our cause to the care and keeping of the Grand Master of the Universe.

37. Delany refers to the pre-Socratic Greek philosopher and mathematician Pythago-ras (c.582–c.507 B.C.), who spent a number of years traveling through Asia and Africa, and the Greek mathematician Euclid (c.300 B.C.). Pythagoras supposedly proclaimed "Eureka" (Greek for "I have found it") when he intuited the truth that would be codified in Euclid's forty-seventh problem, that the sum of the squares of the sides of any right-angle triangle always exactly equals the square of the line, the hypotenuse, connecting their ends ($a^2 + b^2 = c^2$). For Masons, geometrical laws and rules symbolize the power, beauty, morality, and wisdom of the Great Architect of the Universe.

Part Two.
The *North Star*

MARTIN DELANY MET William Lloyd Garrison and Frederick Douglass in August 1847, when the white abolitionist leader and his most renowned black speaker came to Pittsburgh to lead five antislavery meetings. Delany spoke at one of those meetings and made a highly favorable impression. Garrison described Delany to his wife as "editor of the Mystery, black as jet, and a fine fellow of great energy and spirit," and Douglass termed him in a dispatch to the *Pennsylvania Freeman* as "one of the most open, free, generous and zealous laborers in the cause of our enslaved brethren, which I have met for a long time."[1] So impressed were Garrison and Douglass with Delany that they invited him to speak with them at their upcoming stops in western Pennsylvania and Ohio. During this tour, Douglass talked to Delany about founding an African American newspaper that would exist independently of Garrison's *Liberator* and quickly convinced him to become coeditor of this new newspaper, the *North Star*. In accepting the coeditorship, Delany revealed his readiness to address a new and significantly wider audience than he had as editor of the *Mystery*. Consistent with Douglass's Garrisonianism, the readership that the coeditors aspired toward was a mix of black and white abolitionists committed to moral suasion as the best way to bring about the end of slavery. Douglass and Delany published the first issue of the *North Star* on 3 December 1847, and Delany would remain Douglass's coeditor until June 1849. During that time Delany contributed numerous letters and over twelve essays to the newspaper, spoke regularly at antislavery meetings about the importance of the *North Star* to abolitionism and black uplift, and remained an essential, if not terribly effective, fund-raiser for the financially struggling paper.

As editor of the *Mystery*, Delany championed black racial pride and the value of developing black institutions, such as schools, churches, and fraternal organizations. As coeditor of the *North Star*, Delany was expected to take a somewhat different approach, combining black self-help with appeals to whites and blacks alike to work not only for the antislavery cause but also for a range of social reforms. As was consistent with Douglass's moral-suasionist position at that time, he was also expected to resist calls for violence and to regard the Constitution as a proslavery document that lacked a binding force on those individuals who put their faith in "higher laws" than those found in a corrupt, man-made document. At times Delany appeared reluctant to support these Garrisonian premises. As several of his letters to Douglass reveal, he regarded black violence as a proper response to white violence; he continued to take a special interest in building alliances with black communities; and as he suggested in his discussion of the Crosswhite case (see "Western Tour for the *North Star*"), he viewed the Constitution as a flexible document that was open to interpretation.

But even as he now and again expressed differences with Douglass, it is important to emphasize that Delany made every effort during this period, particularly during his first year at the *North Star*, to find common ground with his coeditor. Though they would openly conflict with each other during the 1850s, the fact is that during the late months of 1847 and through most of 1848, Delany was for the most part in Douglass's camp. Or perhaps it would be just as accurate to say that Douglass was in Delany's camp. During the late 1840s, both of these charismatic black leaders argued for the importance of African Americans endeavoring to raise themselves socially, economically, and morally in the United States; both had a national vision of black and white abolitionists working together through moral suasion and social action to bring about the end of slavery; both saw the *North Star* as a unifying force on a national level; and both regarded the revolutionary developments in Europe as signs that revolutionary change was possible in the United States. But as hopeful as these leaders were about the possibilities of change, they retained a clear sense of the social and legal barriers that stood in the way of abolition and black uplift. Delany and Douglass were never glib in their hopefulness. They were realists who believed that almost daily activist interventions were needed to bring about the changes they desired. Theirs was an ongoing struggle that for eighteen months they saw fit to wage together.

Delany's *North Star* years are crucial to an understanding of the shape of his career, particularly the recurrence in that career of optimism about blacks' prospects for achieving citizenship and equality within a multiracial United States. The Delany who regarded the Civil War as a war of emancipation, and subsequently worked at South Carolina's Freedmen's Bureau, has close connections to the Delany who worked as coeditor of the *North Star*. As will be seen in subsequent sections of this book, particularly Part 3, Delany's *North Star* years were also crucial to his thinking about black leadership. For Delany, black leadership was centrally tied to conceptions of racial identity and pride. One of the implicit (and sometimes explicit) themes in his *North Star* writings to Douglass is that he, Delany, was the more appropriate leader of African Americans because his skin was darker than Douglass's. A leader with black skin, black racial pride, and strong connections to the black community, Delany believed, would inevitably make the most compelling case to whites about the capabilities of African Americans. Delany took pains in his 1849 and 1850 writings for the *North Star* to downplay his own desires for leadership, but clearly he protested too much. As a result of his eighteen-month coeditorship with Douglass, he ultimately did come to position himself against a man regarded by many as *the* representative leader of free and enslaved blacks. Delany's concern, which was tacitly suggested during the 1840s and then explicitly articulated during the 1850s, was that in assuming leadership, Douglass had overly accommodated himself (and the African Americans he purported to represent) with racist whites.

Although increasingly at odds with Douglass, Delany nevertheless did some of his best writing when he conceived of himself as linked with Douglass. Among the most compelling work he contributed to the *North Star* were the letters of his "Western Tour for the *North Star*," over twenty interlinked letters he wrote to Douglass between 14 January 1848 and 24 February 1849 as he toured the "West"—Pittsburgh, Columbus, Cincinnati, Cleveland, Detroit, and many other towns and cities—in search of free black subscribers for the *North Star*. From Douglass's point of view, Delany's work as a subscription agent was not particularly successful, and in the issue of 5 May 1848 he printed a piece, "To the Friends and Readers of the North Star," in which he stated that he and Delany were "reluctantly compelled to call upon you for pecuniary assistance" (p. 2). He also ran regular squibs urging Delany to return to Rochester, New York, and help with the job of actually running the newspaper (for example: "'Mr. M. R. DELANY is requested so to shape his appointments as to reach Rochester by the 1st of June. The interest of the North Star will require his presence by that time'" [*North Star*, 5 May 1848, p. 2]).

When Delany finally returned to New York in mid-August, he joined Douglass at a number of rallies and conventions, including the Free-Soil Party convention in Buffalo on 9 August 1848 and five subsequent antislavery meetings in New York State (for Douglass's account of these meetings, see "In the Lecturing Field Again," *North Star*, 25 August 1848, p. 2). But the coeditors of the *North Star* regarded the National Convention of Colored Freemen held in Cleveland on 6–8 September 1848 to be their most important engagement. Douglass served as president of the convention, and Delany served as chairman of the business committee. Overall, the delegates achieved consensus on a number of resolutions on the importance of continuing efforts at black uplift and antislavery. Nonetheless, there was clearly some friction between the coeditors when Delany declaimed against African Americans who took jobs as servants and Douglass

called for a more moderate, pragmatic approach to those blacks driven by economic necessity to assume menial positions.[2] Shortly after their relatively quiet
disagreement at this convention, Douglass printed a squib in the 15 September
1848 *North Star* stating that he and Delany would henceforth be initialing their
respective articles, an arrangement, he assured his readers, that was "adopted
solely to gratify our readers, and not because there is the slightest division of
sentiment between ourselves" (p. 2). By late 1848 Delany had recommenced
writing letters to Douglass as part of his "tour," but he had also begun to write
more expansive essays on social and political topics. Eight of Delany's essays on
black elevation, Liberia, Cuba, and other political and social matters are included in Part 2.

Delany's association with the *North Star* came to an end in June 1849. Douglass announced in the issue of 29 June 1849 that he had reached "a mutual understanding with our esteemed friend and coadjutor, M. R. DELANY" and that
the "whole responsibility of editing and publishing the NORTH STAR, will de-
volve upon myself" (p. 2). Delany subsequently returned to his medical apprenticing and practice in Pittsburgh and prepared to apply to medical colleges for a
formal degree. But he continued to read and contribute to the *North Star*, publishing several additional essays and several letters that addressed issues of black
leadership. Though he may have felt estranged from Douglass during this time,
he encouraged his fellow black abolitionists in Ohio to "rally around the *North
Star*" (see the letter to M. H. Burnham below). In 1850, however, the rift between
Douglass and Delany came openly into view with their letter exchange on Samuel R. Ward. Their angry debate on questions of race, leadership, and political
strategy presaged battles to come.

Notes

1. William Lloyd Garrison to Helen E. Garrison, 13 August 1847, *The Letters of William
Lloyd Garrison: No Union with Slaveholders, 1841–1849*, ed. William M. Merrill (Cambridge: Harvard University Press, 1973), 3:509; Dorothy Sterling, *The Making of an Afro-
American: Martin Robison Delany, 1812–1885* (Garden City, New York: Doubleday, 1971),
p. 96.

2. According to the convention proceedings, Delany proclaimed "that he would rather
receive a telegraphic despatch that his wife and two children had fallen victims to a loath-
some disease, than to hear that they had become the servants of any man," while Douglass countered, "Let us say what is necessary to be done, is honorable to do—and leave
situations in which we are considered degraded, as soon as necessity ceases" ("Proceedings of the Colored Convention," *North Star*, 29 September 1848, p. 1).

Western Tour for the *North Star*

SEVERAL MONTHS AFTER agreeing to become coeditor of the *North Star*, Delany departed on what he called his "Western Tour for the *North Star*"—a tour of the free states west of New York in search of subscribers for the financially struggling newspaper. During this stint as lecturing and subscription agent, Delany wrote Douglass twenty-three letters between 14 January 1848 and 24 February 1849 that were published in the *North Star*. All of the letters Delany wrote Douglass while on his western tour, and all of the letters he wrote during a later extension of that tour into Pennsylvania and Delaware, are included here. Taken together, these letters constitute a major African American travel narrative. A travel narrative by a free black that addresses the situation of antebellum free blacks, the letters of Delany's "Western Tour" are considerably different from the slave narratives that have come to be regarded as the representative African American texts of the period. In his letters to Douglass, Delany discusses his travels to the free black communities of what is now the Midwest, describing his visits to schools, churches, and other institutions he conceives of as central to blacks' efforts to attain moral, spiritual, financial, and political elevation. At the same time, he keeps a highly critical eye on the political developments, institutions, and racism of the dominant white culture that work to thwart those efforts. As is typical of travel writing, the letters "journey" widely, ranging from accounts of friends Delany meets along the way to meditations on a slave suicide and an analysis of a key court case. Alternately ironic, hortatory, genteel, prophetic, dramatic, and poetic, Delany emerges in these letters as a shrewd participant in and critical observer of antebellum culture.

PITTSBURGH, January 14, 1848

DEAR DOUGLASS:—I am still in Pittsburgh, getting ready, as fast as possible, to start out on my Western tour for the *North Star*. I have just begun to work here, and do something for our paper, which, as far as it has been seen, has met a cordial welcome.

The proprietors of the "Mystery," my old paper, are, as you have seen, making industrious efforts to sustain their little favorite, which they ought to do, and for which I know you will readily join with me in commending them. This they can do, by making the Mystery more of a home paper; because, in Pittsburgh, there are, alone, sufficient colored people to sustain it, if each family but do their duty.

The "Saturday Visiter [sic]," a new anti-slavery paper, recently commenced in this city, edited, by the distinguished and eccentric Mrs. SWISSHELM,[1] with the wonted ability of that amiable lady, is at present engaging the attention of the anti-slavery community and others here. There is scarcely aught else, of interest, transpiring at present, to name to you. There is, on next Tuesday, the 18th, a "Levee" to be held in Philo Hall,[2] in this city, for the benefit of the Mystery. This is the divine work of the Ladies. God bless them!

Steamboat explosions, as you have doubtless ere this seen, are most awfully and fearfully frequent. This, I opine, *must* be the result of the sheerest and most reprehensible carelessness, meriting the utmost severity of the laws, which now lie a dead letter. A person, now-a-days, taking passage upon a Western steamboat, might be viewed in the light of a child thrown upon the Ganges[3]—a victim to the element. None of these boats, however, I am proud to acknowledge, are of Pittsburgh build, but belong "below." The slaveholders make nothing good but *slaves*: these they appear to be better at manufacturing than anything else.

I was not aware, when I noticed the departure of Mr. GEORGE B. VASHON,[4] that he had been *refused* (even on examination by the committee) admittance to the bar. But, sir, this was even so: although I am credibly informed, that his able and distinguished preceptor, Hon. WALTER FORWARD,[5] made every effort in his

1. Born in Pittsburgh, Jane Grey Swisshelm (1815–84) embraced antislavery during the 1830s and in 1848 founded the *Pittsburgh Saturday Visiter*, which promoted antislavery and women's rights. In 1850, as a columnist for the *New York Tribune*, she was the first woman permitted to sit in the Senate press gallery.

2. Built in 1840, Philo Hall was Pittsburgh's first large hall for public gatherings.

3. An approximately 1,500-mile-long river in India, regarded as sacred by Hindus.

4. A distinguished lawyer and the first African American to receive the B.A. from Oberlin College, George Boyer Vashon (1824–78) worked closely with Delany in Pittsburgh during the 1840s, helping him to publish the *Mystery*. As Delany notes in his letters, Vashon, because of his race, was denied the right to take the bar exam in Pennsylvania. He eventually passed the exam in New York and became the first licensed black attorney in that state. During 1848–50, he taught at the Collège Faustin in Haiti. Upon his return, he devoted himself to antislavery activities, eventually rejecting Delany's emigrationism of the 1850s.

5. A lawyer and judge in Pittsburgh, Walter Forward (1786–1852) was one of the

behalf; but all of no avail. The infernal spirit of proscription and intolerance, fostered among a certain class, found full vent, being proven to have been nestled at the *Pittsburgh bar*; and, like the lava bursting from the crater of hell, they heaved it forth in one damning eruption, sending its fire and smoke hissing and foaming throughout the neighborhood, until a vast portion of Western Pennsylvania has become tarnished by reason thereof. Yes, sir, this is true. The judge, Walter H. Lowrie, Esq., of the District Court, before whom application was made to sue out a rule of court to show cause why Mr. Vashon was not examined, assigned as his reason, that Chief Justice Gibson, of Pennsylvania, had decided against colored people being citizens; therefore *he* would never consent thereto.[6] This, truly, was the decision of Judge Gibson; an insult upon our manhood which all true men hold in utter contempt.

Mr. Vashon, on his tour, stopped in the city of New York; and, as I learn by a recent letter, was on the eve of an examination before the Supreme Court in that city; and, ere this, probably has been admitted to practice.

What a contrast between the smoky Iron City, and the Gothic Metropolis of the Nation! A burning stigma, an indelible disgrace, is this, upon the once liberal, but now retrograding Pennsylvania! But to measure Pittsburgh, or I may even say, the entire state of Pennsylvania, by this miserable example, would be gross injustice.

The example of the medical faculty, alone, would have been sufficient to have taught the apostate disciples of Justin[7] a lesson; and the editorial corps, as well as many other respectable professions I could mention, even here, in our midst, all put, most palpably, these colorphobites of the Pittsburgh bar, to the blush.

David J. Peck, M.D.,[8] is doing well in Philadelphia, having a fine office in "In-

---

founders of the Whig Party during the 1830s. In 1849 he was named chargé d'affaires to Denmark by President Zachary Taylor.

6. In 1838, a Pennsylvania state constitutional convention ruled that blacks were not "freemen," as defined in the 1790 state constitution, and therefore could not vote; that ruling was upheld by white voters in October 1838. The rulings by Walter H. Lowrie (1807–76) and Chief Justice John Bannister Gibson (1807–76) took as their precedent that change in the state constitution. In his attack on Gibson, Delany may also have been referring to his ruling on *Prigg v. Pennsylvania* (1842), in which the Pennsylvania Supreme Court upheld Congress's Fugitive Slave Law of 1793, denying Pennsylvania the right to develop its own legislation on fugitive slaves.

7. A reference to the Byzantine emperor Justinan I (483–565), who codified Roman law and came to be known as a founder of legal history and practice.

8. The son of the Pittsburgh black abolitionist John Peck, the physician David Peck was active in antislavery circles during the late 1840s. Early in 1850 he met Delany in New York City and, embracing his plan of black emigration to Central America, chose to spend several years as a doctor and politician in San Juan del Norte before returning to Pennsylvania in the late 1850s.

stitute Buildings," where he is receiving the calls and attention of the most polished practitioners and professors of the medical schools. This is as it should be,
and shows most conclusively that *law* has as much to do with the hideous monster, slavery, as medicine, or any other respectable business.[9] And it is a fact, well
worthy of remark, that, other than that of law, any combination with slavery is
considered a blighting disgrace to the participants. How stand the law, then, and
lawyers, when favoring the oppressor! I know that you will answer, They are
supporters of tyranny and despotism.

I will write you once a week.

Yours, in behalf of our oppressed and down-trodden countrymen,
M. R. D.

(*North Star*, 28 January 1848, p. 2)

PITTSBURGH, January 21, 1848

DEAR DOUGLASS:—I promised to give you weekly advices of my movements, whether or not there were anything of interest to communicate.

On last evening, there was an interesting meeting held in Temperance Hall,[10]
a place well known to you, to continue the measures previously entered into, for
the relief of Dr. Mitchell,[11] of Indiana, Pa., a prominent Anti-Slavery friend of
the Liberty Party,[12] who was most unrighteously mulcted in the heavy sum of
fifteen hundred dollars, for no other crime under heaven than that of feeding the
hungry, clothing the naked, and giving shelter to the outcast. Nay, not so much

9. In the 3 March 1848 *North Star*, Delany remarked in a listing of "ERRATA": "In my
first letter, I intended to say, *Law* had *more* to do with slavery than another honorable
calling" (p. 2).

10. A hall in Pittsburgh, at the corner of Smithfield Street and Diamond Alley, regularly used for lectures on temperance and other social reforms.

11. In a case of November 1847 before the Circuit Court of the United States for the
Western District of Pennsylvania, Garrett Van Metre of Virginia sued Dr. Robert Mitchell
(1787–1863), an antislavery activist from Indiana, Pennsylvania, for harboring one of his
fugitive slaves in April 1845. The jury found in favor of Van Metre and awarded him $500.
(In the 3 March 1848 *North Star*, Delany noted in a listing of "ERRATA": "In my second
[letter], speaking of the sum fixed by the Congress of '93, it should read $500, instead of
$1500, as made by the compositor. There were three slaves in the Mitchell case; hence the
sum of $1500 extorted from Dr. Mitchell" [2].)

12. Founded in 1840, the Liberty Party was an antislavery political organization. In
1844, the party's presidential candidate James C. Birney polled 60,000 votes; by late 1848,
the party had merged with the Free-Soil Party.

as this: the Doctor did but permit the weary, outcast creatures to live in an old log cabin on his farm—he employing them to labor. By a despotic act of Congress in '93, this is made a penal offence;[13] and the daring slaveholder may lay his claim at $1,500—the sum fixed by law—and recover the same in any State, even North of Mason and Dixon's line.[14] And yet we are told by the pro-slavery minions, that "the North has nothing to do with slavery!"

The unblushing effrontery and daring impudence of the slaveocracy of this mock-republic, have really become alarming. Whither shall we go for succor?

My kind friend, Mrs. SWISSHELM, of the *Visiter*, was there; by her counsel and smiles, rendering aid and succor.

You have before this seen the announcement of the admittance of GEORGE BOYER VASHON, Esq., at the Bar of the Supreme Court of the State of New York. This is a rebuke to the Bar of Pittsburgh, for which there is no palliation.

Upon this subject, Greeley, of the Tribune,[15] has a word of withering rebuke to Pennsylvania. By the way, Greeley is a noble-hearted fellow; his only objectionable characteristic being the unerring fidelity with which he clings to that arch slaveholder, Henry Clay.[16] But for this, Greeley would be unexceptionable.[17] It would seem, that such is Greeley's love for Clay, that were he to fasten his monster grasp on him and his, he (Greeley) would still essay to justify him, on the ground that it must be right, or he would not have done so. . . .

Liberia, the creature of Colonization, as you have seen, has declared her independence, (for which I commend her, that is, provided she is determined to exist without a *master* and *overseer*,) and for this, she is lauded to the skies as an evidence of the capacity of the colored man for self-government.[18] The proud

13. A reference to the Fugitive Slave Law of 1793, a forerunner of the Fugitive Slave Law of 1850.

14. Running between Pennsylvania and Maryland, the Mason-Dixon line was surveyed by Charles Mason (1730?–87) and Jeremiah Dixon (1733–79) between 1763 and 1767. By the early nineteenth century, the line was taken to mark the boundary between the free and slaveholding states.

15. Founder of the *New York Tribune* in 1841, the influential Whig leader Horace Greeley (1811–72) emerged during the 1850s as a significant antislavery voice, opposing the Kansas-Nebraska Act of 1854 and eventually calling on Lincoln to emancipate the slaves.

16. Congressman, nationalist, and perennial presidential candidate from the slave state of Kentucky, Henry Clay (1777–1852) was one of the principal architects of the Compromise of 1850. He helped to found the American Colonization Society and served as its president from 1836 until his death in 1852.

17. Delany probably meant "unobjectionable" here, or "exceptional."

18. Founded in the early 1820s by the American Colonization Society, which sought to ship U.S. free blacks to Africa, Liberia became an independent republic in 1847. However, many Liberians maintained close ties with American colonizationists.

little Republic of Hayti has for the last fifty years fully demonstrated this truth;[19] yet our *quasi* philanthropists are so *far*-sighted, that this fact is too near and apparent to come within the reach of their vision.

I see that you and Mr. Nell, as well as our dear friend Remond, have been fortunate in being among the chosen of the great Gerrit Smith.[20] For this I am well pleased, as I do not think that his generosity could have been extended to any more meritorious.

The scintillating rays of the NORTH STAR, are just beginning to beam on the west; which brightens the horizon with cheering hopes.

Yours, in behalf of our oppressed and down-trodden countrymen,
M. R. D.

(*North Star*, 4 February 1848, p. 2)

PITTSBURGH, January 28, 1848

DEAR DOUGLASS:—Since I last wrote, nothing of interest has transpired. Anti-Slavery seems to be at a low ebb in this county; at least if present appearances are a test of the reality. We cannot get up a meeting of any considerable number here; nevertheless, the true and real friends of the slave stand firmly to their integrity. . . .

The scheme, now freely and openly discussed, concerning the incorporation of Mexico with the United States, is a project the most frightful and monstrous within the pale of human conception.[21] And even Dr. Bailey, of the *Era*,[22] and

19. Following its bloody rebellion (1791–1803) against French colonial authority, Haiti emerged as an independent black republic in 1804.

20. President of the New York Anti-Slavery Society and a founder of the Liberty Party, the philanthropist and abolitionist Gerrit Smith (1797–1874) during 1847–48 donated 140,000 acres in upstate New York to approximately 3,000 black settlers. Most of the recipients of Smith's gift found the land impossible to cultivate. William C. Nell (1816–74) was a Boston-based black abolitionist who worked closely with William Lloyd Garrison and Frederick Douglass; Charles Lenox Remond (1810–73) was a pioneering African American abolitionist, best known for his work as a lecturing agent for William Lloyd Garrison's Massachusetts Anti-Slavery Society.

21. The Mexican War of 1846–48 was precipitated by the U.S. annexation of Texas in December 1845, and resulted in the United States gaining approximately 40 percent of Mexico's former territory.

22. The *National Era* was an antislavery weekly published in Washington, D.C., by the New Jersey–born abolitionist Gamaliel Bailey (1807–59). Bailey serialized Harriet Beecher Stowe's *Uncle Tom's Cabin* in the *Era* from 1851 to 1852.

some others who call themselves Abolitionists, favor and contend for a consummation of this project. They argue that it will facilitate the overthrow of American Slavery, and forsooth, bring the Mexicans under a more settled and stable government.

But what are the facts in the case? But a glance will suffice to show the fallacy and duplicity of this whole nefarious scheme.

Mexico is peopled by *ten millions* of inhabitants; but fifteen hundred thousand, or three-twentieths of whom are whites, the rest, seventeen-twentieths, or seven and a half millions, are Indians and mixed colors—from the black to the fairest quadroon. According to the *Christian* usages, laws and customs of this *free* republic, no colored person—that is to say, black, mulatto, or Indian—is eligible to the privileges secured to and enjoyed by the whites. Such being the case, should this high-handed project succeed, while it might in reality speed the overthrow of slavery, as such, in the South, yet in doing so, would bring with it degradation and servility to nearly eight millions of freemen, heretofore enjoying the rights and privileges of a free and equal people, common to all, of whatever origin; while but one and a half million would retain those rights, enjoyed in common heretofore by all! And this is what we are asked to subscribe to! How superlatively devilish is this whole scheme! Nay, rather than this, let all Mexico be engulfed in the horrors of an earthquake! . . .

The North Star comes, to the pleasure and approbation of all who receive it. I am receiving many letters from the West, in which it is hailed as a great beacon-light, wherever it has cast its refulgence. I hope soon to be on my Western tour, and wish you to say to our Western friends, that they may all be prepared for subscription, as I shall give them a general visit. I shall hold at least one meeting every place I go, if I can get an audience, although I shall make my stay very short in each place. I omitted to mention in my former correspondence, that the cause of my long silence was owing to indisposition in my family, at which time I am little prepared for writing, especially when fatigued, at the bedside of a tender and interesting child.[23] You shall hear from me soon again.

Yours, in behalf of our oppressed and down-trodden countrymen,
M. R. D.

(*North Star*, 11 February 1848, p. 2)

---

23. An infant daughter, born sometime after Toussaint L'Ouverture Delany (b. 1846), who would die several months later (as reported in his letter to Douglass of 15 April 1848).

PITTSBURGH, February 6, 1848

DEAR DOUGLASS:—I am now a constant recipient of our luminary, the North Star, and find it all that I could desire—a paper of vast interest and usefulness—and I pray you, as I know you will do, keep it so; with its present character as a liberal, high moral, antisectarian, independent, unyielding and uncompromising enemy to that most blighting of all curses, and "abominations of abominations"—Slavery. Whether shielded by the statutes of despotism and tyranny, covered by the sarcedotal garbs of a miserable and false religion, or guarded by the point of the bayonet, it must be a terror to the evil doers of our land, and the beacon-hope of the bondman. . . .

There was held in this city, in the Lafayette Assembly Rooms, on Tuesday last, a mass Clay Meeting, of course to enter into measures preparatory to the nomination of the "Sage of Ashland."[24] It was a full meeting, and you must not think it strange to hear me so express myself about Whiggery,[25] when I assure you that I never attended a meeting, not even Anti-slavery, in which more consistent and greater truths were uttered, by all speakers, concerning the character of their favorite, than did the speakers at this meeting express concerning Mr. Clay. Every orator who mounted the rostrum, declared that he *is the embodiment of Whig principles*. Is this not true to the letter? Who dare dispute it?

The Daily Post of this city, the sub-Government organ, has become the "Deputy bloodhound," and whining spaniel for its Southern masters. The editor has recently been to Washington City, crouching at the feet of his Southern superiors, and has probably received from them, or the hands of that miserable old man, Ritchie, of the Union, the Privy Counsellor of James K. Polk, a right to be the watch-dog and principal hound in this region, on the running trail after fugitive men and women, fleeing from the cruelties of American slavery.[26] This same Daily Post, in the face of a church-going and professedly religious community, in open daylight, under a glaring noon-day sun, and the disapprobation of high Heaven, dares to advertise in the columns of his paper, a *Reward for*

24. A sarcastic reference to Henry Clay, who hailed from Ashland, Kentucky.

25. A reference to the American Whig Party, which was founded in 1834 in opposition to Andrew Jackson and the Democratic Party. Henry Clay was the Whig's most prominent leader. The Whigs committed themselves to national entrepreneurial projects, valuing the legislative over the executive branch.

26. In 1845, with the support of President James Knox Polk (1795–1849), Thomas Ritchie (1778–1854) of the Richmond *Enquirer* purchased the *Globe*, a paper published in Washington, D.C., changed its name to the Washington *Union*, and made it into the house organ for the newly elected president and the Democratic Party. Because of its support for labor, the Pittsburgh *Post* was regarded as the most progressive daily in Pittsburgh, despite its position on fugitive slaves.

Runaway Slaves! and these persons, too, having been brought into the State by the steamer Grey Eagle, from which they escaped. There were three of them, two of whom escaped; who, by a late act of Assembly, were free the moment their foot touched Pennsylvanian soil.[27] But were they taken, justice to them could not be expected, since it appears that the Judges of the Pennsylvania Courts, with a few honorable exceptions, are but the *pledged* minions of the slave power in this country. How contemptibly servile—how disgustingly crouching, is the conduct of these men of the Post, who have fully proved themselves capable of the meanest and lowest set of pimping! They have consigned themselves to that infamy which all such creatures merit, as nobly and fearlessly shown by the respective notices of the daily papers, especially the Dispatch, and Telegraph, of this city.[28]

In this animadversion, you may account me severe; but while the fact exists that the infernal monster, Slavery, has its ponderous grasp upon the throats of mothers, sisters, and wives; that ourselves, old men and children, are but stall-fed cattle for the market; that the denuded persons of the female are daily exhibited in the Southern markets and public places; that the groans and cries of the degraded millions are hourly sent up to Heaven for deliverance; that one-sixth of the whole *American women* are subject to the brute will and lust of five-sixths of American men; and that the object of these worse than land-pirates was to bring back those flying, panting victims to this wretched condition; can I—dare I—speak in any other than thunder tones upon this subject? No, no!—not I. You being my helper, and God the mainstay of us both, I will never cease to cry aloud, and spare not, until you, and I, and every wronged and oppressed son and daughter of America and the world, stand up in the living image and dignity of manhood, in the full possession of all those rights and privileges common to our nature, made sacred by the God of Love! Tell me, when the ruthless slaveholder has fully prostrated before him his struggling victim in the person of my wife, mother, or sister, piteously crying, "Help! help!" that I should stop to address him with a kind of formal politeness or placid arguments, lest I only aggravate him and fail in my effort? Do you subscribe to doctrine such as this? Tell this to others, but tell it not to me. Should I not arrest his outrageous grasp, by any effective means within my power, in which the laws of Nature's God would justify me?

27. The Pennsylvania State Legislature passed an act of 1847 that made it a criminal offense for state officials to enforce the federal fugitive slave law of 1793.

28. Founded in 1846 and known for its independence, the Pittsburgh *Dispatch* was the first successful penny paper in the west. The *Telegraph* had a considerably smaller circulation.

I regret to see that rather wrong-spirited allusion, concerning the North Star, which appeared in the last number of the "Mystery;" there being no just cause for such a thing.[29] I simply notice this matter, that it may correct a wrong impression, which might arise from it. One thing is, however, certain. All who are acquainted with you and me, certainly, if they know anything of us at all, know us to be incapable of meriting that reflection.

Your "charge" upon the Mexican War, and comments upon the Colonization speech of Henry Clay, are a triumphant vindication of right against wrong; truth against falsehood; and of the undefended against the vilest malignity.[30] To use a homely figure, you completely "floored your man." Do you know, Douglass, that you have been grappling with one who possesses attributes known to no other human being—attributes which render him truly "God-like," as his admirers declare him to be? This can be illustrated to a demonstration, and the great embodiment proved to be a Trinity. He is the embodiment of Colonization, the embodiment of Whiggery, and the embodiment of Slavery. Is he not a very Deity?—and how little were you aware with whom you struggled!

I see that our good friend Joseph Cassey,[31] of Philadelphia, has gone the way of all flesh. I concur with you in sympathy with his amiable widow and interesting family for the loss of so good a friend as he; but his relict and children have been left well provided with the good things of this life. This, Mrs. Cassey merited, as her name was always among the first of those untiring friends of the slave, who so assiduously labored for the Anti-Slavery cause.

I prefer thus to give you a summary of passing events, than one long article on the subject of Slavery; as I know full well that you will attend to that particular department, and that, too, with the pen of a ready writer.

Yours, in behalf of our oppressed and down-trodden countrymen,
M. R. D.

(*North Star*, 18 February 1848, p. 2)

---

29. That issue is not extant, but one imagines that the editors of the *Mystery* remained upset about Delany's departure for the *North Star*.

30. See Douglass's "The War with Mexico," *North Star*, 21 January 1848, p. 2, and his "Henry Clay," *North Star*, 28 January 1848, p. 2.

31. A native of the French West Indies, Joseph R. Cassey (1789–1848) came to Philadelphia in 1808, where he soon embraced a number of antislavery and moral reform causes, such as the black convention movement and the American Anti-Slavery Society. He served on the board of managers of the society from 1834 to 1837.

PITTSBURGH, February 19, 1848

DEAR DOUGLASS:— . . . The Underground Railroad is in high flight, and doing a fair business here; and while I write, a panting fugitive enters my room, in company with a brother, seeking aid and advice. Of course I immediately sent the brother out for aid. He returns—a ticket is obtained—and another moment, and he is on his way rejoicing!

"Ho, the car Emancipation,
Rides majestic through our nation!"[32]

The Whigs have another long and loud call for a candidate meeting in this city. Scott is the choice of this call. What in the world they intend doing with all their nominees, they only know. There is also a suggestion for a Taylor meeting. It is thought that there is not much difference between the Clay and Taylorites, as the aim of both parties seems to be to support a *slaveholder* at all hazards.[33] "When a house is divided against itself, it cannot stand."[34] I am in hopes that the Whigs will stand long enough to overthrow the pro-slavery Democrats, then fall themselves, never more to rise, until this whole slaveocratic nation shall have become regenerated.

The Mexicans, it would appear, are not yet conquered; so far is this from being the case, that they, if army reports are at all reliable authority, have now in the field an army of 90,000 able-bodied men, ready to make, or receive any demonstrations which may be made upon them. It is true, there are rumors of peace, but all without the shadow of a foundation; so, without doubt, there is fighting yet to be done in Mexico;—nay, without a speedy issue of peace, the struggle is scarcely begun.

Hayti, according to foreign reports, is now in quite a prosperous condition. The President[35] is very popular with the people, and all departments of the Government harmonize.

32. From "Get off the Track!" (1844), composed and performed by the "Singing Hutchinsons," a popular family of antislavery singers from New Hampshire.
33. Henry Clay had been the Whig presidential nominee in 1844. In 1848, the Whigs nominated general Zachary Taylor (1784–1850), who was celebrated for his victories in Monterrey and Buena Vista during the Mexican War. He won the election but served only a little more than a year as the twelfth president of the United States before his death in July 1850. Another hero of the Mexican War, General Winfield Scott (1786–1866), was considered for the the Whig presidential nomination in 1848 and received it in 1852, losing to Franklin Pierce.
34. Mark 3:25.
35. Faustin-Élie Souloque (1782?–1867); see note 83 below.

I see that that most infamous personage, O'Donnell,[36] Governor of Cuba, is to be succeeded by one whose cup of iniquity, [it] is to be hoped, will never equal in fullness that of this man. O'Donnell is one of, if not the largest African slaveholder in the world, and next to Pedro Blanco,[37] the wretched proprietor of the slave factories on the coast of Africa, is the greatest slave trader living. Perhaps there is not a slave of the hundreds which sail out of Cuba, that is not partly owned by O'Donnell. So wealthy has he become by this infernal traffic in human beings, that the crown of Spain is alarmed at his influence over the Colony. He is the same, it will be remembered, who, when the Memorial from the World's Convention, for the abolition of slavery,[38] went forth, invoking the immediate action of the crowned heads of Europe, and the sovereignties of the world, in aid of the great cause, declared, "that though an act were passed by the Cortes Councils, sanctioned by the Sovereign, for the abolition of slavery in the Spanish Colonies, he would never, while acting as the Chief Magistrate of that Island, permit such an act to take effect there." This stand was taken by him in an official proclamation to the slaveholders of Cuba.

It may be well, in this connection, to name the fact that Trist, who is now in Mexico, as the Representative of this Republic, endeavoring to treat with an Anti-Slavery nation, is also a slaveholder, and the same who, as the resident Consul of the U.S., endeavored his utmost to effect the re-enslavement of the Amistad captives.[39] Trist is a fast friend of O'Donnell, and also enters, it is said, and I doubt not the report is correct, largely into the foreign slave-trade. His immediate interest is in the barracoons or slave factories of Cuba, and instead of being, as he now is, in Mexico, the representative of a nation making high pre-

36. The Spanish general Leopoldo O'Donnell (1809–67), a notorious slave trader, served as governor of Cuba from 1844 to 1848.

37. The Cuban Pedro Blanco (1795–1854) set up slave trading "factories" in Africa during the 1820s and by the late 1830s had a network of factories on the Gallinas and along the region's coast. To market the slaves, he had headquarters in Havana, agents in Puerto Rico, Trinidad, and Texas, and bills of credit established in London and New York. His firm failed in 1848.

38. The World Antislavery Convention was held in London in the summer of 1843.

39. In July 1839, the fifty-three enslaved Africans on board the *Amistad*, a Spanish slaver, violently rebelled against the white masters, took control of the ship, which had illegally sailed out of Cuba, and sailed into the high seas. The ship was seized by the U.S. navy off Long Island, New York, and the case eventually came before the U.S. Supreme Court. In March 1841 the Court granted the rebels their freedom, and abolitionists subsequently helped to finance the blacks' return to West Africa. Nicholas Trist (1800–1874), U.S. consul in Havana from 1833 to 1841, supported Cuba's efforts to regain control of the rebels. At the time that Delany wrote this letter, Trist was chief clerk of the Department of State and had been sent to Mexico to negotiate an end to the Mexican War. On his own, he negotiated the Treaty of Guadalupe Hidalgo.

tensions to justice, he, by their own laws, the act of Congress, 1808, should be branded as a felon and pirate. If we except Pedro Blanco and O'Donnell, there is no one who is more our enemy than Mr. Trist. . . .

England, at present, is the master-spirit of the world. Her every example is to promote the cause of Freedom; and had she possessed the same principles during the revolutionary period, in every place that she possessed, slavery would have been abolished. Hence, slavery in this country could not have stood; for the slave once tasting freedom, all the powers of earth and hell could not have reduced him again to servitude.

But how with France? She is a slaveholding power, deeply engaged in human traffic, favoring and fostering the institution of slavery wherever she holds the power or influence; and with the able politician and learned statesman, Guizot, at the helm of affairs, the cause and progress of liberty would be retarded for years.[40]

Yours, in behalf of our oppressed and down-trodden countrymen,
M. R. D.

(*North Star*, 3 March 1848, p. 2)

NEW LISBON, O[hio], March 22, '48

DEAR DOUGLASS:—Here I am. I left Pittsburgh, after an effectual settlement of my business and domestic affairs, on Monday, the 13th inst., on my western tour for the North Star. . . .

I am now, as you know, in the region of the "Anti-Slavery Bugle," a well-conducted paper, under the editorial management of our kind friends, Benj. and Elizabeth Jones.[41] I shall leave this morning for Hanover, thence shape my course South-westerly, touching the most important places and settlements of the friends of humanity, both white and colored, until I reach Cincinnati. I have had a loud call to this city—I am in hopes it will not be in vain.

I have met thus far in my travels, with courtesy and kindness, the friends invariably keeping me clear of expense, and wherever I stopped at hotels, I fared, as common sense would have it, equally with the others.

40. The conservative François Guizot (1787–1874), who became premier of France in 1847, was overthrown in February during the Revolution of 1848.

41. A Garrisonian antislavery newspaper published in Salem, Ohio, by the Western Anti-Slavery Society, the *Anti-Slavery Bugle* (1845–61) was coedited by Jane Elizabeth Hitchcock Jones (1813–96) and Benjamin S. Jones (1812–62) from 1845 to 1849, and again from 1859 to 1861.

Of all the places I have as yet visited in Ohio, I find New Lisbon to be the most under pro-slavery influence. There are, it is true, some noble spirits here, such as the Garretsons, and others whom I could name; but, aside from these, there is an assumed mock-aristocracy, who endeavor to mould everything to suit their own caprices; and such is the influence they exert, that what is termed the "poor men," or common men, in walking along the streets, look and act the very slave. For instance, a respectable looking strange colored man, is assailed and assaulted on every side as he passes through the streets, with all manner of low and disparaging epithets, and those who do it, like spaniels fawning upon their masters, look about towards the doors of the stores and offices, to receive the grinning approbation of the hidden inmate, who, too proud to do the dirty work himself, sits or stands within the doors, and commands his miserable serfs without.

So prevalent is this serfdom of prejudice, that there is scarcely a child in the place able to lisp a name, but it flips out disparagement against the colored stranger—even the children of some who call themselves abolitionists. This proves, that such persons are so crushed with the prevailing influence of the place, that they readily yield to its base mandates, rather than fall victims to the odium consequent upon a contrary course. There are, however, but few such, as the majority of the abolitionists here, especially the Friends, are themselves wealthy, and (aside from their abolition) influential, and above the influences in question.

There is here a Sewing Circle, but few in number, though great in acting and the good they effect. I expect much good to the slave and the cause of bleeding humanity, to be effected by the efforts of these good Ladies. God bless them! Notwithstanding petty prejudices, this is a great field for Anti-Slavery labor, and I had a very large meeting, though there were several important meetings in session, together with a night session of the court, upon a very interesting case. Of course this manifests a desire on the part of the people to search after anti-slavery truths. Considering that this place is the seat of the county court house, you may not wonder at the servility of the lower classes, because where there is in this country the most law, there is the least liberty. . . .

Having now made a beginning, I shall, while on my tour, give you weekly advices of my whereabouts.

Yours in the cause of God and humanity,
M. R. D.

(*North Star*, 7 April 1848, p. 2)

HANOVER, O[hio], March 27, 1848

DEAR DOUGLASS:— . . . Yesterday, a wagon load of us, male and female, some eight persons altogether, went some distance into the country, where we held a most effective Anti-Slavery meeting in a private farm-house, where were collected a crowd of intelligent people, of all sexes and ages, to sympathize with the suffering slave. Coming back, we were completely drenched in the rain, when some one observing the fact—"What is that," answered one of the females, "to the sufferings of the downtrodden bondsman?" Sure enough, what was it compared with theirs?

I have, up to the present, been treated like a man, without exception, at every hotel at which I stopped since travelling in this State (Ohio.) At New Garden, the proprietor of the hotel, Mr. Ayer, while I stopped, kept my horse, and otherwise treated me with kind favors, and refused to take pay. The friends of the slave are many in this place, and like all other places where I have visited in this State, I myself staid among them. I shared, in this instance, the hospitality of our friend Pickens.

There is some hope of my leaving here today for Augusta, where I am to hold a meeting to-morrow evening. From there I proceed to Carrolton, Leesburg, Cadiz, New Athens, Georgetown, Lloydsville, Concord, Zanesville, with all important places and settlements, to Columbus, thence to Cincinnati, from whence I shall be able to give you another description of my course. In and about this neighborhood there are several colored families, all of the most respectable and praiseworthy kind. They are generally farmers. Of them I shall have occasion here-after to say much more.

Yours, in behalf of our oppressed countrymen,
M. R. D.

(*North Star*, 14 April 1848, p. 2)

COLUMBUS, April 15, 1848

DEAR DOUGLASS:— . . . In the neighborhood of Hanover and the Cyrus Settlement,[42] there are a good number of colored residents, the most of whom are new settlers, but all industrious and respectable, the greater part farmers, and some mechanics among them, doing a good and promising business. The principal mechanics are carpenters and house joiners, and stone-cutters and ma-

---

42. A Quaker settlement near Columbus, Ohio.

sons; and I invariably find that the farmers and mechanics among our colored brethren, command the same civil respect of their neighbors that others do. Their sociability is carried out to a much greater extent than possibly could or would be the case under other circumstances. It is no unfrequent occurrence for the colored residents to receive the civilities of their white neighbors to attend parties and weddings, and *vice versa*; while in other capacities, such as doing their inferior domestic offices, they are neither noticed nor thought of. I wish to heaven that our brethren would see this matter as they should. . . .

There are a large number of respectable and well-doing colored people in Columbus, some quite wealthy, among whom are many good mechanics, who find constant employment and plenty to do. Several are proprietors of business, and others find no difficulty in getting employment among their white fellow-citizens. The most prominent of these tradesmen are shoemakers, carpenters, painters, of whom there is a very large number, plasterers, bricklayers, and several others. There are many owners of real estate in the city, decidedly more for the size of the place and number of the people, than any place I have ever yet visited. These things speak well for the spirit and industry of the colored Columbians, and I have been thus explicit in naming them, because, in my judgment, they are among the essential means by which, as a nominally free but oppressed people, we are to be elevated. We *must* become mechanics—we must become tradesmen—we must become farmers—we must be educated if we ever expect to become elevated, even after we have gained our liberty. I do not desire it to be thought that I look upon these things as essential to liberty and freedom as such, as a fundamental basis, but I wish to be distinctly understood when I repeat that they are essential to elevation. Whatever is necessary for others, is necessary for us. These things are necessary for the elevation of others, therefore they are necessary for our elevation. I would that our people could be made sensible of these facts, and fewer of them would be found in the domestic departments of hotels and private families, as a matter of choice, than there now are.

I should have stated that there are a number of persons in this city who own good farms in the country.

The cause of education among them is not so forward as I could wish, but they are generally intelligent, having two or three good common schools, supported mainly by themselves, the odious provisions of the infernal black-laws[43] prohibiting a large portion of the colored children from a participation in the

43. Ohio's notorious black laws, which dated back to the early nineteenth century, drastically abridged blacks' civil rights and contributed to racial segregation in "free" Ohio. See Douglass's blistering attack, "Ohio Black Laws," *North Star*, 10 March 1848, p. 2.

benefits of the State school fund, as provided by law. The last session of the Legislature made a kind of provision, which is so pro-slavery in its character that I consider the chances worse than before. It has completely shut the door against the colored people for years. The act provides that where there are less than twenty colored children in any school district, they may enter the same school in that district with the white children, enjoying all the privileges of the school, provided there is no objection on the part of any white tax-payer, or any person sending his children to the same school! In a word, there must be an unanimous consent of all the tax-payers and parents who send children in that district, before a colored child can be permitted to go. In all cases where there are over twenty colored children, they must have a separate school, with their own directors and teachers, when the State will allow to be appropriated the amount of school tax assessed on the number of colored residents in that district to said colored school, which assessment, I have learned on inquiry, in the school district in the State, will be sufficient for the education of one dozen of children one quarter!

With the present prejudices of the whites, according to this act of the Legislature of Ohio, cannot every one see that no colored children will ever be educated in the common schools of Ohio? The tendency of the act is to deceive the common people, and lull to an indifference the colored people themselves, and the friends of freedom and equal rights, by inducing them to believe that equal justice had been done to the colored people. Let their acts of wickedness and despotism be exposed upon the house-top, until they shall learn to respect the rights of man, and administer equal and even-handed justice to all.

The females among the colored people, also many, are doing their part. There are two teachers, and many seamstresses among them, who make their livelihood by their profession. This also is praiseworthy. The population of Columbus is 10,000 souls; colored 1,000, or one-tenth of the whole city. Anti-Slavery appears to be at low tide here, except among the colored people, and even some of them are pro-slavery. This, however, in the main, I look upon as more the effects of ignorance than wickedness. They require anti-slavery light doubtless.

Monday, April 17th.—Visited the Blind Asylum; Superintendent, Mr. McMillen. This gentleman has recently taken charge of the institution, and is quite polite. The inmates number 68 pupils—young women and men, lads and lasses. Among them, and decidedly the most attractive and intelligent, is Lucinda Shaw, from Pickaway county. She acted as my guide and conductor, (this being her office,) taking me through all parts of the Asylum, showing me everything connected with it. One would scarcely believe with what facility she trips from room to room, and apartment to apartment, telling to a certainty what is carried on here and what there, pointing out the different articles, distinguishing their quality, and naming their prices. When ascending or descending a stair-way, especially the latter, I invariably found myself far in the rear, and her wait-ing at the threshold for my arrival! She sang for my entertainment, and played sweetly upon the piano. Her singing was painfully effective—her first air being the "Rose-bud,"[44] some of the words of which lamented its being "nipped in the bud," coming as it did in the instant of the reception of the intelligence of the death of my dear little daughter, appeared like piercing my heart with a *golden* spear, or riddling my breast with *precious* stones! It seemed as though the inno-cent and unconscious young Lucinda, selected that song intentionally. It was painfully singular how I enjoyed it. I would that she had sung it again, and yet I would that she had not sung it at all. The institution is well-conducted, well-furnished and handsome; the pupils all well dressed, clean and cheerful. But whatever the other merits of this institution, the poor blind colored youth can find no sympathy there.

This evening, delivered a lecture before an institution of colored ladies and gentlemen. Tomorrow evening to lecture in the Colored Methodist Church.

Tuesday evening, April 18th, lectured in the colored Methodist Church, to a tolerable audience. There is some pro-slavery among the colored people here, and, I am fearful, not the best of union. But of this I may probably speak again. I leave for Circleville and Chillecothe.

Yours for God and humanity,
M. R. D.

P.S.—There has been a fall of snow, and a cold north-westerly winterly blast. Great fears for the fruit.

M. R. D.

(*North Star*, 28 April 1848, p. 2)

CHILLICOTHE, April 20, 1848

DEAR DOUGLASS:—I arrived here from Columbus to-day, after holding two meetings among the colored citizens alone, having vainly endeavored to effect a meeting among the citizens of the place generally. When upon the eve of leav-ing, I was informed by a gentleman, that provided I staid another day, a meeting could be effected. But my time being precious, and having already spent suffi-

44. In all likelihood, a reference to the popular song "The Virginia Rose-Bud; or, The Lost Child."

cient in the place, I could not consent. I am of opinion, that the failure in the first place was more the effect of timidity on the part of the applicants than anything else.

For want of room in my last, I omitted to mention some incidents peculiar to the National Road,[45] which came under my notice, traveling from Lloydsville to Columbus. . . . Although I have met with enough to rebuke in almost every place I have visited, yet have never met, nor did I expect to meet, with anything like the miserable truckling to the slave-power, and low servility manifested at most every house upon the road, and in every town through which I passed. Indeed, I cannot permit myself to believe that there is in either Asia or Africa, short of the most consummately ignorant, and degradedly barbarous, a tribe or clan of heathen that can be found, among whom a stranger, of whatever nation or clime, would not meet with more civility, than a colored person—at least than I received from Lloydsville to Zanesville upon this "National Road," and that, too, a road which is one of the greatest highway thoroughfares in the country— a thoroughfare along which people of all kinds and grades are continually passing. There is a manifest depravity on the part of many of the people in this country, which, if it be not speedily remedied, will as is now apparent militate greatly to the detriment of the National prosperity. It is the reckless disregard of the rights of individuals that causes the tottering fabrics of nations to fall. This constant and unmitigated rioting upon the rights of man cannot continue forever. No! there is a just God in heaven, and His justice cannot forever sleep.

Aged men and women, young men and maidens; yes, young *ladies* and *gentlemen*, (or those who pass for such;) the mechanics in their shops, the farmer in the field; all, as if by a single truth of magnetic influence, along the whole road, were continual participants in these scenes of moral and civil outrage. Hallowing, disparaging, and frequently vulgar epithets, gestures, the pointing of the finger full in one's face, and such like, and even in several instances throwing stones and blocks, are among the indignities a colored person meets with from these National Road turnpike American Republican Christians! Respectable looking women, standing in the doors of fine-looking houses, would call out, full in one's hearing, "Come, here goes a *nigger!*" when a swarm of little children would answer to the call, who, poor little dears—the manner which they spread their innocent little mouths and showed their teeth manifested evidences of great emotion for the absence of their mother's *brains*. I should be recreant to the cause I have espoused, did I fail to rebuke this insufferable despotism, which

45. Constructed over several decades beginning in 1815, the National Road extended from Cumberland, Maryland, to St. Louis, Missouri, and was championed as an "internal improvement" that linked the states and encouraged western emigration.

only requires the permission of law, to come forth in all its hideous deformity, and terrible consequences. I, and not you, am alone responsible for what I write. . . .

There are quite a number of respectable colored mechanics in Chillicothe, all industriously employed; also, a large number of free-holders; and more farmers round about in this neighborhood than I have ever yet met with. This is highly creditable to the colored inhabitants, and will do more towards elevating us, than all other human efforts this side of Mason and Dixon's line.

I would observe that altogether the young society in this place is not quite so commendable now as when I visited here four years since. There are some most excellent exceptions to this; but there is great room in general for improvement. There does not appear to be the general intelligence here now that there was then, though the manner in which they, as well as the old people, crowded to the churches, attentively listening to discourses upon their moral elevation, certainly manifested the greatest desire to gain information. There are now no good schools—indeed, no school at all for colored youth in Chillicothe; and upon the heads of the authors of the abominable Black Laws let the execrations of outraged humanity rest. It should be borne in mind that all the schools, or nearly so, among the colored people of Ohio, are supported at their own private expense, while they are shamefully and tyrannically compelled to pay taxes for the education of the whites.

There are some rare spirits among the young men and women, who are endeavoring to get an efficient library, to supply them with useful information, and improve their time and talents. I have appointed here, as in Columbus, male and female agencies for the North Star.

Of those ladies and gentlemen who render me service, I will write more particularly hereafter. I leave in the morning, *en route* for Cincinnati.

Yours for God and humanity,
M. R. D.

(*North Star*, 12 May 1848, p. 2)

CINCINNATI, May 7, 1848

DEAR DOUGLASS:—I arrived here on this day week; and have held four meetings on as many different evenings, in two of the churches, all of which meetings have been attended by crowds of anxious listeners. . . .

There is quite a large population of colored residents in Cincinnati, I suppose about 5,000. Among them there are many families of wealth; and among the young people in particular, there is much intelligence. There are several young men here who have talents of the very highest order, oratory and poetry being familiar themes in their literary course, and many young women who would be an ornament to any society. The intelligence of the more youthful of the children, is particularly attractive, many of them giving the promise of an intellect which, if properly cultivated, may beam forth in future with brilliancy. The young men and women generally, who are the most intelligent and the best qualified, are mainly indebted for their qualifications to their own exertions. This is highly praiseworthy, and commends itself to every lover of the human family. Still, the young people, as such, especially the young men, have not in general come up to that standard of duty which the three millions of American slaves, and six hundred thousand nominally free colored people of the non-slaveholding States, so loudly call for and imperatively demand.

The young people, I have said, do not keep pace with the spirit of the age, though there is much to commend among them. The aged generally are the capitalists, but not having had in their youth the advantages of education, cannot make much investment, and enter into such enterprises with their money, as are necessary for the advancement of society. This, of course, is the legitimate business, and expected of their sons and daughters. Now if their children manifest no such inclination, but, on the contrary, appear indifferent to the import and insensible of the advantages to be derived from such a course of domestic enterprise, it is apparent that there is much cause for censure or reproof. . . .

Anti-slavery is but a *beggarly* element in this region, and, save a few exceptions, in which our friends of the [Cincinnati] Herald are included, an Eastern anti-slavery man might well suppose himself to be in Kentucky. Of course, in this I except the colored residents, who, while they are all anti-slavery, have not, as yet, given the subject, aside from its political aspects, any or much thought. I am pleased to see the readiness with which the greater part admit the truthfulness of our position, and subscribe to many of our views; and while many believe in the ballot-box as one of the most effectual means of attaining the great end sought—the overthrow of the infernal system of American slavery; yet they do not hesitate to acknowledge that moral suasion is accomplishing, practically, what it will take ages for politics to do—that is, social equality. . . .

There is now here a Rev. Mr. King,[46] formerly of Scotland, who fell heir to sev-

---

46. Educated at Glasgow University, the Irishman William King (1812–95) immigrated to the United States in 1833 and soon after married the daughter of a Louisiana plantation owner, thereby acquiring several slaves. During the 1840s he was ordained into the Presbyterian clergy, and when Delany first met him he had manumitted his slaves and was in the process of moving to Canada to begin missionary and antislavery work there.

eral slaves, men, women and children, and who determined on settling them in Canada on land of their own, and has arrived thus far on his way, in company with them, and has held several meetings in the famous Dr. Rice's church.[47] Being constantly engaged, I have not had time to hear him or to see his people, which I design doing if possible.

The Ohio river is very high just now, and commerce brisk.

Yours, for God and Humanity,
M. R. D.

(*North Star*, 26 May 1848, p. 2)

CINCINNATI, May 20, 1848

DEAR DOUGLASS:— . . . There are various mechanics among the colored people [of Cincinnati], some of whom are doing fine business. Among them I perceive extensive smithing establishments, many carpenters, shoe-makers, bricklayers, plasterers, and, indeed, most of the mechanical trades, amply demonstrating our capacity to take care of ourselves. There are among the respectable mechanics, none who stand more conspicuously than Henry Boyd,[48] frequently spoken of, and whose name is widely known among abolitionists. His establishment is on the corner of Sycamore and Eighth streets, and is quite an extensive furniture manufactory. He gives constant employment to eight or ten hands in his establishment, and sells off his furniture as fast as they can make it. Bedsteads are the staple article, and these rate in price from $8 to $125. I saw in his furniture rooms some of the finest articles. Mr. Boyd, a few years ago, as you have noticed, was a slave; and now is not only able to take care of himself, but give constant employment to some five or six white men, (as well as a number of colored, there being both employed,) thereby enabling them (the white men) to "take care of themselves." Mr. Boyd, I believe, takes no active part among the colored people. This I regret, as he might be very useful. He is a subscriber to the North Star. . . .

King is best known for establishing the Elgin settlement, a highly successful black agricultural community in Canada West. King supported Delany's African project during the late 1850s.

47. Nathaniel Lewis Rice (1802–77), author of *Lectures on Slavery Delivered at the First Presbyterian Church Cincinnati* (1845) and *Ten Lectures on the Subject of Slavery* (1855).

48. Born a slave in Kentucky, Henry Boyd (1802–86) bought his freedom and moved to Cincinnati, where he invented the Boyd Bedstead, a corded bed, which he patented in 1833.

There is a fine school taught here by Mrs. Eleanor Thomas, (formerly Miss Henderson,) a young lady of acquired accomplishments, a student of Oberlin.[49] Mrs. Thomas has some 50 or more pupils in her school, all colored, of course, and as she is herself of the proscribed race, does credit to it as a literary teacher.

The High School, formerly under the charge of Rev. Hiram Gilmore,[50] I did not find in the condition I expected. Aside from the location and arrangement of buildings, I was disappointed in many respects. The principal school-room is above the True Wesleyan Church, a fine building of medium size, on Harrison street, entrance from the back yard. For the purpose of making room, an adjacent back building has been erected, but these, as well as the main apartment, have its access by a flight of high stairways from the yard, which reduces the story to a mere loft comparatively. I should have no objection to this arrangement, had it been the result of necessity; but knowing, as I do, that it was selected as a matter of choice, and that, too, in the neighborhood of so many preferable spots that might have been obtained, as the purchasers had ample means, I cannot but give my disapprobation to the selection of the place, as not at all being such as would have been made by any person who had in charge a High School for white children, instead of colored. The location is an out-of-the-way, back-ground place, and appears as though it were chosen to hide the pupils from public view. If it be argued that there would have been a difficulty in obtaining a more eligible spot for such a purpose, I answer, that the success would have been as probable as that of the colored Orphan Asylum, in a fine central part of the city, and many of the colored churches.

The former pupils of the Cincinnati High School are not what I expected to find them. I here most cheerfully admit that there has been some progress on the part of many, several little misses having learned music—an excellent accomplishment; and two or three youths, on whom particular pains has been taken, qualified to some extent in the useful branches of a business education; but the most of them have learned comparatively nothing. Instead of a substantial qualification, such as I expected to find in these pupils, a respectable knowledge of the elements of science generally, sorry am I to say it, that the most of those that I have seen and examined, know but little about those branches of education.

Composition, or the correct construction of sentences, appears to be foreign

49. Founded in 1833, Oberlin College, in Oberlin, Ohio, became a center of abolitionist activity beginning in 1834, when students at Ohio's Lane Seminary left the school to protest the trustees' support for colonizationism and enrolled at Oberlin. It was one of the few colleges in the antebellum period that enrolled free blacks.

50. The Reverend Hiram S. Gilmore established a school for blacks, the "Cincinnati High School," in 1844; it was discontinued in 1854.

to the former pupils of this High School. Many of them now, after having "finished" (!) their education, as it is termed by many, when putting their hand to paper, write as though there was no such letter as a capital I. This I much regret, and it would appear as though the greater part of the time of the pupils was spent in preparing for exhibitions, which of course make great displays of seeming qualification, whether or not there be anything real. I am borne out in this opinion by the display of music on the part of many of the little misses, the whole of whom play the same pieces, and when done with these, go no farther. Besides, the parents of several of them quaintly observed, that their daughters were rather indifferent about music, although they had great talents for it, (and certain, I can say they have in reality,) but the secret of the matter was, that these misses had been taught for the purpose of exhibiting in the school, and so soon as they have done with their exhibition exercises, all is done in the main.

I expect here to meet a rebut on the part of the friends of the school, but cannot help it. My mission is to assist in the elevation of the oppressed and downtrodden of our land, in order faithfully to do which we must speak the truth and expose error, and this I shall do, though the "heavens fall."

I wish it not to be thought that I would not award to Mr. Gilmore what is due him — far be it from me, and I disclaim all or any such intention. I thank Mr. Gilmore, most heartily thank him, for the motives which prompted him, but really think that he fell far short of attaining the object of his project, or even adopting the proper method for his attainment. In the estimation of Cincinnatians generally, it was a very good colored school; viewing it in the light of a colored school, it probably was very good, not having it in my power to determine what qualifies a *colored school*; but one thing I do know — it was very far from being a good school. . . .

The colored citizens of Cincinnati have a fine cemetery, which was consecrated with ceremony by Rev. Samuel Lewis, on the 8th inst. I was to have spoken also on the occasion, but by some mishap, did not arrive in time, but like the foolish virgins, found the "doors closed"[51] when I arrived; or in other words, the ceremony over, and the people coming away. This truly is a lovely spot, two and a half miles from the city, on a beautiful Macadamised road, leading North. It was purchased by a company of gentlemen of the "United Colored American Association," laid off in several hundred family lots, with a reserved tract for promiscuous interments. This is a most praiseworthy undertaking on the part of the colored citizens; and how shameful the necessity of a separate burial-place for the dead! America is drinking a double draught of infamy!

A most heart-rending occurrence took place in Covington, Ky., opposite this

51. See Matthew 25:1–12.

city, on Friday morning last, as follows: A slave-holder named Mullin, back of Covington, in Grant county, sold to an infamous soul-driver, by the name of Rust, a man, woman and child, who were placed in Covington *slave-prison*—for such it is in reality—for safe keeping, previous to his going down the river. By some means the parents learned that their darling babe, but twenty months old, was to have been left behind. The frantic and heroic mother—God bless her!—asked her husband for his pocket-knife, which was very small—cut the throat of her child—held her neck to her husband while he deliberately cut her throat—then—O! yes, then like a man and a hero, deliberately cut his own throat, but owing to the smallness of the knife, did not succeed in quite taking his own life. A noble woman!—more deserving of fame than the Queen of the Amazons, or a Semaramis—worthy, thrice worthy to be associated in history with the noble wife of Asdrubal!—Most noble man!—a Virginius![52]—the manly and heroic deed that thou hast perpetrated shall live in the heart of every true friend of humanity and lover of liberty! God grant that thy spirit may take its flight to realms beyond this nation of oppressors and land of slaveholders, robbers of the dearest social ties, and ruthless despoilers of the most sacred family connection! The names of the three whose precious lives were offered as a sacrifice on the hallowed altar of liberty and virtue, shall become the theme and panegyric of the poet, when those of the two infamous dealers in human flesh shall only be remembered to be despised and derided.

Do you call this severity! "Oppression maketh man mad!"[53]

I leave here on Monday morning for Ripley, the residence of that faithful philanthropist, Rev. John Rankin,[54] where I shall hold two meetings on Monday and Tuesday evenings; returning back again on Wednesday, holding a meeting here on that evening, which I expect to be my last; after which, I shall pursue my course in a Northern direction through the State, visiting the best places in my route.

Yours, for God and Humanity,
M. R. D.

(*North Star*, 9 June 1848, pp. 2–3)

---

52. A mythical Assyrian Queen, Semiramis killed her husband, Ninus, founded Babylon, and vanished from earth in the shape of a dove; the wife of Asdrubal, a Carthaginian general, chose to kill herself and her children (according to Herodotus) when Carthage was destroyed by the Romans in the fifth century B.C.; the daughter of the Roman knight Virginius (as recounted by Livy and Chaucer) commanded her father to behead her after she had been raped by Apius, the governor of their province.

53. Ecclesiastes 7:7.

54. The Presbyterian minister John Rankin (1793–1886), author of *Letters on American*

CINCINNATI, June 4, 1848

DEAR DOUGLASS:—I send you my last epistle from this city for the present. Since I last wrote you, I have held several meetings, all of which, like the preceding, were full of interest, by the presence of numerous anxious listeners— the ladies as usual, forming the largest part of the assembly.

I have also been to Ripley, 50 miles above Cincinnati, in Brown county, where I held one meeting in the church of the famous Dr. John Rankin, long and favorably known to the friends of humanity in this country as a firm friend of the panting fugitive. His house has been made the resting place for the way-worn and weary for years, to the great chagrin of the slaveocrats of his neighborhood, and the slaveholders of Kentucky. One friend informs me, and it certainly appears like an over-estimate, that he has known as many as forty to be there at a time! "packed away" in the underground depot. This depot, as a matter of course, is not in the house of Dr. Rankin, but situated in a cavern about two miles south, of the whereabouts of which none but abolitionists are aware. This accounts for the great mistake on the part of the soul-seekers, who frequently, or at least have at different times, by brute force, entered the house of this aged gentleman, when they knew him to be unprotected—his eldest son being absent, and none but children and females at home—in search of their victims, but without success. 'Twas well it was the house of Rev. John Rankin they dared enter, and not some I wot of—yes, very well! . . .

I return again to Cincinnati, in which place I find many things of interest. . . . The young women of Cincinnati, of the colored class, are far in advance of those of any other place that I have visited. Nearly the whole of them have trades, and have continually as much employment as they can attend to. Those who are not employed by others, and do not employ, take business into their own houses, and thus gain a respectable livelihood, with all the advantages of domestic comfort and social happiness. There is scarcely such a class to be found as colored servant girls in Cincinnati, from the fact that nearly all have trades. The white girls, such as those of "oriental" extraction, are the complete monopolists of female menialism in this city. Nor do the young women find any difficulty in getting employment in establishments controlled and owned by white persons. There is one establishment, in particular, perhaps the largest and finest in the city, for the manufacture of linen and corsets, and all kinds of linens and muslin gowns, where there are some twelve or eighteen young colored women, constantly and profitably employed. How many places may be expected

---

Slavery (1833), became legendary in antislavery circles for establishing his home in Ripley, Ohio, as one of the main stops for fugitive slaves on the Underground Railroad.

to follow the praiseworthy example of the young colored ladies of Cincinnati? Cannot every place measurably come up to this standard? Determination and self-resolution only are necessary—determination to do—to "act, act, in the living presence act."[55]

To an already elevated, and refined, and enlightened people, there might appear, in this notice and encomium upon mechanics, tradesmen, and the course of the young colored women, scarcely aught to applaud or merit notice in an editorial correspondence; but when it is borne in mind that we are but in a primitive State—a people, as it were, who, like the ancient Greeks and Romans, when visited by the *literati* and philosophers of Africa, are just beginning to receive the germs of enlightened civilization; then the appropriateness of the course will readily be acknowledged. A practical precept of one sentence is worth a page of unintelligible jargon. The elevation of our race in general, and class in particular, is the ultimatum of our aim, and whatever respectfully and honorably contributes to this end, is among the means to be used for its accomplishment. I cannot agree with some writers, that great matters, or in other words, great things, expressed by great words, are alone worthy of great minds, or the notice of great persons. We are a small people—occupy a small sphere—constituting a small number compared with those by whom we are surrounded; also, the greater part of whom, at present, have but a small conception of things. Now, to my mind, the greatest effort that can be made is, to suitably adapt ourselves to their understanding, imparting to them a correct knowledge of things, though the language may appear homely and void of refinement, but proper. You know I care little for precedent, and therefore discard the frivolous rules of formality, conforming always to principle, suggested by conscience, and guided by the light of reason. . . .

I leave on Monday for Dayton.

Yours for God and humanity,
M. R. D.

(*North Star*, 16 June 1848, p. 2)

MILTON, O., June 18, 1848

DEAR DOUGLASS:—I have, since my last letter, held meetings in Hamilton, Dayton, Springfield, Troy, and Milton, the place from which I now write, all of which, with the exception of one place, (Springfield,) were well attended. In Hamilton, by some mistake, my notice did not reach the persons to whom it was

---

55 Henry Wadsworth Longfellow (1807–82), "A Psalm of Life" (1838).

directed, hence no meeting was in readiness when I arrived; but the colored citizens who had heard of my coming, although it was sun-set when I arrived, immediately got up a good meeting, several of whom subscribed for the Star after
the lecture. They are few in number, but the most intelligent, industrious, and
spirited people, for the size of the place, of any with whom I have met. Their
taste and style of living, is worthy of example—the neatness and cleanliness of
their handsome little cottages being among the most prominent features of
their praiseworthiness. Of all things in this world, for heaven's sake, give me
cleanliness. Let circumstances be what they may, I see no good reason why people may not be cleanly about their houses and with their persons; but it is a fact,
much to be regretted and unsparingly reproved, that a great many families, of .
humble pretensions, and others, too, residing in many of those country towns
and villages, almost entirely neglect the observance of both. There are a number
of respectable farmers in this neighborhood, and some good mechanics round
about the place.

From Hamilton, I went to Dayton, which place I reached at sunset of the day
that I was to speak. It will be scarcely necessary for me to state that this is a very
pro-slavery community, as it has been long known for the mobocratic spirit
which in former days prevailed in the place. . . .

Dayton is an inland city, of above thirteen thousand inhabitants, and was
originally settled by wealthy Kentuckians, some of whom even brought slaves
with them; hence, it was hard and difficult to overcome these human flesh-
mongers. The preponderance, however, of the population are descendants of
Pennsylvania Dutch, who are infinitely worse than Kentuckians. The inter-
spersing of the population with New Englanders and New Yorkers, has made
Dayton the place of civility that it now is.

I had a good meeting and attentive audience of ladies and gentlemen on this
evening, but in consequence of the anxiety of the people to hear, the church
being thought too small, the City Hall was proposed for the next evening, which
was also filled with an attentive assemblage of intelligent listeners.

June 8th.—Lectured again in the City Hall, which was filled to the utmost capacity, vestibule and aisles, which, when thus filled, is said to contain about
eleven hundred people. Like the former, this meeting was equally listful and attentive, breaking up in the best of order and apparent satisfaction. I have been
since informed, that a very good impression has been produced in Dayton. Our
good colaborer, Henry Bibb,[56] lectured in Dayton one week previous to my

56. Born a slave in Kentucky, Henry Bibb (1815–54) escaped from slavery in 1841, settled in Detroit in 1842, and became a prominent antislavery lecturer and writer. His *Narrative of the Life and Adventures of Henry Bibb* was published in 1849. Following the passage of the Fugitive Slave Law, he fled to Canada and there established the antislavery
weekly *Voice of the Fugitive* and promoted black emigration to Canada.

coming—a place where he has several times previously spoken, and [been] much admired; but whatever merit there is in Mr. Bibb, they have always found it very applicable to attribute it to his *whiteness*—that is, they say that his talents emanate from the preponderance of *white* blood in him. This it will puzzle them to say of me!

On Thursday afternoon and evening of the 8th, I held good meetings in the Hall, the meeting in the evening being a very jam. . . .

Monday 14th.—Lectured in Troy to a good assemblage of ladies and gentlemen in the Town Hall. . . .

In and about this place, reside a portion of the Randolph people,[57] driven by mob violence from the land purchased for them near Pickaway. Here resides the wife and daughter of the old and faithful groom of John Randolph, Juba Taylor—known as Juba. She is new married to a nephew of her former husband, Juba, who calls himself Rial Randolph, and who is evidently several years younger than his wife and aunt, Cecilia Taylor, the wife of Juba. She possesses that kind of intelligence that the wife of an illiterate slave, like Juba, might be expected to possess. Susan is the name of Juba's daughter, who is about 16 years of age, and said to be the image of her father. If so, Juba was a pure Guinean, small features and intelligent expression. His wife informed me that he has been dead some six or seven years, and denies that he could either read or write, and all say that John Randolph would not permit a slave to be taught to read. These people generally are very ignorant, though some of their children have learned to read during the short time they have been in Ohio, and that, too, under the most disadvantageous circumstances.

I met here a rare genius in the person of a little boy, but fourteen years of age, by the name of Simon Foreman Laundrey, a natural Phrenologist,[58] who examines heads, reads out the organs, and delivers lectures on the science. He has had but comparatively little schooling, and what his qualifications are I do not know; but he speaks properly, and his examinations compare well with experienced and competent professors of the science of phrenology. Of course he is defective yet, but if care be taken to give him an education, some day he will be at the head of his profession.

57. The Virginian political leader John Randolph (1773–1833) was a fiery advocate of the doctrine of states' rights and the owner of one of Virginia's largest slave plantations. Nevertheless, he went on record opposing slavery, and in his will he freed his slaves, stipulating his executor to purchase land in a free state where his former slaves could reside in an agricultural community. The executor purchased 3,200 acres in Mercer County, Ohio, to be divided among Randolph's approximately 350 ex-slaves. When they moved there, the blacks met with a hostile reception; many then moved to Milton, Ohio.

58. Influenced by the theories of the Viennese physician Franz Joseph Gall (1758–1828), antebellum phrenologists claimed that they could determine character traits and mental faculties from the shape of the human skull.

The little genius lectures also on Dentistry—the anatomy, physiology and disease of the teeth. He informed me that he is preparing a work of some 50 or sixty pages, which he expects to bring out "after harvest," on the "Geography of the Brain," which is to be the title of his work.

He offered his services to examine my cranium, and passed his little hands over the organs, reading them with as much facility as Fowler or Melrose.[59] I advised this child to travel through the country, in company with his mother or some other adult relative, which from the novelty of his age and all the connecting circumstances, would secure him a patronage, from the proceeds of which, in a few months, he would gain sufficient to educate himself at Oberlin, or some other literary institution. His father resides at Harrisburg, O[hio], a poor man, a blacksmith by trade, having a family of several children, none of whom, says Simon, save himself, appear inclined to literature, or manifest more than ordinary intellect.

On Friday, I held a meeting in the M.E. Church at Milton, according to previous notice, which was full and attentive. I lectured again on Saturday (yesterday) evening, the 17th, to a good audience. In the morning, I went out of Milton about three miles, to a settlement of the other part of the Randolph people, whom I addressed in a kind of bush meeting, in the woods, where a number of them, of all ages and both sexes, collected together with many of the white neighbors. We adapted our discourse and language to their comprehension, speaking to them with the most childlike simplicity. Mr. C. H. Langston,[60] a talented young colored gentleman, who volunteered his services to travel with and assist me for a while, was in company, and also spoke to them.

Here I met with a brother and uncle of John White, the old and faithful page of John Randolph, known as his man John. John White, becoming discouraged—as well he might—at the outrages perpetrated against himself and comrades in Ohio, left the State and went back to Virginia; but the laws or ordinances not permitting him to remain in that State, his people inform me, he has removed to Philadelphia, where, I have since been informed by a gentleman, who says he has good authority for saying that he is busily engaged narrating the Life of John Randolph, for some Virginia historian, who is preparing to bring out the life of this singular man—the "Lord of Roanoak." What John is

59. The brothers Orson Fowler (1809–87) and Lorenzo Fowler (1811–96) popularized phrenology in the United States through their wide publications, such as *Phrenology Proved, Illustrated, and Applied* (1837); Melrose is obscure.

60. Born a slave in Virginia, Charles Henry Langston (1817–92) gained his freedom in 1834, attended Oberlin College, and had an important role in the antislavery movement. He participated in the Liberty Party and Ohio Anti-Slavery Society and edited the antislavery journal *Palladium of Liberty*.

to receive for his services, I have not heard, but hope he is to be properly recompensed.

These people generally appear much more intelligent than those at Troy, and several of their children also read. All, however, readily join in saying that John Randolph was a "good master." If these poor, ignorant, dejected and degraded people are—and they most surely are such—the evidences of a good master, or slaveholder, in the name of heaven, what must be the condition of those generally who claim no such character for the "master?" God protect the poor bondman of America! ...

There is a school taught among the Randolph people in this settlement, by Lucy Coates, an amiable young lady of the denomination of Friends. This I conceive to be quite self-sacrificing on the part of Miss Coates, as she could do much better by teaching other schools. There are some few white children [who] go to this school, it is true, but the greater part by far, are of the Randolph people, who are very poor, having been cheated out of the legacy left them by Mr. Randolph. They have nothing now but what they earn by hard labor; this portion of them being by far, if there can be such a difference, the most intelligent and in the most comfortable circumstances; those near Troy, ten miles distant, appearing quite dissatisfied and dejected. And no wonder they should be so, as it appears to be familiar to all that at the death of Randolph they were to obtain their liberty and fall heir to his estate. Thus have they been robbed and cheated, and why should they not be dejected? I would not appear uncharitable, but I am disposed to believe, viewing all the circumstances, that there was collusion between the parties in the purchase and sale of this land for the Randolph people. It will be remembered that after the purchase, immediately at the instance of an attempt on the part of the people to settle on their land, bought and paid for, the mob was raised, composed of the very men from whom the purchase was made; and singular that during all this imposition and outrage on the part of these Ohioans, we see neither executor nor agent enter litigation in the case, but like good peaceful Christians, fold their arms, and express their regret at the occurrence. And be it further remembered, that so soon as the people are effectually repulsed, discouraged and scattered, those who rejected them, immediately waive all objections, and invite them to come and settle on their lands.

And what then? Why, no sooner is this done, than the executor refuses them permission, for the reasons I have already stated! What means all this? Remember what I now predict—the secrets of this nefarious transaction will yet be revealed.

I am aware that I shall be subject to censure, by both friends and foes, for the course I have pursued in thus liberally expressing my opinion; but as I have taken my stand as one of the sentinels on the watch-tower of the liberties of our brethren, I never intend to leave the ramparts, nor suffer an approach of the enemy unmolested, until my colors first be grounded in the hands of the fallen helpless victims, who dared, in the midst of a tempest of oppression, such as now surrounds us, stand upon the citadel, and unfurl its proud drapery to the gaze and dismay of the enemies of our race, and the dearest rights of man.

I shall leave here to-day, in order to meet those two great conventions to assemble at Columbus on the 21st and 22d. The one, an independent gathering of all parties favorable to the nomination of a Northern man, opposed to slavery, for the Presidency; immediately after which a State Liberty Party Convention meets. These are important movements, and as I am but a day and a half travel from the point of meeting, and shall rather gain than lose in the new route, I shall proceed thence; from whence, I shall proceed through the most available places to the Mercer and Shelby settlements, *en route* to Detroit.

The peach and plum crops have failed in all the southern states of Ohio, but all other fruits appear abundant. Grain is fine—the corn crop is great, and oats promise all that is desired.

Yours, for God and humanity,
M. R. D.

(*North Star*, 7 July 1848, pp. 2–3)

SANDUSKY, July 1st, 1848[61]

DEAR DOUGLASS:—I have arrived thus far on my journey from the two great Conventions—the one an independent gathering of the people, irrespective of party ties and basis, opposed to the regular nominees of the Baltimore and Philadelphia Conventions, Cass and Taylor;[62] the first a most unscrupulous pro-slaveryite; the second, an unconscionable slave-holder—and the Liberty Party Convention, which took place immediately on the adjournment of the Independent. . . .

I cannot countenance and tolerate in Liberty men that which I have ever condemned in the old conservative parties; and I shall say here, as I have and shall ever say elsewhere, that I hope that our Liberty party brethren may never lose

61. The letter's date is printed incorrectly in the *North Star* as "June 1st, 1848."
62. Lewis Cass (1782–1866) was the nominee of the Democratic Party for president, and Martin Van Buren (1782–1862) was the nominee of the Liberty Party; they were defeated by the Whig's Zachary Taylor.

sight of the fundamental and primary object of their party, at least of Anti-slavery organizations; because so soon as they become conservative, they cease to be the friends of the oppressed, and, like the other parties, stand as despots and tyrants, resting in very indifference, with their horrible weight upon crushed and outraged humanity. I earnestly entreat our Liberty brethren, in their deliberations, to think and say more about the slave and the *condition* of the free colored people. If these be discarded—if, as I have heard it asserted, these form no essential part of the Liberty party—if, indeed, these form not the foundation upon which rests the Liberty temple—then let it, with the other parties, be scattered to the four winds of heaven, and by every colored person loathed as a monster in disguise, like the "Liberty boys" of seventy-six, only requiring power to carry their designs into execution. But we must, and shall hope and believe differently, until the contrary be fully proven; and then, and not till then, shall we lift up the battle-axe in vindictive warfare against it. But our friends, if they desire our co-operation or approbation, must not forget or neglect our interest. This is imperative. We have been duped and cajoled now quite sufficient. . . .

Wednesday the 28th.—This evening, after sunset, I arrived in a small village of between four and five hundred inhabitants, called Marseilles. On entering the street, I found a number of persons, who, from their appearance, looked as though they were among the principal men of the place, "pitching quoits"[63] in the centre of the principal street. As soon as I was discovered, they suspended their sport, all, or nearly so, to the hotel at which I stopped, as usual in those country places West, being attracted there by the novelty of strangers, yet apprehended nothing more than usual in such cases. I was soon, in a polite manner, questioned by the proprietor of the hotel, whom I found to be a Liberty man, who, suspecting our mission, and who had attended the recent Columbus Convention, and withal a very clever man. Finding who I was, and learning my mission, a meeting was immediately proposed by this gentleman, whose name, neglecting to note down, I have since forgotten.

Consultation being had with several persons, especially one person pretending to be an abolitionist, who sat in the room with us, making many inquiries about Douglass, Garrison and Remond, arrangements were effected, and a meeting determined upon. The house being lighted, in a few minutes, as it was now dark, Mr. Langston and I went off to the place of meeting, the school house. On passing along the streets, the side-ways were strung along with young men, lads and boys, among whom were those who were the most eager for the meeting, and had lighted up the house, who, as we passed, scoffed and used disrespectful language, falling in the train immediately behind us and close to our

---

63. A game much like horseshoes, played with flat rings of iron.

heels, until we entered the school-house, which we found empty, with the exception of some three or four respectable-looking men, who appeared as if they came for the sake of the meeting. We had barely entered the house, when they came pouring in, boys and men, to the number of perhaps forty or fifty, looking ready and eager for any and every mischief. To this, however, I make the exception of about half a dozen gentlemen, among whom are included our host of the hotel, and a book-binder, who sojourned at the same house. When on our way to the school-house, I turned back for a copy of the paper, Mr. Langston stopping by the wayside to wait for me, who being so light in color, that many of them mistook him to be what is called "white": hence, he had a favorable opportunity to hear their schemes and language concerning us. On my return to Mr. Langston, he immediately related to me what he had heard, peremptorily refusing, in consequence of the disrespectful spirit manifested and the conduct of the persons present, to speak at all on the occasion.

I rose up, and in a respectful manner declined to speak under the circumstances. The house, it is true, was quiet, and may have, for aught I know, remained so until I had finished a long discourse, at least, until some position was taken which displeased them, when, from what really followed, it would not then be difficult to determine the consequence. The host of the hotel, and one other gentleman, whose motives, there is no doubt, were the best, hoped that I would give them a lecture, they having no idea of the cause of my refusal. Instanter, a man rose up, the identical person who had previously, Judas-like, manifested at the hotel such friendly feelings, and observed: "I move that we adjourn, by considering this a *darkey* burlesque!" This was but food for the rabble; all leaving the house, with a loud shout of "darkey burlesque!" and this repeated continually, with many other epithets of disparagement, until we reached the hotel.

But nothing less than a MOB would satisfy these craven wretches. They had come to the meeting with the full intention, and were now ready to destroy us, by the aid of "any hand that would administer to their wrath and second their vengeance." The more effectually to accomplish their object, a brass drum, tamborine, clarionet, violin, jaw-bone of a horse, castanets, and a number of other instruments, or whatever would tend to excite and rally a formidable mob, did these miserable outlaws resort to.

The crowd, which consisted well nigh of all the men and boys in the neighborhood, who were able to throw a brickbat, being now assembled, "the tar and feathers" were demanded, with a tone which told forcibly the determination with which they intended carrying out their threats. A tar barrel was procured, and after many yelps and howls which rent the air around, they succeeded, in the course of some twenty minutes, in staving in the head. But it appeared that this barrel had been too closely drained of its contents, and as the village was but small, there was none other in the place, as the barrel was obtained from the principal store, directly opposite the hotel, which place was the general head-quarters of the rowdies for the night. Failing to find tar sufficient in which to saturate us, they resorted to another expedient, which they were certain would have the desired effect.

A torch was brought, and the tar barrel set in a flame, when store boxes were piled upon it, which produced a fire that must have been seen several miles around. The fire was built in the middle of the street, directly opposite the hotel in which we staid. Then came the cry, "Burn them alive!—kill the niggers!—they shall never leave this place!—bring them out!—rush in and take them!—Which is their room? Niggers! come out, or we will burn down the house over your heads!" A consultation was held, the result of which was, that they would rush into our room, drag us out, tie and hand-cuff us, and take us immediately to the South and sell us! declaring that I would bring "fifteen hundred dollars, cash"! Turning to a blacksmith in the crowd, they asked him whether he would make the "hand-cuffs," he, slavelike, answered, "yes, any moment." This, I would observe, was the language of men, and not of lads and boys, who formed no in-considerable part of this gang of rowdies. Our position was such that we could look down upon them, reconnoitre their every movement, and hear all that was said. This position we occupied with as much coolness and deliberation as though nothing was transpiring below, fully determined not to leave it only with the loss of our life. We had done nothing worthy of such treatment, and, therefore, under no circumstances, could submit to personal violence. My friends may censure me—even both of us—for this, but we cannot help it. We are not slaves, nor will we tamely suffer the treatment of slaves, let it come from a high or low source, or from wherever it may.

Then came the most horrible howling and yelling, cursing and blasphemy, every disparaging, reproachful, degrading, vile and vulgar epithet that could be conceived by the most vitiated imaginations, which bedlam of shocking discord was kept up from nine until one o'clock at night. There is no tongue can express nor mind conceive the terrible uproar and ferocious blackguardism of this night's proceedings. Hallooing, cursing, and swearing, blackguardism—the roaring of drums, beating of tamborines, blowing of instruments and horns, the rattling of bones, smashing of store boxes and boards for the fire—all going on at once and the same time, incessantly for the space of four hours, by far exceeding any-thing of a similar nature which I have ever witnessed. If "all pandemonium had been let loose,"[64] and every imp had been a demon, each demon possessing a thousand tongues, each tongue capable of uttering a thousand demoniac howls,

---

64. Probably an allusion to John Milton (1608–74), *Paradise Lost* (1667), wherein he refers to "Pandoemomium, the high capital / Of Satan and his peers" (Book I, 756).

it could not have increased the infernal turmoil of this night's proceedings. The wretches, not possessing courage sufficient to drag us by force into the street, where to execute, in the midst of their assembled hundreds, their hellish designs, conceived the plot of disfiguring and disabling our horse, and breaking the buggy to pieces. Two or three gentlemen, who overhearing their plot, cautiously secreted the horse and buggy in the barn of a neighbor, which prevented this nefarious scheme from being put into execution. I would observe, that during all this midnight outrage, the proprietor of the hotel acted like a man, and I have no doubt but his influence contributed much, in the morning, toward bringing them to a sober reflection.

The mob eventually concluded, after rioting around the hotel until past one o'clock, having burnt, in all probability, all the spare store boxes, to retire until morning; but not, however, without giving strict instructions to the ostler boy, who slept in the bar-room of the hotel, that should we in the night attempt to flee, to give the storekeeper near the hotel speedy notice, who was to call up his troop by the beating of the brass drum, as they, like the forty Jews against Paul, declared that they would neither eat nor drink until they took our lives;[65] and be this remembered, it was not for anything that had been said, but simply for what we did not say. We gave them no pretext for a mob, but to have one they were determined.

In the morning early, there were six only of them on the ground, among them a store keeper, as I learned, who howled and yelped as we left the hotel, two of whom secreted themselves in a shed, and stoned us, striking the horse and buggy, fortunately without injury to either. I have no doubt had they not feared the consequences, and probably from their blackguardism the night previous, been ashamed to be seen, though early in the morning, and identified, but they would have endeavored, at least, to do us some serious injury. Those who were present threatened us in the name of the town, that should either of us pass that way again our doom was fixed. Unfortunately, I could not learn the name of one of these insufferable villains. We left this place unharmed, and even unfrightened, as we were reconciled as to the course we should pursue.

We arrived in Sandusky City on Friday evening the 30th inst., and shall proceed from here to Detroit city, where there is now a very interesting slave case pending before the U.S. Court, Judges McLean and Wilkins. I shall report you concerning this case from Detroit.

Yours, for God and Humanity,
M. R. D.

(*North Star*, 14 July 1848, pp. 2–3)

65. See Acts 23.

DETROIT, MICHIGAN, July 14, 1848

DEAR DOUGLASS:—I arrived here on the 3d inst., from Sandusky City, at which place was arrived on the 29th ult., but were unable to leave sooner. At this place we held no meeting, for the reason that every hour a boat was expected up the lake, we holding ourselves in readiness. At length on Sabbath morning one came, the Pacific; but as we afterwards discovered, having it expressly stated on their bill, "Built expressly for the accommodation of Southern passengers," I and my friend Langston were, by the pitiful Northern slaves to Southern masters, even on the pure and uncontaminated waters of Lake Erie, refused a cabin passage by the vassal clerk of this meaner than slaver, Pacific. Although noted as was the clerk by that extremely polite and humble demeanor which ever characterizes the mean and unprincipled; yet so contemptuously indignant did we feel toward the whole concern, that we even did not inquire of the captain into the rules of the boat. There is no doubt but this is the established rule of the Pacific—a name which I desire the friends of freedom to remember—and neither captain nor clerk had manliness sufficient candidly to state their reasons for the establishment of such odious rules. The truth of the matter is, they are *slaves*—voluntary slaves, and as such, ashamed to acknowledge it. We did not get passage until Monday morning, on the Gen. Scott, a Sandusky and Detroit packet. . . .

As intimated in my last, on arriving in this city [Detroit], we found in session the Circuit Court of the U.S. Judge John McClean, of Ohio, President, and Hon. Ross Wilkins, of the District Court, assistant.[66]

This was a suit brought at the instance of Troutman, who is also a practicing lawyer in Kentucky, Agent of Francis Giltner, of Carroll county, Ky., for damages for payment by the law of '93, for loss of the Crosswhite family of fugitives, who effected their escape on the 9th day of August, 1843, and located near Marshall, Calhoun county, Michigan, against Chas. T. Gorham, Dr. Oliver C. Comstock, Mr. Hurd, and three colored men—Charles Bergen, Planter Moss, and Nelson Hackett.[67]

66. As was standard practice before the Civil War, an associate justice of the U.S. Supreme Court, Judge John McLean (1785–1861), was presiding over a state district court. McLean had served in the House of Representatives from 1813 to 1816, and had been an associate justice on the Ohio Supreme Court from 1816 to 1822. He was appointed to the U.S. Supreme Court by Andrew Jackson in 1829. Ross Wilkins (1799–1872) served as one of ten territorial judges of Michigan from 1832 to 1837. Soon after Michigan was admitted as a state in 1837, he was appointed U.S. district judge of Michigan. He was a close friend of McLean's.

67. A crucial test of the federal fugitive slave law of 1793, which would be strengthened by the Fugitive Slave Law of 1850, the Crosswhite case is not even mentioned in the major

The investigation continued about four weeks, and upwards of sixty witnesses were examined.

On the 27th day of January, 1847, early in the morning, about daylight, Troutman, David Giltner, and Francis Lee, went to the house of the Crosswhite family, consisting of the old man, his wife and four children, forced their way in, presented arms, asserting their intention of taking them back to Kentucky; whereupon the old man or one of his sons cried out, "Kidnappers! kidnappers!"—This had the desired effect of arousing the neighborhood. A colored man, one of the defendants, was the first who came to their aid, upon whom Troutman instantly drew a revolving pistol, commanding him for the life to stand back. When the news got fully spread, an old gentleman mounted his horse, rode through the streets ringing a bell, crying "Kidnappers!—the Crosswhite family!" and so forth, until the whole town was gathered together about the house of the fugitives, whom, up to this time, it was not proven in evidence, that the people of the peaceful village of Marshall *knew* to be fugitives. The family was very respectable, and well thought of by all the people of Marshall.

Messrs. Gorham, Hurd, and Dr. Comstock severally came upon the ground, each of whom at different times endeavored to remonstrate with Troutman and his fellows; during which time they were swaggering and boasting of what they intended doing, not only with the gentlemen who attempted expostulation, but with all on the ground. Not satisfied with this overbearing Southern insolence, Troutman mounted a large stone, and commenced a harangue of arrogance which, had the same been attempted by a Northern man in Kentucky, would have cost him at least his neck, upon the highest stake in the neighborhood; at the conclusion of which, he offered a resolution, which received a unanimous negative, except the four Kentuckians, who voted in favor of their own resolution.

Mr. Gorham offered a resolution to this effect:

"Resolved, That these Kentuckians be prevented from taking away the Crosswhite family, by moral, legal, or physical force, and that they leave the State in two hours, or be subject to a prosecution for breach of the peace."

This received a unanimous aye.

Dr. Comstock, addressing Troutman, remarked: "My good sir, you must see

---

study of McLean, Francis P. Weisenburger's *The Life of John McLean* (1937; reprint, New York: Da Capo Press, 1971), and most of the participants in the case remain relatively obscure. However, for Delany, the Crosswhite case was one of the major cases of the period and a case that revealed McLean's hypocrisy and mendacity. Delany told his biographer Frances Rollin that his letters in the *North Star* on the Crosswhite case led the Free-Soil Party in 1848 to choose Martin Van Buren over McClean as its presidential candidate. To his credit, McLean offered a dissenting opinion in the Dred Scott case of 1857.

that you cannot take these people by moral, legal, or physical force." Troutman insolently inquired, "What! do you say I shall not take them?" To which replied Dr. Comstock, "No, sir, I do not say so; but I say, according to the appearance of things, an excited crowd around you, that you must see the impossibility of taking them by moral, legal, or physical force." Messrs. Gorham and Hurd made similar remarks. With a degree of impudence which could emanate alone from those accustomed to domineer over slaves, Troutman demanded the names instantly of Gorham, Comstock, and Hurd, demanding of the crowd to know whether or not they were responsible men, which being answered in the affirmative, he proceeded to write down. Mr. Gorham, in giving his name, observed, "My name is Charles T. Gorham; write it in capitals, and bear it back with you to Kentucky." Dr. Comstock, also remarked, in giving his: "My name is Oliver Comstock, Jr. Be sure to write Junior, as I bear the name of my father, and do not wish him to be responsible for me." There is no doubt but both of these gentlemen, as well they might be, were somewhat irritated at the overbearing and insolent demands of these Kentucky ruffians.

The Kentuckians had a wagon in which to bear off their victims; but failing of success, as a last resort, endeavored to get them before Esquire Sherman, a Justice of the Peace. To this there was little objection; but before its accomplishment, the ever-vigilant colored men, true to their trust, themselves, humanity and their God, "spirited away the whole family on the Underground." This is a fair statement of the case.

Messrs. Pratt and Norvell appeared for the plaintiffs; Messrs. Romain, Emmons, Wells and Clarke for defendants.[68] Mr. Emmons did justice to his cause, and credit to himself. He assumed as his foundation an elevated position, manfully and fearlessly, in a strain of seven hours, (one and a half the first day, and five and a half the second,) ably vindicated the right, the cause of humanity, and the liberties of the North.

In his eloquent plea, he severely castigated the serf-like servility of Dixon, the acting Deputy Sheriff of Calhoun County, who, for the sum of five dollars, dared, in the absence of all legal injunction, undertake, at the bidding of Troutman, to arrest the Crosswhite family. It was admitted in his own testimony that he knew he had no authority for so doing; but observed he, in justification of the act, "Mr. Troutman insisted on my doing so, saying that he would be responsible for it." It will be gratifying to the friends of humanity to learn that the

---

68. The best known of the government's lawyers was John Norvell (1821–50), who served in the U.S. Senate from 1836 to 1841 and was appointed U.S. district attorney in 1845. The best known of the defense lawyers was Halmer Hull Emmons (1815–77), who had a law practice in Detroit.

High Sheriff of Calhoun county promptly discharged the wretch Dixon from the services of his office. Mr. Wells, who is quite a young man, acquitted himself well and manfully—Mr. Romain, making the closing plea, which was summed up without fear, favor, or affection; with this exception, that he did not take quite so high ground on the subject of human rights as his colleague, the fearless and independent Mr. Emmons.

Mr. Norvell, U.S. Attorney, who opened for the prosecution, made a blustering noise about "Southern Chivalry and gallantry, liberality and patriotism," and all that. To this Mr. Emmons dealt out the severest and most blistering sarcasm.

"The counsel," said he, "talks of chivalry, gallantry, patriotism, and liberality!—Yes, the Southerner is always chivalric—when standing before the crouching slave, who is taught that submission is of the Divine will—he is always gallant, when his only antagonist is the trembling bondman—he might well be patriotic in lifting that arm in defence of his country which has never been nerved by toil—well may his heart be liberal, as the prodigal son's is liberal, when lavishly casting away the means and property of a father, gained by years of care and labor; his being wrung from the hopeless slave!"

Mr. Pratt, who resides at Marshall, closed for the prosecution; and in support of his position, brought forward a written argument—an old, lame, pro-slavery, colonization argument, long since exploded—to prove that slavery was a Divine Institution, sanctioned by the Bible. He talked about Jewish servitude, Joseph in Egypt, Paul and Onesimus,[69] and the like; declaring that these things were true—slavery was an institution sanctioned by God, or the Bible was not true, and should immediately be abandoned as the guide of our faith.

Adverting to his antagonist, Mr. Emmons, he observed that the counsel had brought in books to prove certain positions in law, which did not a student after six months studying know, deserved to be discharged from the profession.

To this, I have but to reply, that if any boy of seven years old knew no better than to believe such silly stuff as that brought forward by Counsellor Pratt, which evidently gained the approbation and sanction of many pro-slavery votaries present, opposed as I am to the corporeal punishment, I do think he should be severely castigated for his ignorance. The position of Counsellor Pratt was both mean and dastardly, and never did a slave more earnestly labor for his master, than Mr. Pratt for these slave catchers, by whom he was employed.

In several respects, the servility manifested during the litigation, was in the extreme humiliating. It is true that there are few in Detroit to be found quite so debased; but there were several, and my attention was called by a gentleman at my side, while sitting in the Court room, to the fact that as the insolent upstart

69. Genesis 37; Paul 1:9–10.

young slaveholder, Troutman, would swagger through the Court Chamber, with his curved staff hanging on his arm, some persons present would smile and bow very obedience to him, although his attention was turned in another direction. They appeared to receive it as a compliment merely to catch a glance of his eye. So accustomed is the North to Southern rule, that it has become second nature. How exceedingly mortifying to see Northern men thus "basely bowing their necks to the dark spirit of slavery!"

The charge of Judge McClean to the Jury, I look upon as decidedly partial, weighing heavily in the scale on the side of slavery. The course of the old gentleman throughout the prosecution, I viewed in the same light. It is true that he asserted the wrongs of slavery in the abstract, declaring that it had "no existence, either in the national law, or law of nations." It was "limited in its existence, and local in its character," deriving its whole strength from "municipal authority." He did not venture, after the Bible argument of Mr. Pratt, who, to all appearance, dared him to the task, once make the declaration, that slavery had no existence in the Law of God! I was much disappointed in Judge McClean, and did not find him that independent and liberal-minded jurist that, from all I had heard of him, I had a reason to expect. During the charge he did not once express his abhorrence of slavery, but modestly evaded commitment on that point, by simply saying, "Whatever may be our feelings," and so forth, "the law" is thus and so. Mr. Pratt, a pro-slavery man, and attorney for the plaintiff, frequently during his pleading declared that he was as much opposed to slavery as anybody, while at the same time he used his might to prove its scripture authority. The anti-slavery references, also, of Judge McClean prove nothing, so far as his sentiments are concerned.

It may be contended that the law is directly against the feelings of the Judge, and, of himself, he can do nothing. This I readily concede; and while so doing, alone hold him responsible for *his own* opinions, independent of Constitutional or State provisions. Such opinions, when emanating from the bench, become the actual law of the land, and are so received and considered in our Courts of Judicature.

This extraordinary opinion of Judge McClean, to which I call your particular attention, announced from the Bench as an essential point in civil jurisprudence, is, to my mind, without precedence in the history of modern—at least enlightened, judicial procedure.

Indeed, in me it may be the result of ignorance of the law of the land, for so thinking and expressing myself, for which I may even be rebuked; but if this is the law of the country in which we live, then is liberty but a byword—litigation for protection a sham, and all judicial proceedings a farce, that should immediately be abolished.

Unexpectedly to every one, either plaintiffs, defendants, or their friends, in his charge to the Jury, giving a definition of a criminal in this and all similar cases—the charge being brought for "harboring, concealing, hindering and obstructing," in the language of the act of Congress, "knowing them to be slaves," &c., "shall forfeit and pay for *each* slave, the sum of five hundred dollars," &c.; unequivocally asserted, repeatedly, that it was not necessary to the offence that the person interfering with the rights of the slave-catcher should *know* that the person or persons so claimed were slaves. If the slave-catcher did but *assert* his intention, declaring that the persons so claimed were his property, which declaration might be made in the absence of any slave, save the persons claimed, it was sufficient.

The merest interference after this declaration, will suffice to criminate. To make this plain, in reply to an interrogatory by one of the counsel for defence, the Judge remarked: "I wish the Jury to understand me. It is not necessary that the persons interfering should know that the persons claimed *are* slaves. If the claimant has made the declaration that they are such, though he should only assert it to the fugitives themselves—indeed, it could not be expected that the claimant would be required the trouble of repeating this to persons who might be disposed to interfere—should any one interfere at all, after the declaration of the claimant, he is liable and responsible to the provisions of the law in such cases."

Here, then, is the decision of the highest Judiciary in the land, upon the subject of *our* liberties; and that, too, by one whom his friends call a friend to humanity. To my judgment, such a decision is neither in accordance with philosophy nor common sense.

Moral philosophy teaches, as common sense dictates, that no act can be considered criminal, where there is not a criminal intention; hence the distinction between killing and murder. A person, through mistake, under the impression that he is aiming at a beast, may shoot and kill a man in the bush; though he actually kills the man, he does not therefore commit murder, because there was no intention of murdering—the object shot at being a beast and not a man.

But in the position assumed by Judge McLean, common sense is set at naught, and philosophy at defiance. Though, says the Judge, a person aims at the rescue of a freeman from the hands of a kidnapper, he must be responsible for an unlawful interference between *master* and *slave!* Nor did he make any allowance for the presumption in favor of freedom, until the contrary is proven. It is enough for one to know that the slave-catcher attempted to arrest his victim, and the presumption must be in favor of the master! Truly, this is the law of the land—law by which you and I must abide!

There is now but one important view to be taken of this matter. Previous to this decision, colored persons had some slight semblance of liberty, but now every vestige has been wrested from us—each and all of us reduced to the mercy or discretion of any white man in the country, and like the colored man in the South without a "Pass,"[70] as it is termed, may at any moment be arrested as the *property* of another!

Nay, more. While upon the coast of Africa, the seizure of a person is, so, considered, and treated in this country as piracy, kidnapping, by the act of Congress and the decision of American Judges, has been legalized; and none dare, under the most burdensome penalty, even utter a word of counsel, or lend a helping hand! I call upon our oppressed fellow-countrymen to look at this law as it now stands; and in so doing, I declare that every colored man in the nominally free States, under it, is reduced to abject slavery; because all slavery is but the arbitrary will of one person over another. This law is nothing more nor less.

To the above, personally, I have but one remark to make. In an attempt, under such pretext, to seize upon the person of myself, I shall know no other law than that suggested by the first impulse of my nature—self-protection!

The case was submitted to the jury, in the presence of a crowd of anxious spectators, who, after an absence of several hours, returned—disagreed; eleven for conviction, and one against. Mr. Charles M. Humphrey, the Foreman, declared that he would, rather than be instrumental in thus sacrificing Liberty on the infamous shrine of slavery, hold out forever! Worthy Freeman!

As a combat between Liberty and Slavery in this country must always terminate in favor of the latter, the slaveholders determined not to be outdone; and taking courage by the result of the Mitchell case in Pennsylvania,[71] have renewed the suit, to come on at the October term; and now Troutman is known to boast about the city that he can bring to his aid, if necessary, $50,000. This case has been made the subject of special action by the Legislature of Kentucky, and the Senate of the U.S., in which the former appropriated $2,000 to aid the prosecution, which money was expended in the present litigation.

Mr. Haskett, one of the colored defendants, recovered, before a magistrate at Marshall, damages of one hundred dollars against Troutman. This they also wish to recover. The citizens of Detroit, at the renewal of the suit, raised instantly, by subscription, in one afternoon, seven hundred dollars, to aid the defence, declaring that they shall lose nothing. In my next, I shall notice Detroit city.

The people call loudly for a National Convention to sit on the sixth of September next, in Cleveland, for which I sent you the call for publication.[72]

70. Slaveowners would give their slaves "passes" when permitting them to leave the plantation (often to perform duties for the master); the pass would assert ownership.

71. See note 11 above.

72. Both Delany and Douglass would attend the Colored National Convention in Cleveland on 6 September 1848; see "The National Convention of Colored Freemen, 1848" below.

Many of the Mexican soldiers are returning. Several furniture wagon, cart, wagon, and dray loads of them are continually passing through the streets, "all covered with glory"—the most miserable-looking specimens of freemen I ever beheld—the most perfect specimen of the inmates of the hospital of "San Lazaro."[73]

My friend Langston here leaves me for the East, via Rochester.

On the verge of closing, I received your kind favor. You may look for me to a certainty to celebrate with you the approaching first of August.[74] I shall write once more before my return.

Yours, for God and Humanity,
M. R. D.

(*North Star*, 28 July 1848, pp. 2–3)

CLEVELAND, July 24, 1848

DEAR DOUGLASS:—Having left Detroit on the 19th inst., I have thus far arrived, *en route* for Rochester, where I shall meet you on or before the glorious first of August—that day which, in a trice, struck the shackles from the limbs of eight hundred thousand chattelized beings in human form, who instantly, in the majesty of manhood, stood erect in the image of their God.

I held, among the colored citizens, during my stay, a series of meetings in Detroit, which were as well attended as reasonably could be expected under the circumstances. One I held for the citizens generally, in the "Presbyterian Session Room," a notice of which, through the papers, having been neglected, there were comparatively few in attendance, at which time I took the opportunity of answering some positions taken that day in the U.S. Supreme Court, by Mr. Pratt, one of the counsel for plaintiff, in his pro-slavery Bible argument. . . .

I came by Oberlin, where I found many excellent spirits and good people. I did not find as many young colored men and women at this Institute as I could have wished. There are but three young men in College, and I believe two young women, one of whom is one of the Amistad captives, preparing to act as a missionary in her own dear native land, among her benighted brethren. May success attend her every effort! I had some conversation with her. She was one of

---

73. San Lázaro is a city in Baja California, the peninsular region of California retained by Mexico in the wake of the U.S.-Mexican war.

74. Abolitionists staged First of August celebrations to commemorate the end of slavery in the British Empire on 1 August 1834.

the three little girls whom Cinque took to his arms and embraced when seized by the "brave" and ever-to-be remembered, Lieut. Meades, of the U.S. Squadron.[75] Those in College are said to be quite promising. There are a number in preparatory schools.

I was most agreeably disappointed in the arrangement of things at Oberlin Institute. Instead of that distant coldness with which the Professors are said to treat the students, the contrary is the fact—kindness and friendship being the traits most prominent—and in many instances the most familiar sociability existing among them. One thing I discovered—the students *love the Professors*; and I desire no greater evidence of the character of the Institute. I visited several of the Professors' families, and found them all that could be desired.

I also visited several of the recitations, and instead of confused awkwardness, as is usually the case among students, I found them ready and cheerful, full of life, with kind and smiling professors and tutors. I greatly admire the regulation and management of Oberlin Institute. . . .

Cleveland is a handsome and pleasant place, as you know; but not yet having seen the people, I cannot say much about them. Last night there was an anti-slavery address. Tonight, Mr. Fitzgerald holds an emigration meeting among his colored brethren. I shall be there; and to-morrow leave for Rochester.

Yours for God and humanity,
M. R. D.

(*North Star*, 4 August 1848, pp. 2–3)

PHILADELPHIA, Sept. 25, 1848

DEAR STAR[76]:—I am now in Philadelphia, after a stay of one week with my dear family, in Alleghany county, Pennsylvania, whom I had not seen for six months. I left Pittsburgh on the nineteenth instant, which place I shall give you an account of on my return, arriving here on the evening of the 21st, where I found a large assemblage in waiting in the "Big Wesley" Church, Lombard st., being ably and eloquently addressed by that untiring friend of the slave, Charles

75. Joseph Cinqué was the leader of the slave rebellion on the *Amistad*. (See note 39 above.) After taking conrol of the ship, Cinqué and his compatriots sailed for several weeks before being captured off the Long Island coast by a naval ship under the command of Lieutenants D. D. Porter and Richard W. Meade.

76. *North Star*. Delany addressed the newspaper because Douglass was there with him in Philadelphia.

Lenox Remond. The meeting of myself and Remond, at such a time and on such an occasion, was certainly a most glorious one, and long to be remembered.

On Friday evening, I attended and addressed a meeting in Hamilton village, across the Schuylkill; and on Sabbath evening a full house in "Little Wesley." On Monday night, C. L. Remond and myself addressed a meeting in the Institute Hall, at which meeting the citizens appointed a committee of 50 for the reception and escort of my unflinching and faithful colleague, Frederick Douglass. On Monday at 11 o'clock, the committee were in waiting at the Walnut street wharf, when the steamer arrived, bearing with it my excellent friend and brother, escorting him to Institute Hall, where the Chairman, Dr. J. J. G. Bias,[77] poured forth the sentiments of fraternal eloquence, which were responded to with a most feeling and happy effort by brother Douglass. Rev. W. T. Catto,[78] an able and eloquent gentleman, Rt. Rev. George Galbraith, and several other gentlemen, addressed the meeting. Mr. Douglass having announced that he casually learned that that most noble specimen of a man, Henry H. Garnet,[79] would arrive in the next train, the same committee was immediately appointed to escort Mr. Garnet to the same Hall.

Mr. Garnet arrived in the course of an hour, escorted to the Hall by the Committee, where Dr. Bias again filled every ear, as well as the soul of his distinguished guest, with the sound of his eloquent voice. Several gentlemen addressed the meeting. Here, before this meeting closed, Garnet, Douglass, Remond, and myself, all had the pleasure, for the first time in our lives, of meeting and shaking glad hands together! This was a meeting the remembrance of which can never be effaced. Truly, the God of Liberty, in this instance, was lavish with favors. This evening, we had a glorious meeting at the Shilo Baptist Church, crowded to overflowing, hundreds having to go away, unable to gain admittance, which meeting had been previously appointed for myself, with the assistance of C. L. Remond. At this, as at the other meetings, subscribers were ob-

77. James J. G. Bias (?–1860) was a prominent leader of the African American community in Philadelphia. In 1850 he chaired a meeting of black Philadelphians opposed to the Fugitive Slave Law; the resulting "Resolutions by a Committee of Philadelphia Blacks" appeared in the 31 October 1850 *Pennsylvania Freeman.*

78. A prominent African Methodist Episcopal Presbyterian preacher, the Reverend William T. Catto (1809–69) was born and educated in Charleston, South Carolina, and moved to Philadelphia in 1848.

79. A radical in the antislavery movement, the New York black abolitionist Henry Highland Garnet (1815–82) rejected the moral suasion position of the Garrisonians in favor of the political abolitionism of the Liberty Party. At the 1843 National Convention of Colored Citizens held in Buffalo, New York, Garnet delivered his famous speech, "An Address to the Slaves of the United States of America," which presented slave resistance as an act of patriotism and self-defense.

tained; also a large number of ladies, married and maidens, offered their services to obtain subscribers, which they are now doing. At this meeting, Remond, Garnet, and Douglass spoke, I having lost the present use of my voice by hoarseness, from cold and speaking.

Yesterday evening, the 26th, our meeting was held in the Lombard street Church, ("Big Wesley,") which was crowded from the gallery to the pavement, the yard being actually filled with females, unable to enter, who remained, endeavoring to catch a sound, a glorious sound of Liberty—a word for God and humanity, and hundreds actually left, because it is against the city ordinance, else the street would have been filled. Here Remond, Garnet and Douglass poured forth the most thrilling peals of eloquence, which were repeatedly loudly responded to by the mutual aspirations of assembled hundreds. I did not speak on this occasion, for the same reason as on the last. This evening, Mr. Garnet speaks in "Little Wesley," and to-morrow evening we shall all speak in Zoar Methodist Church, Hamilton village.

Monday and Tuesday next, we hold a series of protracted Anti-Slavery meetings, day and night; and never was there a time before in the history of our people, when so much interest was felt and manifested by themselves in the anti-slavery movement. The cause of the slave is now in their own hands, assisted by our friends, and as I have oft repeated and long urged, when Liberty is fully appreciated and her cause espoused by us, slavery, that accursed monster, must fall. With the master-grasp of Garnet, Remond, Douglass, Purvis, and others, who are nobly fighting side by side with us, upon his infernal throttle, with the host of noble men and women at their backs, with the feeble aid that I shall render, the monster now staggers, and must soon fall—yea, *shall fall*, to rise no more! Could a place be obtained large enough to contain ten thousand people, at present, it could be filled, such is the interest manifested. A proud day indeed will it be for us, and a terrible day for slavery, when the colored people—when we shall stand up in the might and majesty of manhood, and declare by our strength, that slavery shall cease. When we thus determine, then, and not until then, will the day of our redemption come. Let us have but one mind, one purpose, one cause, and one determination—yea, and but one watch-word—Let my people go!

There are indeed a great number of colored people in this city, sufficient, if their efforts were properly concentrated and directed, to effect anything within the possibility of man; but unfortunately, with a few exceptions, though there are very many fine people of both sexes, like our brethren generally in this country, this is not the case. Though many are the praiseworthy, industrious mechanics, perhaps of every description to be found, still, young gentlemen of capital and fortunes do not invest their means in trading and business as we could desire, and which is necessary to give us equal importance with the whites. I would to God it were otherwise.

The present state of the anti-slavery cause here, demands our protracted stay, and to leave the city at this time, would be to forego one of the most favorable opportunities that has ever presented itself for doing good among our people. Consequently, Mr. Douglass will remain until next week, when he will leave about the middle for home. On Saturday next, Douglass, Remond and myself go to Wilmington, Delaware, to hold an Anti-Slavery meeting, though a slave State. Thus you perceive we intend to "beard the lion in his den."[80] Wilmington is the place where Thompson, the man who endeavored to discredit the Narrative of Douglass, resides, and whom Douglass so successfully refuted in an able letter from Scotland.[81] Thus gloriously goes onward our march to certain victory. . . .

There are now in Philadelphia, or the neighborhood, Mons. Dupee, Ex-Secretary of State of Haiti, a Haitian Senator, a fine-looking man, and a merchant, the last two of whom I have seen, and had much conversation with the merchant, who is a very intelligent gentleman, and speaks English well.

Although a fugitive prisoner, condemned, as he informed me, to four years' imprisonment, he repudiates, with contempt and scorn, the imputation upon the Haitian Republic, as charged by the miserable corrupts of the American press, and denies, positively, that the disturbance is based upon color or complexion. He referred me to France, and observed, in a tone and spirit which I shall never forget, "As well might you charge the present revolution in France[82] as being based upon color;" observing that the partizans were made up irrespective of color, and that the President's guard were principally mulattoes. Soulouque,[83] he says, who is black, is a very ignorant man, one who had never been accustomed to good society, and only known as an old soldier, who, two years ago, was elected general of one of the Arondissmal regiments—the same as our military regiments. A clique, he says, of politicians, forced him on the people, as a no-party man, in opposition to men of splendid talents and quali-

---

80. See Daniel 6; Psalms 10:9.

81. A. C. C. Thompson (1822–?) published a letter in an 1845 issue of the *Delaware Republican* questioning Douglass's authorship of his *Narrative*. Douglass responded to Thompson in "A Few Facts and Personal Observations of Slavery" (1846).

82. Inspired by class and economic conflicts, the French Revolution of February 1848 overthrew the monarchy of Louis Philippe and established the Second Republic.

83. Faustin-Élie Soulouque, a former slave, became president of Haiti in 1847 and in 1849 declared himself emperor Faustin I. An authoritarian and corrupt ruler, he was overthrown by a revolution led by Nicholas Fabre Geffrard in 1859.

fications, blacks and mulattoes, many of whom were the first choice of all the intelligent citizens. As soon as the people expressed themselves against his defective administration, he became offended, and, like ignorance generally, determined on being avenged, immediately discarded the Constitution, declared it null and void, thus assuming the powers of government. However, this amounts but to a temporary matter, much as we regret it, he says, and will last no longer than the power of the present man continues, when all those who have left will return. It is only offensive to those who are terrified to leave, and these consist of blacks and mulattoes. His family is in Haiti, consisting of a wife and four interesting daughters, about whom he has no concern further than the social enjoyment of their society. No women nor children are interfered with, and all the persons condemned to death, according to his account, as far as he could recollect, were—14 in Aux Cayes, 5 in St. Domingo, 1 in Jeremie, which, added to the 12 in Porte Repubcan, will make an aggregate falling far short of the number killed in the Cincinnati mob of 1842.[84]

Haiti, our informant tells us, is an excellent country, and he leaves here shortly for Jamaica.

I will write again next week, when I shall have more to say of Philadelphia, men and things. Until then, I am faithfully for God and humanity,

M. R. D.

(*North Star*, 6 October 1848, p. 2)

PITTSBURGH, Nov. 5, 1848

DEAR DOUGLASS:—I hastily left Philadelphia, on the afternoon of Saturday, the 28th ult., having been telegraphed for in consequence of indisposition in the family, and arrived here on Tuesday morning, the 31st, at five o'clock. One of the stage horses having given out, all the male passengers had to walk, and for some distance to push the coach up a considerable hill. The night being dark and the road muddy, it reminded me of "Paddy on the tow-path," working his passage by *walking* and *leading* the horses.

In this city, there is little or nothing doing in the cause of Anti-Slavery. I believe I am safe in saying that I never saw it at so low an ebb as now. . . .

84. In 1829 and 1841, riotous white proslavery mobs attacked "Bucktown," a black neighborhood in Cincinnati, driving blacks from their homes and killing resisters.

In Philadelphia, up to the time of my leaving, the meetings continued with unabated interest. On Friday evening, the 27th ult., the last meeting, I held in the Shiloh Church, assisted by that distinguished patriot and orator, Henry Garnet, which, like all preceding meetings, was filled to the utmost capacity. . . .

While in Philadelphia, something like thirty fugitives, men, women, and children, passed through the city, effecting their escape from the American prison-house of bondage. Oh! it was a joyful sight to see in one meeting fourteen of these, our panting brethren and sisters, all sitting in front of the altar, some of them handsome young girls, whose mothers had long since been sold away from them, into the cotton fields and rice swamps of Alabama and Georgia.

There they sat in breathless silence, with countenances lighted with joy and surprise, as they for the first time witnessed the proceedings of an Anti-Slavery meeting; and with what astonishment did they gaze as they listened to our righteous denunciation of the man-degrading, heaven-daring man-thieves of this mock Republic; and when peal after peal, in words of living truth, the tones of eloquence escaped the lips of the distinguished Henry H. Garnet. It was a proud day for these our brethren, and one of them whispered in our ear, as he grasped our hand with gratitude, "We only want such men as you and Mr. Garnet in the South to head us!" I name these facts in order to show the man-thieves that the slave has still a soul within him, and we forewarn them to be careful how they attempt longer to trifle with and trample upon the unsubdued spirit of manhood. We forewarn him to look to Europe, and profit by the example there set. We beseech him to stop before it be too late. If he will continue his infamous deeds of outrage upon humanity, by and by, tortured and aggravated to desperation, the slave will rise in the majesty of manhood and the grandeur of his nature, when a terrible day it will be to the evil-doer and despoiler of his rights!

I intend everywhere to induce and urge the necessity among our people of the formation of Anti-Slavery Societies, for the assistance of newspapers and competent lecturers among us. While we do not mean to be exclusive, it is necessary to make our people dependent upon themselves, and cease to look to others to do for them. I would that they could all see and understand this principle as they should.

I want our ladies in particular to understand this matter properly. Among our white Anti-Slavery friends, the ladies, by their industry and perseverance, hold Fairs annually, by which their newspapers and faithful lecturers are sustained. Were it not for these efforts on the part of the ladies and societies, the Anti-Slavery papers which for years have done such great service in the cause of suffering humanity, would have long since ceased to exist, and the noble, untiring friends of the slave and man, who conducted them, been consigned to the seclusion of oblivion. My constant advice to our brethren shall be—Elevate yourselves!

Yours for God and Humanity,
M. R. D.

(*North Star*, 17 November 1848, p. 2)

HARRISBURG, Pa., Nov. 18, 1848

DEAR DOUGLASS:—I arrived here on Tuesday morning the 14th, having left Pittsburgh Friday the 10th. On Monday evening, I held a meeting in Carlisle, 18 miles west of here, where I endeavored to spread light and truth on the great and important subject of the Elevation of the colored citizens of this oppressive Republic, and circulate the North Star as a medium and means of reaching them and the public at large, when they can be reached by no other instrumentality.

Here they gave the best of attention, the house being as well filled as could be expected under the circumstances, they being but few in number in the place. The people here, with but one exception, are poor, and consequently unable to do much. Indeed, this adjective may be applied in general terms to our people, but here I apply it in a comparative sense to the masses, which makes the application even more positive. Hence, they did all they possibly could—gave the "widow's mite."[85]

Notwithstanding this, there is an excellent school for colored children, supported by the public fund, taught by Miss Bell, an amiable and quite accomplished teacher—one who is qualified to teach the children the higher as well as the practical branches of education, which has long been and is still much wanted in many of the schools in this country established for colored children.

Miss Bell took several classes through their various exercises, several of which had embraced the branches upon which they were examined as late as September, but three months since, many of the pupils of which are quite small; yet all, both male and female, went through their task with an ease and pleasantness which satisfied me that they were familiar with their subjects, which familiarity is absolutely necessary before the knowledge obtained can be of practical use. In arithmetic, they wrote down upon the black-board and worked out sums with the facility of a counting-house clerk—geography, grammar and Bible studies, all being demonstrated with equal satisfaction.

85. Small charitable offering coming from someone who can ill afford it (see Mark 12:41–44).

How different will be the intelligence of these pupils, when leaving school, to those generally dismissed from the common schools among us, having finished their education, or "done going to school," as it is properly termed; when on examination of the scholar, you find that he or she can "read and write," and that too in the most incorrect and imperfect manner, totally incapable of making a practical application of any branch of study which they profess to have gone through with at school. Incredible as this may appear to those unacquainted with schools kept for colored children, yet it is nevertheless true, that nine-tenths of our youth are turned out upon the world as having finished their education, with such an education as this, which in all conscience will be acknowledged a very bad education. Seldom can be found in our country towns and small cities, a colored youth or maiden who can practically apply to business purposes the arithmetic they have learned at school, or who is able to write a correct sentence. Even the first rule of composition is generally violated by them—which is, to begin every sentence with a capital letter; also, that which may be called the second, and one of the most obvious rules—that the pronoun **I**, and all proper or particular names, as the name of God and all human beings, as well as many other things, which the sense will suggest to any one who has simply read these rules, should be written with a capital.

You may think it somewhat singular, and altogether misplaced, to lecture the readers of the North Star, in an editorial correspondence on English grammar, but when you reflect on the manner in which we, as conductors of a public press, are continually bored by young writers, aspirants for literary fame, who openly and palpably violate all these rules, you cannot think the strictures amiss in this place.

Miss Bell has frequently been offered a better school and higher salary, to teach white children, but refuses to leave the colored school on any conditions. Some of Miss Bell's pronunciations were not in accordance with my taste or idea of euphony; for instance, too much stress was placed on the definite article wherever it occurred in the reading, thus—"*The* Lord spake unto Moses, saying, Speak unto *the* children of Israel," &c.; also in reading, I thought that their punctuations were not properly observed. However, as accent and punctuation are among the most arbitrary rules of our language, especially the former, continually undergoing changes, I consider this no very serious matter, as doubtless Miss Bell teaches according to some rule, adopting the system of some literary standard or lexicographer. Thanks, many thanks, from the friends of humanity, especially the colored people, to Miss Bell, for the excellent manner in which she conducts this school of the oppressed children of Carlisle. Her name will be treasured up in the bosoms of the grateful, to be honored and revered by the rising generation....

In Harrisburg, I have held three meetings—on Wednesday, Thursday and

Friday evening—endeavoring to awaken an interest among our brethren in their own welfare, by showing them the necessity of acting and doing for themselves—that we must, in fact, become our own representatives in presenting our own claims, and making known our own wrongs. . . .

I leave Harrisburg in the morning for York.

Yours for God and Humanity,

M. R. DELANY

(*North Star*, 1 December 1848, p. 2)

WILMINGTON, Del., Nov. 30, 1848

DEAR DOUGLASS:—. . . On Friday morning the 23d, I arrived at Columbia,[86] where I met for the first time, the untiring friend and advocate of his enslaved fellow-countrymen, W. W. Brown,[87] the St. Louis fugitive, with whom I am well pleased, and Isaac S. Flint of Delaware, who purchased, on the auction block under the hammer, sold one year for his jail-fees in New Castle, our friend and brother, Samuel D. Burris, imprisoned on a charge of aiding the escape of slaves out of the State.[88] We held meetings on the afternoon and evenings of this day, our ever-ready friend, W. W. Brown, participating in the effort to obtain subscribers to the North Star.

Monday, the 26th, I held another meeting here, in which there was much interest manifested, both in our condition and the prosperity of the paper. In Columbia reside the most extensive business colored men, north of Mason and Dixon's line in this country. Smith and Whipper,[89] the former of whom resides

---

86. Town in Lancaster County by the Susquehanna River, east of Harrisburg.

87. Best known at the time Delany first met him as the author of *The Narrative of the William W. Brown, A Fugitive Slave*, the antislavery lecturer and writer William Wells Brown (1814–84) would go on to publish numerous works, including the novel *Clotel* (1853), a play, and several histories of blacks in the United States.

88. In 1848, Isaac Flint, a white Quaker abolitionist from Wilmington, came to the rescue of the free black Samuel D. Burris (?–1855) of Delaware, who, after serving a ten-month jail term for aiding fugitive slaves, was sentenced to be sold into slavery. Flint disguised himself as a slave trader, purchased Burris, and then freed him.

89. William Whipper (ca. 1804–76) and Stephen Smith (ca. 1797–1873) formed a partnership in the 1830s, investing in a lumberyard, railroad cars, ships, and real estate in Pennsylvania and Canada. They also committed themselves to antislavery and antiracist programs. Delany celebrated their accomplishments as black entrepreneurs and antislavery activists in *The Condition, Elevation, Emigration and Destiny of the Colored People of the United States* (1852).

in Philadelphia, have, exclusive of lumber-trucks, some twenty-two of the finest freight-cars upon the road, plying between Columbia and Philadelphia, transporting continually every description of merchandize. They have also at present, in store, four thousand tons of coal, and upwards of two millions five hundred thousand feet of lumber in their depository, forming an area of about one hundred and fifty by five hundred feet. The perseverance and industry of these gentlemen, have had a very salutary effect upon the whole colored population round about the neighborhood. Mr. Burrells, a gentleman formerly a laboring hand in their employ, has now some ten fine freight cars on the track, conducted by himself and sons, doing a good business; and more colored men can be seen employed about warehouses, factories and furnaces, than in any other part in which I have been. Here, instead of seeking house service, colored men, like MEN, seek for and obtain those employments generally discarded by them, and readily grasped by white men, in western Pennsylvania and many other places. I was pleased to see at and about all the furnaces in this section of country, colored men laboring side by side with white—digging ore, boating coal, standing at the helm of burden boats, piling blooms, pigs, and the like. This is just what I desire to see, and is what will make men respected as men.

Messrs. Smith and Whipper keep constantly employed some nineteen or twenty hands, chiefly colored men, besides the hauling from their extensive coal and lumber-yard, which gives employment more or less to every white man who runs a team, cart or drag, about the town. Such men as these are truly beneficial to any community in which they may live, and I would that we had more of them. . . .

I shall leave here for Chester and Westchester, when I shall write soon again.

Yours for God and Humanity,
M. R. D.

(*North Star*, 15 December 1848, pp. 2–3)

LANCASTER CITY, Pa., Dec. 18, 1848

DEAR DOUGLASS:—Since my last, I have held meetings in Wilmington, Delaware, from which place I wrote; West Chester, Pa., and Philadelphia, at which place I was assisted by our worthy friend and co-laborer, Wm. W. Brown, the "noble fugitive."

There are some two thousand of a colored population in Wilmington, all of whom appear to be quite an industrious and laboring people, but seem not to have been instilled with the higher incentives of life. Education, as heretofore, has been greatly neglected and probably but little cared for by the colored people; hence, the characteristics of the slave stand prominently, and a stranger passing through the place, might well mistake four-fifths of the colored persons whom he would see in the streets to be slaves. But such is not the case. Although in a slave State, there are but few slaves in Wilmington, since, like in Wheeling, Virginia, they have nearly all run off and left the place. On Sunday evening while I was there, two slaves took the underground railroad, making good their escape, as I was informed. . . .

Tuesday and Wednesday evenings, the 5th and 6th, I held meetings in West Chester, Pa., which were well attended by both classes. Notwithstanding the almost entire absence of anti-slavery feeling in the place, the colored people took great interest in the meetings, filling the house at an early hour. This perhaps is attributable to the fact, that Mr. A. D. Shadd,[90] an old and tried friend in the cause of suffering humanity and the elevation of the nominally free brethren, resides here, whose excellent character must have exercised a very salutary influence over the people generally. Mr. Shadd is among the soundest and best minded men in our country, and was among the patriotic few who, in 1830, assembled together in the capacity of a National Convention of Colored Freemen, in Philadelphia, when S. Joscelin [*sic*], A. Tappan, and W. L. Garrison, being then Colonizationists, and visiting this Convention, were forced, by reason of the talent there displayed, to "turn from the error of their way," and embrace the cause of the perishing slave and American bondman—of God and humanity.[91] I think I am not wrongly advised in the above allegation; at least, it is what colored men generally claim. If wrong, of course I will be kindly corrected.

There are several good mechanics in West Chester, doing well, and a number of good, well-doing farmers in the neighborhood, working their own lands. I suppose this county embraces more farmers among the colored people, than any other county in Pennsylvania. I would that every county throughout the State contained a *pro rata* of colored farmers. What a different aspect it would present to the affairs of our brethren in this State. Our people must become me-

90. The father of Mary Ann Shadd Cary, the Pennsylvania free black Abraham D. Shadd (1801–82) helped to inspire the black convention movement of the 1830s. Before emigrating to Canada West in 1851, he lived in Wilmington, Delaware, and West Chester, Pennsylvania, where his residences were stops on the Underground Railroad.

91. Noted white abolitionists Simeon S. Jocelyn (1799–1879), Arthur Tappan (1786–1865), and William Lloyd Garrison (1805–79) attended the first black national convention in Philadelphia in 1830. Garrison inaugurated his antislavery newspaper, *The Liberator*, in 1831 and in 1833 published *Thoughts on African Colonization*, which vigorously attacked the American Colonization Society's project of shipping free U.S. blacks to Africa.

chanics and farmers—producers instead of consumers, if we ever expect to be elevated on a level with those who now predominate and rule over us.

Go, brethren—go, young men and women, to the level lands of the West— go to the beautiful plains of Michigan, Iowa, or Wisconsin, lands in themselves, promised by God and blessed of heaven—lands which now be suffering for the healing hand of the skilful cultivator. Will you not go? God grant that you may be brought to see your duty. . . .

On the 7th, 8th and 11th, I addressed meetings in Philadelphia, promising to return there on Christmas, to be present at the Fair got up by the ladies, for the benefit of the North Star and fugitive slaves making their escape.

Tuesday, I left Philadelphia, in company with a large delegation from that county, to attend a State Convention of the Colored Friends of the Common-wealth, to assemble in Harrisburg, the Capital, on Wednesday the 13th inst. This body was organized in the afternoon of the first day's sitting, (the 13th) by the selection of a President, thirteen Vice-Presidents, and four Secretaries, the memorandum of which I have lost, but which, ere this, you have received an official report of. This was a praiseworthy gathering, and the Convention did much credit to their constituents and honor to themselves. Indeed, it was good to witness the assemblage of so respectable a body of colored freemen, manfully legislating for their rights, and the rights of their wives and children, in com-mon with others of their fellow-citizens. The delegates were composed of farm-ers, mechanics and laborers, and much talent was displayed in the discussion of the questions brought before that body. Many of the most distinguished white citizens of the Capital, and several distinguished men of Philadelphia, were in continual attendance. C. L. Remond and myself were favored with a seat as hon-orary members. The Convention sat in the Shakespear Saloon.

Among the most important things done in the Convention, was the adoption of a Constitution and the establishment of a State Executive Board, which is lo-cated in Philadelphia, to have its auxiliaries in every county throughout the Commonwealth. Each member of these societies is taxed the sum of one dollar per annum, for the purpose of raising a fund; the object of which fund is, the es-tablishment of a political temporary newspaper, to be known as a "campaigner," to be issued every year during an electioneering canvass and the session of the Legislature, for the purpose of agitating the great question of the enfranchise-ment and political rights of the colored freemen of Pennsylvania; also the em-ployment of suitable persons to tour the State as agents, and keep up the inter-est before the people. I opine that an agent will be immediately placed in the field. I think it probable that the Board may take some action in recommend-ing the North Star as a permanent organ for our people in this State. This move would be well advised, since now that the North Star has quite a general circu-

lation in the principal places through Pennsylvania; hence, whatever goes into
its columns, will reach our people in this State generally. Large sums of money
were pledged to carry out the above measures. The Convention adjourned *sine
die* on the evening of the 14th.

Friday morning, the 15th, a large number, as a Committee from the Convention, headed by Mr. J. B. Vashon, President of the Convention, and Robert Purvis,[92] Esq., as orator, (C. L. Remond and myself being kindly invited to accompany the Committee,) called in a body, at 11 o'clock, A.M., on his Excellency,
Wm. M. Johnston,[93] Governor of the Commonwealth, at the Executive Chamber, State Capital, as an act of civility due the Chief Magistrate from a portion of
his constituents, though the humblest portion they may be.

On entering the department, the Governor was seated, who immediately
arose and advanced, to the centre of the chamber, the delegation quite filling the
interior of the room, forming a semi-circle, his Excellency in the centre, who
gracefully turned to either side, bowing with an earnest expression of countenance. We all bowed in return; when Robert Purvis, in behalf of the delegation,
made a few neat and appropriate, yet eloquent remarks, by the way of salutation, as nearly as I can recollect in the following words:—"Your Excellency:—
On behalf of the Committee, a delegation from a disenfranchised portion of
your constituents, recently sitting in Convention in this borough, I present you,
sir, our most cordial congratulations. We feel, sir, in common with the rest of
your fellow-citizens, a deep interest in all that concerns the welfare of the Commonwealth, and hope to participate in all the privileges enjoyed by others," &c.

To this the Governor replied:—"Gentlemen and Fellow Human Beings:—I
feel grateful at all times for such marks of personal respect and attention from
any portion of the human family; and had I the framing of the fundamental
laws, there would be none of God's creatures deprived of their liberty. So far as
my authority is concerned, I do assure you that nothing shall be wanting in the
faithful execution of justice to all."

To this his Excellency gracefully bowed, the delegation simultaneously returning the civility; when we left the department. The Governor is a statesman,
having great discretion, without which no man is suitable for the office he fills.
Caution is a prominent faculty in the Governor, as you will perceive that he was

92. One of the best-known abolitionists of Philadelphia's black community, Robert
Purvis (1810–98) helped to organize the American Anti-Slavery Society in 1833 and led
the attack on the Pennsylvania legislature's 1838 decision to take the vote from Pennsylvania's black citizens.

93. William Freame Johnston (1808–72) was governor of Pennsylvania from 1848 to
1852. A Whig with Free-Soil leanings, he opposed the Fugitive Slave Law, a political position that may have cost him the election of 1852.

very careful in the selection of his words. He is a fine-looking man, standing full six feet — gentlemanly in his deportment, with a grave and serious expression of countenance, rather ten years the senior of what his portrait would import. . . .

This and to-morrow evenings, I hold meetings in this place, when I shall leave on Wednesday morning for Reading, Berks county, where I expect to spend the remainder of the week, and be in Philadelphia Christmas morning. There is truly a great interest now being awakened among our people wherever I go; indeed, they hail my visits with gratitude, declaring, as an intelligent body rose up in a meeting, after I had done speaking, and eloquently expressed it, that my lectures on the moral elevation of the colored people, was "the very food, for the want of which the people's minds are starving to death." This subject appears to be to the minds of the people generally, what electricity is to the great area of nature. But a single flash is necessary to light up the whole in a brilliant flame, reflecting light in every direction, which startles the most torpid and indifferent. It is the great sensitive nerve, but a touch of which arouses every fibre throughout the system.

What a reflection for the colored people of this country, that while the oppressed of France, Denmark, Sweden, Wallachia, Tunis, and even Bohemia, as well as several other places, have demanded a restitution of wrongs, demanded liberty and had it conceded, we are comparatively standing fast, not yet having made the first stride towards it. And yet our efforts are but moral, our weapons Truth and Justice.

> "If every foe stood marshaled in the van,
> I'd fight them single combat, man to man!"

Yours for God and Humanity,
M. R. D.

(*North Star*, 5 January 1849, pp. 2–3)

PHILADELPHIA, Jan. 16, 1849

DEAR DOUGLASS:—Since my last, I have held meetings in Lancaster City, from which place I wrote; and on Thursday and Friday, the 21st and 22d, in the city of Reading, Berks county. . . .

On the 22d, 23d, 24th, 25th and 26th, there was a Convention of the colored citizens of the city and county of Philadelphia, held in Hurst street Wesley Church, removing after the first day's session to Institute Hall. This was a political convention, held in obedience to the State Convention recently held at Harrisburg, for the restoration of the elective franchise to our politically degraded brethren of this Commonwealth—a Commonwealth of which I once felt proud to be numbered as one of her free enfranchised sons. But alas! that miserable gathering, misnamed "Reformed Convention," of 1838, which ended its session in this city, despotically wrested from the colored citizen his citizenship, degrading him to the condition of an alien! Thus were we stripped and disarmed of our manhood, and left to the mercy of the most consummate demagogue. . . .

On the 25th, 26th, 29th and 30th, I again held meetings in Wilmington, Delaware, and consequently left the Convention in Philadelphia on the afternoon of the day next to that of adjournment. Our brethren of this place were much interested in my first visit; hence; I could not escape the anxious and continued solicitations to return at a given time, which according to arrangement was fixed on the 25th inst.

The meetings held during this visit were interesting in a high degree—many, very many of the young people entering into the spirit and measures of reform, being stimulated to act and do for themselves, instead of waiting for others to do for them, or like the man in the fable, looking up to Jupiter to do that for them which God has given them strength and means to accomplish for themselves. The impression made I hope is a lasting one, and will only require renewed efforts to keep up the sensibility or alive the sensation.

Among the young people, a choice character is found in the person of Mrs. Mary Ann Shadd,[94] niece of the lady of whom I spoke in my letter, rising up in the meeting and declaring that the subject upon which I spoke was the "very food for which the people's minds in Wilmington were starving to death," and daughter of that most excellent man, A. D. Shadd, of Chester county, Pa. Miss Shadd is the author of a work, now in press, on the elevation of our people.[95] I had the favor of examining this pamphlet in manuscript before it went to press, and take pleasure in saying and recommending it as a creditable production, and an excellent introduction to that great subject, the Moral Elevation of the colored people. This pamphlet will be deposited, as soon as published, at the book store and anti-slavery office of G. W. Goines, 198 S. Sixth street, Philadelphia, also at the grocery store of A. J. Williams, French st., Wilmington, Delaware; price, 12 1-2 cents. Miss Shadd is an excellent girl, and will henceforth give her whole attention to writing.

94. Educated at schools for free blacks run by the African School Society and the Quakers, Mary Ann Shadd Cary (1823–93) taught at black schools for a number of years before immigrating to Canada West in 1851. There she emerged as an influential editor of the Canadian black journal the *Provincial Freeman*. See Delany's "What Does It Mean?" in Part 4 below.

95. *Hints for the Colored People of the North* (1849).

There is one difficulty and grievous wrong under which the colored people of Wilmington labor—a difficulty in getting the North Star from the post office. One half of the papers that are sent never reach the subscribers in this place, they being told by those attending the office sometimes one thing and sometimes another—sometimes that we are "impostors and have got their money," and don't intend to send the paper—that there is no other 'North Star' in existence than that in the heavens—that the paper is sent by mistake to Baltimore—that only one or two papers came 'this time'—that the paper is not published—sometimes actually giving one person's paper to another; all of these outrages and impositions are practised with impunity upon the colored subscribers to our paper in Wilmington, and that too by persons in the employment of the United States, whose business is to serve the people, instead of trampling upon their rights.

But what better can be expected in a slave State, where the will of every white man is the law—at least over a colored person? Such numbers of the North Star as they think unfit for the eye of the colored people, they read themselves, and then destroy. We shall take advantage of this baseness, and send our Wilmington package by another arrangement. . . .

Having several meetings to attend between this and Monday, I shall leave here on Tuesday next for the West, *en route* to Rochester, where I expect to be in March.

Our much-esteemed, long-tried and faithful friend of the slave and his oppressed country, and of man, Robert Douglass, senior,[96] has gone from labor to reward. He departed this life on the 28th of January, after a tedious affliction of protracted duration, in the 78th year of his age—ripe in years, and ripe in the fruitfulness of works of goodness. He died the death of the righteous. I frequently called to see him before his demise, and in one instance had a long conversation with him. He lamented much, and shed tears at the thought, that the young laborers in the cause of philanthropy and reform would so far forget the OLD as to totally neglect them in their hours of seclusion and affliction. This, of course, I endeavored to palliate as well as I could.

Though enfeebled by age, and almost exhausted with disease, at the mere mention of liberty, or the condition of our race, the bosom of the old gentleman would heave, his eyes sparkle, and all the animation of youth and vigor light up

96. Robert Douglass Sr., (1776–1849), one of the founders of the First African Presbyterian Church of Philadelphia, was an important reformer and abolitionist in Philadelphia. He was the father of Robert Douglass Jr., an artist who briefly collaborated with Delany in the late 1850s on his Niger Valley emigration project.

the full expression of his countenance. May the young of the present age live so useful a life, and eventually die as happy a death!

Yours for God and Humanity,
M. R. D.

(*North Star*, 16 February 1849, p. 2)

PITTSBURGH, Feb. 24, 1849

FREDERICK DOUGLASS:—I arrived in Pittsburgh on Wednesday, the 14th inst., having crossed the mountains in perhaps as cold weather as was experienced on the mountain tops. These mountains, though common to every traveller from eastern to western Pennsylvania, and familiar to all who have studied geography; yet they are so novel and romantic in their appearance and arrangement, and withal so tedious to travel, that a cursory description of them here may not be amiss, though I have crossed them frequently in the course of seventeen years, and the fourth and last time in the last five months.

The Alleghany Mountains, on this portion of the Pennsylvania improvements, the Pennsylvania Turnpike, consist of a continuous and contiguous range of seven mountains and thirteen summits in a distance of eighty-six miles, commencing at London, fourteen miles west of Chambersburg, the terminus of the Philadelphia railroad, and half way between Philadelphia and Pittsburgh.

First and second in rank of elevation, is the Cove mountain, seven miles from foot to foot; second, the Scrub Ridge, composed of six summits, or elevated points, and ten miles across; third, Sidling Hill, three and a half miles from foot to foot; fourth, Ray's Hill, two and a half miles; fifth, the Alleghany Mountain, fourteen miles across, the greatest and first in rank of elevation and vastness; sixth, Laurel Hill, the third in rank, six miles across; and seventh and last, Chestnut Ridge, the most westerly, five miles from foot to foot, and forty-five miles east of Pittsburgh.

In some cases the foot of one mountain commences immediately at the foot of the other, as is the case with the Cove Mountain and Scrub Ridge; Scrub Ridge and Sidling Hill; Sidling and Ray's Hill; but a very narrow valley between them, and where this is not the case, there are many little prominences and rugged hills coursing along between the mountains, in the valleys, so that the plains are broken and undulated, making the travel one continuous ascension and descension from the time you strike the foot of the first mountain until you leave the base of the last. Many are the scenes throughout the whole course of these vast mountains and valleys—beautiful, picturesque, grand and sublime, well worthy the pencil of the most accomplished artist. In summer, when clothed with foliage and verdure, the scenery is beyond the most graphic description. It is worth the trip to those who have the means to travel, as the tediousness is lost in contemplation of the scenery around. The soul may here expand in the magnitude of its nature, and soar to the extent of human susceptibility. Indeed, it is only in the mountains that I can fully appreciate my existence as a man in America, my own native land. It is then and there my soul is lifted up, my bosom caused to swell with emotion, and I am lost in wonder at the dignity of my own nature. I see in the works of nature around me, the wisdom and goodness of God. I contemplate them, and conscious that he has endowed me with faculties to comprehend them, I then perceive the likeness I bear to him. What a being is man!—of how much importance!—created in the impress image of his Maker; and how debased is God, and outraged his divinity in the person of the oppressed colored people of America! The thunders of his mighty wrath must sooner or later break forth, with all of its terrible consequences and scourge this guilty nation, for the endless outrages and cruelty committed upon an innocent and unoffending people. I invoke the aid of Jehovah, in this mighty work of chastisement. If two she bears were sent forth from the mountain to slay forty or more children, who in all probability were taught no better, for mocking Jehovah, in the person of the good old "bald-headed" prophet Elijah,[97] then should there, for mocking Him in the person of three millions of his black children, be let loose the fiery dragons of heaven, bearing with their approach the vengeance of an angry God! . . .

Thursday and Friday evenings, the seventh and eighth, I held meetings in York, endeavoring to awaken an interest among the quite interesting people of that place. I am sorry to see that a party spirit has crept even into that little place among our brethren, and would advise them as soon as possible to do it away, as it has, as heretofore, been the very curse of all our moral efforts. It is of infernal origin—its father is Beelzebub, the prince of devils. I left York on Monday, the 12th, passing on to Pittsburgh, without making any other stay on the way.

On Thursday, the 15th inst., it was rumored that Gen. Taylor, of Florida-war, Indian-murder, bloodhound, and Mexican-slaughter notoriety, President of the United States, was to be in the city, whose approach was to be announced by the thunders of a great cannon, placed upon Coal Hill,[98] overlooking the whole

97. See 2 Kings 2:24.
98. Now named Mount Washington, Coal Hill, located in the Pittsburgh coal seam, was the site of the first recorded coal mining in Pennsylvania (1761). For Delany's attack on the election of Taylor, whom he terms "an uncompromising slaveholder," see "The End Is Not Yet," *North Star*, 1 December 1848, p. 2.

neighborhood, as a signal-gun. The firing commenced about 8 o'clock at night, continuing at intervals for several hours. In the morning, however, it was ascertained that his bloody excellency had not arrived, but had telegraphed that he could not make it convenient to come by this way, then being at Wheeling, Va. This appeared to be glory enough for the people of the Smoky City—even that he had condescended to notice them; hence, the firing of cannon in honor of his refusal! The force of his non-compliance may be the better realized, when it is known that on his way up the river he was particular to stop at all slaveholding intermediate ports, going out of his way several hundred miles, up the Cumberland River to Nashville, and down again. Cincinnati, I believe, was the only "free town" he honored with a visit on his way up!

Such was the infatuation and enthusiasm said to have been manifested on the occasion of his approach, that at Memphis, Tenn., one man had his arm shot off; at Louisville, Ky., one man lost his life; at Cincinnati, there was one wounded; at Covington, Ky., one had an arm shot off; at Nashville, Ky., another lost an arm. On arriving at Captina, Va., the ice not permitting the steamer to ascend further up, a sleigh was appropriated for his special use. When passing along, although four men held, two on each side, to prevent accident, such was the wish to see him that the sleigh was upset, and the General tumbled heels-over-head down a precipice of a few feet, not sufficient to do serious injury, but enough to frighten the brave old hero of three hundred slaves and a Mississippi cotton plantation, and make the whole thing ridiculous, and slightly injure him.—Hence, his letter to Hon. Walter Forward, that night sent to Wheeling, that in consequence of an "accident and injury received," he was "unable to visit Pittsburgh at present." I suppose at the moment when the old non-surrender was tumbling over the declivity, he felt more like *going to* _____! than "giving the Mexicans hell!" It is also said that such was the crowd upon the boat in which he came passenger to Captina, that the provisions were all consumed, actually depriving the President of three meals. Thus did they not only show their high regard and love for the general, by killing several persons, but were well nigh killing him by starvation and dashing him to pieces.

The extent to which the American people carry this glorification of military crusaders, is beyond a parallel, except in the days of Roman extravaganza, which was but a foreboding of the end of her glory and speedy downfall of that haughty, insolent empire and commonwealth. The extent to which this homage is carried, ceases to be respectful, since it is neither kind nor complimentary, but like the homage of the serf to the noble, or the vassal to his lord, it is ludicrous. It is unfit for freemen, and only worthy of slaves—it is a flagrant outrage upon common sense and propriety.

I intend to hold a series of meetings among the colored citizens here, and shall write once more previous to my setting out for Rochester; where I shall give you an account of the state and condition of people and things about Pittsburgh.[99]

Yours, for God and Humanity,
M. R. D.

(*North Star*, 9 March 1849, p. 3)

99. Delany's essays on the "Colored Citizens of Pittsburgh" appeared in the 6 July 1849 and 13 July 1849 issues of the *North Star*. He contributed several other letters and short pieces closely related to his "Western Tour" before breaking his connection with the *North Star*; see, for example, "American Civilization: Treatment of the Colored People of the U. States," which appeared in the 30 March 1849 issue, and "Colored People of Cincinnati," which appeared in the 15 June 1849 and 22 June 1849 issues.

True Patriotism

WHEN DELANY RESUMED his tour for the *North Star* after the Cleveland convention of September 1848, he cut back on his letters to Douglass, perhaps because he felt himself at an increasing distance from his coeditor following their dispute on black servantry (see the introduction to Part 2). Clearly, Douglass felt himself at an increasing distance from Delany, for he announced in the 15 September 1848 *North Star* that henceforth the coeditors would initial their respective editorials and essays. Before resigning his coeditorship in June 1849, Delany would contribute over ten essays to the newspaper, including "True Patriotism."

Patriotism consists not in a mere professed love of country, the place of one's birth—an endearment to the scenery, however delightful and interesting, of such country; nor simply the laws and political policy by which such country is governed; but a pure and unsophisticated interest felt and manifested for man—an impartial love and desire for the promotion and elevation of every member of the body politic, their eligibility to all the rights and privileges of society. This, and other than this, fails to establish the claims of true patriotism.

From periods the most remote, the most improper application has been made of the endearing term Patriot. Whether the most absolute monarch, crowned with the hereditary diadem, armed with an unlimited sceptre—the most intolerable despot bearing the title of sovereign—the most cruel and heartless oppressor and slaveholder under the boasted title of President—the most relentless butcher and murderer called Commander-in-Chief—the most haughty and scornful aristocrat who tramples upon the people's rights in the halls of legislation—the most reckless and unprincipled statesman "rioting upon the spoils of a plundered revenue;"[1]—whether Phillips, Curran or Grattan, in defence of Irish constitutional liberty—Emmet upon the scaffold, refusing to let his epitaph be written until Ireland was free—William Tell, under sentence of death, baffling the schemes of the German tyrant, Gesler—the

1. A possible source is 2 Corinthians 16:14.

French baron, Lafayette, leaving his native country and princely fortune, to share in common the fate of the struggling American—Washington, as the leader of his country's destiny—O'Connell, as the Liberator—Thomas Jefferson, Patrick Henry, or John Quincy Adams, standing in the frontal ranks as defenders of American rights, or Mitchell and O'Brien, who sacrificed their all, being forever divorced and exiled from the most tender ties of domestic affections, by the severity of the laws of their country, for daring to discard provisions deemed pernicious to the welfare of their countrymen; all have laid equal claim to a share of the popular gratitude, and been endowed with the loved title of patriot.[2]

A patriot may exist, whether blessed with the privileges of a country, favored with a free constituency, or flying before his pursuers, [and] roam an exile, the declared outlaw of the power that besets him. Love to man, and uncompromising hostility to that which interferes with his divine God-given rights, are the only traits which distinguish the true patriot. To be patriotic, is to be philanthropic; to be which, is necessary to love *all men*, regarding their humanity with equal importance.

Much has been the interest felt and manifested in this country in every movement, with exceptions to be named, whether home or abroad, in favor of human liberty, and those who were foremost in the struggle, bequeathed their names to present and future time, to become the subject of the poet and the theme of the historian. Spain, Italy, Greece, Poland, Germany, France, England, Scotland and Ireland, of modern date, all, have had their patriots, each of whom in succession, has shared largely of America's eulogium. And of all who have scanned the ordeal before them, there were none perhaps for whom there has been expressed more sympathy, than the late victims of British displeasure, the Irish patriots and convicts, Mitchell and O'Brien, especially the latter, the severity of whose sentence aroused every feeling and expression of opposition to the execution of the sentence.

To witness the public demonstrations, as manifested in favor of the Irish struggle, in which Mayors of cities, Judges of Courts, sons of Ex-Presidents and Ex-Governors participated, and the universal interest felt in the result, is well tended to deceive, and betray into the idea those not otherwise advised, that this

2. In addition to well-known American patriots, Delany refers to the Irish nationalists and revolutionaries Charles Phillips (1787?–1859); John Philpot Curran (1750–1817), known for his legal defense of the United Irishmen in the rebellion of 1798; Henry Grattan (1746–1820), who advanced the cause of Catholic emancipation; Robert Emmet (1778–1803), who was executed for his role in planning the insurrection of 1803; Daniel O'Connell (1775–1847), the noted orator and politician who helped to secure the 1829 Catholic Emancipation Act; and John Mitchell (1815–78) and William Smith O'Brien (1803–64), who together helped to organize the ultimately unsuccessful Irish rebellion of

nation is a nation of justice. But how will America stand, when compared with other countries, dark as may be the gloom of their semi-barbarous laws? Condemned must she be in the moral vision of the whole enlightened world. Loud, long, and damning, must be the anathema uttered against her by those whom she treats and so regards in all her legal acknowledgments as aliens and enemies, ere their eyes be opened to a sense of their condition, and she still refuses to succor them.

But how many patriots have lived, toiled, suffered and died, having worn out a life of usefulness, unobtrusively laboring in the cause of suffering humanity, living to the community and the world a life of seclusion, passing to and fro unobserved, amidst the stir and busy scenes of a metropolis, and the throng and bustle of assembled thousands. This class of patriots may be found in every country, but to none are they more common than America, and in no country would they meet with less acceptance than in this Republic. Ever professing the most liberal principles, proclaiming liberty and equality to all mankind, their course of policy gives a glaring contradiction to their pretensions, and the lie to their professions.

Prone as they are to tyrannize and despotize over the liberties of the few, the philanthropist who espouses the cause of the oppressed, is destined to a life of obscurity; instead of commendation and renown, contempt and neglect are the certain and most bitter fruits of his reward. Marked and pointed out by the finger of scorn, he at once becomes the mock of the scoffer, and hiss of the reviler; and affliction heaped upon affliction presses upon him like a mountain weight, until at last he sinks under the mighty pressure, unable longer to bear it up. Yet, galling as this may be, it is a boon for which the downtrodden, oppressed American might anxiously long, compared with his own present miserable, unhappy condition.

Among them have existed, and there do exist, those who are justly entitled to all the claims of true patriotism; but proscription, as infamous as it is wicked, has stamped the seal of degradation upon their brow; and instead of patriots, they become the felon and outlaw. Anticipated and preconcerted by an inquisition of prejudice and slaveholding influence, the colored man of this confederacy, especially the bondman, is doomed to ignominy, whatever may be his merits.

1848 (both were transported to foreign prisons; Mitchell eventually escaped to the United States, where he edited the proslavery journal *Citizen* [1854–55]). Delany also refers to the legendary (perhaps apocryphal) Swiss freedom fighter of the twelfth century, William Tell (Gesler was the evil Austrian bailiff he supposedly triumphed over), and to the Marquis de Lafayette (1757–1834), who came to Philadelphia in 1777 to fight with the American revolutionaries.

Though he has complied with the first demand of a freeman—borne arms in defence of his country—no sooner is victory won, than he is unarmed, not only of his implements, but also of his equality with those among whom he bravely fought side by side for liberty and equality. Mathematician and philosopher he may be, not only furnishing to the country the only correct calendar of time and chronological cycles, but further contribute to its interest, by assisting in the plot and survey of the District of Columbia, without the aid of whose talents it could not at that time have been accomplished with mathematical accuracy; yet no sooner is this effected, than he is forgotten to the nation.[3] Though in a professedly Republican and free Christian country, the yoke is upon his neck, and fetters upon his limbs, and dare he make the attempt to release himself and brethren from a condition little less than death itself, the whole country is solemnly bound, in one confederated band, to riddle his breast with ten thousand balls. Is he a slave the most abject of South America or Cuba, who, rising in the majesty of his nature, with a bold and manly bearing, heads his enslaved brethren, leading them on to a holy contest for the liberty of their wives, mothers, sisters and children, he is, with one universal voice, denounced in this country, as a rebel, insurrectionist, cut-throat; and all the powers of despotism, America in the foremost rank, sallies forth in one united crusade against him.

Many are the untiring, uncompromising, stern and indefatigable enemies of oppression, and friends of God and humanity, now to be found among the nominally free colored people of this slavery-cursed land, at work laboring for the good of all men, though some have recently escaped from the American prison-house of bondage, bearing still fresh upon their quivering flesh the sting of the whip and marks of the lash, many of whom for talents and the qualified ability to write and speak, will favorably compare with the proudest despots and oppressors in the country.

Though they speak, act, petition, remonstrate, pray, and appeal, yet to all this the wickedness of the American people turns a deaf ear, and closed eye. Hence, the American colored patriot lives but to be despised, feared and hated, accordingly as his talents may place him in the community—moving amidst the masses, he passes unobserved, and at last goes down to the grave in obscurity, without a tear to condole his loss, or a breast to heave in sympathy. But the time shall yet come, when the name of the despised, neglected American patriot, in spite of American prejudice, shall rise superior to the spirit that would degrade it, and take its place on the records of merit and fame.—M. R. D.

(*North Star*, 8 December 1848, p. 2)

3. An allusion to the free black polymath Benjamin Banneker (1731–1806), whose almanacs were widely read in the early republic.

Sound the Alarm

THE FREE-SOIL PARTY, a harbinger of the Republican Party, was founded during 1847–48 by northerners who sought to prohibit the spread of slavery into the western territories newly acquired from Mexico. Delany attended the Free-Soil Party Convention in Buffalo in August 1848, which nominated Martin Van Buren for president, and was quickly disillusioned by what he regarded as the Free-Soilers' lack of commitment to abolition in the slave states.

That the question of Free Soil is henceforth to become the great leading political topic of this country, is now admitted by all; and that the true friends of freedom everywhere favor this movement, in preference to all other political movements yet at issue, is no less true. That the colored American entertains a partiality towards the Free Soil party never before manifested by them for any other political party in our country, is worthy of remark. This, perhaps, is not from what this movement "really is, but what it is expected to be."

The great question now should be, What is to be the future course of policy pursued by the Free Soil party? Is it to be sincerely and faithfully urged, and if successful, practically carried out, "Free Soil, Free Territory, Free Speech, and Free Men,"[1] to all men, fundamentally including in this issue the rights of colored men, or all persons on American soil, of whatever origin or descent; or do they simply intend by the alluring cry, "Free Soil, Free Territory, Free Speech, and Free *White* Men"? This, to every friend of freedom and impartial liberty, especially the colored American, should be the great leading thought, adopting as their motto, "Repulsion to every species of Proscription."

It is true that many of the friends of freedom have their hopes perched high upon the prospects of the coming issue; but let them not be deceived. Let them not mistake promises for principles, and political acumen for the propagation of great truths. It is anxiously desired, and sanguinely expected, that the heretofore existing policy will cease to form the political basis upon which the two

---

1. The rallying call of the Free-Soil Party.

great parties acted, and a new policy assumed, based upon Northern and Southern interests. This, even that distant-visioned, lynx-eyed Southern Argus,[2] with jackal-like sagacity and perception, has already predicted. But far-sighted and shrewd as may be that sentinel of American despotism and infamy, John C. Calhoun, there may be those of more moderate pretensions, whose political discernment, if not parallel with his, may be equal to a detection and apprehension of the great national robber and political swindler.

Calhoun has, it is true, predicted, and certainly all who observe the political course of events in this country, believed before he predicted, that such would be the change of policy; but the South, determined on the continuance of slavery, will do "anything and everything, be anything or nothing," to sustain this system of crime and outrage.

The most prominent feature of the American policy is, to preserve inviolate the liberty of the WHITES in this country; and to attempt to deny or disguise this, is both unjust and dishonest. This policy has been the leading measure in the country, and is one of the fundamental principles incorporated in the earliest actions of the American people, as the provisions against the Indians, their expulsion, and the continued wrongs perpetrated against that people show. This should not be lost sight of by the friends of freedom, especially the colored American; and to maintain this liberty to them, a union of the States appeared to be necessary. To preserve this Union, any concession that can, may be made. What then should be expected under such circumstances?

The cry of Free Men was raised, not for the extension of liberty to the black man, but for the protection of the liberty of the white. The liberty of the whites of the North was endangered by the encroachments of the slave power; hence, an alarm was necessary to arouse the North and alarm the South, who determined on the permanent establishment of slavery, as the North is well advised of, is ever ready to compromise, and always able to find one.

To this end, the South will be on the alert—ever watchful over her interests, she will have an eye to the final result; and rather than be instrumental in bringing about so disastrous a result as the dissolution of the Union, the most sure and certain step to emancipation, she will yield to any measure.

The present political movement will assume a new aspect—the South will propose a compromise, and the North will concede. No fears; the South will not propose a secession, except as an only alternative, though in the confusion of alarm they have said it, but will join issue, and make common cause with the Free Soil movement. Pro-slavery Whigs and Democrats in the North will be among the foremost in the measure, while the unsuspecting philanthropist, honest-hearted and inexperienced colored American will be deluded.

2. In classical mythology, Argus was a giant with 100 eyes charged to guard heifer.

The Free Soil party will assume the policy of the National Reformers, whose fundamental principles are based not upon man's rights to himself—his, to them, is of secondary consideration; but upon his natural right to the soil and Homestead Exemption.[3] This does not interfere with the policy of the South, and this they will quickly concede.

Securely concealed behind this veil of deception, and defended by the ramparts of such vast political machinery, the accustomed cry of "Free Soil," will be thundered through the nation, every ear listfully catching the sound, and while the colored people are contentedly waiting for results favorable to their redemption, the rights of the whites will be established, the claims of the slave power conceded, and slavery extended into every new State and Territory South of 36° 30m of the line.[4] This we predict, will be the final result of the present issue, or we very much mistake the American character. Good friends there are who desire otherwise, but these may be set down as pure Christian philanthropists, few in number, and weak in power and means. Politicians we dare not confide in; they have little sympathy with the slave, or concern for the rights of the nominally free colored people and Indians.

These facts the colored people, both North and South, should be hastily apprized of. They should be aroused from their sluggish indifference and drowsy dreaming, in every direction, and faithfully forewarned of the danger that approaches. Sound the alarm! Let the tocsin be heard in the rustling of every wind! Brethren, awake! danger is at your door. Let us not destroy our cause by vain expectations, but stand ready for any emergency that may arise.

Armed with Truth and Justice,
    Onward in the fight,
We'll battle for Freedom's cause,
    "And may God defend the right."

M. R. D.

(*North Star*, 12 January 1849, p. 2)

---

3. Free-Soilers believed that the homestead exemption—the granting of free land to farmers and laborers from the Northeast—would forestall the spread of slavery.

4. The Missouri Compromise of 1820 demarcated the territory north of this dividing line as forbidden to slavery; Free-Soilers wished to extend that ban southward.

Liberia

FOUNDED BY THE American Colonization Society during the early 1820s, the West African country of Liberia achieved its independence in 1847. Delany nonetheless remained suspicious of a country that he believed mainly served the interests of racist U.S. whites desirous of shipping the nation's free blacks to Africa. He would adopt a more favorable opinion of Liberia when he traveled there in 1859.

This country, originally comprising a tract of land obtained by the Colonizationists of the United States, especially for the expatriation of the free colored people from their native land, on the west coast of Africa, may now be regarded as an independency, relatively, according to their own declaration. This infant colony is composed entirely of colored people, not exceeding five thousand in number, and however unfavorable the location, geographically considered, situated as it is about the sixth degree of North latitude, might become a place of note and interest, had those into whose hands the destinies of the nation have fallen, been composed of a different material, morally and qualifiedly.

In speaking upon this subject, we have no sympathy with the degrading, expatriating, insolent, slaveholding scheme of American Colonization, but look upon Liberia, in its present state, as having thwarted the design of the original schemers, its slaveholding founders, which evidently was intended, as they frequently proclaimed it, as a receptacle for the free colored people and superannuated slaves of America; but we view it in the light of a source of subsequent enterprise, which no colored American should permit himself to lose sight of. This being understood, we shall proceed to review the character of some of her prominent citizens, in doing which, we shall select the two heads of Government, Executive and Judicial.

Judge Benedict,[1] chief of the Supreme Judicial department, whatever may be

1. Born a slave in Georgia, Samuel Benedict (1792–1854) became the first chief justice of the Republic of Liberia in 1848.

his literary qualifications, (which, to say the least, are of questionable repute, though perhaps the best that could be obtained, and equal to the emergency,) is a person of no force of character or fixed moral principles. His wife, having been purchased by himself, who, according to the barbarous customs of the South, held a bill of sale against her person, finding a just cause for refusing to him the affections of her bosom, he sailed to Africa without her, where he again endeavored to win her affections to him; but this she refused, unless he agreed to separate his attachment to one who then, and for years before he sailed, which was not discovered by her previous to this time, had occupied the place of violator of her conjugal rights, and impious defiler of her sacred chamber, and who now had claims upon him as strong as the partner of his bosom.

On the peremptory refusal of his wife to live as the partner of her divided affections, he (it is said) actually attempted to sell her to the first purchaser, trader or not, for any purpose for which a slavetrader might obtain a female slave, offering the bill of sale through his Southern agent, the attempt at which so aroused the Southerners of her neighborhood, that they immediately interfered—slaveholders themselves interfering, who brought to their aid and assistance Judge Berrien,[2] who indignantly opposed the act as being inhuman, though probably had it been any other case than an attempt by a husband to sell his wife, the judge, if never before, at this time was certainly a just judge, would have justified the act. And this man Benedict, guilty of the attempt to sell his own wife into hopeless servitude, is an expounder of the Law, and a Moralist—a Minister of Justice, and *model* man of Liberia! The better feelings of our nature recoil at the idea of the toleration of such a wretch in any capacity wherein pends the responsibility of our destiny, or hope of our elevation.

But our intention was more particularly designed to call attention to the course pursued by J. J. Roberts, reputed President of the new Republic,[3] and who, for many years previous to the independence, held the official station of Agent of the American Colonization Society, and Governor of Liberia—a man whom the Colonizationists and slave-holders in the United States extolled to the skies—even that venerable slave-breeder and pre-eminent negro-dreader, the thrice honorable and thrice unlucky Henry Clay,[4] pronounced to be equal to the most eminent executives and statesmen in our country.

A person receiving such high eulogium and commendation, would at least be

2. The lawyer John Macpherson Berrien (1781–1856) of Georgia was elected to the U.S. Senate in 1825 as a Democrat and returned to the Senate in 1840 as a Whig. He served as Andrew Jackson's attorney general from 1828 to 1831.

3. Joseph Jenkins Roberts was elected the first president of the Republic of Liberia in 1848.

4. Clay was defeated in the presidential elections of 1824, 1832, and 1844.

expected to possess, and in his official intercourse especially, to manifest those elevated and ennobling traits of character—a high degree of self-respect, and a high sense of the importance of his position—a demeanor and dignity of purpose commensurate with his station as the Executive of a free, sovereign, independency, and honorable to the nation whose representative he is. This could at least have been hoped and expected of Roberts, whatever contempt we may have entertained toward him as a fawning servilian to the negro-hating Colonizationists.

This we were forced to expect of him, before we could conceive the idea and admit of his fitness for the station he occupied. Whatever prejudices we may have entertained toward him, after the declaration of independence of Liberia, we felt charitably disposed, and endeavored to make ourself believe that Roberts accepted of the position from the American Colonizationists through policy, accepting of their patronage only until a favorable opportunity would ensue for the honorable establishment of a free, independent sovereignty. No one conceived for a moment that Roberts desired degradation, nor would voluntarily solicit submission. Contemptible as we conceived him to be, we never dreamed of the extent of his miserable, crouching baseness.

Immediately subsequent to the independence of Liberia, either for the want of proper qualification on the part of others, or the result of his own political intrigue—most probably the latter—Roberts, though President of the Republic, received the appointment by his country of Envoy Extraordinary, Minister Plenipotentiary, and Commissioner, to negotiate with England, France, Prussia, and other governments, discretionary with himself, for a recognition of the independence of the Republic of Liberia, at present the last of Republics, in the order of their sovereign establishment, and though the smallest, weakest and poorest, we are in hopes that it may yet become the greatest, strongest, and wealthiest on the globe.

Roberts, in his mission to England, met with great success, having treated with Lord Palmerston, receiving many government favors at his hands.[5] In France he met with a like success, with marks of distinction and attention due his rank. Many of the foreign ministers of different courts, much interested themselves in behalf of President Roberts, promising to do all they could with their governments to facilitate the objects of his mission.

5. Immediately after his election to the Liberian presidency in 1848, Roberts attempted to acquire additional territory and international recognition for the new republic. During 1848 he visited England, Belgium, France, and Prussia. While in England he secured funding to purchase land near Liberia frequented by slave traders. The noted Lord Henry John Temple Palmerston (1784–1865), who would become prime minister in 1855, supported Roberts's aims.

Though up to this time, Roberts had been ignorant of the importance of his position and the destiny of his people—though for years he may have existed merely by sufferance, as the servile minion of the misanthropic Colonizationists of the South, and pro-slavery Colonizationists of the North, now that a new arena had been opened to his vision, a new field of action presented itself—an interest of sea and land, having called him into active service, where he stood unfettered and disenthralled, having cast off the menial garb of a slave, posted with the dignity of true manhood, clothed in the paraphernalia of a nation's representative, and armed with the proud panoply of a freeman's rights—these, the new scenes around him, this, his new and elevated position in the world, were, had he been susceptible of it, sufficient in themselves to make him sensible of the respect due to his people, if not his own importance as an equal.

But instead of that manly, dignified, statesmanlike course, such as became a Minister of State, his very first act after the marked distinction and distinguished favors received at the hands of governments and statesmen, is an act of the most pitiable degradation, the most blasting reproach and civil outrage upon his people, that was ever perpetrated by a mendicant.

Like the slave, "cap in hand, obedient to the commands of the dons who employ them," bidden on an errand of his master, President Roberts no sooner concludes the business of his mission, a knowledge and official account of which was alone due to his own government, but he writes to A. G. Phelps,[6] a Colonizationist of the United States, giving him an official report of his proceedings as the Minister of Liberia, an independent nation! If ever the curse of slavery were manifest in the character of man, it has fully exhibited itself in this man Roberts.

The degradation to himself might readily be extenuated, the act being strictly in character with the man; but the insult and disgrace meted to his people should not find palliation in his plea of ignorance. Not content with the stigma thrown into the face of the Liberians by his first report to Phelps, but adding aggravation to insult, promises that so soon as he arrives home to give him "a full and elaborate report" of all his doings.

Here, faithful to the trust reposed in him by his American white masters, this man Roberts discards the people whom he feigns to represent, considering it a condescension so to do, spurns at the idea of reporting to them the result of his mission, but as a serf to his lord, considers it an honor and special privilege to submit his doings first to a white man; hence, that malignant libeller of our race,

6. The wealthy New Yorker Anson Greene Phelps (1781–1853) supported the American Colonization Society from its inception and was one of its principal leaders during the 1840s.

A. G. Phelps, was selected and reported to over the heads of his country and people.

The acts and conduct of Roberts have a bearing not only upon the Liberians as a nation, but upon the whole colored race in America, since having descended from the American colored race, whatever marks the course of progress in his present position, will be seized hold of by the slaveholders and their abettors, as true evidence of the American colored man's character and susceptibility. Hence, we protest against his whole course in regard to his agency and intercourse, either directly or indirectly, with the Colonizationists, especially this crowning act of baseness and servility, in reporting his official doings to A. G. Phelps, a private white man in the United States, instead of his country; averring, that do his government or the national council not impeach him for this act, they are unworthy of freedom, and only fit to be slaves. —M. R. D.

(*North Star*, 2 March 1849, p. 2)

Political Economy

DELANY PRESENTED this essay as a "precursor" to three subsequent essays on domestic economy, which are printed below. In these interlinked essays, as in many other of his writings over the course of his career, Delany called on African Americans to develop strategies for gaining greater access to wealth and power. As he elaborates in the domestic economy essays, he was particularly concerned about the ways in which certain kinds of religious thinking could contribute to passivity and acquiescence.

Our people—the colored people we mean—must give their attention to Political Economy. We do not mean to say, that they must acquire a perfect knowledge of that science, but they must give sufficient attention to it to gain a practical knowledge of its utility. This is within the reach of all, however limited in education, and of whatever lack of experience in business.

Political Economy, properly, is the Science of the Wealth of Nations—practically, the daily application of industry for the purpose of making money. In the present article, we do not design treating this subject scientifically, nor yet elaborately, but simply to reduce it to a plain, easy comprehension of the most obtuse reason. Though the principles of political economy generally apply to a nation, yet the habits of industry apply more particularly to individuals who compose a nation or community.

Nations are but great families; each individual, citizen, or inhabitant, constitutes the members who compose that family. Communities, such as cities, towns, villages, and counties, may be compared to firms, or partnership companies.

All well-bred, well-regulated families, have some great fixed principle as a general rule of conduct, and high incentive as the proper guidance of their children and the individual members of their household. These rules being fully established, the principles fixed, and the incentives to the higher attainments well instilled, the character of the family becomes established, which marks each individual in his walks through life. An improper departure from rules of a well-bred family is always noticed with regret by the observer.

As it is with families, so it is with nations. Whatever characteristics distinguish a nation, each citizen or inhabitant thereof should more or less partake of this character. Each citizen of a nation should bear the same resemblance to the great leading traits which mark the enterprise of that people, as the individual members do to the family to which they belong.

When partnerships are formed, it is intended for mutual benefit. Each member of the firm is required to make an investment, either of capital or labor—that is, money or work.

Now suppose that A, B and C go into partnership. A invests eleven hundred dollars, B ten hundred, and C has no money. How can C be beneficial to the concern? He must give his services, his personal attention to the business, in such a manner as to make it an object with the other partners to have him, else he is worth nothing to them. But in order to be serviceable, he must be qualified to do business; otherwise he will be of no use. It will be seen by this, that qualification and capital, or labor and money, are set as an equivalent against each other.

We, then, as colored people—for it is to the colored people we address ourselves—may be regarded in position, taking the class for the individual, as the partner in a firm, without capital, having made no available investment, and totally unqualified to render valuable and useful service, the other members or partners in the concern bearing the whole burden of business, with us hanging upon their shoulders for daily support. This is precisely, as a general rule, our relation to each other, comparing the blacks and whites as we now exist. This, our brethren must remember, is our own admission, and does not necessarily involve us in disparagement, as our object and determination is to call attention to that fact for the purpose of effecting a speedy change in so objectionable a relation. This much, we deem necessary to say, as a mere precursor to an article every week upon Domestic Economy, or Practical Industry, and money-making business enterprises. What the colored people at present most need, is a knowledge *how to live in this world.* This we must do—this we must be willing to do, or all efforts at regaining our trampled rights in this country or elsewhere, will prove unavailing.—M. R. D.

(*North Star*, 16 March 1849, p. 2)

Domestic Economy

I

. . . The white man is the ruler—the colored man the subject; the white man is ambitious for the mastery—the colored man submits to be the servant. The white man will not live without a country, though he must gain it by usurpation and blood—the colored man is content to sojourn, as it were, denied of every right and privilege tending to make him equal to his fellows. The white man and woman are not satisfied without a large portion of this world's goods, and the fullness of their enjoyment; but the colored man and woman are perfectly satisfied, "contented and happy," in the language of the slaveholder, to live in the service of God, and eventually die and get to heaven. The white man possesses ALL the earth, with a fair prospect of heaven—the colored man has nothing of this earth, with only the same prospect of the white man. Man's mission is an earthly one, and God intended that we should take an equal part in the discharge of its various duties. To do this, we must have means; and to obtain them, we, the colored people, must pursue the same course in the various departments of life that others do.

We must be willing, because it is as contrary to nature as the blending of light and darkness, to cease looking to Providence to do that for us which God has given us the ability and means to do for ourselves. God works by means, and not by miracles. He has placed within our reach means for the accomplishment of certain ends; the application of these means will attain the end aimed at or desired. We must therefore become a business, money-making people. Prayer and praises only fill one's soul with emotion, but can never fill his mouth with bread, nor his pocket with money. Whilst colored people are HOPING, the white man is DOING. We must also DO, if we desire the same enjoyments and possessions of this life. We must learn how to gain a living, to make our bread, the first lesson of which has not yet been taught us. We have not yet lost the feeling common to master and servant; and until this is the case, we are only fit for slaves. Colored people must cease their servile occupations, and get into business, respectable occupations, and thereby cease to be "boys" and "girls," taking their places among men and women in society.

We shall next show the laws by which God governs the destinies of man, the possibility and impossibility of man's attaining certain ends, and that all men may attain the same end by the application of certain means; hence, it is possible for colored people to attain all that the whites have attained.[1]

II

. . . Prayer, we are taught, is all-sufficient for *all* things. This, we also assure our readers, is not the case. Never was there a grosser, or more palpable absurdity; and the writer of this is perfectly willing to hazard his reputation, for the good of his brethren, and run the risk of being branded by bigots and hypocrites as a sceptic and infidel, in giving this a positive contradiction. It may be orthodox, so to believe, but it is not in accordance with common sense,—it may be enjoined as revelation, but it is at variance with truth, and contrary to reason and fact.

. . . The slave may, in the agony of his wounded soul, and goodness of a believing heart, fall upon his knees, and clasping his hands, cry out, "pray, master, forgive me this offence!" then, raising his eyes to heaven, "How long, O Lord! most mighty—how long, shall I thus continue to suffer! O! when shall the day of my deliverance come!" and while he is thus, pathetically supplicating, rending both heaven and earth, with his appeals of misery, the infernal monster, with the blasphemy of hell upon his polluted lips, and the punishing rod of a fiend in his hand, deaf to all entreaties and cries of mercy, will continue to lacerate, scourge, and lay open the naked flesh, until the bleeding, mangled victim falls exhausted at his feet! All this is actually done, yea, daily takes place, somewhere in the South, while the simple-hearted, ignorant slave is calling upon high heaven for aid and assistance!

And why, we ask, in the name of God, and all "the just made perfect,"[2] why are not these prayers and supplications answered? Simply, because prayer and faith are not the means to be made use of, in such a case.

Prayer is a spiritual means, intended only to answer spiritual ends. When the

1. In response to this article, George Weir Jr., in a letter of 29 March 1849, complained that Delany's seeming advocation of business practices over and above spiritual concerns threatened to make African Americans' "hearts . . . more hardened, and their obdurate wills more prone to evil, than what was ever before known" (*North Star*, 7 April 1849, p. 3). Delany responded in an open letter to Weir: "[A]ll that we desire, is to refute the idea so generally entertained, on the part of our people particularly, that by first seeking the kingdom of heaven, that is, if they only become religious people, God will give them everything else. Every intelligent person must see the fallacy and absurdity of this idea" (*North Star*, 27 April 1849, p. 3).
2. Hebrews 12:23.

slave called upon God, from the depths of his soul, to forgive and pardon his sins, to comfort and refresh his spirits, God heard and answered him. But, in this prayer and supplication for deliverance from the iron grasp of a hard-hearted task master, and ruthless tyrant, God answered not his prayer, because it was improperly applied; it was the wrong means to be used, in such a case.

The inhuman despotism of the demon master, toward the slave, was a temporal and physical act, and required temporal and physical means to prevent it. The master and slave are both human beings, endowed with the same faculties—a corporeal or physical system, with limbs having bones, muscles, and tendons, which give strength to the system. As the punishment of the slave was physical, inflicted by strength, so should it have been met by physical force, and prevented by strength. Had the slave, instead of falling upon his knees, looking up to heaven for assistance, have seized his master, held him fast, thrust him aside, or taken to his heels,—in all or either of these cases, he may have been successful in arresting the punishment. The proper means to be made use of in such a case. Physical ends, we honestly and sincerely assure you, brethren, can only be successfully attained by physical means, and it is the height of folly—it is blind madness to believe any thing else.

Further argument is useless; we have now transcended the bounds, to which we had limited ourselves. Our sole, and only object is to disabuse the minds of our brethren, of the miserable heresies, which they have been taught, by the enemies of our race; to unplug their ears, and tear away the veil from their eyes, to the scenes, the sufferings, the groans and wailings, of outraged and down-trodden humanity. The slaveholding and pro-slavery high priests of infamy may, for sinister motives, so teach, as true doctrine, and sound orthodoxy; the white theologian may, if he can, induce colored people to depend upon faith and prayer, to accomplish their earthly desires for them, believing them to be the means; and our brethren may, if they will so stubbornly persist in believing; but we can assure them, that the whites, who so teach, do not believe it themselves; but, if they did, it is not the truth, being at variance with every known fact, and all human experience. It is high time, brethren, we had begun to think for ourselves; we have had others long enough, to think for us. While the pro-slavery whites can keep us satisfied, in depending upon prayer, and looking to heaven for all we desire in this world, there are no fears that we will ever be in their way, other than as a nuisance, when it is the easiest thing in the world, to get rid of us, by sending us away to distant parts. Things should be dealt with just as persons please, and if we will be things, why let us be accordingly dealt with. Brethren, our object is to set you to thinking—thinking *for* yourselves. All that you know, in morals and religion, you have learned from your oppressors, and those for the most part, slave-holders, as the colored people in this country, generally come from the South. An "evil tree cannot bring forth good fruit,"[3] how, then, can such corrupt wretches, as many of these, do otherwise than wrongly teach you? Having removed, as we hope, this difficulty, hoping that you may profit by the same, we shall endeavor to continue, every week, to say something to you, on domestic economy and business.

III

Having previously shown that effects are only equal to the causes that produce them, and that ends can be equal only to the means that are used for their attainment, and that all human affairs are regulated or brought about in accordance with some of the three regular laws of Deity, the *Spiritual, Moral* and *Physical*, and that a compliance with or a violation of either of these laws determines the result of all human affairs; we shall proceed to offer some practical common sense remarks on the subject of business enterprize and industry.

Oppressed, enslaved, degraded, and deprived of all knowledge, consequently knowing nothing but that which we learned from our oppressors, we have been long wont to mourn and sigh over our condition, unable to divine the reason why it is that the slave and colored people generally, with all their religion, moral honesty, and goodness of heart, so far as they know how and understood, strictly doing the will of God, and yet by him have been permitted to continue under the oppression of those who in the majority of instances violate every injunction and *spiritual* precept of the divine will. This we say has been the great barrier in our pathway, and the most difficult point to pass in our efforts at self-elevation. Such a wilderness did this open to our view—such an insurmountable obstacle did it appear to place before us, that disheartened and discouraged by the way side, stopping short—the only, what seemed to us reasonable conclusion we could come to was, instead of pressing onward, to "stand still, and see the salvation of God," honestly believing that He *required* this passiveness and indifference on our part. His declaration to us that "*now* is the *accepted* time, *to-day* is the *day* of salvation,"[4] is equally as imperative, and more forcibly binding upon us, because the first was the injunction of Moses, a man given to the children of Israel more than three thousand years ago, while the second is a divine admonition given by Christ-God himself for the guidance of man since Moses recorded his. Whom shall we obey, Christ or Moses—God or man? Decide for yourselves.

We are anxious to remove those false impressions made by erroneous reli-

3. See Matthew 7:17.
4. Exodus 14:13; 2 Corinthians 6:2.

gious doctrine at the instigation of our oppressors, and continued by us through ignorance.

But why do the wicked slaveholders and blasphemous oppressors of our race succeed against those who are really righteous? Why are *they* intelligent, powerful, and wealthy, having every necessary comfort of life, while we, the colored people, the greater part of whom though religious, are ignorant, powerless, and poor, possessing but few of the comforts of this life, scarcely enough to keep body and soul together?

The reason is obvious; it is this, we make use of heavenly means for the attainment of earthly ends, while our oppressors make use of earthly means for the attainment of earthly ends. The *spiritual* laws, as previously suggested, only pertain to the things of heaven, and were never intended by their Great Author for any other purpose. The physical and moral laws pertain to earthly ends, and by them only can all things temporal be effected. However wicked or perverse may be the person, does he conform to God's law, a favorable result must be the consequence; hence, the reason of the success, frequently, of the wicked over the righteous—the sinner over the saint—the infidel oppressor and slaveholder over the religious colored slaves of America.

Nothing can be accomplished without the proper means being used, therefore all earthly ends can only be obtained by earthly means. Let us then at once, get to business, brethren; let us cease to mourn over what we have been taught to call the *will* of Providence, and raise up our heads like men, embracing the various occupations of society—entering into the various enterprizes, braving every consequence, let these be what they may. Our *masters* have been so accustomed to teach us how to live in the world to come, that they have forgotten to teach us how to live in this world; but are always very careful to teach their own children and themselves, however religious they may be, how to make a living *here*, while in this world.

These things we must also learn and delight in doing, and if you object to them as unworthy of you as Christians, then indeed is this world unfit for your abiding place, your Creator having made a great mistake in placing you here, when you more fittingly should have been uncreated "angels."

We want business men and women among us and must have them in every place. We have been heretofore taught that these things were unfit for us, as they interfered with our prospects of heaven. This our oppressors taught us to prevent us from competing with them in business; and being ignorant, we believed it. Let this henceforth be no longer the case. Industry as much belongs to us, as to them. Surely if we can work for them, and do their drudgery—go at their bidding, and come at their command—spend our money with them in buying from them; if they can advise with us in religion, in medicine, and law, then may we also, if we only determine that it shall be so, sell to them as well as buy from them; give advice to them in matters of religion, medicine, and law, as well as receive advice from them in all these matters. But we must qualify ourselves for these various departments first, which is comparatively an easy matter. We must have farmers, mechanics, and shopkeepers generally among us. By these occupations we make money—these are the true sources of wealth. Give us wealth, and we can obtain all the rest.—M. R. D.

(*North Star*, 23 March 1849, p. 2; 13 April 1849, p. 2; 20 April 1849, p. 2)

Southern Customs — Madame Chevalier

THROUGHOUT HIS CAREER, Delany was prideful of his black skin and scornful of lighter-skinned African Americans who adopted the antiblack racism of their white oppressors.

"Madame Chevalier" as she is called, is a dark mulatto woman of what the Spanish creoles term as sambo color, and takes her name from a slaveholding cotton planter in the Red river county not far distant above Compte[1] by the name of Chevalier. This woman has had a young and interesting daughter, (whose name we forbear to mention at present lest it may hereafter become a source of annoyance to her, should she as she solemnly declares she will do, if an honorable opportunity ever occurs, come to the North again to reside,) for several years at school in the city of Cincinnati, who during the period of Gilmer's "High School"[2] was a pupil of that institution. I—— is a comely and interesting young girl now about fifteen years of age, a pure Louisiana quadroon of the Japanese complexion. The mother who is a native Virginian having been taken south when young, eventually falling into the hands of this man Chevalier, who at once adopted her as his paramour, for the first time came to Cincinnati in May bringing two sons, handsome youths of twelve and fourteen with her, for the purpose of placing them at school at Oberlin and taking her daughter home with her, as she alleged, to finish her education in a French Seminary at New Orleans.

The daughter, as is customary with Southerners, was sent to Cincinnati without the mother, the father coming and making arrangements in person, during which period she has been under the protection and boarded in the family of a very respectable colored lady, Mrs. T—— who keeps a reserved private board-

1. Deriving its name from an eighteenth-century French fort, Compte refers to an area in southeastern Louisiana; the Red River extends from Texas through Oklahoma to Louisiana.

2. Hiram S. Gilmore's "Cincinnati High School." See "Western Tour for the *North Star*," note 50.

ing house, while her husband, an enterprising industrious man, trades on the river. But an absence of nearly five years began to give the mother impressions concerning the daughter, which she at once determined to realise—hence the reason of her coming instead of the father, to make arrangements for the education of her boys. Although the paramour and mistress, being herself a slave, like the slaves generally she was uneducated, and if we mistake not unable to read; consequently so incompetent to discharge duties necessary in making arrangements for the education of her boys, that she declined to discharge that duty herself, employing Mrs. T——, the guardian of her daughter, to take the youths to Oberlin and make arrangements for their education.

Notwithstanding the ignorance and enslavement of this woman, added to which was the double degradation of her situation in concubinage—yet this wreck of a woman—this creature—this victim of human depravity had great fault to find with Mrs. T——, not for any delinquency on her part of attention to the daughter, but forsooth, because she did not prohibit her from the company and society of colored people altogether, except the necessary association with her class at school; with an effrontery only befitting that ignorance the natural offspring of self degradation, this woman, observed to Mrs. T——, with indignance—"Me let my daughter associate with such people indeed! why I have *slaves* at home as goodlooking as they!" the pitiable creature, forgetting that she herself at the same time was a slave—intimating, as we learned, although she did not express it in so many words, that she would prefer to see her daughter in *concubinage* to a white, than respectably married to a colored man! Who could believe that slavery was capable of thus reducing to the deepest abyss of degradation the image of God, created a little lower than the angels?—capable of so obscuring the human vision as to induce it to voluntarily close the windows of the soul and shut out the glaring light of Heaven, preferring darkness to light—preferring ignorance to intelligence—preferring disgrace to respectability—misery to happiness, because their deeds are evil and full of corruption.

But why reflect and animadvert upon the conduct of this miserable wretched woman—she is an ignorant bondee—she knew no better, and if she did, she acted precisely as she had been taught by her master and paramour, who in all probability, is but training up the daughter as a superior *rival* to her *mother*. This will not be thought improbable by those acquainted with Southern customs, but the ignorant slave mother little suspects such an event. She is but a type of hundreds of such poor miserable beings who coming to the North disseminate the prejudices instilled into them at the South by the wily slave-holder, whose only object is to effectually prevent concord and union among the colored people. Hence, the frequent silly attempts at the establishment of "Quadroon Societies," "Dead-head Societies," as one in existence we believe is now termed, and such like ridiculous feints at superiority of descent.[3] But all this has emanated from slavery, ignorance, and arrogance; hence, the impudence and in-famy of Madam Chevalier can easily be extenuated, although we may not be so charitably disposed towards those who under far more favorable auspices in the non-slaveholding states, endorse the doctrine and adopt this hideously de-formed creature of our oppressors, endeavoring to rear it up in our midst. All that is necessary for us to do is to stamp our foot upon it and crush it level to the earth. We conversed with the young girl of doubtful destination, giving her some good advice, who promised us with tears in her eyes, that if possible, she would return to the embraces of virtue and respectability—protesting that it was not her desire at all to return South, laying the charge of all the conse-quences upon the shoulders of her mother!

M. R. D.

(*North Star*, 22 June 1849, p. 2)

---

3. Scornful references to blacks who attempted to "pass" as whites or assert themselves as superior to full-blooded blacks; a "quadroon" was regarded as one-fourth (or less) "black."

Annexation of Cuba

IN HIS NOVEL, *Blake* (1859, 1861–62), Delany imagined the possibility of a hemispheric slave revolution that would have Cuba at its epicenter. Delany had a long-standing interest in Cuba, which remained an important site for the slave trade in the Americas well into the nineteenth century. He regarded the political situation there as yet another distressing instance of white colonial subjugation of peoples of color. He was also concerned, in the light of the recent war with Mexico, that Cuba would eventually fall into the hands of U.S. slave expansionists. But given the sheer number of peoples of color in Cuba, and the evidence of their discontent, Delany remained hopeful that the oppressed peoples of Cuba, as in Haiti, could overthrow the white ruling class and achieve their independence. Delany's two essays on Cuba in the *North Star*, "Annexation of Cuba" and "The Redemption of Cuba," provide valuable commentary on the politics of race and slavery in the Americas in the late 1840s and provide as well crucial contexts for reading his later novel of black revolutionism.

There are few persons in any country, who are close or critical observers of political movements; the masses passing along quite unconcernedly until the crisis comes on them with all its anxious uncertainties—its hopes and its fears—its doubts and prospects, which in the American system-politic, usually terminates like an epidemic, not only disastrous to the individual, but spreads its malady with the most fearful consequences, infecting all in contiguity with it.

That there is a deep-concerted scheme for the annexation of Cuba to the United States is not a matter of question, and that the American people in general, and colored people in particular should be timely advised of this perfidious wicked design is not more questionable.

When the nefarious scheme of the annexation of Texas was proposed,[1] no one believed in the possibility of its consummation—not even the Southerners themselves, who doubtless at first proposed it merely as a ruse by which to

---

1. The annexation of Texas in 1845 precipitated the Mexican War.

alarm the North at the time, in order thereby to effect a compromise on the slavery question, which was then in agitation before the councils of the nation. But so little import was given to the measure, that the opponents of the project were ill-aware of it until the startling reality was full upon them despite every effort to stay it.

This we forewarn the friends of freedom, without the most vigorous united effort to stop it, will be the reality in the case of Cuba, an island possessing triple-fold advantages to the United States as a territory, to that of Texas.

Cuba is the great key-of-entry to the United States from the East, possessing one of the strongest forts in the western hemisphere, that of Vera Cruz not excepted, and being an old established place has grown to be of great commercial importance, populated with several considerable cities and ports, Havana the greatest of which, the present seat of the Viceroy, is probably not inferior to New Orleans in trade and population. Besides it is said that there are more Americans directly interested in possessions in the isle of Cuba than in any other foreign territory. Perhaps there is not a large commercial city in the United States, North or South, at least a maritime city, with many others in which there are not capitalists who are more or less interested by investments in Cuba. Boston, New York, Philadelphia, Wilmington, Baltimore, Washington City, and Georgetown, (the three last, *largely*,) Annapolis, Norfolk, Richmond, Charleston, (the two last *largely*) Mobile, New Orleans, largely, Natchez, largely, Nashville, St. Louis, Louisville, Cincinnati, Wheeling, and Pittsburgh, all have large interests there.

But there is a tie doubly as strong as all the other commercial interests taken in the aggregate, which binds this foreign child in embryo to a most sympathizing mother — it is the iron-linked and yet unbroken chain of slavery. Here is the deep and abiding interest.

Cuba is the great western slave mart of the world, containing the barracoons or refining shops to the slave factories of Pedro Blanco,[2] and other pirates on the western coast of Africa. It is the great channel through which slaves are imported annually into the United States, contrary to the law of the land, and the sovereign power by which the constitutional power of 1808 is stricken down, and made null and void at the will of the slaveholder. Into this island are there annually imported more than fifty thousand slaves, expressly for the human market, and being contiguous to the United States, vessels from Baltimore, Washington city, Richmond, and other American slave-markets usually after shipping a *few* slaves purchased in those particular places, sail to the isle of Cuba under the pretext of touching by Havana for trade. When they enter the barracoons, the traders to whom the slaves on board belong, frequently the master

2. See "Western Tour for the *North Star*," note 37.

and owner of the vessel being concerned in the traffic, purchase a full cargo of slaves, sail to New Orleans where they are sold out to the highest bidder, at the slave market there, from whence they are taken to all parts of the South. In this high-handed manner is the provision prohibiting the importation of slaves into the United States after the year 1808,[3] openly and constantly trampled under foot; and those in power, the supreme Judicial and Executive authorities being generally slaveholders or their abettors, well know these facts, and by keeping silence wink at and encourage such undisguised, infamous deeds of daring.

There are at present in Cuba, probably not less than 600,000 slaves, there being in 1830 nearly twenty years ago, 450,000, with a yearly increase of trade in the slave products. These human souls, computed at the lowest estimate of $250 a-piece would amount to the sum of $150,000,000 which added to the land possessions, would bring into this country if annexed to it, no inconsiderable wealth to be at once added to its resources as a nation. Besides, the imports and expenditures with foreign nations would, according to the American policy of encouragement to home manufactures, as far as possible be turned to the domestic market.

For the consummation of an object, to them so desirable as the annexation of Cuba, the late administration, James K. Polk, who if not the projector, was the accomplisher of the unequalled scheme of the annexation of Texas, gave instructions and authority to Mr. Saunders, acting Minister at the Court of Spain, to negotiate with that Government for the payment of the Spanish debt to England, receiving as an equivalent, a mortgage on Cuba, which would at once place fairly in the American power the island as an American territory.[4] And the principal objection to this project appears to have been made by the Spanish subjects resident on the island, who becoming alarmed at the prospect of the passage of the Wilmot proviso[5] and the fear of the prohibition of the slave trade being extended over them, would prefer to remain an integral portion of Spain, to that of becoming a fractional part of the United States government.

The project being once determined on, as we really believe it has been, the slave-holders and their compatriots in the North will find no difficulty in effect-

3. Article I, Section IX, of the Constitution banned slave importation beginning in the year 1808.

4. Delany's account here is fairly accurate. Following a 17 June 1848 meeting with his cabinet, which approved the plan, President James Polk instructed Romulus Mitchell Saunders (1791–1867), U.S. minister to Spain, to offer Spain up to 100 million dollars for Cuba.

5. In 1846, David Wilmot (1814–68), a democrat from Pennsylvania, put before the U.S. House of Representatives a bill banning slavery in any territory acquired from the Mexican War. The bill passed the House but not the Senate.

ing a removal of these objections, since their whole studied policy is to dupe the country into their interested measures which they will most probably succeed in. The objections to Texan annexation were once as strong even on the part of Texans themselves, and as apparently improbable as that of the projected annexation of Cuba. But how soon were such objections dissipated! a large majority of Texans over-ruling the others, and the proposition passing the Congress of the United States, with one or two honorable exceptions, with scarcely a respectable opposition.

It is surmised that the interposition of Great Britain would be brought to bear, to prevent the accomplishment of this scheme of Cuban annexation. Let none deceive themselves on this point. Great Britain does not desire a war with any nation at present, and only wages war when she cannot avoid it. Her first resource is negotiation by treaty; when this does not avail, her last is a resort to arms. She will never concern herself with the affairs of other nations when she is not particularly interested; and her relations with Cuba are such that they may easily be adjusted by negociation, which is as compatible with the British policy as warfaring. To suppose that England will interfere mainly on account of the regard she has for the colored people and slaves of the island is also a great mistake. Although purely an antislavery nation and tried and proven friend of the African race, yet she has no greater love for black than white, and may not be expected to interfere except as her interest and commercial relations demand it. Such men as Lord Palmerston, the earl of Aberdeen, Henry Lord Brougham, Sir Robert Peel, and Lord John Russell,[6] will not remain silent and see a nation of thirty five million involved in a terrible war, for the sake of six hundred thousand slaves, in whom they have no interest, when they possess the heads to prevent it.

Another important consideration. Did England desire to war with the United States, there is an almost insurmountable difficulty in the way of her doing so, and this fact may as well be known now as hereafter, as it is a fact that must and will be known. The United States, like the great prostitute of Revelation, who sat at her door inducing all who passed along,[7] has been for the last three quarters of a century sitting upon the highway of political and historical fame, with the enchanting words of Justice, Freedom, Liberty, Equality, Democracy, and Re-

6. Delany lists some of the leading reform politicians of Great Britain: Henry Temple, Lord Palmerston (1784–1865), George Hamilton Gordon, 4th earl of Aberdeen (1784–1860), Henry Peter, Lord Brougham (1778–1868), Sir Robert Peel (1788–1850), and Lord John Russell (1792–1878). In 1860, Delany would be saluted by Brougham in what would become an international incident; see "The International Statistical Congress" in Part 4 below.

7. See Revelation 17.

publicanism on her tongue, which has been sounding through the earth, inviting the oppressed of all countries to seek a home under the hospitality of her covering, until the peasant-subjects of every nation of Europe have caught the sound, and learned to love the name of America; and now, almost a universal revolution has been produced throughout all the European nations, those who have not struck the blow being only deterred by fear, so that they have really rebelled in heart; and under such circumstances, depend upon it, it is next to impossible to muster an army in England or any other European nation, who would be willing to wage war *against* the United States.

In the event of such an issue, the only reliable hope of England would be her black subjects in the West Indies and other British colonies, as the white peasantry could not be depended upon, having white friends, especially the Irish who constitute a large portion of her soldiery, scattered over this extensive country, filling offices both civil and military, and completely incorporated in all the various ramifications of the country and nation, they would not fight against them. And we are not quite certain that England is ready to place her black soldiery in the front ranks of battle array, although they are formidable and trustworthy to a man.

England, then, may not be expected to interfere further than to secure the debt due to her by Spain, and this the United States will manage by negotiation and "compromise" to secure in "good faith."

To have Cuba as a United States territory the Americans are determined, if within the bounds of possibility. But what is to be done to prevent a scheme fraught with such fearful consequences as this project of annexation of Cuba? There is but one party more interested than all others, who are able to prevent at least the consummation of this deep-seated design—the colored people themselves, and to them we make the appeal. We heartily believe with the Spanish Sancho,[8] chief of a delegation of Commissioners, who, sent some ten or twelve years since, by the Cortez council of the nation, to investigate the affairs of the colony, reported that "Cuba must cease to be a Spanish colony and become a Negro government, for the reason there is no power under heaven capable of subduing four hundred thousand negroes, if they deliberately determined that they *will not* be oppressed by them."

There are now six hundred thousand human souls, held in abject bondage in

---

8. In all likelihood Delany refers to the Spanish editor José Antonio Saco (1797–1879), who published a widely discussed article in an 1833 issue of his newly founded Cuban magazine, *Rivesta Bimestre Cubana*, warning that the growth of the slave population in Cuba threatened to bring about a slave revolution on the order of Haiti's. His assessment angered Spanish authorities, who forced him into exile.

Cuba, all of whom must ere long be disenthralled by the very nature of things, but for this American interference. And shall we who are nominally free, as mute as the dumb-gagged slave, remain silent at the approach of such an alarming usurpation, and not utter our voices against it? Shall we whose duty it is to give the strongest opposition to these inroads upon right, be the most indifferent to them? No, we should not. The cause is ours—we are the interested party, and every colored man should make common cause of it, uniting in mind, heart, sentiment, and action, sending up one united voice of solemn indignation against this and every such scheme, and by every means in his power enlighten his brethren in slavery upon the subject of their inalienable God-given rights; this we conceive to be, as freemen, our heaven-required duty, and should use every possible means to accomplish it.

While the oppressed of every nation have risen up, and are arousing the world with their struggles for liberty—braving every consequence,—caring for, and fearing nothing, in defence of their rights,—shall the American slave remain in abject bondage, waiting patiently, toiling on and suffering on, having nothing in prospect but the hope of his heartless relentless master's good will? Never. Let him be taught that he dare strike for liberty,—let him know this, and he at once rises up disenthralled—a captive redeemed from the portals of infamy to the true dignity of his nature—an elevated freeman. A determined opposition to the increase of the slave power, and encroachments upon their God-given rights, should signalize the bondman everywhere, and they should at this juncture be taught, we care not how, by whom or in what manner it is imparted to them, that on the attempt at such an effort they should hold themselves in readiness, and at the instant of the annexation of Cuba to these United States, it should be the signal for simultaneous rebellion of all the slaves in the Southern States, and throughout that island. The author of this article, alone, is responsible for the sentiments therein contained.

"Were I a slave, I would be free,
I would not live to live a slave,
But boldly strike for liberty—
For freedom, or a martyr's grave.

One look upon the tyrant's chains
Would draw my sabre from its sheath,
And drive the hot blood thro' my veins
To rush for liberty or death.

One look upon my tortured wife,
Shrieking beneath the driver's blow,

Would nerve me on to desp'rate strife;
Nor would I spare her dastard foe.

Away the unavailing plea
Of peace, the tyrant's blood to spare;
If you would set the bondman free,
Teach him for freedom bold to dare.

To throw his galling shackles by,—
To wing the cry on every breath,
Determined, manhood's conquering cry
For Justice—Liberty—or Death."—M. R. D.

(*North Star*, 27 April 1849, p. 2)

The Redemption of Cuba

Of the many who speculate on the affairs of this country, there are but few who understand its real state and condition—its population and resources—the strength and means for success on the part of the oppressed whenever the time comes—the decisive hour—that eventful moment, which as certain as the heavens must and will come, when the oppressed and bondmen of every origin, grade, and hue under the despotism of the white race, shall determine to strike the fatal blow and rend the yoke from every neck! . . .

Let the colored races look well to their own interests—let them act for themselves. This we have determined ever to do. Three millions of our brethren and kinsmen groan in servitude in the United States of America—in bondage and degradation unsurpassed by any that ever disgraced the world and outraged humanity. For these there are many moral agents now at work, by which means we shall hope and trust for success, and by whom we shall ever stand and never yield, while the stench of their affliction continues to pollute the air, administering to their necessities as far as in our power lies to reach them by the balm of moral consolation, until every fetter shall be riven, and every shackle shall be shattered, and the bondman of America is made every whit whole. But the oppressed of Cuba have not this moral consolation at hand—no moral agencies at work directly for them. They *must take their cause in their own hands,* and use the means adequate to the ends—the means within *their reach.* These means they have. Let them but remember the masterly and noble reply of Henry Christophe,[1] one of the oppressed of St. Domingo, who in answer to general Leclerc,[2] the able captain and brother-in-law of the emperor Napoleon, said, "It is needless to count on numbers or means. My determination to be a man and *freeman,* is the sum of my arithmetic!" But let them come to this noble determination and conclusion, and the colored races of Cuba are *free!*—Slavery must

1. Henri Christophe (1760–1820), a freed black slave, was one of the leaders of the Haitian revolution against French colonial authority.

2. In 1802 Napoleon sent his brother-in-law, general Charles Victor Emmanuel LeClerc (1772–1802), to Haiti to subdue the black revolutionaries. LeClerc died of yellow fever shortly after he deported the revolutionary leader Toussaint L'Ouverture to France.

and will fall!—The slaveholders' doom is irrevocably sealed!—Sealed forever
there! The blood of the murdered Placido[3] and his brave compatriots, still cries
aloud for justice, and vengeance must sooner or later overtake their guilty oppressors and inquisitors of that memorable event. Take courage—courage, dis-
comfited bondman of Cuba—your redemption draweth nigh! Already is that
anxious and eventful morning approaching—its dawn is visible in the distant
horizon—the day-star appears in the midst and gives additional splendor to its
brilliancy. Hold up your heads—cheer up your spirits—let your hearts even be
glad. Brace your muscles—nerve your arms with a full determination to strike
for Liberty, and never cease until you have gained it.

Send up your aspirations to high heaven—invoke the aid of the Lord of
hosts—beseech him in righteous solicitude to satisfy you whether or not it be
his will to.

> "See Afric's sons and daughters toil,
> Day after day, year after year,
> Upon this blood bemoistened soil,
> And to their cries turn a deaf ear?
> Canst thou the white oppressor bless
> With verdant hills and fruitful plains,
> Regardless of the slave's distress—
> Unmindful of the black man's chains?"

No, the day has arrived when the colored race must advocate their own
cause—when we must defend ourselves and the cause of our brethren, regardless of consequences.

Too long have we been diffident upon this subject, and fearful to speak—too
long have we submitted to be gulled by our white oppressors by permitting ourselves to believe that to be criminal in us which is commendable in them—
vicious in us which is virtuous in them. Let this no longer be the case, but whenever you are ready, hoist the flag, and draw the sword of revolution, and put your
oppressors in Cuba to a terrible flight. In this you will have the prayers and approbation of all the assimilated oppressed throughout the world in general and
in America in particular. And so far as is consistent with our idea of right, our
aid in approbation, encouragement, advice and *counsel*, were it possible to give
it, shall ever be at your service. If it were just and right for Poland, Greece,
France and Rome,[4] to strike down tyranny and assert their right to civil lib-

---

3. Cuban poet executed by Spanish authorities in 1844 for alleged treasonous activities;
for more on Placido (1809–44), see the selection from *Blake* in Part 3.

4. Delany refers to the Polish revolution of 1831; the Greek war of independence beginning in 1821; the French Revolution of the late eighteenth century; and the Roman republican revolution of 1848.

erty—if it were an act in France, worthy the commendation, praise, and honor of the American people, to strike down the oppressor, throw off the burden of an unjust government, and declare in favor of "Liberty, Equality, Fraternity,"[5] then will it be just and right in you.

> "Armed with the vindicating brand—
> For once the tyrant's heart should feel,
> No milk-sop plea should stay my hand—
> The slave's great wrong, would drive the steel!"

And should ever the time come when we become so recreant to the cause of our oppressed brethren as to refuse them our aid in the righteous and sacred cause of liberty—may the earth—the grave refuse our body a resting place, and "vaulted heaven" our spirit a home.

> "How long oh Lord! ere thou wilt speak
> In thy Almighty—thundering voice,
> To bid the oppressors' fetters break,
> And Ethiopia's sons rejoice?"

M. R. D.

(*North Star*, 20 July 1849, p. 3)

---

5. The Jacobins' rallying cry during the French Revolution.

Letter to M. H. Burnham, 5 October 1849

IN SEPTEMBER 1849, M. H. Burnham, a relatively obscure black abolitionist from Lanesville, Ohio, requested Delany's help in establishing a black newspaper in Ohio. Despite his apparent disaffection with Douglass, Delany pragmatically urged blacks to support the *North Star*. He also revealed some of his frustrations with the public and economic dimensions of his antislavery work of the 1840s.

DEAR SIR:—I have received your letter dated Sept. 5th, in which you suggest the enterprise of establishing a newspaper to be located at some eligible point in the State as an organ of the colored people of Ohio, soliciting my advice and opinion on the subject, and also my services at the head of the enterprise as *editor* and *conductor* of such paper, should it [be] established.

I am fully sensible of the purity of the motives and the pressing demands which prompted the faithful enterprising gentlemen, our brethren, to suggest such a movement, and should be stupidly vain indeed, did I not acknowledge the compliment and deference paid, and the confidence reposed in me, by selecting me to head the noble band of colored freemen of your State, in an enterprise, laudable, honorable, philanthropic, and inevitably glorious, could the project be successfully carried out. You set an estimate upon my knowledge of the State, and ask my opinion accordingly. I shall at once proceed to give that opinion unreserved and unrestrained.

Having traversed the length and breadth of your State during five months of the last year, I acquired a tolerable knowledge of the condition and resources of our brethren of Ohio, and their probability of success in the event of such an issue.

The colored population of the State, is now rising twenty thousand, a body of people, in all conscience much too great to be without an organ or special advocate. Making the allowance of one sixth of this number only, it gives three thousand, three hundred and thirty-three families, who should be sufficiently adequate to the sustenance of any single newspaper. These families it must be admitted are generally well to do—being industrious; they are mostly property holders, many of whom are farmers and mechanics, and consequently, men and women of means and money.

But there is another consideration. In no one community in the State, is there a thousand of a population of colored people save Cincinnati and Columbus, the former of which is rising five thousand, and the latter one. Again, to ensure the success of a newspaper, two things are necessary—a reading and a business community. The first to ensure subscriptions, and the other support by advertisements. These are what give life to and ensure the existence of the various public journals of the country, except the reformatory, which are always a drag and burden to their conductors, drooping through a period of beggarly existence, coming at last to a pitiable end. Such a result should be henceforth studiously avoided by us in every enterprise, having ever occupied a beggarly position, and God knows, only regarded as the objects of pity.

In any given number of colored families where the heads consist of elderly persons, there is always a ratio of two thirds who cannot read, leaving but one third, but a portion of whom are in circumstances that will justify them in supporting a paper; but a fraction of which portion again may be willing, allowing all reasonable excuses and objections so common among our people. This estimate will hold good particularly among the three thousand families in Ohio, (Cincinnati being an exception,) as the greater part are immigrants from different parts of the South.

Three thousand families, remotely scattered over the State, with no one community sufficient to sustain such a project; with all their various misconceptions and prejudices—predilections and biases, imbibed and instilled in the South, and the difficulty in obtaining suitable agents to secure subscribers and collect money sufficient to sustain the enterprise, renders the undertaking at once so difficult, that it looks in the distance to be insurmountable; and having had seven years' experience in editing and conducting newspapers, and an extensive acquaintance among our people—with their situation, condition, and otherwise, in other places as well as Ohio, I unhesitatingly express my doubt of the ultimate success of the project, believing that it would end with great losses to the undertakers, and in its failure, produce consequences that would give much cause for future regret.[1]

There are at present two or more newspapers in existence published by colored men,[2] devoted to the cause of our people; all of which are merely dogging

1. On the difficulty of sustaining an African American newspaper, see also Delany's "Highly Important Statistics—Our Cause and Our Destiny—Endowment of a Newspaper," *North Star*, 13 April 1849, p. 2.

2. African American newspapers published around the time Delany wrote Burnham

at the threshold of doubts and fears—asking aid at the gateway of impatient benevolence—their conductors depending upon personal friends, to whom they are almost compelled from necessity to cater and pander for their scanty means of subsistence. If one or two papers cannot be sustained, surely an additional number must make the prospects still the less; and in my humble opinion, I should much prefer that we would support one good paper, ably and properly conducted, adapted to our demands, wants and condition; than to have several in existence, barely floating with exhausted wings upon the ebbing-tide and worn out patience of Philanthropy—gouging to the vitals, and obstructing the very life-blood of the charity of the public and community in which they exist.

I have, Sir, other and personal objections to entering into such an enterprise. I have never been sufficiently successful in the cause of our brethren to have a value set upon my efforts. I have labored for nought, and received nothing. If I except the use of fifty dollars borrowed from a donation of one hundred dollars, presented by the Ladies' Fair to the *North Star*, which sum I have still to pay, the present of a sum of ten dollars, and various articles of clothing for myself and wife and little children, during my stay in Philadelphia last winter, by several excellent colored ladies, is more than I ever before realised, during seven years labor as editor of different papers, the last eighteen months of which time, were devoted entirely to the cause.

I am fully persuaded, that to embark in a new enterprise of this kind, would be heedless in me, and the last precipitous stride and gasping struggle to the certain starvation of my family, whom I am bound by all the ties of consanguinity and self-respect, and what is stronger than self-love—of conjugal and filial affection, to protect and support—protect alike against starvation as well as oppression and personal injury and abuse. This I hope will constitute sufficient reason for my personal objection to entering into such an enterprise, though there are others I might give. My ardent desire for the elevation of our race, has caused me to sacrifice more than I was able to bear—more than my share.

I would therefore most cordially recommend to our people throughout this country, to rally around the *North Star*, a paper upon which large sums of money, much means, time and talent have been and are still being expended, published in Rochester, N.Y., and ably edited by Frederick Douglass, a brother, who has "borne the heat and burden of the day"[3] of oppression—tasted the wormwood and gall of slavery—a self-made freeman—a self-taught man.

included Stephen Myers's *Northern Star and Freeman's Advocate* (Albany, New York), William Hodge's *Ram's Horn* (New York City), and Samuel Ward's *True American* (Cortland, New York).
   3. Matthew 20:12.

Should any be disposed to object to the Star on the ground of its not being what they desire—send on your request, and demand of Frederick Douglass in the name of a common cause, of mutual oppression—in the name of his out-raged kinsmen—in the name of discarded manhood, outraged humanity, and insulted intelligence, to pursue that course which you conceive to be the best adapted to the end to be attained. If you be so dissatisfied, do this—until then, you will have failed to do your duty, and a brother justice.

If the whole can be sustained or any part of them, now in existence, then do. I heartily join in recommending them to be supported, until there shall have been brought about a different state of society; our people having become more improved in all their various relations, and consequently be able to appreciate such enterprises, and the labors of those of their brethren who are willing to sacrifice their all, and wear out their lives in the service of their people and cause of their race and humanity.

I say rally around the *North Star*, because of the several papers now in exis-tence, it is on the firmest basis, having the greatest prospects of success, and if it cannot be sustained, the hope for the continuance of others is as the distant glimmering of an expended meteor. We are not yet in a condition in this coun-try to support more than one efficient newspaper. This I have stated on a former occasion, when connected with the *North Star*, and my present relation to the paper makes the fact none the less truthful.

I have no other desire than to do that which I conceive to be just and right to-wards God and man—to justify myself without wronging my neighbor. I detest that dog-in-the-manger ambition, which, because I cannot eat the hay myself, will suffer no other one to eat it; and that Pharisaical philanthropy, which be-cause Israel cannot be gathered together, would prevent Jacob[4] from receiving *his* reward. No, thank God, I have a different object and higher aim in view— the elevation of our race—I care not by whom it be effected so that it be prop-erly done: Let it be Henry Highland Garnet, Samuel R. Ward,[5] W. W. Brown, Henry Bibb, Charles Lenox Remond, Frederick Douglass, or whom.

I have no ambition whatever for popular fame and personal distinction in the heaven-decreed pursuit of philanthropy. It admits of no such rivalry. That which partakes of the nature of Deity, can possess neither hatred nor envy. It is an assumption to force one's services where they are not wanted, especially

4. Also known as Israel, Jacob was the father of the patriarchs of the twelve tribes of Is-rael; see Genesis 25–50.

5. The New York black abolitionist Samuel Ringgold Ward (1817–ca. 1866), known as a commanding lecturer, founded two antislavery newspapers and authored *Autobiogra-phy of a Fugitive Negro* (1855). In 1851 he fled to Canada after his involvement with the res-cue of the fugitive slave William "Jerry" McHenry. He emigrated to Jamaica in the late 1850s.

when they are useless; and he who does it is an intruder, if not a usurper. This being my case, I have determined to remain in the seclusion of obscurity, where I have ever been, wishing God-speed to our public great men, in every good and laudable undertaking in which they may embark.

You will herewith receive my humble advice against the establishment of a paper in Ohio, feeling fully assured that it will result in serious losses to the proprietors; and should such a project be carried out, though I may possibly at some future day become a resident of your great promising State, in a professional capacity I must respectfully decline the honor suggested to me, of becoming the Editor of your paper, or in any way responsibly interested in it.[6]

M. R. DELANY

(*North Star*, 5 October 1849, p. 3)

6. Distressed that Delany made his personal letter public business, Burnham responded with an open letter to Delany in the *North Star* (16 November 1849, p. 2). He maintained that "the establishment of a paper West would not affect, in the least, as I think, the interest of the Star," and he complained that "the Star is not effecting that amount of good in and among Ohioans that we might derive from a sectional organ."

Delany and Frederick Douglass on Samuel R. Ward

IN 1849 FREDERICK DOUGLASS several times debated the prominent black abolitionist Samuel Ringgold Ward on the nature of the U.S. Constitution, with Ward arguing that it was an antislavery document while Douglass argued that it was proslavery. (By 1851, Douglass would come to agree with Ward.) Though their debates had been cordial, Douglass in an "Extra" of the May 1850 *North Star* vociferously attacked Ward for allegedly complying with white racist practices during an antislavery meeting at a black church. In a letter to Ward printed in the *North Star*, Delany defended Ward, though at times he seemed to be commenting more on his own relationship with Douglass than on the conflict between Douglass and Ward. Delany's letter prompted a response from Douglass, which prompted another letter from Delany. The three letters are printed below, beginning with Delany's letter to Ward.

To Samuel R. Ward

MY DEAR FRIEND: I have recently seen the extra "North Star," issued by Frederick Douglass, an old friend and oppressed brother, and I regret to learn that in you the cause of our downtrodden people has recently experienced a sad and mortifying damper.

The charges made against you were in consequence of a handbill calling a meeting, gotten up in Philadelphia by the whites, expressly for yourself, the conditions of which were degrading to the colored people, altho' the meeting was to be held in a church belonging exclusively to themselves, having colored trustees and a colored pastor—the offensive part of which read thus: "The lower part of the house will be reserved exclusively for white persons, who are particularly invited to attend." The complaint against you is, that concerning this most palpable insult to your intelligence, you were silent during your address. . . .

You cannot find, in the history of enlightened deliberations, where great men, distinguished for their talents, however opposed to each other in position, have made such bitter personal attacks, in denunciation of each other, as have passed between you, especially in this instance by Mr. Douglass. None, I think, can be found, except it should be the uncivilized, vulgar attacks of the Mississippi ruffian Foote, of the U.S. Senate, to whom I will liken neither of you, in his outlandish assaults upon the hoary sage of Missouri—Benton, and upon other advocates of liberty in the councils of the nation.[1] This and similar cases are the only instances, and these men are wholly without character or reputation, save their heathenish ferocity and daring impudence.

It will not do to justify these things in us, because they are done by the whites. This is no excuse for us. I deny that the same things are done by white men, under similar circumstances, occupying the same position among their people as you occupy among us. A people wholly oppressed, all making struggling efforts for liberty and elevation among their oppressors, have no time to spend in personal hostility towards each other, especially among their leaders. *We cannot afford to be divided—it costs too much.* The expense is greater than we can bear. It may do for others, but it will not do for us nor any people circumstanced as we are. We must learn adaptation—learn to suit ourselves to the time or the occasion, and be equal to any emergency. Let others do as they may—this we must do for ourselves, if we ever expect success in the glorious cause of self-elevation.

In the American struggle for liberty against British despotism, supposing Washington, Warren, Hancock,[2] Jefferson, and other great men, leaders among the people, had ceased their mutual counsel and co-operation, and commenced hostility among themselves, because of a mere difference of opinion, what would have become of the common people, both civil and military, and the cause of American liberty? This cause being in the hands of the leaders, it is not hard to determine. And shall our cause suffer violence in our first tottering steps at advancement? Just Heaven decree otherwise!

The injury done to our people at large by these proceedings, and the sacred cause in which you have embarked, is perhaps beyond your conception. It was on the very morning of the reception of the extra, favored by a friend in Philadelphia, and before opening it, that a gentleman stepped up to me, suggesting the idea of "sending for S. R. Ward, to pay Pittsburgh a visit." When on

1. During the debates on the Compromise of 1850, which the antislavery senator from Missouri Thomas Hart Benton (1782–1858) opposed, Henry Stuart Foote (1804–80), proslavery senator from Mississippi, drew a five-chambered loaded revolver on Benton and taunted him. In response, Benton marched toward Foote, challenging him to shoot. Order was eventually restored.
2. The Massachusetts patriots Joseph Warren (1741–75) and John Hancock (1737–93).

opening the package I held in my hand, "what a tale did it unfold!" This, of course, had its effect. Thus, while others are writing you into fame, you are writing each other down!

The public has pronounced upon you as aspirants—jealous of each other's popularity—rivals, contending for precedence in the annals of fame, with a determination to accomplish the design of personal ambition, though it be done over the ragged fragments of the liberties of your almost hopeless, struggling people. The friends of Mr. Douglass say, "Ward is jealous of Douglass' popularity," while the friends of Mr. Ward, on the other hand, say, "Douglass is jealous of Ward and Garnet, lest they become as popular throughout the country as himself." And this, sir, you give them good reason to say, while you continue this personal hostility towards each other; for a division among you, causes a division of sentiment among the people in regard to you, who should and otherwise would be united in a oneness of feeling toward you.

Aside from these bickerings, the noble efforts of you both in the holy cause of your oppressed brethren and downtrodden humanity, have been praiseworthy indeed. Proud indeed, would I feel at the thought, that even in a life-time, it were possible for me to attain half the high-standing and respect that is now either of your privilege to enjoy; but whatever estimate I may set upon such a proud privilege, I had rather remain in obscurity as I am, than attain such a position at the expense of another's destiny. Nay, palsied be the hand that holds this pen—stultified be the intellect that suggests the thought—and hushed in the stillness of death first be this voice, before giving utterance to such an expression. God, our common Father, has ordained otherwise—let us do as he would that we should truly love one another; then, and not until then, shall this selfishness cease to find existence among us. Love would imply a common liking for each other—a heart-felt interest in each other's welfare, and a desire for each other's prosperity. This is that love which God speaks of—this is the love we should have one to another. . . .

With a full reliance that the eminence sustained by both of you, will induce you liberally to forgive the liberty taken in this instance, by an humble individual, I am gratefully your sincere friend in the cause of God and humanity,

MARTIN R. DELANY

Pittsburgh, June 13, 1850.

(*North Star*, 27 June 1850, p. 2)

Douglass's response appeared in the same issue of the *North Star*, strategically placed as a preface to Delany's letter.

. . . We have re-examined what we said in "The North Star," to which Mr. Delany takes exception, and we find nothing in it so grossly personal as to justify the implied censure which our friend Delany has so freely lavished upon us. One must be struck, on reading his letter, with the appropriateness of his advice, if applied to himself. In correcting our errors he has followed the example of many others who have presumed to give advice; by doing the very thing himself, which he disallows in us. He compares our comments upon Mr. Ward's handbill, to the "*uncivilized, vulgar,* attacks of the Mississippi *ruffian,*" and he goes on imputing, (by implication to be sure,) such base motives for our conduct, as jealousy, envy, and mean ambition—all of which we think quite gratuitous, and uncalled for. We undertake to affirm that our whole course of conduct towards Mr. Ward, (and we think that the columns of the North Star will bear us out in our affirmation,) up to his recent visit to Philadelphia, has displayed marked admiration of his very superior talents; and a high appreciation of his character, as a man. . . . If we differ with him now, it is not that we *love him less,* but freedom and equality more. And if M. R. Delany should ever venture to hold a public meeting in the City of Rochester, or elsewhere, on the pro-slavery conditions of driving the Negro into a separate pew, he shall find us equally ready to denounce such conduct on his part. Persons must be respected, but principles are above persons, and we must follow the latter, though they bring us into conflict with the whole world.—F. D.

(*North Star*, 27 June 1850, p. 2)

* * *

To Frederick Douglass

Two weeks later, Douglass printed Delany's apologetic letter.

MY DEAR FRIEND:—On perusing your remarks on my letter to Mr. Ward, I perceive that your feelings have been wounded because of the impression you are under that my strictures were intended to apply entirely to yourself, and that

I compared you to the "Mississippi ruffian." This was not the case; and no one, I am persuaded, who reads that letter will place any such construction upon it.

It would be useless here for me to state the estimate that I set upon your talents and ability as a man among us. I have often announced that with pen and voice, and have ever felt proud that we had so noble a specimen of our oppressed and enslaved brethren, who, with a righteous indignation, cursed the slaveholder, spurned slavery, and, with the power of a Hercules, had riven the contemptible fetters that bound his manly form, dashing them to atoms, and walked forth untrammeled as nature had designed him, a god-like native nobleman. . . .

What I have written has been done in love, as an act of justice, not only to yourself and our dear and esteemed friends and brothers, Ward and Garnet, but also our people at large and the cause in which you have embarked.

Let me repeat again, that what I have said in humbleness is exempt from all attempts of censure, believing that whatever errors do exist are the result of oversight and not design; and that a suggestion alone is sufficient to induce a sufficient remedy; and that greatness should fully appreciate the design of one, however humble and obscure, when approaching you with every manifestation of kindred sincerity.

With every hope and desire for your continuance, prosperity and eventual success in the sacred cause of our elevation,

I am, dear sir,
Yours for God and humanity,
M. R. DELANY

Pittsburgh, July 1, 1850.

(*North Star*, 11 July 1850, p. 2)

Part Three.
Debating Black Emigration

DURING HIS *North Star* association with Frederick Douglass of the late 1840s, Delany for the most part shared Douglass's and other black Garrisonians' commitments to moral suasion and black uplift. As Delany made clear in his "Western Tour" letters, he thought, as Douglass did, that regular pronouncements to the white majority on the moral iniquity of slavery, coupled with appeals to the free blacks to demonstrate their ability to rise and prosper in the marketplace, represented the best possible hope for bringing about the end of slavery in the United States. Of course Delany was hardly naive about antislavery reform. As his letters to Douglass also made clear, he recognized the crucial role of legal and social institutions, along with a seemingly intractable white racism, in perpetuating U.S. slave culture. Nevertheless, during this period Delany put special emphasis on the importance of black uplift, arguing that African Americans needed to empower themselves in capitalist culture. The existence of thriving black communities, he believed, would offer indisputable evidence of blacks' equality with whites, evidence that, when assessed by rational whites, could not help but bring about social change.

Such optimistic scenarios for social change through moral suasion and black uplift came under challenge during the 1850s as the result of three major political developments: the Compromise of 1850, the Kansas-Nebraska Act of 1854, and the Supreme Court's Dred Scott decision of 1857. The Compromise of 1850 admitted new slave states and, through its toughened Fugitive Slave Law, legally compelled northerners to aid southerners in capturing fugitive slaves. The Kansas-Nebraska Act repealed the limits on the spread of slavery established by the Missouri Compromise of 1820–21 and essentially granted white settlers of any new territory the right to constitute themselves as a slave state should that be the desire of the majority of voters. With this new act, antislavery advocates feared that the sectional balance ensured by the Compromise of 1850 would eventually be skewed in the direction of the slave states. Finally, when Chief Justice Roger B. Taney presented the majority ruling in *Dred Scott v. Sanford* that African Americans had no rights consistent with citizenship, even the optimistic

Frederick Douglass came to despair about blacks' prospects in the United States, declaring in a speech of 3 August 1857 that the "highest satisfaction of our oppressors, is to see the negro degraded, divested of public spirit, insensible to patriotism, and to all concern for the freedom, elevation, and respectability of the race."[1]

In response to the dire developments of the 1850s, Douglass abandoned Garrisonian moral suasion for a political abolitionism grounded in an antislavery reading of the Constitution and continued his efforts to achieve emancipation and black elevation in the United States. But Douglass's "representative" status as the most prominent black leader of the 1850s should not obscure the fact that there were ongoing debates among free black leaders during this time about the advisability of remaining in a nation where slavery was the law of the land and African Americans were regarded as having the same legal status as property. Increasingly during the 1850s there were calls for the free blacks to emigrate from the United States. This was not the first decade in which black leaders had argued for black emigration. During the 1810s, Paul Cuffe had initiated a program of black emigration to Africa, which gained support in the late 1820s from John Russwurm, coeditor of the first black newspaper, *Freedom's Journal.* During the 1830s Lewis Woodson, one of Delany's teachers in Pittsburgh, advocated black emigration to Canada or the British West Indies.[2] Most free blacks resisted calls for emigration, convinced that they, and the slaves, deserved the same legal rights to citizenship as whites. But perhaps the greatest check on the black emigration movement was the formation in December 1816 of the American Colonization Society (ACS), a reformist "antislavery" organization that, as noted in Part 2, was committed to the idea that the United States would function best as an all-white nation. As the ACS gained in numbers and financial strength, African American leaders were reluctant to appear to support the aims of an organization that sought nothing less than their eventual removal from the United States.

By the late 1840s and early 1850s, however, many African Americans insisted that there were significant distinctions between the colonization agenda of the ACS and black emigration, insofar as colonization was imposed upon blacks while emigration resulted from black agency. In response to the Compromise of 1850, then, a number of African American leaders, most notably Henry Bibb and Mary Ann Shadd Cary, argued for black emigration to Canada; and in response to the Kansas-Nebraska Act and the Dred Scott decision, a number of African American leaders, most notably James Holly and William Wells Brown, argued for black emigration to Haiti. There was also a renewed interest in black emigration to Africa, as advocated in the late 1850s and early 1860s by Henry Highland Garnet and Delany (see Part 4).

Martin Delany was at the forefront of the debate on black emigration during the 1850s, despite his 1849 assertion to M. H. Burnham that he was "no public man." In 1852 Delany published *The Condition, Elevation, Emigration and Destiny of the Colored People of the United States*, which argued for black emigration to Central and South America or the Caribbean; and in 1854 he convened in Cleveland, Ohio, the National Emigration Convention of Colored Men, where he delivered the keynote address, "Political Destiny of the Colored Race on the American Continent," arguably the most eloquent and influential call for black emigration of the antebellum period. In 1856 he moved to Canada, where he initially continued to work for black emigration to the southern Americas, though by the late 1850s he was using his Canadian base to champion black emigration to Africa. Delany's emigrationist philosophy influenced the Haitian emigration movement of the late 1850s and early 1860s; and his transplantation to Canada influenced the Canadian emigration movement as well. It is not excessive to claim that Delany was the most important African American emigrationist of the 1850s.

Delany had expressed some interest in black emigration prior to the early 1850s. In 1838 he drafted a proposal for emigration to Africa (see "A Project for an Expedition of Adventure, to the Eastern Coast of Africa," in Part 4), and while undertaking his western tour for the *North Star* he reported in a letter of 24 July 1848 on his visit to "an emigration meeting" in Cleveland. Key events of late 1850 contributed to his disillusionment with moral suasion and black uplift and his adoption of a public politics of black emigrationism. In response to the adoption of the Compromise of 1850, with its infamous Fugitive Slave Law, Delany bade farewell to moral suasion. Addressing an antislavery meeting in Allegheny City, Pennsylvania, on 30 September 1850, twelve days after the passage of the Fugitive Slave Law, Delany, as reported in Frances Rollin's biography, proclaimed to the white politicians assembled at that gathering:

> Honorable Mayor, whatever ideas of liberty I may have, have been received from reading the lives of your revolutionary fathers. I have therein learned that a man has a right to defend his castle with his life, even unto the taking of life. Sir, my house is my castle; in that castle are none but my wife and my children, as free as the angels of heaven, and whose liberty is as sacred as the pillars of God. If any man approaches that house in search of a slave,—I care not who he may be, whether constable or sheriff, magistrate or even judge of the Supreme Court—nay, let it be he who sanctioned this act to become a law [President Millard Filmore], surrounded by his cabinet as his body-guard, with the Declaration of Independence waving above his head as his banner, and the constitution of his country upon his breast

as his shield,—if he crosses the threshold of my door, and I do not lay him
a lifeless corpse at my feet, I hope the grave may refuse my body a resting-
place, and righteous Heaven my spirit a home.[3]

Shortly after delivering this defiant and angry speech, Delany set off for Harvard
Medical School in Cambridge, Massachusetts, with a set of superlative letters
of recommendation from Pennsylvania physicians. The dean of the medical
school, Oliver Wendell Holmes (1809–94), admitted Delany in November 1850.
But at this hotbed of resistance to the Fugitive Slave Law, the majority of students at Harvard petitioned the medical faculty to dismiss Delany and two
other black students sponsored by the Massachusetts Colonization Society, because, as the students put it in their petition of 10 December 1850, "we deem the
admission of blacks to the medical Lectures highly detrimental to the interests
and welfare, of the Institution of which we are members, calculated alike to
lower its reputation in this and other parts of the country."[4] Guided by advice
from the medical faculty, Holmes capitulated to the students' demands that
Harvard remain an all-white institution and dismissed Delany in late December. Delany departed from Massachusetts in March 1851, three months before
Harriet Beecher Stowe's *Uncle Tom's Cabin* began to appear serially in the *National Era.*

As a result of these developments, Delany moved toward but did not immediately adopt emigrationism, and in fact he resisted that option in 1851. Arguably, during the 1850s he debated black emigration not only with Douglass
and his allies but also with himself, for he remained committed throughout the
decade to the notion that African Americans *should* have full rights as U.S. citizens. Nevertheless, it was during 1851 that he persuaded one of his friends, David
Peck, to journey to Greytown and become involved in the local politics of
Nicaragua, and by early 1852 he had publicly called on U.S. blacks, in his controversial *Condition,* to consider emigration to Central and South America.[5] He
made this call at a time when many African Americans had been energized by
the 1852 publication of Stowe's *Uncle Tom's Cabin,* a book that Frederick Douglass and others regarded as offering renewed hopes that slavery and antiblack
racism would come to an end in the United States. And this despite the fact that
the novel concludes with an apparent endorsement of African colonization.

The documents in Part 3 present a documentary account of Delany's emergence as the major proponent of black emigration during the 1850s, showing
how his advocacy of emigrationism occurred in the personal and cultural context of debate. The first document in this section, from the 1851 North American
Convention in Toronto, reveals Delany as an antiemigrationist not too long before he wrote *Condition.* In his 1852 letter to Garrison, and in parts of *Condition,*

one senses Delany's disappointment at the necessity of having to consider emigration. That said, there was no advocate of black emigration during the 1850s more impassioned than Delany, and no advocate more skillfully strategic in disseminating his ideas. Through his letters to Oliver Johnson, Frederick Douglass, and other antislavery leaders of the 1850s, Delany, despite not having his own newspaper during this time, managed to create a forum in the abolitionist newspapers for his views on the possibilities of black emigration. We see Delany most eloquent on the topic of black emigration at the 1854 National Emigration Convention, where he delivered "Political Destiny." Delany's major emigrationist statement of the 1850s is presented in this section in its entirety.

Delany continued his advocacy of black emigration when he moved to Canada in 1856. In a letter of 29 May 1856 to William C. Munroe, printed in the Canadian black newspaper *The Provincial Freeman*, Delany called for "a great Continental Convention of colored men" that would meet in "KINGSTON on the Isle of Jamaica, West Indies."[6] This section prints several of his writings from that newspaper, and it prints a letter about, and a selection from, Delany's novel of 1859–62, *Blake*. Though not directly linked to his emigrationism (the novel imagines a hemispheric slave insurrection extending from Cuba into the United States), *Blake* was written in an effort to gain funding for his emigration projects, and it certainly speaks to Delany's claims, as elaborated in "Political Destiny," that blacks possessed the numbers and power to take control of the Americas. The concluding selection, "Comets" (1859), was written shortly after Delany shifted from an emigrationist program emphasizing Central and South America to an emigrationist program emphasizing Africa. It can be read as a semiautobiographical account of Delany's sense of himself as a force in a "constant state of action," supplying "life, action, health and vigor" during a time of "continual loss."

Notes

1. Frederick Douglass, "The Significance of Emancipation in the West Indies," in *The Frederick Douglass Papers*, ser. 1, *Speeches, Debates, and Interviews*, vol. 3, ed. John W. Blassingame et al. (New Haven: Yale University Press, 1985), p. 201.

2. For an excellent account of black emigration movements during the early national and antebellum periods, see Floyd J. Miller, *The Search for a Black Nationality: Black Emigration and Colonization, 1787–1863* (Urbana: University of Illinois Press, 1975).

3. Francis [Frances] A. Rollin, *Life and Public Services of Martin R. Delany* (Boston: Lee and Shepard, 1868), p. 76.

4. See Dorothy Sterling, *The Making of an Afro-American: Martin Robison Delany, 1812–1885* (Garden City, New York: Doubleday, 1971), p. 130. Also useful is Philip Cash, "Pride, Prejudice, and Politics," in *Blacks at Harvard: A Documentary History of African-American Experience at Harvard and Radcliffe*, ed. Werner Sollors, Caldwell Titcomb, and Thomas A. Underwood (New York: New York University Press, 1993), pp. 18–31.

5. Indicative of Delany's conflicted views on emigration, in April 1852, as *Condition* was being printed, he chaired a meeting in Philadelphia that, according to Miller, "endorsed two resolutions opposing emigration in general" (*Search for a Black Nationality*, p. 129).

6. Letter to William C. Munroe, 29 March 1856, in the *Provincial Freeman*, 31 May 1856, vol. 3, p. 26. Munroe, a black abolitionist from Detroit, Michigan, had served as president of Delany's 1854 Cleveland emigration convention. Delany's plans for a Kingston convention fell through, and instead a small convention, chaired by Munroe, was held 27–28 August 1856 in the A.M.E. Church in Cleveland; Delany was unable to attend.

Protest against the First Resolution of the North American Convention

IN A LETTER TO HIS FRIEND Charles H. Langston, printed in the 3 April 1851 issue of the *North Star*, Delany expressed his concerns about Langston's proposal to convene a national black convention in September 1851. Though this particular convention did not transpire, Delany would overcome his hesitations and attend a black convention in Toronto the same month that Langston had proposed for his. Organized by Henry Bibb, who was residing in Canada West, the North American Convention in Toronto of 11–13 September 1851 brought together fifty-three black leaders from Canada and the United States, the majority of whom voted to encourage blacks of the United States to emigrate to Canada. As reported in the convention's proceedings, printed in the 24 September 1851 issue of Bibb's newspaper, *Voice of the Fugitive*, the first adopted resolution broadly urged U.S. blacks to emigrate: "1. Resolved, that the infamous fugitive slave enactment of the American Government—whether constitutional or unconstitutional, is an insult to God, and an outrage upon humanity, not to be endured by any people; we therefore earnestly entreat our brethren of the northern and southern states to come out from under the jurisdiction of those wicked laws—from the power of a Government whose tender mercies, towards the colored people, are cruel" (p. 2). The proceedings also reported that Martin Delany and three other delegates filed an official dissent.

The following protest against the first resolution was entered by the undersigned delegates:

Whereas, the convention, in adopting the first resolution, inviting the colored people to leave the northern part of the United States, has done so contrary to the desires and wishes of those of us, from the States, who believe it to be impolitic and contrary to our professed policy in opposing the infamous fugitive slave laws, and schemes of American colonization;[1] therefore we do hereby enter our solemn disapprobation and protest against this part of the said resolution.

M. R. Delany, Penn.
Wm. H. Topp, New York
Henry F. Stanton, Ohio
Payton Harris, New York[2]

(*Voice of the Fugitive*, 24 September 1851, p. 2)

1. A reference to the American Colonization Society's project of colonizing the free blacks to Africa.

2. Delany's co-signers were William Topp (1812–57), a tailor and antislavery organizer from Albany; Henry Stanton (1824–?), a barber and musician from Toledo; and Payton Harris (1794–?), a tailor and antislavery activist from Buffalo.

The Condition, Elevation, Emigration and Destiny of the Colored People of the United States

1852

IN HIS PREFACE TO *The Condition, Elevation, Emigration and Destiny of the Colored People of the United States*, Delany claimed that he wrote the book "inside of one month" while detained in New York on business. But in 1867 he told his biographer Frances Rollin that he worked on the book over eight months of 1851 and 1852. The years 1851–52 were a busy time for Delany, who was lecturing on comparative anatomy in New York and Ohio, fighting the Fugitive Slave Law, attempting to obtain a patent for a train-engine component, and becoming increasingly involved in the politics of Nicaragua's Greytown. In 1851 he encouraged his friend David J. Peck to travel there, and early in 1852 he learned that Peck had helped to organize an election that resulted in Delany's election as mayor. Delany accepted the position but never actually went to Greytown, perhaps because he remained conflicted about the value of black emigration. That conflict came to inform *Condition*, which was published in April 1852, several weeks after the publication of *Uncle Tom's Cabin*. On the one hand, the book called on blacks to emigrate to Central and South America; on the other, the book celebrated the achievements of African Americans and made a passionate moral and legal case for black citizenship in the United States. Self-published by Delany, the 215-page book consists of twenty-three chapters, a preface, and an appendix. The excerpts provide a significant sampling of Delany's main arguments.

Chapter I. Condition of Many Classes in Europe Considered.

THAT there have been in all ages and in all countries, in every quarter of the habitable globe, especially among those nations laying the greatest claim to civilization and enlightenment, classes of people who have been deprived of equal privileges, political, religious and social, cannot be denied, and that this deprivation on the part of the ruling classes is cruel and unjust, is also equally true.

Such classes have ever been looked upon as inferior to their oppressors, and have ever been mainly the domestics and menials of society, doing the low offices and drudgery of those among whom they lived, moving about and existing by mere sufferance, having no rights nor privileges but those conceded by the common consent of their political superiors. These are historical facts that cannot be controverted, and therefore proclaim in tones more eloquently than thunder, the listful attention of every oppressed man, woman, and child under the government of the people of the United States of America.

In past ages there were many such classes, as the Israelites in Egypt, the Gladiators in Rome, and similar classes in Greece; and in the present age, the Gipsies in Italy and Greece, the Cossacs in Russia and Turkey, the Sclaves and Croats in the Germanic States, and the Welsh and Irish among the British, to say nothing of various other classes among other nations.

That there have in all ages, in almost every nation, existed a nation within a nation—a people who although forming a part and parcel of the population, yet were from force of circumstances, known by the peculiar position they occupied, forming in fact, by the deprivation of political equality with others, no part, and if any, but a restricted part of the body politic of such nations, is also true.

Such then are the Poles in Russia, the Hungarians in Austria, the Scotch, Irish, and Welsh in the United Kingdom, and such also are the Jews, scattered throughout not only the length and breadth of Europe, but almost the habitable globe, maintaining their national characteristics, and looking forward in high hopes of seeing the day when they may return to their former national position of self-government and independence, let that be in whatever part of the habitable world it may. This is the lot of these various classes of people in Europe, and it is not our intention here, to discuss the justice or injustice of the causes that have contributed to their degradation, but simply to set forth the undeniable facts, which are as glaring as the rays of a noon-day's sun, thereby to impress them indelibly on the mind of every reader of this pamphlet.

It is not enough, that these people are deprived of equal privileges by their rulers, but, the more effectually to succeed, the equality of these classes must be denied, and their inferiority by nature as distinct races, actually asserted. This policy is necessary to appease the opposition that might be interposed in their behalf. Wherever there is arbitrary rule, there must of necessity, on the part of the dominant classes, superiority be assumed. To assume superiority, is to deny the equality of others, and to deny their equality, is to premise their incapacity for self-government. Let this once be conceded, and there will be little or no sympathy for the oppressed, the oppressor being left to prescribe whatever terms at discretion for their government, suits his own purpose.

Such then is the condition of various classes in Europe; yes, nations, for centuries within nations, even without the hope of redemption among those who oppress them. And however unfavorable their condition, there is none more so than that of the colored people of the United States.

Chapter II. Comparative Condition of the Colored People of the United States.

THE United States, untrue to her trust and unfaithful to her professed principles of republican equality, has also pursued a policy of political degradation to a large portion of her native born countrymen, and that class is the Colored People. Denied an equality not only of political, but of natural rights, in common with the rest of our fellow citizens, there is no species of degradation to which we are not subject.

Reduced to abject slavery is not enough, the very thought of which should awaken every sensibility of our common nature; but those of their descendants who are freemen even in the non-slaveholding States, occupy the very same position politically, religiously, civilly and socially, (with but few exceptions,) as the bondman occupies in the slave States.

In those States, the bondman is disenfranchised, and for the most part, so are we. He is denied all civil, religious, and social privileges, except such as he gets by mere sufferance, and so are we. They have no part nor lot in the government of the country, neither have we. They are ruled and governed without representation, existing as mere nonentities among the citizens, and excrescences on the body politic—a mere dreg in community, and so are we. Where then is our political superiority to the enslaved? none, neither are we superior in any other relation to society, except that we are de facto masters of ourselves and joint rulers of our own domestic household, while the bondman's self is claimed by another, and his relation to his family denied him. What the unfortunate classes are in Europe, such are we in the United States, which is folly to deny, insanity not to understand, blindness not to see, and surely now full time that our eyes were opened to these startling truths, which for ages have stared us full in the face.

It is time that we had become politicians, we mean, to understand the political economy and domestic policy of nations; that we had become as well as moral theorists, also the practical demonstrators of equal rights and self-government. Except we do, it is idle to talk about rights, it is mere chattering for the sake of being seen and heard—like the slave, saying something because his so called "master" said it, and saying just what he told him to say. Have we not now sufficient intelligence among us to understand our true position, to realise our actual condition, and determine for ourselves what is best to be done? If we have not now, we never shall have, and should at once cease prating about our equality, capacity, and all that. . . .

. . . [A]s a policy, we the colored people were selected as the subordinate class in this country, not on account of any actual or supposed inferiority on their part, but simply because, in view of all the circumstances of the case, they were the very best class that could be selected. They would have as readily had any other class as subordinates in the country, as the colored people, but the condition of society *at the time*, would not admit of it. In the struggle for American Independence, there were among those who performed the most distinguished parts, the most common-place peasantry of the Provinces. English, Danish, Irish, Scotch, and others, were among those whose names blazoned forth as heroes in the American Revolution. But a single reflection will convince us, that no course of policy could have induced the proscription of the parentage and relatives of such men as Benjamin Franklin the printer, Roger Sherman the cobbler,[1] the tinkers, and others of the signers of the Declaration of Independence. But as they were determined to have a subservient class, it will readily be conceived, that according to the state of society at the time, the better policy on their part was, to select some class, who from their political position—however much they may have contributed their aid as we certainly did, in the general struggle for liberty by force of arms—who had the least claims upon them, or who had the *least chance* or was the *least potent* in urging their claims. This class of course was the colored people and Indians.

The Indians who in the early settlement of the continent, before an African captive had ever been introduced thereon, were reduced to the most abject slavery, toiling day and night in the mines, under the relentless hands of heartless Spanish taskmasters, but being a race of people raised to the sports of fishing, the chase, and of war, were wholly unaccustomed to labor, and therefore sunk under the insupportable weight, two millions and a half having fallen victims to the cruelty of oppression and toil suddenly placed upon their shoulders. And it was only this that prevented their farther enslavement as a class, after the provinces were absolved from the British Crown. It is true that their general enslavement took place on the islands and in the mining districts of South America, where indeed, the Europeans continued to enslave them, until a comparatively recent period; still, the design, the feeling, and inclination from policy, was the same to do so here, in this section of the continent.

Nor was it until their influence became too great, by the political position occupied by their brethren in the new republic, that the German and Irish peas-

---

1. Benjamin Franklin (1706–90) and the Connecticut political leader Roger Sherman (1721–93) helped to draft and were among the signers of the Declaration of Independence.

antry ceased to be sold as slaves for a term of years fixed by law, for the repay-
ment of their passage-money,[2] the descendants of these classes of people for a
long time being held as inferiors, in the estimation of the ruling class, and it was
not until they assumed the rights and privileges guaranteed to them by the established policy of the country, among the leading spirits of whom were their
relatives, that the policy towards them was discovered to be a bad one, and accordingly changed. Nor was it, as is frequently very erroneously asserted, by colored as well as white persons, that it was on account of hatred to the African, or
in other words, on account of hatred to his color, that the African was selected
as the subject of oppression in this country. This is sheer nonsense; being based
on policy and nothing else, as shown in another place. The Indians, who being
the most foreign to the sympathies of the Europeans on this continent, were selected in the first place, who, being unable to withstand the hardships, gave way
before them.

But the African race had long been known to Europeans, in all ages of the
world's history, as a long-lived, hardy race, subject to toil and labor of various
kinds, subsisting mainly by traffic, trade, and industry, and consequently being
as foreign to the sympathies of the invaders of the continent as the Indians, they
were selected, captured, brought here as a laboring class, and as a matter of policy held as such. Nor was the absurd idea of natural inferiority of the African
ever dreamed of, until recently adduced by the slave-holders and their abettors,
in justification of their policy. This, with contemptuous indignation, we fling
back into their face, as a scorpion to a vulture. And so did our patriots and leaders in the cause of regeneration know better, and never for a moment yielded to
the base doctrine. But they had discovered the great fact, that a cruel policy was
pursued towards our people, and that they possessed distinctive characteristics
which made them the objects of proscription. These characteristics being
strongly marked in the colored people, as in the Indians, by color, character of
hair and so on, made them the more easily distinguished from other Americans,
and the policies more effectually urged against us. . . .

———

Chapter IX. Capacity of Colored Men and Women as Citizen Members of Community.

THE utility of men in their private capacity as citizens, is of no less import
than that of any other department of the community in which they live; indeed,
the fitness of men for positions in the body politic, can only be justly measured

2. A reference to indentured servants, who agreed to work for a period of time, usually
seven years, in exchange for passage and food and shelter.

by their qualification as citizens. And we may safely venture the declaration, that in the history of the world, there has never been a nation, that among the oppressed class of inhabitants—a class entirely ineligible to any political position of honor, profit or trust—wholly discarded from the recognition of citizens' rights—not even permitted to carry the mail, nor drive a mail coach—there never has, in the history of nations, been any people thus situated, who has made equal progress in attainments with the colored people of the United States. It would be as unnecessary as it is impossible, to particularize all the individuals; we shall therefore be satisfied, with a classification and a few individual cases. Our history in this country is well known, and quite sufficiently treated on in these pages already, without the necessity of repetition here; it is enough to know that by the most cruel acts of injustice and crime, our forefathers were forced by small numbers, and enslaved in the country—the great body now to the number of three millions and a half, still groaning in bondage—that the half million now free, are the descendants of the few who by various means, are fortunate enough to gain their liberty from Southern bondage—that no act of general emancipation has ever taken place, and no chance as yet for a general rebellion—we say in view of all these facts, we proceed to give a cursory history of the attainments—the civil, social, business and professional, and literary attainments of colored men and women, and challenge comparison with the world—according to circumstances—in times past and present.

Though shorn of their strength, disarmed of manhood, and stripped of every right, encouraged by the part performed by their brethren and fathers in the Revolutionary struggle—with no records of their deeds in history, and no means of knowing them save orally, as overheard from the mouths of their oppressors, and tradition as kept up among themselves—that memorable event, had not yet ceased its thrill through the new-born nation, until a glimmer of hope—a ray of light had beamed forth, and enlightened minds thought to be in total darkness. Minds of no ordinary character, but those which embraced business, professions, and literature—minds, which at once grasped the earth, encompassed the seas, soared into the air, and mounted the skies. And it is none the less creditable to the colored people, that among those who have stood the most conspicuous and shone the brightest in the earliest period of our history, there are those of pure and unmixed African blood. A credit—but that which is creditable to the African, cannot disgrace any into whose veins his blood may chance to flow. The elevation of the colored man can only be completed by the elevation of the pure descendants of Africa; because to deny his equality, is to deny in alike proportion, the equality of all those mixed with the African organization; and to establish his inferiority, will be to degrade every person related to him by consanguinity; therefore, to establish the equality of the African

with the European race, establishes the equality of every person intermediate
between the two races. This establishes beyond contradiction, the general equality of men.

In the year 1773, though held in servitude, and without the advantages or
privileges of the schools of the day, accomplishing herself by her own perseverance, Phillis Wheatley appeared in the arena,[3] the brilliancy of whose genius, as
a poetess, delighted Europe and astonished America, and by a special act of the
British Parliament, 1773, her productions were published for the Crown. She was
an admirer of President Washington, and addressed to him lines, which elicited
from the Father of his country, a complimentary and courteous reply. In the absence of the poem addressed to General Washington, which was not written
until after her work was published, we insert a stanza from one addressed (intended for the students) "To the University at Cambridge." We may further remark, that the poems were originally written, not with the most distant idea of
publication, but simply for the amusement and during the leisure moments of
the author.

"Improve your privileges while they stay,
Ye pupils, and each hour redeem, that bears
Or good or bad report of you to heav'n.
Let sin, that baneful evil of the soul,
By you be shunn'd, nor once remit your guard;
Suppress the deadly serpent in its egg.
Ye blooming plants of human race divine,
An *Ethiop* tells you 'tis your greatest foe;
Its transient sweetness turns to endless pain,
And in immense perdition sinks the soul."

"CAMBRIDGE, FEBRUARY 28, 1776.

"MISS PHILLIS:

"Your favor of the 26th of October, did not reach my hands till the middle of December. Time enough, you will say, to have given an answer ere

---

3. Brought from West Africa to Boston, where she was purchased as a slave by the
Wheatley family in 1761, Phillis Wheatley (1753–84) emerged as a prodigy who at an early
age published several poems in newspapers. The Wheatleys sent Phillis to England in
1773, where she was lauded as a black poet whose artistry confuted racist stereotypes; her
Poems (1773), which were published in England, went through at least four printings. In
Notes on the State of Virginia (1785), Thomas Jefferson asserted that her poetry was
"below the dignity of criticism."

this. Granted. But a variety of important occurrences, continually inter-
posing to divert the mind and withdraw the attention, I hope will apolo-
gise for the delay, and plead my excuse for the seeming, but not real neglect. I thank you most sincerely for your polite notice of me, in the elegant
lines you enclosed; and however undeserving I may be of such encomium
and panegyric, the style and manner exhibit a striking proof of your poetic
talents; in honor of which, and as a tribute justly due to you, I would have
published the poem, had I not been apprehensive, that, while I only meant
to give the world this new instance of your genius, I might have incurred
the imputation of vanity. This, and nothing else, determined me not to
give it place in the public prints.

"If you should ever come to Cambridge, or near head-quarters, I shall be
happy to see a person so favored by the Muses, and to whom Nature has
been so liberal and beneficent in her dispensations.

"I am, with great respect, your obedient servant,
"GEORGE WASHINGTON.

"Miss Phillis Wheatley."

The tenor, style, and manner of President Washington's letter to Miss Wheatley—the publication of her works, together with an accompanying likeness of
the author, and her inscription and dedication of the volume to the "Right Honorable the Countess of Huntingdon,"[4] show, that she, though young, was a person of no ordinary mind, no common attainments; but at the time, one of the
brightest ornaments among the American literati. She also was well versed in
Latin, in which language she composed several pieces. Miss Wheatley died in
1780, at the age of 26 years, being seven years of age when brought to this country in 1761.

Doctor Peter, who married Miss Wheatley, 1775, was a man of business, tact,
and talents—being first a grocer, and afterwards studied law, which he practised with great success, becoming quite wealthy by defending the cause of the
oppressed before the different tribunals of the country. And who shone brighter
in his day, than Benjamin Bannaker [sic], of Baltimore county, Maryland, who
by industry and force of character, became a distinguished mathematician and
astronomer,—"for many years," says Davenport's Biographical Dictionary, "cal-

4. Selina, the countess of Huntingdon (1707–91), was instrumental in helping Wheatley to publish *Poems* in England.

culated and published the Maryland Ephemerides."[5] He was a correspondent of
the Honorable Thomas Jefferson, Secretary of State of the United States, taking
the earliest opportunity of his acquaintanceship, to call his attention to the evils
of American slavery, and doubtless his acquaintance with the apostle of American Democracy, had much to do with his reflections on that most pernicious
evil in this country.[6] Mr. Bannaker was also a naturalist, and wrote a treatise on
locusts. He was invited by the Commission of United States Civil Engineers, to
assist in the survey of the Ten Miles Square, for the District of Columbia. He assisted the Board, who, it is thought, could not have succeeded without him. His
Almanac was preferred to that of Leadbeater,[7] or any other calculator cotemporary with himself. He had no family, and resided in a house alone, but principally made his home with the Elliott family. He was upright, honorable, and virtuous; entertaining religious scruples similar to the Friends. He died in 1807, near
Baltimore. Honorable John H. B. Latrobe, Esq., of Baltimore, is his biographer.

In 1812, Captain Paul Cuffy[8] was an extensive trader and mariner, sailing out
of Boston, to the West Indies and Europe, by which enterprise, he amassed an
immense fortune. He was known to the commercial world of his day, and, if not
so wealthy, stood quite as fair, and as much respected, as Captain George Laws
or Commodore Vanderbilt, the Cunards of America.[9] Captain Cuffy went to
Africa, where he died in a few years.

James Durham, originally of Philadelphia, in 1778, at the early age of twenty-one, was the most learned physician in New Orleans. He spoke English, French
and Spanish, learnedly, and the great Dr. Rush said of him, "I conversed with
him on medicine, and found him very learned. I thought I could give him information concerning the treatment of diseases; but I learned from him more

5. See R. A. Davenport, *A Dictionary of Biography* (1846). The free black Benjamin Banneker (1731–1806), as Delany makes clear, was an extraordinarily gifted mathematician, astronomer, inventor, and natural historian. "Ephemerides" are the tables found in astronomical almanacs.

6. Banneker wrote Jefferson on 19 August 1791, and Jefferson replied on 30 August 1791.

7. Probably a reference to Charles Leadbetter, author of *Astronomy* (1727) and *Compleat System of Astronomy* (1742).

8. A merchant and seaman, Paul Cuffe (1759–1817) fought for a law granting free blacks the right to vote in Massachusetts, which was approved in 1783. In 1815, disillusioned by white racism in the United States, Cuffe, who was part black and part Native American, financed and commanded a voyage to Sierre Leone of thirty-eight black emigrants.

9. Sir Samuel Cunard (1787–1865) of Canada helped to pioneer transatlantic steam navigation; Cornelius Vanderbilt (1794–1877) developed shipping lines from the East Coast to California; George Laws was president of the United States Mail Steamship Company.

than he could expect from me." And it must be admitted, he must have been learned in his profession, to have elicited such an encomium from Dr. Rush, who stood then at the head of his profession in the country.[10]

We have designed nothing here, but merely to give an individual case of the various developments of talents and acquirements in the several departments of respectability, discarding generalization, and naming none but the Africo-American of an unmixed extraction, who rose into note subsequent to the American Revolution. In the persons of note and distinction hereafter to be given, we shall not confine ourselves to any such narrow selections, but shall name persons, male and female, regardless of their extraction, so that they are colored persons, which is quite enough for our purpose. And our only excuse for the policy in the above course is, that we desire to disarm the villifiers of our race, who disparage us, giving themselves credit for whatever is commendable that may emanate from us, if there be the least opportunity of claiming it by "blood." We shall now proceed to review the attainments of colored men and women of the present day.

————

Chapter XVI. National Disfranchisement of Colored People.

WE give below the Act of Congress, known as the "Fugitive Slave Law," for the benefit of the reader, as there are thousands of the American people of all classes, who have never read the provisions of this enactment; and consequently, have no conception of its enormity. We had originally intended, also, to have inserted here, the Act of Congress of 1793, but since this Bill includes all the provisions of that Act, in fact, although called a "supplement," is a substitute, *de facto*, it would be superfluous; therefore, we insert the Bill alone, with explanations following:—

AN ACT TO AMEND, AND SUPPLEMENTARY TO THE ACT, ENTITLED, "AN ACT RESPECTING FUGITIVES FROM JUSTICE, AND PERSONS ESCAPING FROM THE SERVICE OF THEIR MASTERS, APPROVED FEBRUARY 12, 1793.

Be it enacted by the Senate and House of Representatives of the United States of America in Congress assembled, . . .

. . . That when a person held to service or labor in any State or Territory

10. Benjamin Rush (1745?–1813), an important scientist, doctor, and civic leader in Philadelphia, corresponded with James Durham (1762?–1805?) between 1788 and 1803 (see Betty L. Plummer, "Letters of James Durham and Benjamin Rush," *Journal of Negro History* 65 [1980]: 261–69). The more obscure Durham was born a slave in Philadelphia, and he vanished from the historical record after he moved to New Orleans in 1803. Some regard him as the first black physician in the United States.

of the United States has heretofore or shall hereafter escape into another State or Territory of the United States, the person or persons to whom such service or labor may be due, or his, her, or their agent or attorney, duly authorized, by power of attorney, in writing, acknowledged and certified under the seal of some legal office or court of the State or Territory in which the same may be executed, may pursue and reclaim such fugitive person, either by procuring a warrant from some one of the courts, judges, or commissioners aforesaid, of the proper circuit, district or county, for the apprehension of such fugitive from service or labor, or by seizing and arresting such fugitive, where the same can be done without process, and by taking and causing such person to be taken forthwith before such court, judge or commissioner, whose duty it shall be to hear and determine the case of such claimant in a summary manner; and upon satisfactory proof being made, by deposition or affidavit, in writing, to be taken and certified by such court, judge, or commissioner, or by other satisfactory testimony, duly taken and certified by some court, magistrate, justice of the peace, or other legal officer authorized to administer an oath, and take depositions under the laws of the State or Territory from which such person owing service or labor may have escaped, with a certificate of such magistracy or other authority, as aforesaid, with the seal of the proper court or officer thereto attached, which seal shall be sufficient to establish the competency of the proof, and with proof, also by affidavit, of the identity of the person whose service or labor is claimed to be due as aforesaid, that the person so arrested does in fact owe service or labor to the person or persons claiming him or her, in the State of Territory from which such fugitive may have escaped as aforesaid, and that said person escaped, to make out and deliver to such claimant, his or her agent or attorney, a certificate setting forth the substantial facts as to the service or labor due from such fugitive to the claimant, and of his or her escape from the State or Territory in which such service or labor was due to the State or Territory in which he or she was arrested, with authority to such claimant, or his or her agent or attorney to use such reasonable force and restraint as may be necessary under the circumstances of the case, to take and remove such fugitive person back to the State or Territory from whence he or she may have escaped as aforesaid. In no trial or hearing under this act shall the testimony of such alleged fugitive be admitted in evidence; and the certificates in this and the first section mentioned shall be conclusive of the right of the person or persons in whose favor granted to remove such fugitive to the State or Territory from which he escaped, and shall prevent all molestation of said person or persons by any process issued by any court, judge, magistrate, or other person whomsoever. . . .

HOWELL COBB,
  Speaker of the House of Representatives.
William R. King,
  President of the Senate, pro tempore.

Approved September 18, 1850.

MILLARD FILMORE[11]

The most prominent provisions of the Constitution of the United States, and those which form the fundamental basis of personal security, are they which provide, that every person shall be secure in their person and property: that no person may be deprived of liberty without due process of law, and that for crime or misdemeanor; that there may be no process of law that shall work corruption of blood. By corruption of blood is meant, that process, by which a person is *degraded* and deprived of rights common to the enfranchised citizen—of the rights of an elector, and of eligibility to the office of a representative of the people; in a word, that no person nor their posterity, may ever be debased beneath the level of the recognised basis of American citizenship. This debasement and degradation is "corruption of blood;" politically understood—a legal acknowledgement of inferiority at birth.

Heretofore, it ever has been denied, that the United States recognised or knew any difference between the people—that the Constitution makes no distinction, but includes in its provisions, all the people alike. This is not true, and certainly is blind absurdity in us at least, who have suffered the dread consequences of this delusion, not now to see it.

By the provisions of this bill, the colored people of the United States are positively degraded beneath the level of the whites—are made liable at any time, in any place, and under all circumstances, to be arrested—and upon the claim of any white person, without the privilege, even of making a defence, sent into endless bondage. Let no visionary nonsense about *habeas corpus,* or a *fair trial,* deceive us; there are no such rights granted in this bill, and except where the commissioner is too ignorant to understand when reading it, or too stupid to enforce it when he does understand, there is no earthly chance—no hope—under

11. Representing distinct regional and political interests, Howell Cobb (1815–68) was a Democratic congressman from Georgia who favored the Whig position on compromise; William R. King (1786–1853) was a Democratic senator from Alabama; and President Millard Filmore (1800–1874) was a Whig from New York.

heaven for the colored person who is brought before one of these officers of the law. Any leniency that may be expected, must proceed from the whims or caprice of the magistrate—in fact, it is optional with them; and our rights and liberty entirely at their disposal.

We are slaves in the midst of freedom, waiting patiently, and unconcernedly—indifferently, and stupidly, for masters to come and lay claim to us, trusting to their generosity, whether or not they will own us and carry us into endless bondage.

The slave is more secure than we; he knows who holds the heel upon his bosom—we know not the wretch who may grasp us by the throat. His master may be a man of some conscientious scruples; ours may be unmerciful. Good or bad, mild or harsh, easy or hard, lenient or severe, saint or satan—whenever that master demands any one of us—even our affectionate wives and darling little children, *we must go into slavery*—there is *no alternative*. The *will* of the man who sits in judgment on our liberty, is the law. To him is given *all power* to say, whether or not we have a right to enjoy freedom. This is the power over the slave in the South—this is now extended to the North. The will of the man who sits in judgment over us is the law; because it is explicitly provided that the *decision* of the commissioner shall be final, from which there can be no appeal.

The freed man of the South is even more secure than the freeborn of the North; because such persons usually have their records in the slave states, bringing their "papers" with them; and the slaveholders will be faithful to their own acts. The Northern freeman knows no records; he despises the "papers."

Depend upon no promised protection of citizens in any quarter. Their own property and liberty are jeopardised, and they will not sacrifice them for us. This we may not expect them to do.

Besides, there are no people who ever lived, love their country and obey their laws as the Americans.

Their country is their Heaven—their Laws their Scriptures—and the decrees of their Magistrates obeyed as the fiat of God. It is the most consummate delusion and misdirected confidence to depend upon them for protection; and for a moment suppose even our children safe while walking in the streets among them.

A people capable of originating and sustaining such a law as this, are not the people to whom we are willing to entrust our liberty at discretion.

What can we do?—What shall we do? This is the great and important question:—Shall we submit to be dragged like brutes before heartless men, and sent into degradation and bondage?—Shall we fly, or shall we resist? Ponder well and reflect.

A learned jurist in the United States, (Chief Justice John Gibson of Pennsylvania,[12]) lays down this as a fundamental right in the United States: that "Every man's house is his castle, and he has the right to defend it unto the taking of life, against any attempt to enter it against his will, except for crime," by well authenticated process.

But we have no such right. It was not intended for us, any more than any other provision of the law, intended for the protection of Americans. The policy is against us—it is useless to contend against it.

This is the law of the land and must be obeyed; and we candidly advise that it is useless for us to contend against it. To suppose its repeal, is to anticipate an overthrow of the Confederative Union; and we must be allowed an expression of opinion, when we say, that candidly we believe, the existence of the Fugitive Slave Law *necessary* to the continuance of the National Compact. This Law is the foundation of the Compromise—remove it, and the consequences are easily determined. We say necessary to the continuance of the National Compact: certainly we will not be understood as meaning that the enactment of such a Law was *really* necessary, or as favoring in the least this political monstrosity of the THIRTY-FIRST CONGRESS of the UNITED STATES OF AMERICA—surely not at all; but we speak logically and politically, leaving morality and right out of the question—taking our position on the acknowledged popular basis of American Policy; arguing from premise to conclusion. We must abandon all vague theory, and look at *facts* as they really are; viewing ourselves in our true political position in the body politic. To imagine ourselves to be included in the body politic, except by express legislation, is at war with common sense, and contrary to fact. Legislation, the administration of the laws of the country, and the exercise of rights by the people, all prove to the contrary. We are politically, not of them, but aliens to the laws and political privileges of the country. These are truths—fixed facts, that quaint theory and exhausted moralising, are impregnable to, and fall harmlessly before.

It is useless to talk about our rights in individual States: we can have no rights there as citizens, not recognised in our common country; as the citizens of one State, are entitled to all the rights and privileges of an American citizen in all the States—the nullity of the one necessarily implying the nullity of the other. These provisions then do not include the colored people of the United States; since there is no power left in them, whereby they may protect us as their own citizens. Our descent, by the laws of the country, stamps us with inferiority— upon us has this law worked *corruption of blood.* We are in the hands of the Gen-

---

12. John Bannister Gibson (1780–1853) became chief justice of the Pennsylvania Supreme Court in 1827; he was a widely quoted and admired jurist.

eral Government, and no State can rescue us. The Army and Navy stand at the service of our enslavers, the whole force of which, may at any moment—even in the dead of night, as has been done—when sunk in the depth of slumber, called out for the purpose of forcing our mothers, sisters, wives, and children, or ourselves, into hopeless servitude, there to weary out a miserable life, a relief from which, death would be hailed with joy. Heaven and earth—God and Humanity!—are not these sufficient to arouse the most worthless among mankind, of whatever descent, to a sense of their true position? These laws apply to us—shall we not be aroused?

What then shall we do?—what is the remedy—is the important question to be answered?

This important inquiry we shall answer, and find a remedy in when treating of the emigration of the colored people.

Chapter XVII. Emigration of the Colored People of the United States.

That there have been people in all ages under certain circumstances, that may be benefited by emigration, will be admitted; and that there are circumstances under which emigration is absolutely necessary to their political elevation, cannot be disputed.

This we see in the Exodus of the Jews from Egypt to the land of Judea; in the expedition of Dido and her followers from Tyre to Mauritania;[13] and not to dwell upon hundreds of modern European examples—also in the ever memorable emigration of the Puritans, in 1620, from Great Britain, the land of their birth, to the wilderness of the New World, at which may be fixed the beginning of emigration to this continent as a permanent residence.

This may be acknowledged; but to advocate the emigration of the colored people of the United States from their native homes, is a new feature in our history, and at first view, may be considered objectionable, as pernicious to our interests. This objection is at once removed, when reflecting on our condition as incontrovertibly shown in a foregoing part of this work. And we shall proceed at once to give the advantages to be derived from emigration, to us as a people, in preference to any other policy that we may adopt. This granted, the question will then be, Where shall we go? This we conceive to be all-important—of paramount consideration, and shall endeavor to show the most advantageous locality; and premise the recommendation, with the strictest advice against any

13. According to Roman mythology, Dido, queen of Carthage, fled Tyre after her brother, Pygmalion, murdered her husband.

countenance whatever, to the emigration scheme of the so called Republic of
Liberia.[14]

Chapter XVIII. "Republic of Liberia."

That we desire the civilization and enlightenment of Africa—the high and
elevated position of Liberia among the nations of the earth, may not be doubted,
as the writer was among the first, seven or eight years ago, to make the suggestion and call upon the Liberians to hold up their heads like men; take courage,
having confidence in their own capacity to govern themselves, and come out
from their disparaging position, by formally declaring their Independence. . . .

However foreign to the designs of the writer of ever making that country or
any other out of America, his home; had this been done, and honorably maintained, the Republic of Liberia would have met with words of encouragement,
not only from himself, an humble individual, but we dare assert, from the leading spirits among, if not from the whole colored population of the United
States. Because they would have been willing to overlook the circumstances
under which they went there, so that in the end, they were willing to take their
stand as men, and thereby throw off the degradation of slaves, still under the
control of American slave-holders, and American slave-ships. But in this, we
were disappointed—grievously disappointed, and proceed to show in short,
our objections to Liberia.

Its geographical position, in the first place, is objectionable, being located in
the *sixth degree* of latitude North of the equator, in a district signally unhealthy,
rendering it objectionable as a place of destination for the colored people of the
United States. We shall say nothing about other parts of the African coast, and
the reasons for its location where it is: it is enough for us to know the facts as
they are, to justify an unqualified objection to Liberia.

In the second place, it originated in a deep laid scheme of the slaveholders of
the country, to *exterminate* the free colored of the American continent; the origin being sufficient to justify us in impugning the motives.

Thirdly and lastly—Liberia is not an Independent Republic: in fact, *it is not
an independent nation at all; but a poor miserable mockery*—a *burlesque* on
a government—a pitiful dependency on the American Colonizationists, the
Colonization Board at Washington city, in the District of Columbia, being the
Executive and Government, and the principal man, called President, in Liberia,

14. Established by the American Colonization Society in 1821, Liberia declared its independence in 1847, though it retained ties over the next two decades or so to American-
based colonization and emigration societies.

being the echo—a mere parrot of Rev. Robert [*sic*] R. Gurley, Elliott Cresson, Esq., Governor Pinney, and other leaders of the Colonization scheme—to do as they bid, and say what they tell him.[15] This we see in all of his doings.

Does he go to France and England, and enter into solemn treaties of an honorable recognition of the independence of his country; before his own nation has any knowledge of the result, this man called President, dispatches an official report to the Colonizationists of the United States, asking their gracious approval? Does king Grando, or a party of fishermen besiege a village and murder some of the inhabitants, this same "President," dispatches an official report to the American Colonization Board, asking for instructions—who call an Executive Session of the Board, and immediately decide that war must be waged against the enemy, placing ten thousand dollars at his disposal—and war *actually declared in Liberia*, by virtue of the *instructions* of *the American Colonization Society*. A mockery of a government—a disgrace to the office pretended to be held—a parody on the position assumed. Liberia in Africa, is a mere dependency of Southern slaveholders, and American Colonizationists, and unworthy of any respectful consideration from us.

What would be thought of the people of Hayti, and their heads of government, if their instructions emanated from the American Anti-Slavery Society, or the British Foreign Missionary Board? Should they be respected at all as a nation? Would they be worthy of it? Certainly not. We do not expect Liberia to be all that Hayti is; but we ask and expect of her, to have a decent respect for herself—to endeavor to be freemen instead of voluntary slaves. Liberia is no place for the colored freemen of the United States; and we dismiss the subject with a single remark of caution against any advice contained in a pamphlet, which we have not seen, written by Hon. James G. Birney, in favor of Liberian emigration.[16] Mr. Birney is like the generality of white Americans, who suppose that we are too ignorant to understand what we want; whenever they wish to get rid of

15. The American Colonization Society (ACS) was founded in December 1816 with the goal of transporting free blacks to Africa. The colonizationists conceived of themselves as moderate reformers who would bring about an end to racial strife (and eventually slavery) in the United States by shipping the nation's free blacks to their "natural" home in Africa. Delany refers to some of the principal leaders of the ACS: the Presbyterian clergyman Ralph Randolph Gurley (1797–1872), who at one time was vice president of the ACS; the Philadelphia Quaker Elliott Cresson (1796–1854), who served as an ACS agent in the United States and England; and the Presbyterian minister John Book Pinney (1806–82), who served as colonial governor of Liberia during the 1830s.

16. See James Gillespie Birney (1792–1857), *Letter on Colonization* (1838). Delany is somewhat unfair to Birney, for he renounced colonizationism during the 1840s and advocated political action to bring about the end of slavery. In 1840 and 1844 Birney was the presidential candidate of the Liberty Party.

us, would drive us any where, so that we left them. Don't adhere to a word therein contained; we will think for ourselves. Let Mr. Birney go his way, and we will go ours. This is one of those confounded gratuities that is forced in our faces at every turn we make. We dismiss it without further comment—and with it Colonization *in toto*—and Mr. Birney *de facto*.

But to return to emigration: Where shall we go? We must not leave this continent; America is our destination and our home. . . .

Chapter XXI. Central and South America and the West Indies.

Central and South America, are evidently the ultimate destination and future home of the colored race on this continent; the advantages of which in preference to all others, will be apparent when once pointed out.[17]

Geographically, from the Northern extremity of Yucatan, down through Central and South America, to Cape Horn, there is a variation of climate from the twenty-second degree of North latitude, passing through the equatorial region; nowhere as warm as it is in the same latitude in Africa; to the *fifty-fifth degree* of South latitude, including a climate as cold as that of the Hudson Bay country in British America, colder than that of Maine, or any part known to the United States of North America; so that there is every variety of climate in South, as well as North America.

In the productions of grains, fruits, and vegetables, Central and South America are also prolific; and the best of herds are here raised. Indeed, the finest Merino sheep, as well as the principal trade in rice, sugar, cotton, and wheat, which is now preferred in California to any produced in the United States—the Chilian flour—might be carried on by the people of this most favored portion of God's legacy to man. The mineral productions excel all other parts of this

---

17. The native language of all these countries, as well as the greater part of South America, is *Spanish*, which is the easiest of all foreign languages to learn. It is very remarkable and worthy of note, that with a view of going to Mexico or South America, the writer several years ago paid some attention to the Spanish language; and now, a most singular coincidence, without preunderstanding, in almost every town, where there is any intelligence among them, there are some *colored persons* of both sexes, who are studying the Spanish language. Even the Methodist and other clergymen, among them. And we earnestly entreat all colored persons who can, to study, and have their children taught Spanish. No foreign language will be of such *import* to colored people, in a very short time, as the Spanish. Mexico, Central and South America, importune us to speak their language; and if nothing else, the silent indications of Cuba, urge us to learn the Spanish tongue. [Delany's note]

continent; the rivers present the greatest internal advantages, and the commercial prospects, are without a parallel on the coast of the new world.

The advantages to the colored people of the United States, to be derived from emigration to Central, South America, and the West Indies, are incomparably greater than that of any other parts of the world at present.

In the first place, there never have existed in the policy of any of the nations of Central or South America, an inequality on account of race or color, and any prohibition of rights, has generally been to the white, and not to the colored races.[18] To the whites, not because they were white, not on account of their color, but because of the policy pursued by them towards the people of other races than themselves. The population of Central and South America, consist of fifteen millions two hundred and forty thousand, adding the ten millions of Mexico; twenty-five millions two hundred and forty thousand, of which vast population, but *one-seventh* are whites, or the pure European race. Allowing a deduction of one-seventh of this population for the European race that may chance to be in those countries, and we have in South and Central America alone, the vast colored population of *thirteen millions one hundred and seventy-seven thousand*; and including Mexico, a *colored* population on this glorious continent of *twenty-one millions, six hundred and forty thousand.*

This vast number of people, our brethren—because they are precisely the same people as ourselves and share the same fate with us, as the case of numbers of them have proven, who have been adventitiously thrown among us—stand ready and willing to take us by the hand—nay, are anxiously waiting, and earnestly importuning us to come, that they may make common cause with us, and we all share the same fate. There is nothing under heaven in our way—the people stand with open arms ready to receive us. The climate, soil, and productions—the vast rivers and beautiful sea-coast—the scenery of the landscape, and beauty of the starry heavens above—the song of the birds—the voice of the people say come—and God our Father bids us go.—Will we go? Go we must, and go we will, as there is no alternative. To remain here in North America, and be crushed to the earth in vassalage and degradation, we never will.

Talk not about religious biases—we have but one reply to make. We had rather be a Heathen *freeman*, than a Christian *slave*. . . .

18. The Brazilians have formed a Colonization Society, for the purpose of colonizing free blacks to Africa. The Brazilians are Portuguese, the only nation that can be termed white, and the only one that is a real slave holding nation in South America. Even the black and colored men have equal privileges with whites; and the action of this society will probably extend only to the sending back of such captives as may be taken from piratical slavers. . . . [Delany's note]

Chapter XXII. Nicaragua and New Grenada.

As it is not reasonable to suppose, that all who read this volume—especially those whom it is intended most to benefit—understand geography; it is deemed advisable, to name some particular places, as locality of destination.

We consequently, to begin with, select NICARAGUA, in Central America, North, and NEW GRENADA, the Northern part of South America, South of Nicaragua, as the most favorable points at present, in every particular, for us to emigrate to.

In the first place, they are the nearest points to be reached, and countries at which the California adventurers are now touching, on their route to that distant land, and not half the distance of California.

In the second place, the advantages for all kinds of enterprise, are equal if not superior, to almost any other points—the climate being healthy and highly favorable.

In the third place, and by no means the least point of importance, the British nation is bound by solemn treaty, to protect both of those nations from foreign imposition, until they are able to stand alone.

Then there is nothing in the way, but every thing in favor, and opportunities for us to rise to the full stature of manhood. Remember this fact, that in these countries, colored men now fill the highest places in the country: and colored people have the same chances there, that white people have in the United States. All that is necessary to do, is to go, and the moment your foot touches the soil, you have all the opportunities for elevating yourselves as the highest, according to your industry and merits.

Nicaragua and New Grenada, are both Republics, having a President, Senate, and Representatives of the people. The municipal affairs are well conducted; and remember, however much the customs of the country may differ, and appear strange to those you have left behind—remember that you are free; and that many who, at first sight, might think that they could not become reconciled to the new order of things, should recollect, that they were once in a situation in the United States, (in *slavery*,) where they were compelled to be content with customs infinitely more averse to their feelings and desires. And that customs become modified, just in proportion as people of different customs from different parts, settle in the same communities together. All we ask is Liberty—the rest follows as a matter of course.

Chapter XXIII. Things as They Are.

> "And if thou boast TRUTH to utter,
> SPEAK, and leave the rest to God."

In presenting this work, we have but a single object in view, and that is, to inform the minds of the colored people at large, upon many things pertaining to their elevation, that but few among us are acquainted with. Unfortunately for us, as a body, we have been taught to believe, that we must have some person to think for us, instead of thinking for ourselves. So accustomed are we to submission and this kind of training, that it is with difficulty, even among the most intelligent of the colored people, an audience may be elicited for any purpose whatever, if the expounder is to be a colored person; and the introduction of any subject is treated with indifference, if not contempt, when the originator is a colored person. Indeed, the most ordinary white person, is almost revered, while the most qualified colored person is totally neglected. Nothing from them is appreciated.

We have been standing comparatively still for years, following in the footsteps of our friends, believing that what they promise us can be accomplished, just because they say so, although our own knowledge should long since, have satisfied us to the contrary. Because even were it possible, with the present hate and jealousy that the whites have towards us in this country, for us to gain equality of rights with them; we never could have an equality of the exercise and enjoyment of those rights—because, the great odds of numbers are against us. We might indeed, as some at present, have the right of the elective franchise—nay, it is not the *elective franchise*, because the *elective franchise* makes the enfranchised, *eligible* to any position attainable; but we may exercise the right of *voting* only, which to us, is but poor satisfaction; and we by no means care to cherish the privilege of voting somebody into office, to help to make laws to degrade us.

In religion—because they are both *translators* and *commentators*, we must believe nothing, however absurd, but what our oppressors tell us. In Politics, nothing but such as they promulge; in Anti-Slavery, nothing but what our white brethren and friends say we must; in the mode and manner of our elevation, we must do nothing, but that which may be laid down to be done by our white brethren from some quarter or other; and now, even on the subject of emigration, there are some colored people to be found, so lost to their own interest and self-respect, as to be gulled by slave owners and colonizationists, who are led to believe there is no other place in which they can become elevated, but Liberia, a government of American slave-holders, as we have shown—simply, because white men have told them so.

Upon the possibility, means, mode and manner, of our Elevation in the

United States—Our Original Rights and Claims as Citizens—Our Determination not to be Driven from our Native Country—the Difficulties in the Way of Our Elevation—Our Position in Relation to our Anti-Slavery Brethren—the Wicked Design and Injurious Tendency of the American Colonization Society—Objections to Liberia—Objections to Canada—Preferences to South America, &c., &c., all of which we have treated without reserve; expressing our mind freely, and with candor, as we are determined that as far as we can at present do so, the minds of our readers shall be enlightened. The custom of concealing information upon vital and important subjects, in which the interest of the people is involved, we do not agree with, nor favor in the least; we have therefore, laid this cursory treatise before our readers, with the hope that it may prove instrumental in directing the attention of our people in the right way, that leads to their Elevation. Go or stay—of course each is free to do as he pleases—one thing is certain; our Elevation is the work of our own hands. And Mexico, Central America, the West Indies, and South America, all present now, opportunities for the individual enterprise of our young men, who prefer to remain in the United States, in preference to going where they can enjoy real freedom, and equality of rights. Freedom of Religion, as well as of politics, being tolerated in all of these places.

Let our young men and women, prepare themselves for usefulness and business; that the men may enter into merchandise, trading, and other things of importance; the young women may become teachers of various kinds, and otherwise fill places of usefulness. Parents must turn their attention more to the education of their children. We mean, to educate them for useful practical business. Educate them for the Store and the Counting House—to do every-day practical business purposes. Consult the children's propensities, and direct their education according to their inclinations. It may be, that there is too great a desire on the part of parents, to give their children a professional education, before the body of the people, are ready for it. A people must be a business people, and have more to depend upon than mere help in people's houses and Hotels, before they are either able to support, or capable of properly appreciating the services of professional men among them. This has been one of our great mistakes—we have gone in advance of ourselves. We have commenced at the superstructure of the building, instead of the foundation—at the top instead of the bottom. We should first be mechanics and common tradesmen, and professions as a matter of course would grow out of the wealth made thereby. Young men and women, must now prepare for usefulness—the day of our Elevation is at hand—all the world now gazes at us—and Central and South America, and the West Indies, bid us come and be men and women, protected, secure, beloved and Free.

The branches of education most desirable for the preparation of youth, for practical useful every-day life, are Arithmetic and good Penmanship, in order to be Accountants; and a good rudimental knowledge of Geography—which has ever been neglected, and under estimated—and of Political Economy; which without the knowledge of the first, no people can ever become adventurous— nor of the second, never will be an enterprising people. Geography, teaches a knowledge of the world, and Political Economy, a knowledge of the wealth of nations; or how to make money. These are not abstruse sciences, or learning not easily acquired or understood; but simply, common School Primer learning, that every body may get. And, although it is the very Key to prosperity and suc- cess in common life, but few know any thing about it. Unfortunately for our people, so soon as their children learn to read a Chapter in the New Testament, and scribble a miserable hand, they are pronounced to have "Learning enough;" and taken away from School, no use to themselves, nor community. This is ap- parent in our Public Meetings, and Official Church Meetings; of the great num- ber of men present, there are but few capable of filling a Secretaryship. Some of the large cities may be an exception to this. Of the multitudes of Merchants, and Business men throughout this country, Europe, and the world, few are qualified, beyond the branches here laid down by us as necessary for business. What did John Jacob Astor, Stephen Girard,[19] or do the millionaires and the greater part of the merchant princes, and mariners, know about Latin and Greek, and the Classics? Precious few of them know any thing. In proof of this, in 1841, during the Administration of President Tyler, when the mutiny was detected on board of the American Man of War Brig Somers, the names of the Mutineers, were recorded by young S—a Midshipman in Greek. Captain Alexander Slidell McKenzie, Commanding, was unable to read them; and in his despatches to the Government, in justification of his policy in executing the criminals, said that he "discovered some curious characters which he was unable to read," &c.; showing thereby, that that high functionary, did not understand even the Greek Alphabet, which was only necessary, to have been able to read proper names written in Greek.[20]

What we most need then, is a good business practical Education; because, the Classical and Professional education of so many of our young men, before their

19. The New York merchant John Jacob Astor (1763–1848) established the charter for the American Fur Company (1808) and eventually had a monopoly on the fur trade in the United States; the Philadelphia merchant, banker, and philanthropist Stephen Girard (1750–1831) helped to establish the Second Bank of the United States.

20. In November 1842, Captain Alexander Slidell Mackenzie (1803–48) believed he de- tected an incipient mutiny on board the U.S. naval brig *Somers*, and he ordered hanged three sailors, including "S," Philip Spencer (1823–42), the son of President Tyler's secre- tary of war, John Canfield Spencer. The controversial case was widely publicized.

parents are able to support them, and community ready to patronize them, only serves to lull their energy, and cripple the otherwise, praiseworthy efforts they would make in life. A Classical education, is only suited to the wealthy, or those who have a prospect of gaining a livelihood by it. The writer does not wish to be understood, as underrating a Classical and Professional education; this is not his intention; he fully appreciates them, having had some such advantages himself; but he desires to give a proper guide, and put a check to the extravagant idea that is fast obtaining, among our people especially, that a Classical, or as it is termed, a "finished education," is necessary to prepare one for usefulness in life. Let us have an education, that shall practically develope our thinking faculties and manhood; and then, and not until then, shall we be able to vie with our oppressors, go where we may. We as heretofore, have been on the extreme; either no qualification at all, or a Collegiate education. We jumped too far; taking a leap from the deepest abyss to the highest summit; rising from the ridiculous to the sublime; without medium or intermission.

Let our young women have an education; let their minds be well informed; well stored with useful information and practical proficiency, rather than the light superficial acquirements, popularly and fashionably called accomplishments. We desire accomplishments, but they must be *useful*.

Our females must be qualified, because they are to be the mothers of our children. As mothers are the first nurses and instructors of children; from them children consequently, get their first impressions, which being always the most lasting, should be the most correct. Raise the mothers above the level of degradation, and the offspring is elevated with them. In a word, instead of our young women, transcribing in their blank books, recipes for *Cooking*; we desire to see them making the transfer of *Invoices of Merchandise.* Come to our aid then; the *morning* of our *Redemption* from degradation, adorns the horizon.

In our selection of individuals, it will be observed, that we have confined ourself entirely to those who occupy or have occupied positions among the whites, consequently having a more general bearing as useful contributors to society at large. While we do not pretend to give all such worthy cases, we gave such as we possessed information of, and desire it to be understood, that a large number of our most intelligent and worthy men and women, have not been named, because from their more private position in community, it was foreign to the object and design of this work. If we have said aught to offend, "take the will for the deed,"[21] and be assured, that it was given with the purest of motives, and best intention, from a true hearted man and brother; deeply lamenting the sad fate

21. Jonathan Swift, *Polite Conversation* (1738), Dialogue ii.

of his race in this country, and sincerely desiring the elevation of man, and submitted to the serious consideration of all, who favor the promotion of the cause of God and humanity.

Chapter XXIV. A Glance at Ourselves—Conclusion.

With broken hopes—sad devastation;
A race *resigned* to DEGRADATION!

. . . The writer is no "Public Man," in the sense in which this is understood among our people, but simply an humble individual, endeavoring to seek a livelihood by a profession obtained entirely by his own efforts, without relatives and friends able to assist him; except such friends as he gained by the merit of his course and conduct, which he here gratefully acknowledges; and whatever he has accomplished, other young men may, by making corresponding efforts, also accomplish.

We have advised an emigration to Central and South America, and even to Mexico and the West Indies, to those who prefer either of the last named places, all of which are free countries, Brazil being the only real slave-holding State in South America—there being nominal slavery in Dutch Guiana, Peru, Buenos Ayres, Paraguay, and Uraguay, in all of which places colored people have equality in social, civil, political, and religious privileges; Brazil making it punishable with death to import slaves into the empire. . . .

In our own country, the United States, there are *three million five hundred thousand slaves*; and we, the nominally free colored people, are *six hundred thousand* in number; estimating one-sixth to be men, we have *one hundred thousand* able bodied freemen, which will make a powerful auxiliary in any country to which we may become adopted—an ally not to be despised by any power on earth. We love our country, dearly love her, but she don't love us—she despises us, and bids us begone, driving us from her embraces; but we shall not go where she desires us; but when we do go, whatever love we have for her, we shall love the country none the less that receives us as her adopted children.

For the want of business habits and training, our energies have become paralyzed; our young men never think of business, any more than if they were so many bondmen, without the right to pursue any calling they may think most advisable. With our people in this country, dress and good appearances have been made the only test of gentlemen and ladyship, and that vocation which offers the best opportunity to dress and appear well, has generally been preferred, however menial and degrading, by our young people, without even, in the majority of cases, an effort to do better; indeed, in many instances, refusing situations equally lucrative, and superior in position; but which would not allow as much display of dress and personal appearance. This, if we ever expect to rise, must be discarded from among us, and a high and respectable position assumed.

One of our great temporal curses is our consummate poverty. We are the poorest people, as a class, in the world of civilized mankind—abjectly, miserably poor, no one scarcely being able to assist the other. To this, of course, there are noble exceptions; but that which is common to, and the very process by which white men exist, and succeed in life, is unknown to colored men in general. In any and every considerable community may be found, some one of our white fellow-citizens, who is worth more than all the colored people in that community put together. We consequently have little or no efficiency. We must have means to be practically efficient in all the undertakings of life; and to obtain them, it is necessary that we should be engaged in lucrative pursuits, trades, and general business transactions. In order to be thus engaged, it is necessary that we should occupy positions that afford the facilities for such pursuits. To compete now with the mighty odds of wealth, social and religious preferences, and political influences of this country, at this advanced stage of its national existence, we never may expect. A new country, and new beginning, is the only true, rational, politic remedy for our disadvantageous position; and that country we have already pointed out, with triple golden advantages, all things considered, to that of any country to which it has been the province of man to embark.

Every other than we, have at various periods of necessity, been a migratory people, and all when oppressed, shown a greater abhorrence of oppression, if not a greater love of liberty, than we. We cling to our oppressors as the objects of our love. It is true that our enslaved brethren are here, and we have been led to believe that it is necessary for us to remain, on that account. Is it true, that all should remain in degradation, because a part are degraded? We believe no such thing. We believe it to be the duty of the Free, to elevate themselves in the most speedy and effective manner possible; as the redemption of the bondman depends entirely upon the elevation of the freeman; therefore, to elevate the free colored people of America, anywhere upon this continent; forebodes the speedy redemption of the slaves. We shall hope to hear no more of so fallacious a doctrine—the necessity of the free remaining in degradation, for the sake of the oppressed. Let us apply, first, the lever to ourselves; and the force that elevates us to the position of manhood's considerations and honors, will cleft the manacle of every slave in the land.

When such great worth and talents—for want of a better sphere—of men like Rev. Jonathan Robinson, Robert Douglass, Frederick A. Hinton,[22] and a hundred others that might be named, were permitted to expire in a barber-shop; and such living men as may be found in Boston, New York, Philadelphia, Baltimore, Richmond, Washington City, Charleston, (S.C.), New Orleans, Cincinnati, Louisville, St. Louis, Pittsburg, Buffalo, Rochester, Albany, Utica, Cleveland, Detroit, Milwaukie, Chicago, Columbus, Zanesville, Wheeling, and a hundred other places, confining themselves to Barber-shops and waiterships in Hotels; certainly the necessity of such a course as we have pointed out, must be cordially acknowledged; appreciated by every brother and sister of oppression; and not rejected as heretofore, as though they preferred inferiority to equality. These minds must become "unfettered," and have "space to rise." This cannot be in their present positions. A continuance in any position, becomes what is termed "Second Nature;" it begets an *adaptation*, and *reconciliation* of *mind* to such condition. It changes the whole physiological condition of the system, and adapts man and woman to a higher or lower sphere in the pursuits of life. The offsprings of slaves and peasantry, have the general characteristics of their parents; and nothing but a different course of training and education, will change the character.

The slave may become a lover of his master, and learn to forgive him for continual deeds of maltreatment and abuse; just as the Spaniel would couch and fondle at the feet that kick him; because he has been taught to reverence them, and consequently, becomes adapted in body and mind to his condition. Even the shrubbery-loving Canary, and lofty-soaring Eagle, may be tamed to the cage, and learn to love it from habit of confinement. It has been so with us in our position among our oppressors; we have been so prone to such positions, that we have learned to love them. When reflecting upon this all important, and to us, all absorbing subject, we feel in the agony and anxiety of the moment, as though we could cry out in the language of a Prophet of old: "Oh that my head were waters, and mine eyes a fountain of tears, that I might weep day and night for the" degradation "of my people! Oh that I had in the wilderness a lodging place of way-faring men; that I might leave my people, and go from them!"[23]

The Irishman and German in the United States, are very different persons to what they were when in Ireland and Germany, the countries of their nativity. There their spirits were depressed and downcast; but the instant they set their foot upon unrestricted soil; free to act and untrammeled to move; their physi-

---

22. Robert Douglass and Frederick A. Hinton (1804–49), both of Philadelphia, were prominent black abolitionists who fought for black voting rights in Pennsylvania; Jonathan Robinson was more obscure.

23. Jeremiah 9:1–2.

cal condition undergoes a change, which in time becomes physiological, which is transmitted to the offspring, who when born under such circumstances, is a decidedly different being to what it would have been, had it been born under different circumstances.

A child born under oppression, has all the elements of servility in its constitution; who when born under favorable circumstances, has to the contrary, all the elements of freedom and independence of feeling. Our children then, may not be expected, to maintain that position and manly bearing; born under the unfavorable circumstances with which we are surrounded in this country; that we so much desire. To use the language of the talented Mr. Whipper,[24] "they cannot be raised in this country, without being stoop shouldered." Heaven's pathway stands unobstructed, which will lead us into a Paradise of bliss. Let us go on and possess the land, and the God of Israel will be our God.

The lessons of every school book, the pages of every history, and columns of every newspaper, are so replete with stimuli to nerve us on to manly aspirations, that those of our young people, who will now refuse to enter upon this great theatre of Polynesian adventure, and take their position on the stage of Central and South America, where a brilliant engagement, of certain and most triumphant success, in the drama of human equality awaits them; then, with the blood of *slaves*, write upon the lintel of every door in sterling Capitals,[25] to be gazed and hissed at by every passer by—

> Doomed by the Creator
> To servility and degradation;
> The SERVANT of the *white* man,
> And despised of every nation!

(*The Condition, Elevation, Emigration and Destiny of the Colored People of the United States* [Philadelphia: published by the author, 1852], pp. 11–15, 20–22, 85–92, 147–48, 149–61, 168–71, 178–81, 188–208)

24. The Pennsylvania free black William Whipper (1804?–76) gained prominence during the 1830s for championing moral reform among blacks, but by the 1840s he had modified his position, arguing that the principal problem facing U.S. blacks was white racism. Working with black entrepeneur Stephen Smith, he became one of the wealthiest blacks in the United States, owning a lumberyard, railroad cars, a merchant ship, and extensive property in the United States and Canada West.

25. An ironic reference to Exodus 12:21–23, which describes Moses instructing the Jews to put the blood of the lamb on the lintel of their doorposts so that God will not smite them.

Letter to Oliver Johnson, 30 April 1852

CONDITION WAS GENERALLY criticized or ignored by abolitionists. One of the most scathing reviews came from Oliver Johnson (1809–89), the editor of the antislavery *Pennsylvania Freeman*. Delany refused to ignore Johnson's cutting remarks.

EDITOR OF THE PENNSYLVANIA FREEMAN:—In your paper of Thursday the 29th inst., I find the following:

THE CONDITION, ELEVATION, EMIGRATION AND DESTINY OF THE COLORED PEOPLE OF THE UNITED STATES. Politically considered. By MARTIN ROBINSON [*sic*] DELANY. Philadelphia: Published by the Author.

The preface of this work opens with the following confession:

"The author of this little volume has no other apology for offering it to the public, than the hurried manner in which it has been composed."

This will probably strike our readers, as it did us, as a very singular reason for publishing a book; but if any better exists, we have not been able to discover it in the book itself. It embodies many facts which are in themselves interesting and valuable, which, if they were less bunglingly and egotistically presented and not mixed up with much that is of questionable propriety and utility, might be available to the reader; but the manner in which the author has used his materials deprives his work of all value. We could wish that, for his own credit, and that of the colored people, it had never been published.[1]

That there are a number of palpable errors in this book, is true; which occurred by a neglect to furnish me with a revision proof-sheet—the whole of the

1. Johnson's review appeared in the 29 April 1852 *Pennsylvania Freeman*, p. 2. In the letter he sent to Johnson, Delany apparently copied out the review (which is inserted here), but instead of reprinting the review, Johnson put the following remark in brackets: "See notice of Dr. Delany's work on the Colored People in our last. There is no need of repeating it here.—*Ed. Freeman.*"

present edition being struck off, before I got to revise it—all of which have been ordered to be corrected in the plates, and will stand corrected in the next issue.

But the object of your remarks evidently has been, to disparage me, and endeavor to injure the sale of the book, especially among the colored people —upon whose ignorance you presume, and take advantage by your position— which but furnishes a striking proof of *your* negro-hate, in common with many of your less pretending fellows. There is not an intelligent colored man nor woman in the country—except the most miserable servile and tool—but will indignantly repel this bare-faced insult.

You also charge me with egotism, which is but a prejudicial sneer at a black man, for daring to do anything upon his own responsibility; and is in keeping with Mrs. Stowe's ridicule of Hayti,[2] which you very adroitly avoid in your apology for the objectionable portion of her work, in reply to the manly note of that fearless advocate of his race, Robert Purvis.[3] There is not one word, which to an unprejudiced mind, will be tortured into egotism.

As to your judgment upon my style and taste in composition, I utterly disregard; but under the circumstances, the attack was cowardly. I therefore despise your sneers and defy your influence.

M. R. DELANY.

Philadelphia, April 30th, 1852.

(*Pennsylvania Freeman,* 6 May 1852, p. 2)

2. See *Uncle Tom's Cabin,* vol. 2, chs. 23, 43.

3. In his critical remarks on *Uncle Tom's Cabin,* printed in the same 29 April 1852 issue of the *Pennsylvania Freeman* in which Johnson attacked *Condition,* the black abolitionist Robert Purvis (1810–98) complained about the novel's apparent support for African colonization.

Letter to William Lloyd Garrison, 14 May 1852

IN HIS REVIEW OF *Condition* in the 7 May 1852 *Liberator,* Garrison stated that Delany's book should be widely read for its sketches of notable African Americans, even as he lamented its "tone of despondency" and its "inimical" call for black emigration. He printed Delany's response to the review two weeks later.

PHILADELPHIA, May 14, 1852

MR. GARRISON:

MY DEAR SIR:—I thank you, most kindly, for the very favorable and generous notice you have taken of my hastily written book. This, to many, may appear singular, that the author of a work should send words of thanks to an editor for his notice of him, but this favor of yours came so opportune, that it seems like a God-send.

The errors and deficiencies, which you are pleased to pass by unnoticed—justly taking my prefatory apology as sufficient—I have corrected, and will so appear in the next issue, shortly to come out.[1] The corrections you make concerning *yourself,* I shall add as a Note at the conclusion of the work.

I thank those editors of Philadelphia and elsewhere, who have favorably noticed this work, and would add, that the ever good, generous Gerrit Smith has sent me a letter of approval of the work in general.

I am not in favor of caste, nor a separation of the brotherhood of mankind, and would as willingly live among white men as black, if I had an *equal possession and enjoyment* of privileges; but shall never be reconciled to live among them, subservient to their will—existing by mere *sufferance,* as we, the colored people, do in this country. The majority of white men cannot see why colored men cannot be satisfied with their condition in Massachusetts—what they desire more than the *granted* right of citizenship. Blind selfishness on the one

---

1. Delany never published a revised *Condition.*

hand, and deep prejudice on the other, will not permit them to understand that we desire the *exercise* and *enjoyment* of these rights, as well as the *name* of their possession. If there were any probability of this, I should be willing to remain in the country, fighting and struggling on, the good fight of faith. But I must admit, that I have no hopes in this country—no confidence in the American people—with a *few* excellent exceptions—therefore, I have written as I have done. Heathenism and Liberty, before Christianity and Slavery.

> "Were I a slave, I would be free,
>   I would not live to live a slave;
> But boldly *strike* for LIBERTY—
>   For FREEDOM or a *Martyr's* grave."

Yours for God and Humanity,

M. R. DELANY

(*Liberator*, 21 May 1852, p. 3)

Letter to Frederick Douglass, 10 July 1852

SMARTING FROM HIS conflict with Oliver Johnson, Delany sent Douglass a letter that attempted to prod him to take notice of *Condition* in his newspaper.

NEW YORK CITY, July 10, 1852.

FREDERICK DOUGLASS: SIR:—I send you for publication, an interesting paper, written evidently by a competent person, one very intelligent upon the subject, as a contribution to the *National Intelligencer*, (of Washington City, D.C.,) giving a statistic summary of the five States of CENTRAL AMERICA.[1] Of course, anything said in commendation of this paper, every due allowance is made for the peculiar *Anglo-Saxon prejudices* of the writer, in his allusion to the "superiority" of the white race: a fact well worthy of remark, that wherever found, this same *Anglo-Saxon race*, is the most inveterate enemy of the *colored races*, of whatever origin—whether African, Mongolian, Malayan, or Indian. This is substantially true, (to which there are always individual exceptions,) but is not really the case with any *other* race of the Caucasian type. You will find by this writer's own acknowledgment, that the greater part of the inhabitants of the country are colored people, there being more *whites* in proportion in the little State of Costa Rica, than in any other of the States, and these fall far in the minority.

I am deeply interested in this subject—and you will not charge me with the "egotism," with which a distinguished statesman was charged during the Mexican War with the United States, who said, that he had "studied Humboldt forty years ago"[2]—when I say, that I am equally, if not more familiar with the subject

---

1. Douglass reprints this particular article, from the Washington, D.C., newspaper *National Intelligencer*, in the same issue of *Frederick Douglass' Paper* as Delany's letter.

2. A reference to the German naturalist Alexander von Humboldt (1769–1859), whose *Personal Narrative of Travels to the Equinoctial Regions of the New Continent* (1814–29) helped to establish him as an expert on Latin America.

of these countries, than the most of colored men, having made them a matter of thought, for more than seventeen years, at which time (being very young) I introduced the subject before the young people, and have never since abandoned it. But for my views upon this subject, I refer you and the reader to a work, recently published by myself, on the Condition, Elevation, Emigration, and Destiny of the Colored People of the United States.—This work, a copy of which I sent you in May, on its issue, has never been noticed in the columns of your paper. *This* silence and neglect on your part was unjustifiable, because in noticing it, it was not necessary that you should implicate yourself either with the *errors* or *sentiments* therein contained. You could have given it a circulating notice, by saying such a book had been written by me, (saying anything else about or against it you pleased,) and let those who read it pass their own opinions also. But you heaped upon it a cold and deathly silence. This is not the course you pursue towards any issue, good or bad, sent you by white persons; you have always given them some notice. I desire not here to make an undue allusion, but simply to be treated as justly as you treat them. I care but little, what white men think of what I say, write, or do; my sole desire is, to benefit the colored people; this being done, I am satisfied—the opinion of every white person in the country or the world, to the contrary notwithstanding. This, I believe, so far, my book has accomplished—at least, the *colored people* generally are pleased with it, and that is all I desire in this case. It is true, there are some white men and women whose good opinions I desire and esteem; but these are few—good and tried friends. The remarks I make concerning your neglect, will also apply to Mr. Henry Bibb.[3] I may add, that when it was my province to conduct a *Journal*,[4] I always took pleasure in noticing anything to enhance either of your interests. But no matter.

I desire that our people have light and information upon the available means of bettering their condition; this they must and shall have. We never have, as heretofore, had any settled and established policy of our own—we have always adopted the policies that white men established for themselves without considering their applicability or adaptedness to us. No people can rise in this way. We must have a position, independently of anything pertaining to white men as nations. I weary of our miserable condition, and [am] heartily sick of whimpering, whining and snivelling at the feet of white men, begging for their refuse and

3. In fact, Henry Bibb's antislavery weekly *Voice of the Fugitive*, published in Canada, did not ignore Delany's *Condition*: the 3 June 1852 issue had a short, mostly favorable review of the book.

4. The *Mystery*.

offals existing by mere sufferance. You will please give this an insertion, in any part of the paper, so that the letter and article appear in the same number.

Yours for God and Humanity,
M. R. DELANY

(*Frederick Douglass' Paper*, 23 July 1852, p. 3)

Delany and Douglass on *Uncle Tom's Cabin*

THE YEAR 1852 SAW the publication of Delany's *Condition* and Stowe's *Uncle Tom's Cabin*. Douglass ignored *Condition* and over the next several years championed *Uncle Tom's Cabin* in the pages of *Frederick Douglass' Paper*. Angered that Douglass would choose to advocate an antislavery novel by a white woman over his own book, Delany wrote a series of four letters to Douglass that were highly critical of Stowe. Douglass printed the letters in his newspaper and responded to two of them with editorial commentary. Addressing issues of cross-racial sympathy, antislavery leadership, black violence, and African colonization, the Delany-Douglass debate on *Uncle Tom's Cabin* helped to set the terms of black debate on the novel for decades to come.

PITTSBURGH, March 20, 1853.

FREDERICK DOUGLASS, ESQ: DEAR SIR:—I notice in your paper of March 4th, an article in which you speak of having paid a visit to Mrs. H. E. B. Stowe, for the purpose, as you say, of consulting her, "as to some method which should contribute successfully, and permanently, to the improvement and elevation of the free people of color in the United States."[1] Also, in the number of March 18th, in an article by a writer over the initials of "P. C. S." in reference to the same subject, he concludes by saying, "I await with much interest the suggestions of Mrs. Stowe in this matter."

Now I simply wish to say, that we have always fallen into great errors in efforts of this kind, going to others than the *intelligent* and *experienced* among *ourselves*; and in all due respect and deference to Mrs. Stowe, I beg leave to say, that she *knows nothing about us*, "the Free Colored people of the United States," neither does any other white person—and, consequently, can contrive no successful scheme for our elevation; it must be done by ourselves. I am aware, that I differ

1. See Frederick Douglass, "A Day and a Night in 'Uncle Tom's Cabin,'" *Frederick Douglass' Paper*, 4 March 1853, p. 2.

with many in thus expressing myself, but I cannot help it; though I stand alone, and offend my best friends, so help me God! in a matter of such moment and importance, I will express my opinion. Why, in God's name, don't the leaders among our people make suggestions, and *consult* the most competent among *their own* brethren concerning our elevation? This they do not do; and I have not known one, whose province it was to do so, to go ten miles for such a purpose. We shall never effect anything until this is done.

I accord with the suggestions of H. O. Wagoner for a National Council or Consultation of our people,[2] provided *intelligence, maturity,* and *experience,* in matters among them, could be so gathered together; other than this, would be a mere mockery—like the Convention of 1848,[3] a coming together of rivals, to test their success for the "biggest offices." As God lives, I will never, knowingly, lend my aid to any such work, while our brethren groan in vassalage and bondage, and I and mine under oppression and degradation, such as we now suffer.

I would not give the counsel of one dozen *intelligent colored* freemen of the *right stamp,* for that of all the white and unsuitable colored persons in the land. But something must be done, and that speedily.

The so called free states, by their acts, are now virtually saying to the South, "you *shall not* emancipate; your blacks *must be slaves*; and should they come North, there is no refuge for them." I shall not be surprised to see, at no distant day, a solemn Convention called by the whites in the North, to deliberate on the propriety of changing the whole policy to that of slave states. This will be the remedy to prevent dissolution; *and it will come, mark that!* anything on the part of the American people to *save* their *Union.* Mark me—the non-slaveholding states *will become slave states.*

Yours for God and Humanity.

M. R. DELANY

REMARKS [by Frederick Douglass]—That colored men would agree among themselves to do something for the efficient and permanent aid of themselves

---

2. See *Frederick Douglass' Paper,* 18 March 1853, for a proposal to create a National Council of the Colored People, which was adopted in July 1853 at Douglass's Rochester convention. The council sought to unite black leaders but, as a result of the controversy between emigrationists and antiemigrationists, fell apart by 1855. Henry O. Wagoner (1816–?), a black abolitionist from Chicago, remained a strong advocate of Douglass's antiemigrationism.

3. Colored National Convention, in Cleveland, Ohio, 6 September 1848.

and their race, "is a consummation devoutly to be wished;" but until they do, it is neither wise nor graceful for them, or for any one of them to throw cold water upon plans and efforts made for that purpose by others. To scornfully reject all aid from our white friends, and to denounce them as unworthy of our confidence, looks high and mighty enough on paper; but unless the back ground is filled up with facts demonstrating our independence and self-sustaining power, of what use is such display of self-consequence? Brother DELANY has worked long and hard—he has written vigorously, and spoken eloquently to colored people—beseeching them, in the name of liberty, and all the dearest interests of humanity, to unite their energies, and to encrease their activities in the work of their own elevation; yet where has his voice been heeded? and where is the practical result? Echo answers, where? Is not the field open? Why, then, should any man object to the efforts of Mrs. Stowe, or any one else, who is moved to do anything on our behalf. The assertion that Mrs. Stowe "knows nothing about us," shows that Bro. DELANY knows nothing about Mrs. Stowe; for he certainly would not so violate his moral, or common sense if he did. When Brother DELANY will submit any plan for benefiting the colored people, or will candidly criticise any plan already submitted, he will be heard with pleasure. But we expect no plan from him. He has written a book—and we may say that it is, in many respects, an excellent book—on the condition, character, and destiny of the colored people;[4] but it leaves us just where it finds us, without chart or compass, and in more doubt and perplexity than before we read it.

Brother Delany is one of our strong men; and we are therefore all the more grieved, that at a moment when all our energies should be united in giving effect to the benevolent designs of our friends, his voice should be uplifted to strike a jarring note, or to awaken a feeling of distrust.

In respect to a national convention, we are for it—and will not only go "ten miles," but a thousand, if need be, to attend it. Away, therefore, with all unworthy flings on that score.—ED.

(*Frederick Douglass' Paper*, 1 April 1853, p. 2)

* * *

FREDERICK DOUGLASS, ESQ: MY DEAR SIR:—I have many things to say to you; and as I desire to be as laconic as possible, seeing that you now have many able and interesting correspondents, and not wishing to encumber your valu-

---

4. One of the few mentions in *Frederick Douglass' Paper* of Delany's *Condition*.

able space with such as I have to write, I must make it the subject of three letters. The first, I write now; the second I design writing next week; and the third, the week after. Severally, a brotherly reply, to set you right in your kindly remarks on my letter, in relation to Mrs. Stowe's project, the subject of a *National Council* of colored freemen; and in regard to your article on the business pursuits of our people and *youth*, and the elevation of our people in general—all of which, you know, I highly approve, and have long and generally advocated. I am well pleased with some of the remarks of "B,"[5] in your paper of the 8th inst., which came to hand to-day, and desire to say, whatever difference of opinion there may exist between us, if any there be, in regard to the *means* to be used to attain our long-desired end—the elevation of ourselves and brethren—bond and free—upon the manner in which you treated this subject, we shall never disagree, and to all of what you then said, I give a long and loud Amen! the fretful letter of a mis-taken brother—if *such* he considers *himself*—to the contrary notwithstanding.

But my object just now, was to write you on the subject of *Eliza Greenfield*,[6] the BLACK SWAN, and her confidential friend, *Colonel Wood*,[7] with whom she now travels; than whom, a *meaner*, and more *unprincipled* hater of the black race does not live in this land of oppression. Miss Greenfield's course and con-duct have been equally void of principle, but so induced to act, through this man, Wood, and his friends. Elizabeth Greenfield had engaged herself to a com-petent, and in every respect suitable colored man, who had made ample provi-sions for giving concerts. She had also engaged Mr. D., an accomplished artist and gentleman of Philadelphia, as her private Secretary and treasurer.[8] Mr. D., in November, 1851, had already entered on the discharge of his duties, closing a

5. Perhaps Amos Gerry Beman (1812–74), a black abolitionist clergyman from Con-necticut who, like Wagoner, strongly supported plans for a National Council of the Col-ored People. Delany refers to the essay by "B," "Make Your Sons Mechanics and Farmers, not Waiters, Porters, and Barbers," which appeared in the 8 April 1853 issue of *Frederick Douglass' Paper*, p. 2.

6. Known as the "Black Swan" by her many admirers, Elizabeth Taylor Greenfield (1819?–76) was born a slave in Natchez, Mississippi, and freed in the early 1820s after her mistress took her to Philadelphia and joined the Society of Friends. Greenfield began her musical training in the 1830s, first performed in the 1840s, and during 1851–52 gave ac-claimed public performances in New York, Massachusetts, and Illinois. In 1854 she sang for Queen Victoria in Buckingham Palace.

7. The relatively obscure Colonel J. Wood was briefly associated with P. T. Barnum and became known for his Cincinnati museum. Wood generally refused to let Greenfield per-form before black audiences.

8. In a valuable collection of primary documents, *The Black Swan: Elizabeth T. Green-field, Songstress* (Detroit: privately published, 1969), Arthur R. La Brew includes a copy of a contractual agreement between Elizabeth T. Greenfield and Geo. Davis, "Mr. D.," signed on 16 February 1853 (pp. 88–89), which suggests that Greenfield broke with Wood

good business at an honorable profession, and at his own expense accompanied her from Philadelphia to Western New York. Wood met her in Buffalo, when she broke her contract with the former, totally disappointing him, after his spending much money; and right in the face of Mr. D., and without his knowledge, appointed another person over his head, as her Secretary and Treasurer, Wood telling her that it *would not do* to have a *colored man*, as he would *not* have one about him, *except as a servant,* and actually insulted Mr. D. by telling him and ordering indirectly to do menial services for him; calling Mr. D., when referring to him, in presence of Miss Greenfield, as "That *colored* man," disdaining to treat him with the common politeness of even calling him by his name. When he did so, he dared to use his Christian name with a servant's signification. Of course, after this, Mr. D. left them indignantly.

So little regard had Wood for a colored person, that in presence of Mr. D., standing obliquely behind Miss Greenfield, at a rehearsal with some of his unprincipled friends, he was distinctly seen, and heard to make derisive remarks of her *person* and *color;* then in a low, mean, rowdy-like manner, shrugging up his shoulders, winking and licking out his tongue, step before her, uttering audibly the flattering words, "O! lovely! delightful! isn't she *angelic!*" then stepping back behind her, wink and lick out his tongue again.

She is the merest creature of a slave, in the hands of this fellow Wood, and his associates, and does *not* know what she is getting for her services; as she does not handle her own money, but the person whom Wood appointed, *one of his own troup*, being her *treasurer*, and *holding*, as they *pretend*, the money for her! All that talk about her getting $25,000 a year, is the most barefaced falsehood.

Every letter that she receives is first opened and read by the man Wood, lest she may be advised to her own interest; and he has been known to destroy two or three several letters written to her by the colored contractor, who made the previous engagement with her. When she is in a place, she dare not receive and see colored company, as this imposter Wood uses every devise and low cunning to prevent it.

This Wood is the same mean person, who, three years ago, was proprietor of a museum in Cincinnati, Ohio,[9] and kept a constant notice, that *no colored person would be admitted.* Indeed it is said of him that he has said that he would as

---

around that time. Though Delany presents Greenfield as the pawn of the white racist Colonel Wood, Greenfield in fact performed antislavery songs on her British tour of 1853–54 and linked herself with the National Antislavery Society.

9. Located at the corner of Fifth and Walnut, Wood's Cincinnati Museum was known for its wax models, freak shows, plays, and lectures. It was destroyed by a fire in the early 1850s.

"willingly see a black *dog* coming into his museum, as a colored person;" and this is the man who intends leaving the United States to fill his coffers with the generous contributions of British philanthropy!

I will simply add, that Mr. D., the artist here spoken of, is well known in Great Britain, particularly in Liverpool and London; and Miss Greenfield was fully apprised of the character of Wood, and the superior advantages to her in going to Europe with a suitable colored gentleman and lady. In addition to Wood's other principles of negro hate, he is a most uncompromising supporter of the infamous Fugitive Slave Law. What I write, I do as a duty I owe to our oppressed selves, and stand individually responsible for. In a concert held in Cincinnati, last winter, a year, when Jenny Lind and Parodi had held concerts,[10] and two or three hundred of the colored citizens attended, in common with others, without distinction, this same Col. Wood and Miss Eliza Greenfield objected to colored persons attending. In regard to this unparalleled act of meanness and insult to a large and respectable population, the *Dispatch* of this city, one of the leading *daily* papers,[11] has the following just rebuke:

MEAN SPIRIT.—"We find the following announcement in the Cincinnati *Nonpareil* of Friday:

"'Colored persons are excluded from the Black Swan's concerts at Smith and Nixon's Hall.'

"Then the 'Black Swan,' if she has a particle of true spirit, should *exclude herself* from that same hall. If she consents that her own people shall, on account of their color, be shut out from a room where she sings, the glorious gifts of Genius and of Song have been bestowed on one most unworthy of their possession."

Yours for God and Humanity,

M. R. DELANY

Pittsburgh, April 13, 1853

(*Frederick Douglass' Paper*, 22 April 1853, p. 3)

* * *

10. Born in Stockholm, the wildly popular singer Jenny Lind (1820–87) became known as "the Swedish Nightingale." Under the sponsorship of P. T. Barnum, she gave concerts in over ninety cities in the United States during 1850. Teresa Parodi (1827–78) was a popular Italian soprano who also toured the United States to great acclaim during 1850.

11. Founded in 1846, the Pittsburgh *Dispatch* was the city's first successful penny paper.

FREDERICK DOUGLASS, ESQ: DEAR SIR:—I "throw in" this note, between the three letters which I promised you in regular succession.

It is now certain, that the Rev. JOSIAH HENSON, of Dawn, Canada West, is the real *Uncle Tom*, the Christian hero, in Mrs. Stowe's far-famed book of "Uncle Tom's Cabin."[12] Mr. Henson is well known to both you and I, and what is said of him in Mrs. S.'s "Key,"[13] as far as we are acquainted with the man, and even the opinion we might form of him from our knowledge of his character, we know, or at least believe, to be true to the letter.

Now, what I simply wish to suggest to you, is this: Since Mrs. Stowe and Messrs. Jewett & Co., Publishers, have realized so great an amount of money from the sale of a work founded upon this good old man, whose *living testimony* has to be brought to sustain this great book—and believing that the publishers have realized *five dollars* to the authoress' *one*—would it be expecting too much to suggest, that they—the *publishers*—present Father Henson—for by that name we all know him—with at least *five thous.*—now, I won't name any particular sum—but a portion of the profits? I do not know what you may think about it; but it strikes me that this would be but just and right.

I have always thought that George and Eliza were Mr. Henry Bibb and his first wife, with the character of Mr. Lewis Hayden, his wife Harriet and little son, who also effected their escape from Kentucky, under the auspices of Delia Webster, and that martyr philanthropist, Calvin Fairbanks, now incarcerated in a Kentucky State's prison dungeon.[14] I say the *person* of Bibb with the *character* of Hayden; because, in personal appearance of stature and color, as well as circumstances, Bibb answers precisely to George; while he stood quietly by, as he tells us in his own great narrative[15]—and it is a great book—with a hoe in his hand, begging his master to desist, while he *stripped his wife's clothes off (! ! !)* and lacerated her flesh, until the blood flowed in pools at her feet! To the con-

12. Born a slave in Maryland, Josiah Henson (1789–1883) fled to Canada in 1830 and emerged as a leader of Canada's black community, founding the British-American Institute at Dawn in 1842.

13. Harriet Beecher Stowe, *A Key to Uncle Tom's Cabin; Presenting the Original Facts and Documents upon which the Story Is Founded* (1853).

14. In 1846, two white abolitionists, the Methodist clergyman Calvin Fairbanks (1816–98) and the schoolteacher Delia Webster (1818–1904), who had helped Lewis Hayden (1811–89) escape from slavery in Kentucky in 1844, were imprisoned for their action. Webster was quickly released; Fairbanks served four years in prison. Hayden emerged as a major antislavery activist, a leader of Boston's black community.

15. Henry Bibb, *Narrative of the Life and Adventures of Henry Bibb* (1849).

trary, had this been Hayden—who, by the way, is not like Bibb nearly *white*, but *black*—he would have buried the hoe deep in the master's skull, laying him lifeless at his feet.

I am of the opinion, that Mrs. Stowe has draughted largely on all of the best fugitive slave narratives—at least on Douglass's, Brown's, Bibb's, and perhaps Clark's,[16] as well as the living Household of old Father Henson; but of this I am not competent to judge, not having as yet *read* "Uncle Tom's Cabin," *my wife* having *told* me the most I know about it. But these draughts on your narratives, clothed in Mrs. Stowe's own language, only make her work the more valuable, as it is the more *truthful*.

The "negro language," attributed to Uncle Tom by the authoress, makes the character more natural for a slave; but I would barely state, that Father Josiah Henson makes use of as good language, as any one in a thousand Americans.

The probability is, that either to make the story the more effecting, or to conceal the facts of the old man's still being alive, Mrs. Stowe closed his earthly career in New Orleans; but a fact which the publishers may not know: *Father Henson is still a slave* by the laws of the United States—a fugitive slave in Canada. It may be but justice to him to say, that I have neither seen nor heard directly or indirectly from Father Henson since September, 1851—then, I was in Toronto, Canada.

The person of Father Henson will increase the valuation of Mrs. Stowe's work very much in England, as he is well known, and highly respected there. His son, Josiah Henson, Jr., is still in England, having accompanied his father there in the winter of 1850.

I may perhaps have made freer use of your and the other names herein mentioned, than what was altogether consonant with your feelings; but I didn't ask you—that's all. Yours for God and Humanity,

M. R. DELANY

PITTSBURGH, April 15th, 1853.

(*Frederick Douglass' Paper*, 29 April 1853, p. 3)

* * *

16. Frederick Douglass, *Narrative of the Life of Frederick Douglass* (1845); William Wells Brown, *Narrative of William W. Brown* (1847); Lewis G. Clarke (1815–97), *Narrative of the Sufferings of Lewis Clarke* (1845).

FREDERICK DOUGLASS, ESQ: DEAR SIR:—I send you, according to promise, the second of my series of three letters.[17] In saying in my letter of the 22d of March, that "Mrs. Stowe knows nothing about us—'the *Free* Colored People of the United States'—neither does any white person," I admit the expression to be ironical, and not intended to be taken in its literal sense; but I meant to be understood in so saying, that they know nothing, comparatively, about us, to the intelligent, reflecting, general observers among the Free Colored People of the North. And while I readily admit, that I "know nothing about Mrs. Stowe," I desire very much, to *learn* something of her; and as I could not expect it of Mrs. Stowe, to do so, were she in the country at present, I may at least ask it of brother Douglass, and hope that he will neither consider it derogatory to Mrs. Stowe's position nor attainments, to give me the required information concerning her. I go beyond the mere point of asking it as a favor; I demand it as a right—from you I mean—as I am an interested party, and however humble, may put such reasonable questions to the other party—looking upon you, in this case, as the attorney of said party—as may be necessary to the pending proceedings.

First, then, *assertion*; is not Mrs. Stowe a *Colonizationist?* having so avowed, or at least subscribed to, and recommended their principles in her great work of Uncle Tom.

Secondly; although Mrs. Stowe has ably, eloquently and pathetically portrayed some of the sufferings of the slave, is it any evidence that she has any sympathy for his thrice-morally crucified, semi-free brethren any where, or of the *African race* at all; when in the same world-renowned and widely circulated work, she sneers at Hayti—the only truly free and independent civilized black nation as such, or colored if you please, on the face of the earth—at the same time holding up the little dependent colonization settlement of Liberia in high estimation? I must be permitted to draw my own conclusions, when I say that I can see no other cause for this singular discrepancy in Mrs. Stowe's interest in the colored race, than that one is independent of, and the other subservient to, white men's power.

You will certainly not consider this idea *farfetched*, because it is true American policy; and I do not think it strange, even of Mrs. Stowe, for following in a path so conspicuous, as almost to become the principal public highway. At least, no one will dispute its being a *well-trodden path*.

Thirdly; says brother Douglass, "Why, then, should any man object to the efforts of Mrs. Stowe, or any one else, who is moved to do anything in our behalf?" Bro. Douglass does not mean, and I will not so torture his language, as to make it imply that he means, that we should permit *any body* to undertake

17. As it turned out, this was Delany's final letter to Douglass on Stowe.

measures for our elevation. If so, those of Gurley, Pinney, and other colonizationists, should be acknowledged by us as *acceptable measures*. But are we to accept of colonization measures for our elevation?—Certainly not, you will readily reply. Then, if that be true, and Mrs. Stowe be what I have predicated—which
I hope her friends may prove, satisfactorily, to the contrary—we should reject
the proffers of Mrs. Stowe, as readily as those of any other colonizationist. What!
have our children tutored under colonization measures? God forbid! But why
question Mrs. Stowe's measures? I will tell you. In May last, a colored man,—
humble and common placed, to be sure—chanced to meet with Mrs. Stowe at
the house of Mr. B——, in the city of N——, State of N——, where he had
called with some articles for sale. He informs me that Mrs. Stowe was very indifferent towards him—more so, he thought, than any of the several persons
present; and hearing him speak of his elevation in the United States, she asked,
very seriously, what he expected to gain by any efforts that could be made here;
and when he referred to the West Indies, and South America, &c., as an alternative, she at once asked him, "why he did not go to Liberia"—that moral and political bane of the colored people of this country—manifesting no sympathy
whatever with the tortured feelings, crushed spirits and outraged homes of the
Free Colored people, even the poor wretch who then stood before her. All this
may have been, you may say, and still Mrs. Stowe be all that we could desire. It
may be; but he who can believe such things, has stronger faith and confidence
than I, in our American people. I must admit, that in them *my* confidence is terribly shattered. But, I will suppose a case as parallel with this one.

Mrs. Christian, of Vienna, in Austria, a highly intellectual, pious lady, writes a
book—an excellent work—which is beginning to attract general public attention, for its portrayal of Hungarian wrongs. The deeply-moved sympathies of
the lady's soul seem to teem through every chapter and page, exposing Austrian
oppression, and, impliedly, advocating Hungarian *rights*—as would be reasonably supposed—the right to live freemen in Austria, or, at least, Hungary, their
native part of the Empire. While the public attention is thus aroused, and that
lady's book is almost the only topic of conversation among the people, from
Paris to St. Petersburg, what would be thought of *that* lady if a poor Hungarian
chanced to meet her, and she manifested no sympathy for him, the *present* representative in poverty and obscurity of the very people whose cause she professed to espouse; and when he claimed the right to live in Austria, she would
unconcernedly ask him why he did not go to Siberia, the inhospitable criminal
colony of Russia—answering very well to the Liberia of the American colonizationists, only not so cruel—since Russia sends only her criminals, mostly
deserting soldiers and political offenders, while the United States Colonizationist Society forces innocent men, women and children to go, who never did harm

to any one? Surely, according to the supposition predicated above, the Hungarians would have great cause for fearing, if not suspecting Mrs. Christian's fidelity to their cause.

Lastly; the Industrial Institution in contemplation by Mrs. Stowe, for the tuition of colored youth, proposes, as I understand it, the entire employment of white instructors. This, I strongly object to, as having a tendency to engender in our youth a higher degree of respect and confidence for white persons than for those of their own color; and creates the impression that colored persons are incapable of teaching, and only suited to *subordinate* positions. I have observed carefully, in all of my travels in our country—in all the schools that I visited—colored schools I mean—that in those taught in whole or part by colored persons, the pupils were always the most respectful towards me, and the less menial in their general bearing. I do not object to white teachers in part; but I do say, that wherever competent colored teachers could be obtained for any of the departments, they should be employed. Self-respect begets *due* obedience to others; and obedience is the first step to *self-government* among any people. Certainly, this should be an essential part of the training of our people, separated in interests as we have been, in this country. All the rude and abominable ideas that exist among us, in *preferences for color*, have been engendered *from the whites*; and in God's name, I ask them to do nothing more to increase this absurdity.

Another consideration, is, that all of the pecuniary advantages arising from this position go into the pockets of white men and women, thereby depriving colored persons, so far, of this livelihood. This is the same old song sung over again,

"Dimes and dollars—dollars and dimes;"

And I will say, without the fear of offence, that nothing that has as yet been gotten up by our friends, for the assistance of the colored people of the United States, has even been of any pecuniary benefit to them. Our white friends take care of *that* part. There are, to my knowledge, two exceptions to this allegation—Douglass' printing establishment, and the "Alleghany Institute;"[18] the one having a colored man at the head, and in the other, the assistant being a colored man.

There is an old American story about an Indian and a white man, hunting game together; when they shot wild turkeys and buzzards, agreeing to divide, taking bird about; the white huntsman being the *teller*. In counting, the white

---

18. Founded by the white philanthropist Charles Avery (1784–1858) of Pittsburgh, the Allegheny Institute and Mission Church, which became Avery College when Avery died in 1858, was one of the few schools offering higher education to blacks. Among its board of trustees were a number of blacks, including the abolitionist John Peck (1802–75).

man would say, alternately taking up either bird, "turkey for *me*, and buzzard for *you*—buzzard for *you*, and turkey for *me*." He growing tired of that method of counting the game, soon accosted his friend: "Uh! how's dis? all *buzzard* for me; but you never say, *turkey* for me, once." I feel somewhat as this Indian did; I am growing weary of receiving the *buzzard* as *our* share, while our tellers get all the *turkeys*. That "is not the way to 'tell' it to me."

But I have not yet read the "Key to Uncle Tom's Cabin," and it may be that, in that, Mrs. S.—and I sincerely hope she has—has changed her policy, and renounced Colonization as she had made a public avowal of it; and *apriori*, just so far as her work received favor, her opinions on that subject will also be received.[19]

I am aware that I am saying much more than is allowable, as I do not know of any of our professed anti-slavery friends who have taken public positions, who will permit any of their measures to be questioned by a colored person, except in the fullness of those great and good hearts—W. L. Garrison, Gerrit Smith, and that more than excellent woman, *Mrs. Hester Moore*,[20] of Philadelphia, whose name you now scarcely ever hear of. She is an *abolitionist* of the Garrison and Smith sort; she loves the cause of Hungary for the *sake* of the *Hungarian*.

Let me say another thing, brother Douglass; that is, that no enterprize, institution, or anything else, should be commenced *for us*, or our general benefit, without *first consulting us*. By this, I mean, consulting the various communities of the colored people in the United States, by such a correspondence as should make public the measure, and solicit their general interests and coincidence. In this way, the intelligence and desires of the whole people would be elicited, and an intelligent understanding of their real desires obtained. Other than this, is treating us as slaves, and presupposing us all to be ignorant, and incapable of knowing our own *wants*. Many of the measures of our friends have failed from this very cause; and I am fearful that many more will fail.

In conclusion, brother Douglass, let me say, that I am the last person among us who would wilfully "strike a jarring note, or awaken a feeling of distrust," uncalled for; and although you may pronounce it "unwise, ungraceful, and sounding high and mighty on paper;" as much high respect as an humble simpleminded person should have for them, and as much honored as I should feel in having such names enrolled as our benefactors—associated with our degraded position in society; believe me when I tell you, that I speak it as a son, a brother,

19. Stowe's 1853 *Key* urged whites to help blacks rise in the northern states and said nothing about African colonization. In May 1853 she delivered a note to the New York meeting of the American and Foreign Anti-Slavery Society declaring that she regretted sending George Harris to Liberia at the conclusion of *Uncle Tom's Cabin*.

20. One of the founders of the American Anti-Slavery Society, the Philadelphia Quaker Esther Moore (1774–1854) was a proponent of abolitionism and women's rights.

a husband and a father; I speak it from the consciousness of oppressed humanity, outraged manhood, of a degraded husband and disabled father; I speak it
from the recesses of a wounded bleeding heart—in the name of my wife and
children, who look to me for protection, as the joint partner of our humble fire-
side; I say, if this great fund and aid are to be sent here to foster and aid the
schemes of the American Colonization Society, as I say to you—I say with reverence, and an humbleness of feeling, becoming my position, with a bowed-
down head, that the benevolent, great and good, the Duchess of Sutherland, Mr.
Gurney, their graces the Earl of Shaftesbury and the Earl of Carlisle; had far better retain their money in the Charity Fund of Stafford House,[21] or any other
place, than to send it to the United States for any such unhallowed purposes!—
No person will be more gratified, nor will more readily join in commendation,
than I, of any good measure attempted to be carried out by Mrs. Stowe, if the
contrary of her colonization principles be disproved. I will not accept *chains*
from a king, any sooner than from a peasant; and never shall, willingly, submit
to any measures for my own degradation. I am in hopes, brother Douglass, as
every one else will understand my true position.

Yours for God and down-trodden Humanity,
M. R. DELANY.

PITTSBURGH, April 18th, 1853

* * *

The Letter of M. R. Delany

Douglass printed his response to Delany's letter on the page before Delany's letter.

This letter is premature, unfair, uncalled for, and, withal, needlessly long; but,
happily, it needs not a long reply.
Can brother Delany be the writer of it?—It lacks his generous spirit. The let-

21. Harriet Elizabeth Georgiana Leveson-Gower (1806–68) became duchess of Sutherland in 1833. Her London home, Stafford House, was a well-known meeting place for
philanthropists and social activists. The Quaker evangelist Joseph John Gurney (1788–
1847), Anthony Ashley Cooper, earl of Shaftesbury (1801–85), and George William Frederick Howard, earl of Carlisle (1802–64), shared the duchess of Sutherland's commitment
to antislavery.

ter is premature, because it attacks a plan, the details of which are yet undefined. It is unfair, because it imputes designs (and replies to them) which have never been declared. It is uncalled for, because there is nothing in the position of Mrs. Stowe which should awaken against her a single suspicion of unfriendliness towards the free colored people of the United States; but, on the contrary, there is much in it to inspire confidence in her friendship.

The information for which brother Delany asks concerning Mrs. Stowe, he has given himself. He says *she* is a colonizationist; and we ask, what if she is?— names do not frighten us. A little while ago, brother Delany was a colonizationist. If we do not misremember, in his book he declared in favor of colonizing the eastern coast of Africa.[22] Yet, we never suspected his friendliness to the colored people; nor should we feel called upon to oppose any plan he might submit, for the benefit of the colored people, on that account. We recognize friends wherever we find them.

Whoever will bring a straw's weight of influence to break the chains of our brother bondmen, or whisper one word of encouragement and sympathy to our proscribed race in the North, shall be welcomed by us to that philanthropic field of labor. We shall not, therefore, allow the sentiments put in the brief letter of GEORGE HARRIS, at the close of Uncle Tom's Cabin, to vitiate forever Mrs. Stowe's power to do us good. Who doubts that Mrs. Stowe is more of an abolitionist now than when she wrote that chapter?—We believe that lady to be but at the beginning of her labors for the colored people of this country. . . .

(*Frederick Douglass' Paper*, 6 May 1853, pp. 3, 2)

22. Douglass refers to the appendix to Delany's *Condition*, "A Project for an Expedition of Adventure, to the Eastern Coast of Africa," which is reprinted in Part 4 of this book.

Letter to Douglass, 30 May 1853

BEGINNING IN MAY 1853, Frederick Douglass ran regular calls in his newspaper for a Colored National Convention to be held July 1853 in Rochester, New York. Thirty-three black men were listed as having signed Douglass's call, including Martin Delany. Revealing that his name had been appended to Douglass's "Call" without his permission, and concerned about the timing, Delany nonetheless appeared to be enthusiastic about participating in Douglass's proposed Colored National Convention.

FREDERICK DOUGLASS: DEAR SIR:—I am happy to see the issue of a Call for a National Convention, though my name was attached to it without my consent or knowledge, and the *time* and *place* different to those which I named in my suggestions.

I had said in my letter, (the publication of which has been rendered unnecessary, by the previous issue of this Call,) that some specific object should be had in view, and those things which now form the greatest subjects of interest should be entertained before such a gathering; otherwise, it would be a useless waste of time and means to hold such a gathering.

I am happy to say, that in consequence of the following propositions, I can heartily subscribe to the issue of the Call—which propositions will meet my suggestions precisely:

"Among the matters which will engage the attention of the Convention, will be a proposition to establish a NATIONAL COUNCIL of our people, with a view to a permanent existence. * * * In a word, *the whole field of our interest will be open to enquiry, investigation* and DETERMINATION." This is the thing *precisely*; this, and this alone, is what we now want.

I have but one thing more to mention, which is the *time* specified in the Call—the *place* I do not object to, which is rather more favorable to western men than Syracuse—and could hope that it might be changed to say, Wednesday, the 24th of August, as I know that that time in the season will much better suit the great majority of our western men;[1] and I do not think it asking too much to request that their *convenience* also be consulted. Any season almost will suit eastern and northern men; but not so with us of the West.

I think that I can see the head and hand of my excellent friend, Dr. Pennington,[2] in this carefully written Call; will he change the *time* as suggested above, which should be for *three* consecutive days—24th, 25th and 26th of August? I can assure you that this will meet the general approbation of the entire western people.

I venture to *take* the *responsibility* of ordering the attachment of those names to the Call, which I sent on—except those already published—and venture to say, that there will be no dissenting voice, except it should be in regard to the *time* as now published—the 6th of July. In hopes of a happy gathering,

Yours for God and Humanity,

M. R. DELANY,

PITTSBURGH, May 30th, 1853

(*Frederick Douglass' Paper*, 17 June 1853, p. 3)

---

1. The Colored National Convention was held in Rochester, New York, 6–8 July 1853.
2. The minister J. W. C. Pennington (1807–70), a former slave and widely traveled abolitionist speaker, shared Douglass's views on the importance of black self-help, integrationism, and antiemigrationism. Among his works are *A Textbook of the Origin and History of the Colored People* (1841) and *The Fugitive Blacksmith* (1849).

Call for a National Emigration Convention of Colored Men to Be Held in Cleveland, Ohio, on the 24th, 25th and 26th of August, 1854

SHORTLY AFTER DOUGLASS presided over the Colored National Convention in Rochester in 1853, which Delany did not attend, Delany called for an emigration convention to take place the following year. He regarded emigration as a pragmatic alternative to the integrationism championed by the Rochester convention. Douglass initially ran Delany's call in his paper but soon was unwilling to publicize Delany's emigrationist program. The call was then regularly printed in the *Provincial Freeman* and other black newspapers.

MEN AND BRETHREN:—The time has now fully come, when we, as an oppressed people, should do something effectively, and use those means adequate to the attainment of the great and long desired end. To do something to meet the actual demands of the present, and prospective necessities of the rising generation of our people in this country. To do this, we must occupy a position of entire *equality* of *unrestricted* rights, composed in fact, an acknowledged *necessary* part of the *ruling element* of society in which we live. The policy *necessary* to the *preservation* of this *element* must be *in our favor*, if ever we expect the enjoyment, freedom, sovereignty, and equality of rights anywhere.

For this purpose, and to this end, then.—All colored men in favor of emigration out of the United States, and *opposed* to the American Colonization scheme of leaving the Western Hemisphere, are requested to meet in CLEVELAND, OHIO, on TUESDAY the 24TH DAY of AUGUST, 1854, in a great NATIONAL CONVENTION, then and there, to consider and decide upon the great and important subject of emigration from the United States.

No person will be admitted to a seat in the Convention, who would introduce the subject of emigration to the Eastern Hemisphere—either to Asia, Africa, or Europe—as our object and determination are to consider our claims to the West Indies, Central and South America, and the Canadas. This restriction has no reference to *personal* preferences, or *individual* enterprise; but to the great question of national claims to come before the Convention.

All persons coming to the Convention must bring credentials properly authenticated, or give verbal assurance to the Committee on Credentials—appointed for the purpose—of their fidelity to the measures and objects set forth in this Call; as the Convention is specifically called by, and for the friends of emigration, and NONE OTHERS, and no opposition to them, will be entertained.

The question is not whether our condition can be bettered by emigration, but whether it can be made worse. If not, then, there is no part of the wide-spread universe, where our social and political condition are not better than here in our native country, and nowhere in the world as here, proscribed on account of color.

We are friends, too, and ever will stand shoulder to shoulder by our brethren, and all *true* friends in all good measures adopted by them, for the bettering of our condition in this country, and surrender no rights but with our last breath; but as the subject of emigration is of vital importance, and has ever been shunned by all delegated assemblages of our people as heretofore met, we cannot longer delay, and will not be farther baffled; and deny the right of our most sanguine friend or dearest brother, to prevent an intelligent enquiry to, and the carrying out of these measures, when this can be done, to our entire advantage, as we propose to show in Convention—as the West Indies, Central and South America—the majority of which are peopled by our brethren, or those identified with us in race, and what is more, *destiny* on this continent—all stand with open arms and yearning hearts, importuning us in the name of suffering humanity to come. To make common cause, and share one common fate on the continent.

The Convention will meet without fail, at the time fixed for assembling, as none but those favorable to emigration are admissible; therefore no other gathering may prevent it.

The number of delegates will not be restricted—except in the town where the Convention may be held—and their number will be decided by the Convention when assembled, that they may not too far exceed the other delegations.

The time and place fixed for holding the Convention are ample; affording sufficient time, and a leisure season generally—and as Cleveland is now the centre of all directions—a good and favorable opportunity to all who desire to attend. Therefore, it may reasonably be expected that this will emphatically be the greatest gathering of the colored people ever before assembled in a Convention in the United States.

Colonizationists are advised, that no favors will be shown to them or their expatriating scheme, as we have no sympathy with the enemies of our race.

All colored men, East, West, North and South, favorable to the measures set forth in this Call, will send in their names (post-paid) to M. R. Delany, or Rev. Wm. Webb, Pittsburgh, Pa., that there may be arranged and attached to the Call *five* names from each state.

We must make an issue, create an event, and establish a position *for ourselves.* It is glorious to think of, but far more glorious to carry out.

REV. WM. WEBB
M. R. DELANY[1]

(*Frederick Douglass' Paper*, 26 August 1853, p. 3)

1. Webb's and Delany's names headed a list of twenty-six to sign the "Call." All but three of those signing were from Pennsylvania. An ordained African Methodist Episcopal clergyman of Pennsylvania, William Webb (1812–68) helped Delany to organize the 1854 Cleveland convention.

Letter to Douglass, 7 November 1853

AS DELANY PLANNED HIS black emigration convention, he had to confront the fact that Douglass had a newspaper and he did not. Douglass used his paper from mid-1853 well into 1854 to contest Delany's proposed Cleveland emigration convention. For example, he copied into the 28 October 1853 issue of *Frederick Douglass' Paper* resolutions from an African American convention in Chicago, chaired by John Jones, attacking Delany for creating "a spirit of disunion"; he printed a letter in the issue of 18 November 1853 from one "B. D. J." calling on Delany to leave the United States; and in that same issue he printed a letter from Jones calling Delany "misguided." In a letter to Douglass, Delany responded specifically to Jones.

FREDERICK DOUGLASS, ESQ:—I desire to enquire, through the medium of Mr. John Jones,[1] of Chicago, Ill., by what authority he charges upon me the *spirit* and design of *disunion*, in the issue of the Call for the Emigration Convention? I can submit to any other wrong—as I have ever been doing all my life—from colored men, except that of charging me with a *design* of *injury* to my race; and this I never shall submit to with indifference, from any source, except one too contemptible to merit a notice.

Mr. Jones, and the members of the Illinois Convention, must understand, that I am neither a neophyte, an ephemera, nor a novice in the cause of our elevation, having doubtless aided, either directly or indirectly, in the elevation, morally, of many of the members of that same Convention, as I had the honor of starting and conducting, for five years, the first newspaper ever published or edited by a colored person in the West,[2] which *faithfully* defended the rights of

1. Chicago's most prominent black abolitionist, John Jones (1816–79) emphasized the role of black economic success and social integration in fighting white racism; he served as vice president of Douglass's July 1853 Colored National Convention. Delany would attack him again in a letter to Douglass of 22 November 1853, printed in *Frederick Douglass' Paper*, 2 December 1853, p. 3.
    2. *Mystery.*

our people; and if they can so soon forget the services of some men, because they are in the favor of others whom they are pleased to set a higher estimate upon, it shall not be done by a false representation of my motives and designs.

There seems to have been but one course laid out by the superiors among us—for as such I acknowledge them, with an humble sensibility of my own obscurity—who have taken any public action against this great movement of establishing our nationality, and that is, to *impugn* the motives of myself, and the self-sacrificing men, as several of them are, whose names are attached to the Call. I and they favor *every*thing which may tend to benefit us *here*, and do all we can to further so desirable an end; but neither I nor they can be content, as the greatest aspirations of our bosoms, with the mere smiles, and rubbing elbows with white men, and obtaining limited privileges at their *sufferance*. We are doing all here, than any others of our people are doing, and much more than many who are making much noise about it. It is not all who talk the loudest about *staying* here for the *sake* of the *slave*, who love him or his cause most, or even at all; as I *know* of some who do so, who would not ask a poor panting fugitive into their houses, come along when he would.

But we have no quarrel with those who love to live among the whites better than the blacks, and leave them to the enjoyment of their predilections, and shall continue doing all we can for the elevation of our people and race, let that be through whatever just medium and policy it may.

Yours for God and humanity,

M. R. DELANY

PITTSBURGH, Nov. 7th, 1853.

(*Frederick Douglass' Paper*, 18 November 1853, p. 1)

Political Destiny of the Colored Race on the American Continent

AT THE 1854 National Emigration Convention of Colored Men in Cleveland, Delany, who served as chairman of the business committee, delivered the keynote address, "Political Destiny" (reputedly over a seven-hour period). The address, which is presented here in its entirety, counseled African Americans to emigrate to Central or South America, or the Caribbean, on the grounds that white racists would never allow blacks to become U.S. citizens. But much more is going on in the speech than a call for emigration. "Political Destiny" provides acute political commentary on race relations in the United States and an eloquent Pan-African vision of blacks' potentially regenerative role in the Americas. Infused with a Masonic transnationalism, an Africanist pride, and a pragmatics of nation and place, "Political Destiny" emerged as Delany's best-known statement on black emigration and black nationalism. Ironically, it inspired not only blacks but also whites, particularly "liberal" whites who thought that the problem of race in the United States could be solved by financing the removal of U.S. blacks to Central America. In 1862, when Lincoln and other Republicans contemplated plans to finance such a removal project, Delany's "Political Destiny" was reprinted in the House of Representatives' *Report of the Select Committee on Emancipation and Colonization* (Washington, D.C., 1862).

FELLOW COUNTRYMEN!—The duty assigned us is an important one, comprehending all that pertains to our destiny and that of our posterity—present and prospectively. And while it must be admitted, that the subject is one of the greatest magnitude, requiring all that talents, prudence and wisdom might adduce, and while it would be folly to pretend to give you the combined result of these three agencies, we shall satisfy ourselves with doing our duty to the best of our ability, and that in the plainest, most simple and comprehensive manner.

Our object, then, shall be to place before you our true position in this country—the United States—, the improbability of realizing our desires, and the sure, practicable and infallible remedy for the evils we now endure.

We have not addressed you as *citizens*,—a term desired and ever cherished by us—because such you have never been. We have not addressed you as *freemen*,—because such privileges have never been enjoyed by any colored man in the United States. Why then should we flatter your credulity, by inducing you to believe that which neither has now, nor never before had, an existence? Our oppressors are ever gratified at our manifest satisfaction, especially when that satisfaction is founded upon false premises; an assumption on our part, of the enjoyment of rights and privileges which never have been conceded, and which, according to the present system of the United States policy, we never can enjoy.

The *political policy* of this country was solely borrowed from, and shaped and modelled after, that of Rome. This was strikingly the case in the establishment of immunities, and the application of terms in their Civil and Legal regulations.

The term Citizen—politically considered—is derived from the Roman definition—which was never applied in any other sense—*Cives Ingenui*; which meant, one exempt from restraint of any kind. (*Cives*, a citizen; one who might enjoy the highest honors in his own free town—the town in which he lived—and in the country or commonwealth; and *Ingenui*, *freeborn*—of GOOD EXTRACTION.) All who were deprived of citizenship—that is, the right of enjoying positions of honor and trust—were termed *Hostes* and *Peregrini*; which are public and private *enemies*, and foreigners, or *aliens* to the country. (*Hostis*, a public—and sometimes—private enemy; and *Peregrinus*, an *alien*, *stranger*, or *foreigner*.)

The Romans, from a national pride, to distinguish their inhabitants from those of other countries, termed them all "citizens," but consequently, were under the necessity of specifying four classes of citizens: none but the *Cives Ingenui* being unrestricted in their privileges. There was one class, called the *Jus Quiritium*, or the wailing or *supplicating* citizen—that is, one who was continually *moaning*, *complaining*, or *crying for aid or succor*. This class might also include within themselves, the *jus suffragii*, who had the privilege of *voting*, but no other privilege. They could vote for one of their superiors—the *Cives Ingenui*—but not for themselves.

Such, then, is the condition, precisely, of the black and colored inhabitants of the United States; in some of the States they answering to the latter class, having the privilege of *voting*, to elevate their superiors to positions to which they need never dare aspire, or even hope to attain.

There has, of late years, been a false impression obtained, that the privilege of *voting* constitutes, or necessarily embodies, the *rights of citizenship*. A more radical error never obtained favor among an oppressed people. Suffrage is an ambiguous term, which admits of several definitions. But according to strict political construction, means simply "a vote, voice, approbation." Here, then, you have the whole import of the term suffrage. To have the "right of suffrage," as we rather proudly term it, is simply to have the *privilege*—there is no *right* about it—of giving our *approbation* to that which our *rulers may do*, without the privilege, on our part, of doing the same thing. Where such privileges are granted—privileges which are now exercised in but few of the States by colored men—we have but the privilege granted of saying, in common with others, who shall, for the time being, exercise *rights*, which, in him, are conceded to be *inherent* and *inviolate*: Like the indented[1] apprentice, who is summoned to give his approbation to an act which would be fully binding without his concurrence. Where there is no *acknowledged sovereignty*, there can be no binding power; hence, the suffrage of the black man, independently of the white, would be in this country unavailable.

Much might be adduced on this point to prove the insignificance of the black man, politically considered in this country, but we deem it wholly unnecessary at present, and consequently proceed at once to consider another feature of this important subject.

Let it then be understood, as a great principle of political economy, that no people can be free who themselves do not constitute an essential part of the *ruling element* of the country in which they live. Whether this element be founded upon a true or false, a just or an unjust basis; this position in community is necessary to personal safety. The liberty of no man is secure, who controls not his own political destiny. What is true of an individual, is true of a family; and that which is true of a family, is also true concerning a whole people. To suppose otherwise, is that delusion which at once induces its victim, through a period of long suffering, patiently to submit to every species of wrong; trusting against probability, and hoping against all reasonable grounds of expectation, for the granting of privileges and enjoyment of rights, which never will be attained. This delusion reveals the true secret of the power which holds in peaceable subjection, all the oppressed in every part of the world.

A people, to be free, must necessarily be *their own rulers*: that is, *each individual* must, in himself, embody the *essential ingredient*—so to speak—of the *sovereign principle* which composes the *true basis* of his liberty. This principle, when not exercised by himself, may, at his pleasure, be delegated to another—his true representative.

Said a great French writer: "A free agent, in a free government, should be his own governor;"[2] that is, he must possess within himself the *acknowledged right*

1. Indentured.

2. The most likely source is Benjamin Constant (1767–1830), *Principles of Politics Applicable to All Representative Governments* (1815); see especially ch. 18, "On the Liberty of the Individual."

to govern: this constitutes him a *governor*, though he may delegate to another the power to govern himself.

No one, then, can delegate to another a power he never possessed; that is, he cannot *give an agency* in that which he never had a right. Consequently, the colored man in the United States, being deprived of the right of inherent sovereignty, cannot *confer* a suffrage, because he possesses none to confer. Therefore, where there is no suffrage, there can neither be *freedom* nor *safety* for the disfranchised. And it is a futile hope to suppose that the agent of another's concerns will take a proper interest in the affairs of those to whom he is under no obligations. Having no favors to ask or expect, he therefore has none to lose.

In other periods and parts of the world—as in Europe and Asia—the people being of one common, direct origin of race, though established on the presumption of difference by birth, or what was termed *blood*, yet the distinction between the superior classes and common people, could only be marked by the difference, in the dress and education of the two classes. To effect this, the interposition of government was necessary; consequently, the costume and education of the people became a subject of legal restriction, guarding carefully against the privileges of the common people.

In Rome, the Patrician and Plebeian were orders in the ranks of her people— all of whom were termed citizens (*cives*)—recognized by the laws of the country; their dress and education being determined by law, the better to fix the distinction. In different parts of Europe, at the present day, if not the same, the distinction among the people is similar, only on a modified—and in some kingdoms—probably more tolerant or deceptive policy.

In the United States, our degradation being once—as it has in a hundred instances been done—legally determined, our color is sufficient, independently of costume, education, or other distinguishing marks, to keep up that distinction.

In Europe, when an inferior is elevated to the rank of equality with the superior class, the law first comes to his aid, which, in its decrees, entirely destroys his identity as an inferior, leaving no trace of his former condition visible.

In the United States, among the whites, their color is made, by law and custom, the mark of distinction and superiority; while the color of the blacks is a badge of degradation, acknowledged by statute, organic law, and the common consent of the people.

With this view of the case—which we hold to be correct—to elevate to equality the degraded subject of law and custom, it can only be done, as in Europe, by an entire destruction of the identity of the former condition of the applicant. Even were this desirable—which we by no means admit—with the deep seated prejudices engendered by oppression, with which we have to contend, ages incalculable might reasonably be expected to roll around, before this could honorably be accomplished; otherwise, we should encourage and at once commence an indiscriminate concubinage and immoral commerce, of our mothers, sisters, wives and daughters, revolting to think of, and a physical curse to humanity.

If this state of things be to succeed, then, as in Egypt, under the dread of the inscrutable approach of the destroying angel, to appease the hatred of our oppressors, as a license to the passions of every white, let the lintel of each door of every black man, be stained with the blood of virgin purity and unsullied matron fidelity.[3] Let it be written along the cornice in capitals, "The *will* of the white man is the rule of my household." Remove the protection to our chambers and nurseries, that the places once sacred may henceforth become the unrestrained resort of the vagrant and rabble, always provided that the licensed commissioner of lust shall wear the indisputable impress of a *white* skin.

But we have fully discovered and comprehended the great political disease with which we are affected, the cause of its origin and continuance; and what is now left for us to do is to discover and apply a sovereign remedy—a healing balm to a sorely diseased body—a wrecked but not entirely shattered system. We propose for this disease a remedy. That remedy is Emigration. This Emigration should be well advised, and like remedies applied to remove the disease from the physical system of man, skillfully and carefully applied, within the proper time, directed to operate on that part of the system, whose greatest tendency shall be, to benefit the whole.

Several geographical localities have been named, among which rank the Canadas. These we do not object to as places of temporary relief, especially to the fleeing fugitive—which, like a palliative, soothes for the time being the misery —but cannot commend them as permanent places upon which to fix our destiny, and that of our children, who shall come after us. But in this connection, we would most earnestly recommend to the colored people of the United States generally, to secure by purchase all of the land they possibly can, while selling at low rates, under the British people and government; as that time may come, when, like the lands in the United States territories generally, if not as in Oregon and some other territories and States, they may be prevented entirely from settling or purchasing them;—the preference being given to the white applicant.

And here, we would not deceive you by disguising the facts, that according to political tendency, the Canadas—as all British America—at no very distant day, are destined to come into the United States.

And were this not the case, the odds are against us, because the ruling ele-

3. An allusion to Exodus 12:22–23; see *Condition*, note 25.

ment there, as in the United States, is, and ever must be, white—the population now standing, in all British America, two and a half millions of whites, to but forty thousand of the black race; or sixty-one and a fraction, whites, to one black!—the difference being eleven times greater than in the United States—so that colored people might never hope for anything more than to exist politically by mere sufferance—occupying a secondary position to the whites of the Canadas. The Yankees from this side of the lakes, are fast settling in the Canadas, infusing, with industrious success, all the malignity and negro-hate, inseparable from their very being, as Christian Democrats and American advocates of equality.

Then, to be successful, our attention must be turned in a direction towards those places where the black and colored man comprise, by population, and constitute by necessity of numbers, the *ruling element* of the body politic. And where, when occasion shall require it, the issue can be made and maintained on this basis. Where our political enclosure and national edifice can be reared, established, walled, and proudly defended on this great elementary principle of original identity. Upon this solid foundation rests the fabric of every substantial political structure in the world, which cannot exist without it; and so soon as a people or nation lose their original identity, just so soon must that nation or people become extinct. Powerful though they may have been, they must fall. Because the nucleus which heretofore held them together, becoming extinct, there being no longer a centre of attraction, or basis for a union of the parts, a dissolution must as naturally ensue, as the result of the neutrality of the basis of adhesion among the particles of matter.

This is the secret of the eventful downfall of Egypt, Carthage, Rome, and the former Grecian States, once so powerful—a loss of original identity; and with it, a loss of interest in maintaining their fundamental principles of nationality.

This, also, is the great secret of the present strength of Great Britain, Russia, the United States, and Turkey; and the endurance of the French nation, whatever its strength and power, is attributable only to their identity as Frenchmen.

And doubtless the downfall of Hungary, brave and noble as may be her people, is mainly to be attributed to the want of identity of origin, and, consequently, a union of interests and purpose. This fact it might not have been expected would be admitted by the great Magyar, in his thrilling pleas for the restoration of Hungary, when asking aid, both national and individual, to enable him to throw off the ponderous weight placed upon their shoulders by the House of Hapsburg.[4]

4. Louis Kossuth (1802–94), the "Great Magyar," declared Hungary free of Austrian (Hapsburg) rule in April 1849 and became president of the nation shortly thereafter. But

Hungary consisted of three distinct "races"—as they called themselves—of people, all priding in and claiming rights based on their originality—the Magyars, Celts, and Sclaves. On the encroachment of Austria, each one of these races—declaring for nationality—rose up against the House of Hapsburg, claiming the right of self-government, premised on their origin. Between the three a compromise was effected—the Magyars, being the majority, claimed the precedence. They made an effort, but for the want of a unity of interests—an identity of origin—the noble Hungarians failed. All know the result.

Nor is this the only important consideration. Were we content to remain as we are, sparsely interspersed among our white fellow-countrymen, we never might be expected to equal them in any honorable or respectable competition for a livelihood. For the reason that, according to the customs and policy of the country, we for ages would be kept in a secondary position, every situation of respectability, honor, profit or trust, either as mechanics, clerks, teachers, jurors, councilmen, or legislators, being filled by white men, consequently, our energies must become paralyzed or enervated for the want of proper encouragement.

This example upon our children, and the colored people generally, is pernicious and degrading in the extreme. And how could it otherwise be, when they see every place of respectability filled and occupied by the whites, they pandering to their vanity, and existing among them merely as a thing of conveniency?

Our friends in this and other countries, anxious for our elevation, have for years been erroneously urging us to lose our identity as a distinct race, declaring that we were the same as other people; while at the very same time their own representative was traversing the world and propagating the doctrine in favor of a *universal Anglo-Saxon predominance*. The "Universal Brotherhood," so ably and eloquently advocated by that Polyglot Christian Apostle[5] of this doctrine, had established as its basis, a universal acknowledgment of the Anglo-Saxon rule.

The truth is, we are not identical with the Anglo-Saxon or any other race of the Caucasian or pure white type of the human family, and the sooner we know and acknowledge this truth, the better for ourselves and posterity.

The English, French, Irish, German, Italian, Turk, Persian, Greek, Jew, and all other races, have their native or inherent peculiarities, and why not our race? We

---

by the end of the year Russia had helped Austria to regain control of Hungary, and Kossuth was forced to flee. In the early 1850s he made a celebrated tour of the United States, where he was hailed as a freedom fighter (though abolitionists became increasingly concerned about his unwillingness to speak out against slavery).

5. Elihu Burritt. [Delany's note.] A well-known peace reformer, Burritt (1810–79) founded the League of Universal Brotherhood in 1846.

are not willing, therefore, at all times and under all circumstances to be moulded into various shapes of eccentricity, to suit the caprices and conveniences of every kind of people. We are not more suitable to everybody than everybody is suitable to us; therefore, no more like other people than others are like us.

We have then inherent traits, attributes—so to speak—and native characteristics, peculiar to our race—whether pure or mixed blood—and all that is required of us is to cultivate these and develop them in their purity, to make them desirable and emulated by the rest of the world.

That the colored races have the highest traits of civilization, will not be disputed. They are civil, peaceable and religious to a fault. In mathematics, sculpture and architecture, as arts and sciences, commerce and internal improvements as enterprises, the white race may probably excel; but in languages, oratory, poetry, music, and painting as arts and sciences, and in ethics, metaphysics, theology, and legal jurisprudence; in plain language—in the true principles of morals, correctness of thought, religion, and law or civil government, there is no doubt but the black race will yet instruct the world.

It would be duplicity longer to disguise the fact, that the great issue, sooner or later, upon which must be disputed the world's destiny, will be a question of black and white; and every individual will be called upon for his identity with one or the other. The blacks and colored races are four-sixths of all the population of the world; and these people are fast tending to a common cause with each other. The white races are but one-third of the population of the globe— or one of them to two of us—and it cannot much longer continue that two-thirds will passively submit to the universal domination of this one-third. And it is notorious that the only progress made in territorial domain, in the last three centuries, by the whites, has been a usurpation and encroachment on the rights and native soil of some of the colored races.

The East Indies, Java, Sumatra, the Azores, Madeira, Canary, and Cape Verde Islands; Socotra,[6] Guardifui,[7] and the Isle of France; Algiers, Tunis, Tripoli, Barca[8] and Egypt in the North, Sierra Leone in the West, and Cape Colony in the South of Africa; besides many other Islands and possessions not herein named. Australia, the Ladrone Islands,[9] together with many others of Oceanica;[10] the seizure and appropriation of a great portion of the Western Continent, with all its Islands, were so many encroachments of the whites upon the rights of the colored races. Nor are they yet content, but, intoxicated with the success

6. An island in the Indian Ocean.
7. A cape at East Africa.
8. Cyrenaica—an ancient district in North Africa.
9. Now called the Mariana Islands, a group of fifteen islands east of the Philippines.
10. Islands of the central and south Pacific.

of their career, the Sandwich Islands[11] are now marked out as the next booty to be seized, in the ravages of their exterminating crusade.

We regret the necessity of stating the fact—but duty compels us to the task—that, for more than two thousand years, the determined aim of the whites has been to crush the colored races wherever found. With a determined will they have sought and pursued them in every quarter of the globe. The Anglo-Saxon has taken the lead in this work of universal subjugation. But the Anglo-American stands pre-eminent for deeds of injustice and acts of oppression, unparalleled perhaps in the annals of modern history.

We admit the existence of great and good people in America, England, France, and the rest of Europe, who desire a unity of interests among the whole human family, of whatever origin or race.

But it is neither the moralist, Christian, nor philanthropist whom we now have to meet and combat, but the politician—the civil engineer—and skillful economist, who direct and control the machinery which moves forward with mighty impulse, the nations and powers of the earth. We must, therefore, if possible, meet them on vantage ground, or, at least, with adequate means for the conflict.

Should we encounter an enemy with artillery, a prayer will not stay the cannon shot; neither will the kind words nor smiles of philanthropy shield his spear from piercing us through the heart. We must meet mankind, then, as they meet us—prepared for the worst, though we may hope for the best. Our submission does not gain for us an increase of friends nor respectability—as the white race will only respect those who oppose their usurpation, and acknowledge as equals those who will not submit to their rule. This may be no new discovery in political economy, but it certainly is a subject worthy the consideration of the black race.

After a due consideration of these facts, as herein recounted, shall we stand still and continue inactive—the passive observers of the great events of the times and age in which we live; submitting indifferently to the usurpation, by the white race, of every right belonging to the blacks? Shall the last vestige of an opportunity, outside of the continent of Africa, for the national development of our race, be permitted, in consequence of our slothfulness, to elude our grasp and fall into the possession of the whites? This, may Heaven forbid. May the sturdy, intelligent Africo-American sons of the Western Continent forbid.

Longer to remain inactive, it should be borne in mind, may be to give an opportunity to despoil us of every right and possession sacred to our existence, with which God has endowed us as a heritage on the earth. For let it not be for-

11. Former name of the Hawaiian islands.

gotten, that the white race—who numbers but *one* of them to *two* of us—originally located in Europe, besides possessing all of that continent, have now got
hold of a large portion of Asia, Africa, all North America, a portion of South
America, and all of the great Islands of both Hemispheres, except Paupau, or
New Guinea, inhabited by negroes and Malays, in Oceanica; the Japanese Islands, peopled and ruled by the Japanese; Madagascar, peopled by negroes, near
the coast of Africa; and the Island of Haiti, in the West Indies, peopled by as
brave and noble descendants of Africa, as they who laid the foundation of The-
bias,[12] or constructed the everlasting pyramids and catacombs of Egypt. A people who have freed themselves by the might of their own will, the force of their
own power, the unfailing strength of their own right arms, and their unflinching determination to be free.

Let us, then, not survive the disgrace and ordeal of Almighty displeasure, of
two to one, witnessing the universal possession and control by the whites, of
every habitable portion of the earth. For such must inevitably be the case, and
that, too, at no distant day, if black men do not take advantage of the opportunity, by grasping hold of those places where chance is in their favor, and establishing the rights and power of the colored race.

We must make an issue, create an event, and establish for ourselves a position. This is essentially necessary for our effective elevation as a people, in shap-
ing our national development, directing our destiny, and redeeming ourselves
as a race.

If we but determine it shall be so, it *will* be so; and there is nothing under the
sun can prevent it. We shall then be but in pursuit of our legitimate claims to inherent rights, bequeathed to us by the will of Heaven—the endowment of God,
our common parent. A distinguished economist has truly said, "God has implanted in man an infinite progression in the career of improvement. A soul ca-
pacitated for improvement ought not to be bounded by a tyrant's landmarks."[13]
This sentiment is just and true, the application of which to our case, is adapted
with singular fitness.

Having glanced hastily at our present political position in the world generally,
and the United States in particular—the fundamental disadvantages under
which we exist, and the improbability of ever attaining citizenship and equality
of rights in this country—we call your attention next, to the places of destination to which we shall direct Emigration.

The West Indies, Central and South America, are the countries of our choice,
the advantages of which shall be made apparent to your entire satisfaction.

12. Thebes; an ancient city in Upper Egypt.
13. The probable source is John Locke (1632–1704); see, for example, "Of Slavery," in
Two Treatises on Civil Government (1690).

Though we have designated them as countries, they are in fact but one country—relatively considered—a part of this, the Western Continent.

As now politically divided, they consist of the following classification—each group or division placed under its proper national head:

FRENCH ISLANDS

Consist of:		Square miles.		Population in 1840.
Guadeloupe	...	675	...	124,000
Martinico,	...	260	...	110,000
St. Martin,				
N part,	...	15	...	6,000
Mariegalante,	...	90	...	11,500
Deseada,	...	25	...	1,500

DANISH ISLANDS

Santa Cruz,	...	80	...	34,000
St. Thomas,	...	50	...	15,000
St. John,	...	70	...	3,000

SWEDISH

St. Bartholemew,	...	25	...	8,000

DUTCH

St. Eustatia,	...	10	...	20,000
Curacoa,	...	375	...	12,000
St. Martin, S. Part,	...	10	...	5,000
Saba,	...	20	...	9,000

VENEZUELA

Margarita,	...	00	...	16,000

SPANISH

Cuba,	...	43,500	...	725,000
Porto Rico,	...	4,000	...	325,000

BRITISH

Jamaica,	...	5,520	...	375,000
Barbadoes,	...	164	...	102,000
Trinidad,	...	1,970	...	45,000
Antigua,	...	108	...	36,000

Grenada and the Granadines	...	120	...	29,000
St. Vincent,	...	121	...	36,000
St. Kitts,	...	68	...	24,000
Dominica,	...	275	...	20,000
St. Lucia,	...	275	...	18,000
Tobago,	...	120	...	14,000
Nevis,	...	20	...	12,000
Montserrat,	...	47	...	8,000
Tortola,	...	20	...	7,000
Barbuda,	...	72	...	0,000
Anguilla,	...	90	...	3,000
Bahamas,	...	4,440	...	18,000
Bermudas,	...	20	...	10,000

HAYTIEN NATION

Hayti,	...	000	...	800,00

In addition to these there are a number of smaller Islands, belonging to the Little Antilles, the area and population of which are not known, many of them being unpopulated.

These Islands, in the aggregate, form an area—allowing 40,000 square miles to Haiti and her adjunct islands, and something for those the statistics of which are unknown—of about 103,000, or equal in extent to Rhode Island, New York, New Jersey and Pennsylvania, and little less than the United Kingdoms of England, Scotland, Ireland and the principality of Wales.

The population being on the above date, 1840: 3,115,000—three millions, one hundred and fifteen thousand—and allowing an increase of *ten per cent* in ten years, on the entire population, there are now 3,250,000 (three millions, two hundred and fifty thousand) inhabitants, who comprise the people of these islands.

CENTRAL AMERICA

Consists of—		Population in 1840.
Guatemala,	...	800,000
San Salvador,	...	350,000
Honduras,	...	250,000
Costa Rica,	...	150,000
Nicaragua,	...	250,000

These consist of five States, as shown in the above statistics, the united population of which, in 1840, amounted to 1,800,000 (one million, eight hundred thousand) inhabitants. The number at present being estimated at 2,500,000, (two and a half millions) shows in thirteen years, 700,000, (seven hundred thousand) being one-third and one-eighteenth of an increase in population.

SOUTH AMERICA		
Consists of—	Square miles	Population in 1840.
New Grenada, ...	450,000 ...	1,687,000
Venezuela, ...	420,000 ...	900,000
Ecuador, ...	280,000 ...	600,000
Guiana, ...	160,000 ...	182,000
Brazil, ...	3,390,000 ...	5,000,000
North Peru, ...	300,000 ...	700,000
South Peru, ...	130,000 ...	800,000
Bolivia, ...	450,000 ...	1,716,000
Buenos Ayres, ...	750,000 ...	700,000
Paraguay, ...	88,000 ...	150,000
Uruguay, ...	92,000 ...	75,000
Chili, ...	170,000 ...	1,500,000
Patagonia, ...	370,000 ...	30,000

The total area of these States is 7,050,000 (seven millions and fifty thousand) square miles; but comparatively little (450,000 square miles) less than the whole area of North America, in which we live.

But one State in South America—Brazil—is an abject slave-holding State; and even here, all free men are socially and politically equal, negroes and colored men partly of African descent, holding offices of honor, trust and rank, without restriction. In the other States slavery is not known, all the inhabitants enjoying political equality, restrictions on account of color being entirely unknown, unless, indeed, necessity induces it, when, in all such cases, the preference is given to the colored man, to put a check to European presumption, and insufferable Yankee intrusion and impudence.

The aggregate population was 14,040,000 (fourteen millions and forty thousand) in 1840. Allowing for thirteen years the same ratio of increase as that of the Central American States—being one-third (4,680,000)—and this gives at present a population of 18,720,000 in South America.

Add to this the population of the Antilles and Guatemala, and this gives a population in the West Indies, Central and South America of 24,470,000 (twenty-four millions, four hundred seventy thousand) inhabitants.

But one-seventh of this population, 3,495,714, (three millions, four hundred and ninety-five thousand, seven hundred and fourteen) being white, or of pure European extraction, there is a population throughout this vast area of 20,974,286 (twenty millions, nine hundred and seventy-four thousand, two hundred and eighty-six) colored persons, who constitute, from the immense preponderance of their numbers, the *ruling element* as they ever must be, of those countries.

There are no influences that could be brought to bear to change this most fortunate and Heaven-designed state and condition of things. Nature here has done her own work, which the art of knaves nor the schemes of deep-designing political impostors can ever reach. This is a fixed fact in the zodiac of the political heavens, that the blacks and colored people are the stars which must ever most conspicuously twinkle in the firmament of this division of the Western Hemisphere.

We next invite your attention to a few facts, upon which we predicate the claims of the black race, not only to the tropical regions and *South temperate zone* of this hemisphere, but to the whole Continent, North as well as South. And here we desire it distinctly to be understood, that, in the selection of our places of destination, we do not advocate the *Southern* scheme as a concession, nor yet at the will nor desire of our North American oppressors; but as a policy, by which we must be the greatest political gainers, without the risk or possibility of loss to ourselves. A gain by which the lever of political elevation and machinery of national progress must ever be held and directed by our own hands and heads, to our own will and purposes, in defiance of the obstructions which might be attempted on the part of a dangerous and deep-designing oppressor.

From the year 1492, the discovery of Hispaniola—the first land discovered by Columbus in the New World—to 1502, the short space of ten years, such was the mortality among the natives, that the Spaniards, then holding rule there, "began to employ a few" Africans in the mines of the Island. The experiment was effective—a successful one. The Indian and the African were enslaved together, when the Indian sunk, and the African stood.

It was not until June the 24th, of the year 1498, that the Continent was discovered by John Cabot,[14] a Venetian, who sailed in August of the previous year, 1497, from Bristol, under the patronage of Henry VII, King of England.

In 1517, the short space of but fifteen years from the date of their introduction, Carolus V, King of Spain, by right of a patent, granted permission to a number of persons annually to supply the islands of Hispaniola, (St. Domingo,) Cuba, Jamaica and Porto Rico, with natives of Africa, to the number of four

14. The English explorer John Cabot (1461–98), originally of Venice, "discovered" the North American coast. British claims to North America were based on Cabot's voyage.

thousand annually. John Hawkins,[15] a mercenary Englishman, was the first person known to engage in this general system of debasing our race, and his royal mistress, Queen Elizabeth, was engaged with him in interest and shared the general profits.

The Africans, on their advent into a foreign country, soon experienced the want of their accustomed food, and habits and manner of living.

The aborigines subsisted mainly by game and fish, with a few patches of maize, or Indian corn, near their wigwams, which were generally attended by the women, while the men were absent engaged in the chase, or at war with a hostile tribe. The vegetables, grains and fruits, such as in their native country they had been accustomed to, were not to be obtained among the aborigines, which first induced the African laborer to cultivate "patches" of ground in the neighborhood of the mining operations, for the purpose of raising food for his own sustenance.

This trait in their character was observed and regarded with considerable interest; after which the Spaniards and other colonists, on contracting with the English slave dealers—Captain Hawkins and others—for new supplies of slaves, were careful to request that an adequate quantity of seeds and plants of various kinds, indigenous to the continent of Africa, especially those composing the staple products of the natives, be selected and brought out with the slaves to the New World. Many of these were cultivated to a considerable extent, while those indigenous to America were cultivated with great success.

Shortly after the commencement of the slave trade, under Elizabeth and Hawkins, the Queen granted a license to Sir Walter Raleigh,[16] to search for uninhabited lands, and seize upon all unoccupied by Christians. Sir Walter discovered the coast of North Carolina and Virginia, assigning the name "Virginia" to the whole coast now comprising the old Thirteen States.

A feeble colony was here settled, which did not avail much, and it was not until the month of April, 1607, that the first permanent settlement was made in Virginia, under the patronage of letters patent from James I, King of England, to Thomas Gates and associates. This was the first settlement of North America, and thirteen years anterior to the landing of the Pilgrims on Plymouth Rock.

And we shall now introduce to you, from acknowledged authority, a number of historical extracts, to prove that previous to the introduction of the black race upon this continent, but little enterprise of any kind was successfully carried on.

15. During the 1560s, the British admiral Sir John Hawkins (1532–95), in defiance of Spanish prohibitions, led expeditions to West Africa to capture natives and sell them as slaves.

16. The English explorer and writer Sir Walter Raleigh (1554?–1618), a favorite of Queen Elizabeth, helped to plan colonizing missions to America during the 1580s.

The African or negro was the first *available contributor* to the country, and consequently is by priority of right, and politically should be, entitled to the highest claims of an eligible citizen.

"No permanent settlement was effected in what is now called the United States, till the reign of James the First."—*Ramsay's Hist. U.S.*, Vol. 1. p. 38.[17]

"The month of April, 1607, is the epoch of the first permanent settlement on the coast of Virginia, the name then given to all that extent of country which forms thirteen States."—*Ib.* p. 39.

The whole coast of the country was at this time explored, not for the purpose of trade and agriculture—because there were then no such enterprises in the country, the natives not producing sufficient of the necessities of life, to supply present wants, there being consequently nothing to trade for—but, like their Spanish and Portuguese predecessors, who occupied the Islands and different parts of South America, in search of gold and other precious metals.

Trade and the cultivation of the soil, on coming to the new world, were foreign to their intention or designs, consequently, when failing of success in that enterprise, they were sadly disappointed.

"At a time when the precious metals were conceived to be the peculiar and only valuable productions of the new world, when every mountain was supposed to contain a treasure and every rivulet was searched for its golden sands, this appearance was fondly considered as an infallible indication of the mine. Every hand was eager to dig. * * *

"There was now," says Smith,[18] "no talk, no hope, no work; but dig gold, wash gold, refine gold. With this imaginary wealth, the first vessel returning to England was loaded, while the *culture of the land* and every useful occupation was *totally neglected.*

"The colonists thus left, were in miserable circumstances for want of provisions. The remainder of what they had brought with them was so small in quantity, as to be soon expended—and so damaged, in course of a long voyage, as to be a source of disease.

"* * In their expectation of getting gold, the people were disappointed, the glittering substance they had sent to England, proving to be a valueless mineral. Smith, on his return to Jamestown, found the colony reduced to

17. David Ramsay (1749–1815), *History of the United States, from the First Settlement as English Colonies, in 1607, to the Year 1808* (1816).

18. The British explorer John Smith (1580–1631) was an important leader of the Virginia Company's first colonists and is best known as the author of *The Generall Historie of Virginia, New-England, and the Summer Isles* (1624).

thirty-eight persons, who, in despair, were preparing to abandon the country. He employed caresses, threats, and even violence, in order to prevent them from executing this fatal resolution."—*Ibid*, pp. 45–6.

The Pilgrims or Puritans, in November, 1620, after having organized with solemn vows to the defence of each other, and the maintenance of their civil liberty, made the harbor of Cape Cod, landing safely on "Plymouth Rock," December 20th, about one month subsequently. They were one hundred and one in number, and from the *toils* and *hardships* consequent to a *severe season*, in a *strange country*, in less than six months after their arrival, "forty persons— nearly one-half of their original number"—had died.

"In 1618, in the reign of James I, the British government established a regular trade on the coast of Africa. In the year 1620, negro slaves began to be imported into Virginia, a Dutch ship bringing twenty of them for sale."—*Sampson's Historical Dictionary*, p. 348.[19]

It will be seen by these historical reminiscences, that the Dutch ship landed her cargo at New Bedford, Massachusetts—the whole coast now comprising the old original States, then went by the name of Virginia, being so named by Sir Walter Raleigh, in honor of his royal mistress and patron, Elizabeth, the Virgin Queen of England, under whom he received the patent of his royal commission, to seize all the lands unoccupied by Christians.

Beginning their preparations in the slave trade in 1618, just two years previous,—allowing time against the landing of the first emigrants, for successfully carrying out the project—the African captives and Puritan emigrants—singularly enough!—landed upon the same section of the continent at the same time—1620—the Pilgrims at Plymouth, and the captive slaves at New Bedford, but a few miles, comparatively, south.

"The country at this period, was one vast wilderness. The continent of North America was then one continued forest. * *

"There were no horses, cattle, sheep, hogs, or tame beasts of any kind.* * There were no domestic poultry. * * There were no gardens, orchards, public roads, meadows, or cultivated fields. — * * They often burned the woods that they could advantageously plant their corn. * *

"They had neither spice, salt, bread, butter, cheese, nor milk.—They had no set meals, but eat when they were hungry, or could find anything to satisfy the cravings of nature.

19. Ezra Sampson (1749–1823), *The Youth's Companion; or, An Historical Dictionary* (1813).

"Very little of their food was derived from the earth, except what it spontaneously produced. * * The ground was both their seat and table. * * Their best bed was a skin. * * They had neither iron, steel, nor any metallic instruments."—*Ramsay's Hist.*, pp. 39–40.

We adduce not these extracts to disparage or detract from the real worth of our brother Indian—for we are identical as the subjects of American wrongs, outrages, and oppression; and therefore one in interest—far be it from our designs. Whatever opinion he may entertain of our race—in accordance with the impressions made by the contumely heaped upon us by our mutual oppressor, the American nation—we admire his, for the many deeds of heroic and noble daring with which the brief history of his liberty-loving people is replete. We sympathize with him, because our brethren are the successors of his, in the degradation of American bondage; and we adduce them in evidence against the many aspersions heaped upon the African race, avowing that their inferiority to the other races, and unfitness for a high civil and social position, caused them to be reduced to servitude.

For the purpose of proving their availability and eminent fitness alone,—not to say superiority, and not inferiority—first suggested to Europeans the substitution of African for that of Indian labor in the mines; that their superior adaptation to the difficulties consequent to a new country and different climate, made them preferable to Europeans themselves; and their superior skill, industry, and general thriftiness in all that they did, first suggested to the colonists the propriety of turning their attention to agricultural and other industrial pursuits than those of mining operations.

It is evident, from what has herein been adduced—the settlement of Capt. John Smith being in the course of a few months, reduced to thirty-eight, and that of the Pilgrims at Plymouth, from one hundred and one to fifty-seven, in six months—that the whites nor aborigines were equal to the hard, and to them insurmountable difficulties, which then stood wide-spread before them.

An endless forest—the impenetrable earth—the one to be removed and the other to be excavated. Towns and cities to be built, and farms to be cultivated: all presented difficulties too arduous for the European then here, and entirely unknown to the native of the continent.

At a period such as this, when the natives themselves had fallen victims to the tasks imposed upon them by the usurpers, and the Europeans also were fast sinking beneath the influence and weight of climate and hardships; when food could not be obtained, nor the common conveniences of life procured; when arduous duties of life were to be performed, and none capable of doing them— save those who had previously by their labors, not only in their own country, but in the new, so proven themselves capable—it is very evident, as the most natural consequence, the Africans were resorted to, for the performance of every duty common to domestic life.

There were no laborers known to the Colonists, from Cape Cod to Cape Lookout,[20] than those of the African race. They entered at once into the mines, extracting therefrom the rich treasures which for a thousand ages lay hidden in the earth; when plunging into the depths of the rivers, they culled from their sandy bottoms, to the astonishment of the natives and surprise of the Europeans, minerals and precious stones, which added to the pride and aggrandizement of every throne in Europe.

And from their knowledge of cultivation—an art acquired in their native Africa—the farming interests in the North and planting in the South, were commenced with a prospect never dreamed of before the introduction on the continent of this most interesting, unexampled, hardy race of men. A race capable of the endurance of more toil, fatigue and hunger, than any other branch of the human family.

Though pagans for the most part in their own country, they required not to be taught to work, and how to do it; but it was only necessary to bid them work, and they at once knew what to do, and how it should be done.

Even up to the present day, it is notorious that in the planting States, the blacks themselves are the only skillful cultivators of the soil, the proprietors or planters, as they are termed, knowing little or nothing of the art, save that which they learn from the African husbandman; while the ignorant white overseer, whose duty is to see that the work is attended to, knows still less.

Hemp, cotton, tobacco, corn, rice, sugar, and many other important staple products, are all the result of African skill and labor, in the southern States of this country. The greater number of the mechanics of the South are also black men.

Nor was their skill as herdsmen inferior to their other proficiencies, they being among the most accomplished trainers of horses in the world.

Indeed, to this class of men may be indebted the entire country, for the improvement South, in the breed of horses. And those who have travelled in the southern States could not have failed to observe that the principal trainers, jockeys, riders, and judges of horses, were men of African descent.

These facts alone, are sufficient to establish our claim to this country, as legitimate as that of those who fill the highest stations, by the suffrage of the people.

In no period since the existence of the ancient enlightened nations of Africa, have the prospects of the black race been brighter than now; and at no time dur-

20. Capes in Massachusetts and North Carolina.

ing the Christian era, have there been greater advantages presented for the advancement of any people, than at present, those which offer to the black race, both in the Eastern and Western hemispheres—our election being in the Western.

Despite the efforts to the contrary, in the strenuous endeavors for a supremacy of race, the sympathies of the world in their upward tendency, are in favor of the African and black races of the earth. To be available, *we* must take advantage of these favorable feelings, and strike out for ourselves a bold and manly course, of *independent action* and *position;* otherwise, this pure and uncorrupted sympathy will be reduced to pity and contempt.

Of the countries of our choice, we have stated that one province and two islands were slaveholding places. These, as before named, are Brazil in South America, and Cuba and Porto Rico in the West Indies. There are a few other little islands of minor consideration—the Danish, three—Swedish, one—and Dutch, four.

But in the eight last referred to, slavery is of such a mild type, that—however objectionable as such—it is merely nominal.

In South America and the Antilles, in its worst form, slavery is a blessing almost, compared with the miserable degradation of the slave under our upstart, assumed superiors, the slave-holders of the United States.

In Brazil, color is no badge of condition, and every freeman, whatever his color, is socially and politically equal, there being black gentlemen of pure African descent, filling the highest positions in State, under the Emperor. There is also an established law by the Congress of Brazil, making the crime punishable with death, for the commander of any vessel to bring into the country any human being as a slave.[21]

The following law has passed one branch of the General Legislative Assembly of Brazil, but little doubt being entertained that it will find a like favor in the other branch of that august general legislative body:

1

All children born after the date of this law shall be free.

2

All those shall be considered free who are born in other countries, and come to Brazil after this date.

3

Every one who serves from birth to 7 years of age, any of those included in article 1, or who has to serve so many years, at the end of 14 years shall be emancipated, and live as he chooses.

21. The Querioz Law of 1850 banned the slave trade.

4

Every slave paying for his liberty a sum equal to what he cost his master, or who shall gain it by honorable gratuitous title, the master shall be obliged to give him a free paper, under the penalty of article 179 of the criminal code.

5

Where there is no stipulated price or fixed value of the slave, it shall be determined by arbitrators, one of which shall be the public *promoter* of the town.

6

The government is authorized to give precise regulations for the execution of this law, and also to form establishments necessary for taking care of those who, born after this date, may be abandoned by the owners of slaves.

7

Opposing laws and regulations are repealed.

————

Concerning Cuba, there is an old established law, giving any slave the right of a certain *legal tender*, which, if refused by the slave holder, he, by going to the residence of any parish priest and making known the facts, shall immediately be declared a freeman, the priest or bishop of the parish or diocese giving him his "freedom papers." The legal tender, or sum fixed by law, we think does not exceed two hundred and fifty Spanish dollars. It may be more.

Until the Americans intruded themselves into Cuba, contaminating society wherever they located, black and colored gentlemen and ladies of rank, mingled indiscriminately in society. But since the advent of these negro-haters, the colored people of Cuba have been reduced nearly, if not quite, to the level of the miserable degraded position of the colored people of the United States, who almost consider it a compliment and favor to receive the notice or smiles of a white.

Can we be satisfied, in this enlightened age of the world—amid the advantages which now present themselves to us with the degradation and servility inherited from our fathers in this country?—God forbid. And we think the universal reply will be—We will not.

A half century brings about a mighty change, in the reality of existing things, and events of the world's history. Fifty years ago, our fathers lived: for the most part they were sorely oppressed, debased, ignorant and incapable of comprehending the political relations of mankind; the great machinery and motive power by which the enlightened nations of the earth were impelled forward. They knew but little, and ventured to do nothing to enhance their own interests, beyond that which their oppressors taught them. They lived amidst a continual cloud of moral obscurity—a fog of bewilderment and delusion, by which they were of necessity compelled to confine themselves to a limited space—a *known* locality—lest by one step beyond this, they might have stumbled over a precipice, ruining themselves beyond recovery in the fall.

We are their sons, but not the same individuals; neither do we live in the same period with them. That which suited them, does not suit us; and that with which they may have been contented, will not satisfy us.

Without education, they were ignorant of the world and fearful of adventure. With education, we are conversant with its geography, history and nations, and delight in its enterprises and responsibilities. They once were held as slaves; to such a condition we never could be reduced. They were content with privileges; we will be satisfied with nothing less than rights. They felt themselves happy to be permitted to beg for rights; we demand them as an innate inheritance. They considered themselves favored to live by sufferance; we reject it as a degradation. A subordinate position was all they asked for; we claim entire equality or nothing. The relation of master and slave was innocently acknowledged by them; we deny the right as such, and pronounce the relation as the basest injustice that ever scourged the earth and cursed the human family. They admitted themselves to be inferiors; we barely acknowledge the whites as equals—perhaps not in every particular. They lamented their irrecoverable fate, and incapacity to redeem themselves and their race. We rejoice, that as their sons, it is our happy lot and high mission, to accomplish that which they desired and would have done, but failed for the want of ability to do.

Let no intelligent man or woman, then, among us, be found at the present day, exulting in the degradation that our enslaved parents would gladly have rid themselves, had they have had the intelligence and qualifications to accomplish their designs. Let none be found to shield themselves behind the plea of our brother bondmen in ignorance; that we know not *what* to do, nor *where* to go. We are no longer slaves, as were our fathers, but freemen; fully qualified to meet our oppressors in every relation which belongs to the elevation of man, the establishment, sustenance and perpetuity of a nation. And such a position, by the help of God our common Father, we are determined to take and maintain.

There is but one question presents itself for our serious consideration, upon which we *must* give a decisive reply—Will we transmit, as an inheritance to our children, the blessings of unrestricted civil liberty, or shall we entail upon them, as our only political legacy, the degradation and oppression left us by our fathers?

Shall we be persuaded that we can live and prosper nowhere but under the authority and power of our North American white oppressors; that this (the United States) is the country most—if not the only one—favorable to our improvement and progress? Are we willing to admit that we are incapable of self-government, establishing for ourselves such political privileges, and making such internal improvements as we delight to enjoy, after American white men have made them for themselves?

No! Neither is it true that the United States is the country best adapted to *our* improvement. But that country is the best in which our manhood—morally, mentally and physically—can be *best developed*—in which we have an untrammelled right to the enjoyment of civil and religious liberty; and the West Indies, Central and South America, present now such advantages, superiorly preferable to all other countries.

That the continent of America was designed by Providence a reserved asylum for the various oppressed people of the earth, of all races, to us seems very apparent.

From the earliest period after the discovery, various nations sent a representative here, either as adventurers and speculators, or employed laborers, seamen, or soldiers, hired to work for their employers. And among the earliest and most numerous class who found their way to the new world, were those of the African race. And it has been ascertained to our minds beyond a doubt, that when the Continent was discovered, there were found in the West Indies and Central America, tribes of the black race, fine looking people, having the usual characteristics of color and hair, identifying them as being originally of the African race; no doubt, being a remnant of the Africans who, with the Carthaginian expedition, were adventitiously cast upon this continent, in their memorable adventure to the "Great Island," after sailing many miles distant to the west of the "Pillars of Hercules"—the present Straits of Gibraltar.[22]

We would not be thought to be superstitious, when we say, that in all this we can "see the finger of God." Is it not worthy of a notice here, that while the ingress of foreign whites to this continent has been voluntary and constant, and that of the blacks involuntary and but occasional, yet the whites in the southern part have *decreased* in numbers, *degenerated* in character, and become mentally and physically *enervated* and imbecile; while the blacks and colored people have studiously *increased* in numbers, *regenerated* in character, and have grown mentally and physically vigorous and active, developing every function of their manhood, and are now, in their elementary character, decidedly superior to the white race? So then the white race could never successfully occupy the southern portion of the continent; they must of necessity, every generation, be repeo-

22. A reference to the possible journey of ancient Africans to the New World (the "Great Island"); the Pillars of Hercules are promonotories flanking the east entrance to the Strait of Gilbratar, which is between Europe and Africa.

pled from another quarter of the globe. The fatal error committed by the Spaniards, under Pizarro,[23] was the attempt to exterminate the Incas and Peruvians, and fill their places by European whites. The Peruvian Indians, a hale, hardy, vigorous, intellectual race of people, were succeeded by those who soon became idle, vicious, degenerated and imbecile. But Peru, like all the other South American States, is regaining her former potency, just in proportion as the European race decreases among them. All the labor of the country is performed by the aboriginal natives and the blacks; the few Europeans there, being the merest excrescences on the body politic—consuming drones in the social hive.

Had we no other claims than those set forth in a foregoing part of this Address, they are sufficient to induce every black and colored person to remain on this continent, unshaken and unmoved.

But the West Indians, Central and South Americans, are a noble race of people; generous, sociable, and tractable—just the people with whom we desire to unite, who are susceptible of progress, improvement and reform of every kind. They now desire all the improvements of North America, but being justly jealous of their rights, they have no confidence in the whites of the United States, and consequently peremptorily refuse to permit an indiscriminate settlement among them of this class of people; but placing every confidence in the black and colored people of North America.

The example of the unjust invasion and forcible seizure of a large portion of the territory of Mexico, is still fresh in their memory; and the oppressive disfranchisement of a large number of native Mexicans, by the Americans—because of the color and race of the natives—will continue to rankle in the bosom of the people of those countries, and prove a sufficient barrier henceforth against the inroads of North American whites among them.

Upon the American continent, then, we are determined to remain, despite every opposition that may be urged against us.

You will doubtless be asked—and that, too, with an air of seriousness—why, if desirable to remain on this continent, not be content to remain *in* the United States. The objections to this—and potent reasons, too, in our estimation—have already been clearly shown.

But notwithstanding all this, were there still any rational, nay, even the most futile grounds for hope, we still might be stupid enough to be content to remain, and yet through another period of unexampled patience and suffering, continue meekly to drag the galling yoke and clank the chain of servility and degradation. But whether or not in this, God is to be thanked and Heaven

23. During the 1530s, the Spanish explorer Francisco Pizarro (1476–1541) invaded and conquered Peru.

blessed, we are not permitted, despite our willingness and stupidity, to indulge even the most distant glimmer of a hope of attaining to the level of a well protected slave.

For years we have been studiously and jealously observing the course of political events and policy on the part of this country, both in a national and individual State capacity, as pursued towards the colored people. And he who, in the midst of them, can live without observation, is either excusably ignorant, or reprehensibly deceptious and untrustworthy.

We deem it entirely unnecessary to tax you with anything like the history of even one chapter of the unequalled infamies perpetrated on the part of the various States, and national decrees, by legislation, against us. But we shall call your particular attention to the more recent acts of the United States; because whatever privileges we may enjoy in any individual State, will avail nothing, when not recognized as such by the United States.

When the condition of the inhabitants of any country is fixed by legal grades of distinction, this condition can never be changed except by express legislation. And it is the height of folly to expect such express legislation, except by the inevitable force of some irresistible internal political pressure. The force necessary to this imperative demand on our part, we never can obtain, because of our numerical feebleness.

Were the interests of the common people identical with ours, we, in this, might succeed, because we, as a class, would then be numerically the superior. But this is not a question of the rich against the poor, nor the common people against the higher classes; but a question of white against black—every white person, by legal right, being held superior to a black or colored person.

In Russia, the common people might obtain an equality with the aristocracy; because, of the sixty-five millions of her population, forty-five millions are serfs or peasants—leaving but twenty millions of the higher classes, royalty, nobility and all included.

The rights of no oppressed people have ever yet been obtained by a voluntary act of justice on the part of the oppressors. Christians, philanthropists, and moralists may preach, argue and philosophize as they may to the contrary; facts are against them. Voluntary acts, it is true, which are in themselves just, may sometimes take place on the part of the oppressor; but these are always actuated by the force of some outward circumstances of self-interest, equal to a compulsion.

The boasted liberties of the American people were established by a constitution, borrowed from and modelled after the British *magna charta*. And this great charter of British liberty, so much boasted of and vaunted as a model bill of rights, was obtained only by force and extortion.

The Barons, an order of noblemen, under the reign of King John, becoming dissatisfied at the terms, submitted to by their sovereign, which necessarily brought degradation upon themselves—terms prescribed by the insolent Pope Innocent III, the haughty sovereign Pontiff of Rome; summoned his majesty to meet them on the plains of the memorable meadow of Runnimede, where, presenting to him their own Bill of Rights—a bill dictated by themselves, and drawn up by their own hands—at the unsheathed points of a thousand glittering swords, they commanded him, against his will, to sign the extraordinary document. There was no alternative; he must either do or die. With puerile timidity, he leaned forward his rather commanding but imbecile person, and with a trembling hand, and a single dash of the pen, the name KING JOHN stood forth in bold relief, sending more terror throughout the world, than the mystic hand-writing of Heaven throughout the dominions of Nebuchadnezzar, blazing on the walls of Babylon.[24] A consternation, not because of the *name* of the King, but because of the rights of *others*, which that name acknowledged.

The King, however, soon became dissatisfied, and determining on a revocation of the act—an act done entirely contrary to his will—at the head of a formidable army, spread fire and sword throughout the kingdom.

But the Barons, though compelled to leave their castles—their houses and homes—and fly for their lives, could not be induced to undo that which they had so nobly done; the achievement of their rights and privileges. Hence, the act has stood throughout all succeeding time, because never annulled by those who *willed* it.

It will be seen that the first great modern Bill of Rights was obtained only by a force of arms; a resistance of the people against the injustice and intolerance of their rulers. We say the people—because that which the Barons demanded for themselves, was afterwards extended to the common people. Their only hope was based on their *superiority of numbers*.

But can we in this country hope for as much? Certainly not. Our case is a hopeless one. There was but *one* John, with his few sprigs of adhering royalty; and but *one* heart at which the threatening points of their swords were directed by a thousand Barons; while in our case, there is but a handful of the oppressed, without a sword to point, and *twenty millions* of Johns or Jonathans[25]—as you please—with as many hearts, tenfold more relentless than that of Prince John Lackland, and as deceptious and hypocritical as the Italian heart of Innocent III.

24. An account of King John's initial issuing of the Magna Carta in 1215, under compulsion from the barons and the church. The document, reissued in 1217 and 1225, came to be understood as a freedom document, placing constitutional protections above and beyond the power of the king. Nubuchadnezzar was king of Babylon circa 604–561 B.C. and conqueror of Jerusalem; see II Kings 24, 25.

25. "Jonathan," or "Brother Jonathan," was a colloquial and often deliberately comic name for the typical American, particularly a New Englander.

Where, then, is our hope of success in this country? Upon what is it based? Upon what principle of political policy and sagacious discernment, do our political leaders and acknowledged great men—colored men we mean—justify themselves by telling us, and insisting that we shall believe them, and submit to what they say—to be patient, remain where we are; that there is a "bright prospect and glorious future" before us in this country! May Heaven open our eyes from their Bartimean[26] obscurity.

But we call your attention to another point of our political degradation. The acts of State and general governments.

In a few of the States, as in New York, the colored inhabitants have a partial privilege of voting a white man into office. This privilege is based on a property qualification of two hundred and fifty dollars worth of real estate. In others, as in Ohio, in the absence of organic provision, the privilege is granted by judicial decision, based on a ratio of blood, of an admixture of more than one-half white; while in many of the States, there is no privilege allowed, either partial or unrestricted.

The policy of the above-named States will be seen and detected at a glance, which while seeming to extend immunities, is intended especially for the object of degradation.

In the State of New York, for instance, there is a constitutional distinction created among colored men—almost necessarily compelling one part to feel superior to the other; while among the whites no such distinctions dare be known. Also, in Ohio, there is a legal distinction set up by an upstart judiciary, creating among the colored people, a privileged class by birth! All this must necessarily sever the cords of union among us, creating almost insurmountable prejudices of the most stupid and fatal kind, paralyzing the last bracing nerve which promised to give us strength.

It is upon this same principle, and for the self-same object, that the General Government has long been endeavoring, and is at present knowingly designing to effect a recognition of the independence of the Dominican Republic, while disparagingly refusing to recognize the independence of the Haytien nation— a people four-fold greater in numbers, wealth and power.[27] The Haytiens, it is pretended, are refused because they are *Negroes*; while the Dominicans, as is well

26. A reference to the blind Bartimaeus, who was restored to sight by Jesus; see Matthew 20:29–34, Mark 10:46–52, and Luke 18:35–43.

27. In 1860 the United States recognized the Dominican Republic's authority over the islet of Alta Vela; in 1862 the United States offered diplomatic recognition of Haiti and two years later signed a treaty of friendship with Haiti. Nonetheless, in the decades following the Civil War the United States continued its hostile, interventionist policies toward both nations.

known to all who are familiar with the geography, history, and political relations of that people, are identical — except in language, they speaking the Spanish tongue — with those of the Haytiens; being composed of negroes and a mixed race. The government may shield itself by the plea that it is not familiar with the origin of those people. To this we have but to reply, that if the government is thus ignorant of the relations of its near neighbors, it is the height of presumption, and no small degree of assurance, for it to set up itself as capable of prescribing terms to the one, or conditions to the other.

Should they accomplish their object, they then will have succeeded in forever establishing a barrier of impassable separation, by the creation of a political distinction between those peoples of superiority and inferiority of origin or national existence. Here, then, is another stratagem of this most determined and untiring enemy of our race — the government of the United States.

We come now to the crowning act of infamy on the part of the General Government towards the colored inhabitants of the United States — an act so vile in its nature, that rebellion against its demands should be promptly made, in every attempt to enforce its infernal provisions.

In the history of national existence, there is not to be found a parallel to the tantalising insult and aggravating despotism of the provisions of Millard Fillmore's Fugitive Slave Bill, passed by the thirty-third Congress of the United States, with the approbation of a majority of the American people, in the year of the Gospel of Jesus Christ, eighteen hundred and fifty.

This Bill had but one object in its provisions, which was fully accomplished in its passage; that is, the reduction of every colored person in the United States — save those who carry free papers of emancipation, or bills of sale from former claimants or owners — to a state of relative *slavery;* placing each and every one of us at the *disposal of any and every white* who might choose to *claim* us, and the caprice of any and every upstart knave bearing the title of "Commissioner."

Did any of you, fellow-countrymen, reside in a country the provisions of whose laws were such that any person of a certain class, who, whenever he, she or they pleased, might come forward, lay a claim to, make oath before (it might be,) some stupid and heartless person, authorized to decide in such cases, and take, at their option, your horse, cow, sheep, house and lot, or any other property, bought and paid for by your own earnings — the result of your personal toil and labor — would you be willing, or could you be induced, by any reasoning, however great the source from which it came, to remain in that country? We pause, fellow-countrymen, for a reply.

If there be not one yea, of how much more importance, then, is your *own personal safety*, than that of property? Of how much more concern is the safety of a wife or husband, than that of a cow or horse; a child, than a sheep; the destiny of your family, to that of a house and lot?

And yet this is precisely our condition. Any one of us, at any moment, is liable to be *claimed, seized* and *taken* into custody by any white, as his or her property— and be *enslaved for life*—and there is no remedy, because it is the *law of the land!* And we dare predict, and take this favorable opportunity to forewarn you, fellow-countrymen, that the time is not far distant, when there will be carried on by the white men of this nation, an extensive commerce in the persons of what now compose the free colored people of the North. We forewarn you, that the general enslavement of the whole of this class of people, is now being contemplated by the whites.

At present, we are liable to enslavement at any moment, provided we are taken *away* from our homes. But we dare venture further to forewarn you, that the scheme is in mature contemplation, and has even been mooted in high places, of harmonizing the two discordant political divisions in the country, by again reducing the free to slave States.

The completion of this atrocious scheme, only becomes necessary for each and every one of us to find an owner and master at our own doors. Let the general government but pass such a law, and the States will comply as an act of harmony. Let the South but *demand* it, and the North will comply as a *duty* of compromise.

If Pennsylvania, New York and Massachusetts can be found arming their sons as watch-dogs for southern slave hunters; if the United States may, with impunity, garrison with troops the Court House of the freest city in America; blockade the streets; station armed ruffians of dragoons, and spiked artillery in hostile awe of the people; if free, white, high-born and bred gentlemen of Boston and New York, are smitten down to the earth,[28] refused an entrance on pro-

28. John Jay, Esq., of New York, son of the late distinguished jurist, Hon. Wm. Jay, was, in 1852, as the counsel of a Fugitive Slave, brutally assaulted and struck in the face by the slave catching agent and counsel, Busteed. Also, Mr. Dana, an honorable gentleman, counsel for the fugitive Burns, one of the first literary men of Boston, was arrested on his entrance into the Court House, and not permitted to pass the guard of slave-catchers, till the slave agent and counsel, Loring, together with the overseer, Suttle, *inspected* him, and ordered that he might be *allowed* to pass in! After which, in passing along the street, Mr. Dana was ruffianly assaulted and murderously felled to the earth, by the minions of the dastardly southern overseer. [Delany's note.] In one of the most famous cases of the period, the Virginia slave Anthony Burns (1834–62) escaped to Boston in 1854, and when he was seized in March under the provisions of the Fugitive Slave Law, a group of protesters stormed the Massachusetts Supreme Court in a failed effort to free him. In 1855 his freedom was purchased by the Baptist Church.

fessional business, into the Court Houses, until inspected by a slave hunter and his counsel; all to put down the liberty of the black man; then, indeed, is there no hope for us in this country!

It is, fellow-countrymen, a fixed fact, as indelible as the Covenant of God in the Heavens, that the colored people of these United States, are the slaves of any white person who may choose to claim them!

What safety or guarantee have we for ourselves or families?—Let us, for a moment, examine this point.

Supposing some hired spy of the slave power, residing in Illinois, whom, for illustration, we shall call Stephen A., Counsel B., a mercenary hireling of New York, and Commissioner C., a slave catcher of Pennsylvania, should take umbrage at the acts or doings of any colored person or persons in a free State; they may with impunity, send or go on their knight errands to the South, (as did a hireling of the slave power in New York—a lawyer by profession,) give a description of such person or persons, and an agent with warrants may be immediately despatched to swear them into slavery forever.

We tell you, fellow-countrymen, any one of you here assembled—your humble committee who report to you this address—may, by the laws of this land, be seized, whatever the circumstances of his birth; whether he descends from free or slave parents—whether born North or South of Mason and Dixon's Line—and ere the setting of another sun, be speeding his way to that living sepulchre, and death chamber of our race—the curse and scourge of this country—the Southern part of the United States. This is not idle speculation, but living, naked, undisguised truth.

A member of your committee has received a letter from a gentleman of respectability and standing in the South, who writes to the following effect. We copy his own words:

> "There are at this moment, as I was to-day informed by Colonel W., one of our first magistrates in this city, a gang of from twenty-five to thirty vagabonds of poor white men, who for twenty-five dollars a head, clear of all expenses, are ready and willing to go to the North, make acquaintance with the blacks in various places, send their descriptions to unprincipled slave holders here—for there are many of this kind to be found among the poorer class of masters—and swear them into bondage. So the free blacks, as well as fugitive slaves, will have to keep a sharp watch over themselves to get clear of this scheme to enslave them."

Here, then, you have but a paragraph in the great volume of this political crusade, and legislative pirating by the American people, over the rights and privileges of the colored inhabitants of the country. If this be but a paragraph—for such it is in truth—what must be the contents when the whole history is divulged! Never will the contents of this dreadful record of crime, corruption and oppression be fully revealed, until the Trump of God shall proclaim the universal summons to judgment. Then, and then alone, shall the whole truth be acknowledged, when the doom of the criminal shall be forever sealed.

We desire not to be sentimental, but rather would be political; and therefore call your attention to another point—a point already referred to.

In giving the statistics of various countries, and preferences to many places herein mentioned, as points of destination in emigration, we have said little or nothing concerning the present governments, the various State departments, nor the condition of society among the people.

This is not the province of your committee, but the legitimate office of a Board of Foreign Commissioners, whom there is no doubt will be created by the Convention, with provisions and instructions to report thereon, in due season, of their mission.[29]

With a few additional remarks on the subject of the British Provinces of North America, we shall have done our duty, and completed, for the time being, the arduous, important and momentous task assigned to us.

The British Provinces of North America, especially Canada West—formerly called Upper Canada—in climate, soil, productions, and the usual prospects for internal improvements, are equal, if not superior, to any northern part of the continent. And for these very reasons, aside from their contiguity to the northern part of the United States—and consequent facility for the escape of the slaves from the South—we certainly should prefer them as a place of destination. We love the Canadas, and admire their laws, because as British Provinces, there is no difference known among the people—no distinction of race. And we deem it a duty to recommend, that, for the present, as a temporary asylum, it is certainly advisable for every colored person, who desiring to emigrate, and is not prepared for any other destination, to locate in Canada West.

Every advantage on our part, should be now taken of the opportunity of *obtaining* LANDS, while they are to be had cheap and on the most easy conditions, from the Government.

Even those who never contemplate a removal from this country of chains, it will be their best interest and greatest advantage, to procure lands in the Canadian Provinces. It will be an easy, profitable and safe investment, even should they never occupy nor yet see them. We shall then be but doing what the whites in the United States have for years been engaged in; securing unsettled lands in

29. Established at the National Emigration Convention, the National Board of Commissioners remained operative into the late 1850s.

the territories, previous to their enhancement in value, by the force of settlement and progressive neighboring improvements. There are also at present,
great openings for colored people to enter into the various industrial departments of business operations: laborers, mechanics, teachers, merchants and
shop-keepers, and professional men of every kind. These places are now open,
as much to the colored as the white man, in Canada, with little or no opposition
to his progress; at least in the character of prejudicial preferences on account of
race. And all of these, without any hesitancy, do we most cheerfully recommend
to the colored inhabitants of the United States.

But our preference to other places over the Canadas has been cursorily stated
in the foregoing part of this paper; and since the writing of that part, it would
seem that the predictions or apprehensions concerning the Provinces, are about
to be verified by the British Parliament and Home Government themselves.
They have virtually conceded, and openly expressed it—Lord Brougham in the
lead—that the English Provinces of North America must, ere long, cease to be
a part of the British domain, and become annexed to the United States.[30]

It is needless—however much we may regret the necessity of its acknowledgment—for us to stop our ears, shut our eyes, and stultify our senses against
the truth in this matter; since by so doing, it does not alter the case. Every political movement, both in England and the United States, favors such an issue,
and the sooner we acknowledge it, the better it will be for our cause, ourselves
individually, and the destiny of our people in this country.

These Provinces have long been burdensome to the British nation, and her
statesmen have long since discovered and decided as an indisputable predicate
in political economy, that any province as an independent State, is more profitable in a commercial consideration to a country, than when depending as one
of its colonies. As a child to the parent, or an apprentice to his master, so is a
colony to a State. And as the man who enters into business is to the manufacturer and importer, so is the colony which becomes an independent State, to the
country from which it recedes.

Great Britain is decidedly a commercial and money-making nation, and
counts closely on her commercial relations with any country. That nation or

---

30. In the interest of encouraging blacks to turn southward to Central and South
America, Delany attempted to give credence to rumors that the British would be willing
to allow proslavery interests in the United States to bring about the annexation of
Canada. Though an annexationist movement took hold in Montreal in the late 1840s, the
possibility of annexation remained remote. Moreover, the antislavery Lord Henry Peter
Brougham would have been the last person to accept annexation with such sanguinity;
on Brougham and Delany, see "Delany at the International Statistical Congress" in Part 4.

people which puts the largest amount of money into her coffers, are the people who may expect to obtain her greatest favors. This the Americans do; consequently—and we candidly ask you to mark the prediction—the British will interpose little or no obstructions to the Canadas, Cuba, or any other province or colony contiguous to this country, falling into the American Union; except only in such cases where there would be a compromise of her honor. And in the event of a seizure of any of these, there would be no necessity for such a sacrifice; it could readily be avoided by diplomacy.

Then, there is little hope for us on this continent, short of those places where by reason of their numbers, there is the greatest combination of strength and interests on the part of the colored race.

We have ventured to predict a reduction of the now nominally free into slave States. Already has this "reign of terror" and dreadful work of destruction commenced. We give you the quotation from a Mississippi paper, which will readily be admitted as authority in this case:

> "Two years ago a law was passed by the California Legislature granting *one year* to the owners of slaves carried into the territory previous to the adoption of the Constitution, to remove them beyond the limits of the State. Last year the provision of this law *was extended twelve months longer.* We learn by the late California papers that a bill has just passed the Assembly, by a vote of 33 to 21, *continuing the same law in force until* 1855. The provisions of this bill embraces *slaves who have been carried to California since the adoption of her Constitution,* as well as those who were there previously. The large majority by which it passed, and the opinions advanced during the discussion, *indicates a more favorable state of sentiment in regard to the rights of slave holders in California than we supposed existed."*—(*Mississippian*)

No one who is a general and intelligent observer of the politics of this country, will, after reading this, doubt for a moment the final result.

At present, there is a proposition under consideration in California, to authorize the holding of a Convention to amend the Constitution of that State, which doubtless will be carried into effect; when there is no doubt that a clause will be inserted, granting the right to *hold slaves at discretion* in the State.[31] This being done, it will meet with general favor throughout the country by the

---

31. During the early 1850s, proslavery forces gained strength in the California state legislature. Though California remained a free state, the California Fugitive Slave Law of 1852, upheld by a proslavery Supreme Court, gave whites arbitrary power to return blacks to southern states and allowed slaveowners to bring their slaves into California for unlimited periods of time.

American people, and the *policy be adopted on the State's right principle.*—This alone is necessary, in addition to the insufferable Fugitive Slave Law, and the recent nefarious Nebraska Bill[32]—which is based upon this very boasted American policy of the State's right principle—to reduce the free to slave States, without a murmur from the people. And did not the Nebraska Bill disrespect the feelings and infringe upon the political rights of Northern *white* people, its adoption would be hailed with loud shouts of approbation, from Portland to San Francisco.

That, then, which is left for us to do, is to *secure* our liberty; a position which shall fully *warrant* us *against* the *liability* of such monstrous political crusades and riotous invasions of our rights. Nothing less than a national indemnity, indelibly fixed by virtue of our own sovereign potency, will satisfy us as a redress of grievances for the unparalleled wrongs, undisguised impositions, and unmitigated oppression, which we have suffered at the hands of this American people.

And what wise politician would otherwise conclude and determine? None, we dare say. And a people who are incapable of this discernment and precaution, are incapable of self-government, and incompetent to direct their own political destiny. For our own part, we spurn to treat for liberty on any other terms or conditions.

It may not be inapplicable, in this particular place, to quote from high authority, language which has fallen under our notice, since this report has been under our consideration. The quotation is worth nothing, except to show that the position assumed by us, is a natural one, which constitutes the essential basis of self-protection.

Said Earl Aberdeen[33] recently in the British House of Lords, when referring to the great question which is now agitating Europe:—"One thing alone is certain, that the only way to obtain a sure and honorable peace, is to *acquire a position* which may *command* it; and to gain such a position *every nerve and sinew* of the empire should be strained. The pickpocket who robs us is not to be let off because he offers to restore our purse;" and his Grace might have justly added, "should never thereafter be intrusted or confided in."

The plea doubtless will be, as it already frequently has been raised, that to remove from the United States, our slave brethren would be left without a hope. They already find their way in large companies to the Canadas, and they have

---

32. The Kansas-Nebraska Act of 1854 repealed the territorial limits on slavery established by the Missouri Compromise (1821) and gave settlers of future states the power to vote on whether to legalize slavery in their state constitutions.

33. The earl of Aberdeen, George Hamilton Gordon (1784–1860), became prime minister in 1852; his popular coalition government fell apart when England became involved in the Crimean War of 1854.

only to be made sensible that there is as much freedom for them South, as there is North; as much protection in Mexico as in Canada; and the fugitive slave will find it a much pleasanter journey and more easy of access, to wend his way from Louisiana and Arkansas to Mexico, than thousand of miles through the slave-holders of the South and slave-catchers of the North, to Canada. Once into Mexico, and his farther exit to Central and South America and the West Indies, would be certain. There would be no obstructions whatever. No miserable, half-starved, servile Northern slave-catchers by the way, waiting cap in hand, ready and willing to do the bidding of their contemptible southern masters.

No prisons, nor Court Houses, as slave-pens and garrisons, to secure the fugitive and rendezvous the mercenary gangs, who are bought as military on such occasions. No perjured Marshals, bribed Commissioners, nor hireling counsel, who, spaniel-like, crouch at the feet of Southern slave-holders, and cringingly tremble at the crack of their whip. No, not as may be encountered throughout his northern flight, there are none of these to be found or met with in his travels from the Bravo del Norte to the dashing Orinoco[34]—from the borders of Texas to the boundaries of Peru.

Should anything occur to prevent a successful emigration to the South—Central, South America, and the West Indies—we have no hesitancy, rather than remain in the United States, the merest subordinates and serviles of the whites, should the Canadas still continue separate in their political relations from this country, to recommend to the great body of our people, to remove to Canada West, where being politically equal to the whites, physically united with each other by a concentration of strength; when worse comes to worse, we may be found, not as a scattered, weak and impotent people, as we now are separated from each other throughout the Union, but a united and powerful body of freemen, mighty in politics, and terrible in any conflict which might ensue, in the event of an attempt at the disturbance of our political relations, domestic repose, and peaceful firesides.

Now, fellow-countrymen, we have done. Into your ears have we recounted your own sorrows; before your own eyes have we exhibited your wrongs; into your own hands have we committed your own cause. If these should prove a failure to remedy this dreadful evil, to assuage this terrible curse which has come upon us; the fault will be yours and not ours; since we have offered you a healing balm for every sorely aggravated wound.

(*Proceedings of the National Emigration Convention of Colored People; Held at Cleveland, Ohio, on Thursday, Friday and Saturday, the 24th, 25th and 26th of August, 1854* [Pittsburgh: A. A. Anderson, 1854], pp. 33–70)

---

34. The Bravo del Norte (also known as the Rio Grande) flows between Texas and Mexico; the Orinico flows from the border of Brazil south to the Atlantic.

Political Aspect of the Colored People
of the United States

AT THE 1854 National Emigration Convention, the delegates established a National Board of Commissioners—a committee of nine charged to continue to explore the possibilities of black emigration. When the board met in Pittsburgh one year later, on 24 August 1855, Delany, its president, presented an overview of the political situation of blacks in the Americas.

GENTLEMEN OF THE NATIONAL BOARD OF COMMISSIONERS:

FELLOW COUNTRYMEN—According to the provisions of the Constitution, we have met in the first Annual Council of the Board, to interchange opinions pertaining to the interests of our race, and we wish that it were in our power, to bring before you such suggestions, as might be adequate to the importance of this great and now all absorbing subject; a subject fraught with considerations of greater magnitude, whether relating to our domestic or foreign relations— for such we have indeed—than all others combined; although but seldom if ever so considered by those termed the leading Colored men in the United States, simply because they suffer their interests to be swallowed up in common with those of their oppressors, and content themselves with vociferating the claims that they are part and parcel of the body politic—the sovereign people of this country—and it would seem, judging from their continual acts, desire not to know nor acknowledge a difference.

This most unfortunately is one of those political errors and blunders, so long committed by our political leaders in the different States, especially the free, until it has become the leading established policy among them, though fatal everywhere, in its consequences and results.

Our Domestic Relations should first claim our attention, although we regret to say, that amid the world of matter that should be at our commands, we have but little at hand in this department, to present in a tangible form before you.

We shall first call your attention to the Southern or Slave States.

The Constitutions of Texas and Arkansas prohibit slavery forever from being abolished, thus perpetuating slavery within their boundaries. In neither of these States has the free colored man any privileges, but those permitted by the merest sufferance. Louisiana has provided by law, for the education of her colored children, and also acknowledges the competency of a colored person as witness in a Court of Justice. Yet the same State denies the right of a free colored person entering the state as a sojourner, even as a passenger on the public highway of the great Mississippi. Should they do so, they are seized and imprisoned to await the terrors of the law.

South Carolina also, though her Governor recommends the establishment of the marriage rites among the slave population, and a law prohibiting the separation of families by purchase. Nevertheless, here, as in Louisiana, a free colored person from the free States, whatever may be the business which calls him hither, though he be an American born, or a British subject, cannot enter that State without imprisonment during the stay, should he be employed on a vessel, and the risk of being sold into perpetual slavery if not connected with a vessel.

Georgia, too, a State proverbial for its acts of oppression, and inseparable connection with the slave trade, as associated in the early memory of every colored person in the country, has, during the current year, recommended through her officials the education of the slaves, so that by teaching them to read the bible, they may be prevented from engendering a spirit of insubordination and insurrection. But in all other respects, she is as despotic and hostile to the interests of the free colored people as any other slave-holding confederates.

Virginia opposes the amelioration of the condition of the slave in any respect, but strongly recommends Colonization to Liberia, and the passage of a law, forcibly to expel from the State, every free colored person. This State also, by custom and example (if not by expressed law) encourages distinctions to be made on account of color or admixture of blood, among the colored people, by impressing them with the idea of superiority of the mixed blood, on account of its proximity to white—provided it is more than what is called "half blood." She, as also does Maryland, prohibits the ingress of free colored persons, or even the return of one who may have been a native resident, if intending to remain out of the State over fifteen days. Nor can a colored person pass out of either of those States, on any kind of conveyance, without first obtaining the assurance of some white, that he or she is not the escaping slave of some Southern "master" or "mistress." For a violation of these provisions, they hazard the penalty of being "publicly whipped at the post," imprisoned and sold into slavery at discretion.

Delaware has refused to abolish slavery from her deteriorating soil, and prohibits by a barbarous provision, free colored persons from going into the State, under severe and cruel penalties. During the current year, a free woman was sold for life, for being found in the State contrary to law.

Nor does the Western division of the slave propagating States, present a more favorable aspect in the political horizon. Here the tempest seems to rage with unabated, if not increased fury.

Kentucky, the State once full of hope and expectation, has repudiated the idea of a contemplated act of Emancipation, adopted a new Constitution, providing strongly against the abolition of slavery, with no reasonable hope of a better state of things for ages to come, and now sustains a most ultra pro-slavery legislature, with scarcely a press in the State, which utters a sentiment in favor of freedom. Nor is Tennessee behind Kentucky in her march of retrogation [sic]. And although we cannot refer to any recent acts of newly devised oppression, yet so steeped is she in the elements of despotism, that her march is equal to that of her contiguous Northern sister.

Mississippi still stands a living reality of American infamy. With a constitution also, which prohibits forever the emancipation of the slaves, it has for years been the great barracoon state or slave pen receptacle of all human cattle which embark down the Mississippi valley, where they are gathered in droves preparatory to their final exhibition for the Auctioneer's hammer, or a last resort, the slave bazaar in New Orleans. Missouri vies with the last named State in recent acts of despotism. By cruel enactments she prohibits the ingress of free colored persons from other states and also expels from the State, those of her free colored residents. Forced by measures the most stringent and extreme, the colored inhabitants of that State, especially those resident in St. Louis, have been driven and compelled to fly in every direction.

California by three successive acts of the legislature, has granted to slaveholders the right to take their slaves into the State, for and during the term of three consecutive years; and now seriously contemplates its permanent establishment, which doubtless will be consummated during the next year. In this state the colored people are deprived of the right of testimony in the courts or any case of litigation, wherein their evidence conflicts with that of a white person. By this despotic provision, many of the native Californians, who were a part of the independent sovereign people under Mexico, have been degraded to the humiliating condition of political nonentities. And by a recent decision of the supreme court of that State, given in a case growing out of a suit in which a Mongolian's evidence conflicted with that of a white man's, in which a demurrer was entered, the Chinese stand in the same political position as the black man. He too is degraded to the level of a slave.[1]

Colored children in this State, like that of Louisiana, have to a certain extent, the benefit of funds for the Public Schools.

The non-slaveholding States next claim our attention. In Maine, the people stand on a political level, there being no political distinctions known in her civil code.

Vermont occupies the same proud political position, with the enactment of a personal protection bill by her legislature, which annuls all and every conflicting United States law. In neither of these states it is thought, would be permitted, an execution of the insufferable Fugitive Slave Law. This, however, has yet to be tested, and upon this point, let us not be too sanguine, and expect more than can be warranted.

Massachusetts has twice trailed her lofty Banner in the dust, by yielding obedience to the despotic slave power.[2] But during the last session of her General Court — Legislature — she has somewhat wiped out the stain which so defiled her, by the passage of the "Personal Liberty Bill,"[3] an act which teaches the menacing impudence of the Central Government of Washington, that the consuming fire of Seventy-Six has not yet been extinguished by the dampening showers of the engines of the United States Navy.

Rhode Island too stands untrammelled in regard to the rights of suffrage; in this particular all stand on a political equality. But in other departments of her municipal provisions, we are not so well advised.

Connecticut still lingers under the "Blue Law" influence of witchcraft superstitions,[4] many laws still existing against the colored people, which are both disgraceful and cruel. None of the political privileges exercised and enjoyed by the colored people in the foregoing states — as we are advised of — are exercised and enjoyed by the colored people in this state. There prejudice is a growing ulcer, which seems fast to be penetrating the vitals of the body politic. The colored inhabitants, with praiseworthy efforts, hold state Conventions for the removal of

1. Delany refers to *People v. Hall* (1854), in which the California Supreme Court upheld legislation barring Chinese immigrants from testifying against whites as consistent with laws already on the books barring black testimony against whites. According to the court, "black" was a generic term term relevant to all nonwhites.

2. A reference to the fugitive slave renditions of Thomas Sims (1851) and Anthony Burns (1854).

3. Massachusetts's Personal Liberty Act of 1843 forbade state officials and institutions to support the pursuit of fugitive slaves. The Personal Liberty Bill of 1855 attempted to do the same, though it was in direct conflict with the Fugitive Slave Act of 1850.

4. Laws related to Sabbath observance and other religious practices, mandated by church authorities in the theocratic colony of New Haven during the seventeenth century. The laws got their name from the blue paper they were printed on.

restrictions; but deaf to all entreaties, she still holds with iron grasp her colored brother by the throat.

New York permits her colored people to exercise a humiliating suffrage by the degrading property qualification; and during the last three or four consecutive years, has contemptuously refused to acknowledge their equality. There too have they been industrious and assiduous, calling State Conventions, getting up Petitions, and even in several instances, sending delegates of their own people to the Capitol to urge their claims in person before their rulers. This year they also hold one, for the same political object. In this state the Public school privileges are great—greater perhaps than in any other in the Union—except Massachusetts—but unlike the last named state, they are based on complexional principles, the "Colored school" system prevailing.

New Jersey is still a Slave State, no act of emancipation having passed the legislature; consequently the colored people who enjoy freedom there, do so simply by *passive* indifference on the part of the whites. Of course they have not even the poor privilege of suffrage, and what other privileges politically they enjoy, we are not advised.

In Pennsylvania where at one time colored men did exercise the poor privileges of suffrage—balloting into office their peer and superior—by an alteration of the constitution in 1838, they were totally deprived of that privilege. In 1847, as an offset to the Act of 1793, a law passed the legislature, to protect the free colored people, by prohibiting the discretionate [*sic*] seizure of that class of people, and thereby put a stop to kidnapping. In 1851 a Bill was introduced in the same body, to prohibit colored persons from coming in the state from any direction whatever. The next year, 1852, a Bill passed appropriating two thousand dollars to aid the state Colonization society. This was a bold stagger toward falling on their knees before the uplifted lash of their Southern masters. During the last legislature, by the assiduity and perseverance of the colored people in different parts of the state, and the liberality of several members of that body, a Bill was introduced asking an amendment of the Constitution, and removing the word *white*, so as to extend equal unqualified suffrage. In this we failed; and notwithstanding the many county and state Conventions held by the colored people of this commonwealth, with the most urgent and thrilling appeals for justice, the political heart and conscience appear to be hardened and seared against every claim relative to their manhood. In this state we are still permitted to testify as competent witnesses in courts of litigation. The "Colored school" system also pervades, and in the eastern and interior counties, a stupid prejudice exists against the colored people, which is only equaled by the ignorance of those who manifest it. Notwithstanding all this, there are those among us who cling to Pennsylvania as to a Paradise.

In Ohio, the colored people are acknowledged by law, as competent witnesses in the *Courts*, the disability under which they labored, being removed some three or four years ago, a provision has also been made for the education of their children—the "Colored school system"—and a person of more than half white has the right of suffrage. There, as in several other states mentioned, they hold almost annually State Conventions, for the purpose of obtaining their stricken down rights, but with no more hope of success than their Eastern brethren; although the advantages which they now enjoy may be attributed to their own efforts; the whites having extended such privileges as they conceive might be enjoyed by the blacks may grant no more.

In some of the school Districts, as in Cincinnati, they have their own directors—a body of colored men holding a subordinate position to the white Directors—and although having no discretionary or primary power, they have not the privilege of voting for themselves, but must be selected by the whites.

Humiliating as this is, a large portion of them, bow to it with pleasurable acceptance.

The barbarous laws of Indiana and Illinois still continue to disgrace their statutes,—especially the former, which prohibits blacks and mulattoes from entering the state, on any pretext, provided they are free.

A slaveholder may with impunity pass into the state with his slaves, and meet everywhere with courtesy, smiles and protection.

But very recently a free colored man in the capital of Indiana was seized upon as a fugitive slave, claimed by a Reverend Slaveholder in Missouri, although he had for more than ten years previous, resided in the city of Indianapolis.

But after clearly establishing his freedom by the testimony of an office-holder under the United States Government in Georgia, the United States Court before which he was tried, compelled him to bear the whole expense of litigation,—a sum amounting to considerable above one thousand dollars.[5]

Nor are the Territories free from the curse of oppression. Oregon has instituted a law, prohibiting a colored person from testifying against a white, and also from settling in the Territory. And those who now reside there, do so by the merest sufferance.

The outrages in Kansas, are familiar to every one. To crown their acts of infamy a law has recently passed the legislature making it a crime, punishable with

5. This notorious case occurred in Indianapolis in 1853, when a Missourian named Pleasant Ellington, who claimed to be a Methodist minister, asserted that the Indianapolis free black John Freeman was his slave. Though Freeman eventually proved to the satisfaction of the U.S. commissioner that he had never been Ellington's slave, he was jailed during much of the trial and required to pay court costs, including the salary of his guards. He successfully sued for $2,000 in damages but never received payment.

death, to take into or carry out of that territory, any person held as a slave for the purpose of freeing them. Here upon this point comment would be an idle waste of words and time. It will hereafter be seen whether or not the policy laid down by the Cleveland Convention, of which you are but the agents, was that of political sagacity, and well-advised intellect, guided and directed by intelligent forethought, wisdom, and prudence; or as those who claim to be alone competent to lead and advise us assert a policy pernicious in its tendency, and destructive in its results to us as a people. We are satisfied, that our position is the only tenable ground, and our policy the only feasible scheme or plan of operation, by which to accomplish our elevation from degradation, and redemption from thraldom as a race.

Foreign relations next claim our attention. In this direction there is a hope; if not the genial rays of a sun, to gladden our hearts and brighten our pathway—at least we may descry the twinkling of a distant star, to direct our weary footsteps in our onward march on this long and tiresome journey.

The long anticipated annexation of the Sandwich Islands to the United States has proved a failure, the scheme being overthrown by the far-sightedness and wise precaution of Prince Kamehameha the III, king of the country.[6] This nobleman has not yet forgotten the insults received by him in various parts of this country, while on a mission as Minister Plenipotentiary, Envoy Extraordinary, from the government of his country to the cabinet at Washington. He is a gentleman of distinguished attainments, a shrewd politician, and will never consent to the suicidal scheme of annexation.

A policy devised by a pernicious pro-slavery cabinet at Washington, which if consummated, would end not only in the annihilation of the name of the Sandwich people, but, in the total extinction of every right and privilege belonging to that people, the whole being usurped and swallowed up by the impudent assumption of "white superiority." The Sandwich Islands, then, for the present, may be regarded as safe; and, it is hoped, the people never will so far forget their own national dignity, nor undervalue their own native sovereignty, as to yield to any terms so disparaging and degrading. This may not be feared, while the influence of the excellent man, now their sovereign head, pervades their councils.

The deep seated scheme for the invasion of Hayti has been signally overthrown, and the wretch who was sent as the accredited agent of the White House conclave at Washington, to the Dominican part of the Island, has been driven away dejected and despised; and his American masters at the Federal City, covered with disgrace.[7] Rather than the consummation of such a design—

6. Prince Kamehameha III (1814–54) thwarted annexation efforts in 1840; that same year he established a representative legislature and gave the vote to all male citizens.

7. During the early 1850s, the United States attempted to establish a naval station on

the subjugation of Hayti by the United States—would we see that splendid Isle sunk beneath the swelling waves of the Caribbean Sea forever. But you need entertain no fears in this direction, as the Haytien people are too intelligent and too conversant with the outlandish prejudices of the Americans, for a moment to entertain any such proposition, however pretending, emanating from the whites of this country. And with such men at their head as the distinguished Sovereign who now rules the Empire, and his accomplished Ministers and wise Imperial Senate—the thought is a very insult. Hayti then is safe, doubly fortified; having the two grand elements of virtue and loyalty.

The marauding crusade against Cuba has also failed, the Spanish Government adopting the policy some time since hinted to them, of fortifying the Island by the establishment of colored soldiery.[8] Under such circumstances as those which for five years past have distracted that Island, black military troops must necessarily be the most secure, because the most *reliable* defenders of the country and Spanish interests. More naturally prone to obedience, more loyal and submissive, patient and forgiving, and greater lovers of their nativity and homes than the whites; it is but necessary to make them sensible of their true condition and the relation which they bear to the American haters of the Negro race, with an assurance of equality of rights, and there is not force enough in the United States, to wrest Cuba from the Crown of Spain. With the blacks as guardians and defenders, she must and will stand in defiance of all the schemes and machinations now being planned against Spain in the United States. With the aid of the blacks, Cuba is safe, without it, she must fall a prey to American cupidity.

The despicable puerile attempt by the buccaneer Walker, to overthrow the governments of Lower California and Nicaragua,[9] has resulted in a most signal chastisement of the temerity and impudence of that marauder, by the countries against which he directed his expeditions. But he was not without encouragement from high quarters, as the government of the United States, doubtless in

---

the Dominican Republic, which Delany regarded as evidence that the United States intended to invade Haiti. In late 1854 President Franklin Pierce sent Texas general William Cazneau to negotiate for the station, and Spain, in response, signed a peace treaty with the Dominican Republic that thwarted Pierce's plans.

8. Spain regularly came to Cuba's (and its own) defense during the late 1840s and 1850s in response to U.S. annexationists and filibusterers. In 1851 Spanish forces overcame Narciso López (1797–1851) and his compatriots, and in 1852 the Spanish put down the "Conspiracy of Vuelta Abajo," which had been organized by López's brother-in-law.

9. The most notorious U.S. filibuster of the 1850s, William Walker (1824–60) invaded Lower California in 1853–54 and Nicaragua in June 1855; both invasions met with eventual failure. On 12 September 1860 he was shot by a firing squad in Honduras after another failed effort to conquer Central America.

anticipation fully devised—had forestalled this crusade of Walker, by a barbarous attack upon San Juan or Greytown,[10] but a few months previous, in which an unarmed people without military defence, were stormed, sacked, being cut to pieces by a naval force of the United States.

Nor have they yet done, since through the same national agency, another piratical expedition under one Captain Kinney, a Pennsylvanian, has within a few weeks past, sailed for Nicaragua.[11] Reports inform us, that he and party have reached their destination, doubtless under the protection of the United States; as Wheeler[12] the recently appointed Minister from the Court at Washington to that government, is a slaveholder from North Carolina, who it is but reasonable to suppose, goes under full instructions concerning this expedition, and all other matters pertaining to American interests, whether legitimately the province of his mission or not. But we are informed that the Nicaragua Government is fully advised of their designs, and fully prepared to meet them. We trust this may be so, since the sole object of the Americans in desiring a foot hold in foreign territories, is the servitude and enslavement of the African and colored races.

Already has there been carried on within the last twelve months a commerce by the enslavement of the Chinese, and Yucatan Indians. These have been principally carried into Cuba, and purchased by the parties in league with the filibusters. The Chinese are decoyed under the pretext of apprenticeship, and the Yucatecoes openly sold as prisoners of war.

An advisory Correspondence is now being opened and carried on with foreign countries. On the tenth day of July last an official commissioner sailed from the United States to the dominions of His Imperial Majesty, Faustin I., Emperor of Hayti, as the representative of the colored people of the United States, fully instructed on the subject of his mission.[13] He also holds a discretionary com-

10. In 1854 the U.S. warship *Cyane* bombarded Greytown (San Juan del Norte) in retaliation for damage done to U.S. property in Nicaragua.

11. Backed by New York speculators, Henry Lawrence Kinney (1814–62) set sail with 100 followers in an ultimately failed attempt to set up a slave state in Nicaragua.

12. The proslavery advocate and slaveowner John Hill Wheeler (1806–82) of North Carolina was appointed U.S. minister to Nicaragua in 1854. He enraged Nicaraguans by supporting the efforts of William Walker and other filibusterers who sought to bring parts of Central America and the Caribbean under U.S. control.

13. The black Episcopal priest James Theodore Holly (1829–1911) was commissioned by the delegates of the 1854 National Emigration Convention to travel to Haiti and develop closer ties between U.S. and Haitian blacks. There he met with Faustin Soulouque (1785–1867), who was born a slave in Haiti and became president of the country in 1847. (Soulouque declared himself Emperor Faustin I in 1849.) In 1857 Holly published *Vindication of the Capacity of the Negro Race*, which made the case for black emigration to Haiti.

mission, to Jamaica, St. Thomas, Nassau, Martinique, Guadeloupe and Central America. He is a black gentleman of distinguished qualifications, literary acquirements and political sagacity. One who doubtless will fill his mission with honor and credit, and we may henceforth hope for a medium of communication to be opened between the colored people of the United States and their brethren of foreign countries, never before dreamed of. By this commission will be established the much needed organization of intermediate communication between all of the colored races on the Western Continent. This is a desideratum in the political prospects of our race, "a consummation devotedly to be wished for." Without it, we may hope for little; with it we may expect much.

Emigration strictly is neither domestic nor foreign, but a policy which belongs to both aspects of our political advancement. And while anxiously contemplating the vista in this direction, the threatening storm of oppression is seen giving way, the lowering clouds of despair dispersing, the sunbeam of hope to radiate in every direction, and the clear unobscured sky of promise and joy, spreading fully to our view, dissipating every doubt as to the future prosperity and successful elevation of our race.

The Canadas, from their near proximity, and easiness of access, are made the point of emigration by the colored people of the United States; and notwithstanding the studied opposition made against it by a class of colored gentlemen known and acknowledged as leaders and great men among their people in various parts of the country, those who prefer this country to going elsewhere; the principles of Emigration are fast becoming the leading policy among our people in this country. We are happy to lay before you the intelligence, that the common people generally have entered into this measure with might and main, and whether the "leading and great men," go with us or not—we have fully accomplished our object. We have opened an avenue to the portals of political equality, without which man is but a cipher anywhere.

From every direction, East, West, North and South, our people are flocking into this beautiful country, and substantially settling themselves down by becoming possessors of the soil, as loyal British subjects. There is more real estate owned at this time by the colored people of the Canadas, the greater part of which has been obtained within three years, and since the propagation of the principles of emigration by our agencies, than by all the balance of the colored people in North America together. These are indisputable facts, which figures will demonstrate.

The only successful remedy for the evils we endure, is to place ourselves in a position of potency, independently of our oppressors. All intelligent political economists and historians know this, our oppressors know this, and hence their strenuous opposition to our settlement in the Canadas. And it is a fallacy to talk of remaining here in the United States for the sake of the slave. Our influence must be tenfold greater when forming a part of the sovereign people of any country, whether as an independent people or the constituent part of another nation,—hence the desire to seize upon Hayti, and prevent the emancipation of Cuba. Hence, also, the burning jealousy existing in the United States against the British and French West Indies. We would that our political leaders and great men could be made to see these things.

It will be as fulsome ere long, to see or hear a colored person in this country opposing emigration as a measure of elevation to political equality, as to see or hear a white American opposing his own national Independence.

God surely is in the work—and how singularly is his declaration verified, that he will choose the "poor and ignorant of this world, to teach the great and wise"—and with much thankfulness as to Him who rules and presides over the destiny of nations, we give all the praise and glory—sensible that he has originated so great a project, with the humble and obscure.

We present you not the result of any hasty conclusion, but the work and sequel of serious study, reflection, and experience of years of intelligent maturity.

Pittsburgh, Aug. 24th 1855

M. R. DELANY

(*Provincial Freeman*, 13 October 1855, vol. 2, pp. 97–98)

What Does It Mean?

THE 23 FEBRUARY 1856 issue of the *Provincial Freeman* hailed the "arrival of our esteemed and talented friend, Dr. M. R. Delany, of Pittsburgh, Pa., in this town [Chatham, Canada West], yesterday morning" and featured an advertisement for his new doctor's office on William Street, noting that Delany "practices in Chronic Diseases, and the Diseases of Women and Children, in particular." Less than three months later, the editors announced in the issue of 10 May 1856 that Delany would be added to "our usual force of efficient contributors." Douglass's editorial in the 4 July 1856 issue of *Frederick Douglass' Paper*, which half-heartedly commended the African American community in Canada while warning black Americans against emigrating to Canada en masse, elicited one of Delany's punchiest contributions.

We promised to give in a series of articles, some thoughts to the readers of the *Freeman*, on the leading political measures of the day, both of Europe and America, but have been induced to turn the course of this article, to head off the charming fascinations of a great magnetizer, who like the great boa of the desert, bewitches his victim, just before crushing it between his hideous coils, when belching forth his slaver, covering it all over with slime, swallows it down, before the creature has time to make a struggling resistance.

In *Frederick Douglass' Paper*, a copy of which has just been put into our hands, we find the leading editorial captioned "Canada—Liberia—H. Ford Douglass—Mary A. Shadd."[1]

---

1. See *Frederick Douglass' Paper*, 4 July 1856, p. 2. Hezekiah Ford Douglas (1831–65) escaped from slavery in 1846 and emerged as a leader of the black abolitionist community in Cleveland, Ohio. He embraced emigrationism in 1852 and became coproprietor of the *Provincial Freeman* in 1856. Mary Ann Shadd Cary emigrated to Canada West in 1851 and worked with Samuel Ringgold Ward to publish the first edition of *Provincial Freeman* in 1853. She was instrumental in transforming the newspaper into a weekly, and between 1854 and 1857 served as its principal editor.

The author of this article, commences with the declaration that "as the servant and journalist of our people" it is his duty to "search out and bring to light the awakened mental abilities of individuals connected and identified with our race," and goes on to descant largely upon our identity wherever found on this continent, whether in the United States or Canada, North or South America, or the West Indies, manifesting great regard for us of Canada, sympathizing with our movement, with the declaration that his not having come to Canada, has never prevented him from "looking with a friendly eye upon us," nor doing anything in his power to advance our interests.

Whence comes all at once, all this pretended friendly feeling? Does any one believe the writer to be sincere? For our part, we frankly admit we have no confidence in it.

Miss Mary Ann Shadd (now Mrs. Cary,) is made the special subject of compliment, with traits of talents and literary acquirements, which places her without an equal among the colored ladies of the United States. Is this a recent discovery? Are the talents and acquired ability of Miss Shadd just beginning to develop themselves that this great keen eyed expositor of our "awakened mental abilities" has just discovered them? Is Miss Shadd of to-day any more deserving of a complimentary notice than Miss Shadd of a few years ago whom *Frederick Douglass* never deigned to notice but to disparage?—Fie, fie! it is simply ridiculous, and savors so much of low cunning, that we are constrained to treat it with profound disrespect.

There is another fact somewhat remarkable, that in his sharp discernment of our "awakened mental abilities," this "journalist" whose business he says it is to "bring to light individuals connected with our race," could during a whole year, overlook such a person connected with the *Provincial Freeman*, as the industrious, untiring, indefatigable Publisher of the paper, *Isaac D. Shadd*,[2] whose urbanity and perseverance might well be emulated by Mr. Douglass himself. Mr. Shadd, though a young man and comparatively inexperienced as such, is one of the *Editors* as well as the Publisher of the paper, and gives to his readers occasionally, a very creditable editorial. In fact, he is a *writer* who with more experience and practice, will compare favorably with his cotemporaries of the corpse editorial. But Mr. Shadd was too small for the discernment of a large perception, and therefore must keep in his proper place as many others of us have been made to do, by the silence of the same great voice.

It is familiar with every one, how *Frederick Douglass* denounced the Emigra-

<hr/>

2. Isaac D. Shadd (1829–96) emigrated to Canada West in 1851 with his sister Mary Ann Shadd (Cary) and was involved as a subscription agent, editor, and publisher of the *Provincial Freeman*. In the late 1850s he supported Delany's African emigration project.

tion movement, designating all those concerned in propagating the sentiments as being Colonizationists, and misleading our people, greatly to the detriment of the cause of the slave, and elevation of the free in the United States. In this he was readily and vehemently joined by his adherents and echoes in New Bedford, New York City, Albany, Buffalo, Philadelphia, Columbus, Ohio, Cincinnati, Chicago, and several other places, all of whom seemed to know no other purpose for living, than to move, say and do, as Frederick Douglass moved, said and did, or bade them do.

But what do we now behold? Why this same denouncer of the Emigration movement, making the barefaced declaration, that he has ever looked with a friendly eye upon us! Surely, Emigration must be safe, now that Frederick Douglass has spoken in favor of it!

Again: what more do we see? Why this same denouncer of our movement and policy, actually lauding Colonization to the skies, by eulogising Liberia and Roberts, Benson, and Yates, the favorite pets and supple minions of Colonization.[3] And it is impossible, for either the New York "Colonization Journal," nor the Philadelphia Herald, to give an article more genuine in favor of Colonization than the latter part of the leading article in *Frederick Douglass' Paper*, written by *Frederick Douglass* himself.

Had we or any other Emigrationist have said one tithe—nay even one word in favor of Liberia in the same spirit as the lengthy encomium written by Mr. Douglass, we would have been denounced as the worst enemies of our race, by the very persons who will now drink down as a nectarine draught, all that has been said of that country and its men, the first of whom—J. J. Roberts—has long been accused and suspected, as having been concerned in the *Slave Trade*. But it is enough for them to know, that Mr. Douglass approbates the Colonization scheme, and the *echo* may be heard from New Bedford to Chicago.

The reader will not fail to detect the brazen impudence with which the editor of that paper, always couples the Emigration movement with Colonization. Hence in his subtle attempt at commending Emigrationists, he presumes to draw a curtain before our faces, to hide the hideous deformity of his new position.

But there is something behind this curtain: a monster the construction of whose deformity, will alarm and dismay those heretofore who delighted in the

---

3. Delany refers to black Liberian political leaders, the most notable of whom, Joseph Jenkins Roberts, he had previously attacked in his 1849 essay "Liberia" and elsewhere. Roberts resigned the presidency of Liberia around the time that Delany wrote this article, and Stephen Allen Benson (1816–65), formerly of Maryland, became the second president of the Republic of Liberia. Beverly Page Yates (1811–83) had left Virginia for Liberia in 1829, and he served as vice president under Roberts and Benson.

exhibitions of the performer. And however much we desire in this great move-ment, the co-operation of all of our people—were it possible—the cause is going prosperiously [*sic*] on and will succeed—even without the approbation of the Rochester "journalist." We may here add, that the fling at the circulation of the *Provincial Freeman*, is a confounded gratuity, in harmony with the breath, that gave it utterance. The *Freeman* in fact, has a much larger circulation among the colored people than *Frederick Douglass' Paper*.

But we had quite forgotten our position, and must beg to thank the Editor of *Frederick Douglass' Paper*, for arresting the names of a few Emigrationists from the obscurity to which they were consigned, and showing to the public at large, that they might possibly possess some talents, and thereby merit his notice. For this we are very thankful, and bow uncovered with obsequious reverence!

M. R. D.

(*Provincial Freeman*, 12 July 1856, vol. 3, p. 50)[4]

---

4. On the same page, the editors also reprinted Delany's letter to the *Kent Advertiser* on how to prevent and treat cholera.

Letter to Garrison, 19 February 1859

DELANY'S EMIGRATION projects of the 1850s lacked any sort of significant funding. Thus one could speculate that in authoring a novel, *Blake*, Delany hoped to emulate the financial success of Stowe's *Uncle Tom's Cabin*. Though he probably began *Blake* in 1853 or 1854 as a "response" to Stowe that could help to fund black emigration to Central and South America, in writing to Garrison in 1859, Delany no doubt hoped for profits that would help to finance his new project of establishing an African American–led settlement in the Niger region of Africa (see Part 4).

NEW YORK, Feb 19th '59

MR. GARRISON — My Dear Sir: — I beg to call your attention to the Story of "Blake or The Huts of America" now being published in the "Anglo-African Magazine,"[1] and would wish that you would call the attention of Mssrs Phillips and Quincey [*sic*][2] also to it, gentlemen whom with yourself, have always taken so great an interest in anything emanating from bold people, which you have thought worthy of your attention. I am anxious to get a good publishing house to take it, as I know I could make a penny by it, and the chances for a negro in this department are so small, that unless some disinterested competent persons would indirectly aid in such a step, I almost despair of any chance.

The Story as it proceeds increases naturally in interest, there being no dull nor tame sameness, and whilst I have studiously guarded against harshness and offensiveness, I have given truth its full force in the pictures drawn. I have ma-

1. The *Anglo-African Magazine* was a black monthly published by Thomas Hamilton (1823–65) in New York City. Hamilton printed three sample chapters from *Blake* in the January 1859 issue (chs. 29–31) and then began to serialize the novel starting with the issue of February 1859.
2. Wendell Phillips (1811–84) and Edmund Quincy (1808–77), notable white abolitionists from Massachusetts who worked closely with Garrison.

turely and carefully written this work, and hope that it so far may meet your approbation and approval, that you may recommend it to the consideration of some publisher.

The language used may seem odd, but it is that made use of by the slave. The March No. will begin to open up the story so that you may begin to form some opinion of it. I would like to see your criticism of it so far, in the columns of the "Liberator."

It is written in Parts 2, pp. about 550 [ ],[3] and its course of publication in the Magazine, is not to interfere with its publication in book form whenever I can obtain a publisher.

I hope sir, you will give me just such aid as in your judgment it merits, and no more.

I am dear sir,
Very Respectfully
Your sincere friend,
M. R. Delany

P.S. The three chapters published in the first number of the Magazine, were full of errors, in consequence of the hurried manner in which it was got out, and the whole will be carefully revised and corrected as far as published up to the time, should the work be taken by a publisher.

(Garrison Papers, Boston Public Library/Rare Books Department)

3. At this point in the letter there are several obscure words in the manuscript.

Blake; or, The Huts of America

DELANY'S ONE WORK of fiction, *Blake; or, The Huts of America: A Tale of the Mississippi Valley, the Southern United States, and Cuba*, aspires to provide an uncommonly broad view of the problem of slavery in the Americas by focusing on the efforts of the eponymous hero to bring about a coordinated black revolution in Cuba and the United States. As Delany wrote Garrison, the novel consists of two parts and about eighty chapters. Most of Part I was published in 1859 in the *Anglo-African Magazine*; the novel was then printed in its entirety in the *Weekly Anglo-African* in issues running from November 1861 to late April or May 1862. Seventy-four chapters of the novel have been recovered, but the novel remains incomplete, as scholars have yet to locate the late April and May 1862 issues of the *Weekly Anglo-African*. The novel in its current form, which received its first book publication by Beacon Press in 1970, thus eerily keeps in suspense the question of whether Blake managed to bring about a successful hemispheric black revolution. The haunting final words of the extant novel come from the Cuban black revolutionary Gondolier: "Woe be unto those devils of whites, I say!" (*Weekly Anglo-African*, 20 April 1862, p. 1).

The following selections are taken from Part I, as printed in the *Anglo-African Magazine*, and Part II, as printed in the *Weekly Anglo-African*. In the first selection, "A Shadow," Blake, known at this point in the novel as "Henry Holland," has previously fled Colonel Franks's Mississippi plantation in response to Franks's sale of his wife, Maggie, and now returns to plant the seeds of his conspiracy among Franks's slaves, particularly Andy and Charles. (In the chapter there are also references to Maggie's parents, Mammy Judy and Daddy Joe; the slave woman Ailcey, who acts as a go-between among the slaves; and Blake's son, little Joe.) Though Blake never explicitly states the "secret" of his conspiracy, it becomes clear that he plans to spread word from plantation to plantation of a slave uprising that will occur at a particular agreed-upon moment under his direction. Blake's leadership remains central to the second selection, "Obscurity" and "The Interview," from Part II of the novel. Now in Cuba and newly reunited with his wife, who was known as "Lotty" before Blake purchased her freedom from the Garcia family, Blake announces his plan to lead a black uprising in

Cuba against the white ruling class. In the context of the 1850s, a time when the U.S. government regularly contemplated invading Cuba, Blake's plan for a black conspiracy poses a challenge to both the Cuban and the U.S. slave powers. In a scene that further ratifies Blake's leadership, he enlists in the conspiracy his cousin, the poet Placido (an actual historical figure who had been executed by Cuban authorities in 1844 for alleged insurrectionary activities). The section ends with Blake about to sail to Africa to gain additional recruits for his Pan-African uprising in the Americas.

Part I.

Chapter XI. A Shadow.

'Ah, boys! here you are, true to your promise,' said Henry, as he entered a covert in the thicket adjacent the cotton place, late on Sunday evening, 'have you been waiting long?'

'Not very,' replied Andy, 'not mo' dan two-three ouahs.'

'I was fearful you would not come, or if you did before me, that you would grow weary, and leave.'

'Yeh no call to doubt us Henry, case yeh fine us true as ole steel!'

'I know it,' answered he, 'but you know Andy, that when a slave is once sold at auction, all respect for him—'

'O pshaw! we ain' goin' to heah nothin' like dat a tall! case—'

'No!' interrupted Charles, 'all you got to do Henry, is to tell we boys what you want, an' we're your men.'

'That's the talk for me!'

'Well, what you doin' here?' enquired Charles.

'W'at brought yeh back from Jackson so soon?' farther enquired Andy.

'How did you get word to meet me here?'

'By Ailcey; she give me the stone, an' I give it to Andy, an' we both sent one apiece back. Did'nt you git 'em?'

'Yes, that's the way I knew you intended to meet me,' replied Henry.

'So we thought,' said Charles, 'but tell us Henry, what you want us to do.'

'I suppose you know all about the sale, that they had me on the auction block, but ordered a postponement, and—'

'That's the very pint we cant understand, although I'm in the same family with you,' interrupted Charles.

'But tell us Henry, what yeh doin' here?' impatiently enquired Andy.

'Yes,' added Charles, 'we want to know.'

'Well, I'm a *runaway*, and from this time forth, I swear—I do it religiously—that I'll never again serve any white man living!'

'That's the pint I wanted to git at before,' explained Charles, 'as I cant understan' why you run away, after your release from Jack Harris, an'—'

'Nah I, nuthah!' interrupted Andy.

'It seems to me,' continued Charles, 'that I'd 'ave went before they 'tempted to sell me, an' that you're safer now than before they had you on the block.'

'Dat's da way I look at it,' responded Andy.

'The stopping of the sale was to deceive his wife, mammy, and daddy Joe, as he had privately disposed of me to a regular soul-driver by the name of Crow.'

'I knows Dick Crow,' said Andy, "e come f'om Faginy, whah I did, da same town.'

'So Ailcey said of him. Then you know him without any description from me,' replied Henry.

'Yes, 'n deed! an' I knows 'im to be a inhuman, mean, dead-po' white man, dat's wat I does!'

'Well, I was privately sold to him for two thousand dollars, then ordered back to Franks, as though I was still his slave, and by him given a pass and requested to go to Woodville where there were arrangements to seize me and hold me, till Crow ordered me, which was to have been on Tuesday evening. Crow is not aware of me having been given a pass; Franks gave it to deceive his wife; in case of my not returning, to make the impression that I had run away, when in reality I was sold to the trader.'

'Then our people had their merry-making all for nothin,'' said Charles, 'an' Franks got what 'e didn't deserve—their praise.'

'No, the merry-making was only to deceive Franks, that I might have time to get away. Daddy Joe, Mammy Judy, and Ailcey, knew all about it, and proposed the feast to deceive him.'

'Dat's good! sarve 'im right, da 'sarned ole scamp!' rejoined Andy.

'It couldn't be better!' responded Charles.

'Henry uh wish we was in yo' place an' you none da wus by it,' said Andy.

'Never mind, boys, give yourselves no uneasiness, as it wont be long before we'll all be together.'

'You think so, Henry?' asked Charles.

'Well uh hope so, but den body can haudly 'spect it,' responded Andy.

'Boys,' said Henry, with great caution, and much emotion, 'I am now about to approach an important subject, and as I have always found you true to me—and you can only be true to me by being true to yourselves—I shall not hesitate to impart it! But for Heaven's sake!—perhaps I had better not!'

'Keep nothin' back, Henry,' said Charles, 'as you know that we boys 'll die by our principles, that's settled!'

'Yes, I wants to die right now by mine; right heah, now!' sanctioned Andy.

'Well it is this—close boys! close!' when they gathered in a huddle beneath an underbush, upon their knees, 'you both go with me, but not now. I—'

'Why not now?' anxiously enquired Charles.

'Dat's wat I like to know!' responded Andy.

'Stop boys, till I explain. The plans are mine and you must allow me to know more about them than you. Just here, for once, the slave-holding preacher's advice to the black man is appropriate, "Stand still and see the salvation."'[1]

'Then let us hear it, Henry,' asked Charles.

'Fah God sake!' said Andy, 'let us heah w'at it is, anyhow, Henry; yeh keep a body in 'spence so long, till I's mose crazy to heah it. Dat's no way!'

'You shall have it, but I approach it with caution! Nay, with fear and trembling, at the thought of what has been the fate of all previous matters of this kind. I approach it with religious fear, and hardly think us fit for the task; at least, I know I am not. But as no one has ever originated, or given us anything of the kind, I suppose I may venture.'

'Tell it! tell it!' urged both in a whisper.

'Andy,' said Henry, 'let us have a word of prayer first!' when they bowed low, with their heads to the ground, Andy, who was a preacher of the Baptist persuasion among his slave brethren, offering a solemn and affecting prayer, in whispers to the Most High, to give them knowledge and courage in the undertaking, and success in the effort.

Rising from their knees, Andy commenced an anthem, by which he appeared to be much affected, in the following words:

'About our future destiny,
There need be none debate—
Whilst we ride on the tide,
With our Captain and his mate.'

Clasping each other by the hand, standing in a band together, as a plight of their union and fidelity to each other, Henry said—

'I now impart to you the secret, it is this: I have laid a scheme, and matured a plan for a general insurrection of the slaves in every State, and the successful overthrow of slavery!'

'Amen!' exclaimed Charles.

1. Exodus 14:13.

'God grant it!' responded Andy.

'Tell us, Henry, how's dis to be carried out?' enquired Andy.

'That's the thing which most concerns me, as it seems that it would be hard to do in the present ignorant state of our people in the slave States,' replied Charles.

'Dat's jis wat I feah!' said Andy.

'This difficulty is obviated. It is so simple that the most stupid among the slaves will understand it as well as if he had been instructed for a year.'

'What!' exclaimed Charles.

'Let's heah dat aghin!' asked Andy.

'It is so just as I told you! So simple is it that the trees of the forest or an orchard illustrate it; flocks of birds or domestic cattle, fields of corn hemp or sugar cane; tobacco rice or cotton, the whistling of the wind, rustling of the leaves, flashing of lightning, roaring of thunder, and running of streams all keep it constantly before their eyes and in their memory, so that they cant forget it if they would.'

'Are we to know it now?' enquired Charles.

'I'm boun' to know it dis night befo' I goes home, 'case I been longin' fah ole Pottah dis many day, an' uh mos' think uh got 'im now!'

'Yes boys, you've got to know it before we part, but—'

'That's the talk!' said Charles.

'Good nuff talk fah me!' responded Andy.

'As I was about to say, such is the character of this organization, that punishment and misery are made the instruments for its propagation, so—'

'I cant understan' that part—'

'You know nothing at all about it Charles, and you must—'

'Stan' still an' see da salvation!' interrupted Andy.

'Amen!' responded Charles.

'God help you so to do, brethren!' admonished Henry.

'Go on Henry tell us! give it to us!' they urged.

'Every blow you receive from the oppressor impresses the organization upon your mind, making it so clear that even Whitehead's Jack could understand it as well as his master.'

'We are satisfied! The secret, the secret!' they importuned.

'Well then, first to prayer, and then to the organization. Andy!' said Henry, nodding to him, when they again bowed low with their heads to the ground, whilst each breathed a silent prayer, which was ended with 'Amen' by Andy.

Whilst yet upon their knees, Henry imparted to them the secrets of his organization.

'O, dat's da thing!' exclaimed Andy.

'Capital, capital!' responded Charles, 'what fools we was that we didn't know it long ago!'

'I is mad wid myse'f now!' said Andy.

'Well, well, well! Surely God must be in the work,' continued Charles.

''E's heah; Heaven's nigh! Ah feels it! it's right heah!' responded Andy, placing his hand upon his chest, the tears trickling down his cheeks.

'Brethren,' asked Henry, 'do you understand it?'

'Understand it? Why a child could understand, it's so easy!' replied Charles.

'Yes,' added Andy, 'ah not only undehstan' myse'f, but wid da knowledge I has uv it, ah could make Whitehead's Jack a Moses!'

'Stand still, then, and see!' said he.

'Dat's good Bible talk!' responded Andy.

'Well, what is we to do?' enquired Charles.

'You must now go on and organize continually. It makes no difference when, nor where you are, so that the slaves are true and trustworthy, as the scheme is adapted to all times and places.'

'How we gwine do Henry, 'bout gittin' da things 'mong da boys?' enquired Andy.

'All you have to do, is to find one good man or woman—I don't care which, so that they prove to be the right person—on a single plantation, and hold a seclusion and impart the secret to them, and make them the organizers for their own plantation, and they in like manner impart it to some other next to them, and so on. In this way it will spread like smallpox among them.'

'Henry, you is fit fah leadah ah see,' complimentingly said Andy.

'I greatly mistrust myself, brethren, but if I cant command, I can at least plan.'

'Is they anything else for us to do Henry?' enquired Charles.

'Yes, a very important part of your duties has yet to be stated. I now go as a runaway, and will be suspected of lurking about in the thickets, swamps and caves; then to make the ruse complete, just as often as you think it necessary, to make a good impression, you must kill a shoat, take a lamb, pig, turkey, goose, chickens, ham of bacon from the smoke house, a loaf of bread or crock of butter from the spring house, and throw them down into the old waste well at the back of the old quarters, always leaving the heads of the fowls lying about and the blood of the larger animals. Everything that is missed do not hesitate to lay it upon me, as a runaway, it will only cause them to have the less suspicion of your having such a design.'

'That's it,—the very thing!' said Charles, 'an it so happens that they's an ole waste well on both Franks' and Potter's places, one for both of us.'

'I hope Andy, you have no religious objections to this?'

'It's a paut ah my 'ligion Henry, to do whateveh I bleve right, an' shall sholy do dis, God being my helpah!'

'Now he's talkin'!' said Charles.

'You must make your religion subserve your interests, as your oppressors do theirs!' advised Henry. 'They use the Scriptures to make you submit, by preaching to you the texts of "obedience to your masters"[2] and "standing still to see the salvation," and we must now begin to understand the Bible so as to make it of interest to us.'

'Dat's gospel talk,' sanctioned Andy. 'Is da anything else yeh want tell us boss—I calls 'im *boss*, 'case 'e aint nothing else but "boss"—so we can make 'ase an' git to wuck? 'case I feels like goin' at 'em now, me!'

'Having accomplished our object, I think I have done, and must leave you to-morrow.'

'When shall we hear from you Henry?' enquired Charles.

'Not until you shall see me again; when that will be, I dont know. You may see me in six months, and might not not in eighteen. I am determined, now that I am driven to it, to complete an organization in every slave state before I return, and have fixed two years as my utmost limit.'

'Henry, tell me before we part, do you know anything about little Joe?' enquired Charles.

'I do!'

'Wha's da chile?' enquired Andy.

'He's safe enough, on his way to Canada!' at which Charles and Andy laughed.

'Little Joe on 'is way to Canada?' said Andy, 'mighty young travelah!'

'Yes,' replied Henry with a smile.

'You're a joking Henry?' said Charles, enquiringly.

'I am serious, brethren,' replied he, 'I do not joke in matters of this kind. I smiled because of Andy's surprise.'

'How did 'e go?' farther enquired Andy.

'In company with his "mother" who was waiting on her "mistress"!' replied he quaintly.

'Eh heh!' exclaimed Andy, 'I knows all 'bout it now; but whah'd da "mammy" come f'om?'

'I found one!'

'Aint 'e high!' said Andy.

'Well brethren, my time is drawing to a close,' said Henry, rising to his feet.

'O!' exclaimed Andy, 'ah like to forgot, has yeh any money Henry?'

2. See Paul 6:16.

'Have either of you any?'

'We has.'

'How much?'

'I got two-three hundred dollahs!' replied Andy.

'An so has I, Henry!' added Charles.

'Then keep it, as I have two thousand dollars now around my waist, and you'll find use for all you've got, and more, as you will before long have an opportunity of testing. Keep this studiously in mind and impress it as an important part of the scheme of organization, that they must have money, if they want to get free. Money will obtain them every thing necessary by which to obtain their liberty. The money is within all of their reach if they only knew it was right to take it. God told the Egyptian slaves to "borrow from their neighbors"—meaning their oppressors—"all their jewels;"[3] meaning to take their money and wealth wherever they could lay hands upon it, and depart from Egypt. So you must teach them to take all the money they can get from their masters, to enable them to make the strike without a failure. I'll show you when we leave for the North, what money will do for you, right here in Mississippi. Bear this in mind; it is your certain *passport* through the *white gap*, as I term it.'

'I means to take all ah can git; I bin doin' dat dis some time. Ev'ry time ole Pottah leave 'is money pus, I borrys some, an' 'e all'as lays it on Miss Mary, but 'e think so much uh huh, dat anything she do is right wid 'im. Ef 'e 'spected me, an' Miss Mary say 'twant me, dat would be 'nough fah 'im.'

'That's right!' said Henry, 'I see you have been putting your own interpretation on the Scriptures, Andy, and as Charles will now have to take my place, he'll have still a much better opportunity than you, to "borrow from his master."'

'You needn't fear, I'll make good use of my time!' replied Charles.

The slaves now fell upon their knees in silent communion, all being affected to the shedding of tears, a period being put to their devotion by a sorrowful trembling of Henry's voice singing to the following touching words:

'Farewell, farewell, farewell!
My loving friends farewell!
Farewell old comrades in the cause,
I leave you here, and journey on;
And if I never more return,
Farewell, I'm bound to meet you there!'

'One word before we part,' said Charles. 'If we never should see you again, I suppose you intend to push on this scheme?'

'Yes!

3. See Exodus 11:1–2.

Insurrection shall be my theme!
  My watchword "Freedom or the grave!"
Until from Rappahannock's stream,
  To where the Cuato[4] waters lave,
One simultaneous war cry
  Shall burst upon the midnight air!
And rouse the tyrant but to sigh—
  Mid sadness, wailing, and despair!'

Grasping each eagerly by the hand, the tears gushing from his eyes, with an humble bow, he bid them finally 'farewell!' and the runaway was off through the forest.

———

Part II.

Chapter VII. Obscurity.

On their arrival in Havana, Henry found lodgings for himself and wife in an obscure but very respectable old black family, consisting of man and wife, with a half grown adopted daughter, the wife too aged to do the active services of the family; the husband being a stevedore made his means by superintending the loading of vessels at the quay, by the employment of large numbers of men. The house was in an obscure and retired locality, the family being, seemingly, without acquaintances or visitors.

This evening the Omnipotence of God was satisfactorily verified and established to depart from them 'no more forever,'[5] in the living reality, as they sat together in the neat and comfortable little back-room assigned them in the humble abode of old man Zoda and wife Huldah Guh.

Here was told that unparalleled tale of sorrow, to a husband never expected again to be seen by the wife; and his narrated facts, unequalled in the living history of a slave, concerning the determined efforts of that husband to reach the wife, and rescue her from thraldom at the risk of every consequence.

Goaded and oppressed by a master known to be her own father, under circumstances revolting to humanity, civilization and Christianity, she had been ruthlessly torn from her child, husband, and mother, and sold to a foreign land, all because, by the instincts of nature—if by the honor of a wife and womanhood she had not been justified—she repelled him. Sold again to a severe mis-

4. A river in Cuba [Delany's note].
5. Exodus 14:13.

tress, then to a heartless, cruel man for the worst of designs, by whom she had
been almost daily beaten, frequently knocked down, kicked and stamped on,
once struck and left for dead; and even smoked and burnt to subdue her. During these sufferings and those untold, her faith had often faltered, and she had
staggered at the thought of believing that 'God was no respecter of persons.'[6]

Maddened to desperation at the tearing away of his wife during his absence
from her child and home, he had confronted his master at the hazard of life,
been set upon the auction block in the midst of an assemblage of anxious slave-
traders, escaped being sold, traversed the greater part of the slaveholding States
amid dangers the most imminent; been pursued, taken, and escaped, frequently
during which time he, too, had his faith much shaken, and found his dependence in Divine aid wavering. But God to them, however their unworthiness, had
fully made manifest Himself, and established their faith in His promises, by
again permitting them to meet each other under circumstances so singular and
extraordinary.

The heartbroken look, hopeless countenance, languid eye, and dejected appearance of the gray-haired, apparently aged, sorrow stricken Lotty, the nurse of
Adelaide Garcia, was now succeeded by the buoyant spirit, handsome smile, and
brilliant eyed Maggie Holland, though the sunken sockets, and gray smitten
hairs still remained, which time and circumstances would doubtless much
improve.

'God be thanked for this privilege!' said Henry, as he sat with his wife lean-
ing upon his knees, looking in his face, her right hand resting on his shoulder,
his left supporting her waist.

'God's name be praised!' responded Maggie both laughing and crying at the
same time.

Henry here, as rapidly as possible, detailed to her his plans and schemes; and
the next day imparted his grand design upon Cuba. At this information she was
much alarmed, and could not comprehend that an ordinary man and American
slave such as he, should project such an undertaking.

'Never mind, wife, you will know better by-and-by,' was the only answer he
would give, with a smile, at his wife's searching inquiries.

'Oh, husband don't have anything to do with it; as we are now both free and
happy, let us attend to our own affairs. I think you have done enough.'

'I am not free, wife, by their acknowledgment, as you are, but have escaped;
they can take me whenever they catch me.'

'I think, then, you might let them alone.'

'As God lives, I will avenge your wrongs; and not until they let us alone—

6. Acts 10:34.

cease to steal away our people from their native country and oppress us in their own—will I let them alone. They shall only live while I live, under the most alarming apprehensions. Our whole race among them must be brought to this determination, and then, and not till then, will they fear and respect us.'

'I don't know, husband, I may be wrong, and I expect you will say so; but I think our people had better not attempt any such thing, but be satisfied as we are among the whites, and God, in His appointed time, will do what is required.'

'My dear wife, you have much yet to learn in solving the problem of this great question of the destiny of our race. I'll give you one to work out at your leisure; it is this: Whatever liberty is worth to the whites, it is worth to the blacks; therefore, whatever it cost the whites to obtain it, the blacks would be willing and ready to pay, if they desire it. Work out this question in political arithmetic at your leisure, wife, and by the time you get through and fully understand the rule, then you will be ready to discuss the subject further with me.' Maggie smiled and sighed, but said no more on the subject.

Chapter VIII. The Interview—Blake.

Having placed his money in the keeping of his wife, Henry suggested that, having enjoyed a good rest of two days pleasure in her company, a visit in the city to make some acquaintances was indispensable at such a juncture.

His first object was to find the residence of the distinguished poet of Cuba, Placido;[7] being directed to a large building occupied below, in the upper story of which was the study of the poet. On giving a light tap at the door, a voice in a somewhat suppressed but highly musical tone said, 'Come in!' On entering, the stare of a person of slender form, lean and sinewy, rather morbid, orange-peel complexion, black hair hanging lively quite to the shoulders, heavy deep brow and full moustache, with great expressive black piercing eyes, with pen in hand, sitting with right side to the table looking over the left shoulder toward the door, occupied the study.

'Be seated, sir!' said the yellow gentleman, as Henry politely bowing raised his cap, advancing toward the table.

'I am looking, sir, for the proprietor of the room,' said Henry.

'I am the person,' replied the gentleman.

'The poet, sir, I believe,' continued he.

'I may not answer your expectation, sir!' modestly answered the gentleman.

---

7. A freeborn Cuban mulatto, Placido, the pen name of the poet Gabriel de la Concepción Valdés (1809–44), was charged with high treason by Cuban authorities and executed by firing squad on 28 June 1844. Many U.S. blacks regarded him as a revolutionary hero.

'Your name, sir?' inquired Henry.

'Placido' was the reply; at which Henry rose to his feet, respectfully bowing.

'May I inquire your name?' asked the poet.

'Blacus, sir,' replied he.

'A familiar name to me. Many years ago I had a cousin of that name, an active, intelligent youth, the son of a wealthy black tobacco, cigar, and snuff manufacturer, who left school and went to sea, since when his parents still living, who doted in him with high hopes of his future usefulness, have known nothing of him,' explained Placido.

'What was his Christian name, sir?'

'Carolus Henrico.'

'Cousin, don't you know me?' said Henry in a familiar voice, after nearly twenty years absence. 'I am Carolus Henrico Blacus, your cousin and schoolmate, who nineteen years ago went to the Mediterranean. I dropped Carolus and Anglicised my name to prevent identity, going by the name of Henry Blake.'

'Is it delusion or reality!' replied Placido with emotion.

'It is reality. I am the lost boy of Cuba,' said Henry; when they mutually rushed into each other's arms.

'Where in God's name have you been, cousin Henry—and what have you been doing?'

'My story, Placido, is easily told—the particulars you may get from one who will be more ready than I to give you details.'

'Who is that you—'

'I will tell you presently; but first to my story. When I left father's house at the age of seventeen, I went to sea on what I believed to be a Spanish man-of-war. I was put as apprentice, stood before the mast, the ship standing east for the Western coast of Africa, as I thought for the Mediterranean. On arriving on the coast, she put into the Bight of Benin near Wydah;[8] was freighted with slaves— her true character then being but too well known—when she again put to sea, standing as I thought for Cuba, but instead, put into Key West, where she quickly disposed of her cargo to Americans. My expression of dissatisfaction at being deceived offended the commander, who immediately sold me to a noted trader on the spot—one Col. Franks, of Mississippi, near Natchez. He seized me under loud and solemn protest, collared and choked me, declaring me to be his slave. By recommendations from the commander whose name was Maria Gomez, that I would become a good sailor, I was left with him, to return as apprentice to marine services, making three voyages, returning with as many cargoes, once to

8. The northern arm of the Gulf of Guinea, on the coast of southwest Nigeria. This was a major slave-trading area from the seventeenth into the nineteenth century.

Brazil, once more to Key West, and once to Matanzas, Cuba, each of which times I was put in irons on landing, and kept in close confinement during the vessel's stay lest I ran away. The last cargo was taken to Key West, where Franks was in waiting, when a final settlement of the affairs resulted in my being taken by him to the United States, and there held as a slave, where in a few years I became enamored with a handsome young slave girl, a daughter of his (the mother being a black slave), married, have one living child, and thus entangled, had only to wait and watch an opportunity for years to do what has just now been affected,' narrated Henry to the astonishment of his intelligent auditor, who, during the time, stood pen in hand, with eyes fixed upon him.

'Just God!' exclaimed Placido; 'how merciful He is! Who could have believed it! And you are also a sailor, Henry?'

'I am, cousin; and have served the hardest apprenticeship at the business, I do assure you; I have gone through all the grades, from common seaman to first mate, and always on the coast had full command, as no white men manage vessels in the African waters, that being entirely given up to the blacks.'

'I really was not aware of that before; you surprise me!' said Placido.

'That is so! every vessel of every nation, whether trader or man-of-war, so soon as they enter African waters are manned and managed by native blacks, the whites being unable to stand the climate.'

'That, then, opens up to me an entirely new field of thought.'

'And so it does. It did to me, and I've no doubt it does so to every man of thought, black or white.'

'Give me your hand, Henry'—both clasping hands—'now by the instincts of our nature, and mutual sympathy in the common cause of our race, pledge to me on the hazard of our political destiny what you intend to do.'

'Placido, the hazard is too much! were it lost, the price is too great—I could not pay it. But I read across the water, in a Cuba journal at New Orleans, a lyric from your pen, in which the fire of liberty blazed as from the altar of a freeman's heart. I therefore make no hazard when I this to you impart: I have come to Cuba to help to free my race; and that which I desire here to do, I've done in another place.'

'Amen!' exclaimed Placido. 'Heaven certainly designed it, and directed you here at this most auspicious moment, that the oppressed of Cuba also may "declare the glory of God!"'[9]

'Have you thought much in that direction, Placido?'

'I have, though I've done but little, and had just finished the last word of the last stanza of a short poem intended to be read at a social gathering to be held at

9. Psalms 19:1.

the house of a friend one evening this week, which meets for the express purpose of maturing some plan of action.'

'Read it.'

'I will; tell me what you think of it:

Were I a slave I would be free!
    I would not live to live a slave;
But rise and strike for liberty,
    For Freedom, or a martyr's grave!

One look upon the bloody scourge,
    Would rouse my soul to brave the fight,
And all that's human in me urge,
    To battle for my innate right!

One look upon the tyrant's chains,
    Would draw my sabre from its sheath,
And drive the hot blood through my veins,
    To rush for liberty or death!

One look upon my tortured wife,
    Shrieking beneath the driver's blows,
Would nerve me on to desp'rate strife,
    Nor would I spare her dastard foes!

Arm'd with the vindicating brand,
    For once the tyrant's heart should feel;
No milk-sop plea should stay my hand,
    The slave's great wrong would drive the steel!

Away the unavailing plea!
    Of peace, the tyrant's blood to spare;
If you would set the captive free,
    Teach him for freedom bold to dare!

To throw his galling fetters by,
    To wing the cry on every breath,
Determined manhood's conquering cry,
    For Justice, Liberty, or death!'

'If heaven decreed my advent here—and I believe it did—it was to have my
spirits renewed and soul inspired by that stimulating appeal, such as before
never reached the ear of a poor, weary, faltering bondman, Placido. I thank God
that it has been my lot to hear it, culled fresh from your fertile brain. Were there

but a smoldering spark, nearly extinguished in the smothered embers of my doubts and fears, it is now kindled into a flame, which can only be quenched by the regenerating waters of unconditional emancipation.'

'Ah, cousin, though you consider us here free—those I mean who are not the slaves of some white man—I do assure you, that my soul as much as yours pants for a draft from the fountain of liberty! We are not free, but merely exist by sufferance—a miserable life for intelligent people, to be sure!'

'You, Placido, are the man for the times!'

'Don't flatter, Henry; I'm not.'

'You are, and it's no flattery to say so. The expression of an honest conviction is not flattery. When the spirits of the Christian begin to droop, to hear the word of life, is refreshing to the soul. That is precisely my case at present.'

'Then you have the vital spark in you?'

'Ah, Placido, I often think of the peaceful hours I once enjoyed at the common altar of the professing Christian. I then believed in what was popularly termed religion, as practised in all the slave States of America; I was devoted to my church, and loved to hear on a Sabbath the word of God spoken by him whom I believed to be a man of God. But how sadly have I been deceived! I still believe in God, and have faith in His promises; but serving Him in the way that I was, I had only "the shadow without the substance," the religion of my oppressors. I thank God that He timely opened my eyes.'

'In this, Henry, I believe you are right; I long since saw it, but you are clear on the subject. I had not thought so much as that.'

'Then as we agree, let us at once drop the religion of our oppressors, and take the Scriptures for our guide and Christ as our example.'

'What difference will that make to us? I merely ask for information, seeing you have matured the subject.'

'The difference will be just this, Placido—that we shall not be disciplined in our worship, obedience as slaves to our master, the slaveholders, by associating in our mind with that religion, submission to the oppressor's will.'

'I see, Henry, it is plain; and every day convinces me that we have much yet to learn to fit us for freedom.'

'I differ with you, Placido; we know enough now, and all that remains to be done, is to make ourselves free, and then put what we know into practice. We know much more than we dare attempt to do. We want space for action—elbow room; and in order to obtain it, we must shove our oppressors out of the way.'

'Heaven has indeed, I repeat, decreed your advent here to—'

'Learn of you!' interrupted Henry.

'No; but to teach us just what we needed,' replied Placido.

'God grant us, then, a successful harmony of sentiment!' responded Henry.

'Grant that we may see eye to eye!' exclaimed Placido.

'Amen, amen!' concluded Henry when relinquishing hands they mutually clasped, embracing in each other's arms.

'Tell me now, cousin, to whom did you allude when you first came in, as the person from whom I should obtain details of your life?'

'My wife.'

'Is she here?'

'She is,' replied Henry relating all the particulars of their separation and reunion.

'Where have you got her?'

'At the house of an old family, west of the Plaza; Zoda and Huldah Ghu are their names; the man is a stevedore.'

'She must not remain there.'

'Why?' asked Henry.

'I deem it an unsafe quarter under the circumstances — that's all,' suggested Placido.

'Then she is committed to your charge. Come with me to see her.'

'Gladly will I do so; but tell me this before we leave — whither are you bound, cousin?'

'I go directly to Matanzas, to take out a slaver as sailing-master, with the intention of taking her in mid ocean as a prize for ourselves, as we must have a vessel at our command before we make a strike. She is also freighted with powder for Dahomi, with several fine field pieces, none of which, I learned, were to be disposed of, but safely deposited at the slaver's rendezvous in an island which I know off the African coast, for future use in trade. I am well acquainted with the native Krumen on the coast, many of the heads of whom speak several European tongues, and as sailing-master, I can obtain as many as I wish, who will make a powerful force in carrying out my scheme on the vessel.'

'I thank God for this interview. Henry, I thank God. Come, let's go and see your wife,' said Placido in conclusion, when they left the poet's study for the hut of Zoda Ghu, back of the Plazas.

(*Anglo-African Magazine*, 1 [1859]: 106–10; *Weekly Anglo-African*, 1 February 1862, p. 1)

Comets

DELANY HAD A long-standing fascination with science. As a medical doctor, he was interested in the nature of disease; as a theorist of race, he was interested in anthropology and evolution. His Masonic affiliation contributed to an interest in astronomy, and in 1859 he published two essays on astronomy, "The Attraction of Planets" and "Comets," in the January and February issues of the *Anglo-African Magazine*. In his essay on comets, Delany seems to be describing not only bodies in space but also a circulatory force, like himself, or Blake, attempting to restore harmony and energy to bodies in need of reinvigoration.

What are *Comets*? This probably is the most difficult question known to natural science. Many have been the deductions upon this most interesting subject, learned astronomers giving different views; but as yet there has not been even a plausible theory adduced upon which to settle an opinion. . . .

A comet must be a great sphere of electric fire in a constant state of action, which like the nucleus termed a "thunder bolt," flies darting, blazing and sparkling through space, leaving far behind streams of electricity, similar to lurid flashes of lightning amidst the darkness of clouds.

The momentum of these extraordinary orbs will justify the conclusion that they are electrical. The trail of the last comet, the past autumn, was calculated by some learned men at 65,000,000 of miles in length, or only 30,000,000 less than the distance of the sun from the earth; and when considering the motion necessary to leave such a trail, and comparing this with lightning flashes in the skies, the velocity of these bodies is beyond human conception. No other force than that of electricity, could possibly be the motive power which impels them on with such speed. Unlike the revolutionary planets, which are alternately impelled and retarded by positive and negative influences, the comet, on the contrary, has a continuous succession of accelerated motions, every center it approaches impelling it onward in its course. . . .

The purpose of comets would seem to be to distribute electricity throughout universal space, re-supplying the continual loss that must be sustained to systems and planets by various causes, and thereby giving life, action, health and vigor to both animate and inanimate creation, to this and distant worlds, worlds to us unknown; as it is a point worthy of attention, that on the approach of a comet, whether observed or not, there is always a sensible effect produced on the weather, which sometimes continues during a season.

Thus then, are comets, the source and fountain from which comes supplies of electricity:

"Giving motion to the seas—
Power to the breeze,"
Excitement to vegetation,
And stimulus to animation;

health to mankind, and the indisputable evidence of the existence, mercy, goodness, justice and power of an omnipresent God, whom all should acknowledge, obey, and reverence as the Father of us all, the source of our existence, and the Author of all things.

(*Anglo-African Magazine*, February 1859, pp. 59–60)

Part Four.
Africa

IN "GENEALOGY," the opening chapter of *Life and Public Services of Martin R. Delany*, Frances A. Rollin reports that Delany's "pride of birth is traceable to his maternal as well as to his paternal grandfather, native Africans—on the father's side, pure Golah; on the mother's, Mandingo." She goes on to inform her readers that Delany's "father's father was a chieftain" and that his mother's father "was an African prince, from the Niger Valley regions of Central Africa."[1] Rollin based her genealogical account on Delany's oral testimony of 1867, which he conveyed to her not when he was in Africa, but when he was in the United States working as a commissioner in the Freedmen's Bureau at Hilton Head, South Carolina. In providing Rollin with his "royal" African genealogy in 1867, two years after he was named a major in the Union army, Delany sought to legitimate his leadership position over the newly emancipated blacks, and he sought as well to assert his racial dignity in the face of an inveterate white racism. But for many scholars and critics, Delany's proud assertion to Rollin of his African genealogy provides the key to a *coherent* Delany, a Delany who from the beginning to the end of his career was guided by an Africanist pride and what Cyril E. Griffith terms an "African Dream." As Griffith writes, "the only consistency in his life was the obsession with Africa. From his mid-thirties, Delany's greatest ambition was to live in Africa permanently."[2]

And yet the facts of Delany's career suggest a much more conflicted or tentative relationship to Africa than Griffith and others would allow. During the 1830s and 1840s, Delany worked first and foremost to fight for black elevation in the United States; for most of the 1850s, he worked for black elevation in the Americas; and from 1863 to 1877, as will be seen in Part 5, he worked to make blacks vital citizens of the United States. Delany's specific commitment to African emigration projects between 1857 and 1863 and, later, 1877 to 1879 (see Part 6 below), added up to fewer than ten years of an extraordinary fifty-year career of antislavery and antiracist action. Delany's sense of his and other blacks' connections to Africa may well have contributed to his racial pride, but Africa itself would appear to have had a relatively minor place in the larger shape of his career.

Or did it? The African pride of ancestry evident in Delany's *Mystery*, his black Masonic writings, his journalistic battles with the mulatto Frederick Douglass, his mystical notion of black destiny in "Political Destiny," and so on, indicate that despite the relatively small number of years he devoted to African emigration projects, Africa held a sacred place in his imagination. In this regard, logistical and strategic factors, rather than a lack of interest in Africa, may have had a determining role in limiting his commitment to African emigrationism. The logistical issues are fairly obvious: African emigration, compared to emigration to the southern Americas, was an enormous undertaking requiring a huge influx of capital. The strategic issues are also fairly obvious: As Delany asserted again and again in his pre-1858 writings on the American Colonization Society (ACS) and Liberia, the idea that U.S. blacks "belonged" in Africa only reinforced the racist assumptions of U.S. whites who had their own "American dream" of a nation purged of blackness. Convinced that African Americans had a right to U.S. citizenry, Delany remained wary of advocating an emigration project that would give the appearance of endorsing views similar to those of the ACS. But as revealed in the first document in Part 4, "A Project for an Expedition of Adventure," Delany seems to have first developed plans for African emigration back in the 1830s; and there is also evidence in his *Official Report of the Niger Valley Exploring Party* that Africa was part of what he termed the "secret" deliberations at the 1854 National Emigration Convention in Cleveland.[3]

Whether Africa was Delany's lifelong dream or sporadic interest is ultimately difficult to say, though it would appear that the truth falls somewhere between these two extremes. What is clear is that for around five years, from late 1858 to early 1863, Delany was passionately committed to developing an African American free-labor settlement in West Africa that, as he presented it, would help to regenerate Africa while undercutting the South's monopoly on cotton production. Delany's African project is the focus of the bulk of the selections in Part 4, which, taken together, present a documentary account of Delany's planning, funding, and undertaking of his Niger Valley Exploring Party. Against great odds, he came close to achieving his goals, thwarted in the end by British missionaries and the unexpected emergence of the Civil War as a war of emancipation.

Some background is in order here. Delany well into the 1850s remained skeptical of African emigration, or colonization, as sponsored by the ACS, and in 1855 wrote the introduction to William Nesbit's *Four Months in Liberia*, which presented a highly critical portrait of that nation as still under the dominion of racist whites.[4] And yet not too long after he wrote that introduction, Delany in 1857 or early 1858 abandoned his plans for emigration to the southern Americas and began to formulate a project to send educated African Americans to Africa to work with native Africans to produce cotton on the continent. His large, and rather elitist, hope was that talented African Americans would help to develop a regenerative black nationality in Africa. After failing in his quest to receive funds from the American Missionary Association (see his letter to Beecher), and flirting with the possibility of joining up with John Brown, he presented a proposal for a Niger Valley exploring party to the 1858 National Emigration Convention in Chatham, Canada West, which offered him only tentative support. Delany subsequently attempted to form a group of black scientists, doctors, and explorers who would accompany him to Africa, but lacking in funds, he was able to recruit only Philadelphia schoolteacher Robert Campbell.[5] In April 1859, Campbell went to England on a fund-raising tour, while Delany, funded by the ACS, one month later went directly to Africa on a ship, the *Mendi*, owned by three Liberian blacks from New York City. Delany spent thirty-nine days in Liberia and eventually made his way to the Yoruba region (now southwest Nigeria), where in December he met up with Campbell. There followed a series of negotiations with the Alake (king or chief) of Abeokuta, which culminated in a treaty of December 1859 granting Delany the land he sought for his initial settlement. The treaty also promised a spirit of cooperation between the African American immigrants and the native Egba peoples of Abeokuta.[6]

Several months after negotiating this treaty, Delany and Campbell departed for England, arriving in May 1860 for what would be an enormously successful seven-month tour. Shortly after his arrival, Delany became involved in the local politics of various antislavery organizations, displacing the white leader Reverend Theodore Bourne from his positions of authority in the African Civilization Society and African Aid Society. At various gatherings, Delany lay claim to leadership in African-based economic and missionary projects by virtue of the blackness of his skin, which he presented as a marker of his more authentic relation to Africa.[7] His skin color was at the center of what was arguably the highlight of his tour: his participation at the International Statistical Congress in London in July 1860. Invited to the congress by the great antislavery reformer Lord Brougham, Delany, as the one black participant, emerged at the center of an international controversy when Brougham pointedly introduced him as a "negro" whose very presence at the conference, so Brougham implied, confuted the racist assumptions of the American South. (See "The International Statistical Congress" in this section.) In response to Brougham's provocation, most of the American delegates left the congress.

The British press reported favorably on Delany's poised handling of the controversy, and those widely published reports helped to publicize his subsequent lecture tour. Delany gave numerous public lectures throughout Great Britain on his Abeokuta settlement, proclaiming that if British manufacturers and philanthropists would supply the capital, then he would supply the land and labor that would produce the cotton that would help to reduce British manufacturers' dependency on the American South.[8] Delany thus presented his project as serving both the economic needs of Great Britain and the moral cause of putting an end to slavery. These lectures were for the most part highly successful, bringing much-needed, though still quite modest, funding to Delany's project from the Manchester Cotton Supply Association and other groups and individuals.

Buoyed by the moral and financial support he obtained in Great Britain, Delany sailed from Liverpool in December 1860 and by early 1861 was back in Chatham and working with Reverend William King of the Elgin Settlement to put his emigration plans into operation. Under pressure from Anglican missionaries and the British Foreign Office, however, which resented Delany's presence in areas where they had developed considerable influence, the Alake renounced his treaty with Delany early in 1861. Undeterred, Delany continued his efforts at recruiting black Canadians for African emigration. With the help of Reverend King, he managed to sign up forty blacks willing to make the move to Africa. But with the outbreak of the Civil War, and the Alake's renunciation of the treaty, only two or three families remained interested and funds became even harder to come by.

Also threatening Delany's African project was the upsurge of interest during the late 1850s and early 1860s in Haitian emigration, a form of emigration, ironically enough, that seemed consistent with the emigrationism Delany had espoused in the mid-1850s. For the great promise of Haitian emigrationism was that it would help to develop a black nationality in the Americas, precisely what Delany had argued for in "Political Destiny." In 1859 the new ruler of Haiti, President Fabre Geffrard (1806–79), began actively to encourage African Americans to emigrate to his nation, establishing a Haytian Emigration Bureau in Massachusetts and offering free passage, and room and board for up to eight days, to those African Americans willing to cast their lots with the black republic. James T. Holly and William Wells Brown were among the most influential black leaders who promoted Haitian emigration. During 1861 and 1862 Delany wrote these and other black leaders a number of letters, several of which are reprinted in this section, contesting the value of Haitian emigration and holding firm to his own plans to develop an African American settlement in Africa.

Concerned about the diminishment of interest in his African project, and in quest of new sources of funding, Delany for a short while linked himself with Henry Highland Garnet's African Civilization Society, which had close ties to the American Colonization Society. But with Lincoln's issuing of the Emancipation Proclamation in January 1863, Delany had renewed hopes for African Americans in the United States. In the final selection in Part 4, we see a conflicted Delany in the spring of 1863, garbed in African dress and giving his speech

"The Moral and Social Aspect of Africa," even as he had begun to work for the U.S. government in recruiting troops for the new black regiments of the Union army.

Notes

1. Frank [Frances] A. Rollin, *Life and Public Services of Martin R. Delany* (Boston: Lee and Shepard, 1868), pp. 15, 16.

2. Cyril E. Griffith, *The African Dream: Martin R. Delany and the Emergence of Pan-African Thought* (University Park: Pennsylvania State University Press, 1975), p. 1. Victor Ullman makes a similar argument about the importance of Delany's African genealogy to Delany's conception of his antislavery work (*Martin R. Delany: The Beginnings of Black Nationalism* [Boston: Beacon Press, 1971], pp. 2–5), but I have found no evidence of any public reference by Delany to that genealogy until he provided his account to Rollin.

3. See M. R. Delany, *Official Report of the Niger Valley Exploring Party* (New York: Thomas Hamilton, 1861), p. 9.

4. See William Nesbit, *Four Months in Liberia; or African Colonization Exposed* (Pittsburgh: J. T. Shryock, 1855), pp. 3–8. For a convenient reprinting of the complete Nesbit text, along with Delany's introduction, see *Liberian Dreams: Back-to-Africa Narratives from the 1850s*, ed. Wilson Jeremiah Moses (University Park: Pennsylvania State University Press, 1998), pp. 79–126.

5. Born in Kingston, Jamaica, Robert Campbell (?–1884) moved to Philadelphia in 1855 and began teaching at a Quaker-sponsored school for black children. He and the black abolitionist and artist Robert Douglass Jr. (1809–87) enthusiastically supported Delany's African project, but Douglass's hopes to accompany Delany fell through because of lack of funds. Campbell did considerable fund-raising for Delany's project in New York City in 1858, joined Delany in Africa and England during 1859–60, and in 1861 published his own account of the expedition, *A Pilgrimage to My Motherland: An Account of a Journey among the Egbas and Yorubas of Central Africa, in 1859–60*. He settled in Lagos with his family in 1862.

6. For a fuller account of Delany and Africa, see Floyd J. Miller, *The Search for a Black Nationality: Black Emigration and Colonization, 1787–1863* (Urbana: University of Illinois Press, 1975), ch. 6; Griffith, *African Dream*, chs. 5–6; and Ullman, *Martin R. Delany*, ch. 12.

7. For an excellent analysis of the organizational politics surrounding Delany's stay in England, see R. J. M. Blackett, *Building an Antislavery Wall: Black Americans in the Atlantic Abolitionist Movement, 1830–1860* (Baton Rouge: Louisiana State University Press, 1983), chap. 5.

8. See, for example, Delany's 2 November 1860 "Speech Delivered at the City Hall, Glasgow, Scotland," in *The Black Abolitionist Papers*, vol. 1, ed. C. Peter Ripley et al. (Chapel Hill: University of North Carolina Press, 1985), pp. 488–89.

A Project for an Expedition of Adventure, to the Eastern Coast of Africa

DELANY WROTE IN both his 1852 *Condition* and 1861 *Official Report of the Niger Valley Exploring Party* that he had contemplated African American emigration to Africa as far back as the 1830s. In 1836, he stated, he even drafted a plan for an expedition to the continent's eastern coast, and he appended a revised draft of that plan, "A Project for an Expedition of Adventure," to *Condition*.

Every people should be the originators of their own designs, the projector of their own schemes, and creators of the events that lead to their destiny—the consummation of their desires.

Situated as we are, in the United States, many, and almost insurmountable obstacles present themselves. We are four-and-a-half millions in numbers, free and bond; six hundred thousand free, and three-and-a-half millions bond.

We have native hearts and virtues, just as other nations; which in their pristine purity are noble, potent, and worthy of example. We are a nation within a nation;—as the Poles in Russia, the Hungarians in Austria, the Welsh, Irish, and Scotch in the British dominions.

But we have been, by our oppressors, despoiled of our purity, and corrupted in our native characteristics, so that we have inherited their vices, and but few of their virtues, leaving us in character, really a *broken people*.

Being distinguished by complexion, we are still singled out—although having merged in the habits and customs of our oppressors—as a distinct nation of people; as the Poles, Hungarians, Irish, and others, who still retain their native peculiarities, of language, habits, and various other traits. The claims of no people, according to established policy and usage, are respected by any nation, until they are presented in a national capacity.

To accomplish so great and desirable an end, there should be held, a great representative gathering of the colored people of the United States; not what is termed a National Convention, represented en masse, such as have been, for the last few years, held at various times and places; but a true representation of the intelligence and wisdom of the colored freemen; because it will be futile and an utter failure, to attempt such a project without the highest grade of intelligence.

No great project was ever devised without the consultation of the most mature intelligence, and discreet discernment and precaution.

To effect this, and prevent intrusion and improper representation, there should be a CONFIDENTIAL COUNCIL held; and circulars issued, only to such persons as shall be *known* to the projectors to be equal to the desired object.

The authority from whence the call should originate, to be in this wise:— The originator of the scheme, to impart the contemplated Confidential Council, to a limited number of known, worthy gentlemen, who agreeing with the project, endorse at once the scheme, when becoming joint proprietors in interest, issue a *Confidential Circular*, leaving blanks for *date, time*, and *place* of *holding* the Council; sending them to trusty, worthy, and suitable colored freemen, in all parts of the United States, and the Canadas, inviting them to attend; who when met in Council, have the right to project any scheme they may think proper for the general good of the whole people—provided, that the project is laid before them after its maturity.

By this Council to be appointed, a Board of Commissioners, to consist of three, five, or such reasonable number as may be decided upon, one of whom shall be chosen as Principal or Conductor of the Board, whose duty and business shall be, to go on an expedition to the EASTERN COAST OF AFRICA, to make researches for a suitable location on that section of the coast, for the settlement of colored adventurers from the United States, and elsewhere. Their mission should be to all such places as might meet the approbation of the people; as South America, Mexico, the West Indies, &c.

The Commissioners all to be men of decided qualifications; to embody among them, the qualifications of physician, botanist, chemist, geologist, geographer, and surveyor,—having a sufficient knowledge of these sciences, for practical purposes.

Their business shall be, to make a topographical, geographical, geological, and botanical examination, into such part or parts as they may select, with all other useful information that may be obtained; to be recorded in a journal kept for that purpose.

The Council shall appoint a permanent Board of Directors, to manage and supervise the doings of the Commissioners, and to whom they shall be amenable for their doings, who shall hold their office until successors shall be appointed.

A National Confidential Council, to be held once in three years; and sooner, if necessity or emergency should demand it; the Board of Directors giving at least three months' notice, by circulars and newspapers. And should they fail to perform their duty, twenty-five of the representatives from any six States, of the former Council, may issue a call, authentically bearing their names, as sufficient authority for such a call. But when the Council is held for the reception of the report of the Commissioners, a general mass convention should then take place, by popular representation.

Manner of Raising Funds.

The National Council shall appoint one or two Special Commissioners, to England and France, to solicit, in the name of the Representatives of a Broken Nation, of four-and-a-half millions, the necessary outfit and support, for any period not exceeding three years, of such an expedition. Certainly, what England and France would do, for a little nation—mere nominal nation, of five thousand civilized Liberians, they would be willing and ready to do, for five millions; if they be but authentically represented, in a national capacity. What was due to Greece, enveloped by Turkey, should be due to us, enveloped by the United States; and we believe would be respected, if properly presented. To England and France, we should look for sustenance, and the people of those two nations—as they would have every thing to gain from such an adventure and eventual settlement on the EASTERN COAST OF AFRICA—the opening of an immense trade being the consequence. The whole Continent is rich in minerals, and the most precious metals, as but a superficial notice of the topographical and geological reports from that country, plainly show to any mind versed in the least, in the science of the earth.

The Eastern Coast of Africa has long been neglected, and never but little known, even to the ancients; but has ever been our choice part of the Continent. Bounded by the Red Sea, Arabian Sea, and Indian Ocean, it presents the greatest facilities for an immense trade, with China, Japan, Siam, Hindoostan, in short, all the East Indies—of any other country in the world. With a settlement of enlightened freemen, who with the immense facilities, must soon grow into a powerful nation. In the Province of Berbera, south of the Strait of Babelmandeb,[1] or the great pass, from the Arabian to the Red Sea, the whole commerce of the East must touch this point.

Also, a great rail road could be constructed from here, running with the Mountains of the Moon, clearing them entirely, except making one mountain pass, at the western extremity of the Mountains of the Moon, and the south-

1. Berbera is a seaport in Somalia; Bab el Mandeb is a strait between East Africa and Southwest Arabia.

eastern terminus of the Kong Mountains;[2] entering the Province of Dahomey, and terminating on the Atlantic Ocean West; which would make the GREAT THOROUGHFARE for all the trade with the East Indies and Eastern Coast of Africa, and the Continent of America. All the world would pass through Africa upon this rail road, which would yield a revenue infinitely greater than any other investment in the world.

The means for prosecuting such a project—as stupendous as it may appear—will be fully realized in the prosecution of the work. Every mile of the road, will thrice pay for itself, in the development of the rich treasures that now lie hidden in the bowels of the earth. There is no doubt, that in some one section of twenty-five miles, the developments of gold would more than pay the expenses of any one thousand miles of the work. This calculation may, to those who have never given this subject a thought, appear extravagant, and visionary; but to one who has had his attention in this direction for years, it is clear enough. But a few years will witness a development of gold, precious metals, and minerals in Eastern Africa, the Moon and Kong Mountains, ten-fold greater than all the rich productions of California.

There is one great physiological fact in regard to the colored race—which, while it may not apply to all colored persons, is true of those having black skins—that they can bear *more different* climates than the white race. They bear *all* the temperates and extremes, while the other can only bear the temperates and *one* of the extremes. The black race is endowed with natural properties, that adapt and fit them for temperate, cold, and hot climates; while the white race is only endowed with properties that adapt them to temperate and cold climates; being unable to stand the warmer climates; in them, the white race cannot work, but become perfectly indolent, requiring somebody to work for them—and these, are always people of the black race.

The black race may be found, inhabiting in healthful improvement, every part of the globe where the white race reside; while there are parts of the globe where the black race reside, that the white race cannot live in health.

What part of mankind is the "denizen of every soil, and the lord of terrestrial creation," if it be not the black race? The Creator has indisputably adapted us for the "denizens of *every soil*," all that is left for us to do, is to *make* ourselves the "*lords* of terrestrial creation." The land is ours—there it lies with inexhaustible resources; let us go and possess it. In Eastern Africa must rise up a nation, to whom all the world must pay commercial tribute.

2. The Mountains of the Moon (also called Moon Mountain) are on the western border of Uganda; the Kong Mountain range appeared in western areas of many nineteenth-century European maps of Africa but is now regarded as fictitious (or a misnaming of a variety of hills and mountains).

We must MAKE an ISSUE, CREATE an EVENT, and ESTABLISH a NATIONAL POSITION for OURSELVES; and never may expect to be respected as men and women, until we have undertaken, some fearless, bold, and adventurous deeds of daring—contending against every odds—regardless of every consequence.

(Martin Robison Delany, *The Condition, Elevation, Emigration and Destiny of the Colored People of the United States* [Philadelphia: published by the author, 1852], pp. 209–15)

Letter to Henry Ward Beecher, 17 June 1858

IN LATE 1857 OR EARLY 1858, Delany's emigrationist thought underwent a dramatic transformation: He decided that Africa, not Central and South America, was the best possible place to develop a black nationality. Arguing that talented African Americans could help to regenerate the continent, he developed plans to send an exploring party to West Africa. In search of funds to support that plan, he wrote to the Reverend Henry Ward Beecher (1813–87), Harriet Beecher Stowe's brother and a popular Congregationalist minister in Brooklyn, New York. The antislavery Beecher was loosely associated with the American Missionary Association (A.M.A.), a nonsectarian antislavery organization founded in 1846 that had a mission in West Africa. Though his inveterate suspicion of the American Colonization Society had made him suspicious as well of any white organization sponsoring missions in Africa, Delany put that suspicion aside in an effort to gain access to the funds bequeathed to the A.M.A. by the late Charles Avery. That effort proved to be unsuccessful, as the Reverend George Whipple, corresponding secretary and one of the founders of the A.M.A., eventually turned down Delany's request for financial support, perhaps because he and other A.M.A. leaders distrusted an enterprise headed by a black man.

CHATHAM, C. W. June 17th 1858.

REV. H. W. BEECHER — My Dear Sir: — Not being advised of the names and residence of the Board of Foreign Free Mission Association,[1] I ask the favor of you to communicate to them the following request from me.

A large number of the most respectable Colored People of the United States and the Canadas, intend Emigrating to Africa. We expect to make the rich, healthy, and beautiful Valley of Niger, somewhere our location. We design meeting sometime in August next for our preparatory organization, and hope to be

1. Another name for the American Missionary Association.

able against the early part of the next favorable season (1859) to make the first Emigrant embarkation.

We are select in this movement, so far as the true character of the people is concerned, whom we intend to enlist, at least for the first few years; because, so far as mere <u>laborers</u> are concerned, the Country, as all who are familiar with the accounts of all the late works and letters of Travelers on this continent know, are abundant.

We intend to number among our adventurers, Agriculturers (and we have an abundance of them of all kinds of culture, especially such as the productions of this country,) Mechanics of all kinds, competent Business men of all kinds, Teachers, qualified clergy, Photographer and Artist, Surveyor and Civil Engineer, Physician and Surgeon, Geologist and Chemist, and persons to fill every vocation necessary to an intelligent and progressive community. We shall expect to take out with us one of the best quality of portable sawmills.

I have been solicited to head this expedition or Adventure, and intend at least, to make one of the number. With me dear Sir, this is the conclusion of years of mature reflection.

The arrangement is, that I am to go out to Africa this fall, to select the location—, and Negociate with the Natives for Territory or Land. I should have two other intelligent qualified colored men with me.

I desire to know of the gentlemen, who control the Legacy of the late Rev. C. Avery,[2] left for the Civilization and Enlightenment of Africa, whether they won't aid me or whom we decide to send out to make Negociation, in this one of the greatest of modern projects. Our determination is, to build up an Enlightened and Christian Nationality in the midst of these tractable and docile people, which shall not cease till its influence shall have reached the remotest parts of that extensive and interesting country.

I was an intimate acquaintance of the Legator in Pittsburg, where I resided for twenty seven years; the last two years having resided in this place. . . .

By handing the contents of this Sir, to the Head,[3] you will do me a great favor, and subserve the cause of an oppressed people.

---

2. Delany had known and admired Charles Avery of Pittsburgh, as he indicated in his "Western Tour for the *North Star.*"

3. Beecher forwarded Delany's letter to George Whipple (1805–76), who requested more information from Delany. In a letter to Whipple of July 1858 (A.M.A. Archives, No. F1-482, Amistad Research Center, Tulane University), Delany attempted to align the goals of his African expedition with the religious goals of the A.M.A., but the association remained unconvinced.

Very Respectfully, Sir, your friend,
M. R. Delany

P.S.—Please address M. R. Delany, Chatham, C.W.

(American Missionary Association Archives, No. F1-480, Amistad Research
Center, Tulane University)

Canada. — Captain John Brown

AROUND THE SAME TIME that he was beginning to seek funds for an exploring mission to Africa, Delany met John Brown (1800–1859), who was well known for his militant antislavery activities, most notoriously his involvement in the killing of five proslavery settlers in Kansas in 1856. In October of 1859 Brown would lead twenty-one men, including five blacks, in a failed effort to seize the federal arsenal at Harpers Ferry and inspire a massive slave uprising. Celebrated in the North as a patriotic martyr in the American Revolutionary tradition and reviled in the South, Brown was captured and hanged for treason on 2 December 1859. In 1867, Delany offered an account of his meetings with Brown to his biographer Frances Rollin. At the time, he was a major and an officer at the Freedmen's Bureau at Hilton Head, South Carolina, and thus he may not have wanted to reveal details that would have compromised his image as an American patriot. According to Delany, Harpers Ferry was not part of his conversations with Brown in 1858. Whether that was true or not (and it probably was true), the fact is that he never did commit himself to Brown's enterprises. Perhaps Delany regarded Brown's plans as futile, or perhaps he simply did not want to follow a white leader. But the most compelling explanation for the short-term nature of his relationship with Brown is that he had already committed himself to his African project.

In April [1858], prior to his [Delany's] departure for Africa, while making final completions for his tour, on returning home from a professional visit in the country, Mrs. Delany informed him that an old gentleman had called to see him during his absence. She described him as having a long, white beard, very gray hair, a sad but placid countenance; in speech he was peculiarly solemn; she added, "He looked like one of the old prophets. He would neither come in nor leave his name, but promised to be back in two weeks' time." Unable to obtain any information concerning his mysterious visitor, the circumstance would have probably been forgotten, had not the visitor returned at the appointed time; and not finding him at home a second time, he left a message to the effect that he would call again "*in four days, and must see him then.*" This time the interest in the visitor was heightened, and his call was eagerly awaited. At the expiration of that time, while on the street, he recognized his visitor, by his wife's description, approaching him, accompanied by another gentleman; on the latter introducing him to the former, he exclaimed, "Not Captain John Brown, of Ossawatomie!"[1] not thinking of the grand old hero as being east of Kansas, especially in Canada, as the papers had been giving such contradictory accounts of him during the winter and spring.

"I am, sir," was the reply; "and I have come to Chatham expressly to see you, this being my third visit on the errand. I must see you at once, sir," he continued, with emphasis, "and that, too, in private, as I have much to do and but little time before me. If I am to do nothing here, I want to know it at once." "Going directly to the private parlor of a hotel near by," says Major Delany, "he at once revealed to me that he desired to carry out a great project in his scheme of Kansas emigration, which, to be successful, must be aided and countenanced by the influence of a general convention or council. *That* he was unable to effect in the United States, but had been advised by distinguished friends of his and mine, that, if he could but see me, his object could be attained at once. On my expressing astonishment at the conclusion to which my friends and himself had arrived, with a nervous impatience, he exclaimed, 'Why should you be surprised? Sir, the people of the Northern States are cowards; slavery has made cowards of them all. The whites are afraid of each other, and the blacks are afraid of the whites. You can effect nothing among such people,' he added, with decided emphasis. On assuring him if a council were all that was desired, he could readily obtain it, he replied, 'That is all; but that is a great deal to me. It is men I want, and not money; money I can get plentiful enough, but no men. Money can come without being seen, but men are afraid of identification with me, though they favor my measures. They are cowards, sir! Cowards!' he reiterated. He then fully revealed his designs. With these I found no fault, but fully favored and aided in getting up the convention.

"The convention, when assembled, consisted of Captain John Brown, his son Owen,[2] eleven or twelve of his Kansas followers, all young white men, enthusiastic and able, and probably sixty or seventy colored men, whom I brought together.[3]

1. In 1855, John Brown and his sons staked out a free settlement in the town of Ossawatomie, Kansas.
2. Owen Brown (1824–89), John Brown's third son, enthusiastically supported his father's various antislavery endeavors. He participated in the Harpers Ferry raid and managed to escape.
3. The convention took place at Chatham, Canada West, 8 May 1858.

"His plans were made known to them as soon as he was satisfied that the assemblage could be confided in, which conclusion he was not long in finding, for with few exceptions the whole of these were fugitive slaves, refugees in her Britannic majesty's dominion. His scheme was nothing more than this: To make Kansas, instead of Canada, the terminus of the Underground Railroad; instead of passing off the slave to Canada, to send him to Kansas, and there test, on the soil of the United States territory, whether or not the right to freedom would be maintained where no municipal power had authorized.

"He stated that he had originated a fortification so simple, that twenty men, without the aid of teams or ordnance, could build one in a day that would defy all the artillery that could be brought to bear against it. How it was constructed he would not reveal, and none knew it except his great confidential officer, Kagi[4] (the secretary of war in his contemplated provisional government), a young lawyer of marked talents and singular demeanor."

Major Delany stated that he had proposed, as a cover to the change in the scheme, as Canada had always been known as the terminus of the Underground Railroad, and pursuit of the fugitive was made in that direction, to call it the Subterranean Pass Way, where the initials would stand S. P. W., to note the direction in which he had gone when not sent to Canada. He further stated that the idea of Harper's Ferry was never mentioned, or even hinted in that convention.

Had such been intimated, it is doubtful of its being favorably regarded. Kansas, where he had battled so valiantly for freedom, seemed the proper place for his vantage-ground, and the kind and condition of men for whom he had fought, the men with whom to fight. Hence the favor which the scheme met of making Kansas the terminus of the Subterranean Pass Way, and there fortifying with these fugitives against the Border slaveholders, for personal liberty, with which they had no right to interfere. Thus it is clearly explained that it was no design against the Union, as the slaveholders and their satraps interpreted the movement, and by this means would anticipate their designs.

This also explains the existence of the constitution for a civil government found in the carpet-bag among the effects of Captain Brown, after his capture in Virginia, so inexplicable to the slaveholders, and which proved such a nightmare to Governor Wise,[5] and caused him, as well as many *wiser* than himself,

4. John Henry Kagi (1835–59) of Ohio joined up with Brown in 1857 and became his most trusted associate. He was killed during the raid on Harpers Ferry.

5. Governor of Virginia, Henry Alexander Wise (1806–76). Concerned that the federal courts would act too slowly, Wise had Brown tried in the Virginia state court in Charlestown immediately after his capture. Brown was hanged two weeks after the attack on Harpers Ferry.

to construe it as a contemplated overthrow of the Union. The constitution for a provisional government owes its origin to these facts.[6]

Major Delany says, "The whole matter had been well considered, and at first a state government had been proposed, and in accordance a constitution prepared. This was presented to the convention; and here a difficulty presented itself to the minds of some present, that according to American jurisprudence, negroes, having no rights respected by white men, consequently could have no right to petition, and none to sovereignty.

"Therefore it would be mere mockery to set up a claim as a fundamental right, which in itself was null and void.

"To obviate this, and avoid the charge against them as lawless and unorganized, existing without government, it was proposed that an independent community be established within and under the government of the United States, but without the state sovereignty of the compact, similar to the Cherokee nation of Indians, or the Mormons. To these last named, references were made, as parallel cases, at the time. The necessary changes and modification were made in the constitution, and with such it was printed.

"Captain Brown returned after a week's absence, with a printed copy of the corrected instrument, which, perhaps, was the copy found by Governor Wise."

During the time this grand old reformer of our time was preparing his plans, he often sought Major Delany, desirous of his personal coöperation in carrying forward his work. This was not possible for him to do, as his attention and time were directed entirely to the African Exploration movement, which was planned prior to his meeting Captain Brown. . . .

(Frank [Frances] A. Rollin, *Life and Public Services of Martin R. Delany* [Boston: Lee and Shephard, 1868], pp. 85–89)

6. See the "Journal of the Provisional Constitution Held on Saturday, May 8th, 1858," in "The John Brown Insurrection: The Brown Papers: Copied from the Originals at Charlestown by Order of the Executive Department of the State of Virginia" (16 November 1859), reprinted in *Calendar of Virginia State Papers*, 11 (1893): 271–72. "The John Brown Insurrection: The Brown Papers" also includes a short letter from Delany to John Kagi, dated 16 April 1858, in which Delany writes, "I have been anxiously looking, expecting to see something of Uncle's [John Brown's] movements in the paper, but as yet have seen nothing" (p. 292).

Martin R. Delany in Liberia

UNWILLING TO LINK HIMSELF with John Brown, and failing to gain financial support from either the American Missionary Association or the National Emigration Convention, which convened in Chatham, Canada West, 4–7 August 1858, Delany eventually received a small amount of funding from the American Colonization Society (ACS) and its close cousin, the African Civilization Society. He was also given free passage to the west coast of Africa on the *Mendi*, which was owned by three Liberians who received some funding from the ACS. The *Mendi* landed at Cape Palmas, Liberia, on 10 July 1859. Known as an inveterate critic of Liberia and the ACS, Delany, as reported in the *Liberia Herald*, sought rapprochement with the nation's leaders and populace the day after his arrival. The account in the *Herald* was written by Edward Wilmot Blyden, who in 1851 had emigrated to Liberia from the United States.

The arrival of Martin Robinson [*sic*] Delany in Liberia is an era in the history of African emigration—an event, doubtless, that will long be remembered by hundreds and thousands of Africa's exiled children. The news of the advent to these shores of this far-famed champion for the elevation of colored men in the United States, and this great antagonist to the American Colonization Society, spread throughout the county of Monserrado with astonishing rapidity, and persons from all parts of the county came to Monrovia[1] to see this great man. He arrived in Mesrado Roads on the 11th day of July, 1859, in the barque "Mendi," ladened with a cargo worth $40,000, and owned by three colored men, Messrs. Johnson, Turpin, and Dunbar.

Dr. Delany is on his way to Yoruba. The citizens of Monrovia knowing well the position which Dr. Delany has held for the last twenty-five years with reference to African Colonization, thought it might be well to invite him to deliver a public lecture in order that the people generally might hear some of the reasons which induced this gentleman to turn his face Africa-wards; also to tender

---

1. A seaport and the capital of Liberia.

to him a formal and public welcome. Accordingly an invitation was sent by a committee of gentlemen to the Dr., requesting him to lecture to the citizens of Monrovia, on any evening he might choose to appoint, and upon any subject that he might be pleased to select. The Doctor consented and appointed Monday evening, July 8th.

The evening came, and though the weather was somewhat inclement, large crowds assembled in the M.E. Church to hear Dr. Delany. Dr. Samuel F. McGill, chairman of the meeting, at the time appointed, arose and introduced to the audience Dr. Martin Robinson Delany, of Canada. The subject was the "Political condition and destiny of the African race." The Doctor began with the condition of the colored people in the early history of the anti-slavery movement. He divided their history up to this time, into four periods. 1st. The period of *letter-writing*—when the writing of letters by colored men gave indications to their white fellow-citizens of African intelligence; when letters written by men of color were sent to the city of London as a literary curiosity. He referred especially to the letters of James Forten.[2] 2d. The period of *newspaper publishing*, when colored men directed their attention to the proving to white men that they were as capable as the whites of editing newspapers and scattering their thoughts, expressed in proper shape and form, all over the country, sending their ideas into the parlors and bed-chambers, into the studies and offices of their oppressors. 3d. The period of *lecturing*, when colored men felt it not only their duty to send their thoughts to their oppressors on paper, but to meet them face to face, and prove to them that they had equally with them the ability to advocate *orally* their own cause. 4th. The period of *conventions*, when colored men met to discuss the great question of an African nationality. "We are now in this period," said the Dr., "and it is the desire of an African nationality that has brought me to these shores."

The Dr. spoke at length of the various causes which have conspired to retard the progress of the colored man in the United States. He described the condition of the negro in that country as being stationary, for the reason, said he, that two opposite forces of nearly equal power are brought to bear upon him, Abolitionism and Colonization. He compared the influences of these two institutions to two strong cords passed around the body of the colored man; one would drag him from the land that gave him birth to Africa,—and the other is brought to bear upon him with equal force to keep him in his native land; so that by a well known law of philosophy, being under the influence of two equal forces oper-

---

2. The Philadelphia-based black abolitionist James Forten Jr. (1817–?) wrote articles for the *Liberator* under the pseudonym "F" and during the late 1830s served as secretary of the American Moral Reform Society.

ating in contrary directions, his position must be stationary, while over the heads of his white instigators, he sometimes hurls his fulminations at his brethren in Liberia.

The Doctor then went on to state the proceedings of a Convention held in 1854, in Cleveland, Ohio, where, convinced of the necessity of a separate nationality in order to [bring about] the elevation of the African, he took ground in favor of emigration from the United States, to some country where the colored man might be able to establish a distinct nationality. (Applause.) This gave offense to some with whom he had fought in the same ranks, and Professor Vashon wrote a letter to "Douglass' Paper" opposing his view and maintaining the creed of the anti-slavery leaders—a creed very short, viz: "We were born in America; in America we were reared; in America we will live; in America will we die, and be buried with our fathers and mothers." Professor Martin H. Freeman, of Allegany [sic], replied to Professor Vashon and turned back his creed upon him with crushing force, just by placing the same argument in the mouth of the slaves of some Virginia plantation, supposing them to be at liberty to seek some congenial home, "We were born on massa's plantation; on massa's plantation we were reared; we will live on massa's plantation; (provided he don't send us to Georgia,) we will die on massa's plantation, and be buried with the rest of massa's niggers."[3] (Applause.) We could not help thinking of the truth and justice of the comparison. How astonishing is it that intelligent colored men in the United States, now laboring so hard against the idea of emigrating from the land of their birth, do not take these things into serious consideration.

The Doctor then referred to the reasonings which led him to the conclusion that emigration was the best and only hope of the colored people in the United States. He said he looked around and saw men of all other races fleeing from countries where they were oppressed and seeking shelter wherever liberty was to be found for them. He saw the Irish and Dutch, the Hungarians, and others who forever turned their backs on their native land because it denied them that liberty which was the birthright of man. He made reference to the flaming and patriotic speeches of Louis Kossuth in the United States;[4] and he did not wish for one moment to entertain the idea that the same causes which move the hearts of the white man, and prompt him to energetic action, could not touch and move the colored man. (Applause.)

The Doctor then stated that another reason which induced him to favor em-

3. For the debate between George B. Vashon and Martin H. Freeman, see *Frederick Douglass' Paper*, 15 December 1854, p. 3; 21 December 1854, p. 3; and 4 January 1855, p. 1. Principal of Pittsburgh's Avery Institute for black youth, Freeman would emigrate to Liberia in 1863.

4. See *The Origin and Objects of Ancient Freemasonry*, note 29.

igration grew out of the fact that the colored population of the United States, however highly favored they might become in point of political privilege in that country, could never wield a great influence. He said that at the highest estimate, the whole colored population, slave and free, of the United States, is not over five millions. Now, allowing that they were all free and enfranchised, they could not make more than two States of the size of Pennsylvania; and what could these five millions do with twenty millions of whites, in a land where the government is in the hands of the majority? They could never make themselves felt. He therefore advocated the emigration of the six hundred thousand free colored men of the North, to Africa, where they may join the one hundred and sixty millions of their degraded brethren, assist to elevate them, and from this point — from such a nationality the reflex influence upon America must be felt and must be powerful, in behalf of the slaves. (Applause.) He avowed that his thoughts had been from early youth, ever set on Africa, and that in turning his attention toward her, he had embraced no new convictions nor changed his principles, but simply his policy in the line of duty and course of action. "I will therefore say to you, sir, as Ruth said to Naomi," exclaimed he — "that your people shall be my people, your God shall be my God, yea, more; sir, your *country* shall be *my country*."[5] To this point the Doctor said he had come, and to this point every free colored man in the United States must come before he would consent to leave the land of oppression.

The Dr. then said that as he had detained the audience a long time, he would defer his remarks on the political destiny of the African race to another occasion.[6] He took his seat amid roars of applause. . . .

E[dward] W[ilmot] B[lyden][7]

(from the *Liberia Herald*, reprinted in the *Weekly Anglo-African*, 1 October 1859, p. 1)

---

5. See Ruth 1:16–17.

6. A short account of that lecture appeared on pages 1–2 of the same issue of the *Weekly Anglo-African*.

7. Born in St. Thomas, Edward Wilmot Blyden (1832–1912) traveled to the United States in 1850, but when Rutgers Theological Seminary denied him admission, he sailed to Liberia in 1851. In Liberia he emerged as one of the great intellectual and cultural Pan-African leaders of the nineteenth century, publishing a brief for African cultural nationalism, *Vindication of a Race* (1857), and teaching classics at Liberia College. He was ordained as a Presbyterian clergyman in 1858 and in 1861 became Liberian commissioner to Britain and the United States, eventually serving three terms as Liberian secretary of state (1864–71). Among his best-known works is *Christianity, Islam, and the Negro Race* (1887).

Official Report of the Niger Valley Exploring Party

ON 27 DECEMBER 1859, Delany signed a treaty with the Alake and chiefs of Abeokuta that granted to Delany and his commissioners the right to establish a settlement of African American emigrants on land of the Egba people. That settlement, as the treaty makes clear, would exist apart from the authority of the Alake. Having successfully achieved the main goal of his exploring party, Delany traveled through nearby areas for several months before departing for a tour of Great Britain. Although his account of his African project, *Official Report of the Niger Valley Exploring Party*, was published in 1861, Delany drafted *Official Report* in the early months of 1860, most likely while sailing to England. In the excerpted chapters, Delany describes his treaty-making, provides a firsthand account of West Africa, and elaborates his vision of African regeneration.

Section VIII. Topography, Climate, etc.

Topography, Climate.

The whole face of the country extending through the Aku region or Yoruba,[1] as it is laid down on the large missionary map of Africa, is most beautifully diversified with plains, hills, dales, mountains, and valleys, interlined with numerous streams, some of which are merely temporary or great drains; whilst the greater part are perennial, and more or less irrigating the whole year, supplying well the numerous stocks of cattle and horses with which that country is so well everywhere provided. The climate is most delightful. . . .

Inhabitants.

The people are of fine physical structure and anatomical conformation, well and regularly featured; not varying more in this particular from the best specimen of their own race than the Caucasian or Anglo-Saxon from that of theirs. They are very polite—their language abounding in vowels, and consequently

1. Regarded during the mid-nineteenth century as a kingdom of West Africa, Yoruba is a region of southwest Nigeria.

euphonious and agreeable—affable, sociable, and tractable, seeking information with readiness, and evincing willingness to be taught. They are shrewd, intelligent, and industrious, with high conceptions of the Supreme Being, only using their images generally as mediators. "So soon," said an intelligent missionary, "as you can convince them that there is a mediator to whom you *may talk, but cannot see,* just so soon can you make Christians of them;" their idea being that God is too great to be directly approached; therefore there must be a mediator to whom they must talk that they can see, when God will listen and answer if pleased.

After my arrival at Abbeokuta [*sic*],[2] not going out for two days, they expecting me through information from Mr. Campbell,[3] the third day the Chief Atambala called upon me, inviting me in turn to call and see him. In a few days after, the king had a popular religious festival in the great public space, where there were assembled many chiefs and elders; but, on our approach, the old king sent his messenger to escort us to the porch of the piazza upon which he was seated, eagerly grasping me by the hand, bidding me welcome to Abbeokuta and his court; telling me, pointing to Mr. Campbell, that he was acquainted with him, and had heard of me through him. . . . *(How received by them.)*

Many had been the social, friendly, and official interchanges between us and the king and chiefs during our stay in Abbeokuta, when, on the twenty-seventh, the day after the missionary meeting,[4] the following document was duly executed, with the express understanding that no heterogenous nor promiscuous "masses" or companies, but select and intelligent people of high moral as well as religious character were to be induced to go out. And I am sure that every good and upright person in that region, whether native or foreign missionary, would exceedingly regret to see a reckless set of religion-spurning, God-defying persons sent there—especially by disinterested white societies in America, which interferingly came forward in a measure which was originated solely by ourselves (and that, too, but a few of us), as our only hope for the regeneration of our race from the curse and corrupting influences of our white American oppressors. *(Official transactions.)*

TREATY

This Treaty, made between His Majesty, OKUKENU, Alake; SOMOYE, Ibashorun; SOKENU, OGUBONNA, and ATAMBALA, Chiefs and Balaguns, of Abbeokuta, on the first part; and MARTIN ROBISON DELANY, and ROBERT CAMPBELL, of the Niger Valley Exploring Party, Commissioners

2. A city in southwest Nigeria.
3. On Robert Campbell, see the introduction to Part 4, note 5.
4. Delany had met with the Wesleyan Missionary Society on 26 December 1859.

from the African race, of the United States and the Canadas in America, on
the second part, covenants:

ART. 1. That the King and Chiefs on their part, agree to grant and assign
unto the said Commissioners, on behalf of the African race in America,
the right and privilege of settling in common with the Egba people, on
any part of the territory belonging to Abbeokuta, not otherwise occupied.

ART. 2. That all matters requiring legal investigation among the settlers, be
left to themselves, to be disposed of according to their own custom.

ART. 3. That the Commissioners, on their part, also agree that the settlers
shall bring with them, as an equivalent for the privileges above accorded, Intelligence, Education, a Knowledge of the Arts and Sciences,
Agriculture, and other Mechanical and Industrial Occupations, which
they shall put into immediate operation, by improving the lands, and in
other useful vocations.

ART. 4. That the laws of the Egba people shall be strictly respected by the
settlers; and, in all matters in which both parties are concerned, an equal
number of commissioners, mutually agreed upon, shall be appointed,
who shall have power to settle such matters.

As a pledge of our faith, and the sincerity of our hearts, we each of us
hereunto affix our hand and seal this Twenty-seventh day of December,
Anno Domini, One Thousand Eight Hundred and Fifty-nine.

> His Mark, + OKUKENU, Alake.
> His Mark, + SOMOYE, Ibashorum.
> His Mark, + SOKENU, Balagun.
> His Mark, + OGUBONNA, Balagun.
> His Mark, + ATAMBALA, Balagun.
> His Mark, + OGUSEYE, Anaba.
> His Mark, + NGTABO, Balagun, O.S.O.
> His Mark, + OGUDEMO, Ageoko.

> M. R. DELANY.
> ROBERT CAMPBELL.

Witness — Samuel Crowther, Jun.
Attest — Samuel Crowther, Sen.[5]

---

5. Samuel Crowther (1806–91) was sold into slavery in 1821 and rescued by a British
cruiser in 1822. He was educated at the Church Missionary College in London and ordained as an Anglican priest in 1843. At that time he began his lifelong work as mission-

On the next evening, the 28th, the king, with the executive council of chiefs and elders, met at the palace in Ake, when the treaty was ratified by an unanimous approval. Such general satisfaction ran through the council, that the great chief, his highness Ogubonna, mounting his horse, then at midnight, hastened to the residence of the Surgeon Crowther, aroused his father the missionary and author, and hastily informed him of the action of the council. . . . Executive Council, and Ratification of the Treaty.

A word about slavery. It is simply preposterous to talk about slavery, as that term is understood, either being legalized or existing in this part of Africa. It is nonsense. The system is a patriarchal one, there being no actual difference, socially, between the slave (called by their protector *son* or *daughter*) and the children of the person with whom they live. Such persons intermarry, and frequently become the heads of state; indeed, generally so, as I do not remember at present a king or chief with whom I became acquainted whose entire members of the household, from the lowest domestic to the highest official, did not sustain this relation to him, they calling him *baba* or "father," and he treating them as children. And where this is not the case, it either arises from some innovation among them or those exceptional cases of despotism to be found in every country. Indeed, the term "slave" is unknown to them, only as it has been introduced among them by whites from Europe and America. So far from abject slavery, not even the old feudal system, as known to exist until comparatively recent in enlightened and Christian Europe, exists in this part of Africa. Slavery.

Criminals and prisoners of war are *legally sold* into slavery among themselves, just as was the custom in almost every civilized country in the world till very lately, when nothing but advanced intelligence and progressive Christianity among the people put a stop to it. There is no place, however, but Illorin,[6] a *bona fide* Mohammedan kingdom, where we ever witnessed any exhibition of these facts.

Slaves are abducted by marauding, kidnapping, depraved natives, who, like the organized bands and gangs of robbers in Europe and America, go through the country thieving and stealing helpless women and children, and men who may be overpowered by numbers. Whole villages in this way sometimes fall victims to these human monsters, especially when the strong young men are out in the fields at work, the old of both sexes in such cases being put to death, whilst the young are hurried through some private way down to the slave factories usually kept by Europeans (generally Portuguese and Spaniards) and Ameri- How slaves are obtained.

---

ary in the Niger region; in 1864 he was consecrated bishop of the Niger territory. Crowther's son, Samuel Crowther Jr., was a surgeon and his father's compatriot; both supported Delany's African project.

6. City in southwest Nigeria.

cans, on some secluded part of the coast. And in no instances are the parents and relatives known to sell their own children or people into slavery, except, indeed, in cases of base depravity, and except such miserable despots as the kings of Dahomi and Ashantee; neither are the heads of countries known to sell their own people; but like the marauding kidnapper, obtain them by war on others. . . .

Section IX. Diseases of This Part of Africa, Treatment, Hygiene, Ailment.

Hygiene— Eating.

. . . . The laws of health should be particularly observed in going to Africa. In respect to eating, there need be no material change of food, but each individual observing those nourishments which best agree with him or her. When there is little inclination to eat, eat but little; and when there is none, eat nothing. I am certain that a large percentage of the mortality which occurs may be attributed to too free and too frequent indulgence in eating, as was the case with the Lewis family of five at Clay-Ashland,[7] in Liberia—all of whom died from that cause; as well as others that might be mentioned.

Fruits— Coffee. Air.

So as soon as you have taken your bath and put on your morning wrapper, even before dressing, you may eat one or more sweet oranges, then take a cup of coffee, creamed and sweetened, or not, to your taste. Make your toilet, and walk out and take the cool air, always taking your umbrella or parasol, because no foreigner, until by a long residence more or less acclimated, can expose himself with impunity to a tropical sun. If preferred, coffee should always be taken with cream or milk and sugar, because it is then less irritating to the stomach. One of the symptoms of native fever is said to be *nervous irritability of the stomach*; hence, all exciting causes to irritation of that part should be avoided as much as possible. Such fruits as best agree with each individual should be most indulged in; indeed, all others for the time should be dispensed with; and when it can be done without any apparent risk to the person, a little fruit of some kind might be taken every day by each new comer. Except oranges, taken as directed above, all fruits should be eaten *after*, and *not* before breakfast. The fruits of the country have been described in another place.

Drinks.

Let your habits be strictly temperate, and for human nature's sake, abstain from the erroneous idea that some sort of malt or spirituous drink is necessary. This is not the case; and I am certain that much of the disease and dire mortality charged against Africa, as a "land of pestilence and death," should be charged

7. A town named after the politician Henry Clay of Ashland, Kentucky, who was one of the principal leaders of the American Colonization Society.

against the Christian lands which produce and *send bad spirits* to destroy those who go to Africa. Whenever wine, brandy, whisky, gin, rum, or pure alcohol are required as a medical remedy, no one will object to its use; but, in all cases in which they are used as a beverage in Africa, I have no hesitation in pronouncing them deleterious to the system. The best British porter and ale may, in convalescence from fever, be used to advantage as a tonic, because of the bitter and farinaceous substances they contain—not otherwise is it beneficial to the system in Africa. Water, lemonade, effervescent drinks—a teaspoonful of super carbonate of soda, to a glass of lemonade—all may be drunk in common, when thirsty, with pleasure to the drinker as well as profit. Pure ginger-beer is very beneficial.

Bathing should be strictly observed by every person at least once every day. **Bathing.** Each family should be provided with a large sponge, or one for each room if not for each person, and free application of water to the entire person from head to foot, should be made every morning.

Every person should rise early in Africa, as the air is then coolest, freshest, and **Early Rising—Breezes.** purest; besides the effect upon the senses, the sight and song of the numerous birds to be seen and heard, produce a healthful influence upon the mental and physical system. The land and sea-breezes blow regularly and constantly from half-past three o'clock P.M. till half-past ten o'clock, A.M., when there is a cessation of about five hours, till half-past three again.

The evenings and mornings are always cool and pleasant, never *sultry* and **Never sultry.** oppressive with heat, as frequently in temperate climates during summer and autumn. This wise and beneficent arrangement of Divine Providence makes this country beautifully, in fact, delightfully pleasant; and I have no doubt but in a very few years, so soon as scientific black men, her own sons, who alone must be more interested in her development than any other persons, take the matter in hand, and produce works upon the diseases, remedies, treatment, and sanitary measures of Africa, there will be no more contingency in going to Africa than any other known foreign country. I am certain, even now, that the native fever of Africa is not more trying upon the system, when properly treated, than the native fever of Canada, the Western and Southern States and Territories of the United States of America.

Dress should be regulated according to the feeling, with sometimes more and **Dress.** sometime less clothing. But I think it advisable that adults should wear flannel **Avoid getting wet.** (thin) next to their person always when first going to Africa. It gradually absorbs the moisture, and retaining a proper degree of heat, thus prevents any sudden change of temperature from affecting the system. Avoid getting wet at first, and should this accidentally happen, take a thoroughly good bath, rub the skin dry, and put on dry clothes, and for two or three hours that day, keep out of the sun;

but if at night, go to bed. But when it so happens that you are out from home and cannot change clothing, continue to exercise until the clothes dry on your person. It is the abstraction of heat from the system by evaporation of water from the clothing, which does the mischief in such cases. I have frequently been wet to saturation in Africa, and nothing ever occurred from it, by pursuing the course here laid down. Always sleep in clean clothes.

Sanitary Measures.   I am sure I need inform no one, however ignorant, that all measures of cleanliness of person, places, and things about the residences, contribute largely to health in Africa, as in other countries.

Ventilation of houses.   All dwellings should be *freely ventilated* during the *night*, as well as day, and it is a great mistake to suppose, as in Liberia (where every settler sleeps with every part of his house closely shut—doors, windows, and all) that it is deletereous to have the house ventilated during the evening, although they go out to night meetings, visit each other in the evening, and frequently sit on their porches and piazzas till a late hour in the night, conversing, without any injurious effects whatever. . . .

Sanitary effects of Ants— Termites, and Drivers.   A word about ants in Africa—so much talked of, and so much dreaded— will legitimately be in place here, regarding them as a sanitary means, provided by Divine Providence. The *termites*, bug-a-bug or white double ant, shaped like two ovals somewhat flattened, joined together by a cylinder somewhat smaller in the middle, with a head at one end of one of the ovals, is an herbivorous insect, and much abused as the reputed destroyers of books, papers, and all linen or muslin clothing. They feed mainly on such vegetable matter as is most subject to decay—as soft wood, and many other such, when void of vitality—and there is living herbage upon which they feed, and thereby prove a blessing to a country with a superabundance of rank vegetable matter. It is often asserted that they destroy whole buildings, yet I have never seen a person who knew of such a disaster by them, although they may attack and do as much mischief in such cases at times as the wood-worms of America; and, in regard to clothing, though doubtless there have been instances of their attack upon and destruction of clothing, yet I will venture to assert that there is not one piece of clothing attacked and destroyed by these creatures, to ten thousand by the moths which get into the factories and houses in civilized countries, where woolen goods are kept. In all my travels in Africa, I never had anything attacked by the termite; but during my stay of seven months in Great Britain, I had a suit of woolen clothes completely eaten up by moths in Liverpool.

Drivers.   Drivers, as every person already knows, are black ants, whose reputation is as bad for attacking living animals, and even human beings, as the termites' for attacking clothing. This creature, like its white cousin, is also an instrument in the hands of Providence as a sanitary means, and to the reverse of the other is carnivorous, feeding upon all flesh whether fresh or putrified. Like the white, for the purpose of destroying superabundance of vegetable, certainly these black ants were designed by Providence to destroy the excess of animal life which in the nature of things would be brought forth, with little or no destruction without them; and although much is said about their attacking persons, I will venture the opinion that there is not one of these attacks a person to every ten thousand musquitoes in America, as it is only by chance, and *not by search after it*, that drivers attack persons.

They usually go in search of food in narrow rows, say from half an inch to a hand's breadth, as swiftly as a running stream of water, and may in their search enter a house in their course—if nothing attract them around it—when, in such cases, they spread over the floor, walls, and ceiling; and finding no insect or creeping thing to destroy, they gather again on the floor, and leave the premises in the regular order in which they entered. Should they encounter a person when on these excursions, though in bed, does he but lie still and not disturb them, the good-hearted negro insects will even pass over the person without harm or molestation; but if disturbed, they will retaliate by a sting as readily as a bee when the hive is disturbed, though their sting, so far from being either dangerous or severe, is simply like the severe sting of a musquito. An aged missionary gentleman, of twenty-five years' experience, informed me that an entire myriad (this term is given to a multitude of drivers, as their number can never be less than the thousand—and I am sure that I have seen as many millions together) passed over him one night in bed, without one stinging him. Indeed, both the black and white ants are quite harmless as to personal injury, and very beneficial in a sanitary point. *[margin: How they travel.]*

There is much more in the imagination than the reality about these things; and one important fact I must not omit, that, however great the number of drivers, a simple *light set in the middle of the floor* will clear the room of them in ten minutes. In this case they do not form in column, but go out in hasty confusion, each effecting as quick retreat and safe escape for himself as possible, forming their line of march outside of the house, where they meet from all quarters of their points of escape. *[margin: How to Drive them out of the Houses.]*

Chloride of sodium or common salt (fine), slightly damped, will entirely destroy the termites; and *acetum* or vinegar, or *acetic acid* either, will destroy or chase off the drivers. These means are simple, and within the reach of every person, but aside from this, both classes or races of these creatures disappear before the approach of civilization. In a word, moths, mice, roaches, and musquitoes are much greater domestic annoyances, and certainly much more destructive in America and Europe than the bug-a-bug or driver is in Africa. *[margin: How to Destroy them.]*

I cannot endorse the statement from personal knowledge of the desperate hostility which the drivers manifest towards the termites, as given by Dr. Livingstone,[8] who, calling them "black rascals," says "they stand deliberately and *[margin: Their Pugnacious and Martial Character.]*

watch for the whites, which, on coming out of their holes, they instantly seize, putting them to death." Perhaps the whites were *kidnappers*, in which case they served the white *rascals* right. Though I have never seen an encounter, it is nevertheless true, that the blacks do subdue the whites whenever they meet. In fact, they go, as do no other creatures known to natural science, in immense incalculable numbers—and I do not think that I exaggerate if I say that I have more than once seen more than six hogsheads of them travelling together, had they been measured—and along the entire line of march, stationed on each side of the columns, there are warriors or soldiers to guard them, who stand sentry, closely packed side by side with their heads towards the column, which passes on as rapidly as a flowing stream of water. I have traced a column for more than a mile, whose greatest breadth was more than a yard, and the least not less than a foot. It is inconceivable the distance these creatures travel in a short time. Should anything disturb the lines, the soldiers sally out a few feet in pursuit of the cause, quickly returning to their post when meeting no foe. The guards are much larger than the common drivers, being about the length of a barley-corn, and armed with a pair of curved horns, like those of the large American black beetle, called "pinching bug." There are no bed-bugs here.

Cesspools.   One important fact, never referred to by travellers as such, is that the health of large towns in Africa will certainly be improved by the erection of *cesspools*, whereas now they have none. With the exception of the residences of missionaries and other civilized people, there is no such thing in Africa. Every family, as in civilized countries, should have such conveniences. Our senses are great and good faculties—seeing, hearing, tasting, smelling, and feeling—God has so created them, and designed them for such purposes; therefore, they should neither be perverted nor marred when this can be avoided. Hence, we should beautify, when required, and make pleasing to the sight; modify and make pleasant to the hearing; *cleanse* and *purify* to make *agreeable* to the smelling; improve and make good to the taste; and never violate the feelings whenever any or all of these are at our will or control.

Wild Beasts   A single remark about these. The wild beasts are driven back before the
and Reptiles.   march of civilization, I having seen none, save one leopard; and but four serpents during my entire travels, one three and a half feet long (a water snake); one fourteen inches long; and another ten inches long; the two last being killed by natives—and a tame one around the neck of a charmer at Oyo.[9] During the time I never saw a centipede, and but two tarantulas.

8. The Scottish missionary David Livingstone (1813–73) explored Africa from the early 1840s to the time of his death, which occurred during one of his expeditions. His *Missionary Travels* (1857) was widely read in Europe and the United States.

9. A farming town in southwest Nigeria.

Section X. Missionary Influence.

To deny or overlook the fact, the all-important fact, that the missionary influence had done much good in Africa, would be simply to do injustice, a gross injustice to a good cause.

The advent of the Protestant Missionaries into Africa, has doubtless been effective of much good, though it may reasonably be expected that many have had their short comings. By Protestant, I mean all other Christian denominations than the Roman Catholic. I would not be regarded either a bigot or partialist so far as the rights of humanity are concerned, but facts are tenable in all cases, and whilst I readily admit that a Protestant monarch granted the first letters-patent to steal Africans from their homes to be enslaved by a Protestant people,[10] and subsequently a *bona fide* Protestant nation has been among the most cruel oppressors of the African race, my numerous friends among whom are many Roman Catholics—black as well as white—must bear the test of truth, as I shall apply it in the case of the Missionaries, as my object in visiting my father-land, was to enquire into and learn every fact, which should have a bearing on this, the grandest prospect for the regeneration of a people, that ever was presented in the history of the world.

Protestant Missionaries.

In my entire travels in Africa, either alone or after meeting with Mr. Campbell at Abbeokuta, I have neither seen nor heard of any Roman Catholic Missionaries; but the most surprising and startling fact is, that every slave-trading point on the coast at present (which ports are mainly situated South and East) where the traffic is carried on, are either Roman Catholic trading-ports, or native agencies protected by Roman Catholics; as Canot, formerly at Grand Cape Mount, Pedro Blanco, and Domingo at Wydah in Dahomi.[11] And still more, it is a remarkable and very suggestive reality that at all of those places where the Jesuits or Roman Catholic Missionaries once were stationed, the slave-trade is not only still carried on in its worst form as far as practicable, but slaves are held in Africa by these white foreigners at the old Portuguese settlements along the Southern and Eastern coasts, of Loango and Mozambique for instance; and although some three years have elapsed since the King of Portugal proclaimed, or pretended to proclaim, "Liberty to all the people throughout his dominions," yet I will venture an opinion, that not one in every hundred of native Africans thus

Influence of Roman Catholic Religion in favor of Slavery.

---

10. Under James I, the English government established regular trade in African slaves in 1618.

11. Delany refers to notorious West African slave traders of the first half of the nineteenth century: Theodore Canot (1804–60), Pedro Blanco (1795?–1854), and the more obscure Domingo Martinez. Delany may have been familiar with Brantz Mayer's popular account of the Italian-born French slave trader Canot, *Captain Canot; or, Twenty Years of an African Slaver* (New York: D. Appelton and Company, 1854).

held in bondage on their own soil, are aware of any such "Proclamation." Dr.
Livingstone tells us that he came across many ruins of Roman Catholic Missionary Stations in his travels—especially those in Loando de St. Paul,[12] a city
of some eighteen or twenty thousand of a population—all deserted, and the
buildings appropriated to other uses, as storehouses, and the like. Does not this
seem as though slavery were the legitimate successor of Roman Catholicism, or
slave-traders and holders of the Roman Catholic religion and Missionaries? It
certainly has that appearance to me; and a fact still more glaring is, that the only
professing Christian government which in the light of the present period of
human elevation and national reform, has attempted such a thing, is that of
Roman Catholic Spain, (still persisting in holding Cuba for the wealth accruing
from African Slaves stolen from their native land) which recently expelled every
Protestant Missionary from the African Island of Fernando Po,[13] that they
might command it unmolested by Christian influence, as an export mart for the
African Slave-Trade. To these facts I call the attention of the Christian world,
that no one may murmur when the day of retribution in Africa comes—which
come it must—and is fast hastening, when slave-traders must flee.

Influence of
Protestant Re-
ligion against
Slavery, and
in favor of
civilization.

Wherever the Protestant Missionaries are found, or have been, there are visible evidences of a purer and higher civilization, by the high estimate set upon
the Christian religion by the natives, the deference paid to the missionaries
themselves, and the idea which generally obtains among them, that all missionaries are opposed to slavery, and the faith they have in the moral integrity of
these militant ambassadors of the Living God. Wherever there are missionaries,
there are schools both Sabbath and secular, and the arts and sciences, and manners and customs, more or less of civilized life, are imparted. I have not as yet
visited a missionary station in any part of Africa, where there were not some,
and frequently many natives, both adult and children, who could speak, read,
and write English, as well as read their own language; as all of them, whether Epis-
copalian, Wesleyan, Baptist, or Presbyterian, in the Yoruba country, have Crowther's editions of religious and secular books in the schools and churches,[14] and
all have native agents, interpreters, teachers (assistants) and catechists or readers in the mission. These facts prove indisputably great progress; and I here take
much pleasure in recording them in testimony of those faithful laborers in that
distant vineyard of our heavenly Father in my fatherland. Both male and female
missionaries, all seemed much devoted to their work, and anxiously desirous of
doing more. Indeed, the very fact of there being as many native missionaries as

12. St. Paul de Loando is the capital of Angola.
13. An island in the Bight of Biafra, south of Nigeria.
14. For example, see Crowther's *Grammar of the Yoruba Language* (1852).

there are now to be found holding responsible positions, as elders, deacons, preachers, and priests, among whom there are many finely educated, and several of them authors of works, not only in their own but the English language, as Revs. Crowther, King, Taylor,[15] and Samuel Crowther, Esq., surgeon, all show that there is an advancement for these people beyond the point to which missionary duty can carry them.

I am indebted to the Missionaries generally, wherever met with, whether in Liberia or Central Africa, for their uniform kindness and hospitality. . . .

I would suggest for the benefit of missionaries in general, and those to whom it applies in particular, that there are other measures and ways by which civilization may be imparted than preaching and praying—temporal as well as spiritual means. If all persons who settle among the natives would, as far as it is in their power and comes within their province, induce, by making it a rule of their house or family, every native servant to sit on a stool or chair; eat at a table instead of on the ground; eat with a knife and fork (or *begin* with a spoon) instead of with their fingers; eat in the house instead of going out in the yard, garden, or somewhere else under a tree or shed; and sleep on a bed, instead of on a bare mat on the ground; and have them to wear some sort of a garment to cover the entire person above the knees, should it be but a single shirt or chemise, instead of a loose native cloth thrown around them, to be dropped at pleasure, at any moment exposing the entire upper part of the person—or as in Liberia, where that part of the person is entirely uncovered—I am certain that it would go far toward impressing them with some of the habits of civilized life, as being adapted to them as well as the "white man," whom they so faithfully serve with a will. I know that some may say, this is difficult to do. It certainly could not have been with those who never tried it. Let each henceforth resolve for himself like the son of Nun, "As for me and my house, we will serve the Lord."[16]

I would also suggest that I cannot see the utility of the custom on the part of Missionaries in *changing* the names of native children, and even adults, so soon as they go into their families to live, as though their own were not good enough for them. These native names are generally much more significant, and euphonious than the Saxon, Gælic, or Celtic. Thus, Adenigi means, "Crowns have their shadow." This was the name of a servant boy of ours, whose father was a native cotton trader. It is to be hoped that this custom among Missionaries and other

Kindness of Missionaries and personal acknowledgments.

Hints to those to whom they apply.

Changing names.

15. Reverend William King (1812–95), founder of the Elgin Settlement in Canada West, helped Delany recruit Canadian blacks for his Abeokuta settlement; Reverend Jeremiah Taylor presided over a large African Methodist Episcopal congregation in Canada West.

16. See Joshua 24:15. (Joshua was the son of Nun.)

Christian settlers, of changing the names of the natives, will be stopped, thereby relieving them of the impression, that to embrace the Christian faith, implies a loss of name, and so far loss of identity.

Section XI. What Africa Now Requires.

What Missionary labor has done.

From the foregoing, it is very evident that missionary duty has reached its *ultimatum*. By this, I mean that the native has received all that the missionary was sent to teach, and is now really ready for more than he can or may receive. He sees and knows that the white man, who first carried him the Gospel, which he has learned to a great extent to believe a reality, is of an entirely different race to himself; and has learned to look upon everything which he has, knows and does, which has not yet been imparted to him (especially when he is told by the missionaries, which frequently must be the case, to relieve themselves of the endless teasing enquiries which persons in their position are subject to concerning all and every temporal and secular matter, law, government, commerce, military, and other matters foreign to the teachings of the gospel; that these things he is not sent to teach, but simply the gospel) as peculiarly adapted and belonging to the white man. Of course, there are exceptions to this. Hence, having reached what he conceives to be the *maximum* of the black man's or African's attainments, there must be a re-action in some direction, and if not progressive it will be retrogressive.

How it was done.

The missionary has informed him that the white man's country is great. He builds and resides in great houses; lives in great towns and cities, with great churches and palaver-houses (public and legislative halls); rides in great carriages; manufactures great and beautiful things; has great ships, which go to sea, to all parts of the world, instead of little canoes such as he has paddling up and down the rivers and on the coast; that the wisdom, power, strength, courage, and wealth of the white man and his country are as much greater than him and his, as the big ships are larger and stronger than the little frail canoes; all of which he is made sensible of, either by the exhibition of pictures or the reality.

The result, if not timely aided by legitimate means.

He at once comes to a stand. "Of what use is the white man's religion and 'book knowledge' to me, since it does not give me the knowledge and wisdom nor the wealth and power of the white man, as all these things belong only to him?" "Our young men and women learn their book, and talk on paper (write), and talk to God like white man (worship), but God no hear 'em like he hear white man! Dis religion no use to black man." And so the African *reasonably* reasons when he sees that despite his having yielded up old-established customs, the laws of his fathers, and almost his entire social authority, and the rule of his household to the care and guardianship of the missionary, for the sake of acquiring his knowledge and power—when, after having learned all that his children can, he is doomed to see them sink right back into their old habits, the country continue in the same condition, without the beautiful improvements of the white man—and if a change take place at all, he is doomed to witness what he never expected to see and dies regretting—himself and people entangled in the meshes of the government of a people foreign in kith, kin, and sympathy, when he and his are entirely shoved aside and compelled to take subordinate and inferior positions, if not, indeed, reduced to menialism and bondage. I am justified in asserting that this state of things has brought missionary efforts to their *maximum* and native progress to a pause.

Religion has done its work, and now requires temporal and secular aid to give it another impulse. The improved arts of civilized life must now be brought to bear, and go hand in hand in aid of the missionary efforts which are purely religious in character and teaching. I would not have the standard of religion lowered a single stratum of the common breeze of heaven. No, let it rather be raised, if, indeed, higher it can be. Christianity certainly is the most advanced civilization that man ever attained to, and wherever propagated in its purity, to be effective, law and government must be brought in harmony with it—otherwise it becomes corrupted, and a corresponding degeneracy ensues, placing its votaries even in a worse condition than the primitive. This was exemplified by the Author of our faith, who, so soon as he began to teach, commenced by admonishing the people to a modification of their laws—or rather himself to condemn them. But it is very evident that the social must keep pace with the religious, and the political with the social relations of society, to carry out the great measures of the higher civilization.

Of what avail, then, is advanced intelligence to the African without improved social relations—acquirements and refinement without an opportunity of a practical application of them—society in which they are appreciated? It requires not the most astute reformer and political philosopher to see.

The native sees at once that all the higher social relations are the legitimate result and requirements of a higher intelligence, and naturally enough expects, that when he has attained it, to enjoy the same privileges and blessings. But how sadly mistaken—what dire disappointment!

The habits, manners, and customs of his people, and the social relations all around him are the same; improvements of towns, cities, roads, and methods of travel are the same; implements of husbandry and industry are the same; the methods of conveyance and price of produce (with comparative trifling variation) are the same. All seem dark and gloomy for the future, and he has his

[Marginal notes:]

Missionary aid.

Christianity and Law or Government must harmonize, to be effective of good.

Like seeks like.

Natives desire higher social relations.

Native doubts respecting the eventual good effects of Missionary labor.

doubts and fears as to whether or not he has committed a fatal error in leaving his native social relations for those of foreigners whom he cannot hope to emulate, and who, he thinks, will not assimilate themselves to him.

The proper element as progressive Missionary agencies.

It is clear, then, that essential to the success of civilization, is the establishment of all those social relations and organizations, without which enlightened communities cannot exist. To be successful, these must be carried out by proper agencies, and these agencies must be a *new element* introduced into their midst, possessing all the attainments, socially and politically, morally and religiously, adequate to so important an end. This element must be *homogenous* in all the *natural* characteristics, claims, sentiments, and sympathies—the *descendants of Africa* being the only element that can effect it. To this end, then, a part of the most enlightened of that race in America design to carry out these most desirable measures by the establishment of social and industrial settlements among them, in order at once to introduce, in an effective manner, all the well-regulated pursuits of civilized life.

Precaution against error in the first steps.

That no mis-step be taken and fatal error committed at the commencement, we have determined that the persons to compose this new element to be introduced into Africa, shall be well and most carefully selected in regard to moral integrity, intelligence, acquired attainments, fitness, adaptation, and, as far as practicable, religious sentiments and professions. We are serious in this; and, so far as we are concerned as an individual, it shall be restricted to the letter, and we will most strenuously oppose and set our face against any attempt from any quarter to infringe upon this arrangement and design. Africa is our fatherland and we its legitimate descendants, and we will never agree nor consent to see this—the first voluntary step that has ever been taken for her regeneration by her own descendants—blasted by a disinterested or renegade set, whose only object might be in the one case to get rid of a portion of the colored population, and in the other, make money, though it be done upon the destruction of every hope entertained and measure introduced for the accomplishment of this great and prospectively glorious undertaking. We cannot and will not permit or agree that the result of years of labor and anxiety shall be blasted at one reckless blow, by those who have never spent a day in the cause of our race, or know nothing about our wants and requirements. The descendants of Africa in North America will doubtless, by the census of 1860, reach five millions; those of Africa may number two hundred millions. I have outgrown, long since, the boundaries of North America, and with them have also outgrown the boundaries of their claims. I, therefore, cannot consent to sacrifice the prospects of two hundred millions, that a fraction of five millions may be benefitted, especially since the measures adopted for the many must necessarily benefit the few.

Africa, to become regenerated, must have a national character, and her position among the existing nations of the earth will depend mainly upon the high standard she may gain compared with them in all her relations, morally, religiously, socially, politically, and commercially.

National character essential to the successful regeneration of Africa.

I have determined to leave to my children the inheritance of a country, the possession of territorial domain, the blessings of a national education, and the indisputable right of self-government; that they may not succeed to the servility and degradation bequeathed to us by our fathers. If we have not been born to fortunes, we should impart the seeds which shall germinate and give birth to fortunes for them.

Section XII. To Direct Legitimate Commerce.

As the first great national step in political economy, the selection and security of a location to direct and command commerce legitimately carried on, as an export and import metropolis, is essentially necessary. The facilities for a metropolis should be adequate—a rich, fertile, and productive country surrounding it, with some great staple (which the world requires as a commodity) of exportation. A convenient harbor as an outlet and inlet, and natural facilities for improvement, are among the necessary requirements for such a location.

First steps in political economy.

The basis of great nationality depends upon three elementary principles: first, territory; second, population; third, a great staple production either natural or artificial, or both, as a permanent source of wealth; and Africa comprises these to an almost unlimited extent. The continent is five thousand miles from Cape Bon (north) to the Cape of Good Hope (south), and four thousand at its greatest breadth, from Cape Guardifui (east) to Cape de Verde (west), with an average breadth of two thousand five hundred miles, any three thousand of which within the tropics north and south, including the entire longitude, will produce the staple cotton, also sugar cane, coffee, rice, and all the tropical staples, with two hundred millions of *natives* as an industrial element to work this immense domain. The world is challenged to produce the semblance of a parallel to this. It has no rival in fact. . . .

The Basis of a great Nation— national wealth.

As to the possibility of putting a stop to the slave-trade, I have only to say that we do not leave America and go to Africa to be passive spectators of such a policy as traffic in the flesh and blood of our kindred, nor any other species of the human race—more we might say—that we will not live there and permit it. "Self-preservation is the first law of nature," and we go to Africa to be *self-sustaining*; otherwise we have no business there, or anywhere else, in my opinion. We will bide our time; *but the Slave-trade shall not continue!*

Stopping the Slave Trade.

Means of doing it.

Another important point of attention: that is, the slave-trade ceases in Africa, wherever enlightened Christian civilization gains an influence. And as to the strength and power necessary, we have only to add, that Liberia, with a coast frontier of seven hundred miles, and a sparse population, which at the present only numbers fifteen thousand settlers, has been effective in putting a stop to that infamous traffic along her entire coast. And I here record with pleasure, and state what I know to be the fact, and but simple justice to as noble-hearted antagonists to slavery as live, that the Liberians are uncompromising in their opposition to oppression and the enslavement of their race, or any other part of the human family. I speak of them as a nation or people and ignore entirely their Iscariots,[17] if any there be. What they have accomplished with less means, we, by the help of Providence, may reasonably expect to effect with more—what they did with little, we may do with much. And I speak with confidence when I assert, that if we in this new position but do and act as we are fondly looked to and expected—as I most fondly hope and pray God that, by a prudent, discretionate and well-directed course, dependant upon Him, we may, nay, I am certain we will do—I am sure that there is nothing that may be required to aid in the prosecution and accomplishment of this important and long-desired end, that may not be obtained from the greatest and most potent Christian people and nation that ever graced the world. There is no aid that might be wanted, which may not be obtained through a responsible, just, and equitable negotiation.

Subsidizing the King of Dahomi.

There is some talk by Christians and philanthropists in Great Britain of subsidizing the King of Dahomi.[18] I hope for the sake of humanity, our race, and the cause of progressive civilization, this most injurious measure of compensation for wrong, never will be resorted to nor attempted.

To make such an offering just at a time when we are about to establish a policy of self-regeneration in Africa, which may, by example and precept, effectually check forever the nefarious system, and reform the character of these people, would be to offer inducements to that monster to continue, and a license to other petty chiefs to commence the traffic in human beings, to get a reward of subsidy.

17. Traitors; Iscariot was the surname of Judas, the betrayer of Jesus.
18. Shortly after the Alake was pressured by British missionaries to renounce his treaty with Delany, the king of Dahomey threatened to invade the Yoruba country. Delany and Crowther suspected that the British had prompted this threat.

Section XIII. Cotton Staple.

Cotton grows profusely in all this part of Africa, and is not only produced naturally, but extensively cultivated throughout the Yoruba country. The soil, climate, and the people are the three natural elements combined to produce this indispensable commodity, and with these three natural agencies, no other part of the world can compete. *Natural elements to produce cotton.*

In India there is a difficulty and great expense and outlay of capital required to obtain it. In Australia it is an experiment; and though it may eventually be obtained, it must also involve an immense outlay of capital, and a long time before an adequate supply can be had, as it must be admitted, however reluctantly by those desirous it should be otherwise, that the African, as has been justly said by a Manchester merchant, has in all ages, in all parts of the world, been sought to raise cotton wherever it has been produced. *Africans the only reliable producers.*

In America there are several serious contingencies which must always render a supply of cotton from that quarter problematical and doubtful, and always expensive and subject to sudden, unexpected and unjust advances in prices. In the first place, the land is purchased at large prices; secondly, the people to work it; thirdly, the expense of supporting the people, with the contingencies of sickness and death; fourthly, the uncertainty of climate and contingencies of frost, and a backward season and consequent late or unmatured crop; fifthly, insubordination on the part of the slaves, which is not improbable at any time; sixthly, suspension of friendly relations between the United States and Great Britain; and lastly, a rupture between the American States themselves, which I think no one will be disposed now to consider impossible. All, or any of these circumstances combined, render it impossible for America to compete with Africa in the growth and sale of cotton, for the following reasons: *Serious contingencies and uncertainty in American cotton supply.*

Firstly, landed tenure in Africa is free, the occupant selecting as much as he can cultivate, holding it so long as he uses it, but cannot convey it to another; secondly, the people all being free, can be hired at a price less than the *interest* of the capital invested in land and people to work it—they finding their own food, which is the custom of the country; thirdly, there are no contingencies of frost or irregular weather to mar or blight the crop; and fourthly, we have two regular crops a year, or rather one continuous crop, as while the trees are full of pods of ripe cotton, they are at the same time blooming with fresh flowers. And African cotton is planted only every seven years, whilst the American is replanted every season. Lastly, the average product per acre on the best Mississippi and Louisiana cotton plantations in America, is three hundred and fifty pounds; the average per acre in Africa, a hundred per cent. more, or seven hundred pounds. As the African soil produces two crops a year to one in America, then *Superior advantages of Africa over all other countries in the production of cotton.*

we in Africa produce fourteen hundred pounds to three hundred and fifty in America; the cost of labor a hand being one dollar or four shillings a day to produce it; whilst in Africa at present it is nine hundred per cent. less, being only ten cents or five pence a day for adult labor. At this price the native lives better on the abundance of produce in the country, and has more money left at the end of the week than the European or free American laborer at one dollar a day.

Cotton, as before stated, is the great commodity of the world, entering intimately into, being incorporated with almost every kind of fabric of wearing apparel. All kinds of woolen goods—cloths, flannels, alpacas, merinoes, and even silks, linen, nankin, ginghams, calicoes, muslins, cordages, ship-sails, carpeting, hats, hose, gloves, threads, waddings, paddings, tickings, every description of book and newspaper, writing paper, candle wicks, and what not, all depend upon the article cotton.

Importance of the African Race in the Social and Political Relations of the world.

By this it will be seen and admitted that the African occupies a much more important place in the social and political element of the world than that which has heretofore been assigned him—holding the balance of commercial power, the source of the wealth of nations in his hands. This is indisputably true—undeniable, that cotton cannot be produced without negro labor and skill in raising it.

The African Race sustains Great Britain.

Great Britain alone has directly engaged in the manufacture of pure fabrics from the raw material, five millions of persons; two-thirds more of the population depend upon this commodity indirectly for livelihood. The population (I include in this calculation Ireland) being estimated at 30,000,000, we have then 25,000,000 of people, or five-sixths of the population of this great nation, depending upon the article cotton alone for subsistence, and the black man is the producer of the raw material, and the source from whence it comes. What an important fact to impart to the heretofore despised and underrated negro race, to say nothing of all the other great nations of Europe, as France, for instance, with her extensive manufactures of muslin delaines—which simply mean *cotton and wool*—more or less engaged in the manufacture and consumption of cotton.

The Negro race sustain the whites—able to sustain themselves.

If the negro race—as slaves—can produce cotton as an *exotic* in foreign climes to enrich white men who oppress them, they can, they must, they will, they shall, produce it as an *indigene* in their own-loved native Africa to enrich themselves, and regenerate their race; if a faithful reliance upon the beneficence and promise of God, and an humble submission to his will, as the feeble instruments in his hands through which the work is commenced, shall be available to this end.

Home Trade.

The Liberians must as a policy as much as possible, patronise home manufactured, and home produced articles. Instead of using foreign, they should prefer their own sugar, molasses, and coffee, which is equal to that produced in any other country; and if not, it is the only way to encourage the farmers and manufacturers to improve them. The coffee of Liberia, is equal to any in the world, and I have drunk some of the native article, superior in strength and flavor to Java or Mocca,[19] and I rather solicit competition in judgment of the article of coffee. And singular as it may appear, they are even supplied from abroad with spices and condiments, although their own country as also all Africa, is prolific in the production of all other articles, as allspice, ginger, pepper black and red, mustard and everything else.

They must also turn their attention to supplying the Coast settlements with sugar and molasses, and everything else of their own production which may be in demand. Lagos and the Missionary stations in the interior, now consume much of these articles, the greater part of which — sugar and molasses — are imported from England and America. This trade they might secure in a short time without successful competition, because many of the Liberia merchants now own vessels, and the firm of Johnson, Turpin and Dunbar,[20] own a fine little coasting steamer, and soon they would be able to undersell the foreigners; whilst at present their trade of these articles in America is a mere *favor* through the benevolence of some good hearted gentlemen, personal *friends* of theirs, who receive and dispose of them — sugar and molasses — at a price much above the market value, to encourage them. This can only last while these friends continue, when it must then cease. To succeed as a state or nation, we must become self-reliant, and thereby able to create our own ways and means; and a trade created *in* Africa *by* civilized Africans, would be a national rock of "everlasting ages." *Coast Trade.*

The domestic trade among the natives in the interior of our part of Africa — Yoruba — is very great. Corn meal, Guinea corn flour very fine, and a fine flour made of yams is plentiful in every market, and cooked food can always be had in great abundance from the women at refreshment stands kept in every town and along the highway every few miles when traveling. *Domestic Trade. Corn meal, Guinea corn and Yam flour.*

Molasses candy or "taffy," is carried about and sold by young girls, made from the syrup of sugar cane, which does not differ in appearance and flavor from that of civilized countries. *Candy.*

Hard and soft soap are for sale in every market for domestic uses, made from lye by percolation or dripping of water through ashes in large earthen vessels or "hoppers." *Soap.*

19. Islands of Indonesia and south Yemen known for their coffee.
20. Established by three Liberians, this was also the firm that owned the *Mendi*, the ship that took Delany from New York to Liberia.

Coloring and Dying. Making Indigo. Coloring and dying is carried on very generally, every woman seeming to understand it as almost a domestic necessity; also the manufacturing of indigo, the favorite and most common color of the country. Red comes next to this which is mostly obtained of camwood, another domestic employment of the women. Yellow is the next favorite color. Hence, blue, red, and yellow may be designated as the colors of Yoruba or Central Africa.

Weaving and cloth manufacturing; Leather. The manufactory of cotton cloth is carried on quite extensively among them; and in a ride of an hour through the city of Illorin, we counted one hundred and fifty-seven looms in operation in several different establishments. Beautiful and excellent leather is also manufactured, from which is made sandals, shoes, boots, bridles, saddles, harness-caparisons for horses, and other ornaments and uses. They all wear clothes of their own manufacture. The inhabitants of Abbeokuta are called Egbas, and those of all the other parts of Yoruba are called Yorubas—all speaking the Egba language.

A fixed policy for the blacks, as a fundamental necessity. Our policy must be—and I hazard nothing in promulging it; nay, without this design and feeling, there would be a great deficiency of self-respect, pride of race, and love of country, and we might never expect to challenge the respect of nations—*Africa for the African race, and black men to rule them.* By black men I mean, men of African descent who claim an identity with the race.

Internal medium of Communication. Navigable rivers. So contrary to old geographical notions, Africa abounds with handsome navigable rivers, which during six or eight months in the year, would carry steamers suitably built. Of such are the Gallinos, St. Paul, Junk, and Kavalla of Liberia; the Ogun, Ossa, the great Niger and others of and contiguous to Yoruba; the Gambia, Senegambia, Orange, Zambisi and others of other parts. The Kavalla is a beautiful stream which for one hundred miles is scarcely inferior to the Hudson of New York, in any particular; and all of them equal the rivers of the Southern States of America generally which pour out by steamers the rich wealth of the planting States into the Mississippi. With such prospects as these; with such a people as the Yorubas and others of the best type, as a constituent industrial, social, and political element upon which to establish a national edifice, what is there to prevent success? Nothing in the world.

Native Government. The Governments in this part are generally Patriarchial, the Kings being elective from ancient Royal families by the Council of Elders, which consists of men chosen for life by the people, for their age, wisdom, experience, and service among them. They are a deliberative body, and all cases of great importance; of state, life and death, must be brought before them. The King as well as either of themselves, is subject to trial and punishment for misdemeanor in office, before the Council of Elders.

Lagos is the place of the family residence of that excellent gentleman Aji, or the Rev. Samuel Crowther, the native Missionary; and also his son-in-law Rev.

T. B. Macaulay, who has an excellent school, assisted by his wife an educated native lady.

"Princes shall come out of Egypt; Ethiopia shall soon stretch out her hands unto God."—Ps. lxviii. 31. With the fullest reliance upon this blessed promise, I humbly go forward in—I may repeat—the grandest prospect for the regeneration of a people that ever was presented in the history of the world. The disease has long since been known; we have found and shall apply the remedy. I am indebted to Rev. H. H. Garnet, an eminent black clergyman and scholar, for the construction, that "soon," in the Scriptural passage quoted, "has reference to the period ensuing *from the time of beginning.*" With faith in the promise, and hope from this version, surely there is nothing to doubt or fear.

(M. R. Delany, *Official Report of the Niger Valley Exploring Party* [New York: Thomas Hamilton, 1861], pp. 30, 33–35, 40, 44–46, 47–51, 52–56, 57–62)

The International Statistical Congress

IN MAY 1860, Delany began a five-month lecture tour of Great Britain, the main purpose of which was to gain financial support for his colony in Abeokuta. However, a highlight of that tour, his attendance in July at the International Statistical Congress in London, had very little to do with Abeokuta. At the opening of the congress, a gathering of many of the leading scientists of Europe, Asia, and America, Lord Henry Peter Brougham pointedly introduced Delany to the assembled scientists and His Royal Highness Prince Albert as a "negro" who was "a man." Regarding the introduction as a deliberate insult to the American South, Judge Augustus Longstreet of South Carolina protested by walking out of the congress; George Mifflin Dallas, the American minister to Britain, remained to observe what he regarded as the humiliating spectacle of Delany becoming the center of attention as he reported on his explorations of Africa. The incident was widely reported in the British and American press. Delany regarded his attendance at the congress as one of the key moments of his life, a moment that ratified his accomplishments as a black man. Taken from the extensive chapter on the congress in Frances Rollin's *Life and Public Services of Major Martin R. Delany*, the following is Delany's version of events as told to Rollin in 1867.

"When the time drew near for the arrival of his royal highness,[1] the Congress was organized, the members taking their seats, and the official dignitaries seated on the platform.

"The royal crimson chair, and one on either side reserved for the prince and his associates, vice-presidents, were vacant. Great demonstrations were made, which gave evidence that some important personage approached, when it was soon observed that it was the arrival of the ex-lord high chancellor of England. He was escorted to his seat on the platform.

"Soon after, music was heard, succeeded by the entry of pages, unrolling the

1. Prince Albert (1819–61), the husband of Queen Victoria.

crimson carpet, which preceded the entry of the prince president. At this the whole Congress arose to their feet, with rousing claps of applause. Ascending the platform, his royal highness stood before the chair of state, bowed, and took his seat, when immediately the Hon. George M. Dallas,[2] the American minister, and the Right Hon. Lord Brougham,[3] were conducted by the royal commissioners to the vacant seats on the right and left of his royal highness.

"The prince, with his usual dignity, now arose, bowed, and commenced reading one of the most profound and philosophically simple and comprehensive addresses delivered during the present century.

"In the course of his remarks, he alluded to his former preceptor, Count Vishers,[4] paying great compliments to him. He concluded amidst suppressed applause, suggestive of a feeling which hesitated to show itself, for fear of committing an impropriety before the royal author. That great and generous-hearted gentleman, Lord Brougham, instantly arose, and addressing the Congress, said, 'I rise not to address myself to his royal highness, but to you, my lords and gentlemen of the Congress, not to permit the presence of his royal highness to restrain you from giving vent and full scope to that outburst of applause, which you are desirous of giving in approbation of that great good sense, philosophical and most extraordinary discourse, to which we have had the honor and pleasure, as well as profit, of listening.'

"Immediately taking his seat, the assemblage gave vent to rapturous applause. As it concluded, he again rose to his feet, remarking in general terms that it was a most extraordinary assemblage of the world's wisdom, and that those who were there were fortunate in being members of such a body, presided over by that great personage, the prince consort of England.

"He also made allusions to the presence of the imperial director of public works from France, the representatives from Brazil, Spain, and some other countries, as an evidence of the progress of the age; then taking his seat, and instantly arising in such a hasty manner, as though something important had been omitted, that he attracted the attention of the entire assembly; when, extending his hands almost across his Royal Highness, he remarked, 'I would remind my friend, Mr. Dallas, that there is a negro member of this Congress' (di-

2. A former vice president of the United States (1845–49), George Mifflin Dallas (1792–1864), a Pennsylvania Democrat, was appointed minister to Great Britain in 1856.

3. The indefatigable Lord Henry Peter Brougham (1778–1868), who had helped to bring about West Indies emancipation, was eighty-two at the time of the congress.

4. Count Vishers is obscure, and there is a possibility that Delany got the name wrong. Prince Albert's tutor of fifteen years and lifelong friend and correspondent was Count Christoph Florschütz.

recting his hand towards me): smiling, he resumed his seat. Mr. Dallas, seeming to receive this kindly, bowed and smiled.

"Count Vishers now rose to reply to the compliments made to him by the prince; then followed the director of the public works from France, followed by the Brazilian representative, and concluding with the Spanish diplomatist.

"While I fully comprehended his lordship's interest, meaning, and its extent, the thought flashed instantly across my mind, How will this assembly take it? May it not be mistaken by some, at least, as a want of genuine respect for my presence, by the manner in which the remarks were made? And again, would not my silence be regarded as an inability to comprehend a want of deference on the part of his lordship? Or should I not be accused of regarding as a compliment a disparaging allusion towards me? These thoughts passed through my mind so soon as his lordship concluded his remarks, and as soon as the minister from Spain was seated, I rose in my place, and said,—

" 'I rise, your Royal Highness, to thank, his lordship, the unflinching friend of the negro, for the remarks he has made in reference to myself, and to assure your royal highness and his lordship that *I am a man.*' I then resumed my seat. The clapping of hands commenced on the stage, followed by what the London Times was pleased to call 'the wildest shouts ever manifested in so grave an assemblage.' . . .

"The next day, when the general Congress convened, on calling for the reports from the several sections, which presented the papers for ratification before that body, alphabetically arranged, and by courtesy commencing with America, it was discovered that the entire American representation, except Dr. Jarvis,[5] from Boston, Mass., had withdrawn,—the fact being stated by the doctor, who presented the paper placed in his hands by Judge Longstreet,[6] whose office it was to present it as head of the representation, and only direct national delegate (Dr. Jarvis being only a state delegate). Lord Brougham, the first vicepresident, who, in the absence of the royal president, filled the chair, arose, remarking, 'This reminds me of a statement made in the papers this morning, that I had designedly wounded the feelings of the American minister at this court, which I deny as farthest from my intention, as all who know me (and I appeal to the American minister himself, Mr. Dallas being a friend of mine), whether I have not uniformly stood forth as the friend of that government and

5. Dr. Edward Jarvis (1803–84) of Boston helped to found the American Statistical Society in 1840, and he served as its president from 1852 to 1882.

6. The proslavery southern leader Judge Augustus B. Longstreet (1790–1870) served as president of four southern universities, including Emory and the University of South Carolina. He was also the author of *Georgia Scenes* (1835), which helped to inaugurate the genre of southwestern humor.

people? Now, what is this "*offence*" complained of. Why, on the opening of this August assemblage (possibly the largest in number, and the most learned, that the world ever saw together from different nations, to be among whom any man might feel proud, as an evidence of his advance, civilization, and attainments), what is the fact? Why, here we see, even in this unequalled council, a son of Africa, one of that race whom we have been taught to look upon as inferior. I only alluded to this as one of the most gratifying as well as extraordinary facts of the age.'

"The noble and philanthropic lord then took his seat amidst another *cause of offence.*"

(Frank [Frances] A. Rollin, *Life and Public Services of Martin R. Delany* [Boston: Lee and Shepard, 1868], pp. 116–19)

Africa and the African Race

HAVING ACHIEVED CELEBRITY status at the International Statistical Congress, Delany lectured to large audiences in Great Britain over the next several months. In his lectures on the Abeokuta settlement, he proclaimed that his and other free-labor settlements would help to develop the cotton crop in Africa, thereby freeing British manufacturers from their reliance on cotton from the slave South. His speeches also emphasized the importance of developing a black nationality and black pride in Africa. One of his most popular lectures was "Africa and the African Race," which he delivered at a number of venues, including the United Presbyterian Church on Blacket Street, Newcastle-upon-Tyne. An account of that church lecture of September 1861 appeared in one of the local newspapers.

Dr. Delany, in the first part of his lecture, noticed the domestic animals common to Central Africa, enumerating fowls, Muscovy ducks, and turkeys. In allusion to the animals, he said the swine were the exact type of our Berkshire breed; goats, though not large, were heavy, and their flesh was of good flavour. The horned cattle resembled the Durham ox, and there was also a long-horned variety. With regard to horses, it was generally supposed that the most celebrated were bred in Arabia; but this was a mistake, for the Arabians themselves purchased their horses in Central Africa, and even the sire of the famous Godolphin[1] was not an Arabian, but an African horse. The buildings of Africa were like those of Tyre and Babylon,[2] and were constructed of unburnt brick, and their architectural structures showed they had a high degree of civilisation among them. Some of the chief houses had animals and reptiles depicted on them, such as were represented on the statues brought from Egypt, and on

1. The British financier and statesman Sidney Godolphin, first earl of Godolphin (1645–1712), became one of Queen Anne's most trusted advisers upon her accession in 1702, and was known for his support of the unpopular War of Spanish Succession.
2. Ancient cities in southwest Asia famed for their wealth, culture, and waterways.

columns in Central Africa he had found figures which could not be mistaken as representations of Rameses, Osiris, and Sesostris.[3] He contended that these monarchs were of the negro and not of the Caucasian race, and in support of his statement alluded to the resemblance between the chief idol of the Egyptians and that of the Africans in the present day. The Egyptian god was Jupiter Ammon,[4] and he was adorned with ram's horns, while the African idol "Shango"[5] was now represented by a black ram. The Africans, however, believed in the existence of a superior and invisible god, to whom they prayed through "Shango." The laying out of their dead in the manner of Egyptian mummies, though not embalmed, was another evidence of their descent from the Egyptians. He controverted the statements of Gliddon,[6] the French antiquarian,[7] and others with reference to the ladies originally sepulchered in the pyramids being of the Caucasian race; submitting that in the subsequent overrunning of the country by the Persians, Grecians, and Saracens,[8] these conquerors had removed the original bodies, and interred those of their own race. He then gave traits, illustrating the negro's self-respect, and his capacity for the participation of civilised life; and afterwards discoursed on the commercial advantages which would accrue to them were they embodied into a distinct nationality. He now came to ask England to assist in the restoration of that people, who, as he had shown in a former lecture, had contributed so much to her wealth and to her power. (Applause.) That people wished to establish a civil government. Since 1815 upwards of £15,000,000 had been expended to put down the slave trade, but he had no hesitation in saying that the establishment of a civil government in Africa would do more towards suppressing the slave trade in ten years than all the naval powers that had ever existed. Dr. Delany then mentioned certain arrangements he

3. Ancient Egyptian leaders and gods. Delany's phrasing meant to suggest that the figures on the columns could not be mistaken as anything other than representations of Rameses, Osiris, and Sesostris.

4. Also known as Amon, the ancient Egyptian god regarded as the supreme deity.

5. Central to Yoruba tradition, Shango was worshiped as a patron saint and protector of the people.

6. The Englishman George R. Gliddon (1809–57) examined mummified skulls while serving as vice consul at Cairo and concluded that the ancient Egyptians were white. His research culminated in a book coauthored with Josiah C. Nott (1804–73) of Mobile, Alabama, *Types of Mankind* (1854), a widely disseminated compendium of "facts" about the races that for many British and American readers offered scientific legitimation to those who would argue for blacks' lower place in the social hierarchy.

7. Jean François Champollion (1790–1832), a French Egyptologist known for his pioneering use of the Rosetta stone to decipher hieroglyphics.

8. Nomadic tribes on the Syrian borders of the Roman Empire.

had already made for the carrying out of his national project, and concluded by saying that on the accomplishment of that object the English might be sure of the alliance of a people who would not be of so doubtful a character as that of some people who lived across the Straits of Dover.[9] (Applause.)

(*The Daily Chronicle and Northern Counties Advertiser*, 21 September 1860, p. 2)

9. A strait between England and France connecting the English Channel and the North Sea.

Letter to James T. Holly, 15 January 1861

SHORTLY AFTER RETURNING to Canada in January 1861, Delany wrote the black abolitionist James Holly (1829–1911) to express his misgivings about Haitian emigration, which he feared would undercut his African project. Holly, an Episcopal priest from New York, had attended Delany's National Emigration Convention in Cleveland and by the late 1850s was a leading advocate of black emigration to Haiti. In 1857 he published *Vindication of the Capacity of the Negro Race*, which extolled Haiti as the embodiment of black nationality in the Americas, and in 1859 he began working with the white journalist James Redpath to encourage blacks to make their way to Haiti. Holly himself led an expedition to Haiti of over 100 immigrants from New Haven, Boston, and Canada West in 1861.

KING STREET HUT.
Chatham, C.W., Jan. 15th, 1861.

Rector Holly, my Dear Sir and Friend:—Your kind favor without date in reply to mine written at Liverpool, England, the 11th ult., has just come to hand for which I thank you.

My duty and destiny are in Africa, the great and glorious (even with its defects) land of your and my ancestry. I cannot, I *will not* desert her for all things else in this world, save that of my "own household," and that does not require it, as it will thereby be enhanced.

I have nothing to say against Haytien emigration, except that I am surprised that in the face of the intelligent *black men* who favor it, two of whom have been to that country and one to Jamaica, (yourself, Mr. Harris, and Mr. Garnet),[1] the

---

1. A black antislavery activist from Cleveland, J. Dennis Harris supported black emigration to the Caribbean. In 1860 he published *A Summer on the Borders of the Caribbean Sea*, and shortly thereafter he became a recruiting agent for the Haytian Emigration Bureau.

government would appoint *over them*, to encourage black emigration, a white man,[2] thereby acknowledging negro inferiority, and the charge recently made against them by Dr. J. McCune Smith, that according to their estimation, "next to God is the white man."[3]

You know that this is *not prejudice* in me, as my sentiments endorsed by yourself, and the whole Cleveland Convention are, that the black man should act and do for himself, just as the white man, under like circumstances, would be justifiable in doing—*self reliance*, on the principles of a Black Nationality. These sentiments conceived in my youth, many years ago, matured in manhood, promulgated in a public document in the great Emigration Convention at Cleveland, Ohio, U.S., in 1854,[4] have since been proclaimed in tones unmistakable upon the high seas, in the capital of Liberia, for twenty-five hundred miles along the coast of Africa, in the Metropolis of the world, and through the United Kingdom until they "career against the wind," reverberating from the top, and rippling the surface of Ben and Loch Lomond,[5] the home and haunt of the gallant highlander, where the slogan of the Campbell's and Cameron's, and of the McDonald's have long since been heard,[6] against the strife of battle and the groans of death. If thus uttered amidst my greatest friends and supporters of my scheme and adventure, I cannot I say be charged with prejudice when I object to a black government appointing over black men, a white, when black were competent to act and no policy requires the appointment of a white. I object to white men in such cases, getting all the positions of *honor* and *emoluments*, while the blacks receive only the *subordinate* with little or no pay! I maintain this position as necessary to self respect, and treat with contempt the idea, that it makes no difference in such cases whether the person be white or black, while black men are still occupying inferior positions in the midst of a people who deny their equality in all the relations of life.

My next exception is, that I fear that this movement is too precipitous—not sufficiently *matured*. There should be no *haste*, as such, at the commencement

---

2. In 1859 the Haitian government appointed the white abolitionist James Redpath (1833–91) commissioner of emigration. Redpath opened the Haytian Emigration Bureau in Boston in 1860 and that same year published *A Guide to Hayti* (1860) and founded the emigrationist newspaper the *Pine and the Palm*. Delany would again attack Redpath and the Haitian emigration movement in letters printed in the 16 November 1861 *Weekly Anglo-African*, p. 1, and the 1 February 1862 *Weekly Anglo-African*, p. 2.

3. A prominent black abolitionist who had a medical practice in New York City, James McCune Smith (1813–65) criticized black emigrationism in the 12 January 1861 *Weekly Anglo-African*, from which Delany took the quotation.

4. "Political Destiny of the Colored Race on the American Continent."

5. A mountain and lake near Glasgow, Scotland.

6. Three large highland clans in Scotland's early history.

of such movements, (and this is the commencement of yours) and all attempts at excitement should be avoided.

Neither do I regard or believe Mr. Redpath, the Haytien Government Agent, nor any other white men, competent to judge and decide upon the destiny of the colored people or the fitness of any place for the bettering of their condition, any more than I should be a Frenchman to direct the destiny of Englishmen. If they have not now,—if we with our claim and boasted equality have not yet reached the point of competency to judge and decide for ourselves, what, when, and where is best for us to do or go, but must needs have white men to act for us, then indeed are we wholly unfit to fill the places they claim for us, and should be under white masters.

Do not misunderstand me as objecting to your movement, as conflicting with mine or ours. This is not the case, as we desire no promiscuous or general emigration to Africa, (as the country needs no laborers, these everywhere abounding, industriously employed in various occupations,) but select and intelligent people to guide and direct the industry, and promote civilization by the establishment of higher social organizations and the legitimate development of our inexhaustible commerce, which promises not only certain wealth to us, but all the rest of the world, besides the certainty of thereby putting a stop to the infamous slave trade, with a reflex influence upon the if possible more infamous American slave trade. In this we desire not to shed their (the Southern monsters') blood, but make them shed their tears.

I am, my dear Mr. Holly, very sincerely your friend and co-laborer in the cause of our race, for God and humanity.

M. R. DELANY.

Rev. J. Theodore Holly,
Rector St. Luke's Church,
New Haven, Conn.

(*Chatham Tri-Weekly Planet*, 21 January 1861, p. 2)

Letter to Robert Hamilton, 28 September 1861

UNDER PRESSURE FROM British missionaries, the Alake rescinded his agreement with Delany early in 1861. Later that year, when William Wells Brown toured Canadian black communities in search of recruits for Haitian emigration, he pointedly remarked on the apparent collapse of Delany's African project. In doing so, he hoped to make Haiti appear an even better option than Africa for Canada's potential black emigrants. In his report "The Colored People of Canada" in the 28 September 1861 issue of the Boston-based Haitian emigration newspaper *Pine and Palm*, Brown represented Delany as virtually demented in his rage at African leaders. Delany responded to Brown in a letter to the editor of the *Weekly Anglo-African*.

NEW YORK, Sept. 28th, 1861.

MR. ROBERT HAMILTON:

Dear Sir—I simply notice the letter of Mr. W. Wells Brown in the "Pine and Palm" of the 28th inst., written from Chatham, Canada, to correct a most flagrant and designedly mischievous misrepresentation therein stated; that I in a speech in London (Canada,) had declared that the "first thing" I intended to do after going to Lagos, was to "take off the King's head!"[1]

It is merely necessary for me to pronounce this as false in toto, which I do: as a side[2] from the intimate friendship which exists between me and all the native authorities at Lagos (as my Report now just out will show); but no rational person could be capable of such folly as I am here charged with by Mr. Brown, all glaringly to promote his employer, Haytian Emigration.

1. Brown had written that Delany asserted he would "take off the head of the old king" (*Pine and Palm*, 28 September 1861, p. 3). In Section VII of *Official Report of the Niger Exploring Party*, Delany had reported on his friendly visit with King Docemo of Lagos.
2. Perhaps a compositor's error; for "a side," Delany would seem to mean "at variance."

I have always treated Mr. Brown as a gentleman, and heretofore regarded him as a friend, and would not now notice his uncouth (and certainly unwarranted) attack, only to correct this shameless misrepresentation.

It is not necessary for me to state that my destiny is fixed in Africa, where my family and myself, by God's providence, will soon be happily situated.

Very respectfully your friend,
M. R. DELANY

(*Weekly Anglo-African*, 5 October 1861, p. 2)

Letter to James McCune Smith, 11 January 1862

THE NEW YORK black abolitionist James McCune Smith strongly opposed black emigration and embraced the Civil War as a war against slavery. Despite their differences, Delany respected Smith and sought to work with him to organize an African American convention in 1862.

TO DR. JAMES MCCUNE SMITH—MY DEAR SIR AND FRIEND: I lay aside the form of conventional etiquet and statesman courtesy, and prefer addressing you in a plain, familiar, and friendly manner in such times as these, on a subject of such grave importance.

The present state of the political affairs of the world more than at any period since the establishment of international policies among Christian governments —which policies comprehend and imply all nations and peoples, whether civilised or heathen—call for and imperatively demand our attention as descendants of Africa in whole or part.

I fully concur with and endorse the idea suggested in the "Anglo-African" of the 14th of December and 4th instant, that there should be held at the earliest possible period, in America, a great Council of the leading men among us;[1] and let me not be misunderstood when I say, that such men must be composed of the highest intelligence, otherwise such an effort must be nugatory, and consequently prove an entire failure. As such a Council can only originate and be held by mutual consent, it is not only the right but duty of those who originate it, to say of whom it may be composed. The point to be considered is not whether we are emigrationists or anti-emigrationists; in favor of or opposed to emigration: but whether we cannot agree upon and endorse a general policy which shall favor both; a policy which whilst it admits my right to go when and where I may think best; admits yours to stay wherever you may think best; and at the same time, secures and defends a reciprocal interest in each other's welfare. Such a policy as this, sir, firmly established and fixed by us, will give a status such as

1. This council never came to fruition. In 1864, there was a National Convention of Colored Men in Syracuse, New York, but Delany did not attend.

never has been known to our race since the days of Africa's primitive national prowess. One of the most prominent features in the present conflicts, struggles, and political movements among the nations of the world seems to be: which can reduce us to a condition the best adapted to promote their luxury, wealth, and aggrandizement, to which we as a race, for centuries have contributed more than any other race. Our race throughout the world (the major part of which is in Africa and the western continent) numbers nearly three hundred millions (300,000,000), some thirty millions (30,000,000), more or less, of which is mixed blood. In God's name, must we ever be subordinate to those of another race, both in as well as out of Africa? Is subordination our normal condition? Must we either be abject slaves, the property personal of the Caucasian, or the submissive drudges of their social industrial element, ever ministering as domestics to their pride and arrogance? Is it true that we are not to be permitted anywhere to govern ourselves, but must have white rulers? Have we no other destiny—no other social and political relations in prospect as an inheritance for our children? It is for us to determine whether or not this shall be so; therefore, I suggest to you, sir, to join with me in calling upon our educated men, to assemble at some convenient time and in Council, and determine on a settled policy as a rule of action, by which we shall be guided.

With the light of the age in which we live—with our advantages of educational attainments—with the Divine Promise that "Princes" (Power) "shall come out of Egypt" (from among the African race), "and Ethiopia stretch forth" (from all parts of the world) "her hands unto God"[2]—did we now remain passive, the world should justly condemn us, and posterity curse our names.

Sir, this is no time for quibbling by the men of qualification and mature intelligence among us; and as duty and obligations call me to Africa, I cannot hope to be long on this continent; but can I but be so happy as to meet such a Council before I depart, I shall be willing to entrust the cause in the hands of those men among us of sterling worth, who have ever been found able, true, sincere and faithful to the cause of their brethren, race, and humanity through years of difficult trial. A policy established on principle as a general basis of action, must be our object and aim.

I am, dear sir, for God and humanity, the Redemption of our race, and Regeneration of Africa,

Your friend and Brother,

M. R. DELANY.

97 High street, Brooklyn, L.I.

(*Weekly Anglo-African*, 11 January 1862, p. 2)

2. Psalms 68:31.

Letter to the *Weekly Anglo-African*, 22 January 1862

VEERING FROM THE AGENDA of the African Civilization Society, Henry Highland Garnet increasingly focused his attention on black emigration to Haiti. Undeterred by Garnet's break, and by the increasing commitment of African Americans to the Civil War effort, Delany in 1862 continued to assert that his African emigration project remained intact.

In reply to a letter just received from a distinguished friend, inquiring whether or not the statement made in a letter by a person who visited Chatham during my absence, that I had given up the African movement or in the words of that unprincipled person who must scurrilize his own people and underrate my scheme to please his master,—"the African scheme had blown up?" I simply answer,—not at all, nor never will. I regard it in every possible relation in which it can be considered, touching the destiny of our race as a whole, a thousand to one preferable to any scheme of Emigration from America, and the only one conservative for the AFRICAN RACE.

I, and all those who originally intended to go to Africa, are making vigorous preparations for the consummation of our designs; and I call the attention of all desiring information to read my Report, recently published, of my Travels and Explorations in Liberia and Central Africa.[1]

M. R. DELANY.

New York, Jan. 22d, 1862

(*Weekly Anglo-African*, 25 January 1862, p. 2)

---

1. *Official Report of the Niger Valley Exploring Party* (1861).

The Moral and Social Aspect of Africa

ALTHOUGH HIS Yoruban venture had collapsed by the middle of 1862, Delany continued to lecture on Africa well into 1863. But by the time he gave this May 1863 speech in Massachusetts, as reported in a surprisingly racist account in the *Liberator*, he had been working to recruit black men not for an African settlement but for the Fifty-fourth Massachusetts Regiment. (Delany's son Toussaint L'Ouverture Delany signed up for the regiment in March 1863.) In the wake of the Emancipation Proclamation, Delany, in this and other speeches on Africa in the spring of 1863, was implicitly pointing to the genealogical sources of the moral and social energy that he believed the black troops would bring to the Union's war against slavery.

A lecture by a gentleman of color is a sort of a "rare bird on the earth," and is very like a "black swan." Rare as the thing may be, however, it is not an impossibility, as Dr. Delaney [*sic*], and a few other men of his blood and race, have occasionally proved, although at wide intervals of time and space. We ought not, perhaps, to be surprised at any unusual manifestation of talent in a negro. Toussaint L'Ouverture has redeemed the whole race of blacks by the magnificence of his talents and career. We do not mean to say that Dr. Delaney is a Toussaint L'Ouverture, but we do say that he is a better specimen of his race than any we, for our part, have seen before, and that he is by no means a bad lecturer.

He was not ashamed, he said, to be called a negro. If curly hair and a black face helped to make a negro, then he was a negro, and a full-blooded one at that. He had no need to be ashamed of his type or origin. He has a good head and intelligent face—just the kind of a head which a phrenologist would tell you a man ought to have who makes natural observations and accumulates scientific facts.

The dress which the Doctor wore on the platform was a long dark-colored robe, with curious scrolls upon the neck as a collar. He said it was the wedding dress of a Chief, and that the embroidery was insignia, and had a specific meaning well understood in African high circles. He wore it because he thought it becoming, and fitting the occasion.

He wanted to say what he knew of the negro race, not on the coast of Africa, but of the interior Africans, of whom so little is known — the Africans of the Niger Valley. The audience would be surprised to hear that even the Liberians had never until lately been ten miles beyond their territory; and so nothing could be expected from them. He was sorry to say, too, that American school-books inculcated, notwithstanding recent discoveries, very erroneous notions of the country, describing it as sandy and barren, the soil unproductive, the air full of pestilence, the vegetation poisonous, the very animals unusually ferocious. All this is more or less false, so far as the interior of Africa is concerned. He had travelled three thousand miles in the country, and had seen it in all its phases of social and moral life. The language of a people is a good sign of its civility; and the African language is derived from fixed roots; it is not a jargon, but abounds in vowels, and is very melodious, and capable of expressing a wide range of feel-ing and sentiment. The people speak clearly and well, without hesitation. They are very polite, and make numerous salutations on all occasions, at out-going and in-coming, at bed-time, and in the morning at meals, and generally every-where. The stranger must not reply to each salutation, but when he takes his leave, he makes a long salaam by bowing his head and body, and by a peculiar intonation of the voice.

The Doctor produced a grammar of the language, and made quotations from it. It was written by a native African, who had also composed numerous school-books, and made translations from the Bible.

As specimens of the moral culture of the people, he read some of the African proverbs, which, though doubtless original, have a peculiar Christian flavor. One of them ran very much after the style of the Golden Rule, thus: "He who in-jures another, injures himself." Another reads thus: "The sword does not know the hand of the blacksmith" (who made it).

One of the poets, whilst singing the occupations of the people, has these de-scriptions of them: "The day dawns; the trader takes his goods; the spinner her distaff; the soldier his shield; the hunter his bow and quiver." After giving us these and other specimens of the writing talent of the Africans, the Doctor sud-denly came down on Robert Bonner,[1] his weekly *Ledger*, who said in it, awhile ago, or allowed somebody else to say it, that the African, having no poetic fac-ulty, is incapable of civilization. He reminded his audience of the simple and beautiful extemporaneous song which the negro woman sang over poor Mungo Park, the traveller, when he sat sorrowing by her tent door, and whom she sup-plied, in her womanly kindness, with milk.[2] The truth was, that the African was

---

1. As editor of the New York *Ledger*, Robert Bonner (1824–99) became well known for attracting popular authors, such as E. D. E. N. Southworth, at big salaries.
2. See Mungo Park (1771–1806), *Travels in the Interior of Africa* (1799), ch. 20.

naturally poetic, and expressed his feelings at all times of passion and emotion in musical and rhythmical words. He read some pretty verses composed by African children, which were translated by one of our missionaries on the spot. They were certainly very simple, and at the same time very hopeful products, describing the pleasure they felt at seeing the beauty and color of certain African birds, no description of which, the Doctor said, has appeared in any book on ornithology.

Alluding to the morals of the people, he said there was a mistake about it very current in these parts and elsewhere. It was thought that because polygamy was tolerated amongst them, there must be immorality also. Polygamy was an old and venerable institution, and had a genuine Oriental origin. Solomon was the arch-polygamist of the world, and the Africans who followed his example were no worse than he. It was the rich only, however, who had many wives; the poor could not afford to keep them. But women were universally respected in Africa, and the men paid them chivalrous attention. They were not allowed to do any physical labor whatever, except to draw water; and this they insisted upon as their peculiar right and privilege. This also was an Oriental custom of immemorial usage; and was frequently alluded to in the Scriptures. He had seen seven hundred women coming out of the gates of a city in the evening, carrying water-pots on their heads, as they did in the days of Jacob. Chastity was a sacred thing amongst them, and any one violating or insulting a woman was decapitated. These bigamists had one who was mistress of the household, and had her maids of honor, who attended her, and ministered to the wants of the guests. They loved these wives better than most civilized people often do theirs. A chief who had lost his wife was asked why he did not marry again. "Because," he said, "I shall never find a woman who will love me as she did." There was no savagery in this reply, and it might readily enough have been uttered by a white man.

The betrothal of young people is made at a very early age, and when it is consummated, the maiden wears a bracelet on her arm, which is made of some inscrutable metallic substance, of which the Doctor could give no account.

An African house, belonging to a bigwig negro, was described as an immense building, the windows and doors of which opened on the inside, looking upon the court-yards. These houses often contained hundreds of women, who were called wives by courtesy, but were not so in reality; as the custom of the country required every rich man to support as many females as he could. These were daily occupied in spinning, basket-making, weaving cotton fabrics, &c., which they sold in the markets. They often went far into the country, in groups, selling provisions along with their wares, and the Doctor never heard of any of them being insulted.

From what the lecturer said, the houses of the rich were a sort of factory, where the surplus women were taught to work, and where they were protected.

They supported themselves. One of these houses put our own hotels, which are, nevertheless, "some pumpkins," into a complete shadow. It is owned by a chief, and covers 1200 square feet, and built of unhewn brick. Another contains a thousand females, and is about the rival of Solomon's immense court of concubines.

Women are always admitted to council meetings. He was present at one, when the wife of a chief leaned her head on his shoulder, and made many suggestions. He thought the hint might be taken in countries a long way from Africa.

Another feature of manners was given which we thought very interesting. It was the respect which youth always had to age, no matter whether the person were rich or poor.

In these interior and remote regions, the people were ruled by a king, whom they elected themselves. Kings, and their sons and families, were all amenable to the law. Litigation begins always in the morning, and defendant's counsel has always the last speech.

Numerous examples of the industry of the Africans were given. They cultivated the lands, and made them as productive as gardens. All the staple cereals of a tropical clime were grown in abundance, and every species of fruit. They were workers in iron and other metals, and made excellent leather and glass. They were a religious people naturally; and he never met with a Pagan in all his travels.

At the close of the lecture, various specimens of native manufacture were shown to the audience.

(*Liberator*, 1 May 1863, p. 1)

Part Five.
Civil War and Reconstruction

DELANY IS BEST KNOWN for his emigrationist and black separatist politics circa 1851–62. Though he was commissioned with great fanfare as the first black major in the Union army, his subsequent creative and influential efforts to play a key role in the reconstruction of the South have remained relatively obscure. There are two large reasons for this obscurity: 1) The image of Delany as a U.S. nationalist who sought to find ways that blacks and whites of the South could live together in harmony does not accord with the more familiar image of Delany as a black nationalist separatist. 2) From mid-1865 to his death in 1885, Delany in effect had become a southerner, basing his national politics in local actions in the towns and villages of South Carolina. Perhaps because the South continues to remain a somewhat marginalized subdiscipline of American literary and cultural studies, the preponderance of Delany scholarship can make it seem that around 1866 or so he has moved "offstage" and is no longer worthy of serious consideration.[1] Delany's interactions with the likes of Daniel H. Chamberlain, John T. Green, and Wade Hampton have hardly ranked in importance with his interactions with Frederick Douglass, Henry Highland Garnet, and Mary Ann Shadd Cary.

And yet this period is absolutely central to Delany's career as a black nationalist and race leader. This section prints nineteen Delany documents from 1863 to 1877 and attempts in particular to recuperate his politics and writings of the Reconstruction period (longer than the time he committed to Central American emigration or his Niger project). For Delany, South Carolina was not a distant outpost; it was *the* key testing ground for the possibilities of a reconstructed United States in which blacks would be accorded citizenship and equal rights, and together with the whites of the state would figure out how to live together amicably and productively in a multiracial United States. That Reconstruction "failed" should not dim the importance of Delany's efforts, for that failure, though predictable, was not foreordained. The selections in Part 5 can help us to recover the sense of possibility that Delany saw in Reconstruction, particularly on the local level of South Carolina, before President Hayes withdrew federal troops from the southern states in 1877.

Because the workings of the Freedmen's Bureau and South Carolina's state government are somewhat arcane, the selections in Part 5 are accompanied by fuller, more detailed headnotes. But some broad biographical developments can be elaborated here. In late 1862 and early 1863, as evident in the final selection of Part 4, "The Moral and Social Aspect of Africa," Delany had concurrent (and conflicted) commitments to both Africa and the United States. But it was around this time, in the wake of the Emancipation Proclamation, that Delany decided to commit himself (as he had in the 1830s and 1840s) to a black nationalism linked to a U.S. nationalism. To some extent, then, the year 1863 saw Delany once again tapping into the hopes and aspirations for black elevation in the United States that had informed his coeditorship of the *North Star*. By mid-1863 he had come to believe that the Civil War was indeed a war against slavery and that the war provided an opportunity for black men, as soldiers, to demonstrate their capacity for citizenship. Accordingly, he began to recruit black troops for the Union army,[2] and in a letter of December 1863 attempted to convince Secretary of War Edwin M. Stanton that he could bring about an early end to the war by recruiting black soldiers in the slave South. In February 1865 he managed to arrange a face-to-face interview with Abraham Lincoln, which he dramatically described to Frances Rollin ("The Council-Chamber—President Lincoln"). As a result of that interview, he was named the first black field officer in the U.S. army. Ironically, one of the reasons that Lincoln may have been willing to meet with Delany is that he would have known about his emigrationist "Political Destiny," which was reprinted in the July 1862 congressional *Report of the Select Committee on Emancipation and Colonization* and used by the House committee to support Lincoln's own thinking at that time about the need to colonize blacks to Central and South America.[3] Of course when Lincoln met Delany in 1865, much had changed, but how else explain Lincoln's choice of an African emigrationist and John Brown collaborator as his first black major? That choice was celebrated by African Americans in New York, Ohio, and elsewhere (see "The Colored Citizens of Xenia"). Delany publicly expressed his own gratitude to Lincoln several months later, when, almost immediately after Lincoln's assassination, he was among the first African American leaders calling on U.S. blacks to memorialize Lincoln's emancipatory accomplishments ("Monument to President Lincoln").

Following the war, the still quite eminent Major Delany was assigned to the Freedmen's Bureau at Beaufort, South Carolina, and in August 1865 was officially named assistant subassistant commissioner of the Freedmen's Bureau at Hilton Head, South Carolina. He kept that position until August 1868. In this new leadership role, Delany emerged as one of the more fervent black proponents of Reconstruction. Though white officers at the bureau initially suspected him of encouraging black insurrection,[4] Delany soon refuted such claims by taking on the responsibility of ferreting out possible conspiracies among South Carolina's African Americans. For example, in response to rumors that the blacks of Port Royal Island were planning an uprising on Christmas Eve 1865, Delany requested a detachment of the Twenty-first United States Colored Troops and used a show of force to keep the peace.

As the Port Royal Island incident suggests, Delany at the Freedmen's Bureau was in key respects at a hierarchical remove from African Americans of the region. From Delany's perspective, however, black leadership was a necessary form of racial solidarity that promised to improve the lot of the freed people. Convinced that possibilities for black elevation in the United States had never been better than right after the Civil War, Delany in 1865 developed a plan for what he called a "domestic triple alliance," in effect a copartnership among northern capitalists, southern white landowners, and black labor, with the profits being shared among the three groups (see "Prospects of the Freedmen of Hilton Head" and "Triple Alliance"). Crucial to Delany's efforts to implement that plan over the next several years was his managerial leadership. Despite having a relatively subordinate role at the Freedmen's Bureau, Delany placed himself at the center of negotiations between white capital and black labor. Delany wrote many of the contracts for his district, urged black laborers to renounce alcoholic beverages, established a cotton-gin mill and warehouse on St. Helena Island that allowed black workers to bypass white factors and increase their profits, and even set up his own police force. In a report submitted from the Freedmen's Bureau, Delany stated: "On the Plantations throughout my Bureau District, I have adopted police regulations. On each place the best man selected by the people, is appointed by me as Head man or Chief of Police, with authority to choose four assistants. . . . He is to report all his doings once a month to Head Quarters." Even Delany's sympathetic biographer Ullman remarks that in attempting to oversee relations among capitalists, planters, and freedmen, Delany was "often downright dictatorial."[5]

Whether dictatorial or communitarian, or an amalgam somewhere in between, Delany's suspicions of southern whites led him to seek unconventional ways of empowering the freed people of South Carolina. Central to black empowerment and citizenship, in South Carolina and the nation, Delany believed, was the right to vote, and from the end of the Civil War until the 1870 ratification of the Fifteenth Amendment, he worked tirelessly to promote the enfranchisement of African Americans. In a letter of 25 July 1866 he wrote directly to President Andrew Johnson on the importance of extending the vote to African Americans, and his 1870 *University Pamphlets* was specifically directed at the nation's new black voters. Though insistent on African Americans' right to vote, and on the importance of blacks having proportional representation in the Republican Party through direct elections and patronage (see Delany's and Douglass's letter exchange of 1871), Delany was politic about the dangers of African Americans claiming too much, too quickly. In a letter of 22 February 1866 to a black delegation that had confronted President Johnson earlier that month, he warned of the risks of alienating white leaders. One year later he contested those black leaders who were demanding that a black vice presidential candidate appear on the Republican ticket (see his letter to Garnet). Although he exhibited an uncharacteristic caution with respect to national politics, Delany fully engaged politics on the state level, regarding South Carolina rather than Ohio (where he had his home) as the important test case for national Reconstruction. In 1868 he participated in the South Carolina Constitutional Convention, and in 1870 he accepted an honorary appointment from the Republican governor Robert K. Scott as aide to the commander in chief of the South Carolina militia.

And yet even as he accepted that appointment, Delany was becoming increasingly concerned that graft and other forms of corruption were damaging South Carolina's Republican Party, and in 1872 he resigned his position on the militia. Disillusioned with the Republicans and concerned as well about the need to mollify the many whites who had come to hate the Republicans and their black supporters, Delany in 1874 broke with the state Republican Party, arguing for the importance of preserving minority representation, by which he meant, at the time, white representation, though he envisioned a future in which blacks themselves would be in the minority.[6] Delany's defense of the white minority in 1874 was surely a pragmatic move, indicative of his view that it was in the interest of the state's African Americans to continue to find ways of working with the whites who owned most of the state's land and resources. As a sign of Delany's own such willingness, in 1874 he backed the Independent Republican movement, which on its face was an effort to restore honest government to the state but which was also intended to cut into the Republicans' voting base in the black majority and had the support of many Democrats. Because he remained perhaps the most respected black leader in the state, Delany won the nomination for the position of lieutenant governor at the Independent Republicans' fall convention. His acceptance speech and campaign speeches conveyed his hopes that this new party alignment would help to quell tensions between the races and contribute to the larger national project of Reconstruction (see "Delany for Lieutenant Governor"). Though he and the party's candidate for governor, John T. Green, lost the election, the final tallies were fairly close. Two years later, Delany broke with the Republicans entirely and endorsed the Democratic candidate for governor, Wade Hampton, a former slaveholder.

Delany's endorsement of Hampton and the Democrats in the 1876 election was a stunningly bold move, motivated in large part by his belief, as he elaborated in an 1875 speech in New York City ("The South and Its Foes"), that it was in the best interests of the freed people to work with the former supporters of the Confederacy. In hindsight, as Delany himself acknowledged, his endorsement of the Democrats was also a stunningly naive and wrongheaded move. The once popular Major Delany was reviled by many of South Carolina's blacks, who heckled and even shot at Delany while he stumped for Hampton (see "Politics at Edisto Island"). Hampton won the election and subsequently awarded Delany a position as trial justice, which he kept until 1879. But the election was violent, corrupt, and contested, and both Hampton and Daniel Chamberlain, the Republican incumbent, claimed victory. Though Hampton was inaugurated on 14 December 1876, Chamberlain remained in office and established a rival government.

The national election, of course, was just as closely contested. In what has come to be known as the Compromise of 1877, southern political leaders provided Hayes the electoral votes he needed to defeat Democrat Samuel Tilden in exchange for the withdrawal of federal troops from the southern states. Hampton himself met with Hayes in March 1877 to offer his support for this compromise, and in April 1877, when Hayes was inaugurated, Chamberlain surrendered the governorship to Hampton. Thus, in an irony that reinforces the point that the local is the national, the Compromise of 1877 that brought about the end of Reconstruction had not a little to do with Delany's support for Wade Hampton in the South Carolina governor's race of 1876. Hampton was a "moderate" on race issues, but under his governorship (1877–79) African Americans' rights continued to erode, and by decade's end Delany was once again looking toward Africa.

Notes

1. Victor Ullman's *Martin R. Delany: The Beginnings of Black Nationalism* (Boston: Beacon Press, 1971) remains an important exception to this tendency in Delany studies.

2. Delany also urged his African American friends in Canada to join the Civil War effort; see his letter to Mary Ann Shadd Cary, 7 December 1863, reprinted in C. Peter Ripley et al., eds., *The Black Abolitionist Papers*, vol. 2 (Chapel Hill: University of North Carolina Press, 1986), pp. 520–22.

3. Delany's "Political Destiny" may have also inspired the 1858–59 efforts of Missouri congressman Frank P. Blair (1791–1876) to obtain federal funding in order to colonize African Americans to Central and South America. See Blair's *Destiny of the Races of this Continent: An Address Delivered before the Mercantile Library Association of Boston, Massachusetts, on the 26th of January, 1859* (Washington, D.C.: Buell & Blanchard, 1859), which includes in the appendix a short letter from Delany stating that he had not yet read the speech (p. 34).

4. As reported in the 13 May 1865 *Charleston Courier*, Delany, in a speech at Charles-

ton's Zion Presbyterian Church, the city's largest black congregation, favorably invoked "the great insurrectionary movement in South Carolina under the lead of Denmark Vesey" (p. 2)—a free black whose plot in which Charleston blacks would kill whites, capture the city, and make their way to the Caribbean was exposed by house servants in June 1822. (Vesey and over thirty other of his associates were executed later that year.) On 23 July 1865, Delany spoke to over 500 freedmen at the Brick Church on St. Helena Island, South Carolina, urging his auditors to resist the exploitative practices of northern and southern whites. The commanding officer at Beaufort had sent two officers to observe Delany's speech, and both submitted critical reports to the War Department and the Bureau of Refugees, Freedmen and Abandoned Lands; see Ripley et al., eds., *Black Abolitionist Papers*, 5:350–52.

5. See Ullman, *Martin R. Delany*, p. 368.

6. See "Delany's Last Lesson," *News and Courier*, 28 March 1874, p. 2.

Letter to Edwin M. Stanton, 15 December 1863

SOON AFTER HE COMMITTED himself to the Civil War effort, Delany began to work as a recruiting agent for the Union army, aggressively enlisting black troops in Massachusetts, Ohio, Illinois, and several other states. In late 1863 the state of Connecticut offered him a recruitment contract, and around that same time he wrote to Secretary of War Edward M. Stanton (1814–69) with a plan to use his authority as a black man to recruit black soldiers in occupied areas of the South. Stanton had been one of the first military leaders to advocate the use of black troops, but there is no evidence that Stanton read or responded to Delany's letter. However, the fact that Lincoln would grant Delany an interview early in 1865 (and allow him to recruit freedmen in South Carolina shortly thereafter) suggests that Delany had made himself known and respected in the White House.

Box 764, P.O.
172 Clark St[reet]
Chicago, Ill[inois]
Dec[ember] 15th, 1863

Sir:

The Subject and policy of Black Troops have become of much interest in our Country, and the effective means and method of raising them, is a matter of much importance.

In consideration of this Sir, I embrace the earliest opportunity of asking the privilege of calling the attention of your Department to the fact, that as a policy in perfect harmony with the course of the President and your own enlightened views, that the Agency of intelligent competent black men adapted to the work must be the most effective means of obtaining Black Troops; because knowing and being of that people as a race, they can command such influence as is required to accomplish the object.

I have been successfully engaged as a Recruiting Agent of Black Troops, first

as a Recruiting Agent for Massachusetts 54th Regt. and from the commence-
ment as the Managing Agent in the West and South-West for Rhode Island
Heavy Artillery, which is now nearly full; and now have the Contract from the
State Authorities of Connecticut, for the entire West and South-West, in raising
Colored Troops to fill her quota.

During these engagements, I have had associated with me, Mr. John Jones, a
very respectable and responsible business colored man of this city, and we have
associated ourselves permanently together, in an Agency for raising Black Troops
for all parts of the Country.[1]

We are able sir, to command all of the effective black men as Agents in the
United States, and in the event of an order from your Department giving us the
Authority to recruit Colored Troops in any of the Southern or seceded states, we
will be ready and able to raise a Regiment, or Brigade if required, in a shorter
time than can be otherwise effected.

With the belief sir, that this is one of the measures in which the claims of the
Black Man may be officially recognised, without seemingly infringing upon
those of other citizens, I confidently ask sir, that this humble request, may engage your early notice.

All satisfactory References will be given by both of us.

I have the honor to be sir, Your most obt. Very humble servt.,

M. R. Delany
M. M. Wagoner, Secry.[2]

(Letters Received, RG 94, Adjutant General's Office, U.S. Colored Troops, National Archives, Washington, D.C.; reprinted in C. Peter Ripley et al., eds., *The
Black Abolitionist Papers*, vol. 5 [Chapel Hill: University of North Carolina Press,
1992], pp. 261–62)

1. On Delany's prior disagreements with Jones, see Part 3, "Letter to Douglass, 7 November 1853."
2. The daughter of black abolitionist Henry O. Wagoner, Marcellina M. Wagoner assisted Delany as secretary during 1863–64 when he worked to recruit black troops.

The Council-Chamber. — President Lincoln

FRANCES ROLLIN'S BIOGRAPHY of Major Martin R. Delany presents Delany as committed to the Civil War from the moment of its outset. (She says virtually nothing about his African project.) In 1861, according to Rollin, Delany first talked to Asa Mahan, the former president of Oberlin College, about the strategic value of organizing black troops as a "corps d'Afrique," modeled on a Berber tribe in Algeria, that would use guerrilla tactics to inspire the slaves to rise against their white oppressors. Delany told Rollin that he proposed a similar plan to Abraham Lincoln when he met with him in February 1865 and that Lincoln was so enthusiastic about the plan that he named him the first black major in the Union army. Delany arrived in Washington, D.C., on 6 February 1865 and, after spending one or two nights with Henry Highland Garnet, met with Lincoln on 7 or 8 February. As recounted in chapter 19 of Rollin's biography, Delany's meeting with Lincoln was one of the triumphal moments of his career.

We give in Major Delany's own language his interview with President Lincoln.

He tells us, "On entering the executive chamber, and being introduced to his excellency, a generous grasp and shake of the hand brought me to a seat in front of him. No one could mistake the fact that an able and master spirit was before me. Serious without sadness, and pleasant withal, he was soon seated, placing himself at ease, the better to give me a patient audience. He opened the conversation first.

"'What can I do for you, sir?' he inquired.

"'Nothing, Mr. President,' I replied; 'but I've come to propose something to you, which I think will be beneficial to the nation in this critical hour of her peril.' I shall never forget the expression of his countenance and the inquiring look which he gave me when I answered him.

"'Go on, sir,' he said, as I paused through deference to him. I continued the conversation by reminding him of the full realization of arming the blacks of the South, and the ability of the blacks of the North to defeat it by complicity with those at the South, through the medium of the *Underground Railroad*—a measure known only to themselves.

"I next called his attention to the fact of the heartless and almost relentless prejudice exhibited towards the blacks by the Union army, and that something ought to be done to check this growing feeling against the slave, else nothing that we could do would avail. And if such were not expedited, all might be lost. That the blacks, in every capacity in which they had been called to act, had done their part faithfully and well. To this Mr. Lincoln readily assented. I continued: 'I would call your attention to another fact of great consideration; that is, the position of confidence in which they have been placed, when your officers have been under obligations to them, and in many instances even the army in their power. As pickets, scouts, and guides, you have trusted them, and found them faithful to the duties assigned; and it follows that if you can find them of higher qualifications, they may, with equal credit, fill higher and more important trusts.'

"'*Certainly*,' replied the president, in his most emphatic manner. 'And what do you propose to do?' he inquired.

"I responded, 'I propose this, sir; but first permit me to say that, whatever I may desire for black men in the army, I know that there exists too much prejudice among the whites for the soldiers to serve under a black commander, or the officers to be willing to associate with him. These are facts which must be admitted, and, under the circumstances, must be regarded, as they cannot be ignored. And I propose, as a most effective remedy to prevent enrolment of the blacks in the rebel service, and induce them to run to, instead of from, the Union forces — the commissioning and promotion of black men now in the army, according to merit.'

"Looking at me for a moment, earnestly yet anxiously, he demanded, 'How will you remedy the great difficulty you have just now so justly described, about the objections of white soldiers to colored commanders, and officers to colored associates?'

"I replied, 'I have the remedy, Mr. President, which has not yet been stated; and it is the most important suggestion of my visit to you. And I think it is just what is required to complete the prestige of the Union army. I propose, sir, an army of blacks, commanded entirely by black officers, except such whites as may volunteer to serve; this army to penetrate through the heart of the South, and make conquests, with the banner of Emancipation unfurled, proclaiming freedom as they go, sustaining and protecting it by arming the emancipated, taking them as fresh troops, and leaving a few veterans among the new freedmen, when occasion requires, keeping this banner unfurled until every slave is free, according to the letter of your proclamation. I would also take from those already in the service all that are competent for commission officers, and establish at once in the South a camp of instructions. By this we could have in about three months an army of forty thousand blacks in motion, the presence of which anywhere would itself be a power irresistible. You should have an army of blacks, President Lincoln, commanded entirely by blacks, the sight of which is required to give confidence to the slaves, and retain them to the Union, stop foreign intervention, and speedily bring the war to a close.'

" 'This,' replied the president, 'is the very thing I have been looking and hoping for; but nobody offered it. I have thought it over and over again. I have talked about it; I hoped and prayed for it; but till now it never has been proposed. White men couldn't do this, because they are doing all in that direction now that they can; but we find, for various reasons, it does not meet the case under consideration. The blacks should go to the interior, and the whites be kept on the frontiers.'

" 'Yes, sir,' I interposed; 'they would require but little, as they could subsist on the country as they went along.'

" 'Certainly,' continued he; 'a few light artillery, with the cavalry, would comprise your principal advance, because all the siege work would be on the frontiers and waters, done by the white division of the army. Won't this be a grand thing?' he exclaimed, joyfully. He continued, 'When I issued my Emancipation Proclamation, I had this thing in contemplation. I then gave them a chance by prohibiting any interference on the part of the army; but they did not embrace it,' said he, rather sadly, accompanying the word with an emphatic gesture.

" 'But, Mr. President,' said I, 'these poor people could not read your proclamation, nor could they know anything about it, only, when they did hear, to know that they were free.'

" 'But you of the North I expected to take advantage of it,' he replied.

" 'Our policy, sir,' I answered, 'was directly opposite, supposing that it met your approbation. To this end I published a letter against embarrassing or compromising the government in any manner whatever; for us to remain passive, except in case of foreign intervention, then immediately to raise the slaves to insurrection.'[1]

" 'Ah, I remember the letter,' he said, 'and thought at the time that you mistook my designs. But the effect will be better as it is, by giving character to the blacks, both North and South, as a peaceable, inoffensive people.' Suddenly turning, he said, 'Will you take command?'

" 'If there be none better qualified than I am, sir, by that time I will. While it is my desire to serve, as black men we shall have to prepare ourselves, as we have had no opportunities of experience and practice in the service as officers.'

" 'That matters but little, comparatively,' he replied; 'as some of the finest officers we have never studied the tactics till they entered the army as subordi-

1. Probably a reference to Delany's letter to Stanton of 15 December 1863; see above.

nates. And again,' said he, 'the tactics are easily learned, especially among your people. It is the head that we now require most—men of plans and executive ability.'

"'I thank you, Mr. President,' said I, 'for the—'

"'No—not at all,' he interrupted.

"'I will show you some letters of introduction, sir,' said I, putting my hand in my pocket to get them.

"'Not now,' he interposed; 'I know all about you. I see nothing now to be done but to give you a line of introduction to the secretary of war.'

"Just as he began writing, the cannon commenced booming.

"'Stanton is firing! listen! he is in his glory! noble man!' he exclaimed.

"'What is it, Mr. President?' I asked.

"'The firing!'

"'What is it about, sir,' I reiterated, ignorant of the cause.

"'Why, don't you know? Haven't you heard the news? Charleston is ours!'[2] he answered, straightening up from the table on which he was writing for an instant, and then resuming it. He soon handed me a card, on which was written,—

'February 8, 1865.

'Hon. E. M. Stanton, *Secretary of War.*

'Do not fail to have an interview with this most extraordinary and intelligent black man.

'A. Lincoln.'

"This card showed he perfectly understood my views and feelings; hence he was not content that my color should make its own impression, but he expressed it with emphasis, as though a point was gained. The thing desired presented itself; not simply a man that was *black*, because these had previously presented themselves, in many delegations and committees,—men of the highest intelligence,—for various objects; but that which he had wished and hoped for, their own proposed measures matured in the council-chamber had never been fully presented to them in the person of a black man."

(Frank [Frances] A. Rollin, *Life and Times of Martin R. Delany* [Boston: Lee and Shepard, 1868], pp. 166–71)

2. Confederate troops evacuated Charleston on 18 February 1865.

IN NOVEMBER 1864, shortly before he received his commission as major, Delany and his wife, Catherine, purchased a house and land at Wilberforce, Ohio, near the campus of Wilberforce University, a recently founded college for black youth. The purchase was motivated by the Delanys' desire to provide their children with good opportunities for education in a predominately black community. The commissioning of Delany as major created great excitement among that community, and the excitement crossed state borders: New York's *Weekly Anglo-African*, for example, sold postcard portraits of Delany in full uniform for twenty-five cents. In March 1865, the black citizenry of Wilberforce and nearby Xenia had an opportunity to see Delany himself in full uniform, and the occasion was described by an anonymous white reporter in "The Colored Citizens of Xenia," which appeared in the 17 March 1865 issue of the *Xenia Sentinel.*

A diminutive piece of manuscript, pasted to the wall of the Post Office, last week, announced that on Monday evening of this week Major Delany would "appear in full uniform" and address the people at the Anti-Slavery Church, on east Main street. Accordingly, at the appointed time, we made our way to the above named building.

Those who are not in the habit of visiting the eastern portion of our city— the Africa of our County—will be likely to entertain erroneous opinions of the people who there "live and have their being." The popular idea is that a "nigger" is a very shabby part and particle of Creation. Rags, rough heads, ignorance and uncouthness are supposed to be inseparably connected with a man of black. But the popular belief is far from correct. A visit to the Church on the occasion alluded to, was sufficient to convince one that colored people are men and women, and that it is possible for them to be ladies and gentlemen.

This church is a respectable building. The audience was quite numerous, and composed almost exclusively of colored citizens. They were all well dressed, and appeared to be well behaved.

Major Delany came in according to advertisement, "in full uniform," and was greeted with a fair share of applause. Major Delany is a citizen of Xenia. Before the war he was connected with Wilberforce University.[1] Among colored people, at least, the Major is claimed as learned and scientific. He has travelled considerably in Europe, has a fair idea of men and things in general, and is not entirely ignorant on every point of history. He has been connected with the Union army for some years, just where or in what capacity we are not able to state. He recently received a commission as Major, and is assigned to duty on the staff of General Saxton,[2] at Beaufort.

Major Delany is a negro, having no "visible admixture" of white blood. He is black—black as the blackest—large, heavy set, vigorous, with a bald, sleek head, which shines like a newly polished boot. And he wears brass buttons and shoulder straps! and is an officer in the army of the Union! These sentences record the history of the progress of the country during the war!

We cannot undertake to enumerate the points made by the Major in his speech. They were too numerous, and occurred in too many places! But the speech was a speech—a speech of real magnitude, force and vigor. The speaker gave his opinions in reference to the respective Constitutions of England and America, declaring that of the former to be and to have been progressive; while that of the latter, he affirmed, has always been, until the present war, conservative. Whether his statements in reference to British history agreed in all respects with those of Blackstone and McCaully [sic],[3] we do not affirm. The speaker, however, declared with truth that English liberty has been brought to its present state of perfection by a succession of liberal measures which the people extorted from the crown. In this respect, and to a certain extent, the Government of England has been progressive. The speaker claimed that as the Constitution of the

1. Founded in 1856 by the Methodist Episcopal Church and purchased by the African Methodist Episcopal Church in 1862, Wilberforce University in Wilberforce, Ohio, is the oldest historically black private college in the United States.

2. Rufus B. Saxton (1824–1928) of Massachusetts, Delany's military supervisor, helped to recruit black troops during the Civil War and was named assistant commissioner of the Freedmen's Bureau for South Carolina, Georgia, and Florida at the war's end. Saxton was removed from his position in 1866 because he was regarded as overly zealous in attempting to help blacks retain lands appropriated from the plantation owners.

3. References to the English jurist Sir William Blackstone (1723–80), best known for *Commentaries on the Laws of England* (4 vols., 1765–69), and the English historian Thomas Babington Macauley (1800–1859), best known for *The History of England* (5 vols., 1849–61).

United States has been written, and unchangeable, it has been conservative; but he gloried in the fact, that the Constitution has been "broken," that it has been amended, that slavery has been abolished, and that the Government, like that of the British, has been rendered "progressive."

The speaker claimed that he was authorized to set the Government right before the people! He told his brethren that they had no reason to complain — that the Government intended to deal justly and fairly with them — that it would commission colored officers when they were qualified — that it would treat colored soldiers well — and finally that it intended to make no distinctions between white and black soldiers.

The speaker affirmed that negroes must think more of themselves, that is, have a higher opinion of themselves. They must declare themselves to be the equals of white men, if not their superiors. In no other way could they attain to their proper position in the body politic. The speaker scouted the idea of social equality.

Major Delany is a patriotic man, and will undoubtedly do good battle for this our and his country.

After his speech, several of the colored young men present walked up and gave their names to the roll of the army. Among these, was Rev. Wm. C. Bryant, the minister of the Congregation. In a few patriotic, chaste, and well timed remarks, he announced his decision to leave his pulpit, and fight for his country and his God.

Colored people could not let such an occasion pass without some music, and the audience, as with one accord, took up "We'll Rally Round the Flag,"[4] and rendered it as only negro melodists can sing. Every one, whether old or young, gave his voice to the chorus, and the words and strains of that glorious song were better than ever as they came from negro throats. The audience also sang "John Brown,"[5] not as a mechanical performance, but as an act inspired of the very heart.

We left the house at a late hour. The wave of patriotism was still running high. When the meeting adjourned, or whether it adjourned at all, we have not been informed.

(*Xenia Sentinel*, 17 March 1865, p. 3)

---

4. Also known as "The Battle Cry of Freedom," the song was written in 1862 by the popular Union composer George F. Root (1820–95).

5. The popular song "John Brown's Body," according to legend, was composed by the Second Battalion of the Boston Light Infantry in 1861.

Monument to President Lincoln:
Two Documents

EARLY IN APRIL 1865, Richmond, Virginia, capital of the Confederacy, fell to Union troops. Shortly thereafter, Robert E. Lee's Army of Northern Virginia surrendered at Appomattox to Ulysses S. Grant's Army of the Potomac. Days later, on April 14, Abraham Lincoln was assassinated by John Wilkes Booth at Ford's Theater and Andrew Johnson assumed the presidency. Delany regarded the assassination as a "calamity" and quickly published two appeals in the *Weekly Anglo-African* calling on African Americans to build a monument to Lincoln as a token of their respect and gratitude.

CHARLESTON, S. C., April 20th, '65

EDITOR OF THE ANGLO-AFRICAN[1]:—SIR:—A calamity such as the world never before witnessed—a calamity, the most heart-rending, caused by the perpetration of a deed at the hands of a wretch, the most infamous and atrocious—a calamity as humiliating to America as it is infamous and atrocious—has suddenly brought our country to mourning by the untimely death of the humane, the benevolent, the philanthropic, the generous, the beloved, the able, the wise, great, and good man, the President of the United States, ABRAHAM LINCOLN, the Just. In his fall, a mighty chieftain and statesman has passed away. God, in his inscrutable providence, has suffered this, and we bow with meek and humble resignation to his Divine will, because He does all things well. God's will be done!

I suggest that, as a just and appropriate tribute of respect and lasting gratitude from the colored people of the United States to the memory of President Lincoln, the Father of American Liberty, every individual of our race contribute *one cent*, as this will enable each member of every family to contribute, parents

1. Thomas Hamilton.

paying for every child, allowing all who are able to subscribe any sum they please above this, to such national monument as may hereafter be decided upon by the American people. I hope it may be in Illinois, near his own family residence.

This penny, or one cent contribution, would amount to the handsome sum of forty thousand (40,000) dollars, as a tribute from the black race (I use the generic term,) and would be not at all felt; and I am sure, that so far as the South is concerned, the millions of freedmen will hasten on their contributions.

To this end, then, let proper and well-selected committees be appointed in every community, to whom such contributions will be made, with a record of the name of every family, and the number of inmates, the name of husband and wife simply, and so many children as "George and Elizabeth Parker, and five children, 7 cents."

I would, to this end, name, as the common Treasurer for the funds, to be paid over to the proper officers at the proper time, in their order, Rev. Stephen Smith,[2] Philadelphia, who will make weekly acknowledgments of the aggregate amount received, with the names of the places where received from, simply.

I am certain that every loyal editor in Philadelphia and elsewhere, will gladly publish without cost such an item.

Will Rt. Rev. Dr. Payne,[3] President of Wilberforce University, Rev. Dr. H. H. Garnet, and James McCune Smith, M. D., sanction this proposition? In sorrow,

Yours, M. R. Delany,
Major 104th Regt. U. S. C. T.[4]

(from the *Weekly Anglo-African*, 13 May 1865, reprinted in the *Christian Recorder*, 20 May 1865, p. 2)

* * *

I propose for the National Monument, to which all the colored people of the United States are to contribute each one cent, a design, as the historic represen-

---

2. Stephen Smith (ca. 1797–1873) of Pennsylvania, the son of a slave woman, formed a partnership with the businessman William Whipper during the 1830s and by the 1840s was perhaps the wealthiest African American in the United States. He was ordained as a pastor in the African Methodist Episcopal Church in 1831, and he used his wealth and influence to champion abolition and black voting rights.

3. Named a bishop in the African Methodist Episcopal Church in 1852, Reverend Daniel Alexander Payne emerged as one of the most prominent leaders of the church until his death in 1893. In 1863 he became president of Wilberforce University, the first black-run college in the United States. Delany purchased his home at Wilberforce from Payne in 1864.

4. United States Colored Troops.

tation of the humble offering of our people. On one side of the *base* of the monument (the *south* side for many reasons would be the most appropriate, it being the south from which the great Queen of Ethiopia came with great offerings to the Temple at Jerusalem, the south from which the Ethiopian Ambassador came to worship at Jerusalem,[5] as well as the south from which the greatest part of our offerings come to contribute to this testimonial) shall be an urn, at the side of which shall be a female figure, kneeling on the right knee, the left thigh projecting horizontally, the leg perpendicular to the ground, the leg and thigh forming the angle of a square, the body erect, but little inclined over the urn, the face with eyes upturned to heaven, with distinct tear-drops passing down the face, falling into the urn, which is represented as being full; distinct tear-drops shall be so arranged as to represent the figures 4,000,000 (four million), which shall be emblematical not only of the number of contributors to the monument, but the number of those who shed tears of sorrow for the great and good deliverer of their race from bondage in the United States; the arms and hands extended—the whole figure to represent "Ethiopia stretching forth her hands unto God."[6] A drapery is to cover the whole figure, thrown back, leaving the entire arms and shoulders bare, but drawn up *under* the arms, covering the breast just to the verge of the swell below the neck, falling down full front, but leaving the front of the knee, leg, and foot fully exposed. The lower part of the drapery should be so arranged behind as just to expose the *sole* of the right foot in its projection. The urn should be directly in front of the female figure, so as to give the best possible effect to, or view of, it. This figure is neither to be Grecian, Caucasian, nor Anglo-Saxon, Mongolian nor Indian, but African—*very* African— an ideal representative *genius* of the race, as Europa, Britannia, America, or the Goddess of Liberty, is to the European race.

Will not our clever mutual friend, Patrick Reason,[7] of New York, sketch the outlines of a good representation of this design? This is to be prominently carved or moulded in whatever material the monument is erected of. Let the one-cent contribution at once commence everywhere throughout the United States. I hope the Independent,[8] and all other papers friendly, especially the re-

5. The scenes draw on Acts 8.

6. Psalms 68:31.

7. Patrick Henry Reason (1816–98) was a well-known African American artist and abolitionist from New York City. His best-known work remains his copper engraving of a chained slave, "Am I Not a Man and a Brother?" (1839), which was widely reprinted in abolitionist publications.

8. The New York *Independent* was an antislavery newspaper established in 1848 by New York businessmen and Congregationalist ministers.

ligious and weeklies, will copy my article published in the Anglo-African of the 13th of May; also this article on the design.

In behalf of this great nation,
M. R. DELANY,
Major 104th U. S. C. T.

(from the *Weekly Anglo-African*, 10 June 1865, reprinted in Frank [Frances] A. Rollin, *Life and Public Services of Martin R. Delany* [Boston: Lee and Shephard, 1868], pp. 207–8)

Prospects of the Freedmen of Hilton Head

BY EARLY MAY 1865, Major Delany had succeeded in his efforts to recruit men for the 104th regiment of the United States Colored Troops, and he was ordered to begin recruiting men for the 105th. Those orders were rescinded on 7 June, when it was clear that the Civil War was over. On 7 August 1865, Delany received a formal order to report to the Freedmen's Bureau on Hilton Head Island, South Carolina, where he would serve as assistant subassistant commissioner until August 1868. Though his title of "assistant subassistant" had a demeaning sound to it, Delany quickly assumed a leadership role in the black community. In an effort to influence whites as well, he wrote a series of seven articles for the *New South*, a Sea Islands newspaper widely read by whites, in which he urged southern blacks and whites to work together to restore the southern economy. He placed particular emphasis on the importance of the freedmen owning their own land. The essays, under the title "The Prospects of the Freedmen of Hilton Head," were published anonymously in issues of late 1865. The selection below is the seventh and concluding essay of the series. There are only scattered extant copies of the newspaper; fortunately, Rollin reprinted "Prospects" in her life of Delany.

I propose to conclude the subject of "THE PROSPECTS OF THE FREEDMEN OF HILTON HEAD" with this article, and believe that the prospects of the one are the prospects of the whole population of freedmen throughout the South.

Political economy must stand most prominent as the leading feature of this great question of the elevation of the negro — and it is a great question — in this country, because, however humane and philanthropic, however Christian and philanthropic we may be, except we can be made to see that there is a prospective enhancement of the general wealth of the country,—a pecuniary benefit to accrue by it to society,—the best of us, whatever our pretensions, could scarcely be willing to see him elevated in the United States.

Equality of political rights being the genius of the American government, I shall not spend time with this, as great principles will take care of themselves, and must eventually prevail.

Will the negroes be able to obtain land by which to earn a livelihood? Why should they not? It is a well-known fact to the statisticians of the South that two thirds of the lands have never been cultivated. These lands being mainly owned by but three hundred and twelve thousand persons (according to Helper[1])— one third of which was worked by four millions of slaves, who are now free- men—what better can be done with these lands to make them available and unburdensome to the proprietors, than let them out in small tracts to the freed- men, as well as to employ a portion of the same people, who prefer it, to culti- vate lands for themselves?

It is a fact—probably not so well known as it should be—in political econ- omy, that a given amount of means divided among a greater number of persons, makes a wealthier community than the same amount held or possessed by a few.

For example, there is a community of a small country village of twenty fam- ilies, the (cash) wealth of the community being fifty thousand dollars, and but one family the possessor of it; certainly the community would not be regarded as in good circumstances, much less having available means. But let this amount be possessed by ten families in sums of five thousand dollars each, would not this enhance the wealth of the community? And again, let the whole twenty families be in possession of two thousand five hundred dollars each of the fifty thousand, would not this be still a wealthier community, by placing each fam- ily in easier circumstances, and making these means much more available? Cer- tainly it would. And as to a community or village, so to a state; and as to a state, so to a nation.

This is the solution to the great problem of the difference between the strength of the North and the South in the late rebellion—the North possessing the means within itself without requiring outside help, almost every man being able to aid the national treasury; everybody commanding means, whether earned by a white-wash brush in black hands, or wooden nutmegs in white: all had something to sustain the integrity of the Union. It must be seen by this that the strength of a country—internationally considered—depends greatly upon its wealth; the wealth consisting not in the greatest amount possessed, but the greatest available amount.

Let, then, such lands as belong to the government, by sale from direct taxa- tion, be let or sold to these freedmen, and other poor loyal men of the South, in small tracts of from twenty to forty acres to each head of a family, and large landholders to the same,—the rental and sales of which amply rewarding

1. In the widely read *Impending Crisis of the South* (1857), Hinton Rowen Helper of North Carolina, who regarded blacks as greatly inferior to whites, attacked slavery as damaging to nonslaveholding southern whites.

them,—and there will be no difficulty in the solution of the problem of the future, or prospects of the freedmen, not only of Hilton Head, but of the whole United States.

This increase of the wealth of the country by the greater division of its means is not new to New England, nor to the economists of the North generally. As in Pennsylvania, many years ago, the old farmers commenced dividing their one hundred and one hundred and fifty acre tracts of lands into twenty-five acres each among their sons and daughters, who are known to have realized more available means always among them—though by far greater in numbers—than their parents did, who were comparatively few. And it is now patent as an historic fact, that, leaving behind them the extensive evergreen, fertile plains, and savannas of the South, the rebel armies and raiders continually sought the limited farms of the North to replenish their worn-out cavalry stock and exhausted commissary department—impoverished in cattle for food, and forage for horses.

In the Path Valley of Pennsylvania, on a single march of a radius of thirty-five miles of Chambersburg, Lee's army, besides all the breadstuffs that his three thousand five hundred wagons (as they went empty for the purpose) were able to carry, captured and carried off more than six thousand head of stock, four thousand of which were horses.[2] The wealth of that valley alone, they reported, was more than India fiction, and equal to all of the South put together. And whence this mighty available wealth of Pennsylvania? Simply by its division and possession among the many.

The Rothschilds[3] are said to have once controlled the exchequer of England, compelling (by implication) the premier to comply with their requisition at a time of great peril to the nation, simply because it depended upon them for means; and the same functionaries are reported, during our recent struggle, to have greatly annoyed the Bank of England, by a menace of some kind, which immediately brought the institution to their terms. Whether true or false, the points are sufficiently acute to serve for illustration.

In the apportionment of small farms to the freedmen, an immense amount of means is placed at their command, and thereby a great market opened, a new

---

2. In a notorious incident of 30 July 1864, two cavalry brigades in Lee's army demanded $500,000 from the citizens of Chambersburg, Pennsylvania, in compensation for the Union army's pillaging in Virginia. When the citizens refused to pay, the town was sacked and burned.

3. A prominent Jewish family of bankers, originally from Germany. The most prominent of the British Rothschilds were Nathan Meyer Rothschild (1777–1836) and Baron Lionel Nathan de Rothschild (1808–79). The baron was the first Jewish member of Parliament.

source of consumption of every commodity in demand in free civilized communities. The blacks are great consumers, and four millions of a population, before barefooted, would here make a demand for the single article of shoes. The money heretofore spent in Europe by the old slaveholders would be all disbursed by these new people in their own country. Where but one cotton gin and a limited number of farming utensils were formerly required to the plantation of a thousand acres, every small farm will want a gin and farming implements, the actual valuation of which on the same tract of land would be several fold greater than the other. Huts would give place to beautiful, comfortable cottages, with all their appurtenances, fixtures, and furniture; osnaburgs[4] and rags would give place to genteel apparel becoming a free and industrious people; and even the luxuries, as well as the general comforts, of the table would take the place of black-eye peas and fresh fish, hominy and salt pork, all of which have been mainly the products of their own labor when slaves. They would quickly prove that arduous and faithfully fawning, miserable volunteer advocate of the rebellion and slaveholder's rule in the United States,—the London Times,—an arrant falsifier, when it gratuitously and unbidden came to the aid of its kith and kin, declaring that the great and good President Lincoln's Emancipation Proclamation would not be accepted by the negroes; "that all Cuffee wanted and cared for to make him happy was his hog and his hominy;"[5] but they will neither get land, nor will the old slaveholders give them employment. Don't fear any such absurdity. There are too many political economists among the old leading slaveholders to fear the adoption of any such policy. Neither will the leading statesmen of the country, of any part, North or South, favor any such policy.

We have on record but one instance of such a course in the history of modern states. The silly-brained, foolhardy king of France, Louis V.,[6] taking umbrage at the political course of the artisans and laborers against him, by royal decree expelled them from the country, when they flocked into England, which readily opened her doors to them, transplanting from France to England their arts and industry; ever since which, England, for fabrics, has become the "workshop of the world," to the poverty of France, the government of which is sustained by borrowed capital.

No fears of our country driving into neighboring countries such immense resources as emanate from the peculiar labor of these people; but when worst comes to worst, they have among them educated freemen of their own color

---

4. Coarse cotton fabrics sometimes used for upholstery and draperies.

5. The London *Times* regularly attacked the Emancipation Proclamation; see, for example, the issue of 7 October 1862.

6. Louis V (c. 967–87) reigned as king from 986 to 987.

North, fully competent to lead the way, by making negotiations with foreign states on this continent, which would only be too ready to receive them and theirs.

Place no impediment in the way of the freedman; let his right be equally protected and his chances be equally regarded, and with the facts presented to you in this series of seven articles as the basis, he will stand and thrive, as firmly rooted, not only on the soil of Hilton Head, but in all the South,—though a black,—as any white, or "Live Oak,"[7] as ever was grown in South Carolina, or transplanted to Columbia.

(Frank [Frances] A. Rollin, *Life and Public Services of Martin R. Delany* [Boston: Lee and Shephard, 1868], pp. 237–41)

7. Variety of oak characterized by dark green evergreen leaves and dark red-brown bark.

Triple Alliance—The Restoration of the South— Salvation of Its Political Economy

DELANY REVEALED HIS identity as the author of "Prospects of the Freedmen of Hilton Head" in a signed essay in a December 1865 issue of the *New South*, "Triple Alliance," which can be read as the conclusion to the series of essays constituting "Prospects." Concerned about President Andrew Johnson's plans to restore confiscated property to the white masters, Delany proposed that northern capitalists, southern white landowners, and black laborers work together to develop the South's economy. And he proposed himself as the person best able to negotiate contracts among these three groups. During his three-year tenure at the Freedmen's Bureau, Delany remained true to his vision of a "Triple Alliance," working against great odds to attempt to create equitable terms for black laborers.

The restoration of the industrial prosperity of the South is *certain*, if fixed upon the basis of a domestic triple alliance, which the new order of things requires, invites, and demands.

Capital, land, and labor require a copartnership. The capital can be obtained in the North; the land is in the South, owned by the old planters; and the blacks have the labor. Let, then, the North supply the capital (which no doubt it will do on demand, when known to be desired on this basis), the South the land (which is ready and waiting), and the blacks will readily bring the labor, if only being assured that their services are wanted in so desirable an association of business relations, the net profits being equally shared between the three,—capital, land, and labor,—each receiving one third, of course. The *net* has reference to the expenses incurred after gathering the crop, such as transportation, storage, and commission on sales.

Upon this basis I propose to act, and make contracts between the capitalist, landholder, and laborer, and earnestly invite, and call upon all colored people,— the recent freedmen,—also capitalists and landholders within the limits of my district, to enter at once into a measure the most reasonable and just to all parties concerned, and the very best that can be adopted to meet the demands of the new order and state of society, as nothing can pay better where the blacks cannot get land for themselves.

I am at liberty to name Rev. Dr. Stoney (Episcopal clergyman), Joseph J. Stoney, Esq., Dr. Crowell, Colonel Colcock (late of the Southern army)—all the first gentlemen formerly of wealth and affluence in the State;[1] and Major Roy, of the United States Regular Army, Inspector General of the department; Colonel Green, commanding district, and Lieutenant Colonel Clitz, commanding post, also of the regular army, each having friends interested in planting, who readily indorse this new partnership arrangement. Of course it receives the approval of Major General Saxton.[2]

I am, sir, very respectfully,
Your most obedient servant,
M. R. DELANY,
Major & A.S.A. Commissioner Bureau R.F.A.L.[3]

HILTON HEAD, December 7, 1865

(Frank [Frances] A. Rollin, *Life and Public Services of Martin R. Delany* [Boston: Lee and Shepard, 1868], pp. 242–43)

---

1. The relatively obscure Reverend James Stoney, Colonel Joseph Stoney, Dr. Crowell, and Colonel Charles J Colcock, according to Frances Rollin's biography of Delany, fought in the Confederate army, commanding fortifications at Hilton Head up to the time of its capture. Following the publication of "Triple Alliance," Colcock negotiated a contract with Delany to employ sixty black laborers on his homestead (see Rollin, *Life and Public Services*, pp. 243–44).

2. In Rollin's biography, Delany expresses his indebtedness to Major J. P. Roy, Sixth United States Infantry, who was inspector general of the Department South; Colonel J. D. Green, Sixth United States Infantry, commanding district; and General H. B. Clitz, Sixth United States Infantry and commander of the post at Hilton Head. Brigadier General Rufus Saxton is the best known of the officers mentioned by Delany; see "The Colored Citizens of Xenia," note 2.

3. Major and assistant subassistant commissioner, Bureau of Refugees, Freedmen, and Abandoned Lands.

Letter to the Colored Delegation, 22 February 1866

WHEN ANDREW JOHNSON succeeded Lincoln as president, he almost immediately set himself in opposition to the Radical Republicans. He opposed the work of the Freedmen's Bureau, argued against black enfranchisement, and supported the rights of Confederate leaders to serve in state governments. Frederick Douglass sharply criticized Johnson's policies in speeches of late 1865 and early 1866, and on 7 February 1866, Douglass and several other African American leaders representing the recently concluded Convention of Colored Men in Washington, D.C., obtained an audience with Johnson. At the meeting Johnson was unbending, expressing concerns about the plight of poor southern whites and calling for black colonization as a possible solution to racial conflict in the United States. Douglass blasted Johnson in a letter printed several days later in the *Washington Chronicle*. Perhaps because he was working for the federal government and was acutely aware of tensions between blacks and whites in the South, Delany, in a letter to the black delegation, called for a less confrontational response to Johnson, whom he thought could, over time, develop a more capacious politics of race.

To Messrs. G. T. DOWNING,[1] WILLIAM WHIPPER, FREDERICK DOUGLASS, JOHN JONES, L. H. DOUGLASS,[2] *and others, Colored Delegation representing the Political Interests of the Colored People of the United States, now near the Capital and Government, Washington, D.C.*

1. George Thomas Downing (1819–1903) of New York City was a wealthy black businessman and forceful advocate for black civil rights. He opposed African colonization and emigration movements, particularly Henry Highland Garnet's African Civilization Society, and led protests against segregated schools in Rhode Island and elsewhere.
2. The eldest son of Frederick Douglass, Lewis Henry Douglass (1840–1908) served with the Fifty-Fourth Massachusetts Regiment from March 1863 to May 1864.

My dear Brothers: I have been watching with deep interest your movements at Washington, near the government of your country. I need not repeat to you that which you all know, and that which we have oft repeated to each other privately, in council, and through the public journals,—we are one in interest and destiny in America. I am with you; yea, if your intentions, designs, purposes, matter, and *manner* continue the same as those presented to the chief magistrate of the nation, then I am with you always, even to the end. Be mild, as is the nature of your race; be respectful and deferential, as you will be; and dignified as you have been; but be determined and persevering. Your position before the saged president, and reply after you left him, challenges the admiration of the world. At least it challenges mine, and as a brother you have it.

Do not misjudge the president, but believe, as I do, that he means to do right; that his intentions are good; that he is interested, among those of others of his fellow-citizens, in the welfare of the black man. That he loves Cæsar none the less, but Rome more. Do not expect too much of him—as black men, I mean. Do not forget that you are black and he is white. Make large allowances for this, and take this as the stand-point. Whatever we may think of ourselves, do not forget that we are far in advance of our white American fellow-citizens in that direction. Remember that men are very differently constituted, and what one will dread and shun another will boldly dare and venture; where one would succeed another might fail. Not far from where I am at present posted on the coast of South Carolina, there are several inlets, of which I will name two—Edisto and St. Helena. Of these, one pilot will shun one, and another the other, each taking his vessel easily through that which he enters; while another will not venture into either, but prefers—especially during a storm—to go outside to sea for the safety of the vessel; all reaching, timely, their destination, Hilton Head, in safety.

Here, what one shuns as a danger another regards as a point of safety; and that which one dreads another dares. What General Sherman succeeded in, General Meade might have failed in; while General Grant may have prosecuted either with success.[3] Men must be measured and adjudged according to their temperaments and peculiar constitutional faculties.

Do not grow weary nor discouraged, neither disheartened nor impatient. Do

---

3. The Union general William Tecumseh Sherman (1820–91) was best known for his destructive attacks on Atlanta and other southern cities in late 1864 and early 1865. The Union general George Gordon Meade (1815–72) led the Union army to victory in the battle of Gettysburg (1863), but he was subsequently criticized for failing to follow up with even more crippling attacks on the Confederate army. Meade had official command of the Army of the Potomac, but it was widely known that General Ulysses S. Grant (1822–85) was its true leader.

not forget God. Think, O think how wonderfully he made himself manifest during the war. Only think how he confounded, not only the wisdom of the mighty of this land, but of the world, making them confess that he is the Lord, high over all, and most mighty. He still lives. Put your trust in him. As my soul liveth, you will reap if you faint not. Wait! "The race is not to the swift nor the battle to the strong, but he that endureth to the end."[4] Bide your time.

Since we last met in council great changes have taken place, and much has been gained. The battle-cry has been heard in our midst, a terrible contest of civil war has raged, and a death-struggle for national life summoned every lover of the Union to the combat. We among our fellow-citizens received the message, and eagerly obeyed the call. Our black right arms were stripped, our bosoms bared, and we stood in the front rank of battle. Slavery yielded, the yoke was broken, the manacles shattered, the shackles fell, and we stood forth a race redeemed! Instead of despair, "Glory to God!" rather let us cry. In the cause of our country you and I have done, and still are doing, our part, and a great and just nation will not be unmindful of it. God is just. Stand still and see his salvation.

"Be patient in your misery;
Be meek in your despair;
Be patient, O be patient!
Suffer on, suffer on!"

Your brother in the cause of our common country,
M. R. DELANY

(Frank [Frances] A. Rollin, *Life and Public Services of Martin R. Delany* [Boston: Lee and Shepard, 1868], pp. 281–83)

4. Ecclesiastes 9:11.

Letter to Andrew Johnson, 25 July 1866

ON 9 APRIL 1866 Congress passed the Civil Rights Act over Andrew Johnson's veto, thereby granting citizenship and equal rights to African Americans. Undaunted by Johnson's veto, Delany wrote him directly to urge him to take the next step and support African Americans' right to vote. There is no record of a response from Johnson, who steadfastly resisted efforts to expand the franchise to black men. The Fifteenth Amendment was adopted in 1870 during the presidency of Ulysses S. Grant.

To His Excellency PRESIDENT JOHNSON:

Sir: *I propose, simply* as a black man,—one of the race most directly interested in the question of *enfranchisement* and the *exercise* of suffrage,—*a cursory view of the basis of security for perpetuating the Union.*

When the compact was formed, the British—a foreign nation—threatened the integrity and destruction of the American colonies. This outside pressure drove them together as independent states, and so long as they desired a Union,—appreciating the power of the enemy, and comprehending their own national strength,—it was sufficient security against any attempt at a dissolution or foreign subjugation.

So soon, however, as, mistaking their own strength, or designing an alliance with some other power, a portion of those states became dissatisfied with the Union, and recklessly sought its dissolution by a resort to the sword, so nearly equally divided were the two sections, that foreign intervention or an exhausting continuance of the struggle would most certainly have effected a dissolution of the Union.

But an element, heretofore latent and unthought of,—a power passive and unrecognized,—suddenly presented itself to the American mind, and its arm to the nation. This power was developed in the blacks, heretofore discarded as a national nonentity—a dreg or excrescence on the body politic. Free, without rights, or slaves, mainly,—therefore *things* constructively,—when called to the country's aid they developed a force which proved the balance precisely called for, and essentially necessary as an elementary part of the national strength. Without this force, or its equivalent, the rebellion could not have been subdued, and without it as an inseparable national element, the Union is insecure.

What becomes necessary, then, to secure and perpetuate the integrity of the Union, is simply the *enfranchisement* and recognition of the *political equality* of the power that saved the nation from destruction in a time of imminent peril— a recognition of the *political equality* of the blacks with the whites in all of their relations as American citizens. Therefore, with the elective franchise, and the exercise of suffrage in all of the Southern States recently holding slaves, there is no earthly power able to cope with the United States as a military power; consequently nothing to endanger the national integrity. Nor can there ever arise from this element the same contingency to threaten and disturb the quietude of the country as that which has just been so happily disposed of. Because, believing themselves sufficiently able, either with or without foreign aid, the rebels drew the sword against their country, which developed a power in national means—military, financial, and statesmanship—that astonished the world, and brought them to submission. Hence, whatever their disposition or dissatisfaction, the blacks, nor any other fractional part of the country, with the historic knowledge before them of its prowess, will ever be foolhardy enough to attempt rebellion or secession. And their own political interest will ever keep them true and faithful to the Union, thereby securing their own liberty, and proving a lasting safeguard as a balance in the political scale of the country.

As the fear of the British, as an outside pressure, drove, and for a time kept and held the Union together, so will the fear of the loss of liberty and their political status, as an element in this great nation, serve as the outside pressure *necessary* to secure the fidelity of the blacks to the Union. And this fidelity, unlike that of the rebels, need never be mistrusted; because, unlike them, the blacks have before them the *proofs* of the *power* and *ability* of the Union to maintain unsullied the *prestige* of the national integrity, even were they, like them, traitorously disposed to destroy their country, or see it usurped by foreign nations.

This, sir, seems to me conclusive, and is the main point upon which I base my argument against the contingency of a future dissolution of the American Union, and in favor of its security.

I have the honor to be, sir, your most obedient servant,

M. R. DELANY
Major 104th U.S.C.T.

PORT ROYAL ISLAND, S.C., July 25, 1866.

(Frank [Frances] A. Rollin, *Life and Public Services of Martin R. Delany* [Boston: Lee and Shepard, 1868], pp. 278–80)

Letter to Henry Highland Garnet, 27 July 1867

IN THE SUMMER OF 1867, several Republican leaders called on the party to nominate a black man for vice president at the upcoming Republican convention. At the South Carolina Republican Party convention in July 1867, a young black lawyer, Jonathan J. Wright, answered that call, declaring his readiness to assume the vice presidency. Concerned that the nomination of a black vice president would lead northern whites to abandon the Republican Party, and concerned as well that such a nomination would only further exacerbate southern whites' hostility toward the freedmen, Delany wrote Henry Highland Garnet, then pastor of New York's Shiloh Presbyterian Church, to ask him to join him in urging younger African Americans in particular to temper their demands. Delany's letter to Garnet was printed in the *New York Tribune* under the title "Colored Men as Office-Holders."

MY DEAR SIR: At such times as these it requires men of the greatest practical experience, acquired ability, mature intelligence, and discretional wisdom, to speak and act for the race now an integral part and essential element in the body politic of the nation. Therefore I do most sincerely hope that you and the other leading minds among our people may take your stand, speak out, and define your true sentiments in relation to the great points now agitating the public mind, especially the black man's claims to office.[1]

The great principle always advocated by our leading men has been to claim for us, as a race, all the rights and privileges belonging to an American citizen of the most favored race. But I do not think that those who have so long, so steadily, and determinedly stood up as you and others of us have done, even to a national concession of these claims, ever contemplated taking any position

1. Like Delany, Garnet had abandoned his African emigration plans during the Civil War. He helped to recruit black troops, and following the war he campaigned for black civil rights. In 1865 he was the first African American to deliver a sermon before the U.S. House of Representatives.

among our fellow-citizens, till *we* at least should be *ready* and *qualified*. It follows, as a matter of course, that *more* than we should be ready, before it is *possible* to attain to such positions. I am sure that upon this point, there will be but one sentiment among the old-line leading men of our race, cotemporaneous with us, when the subject is placed before them.

I have been induced to pen this letter to you by seeing in the telegraph proceedings of the Columbia, S.C., Convention a claim put forth by Mr. J. J. Wright,[2] in behalf of our race, for the Vice-Presidency of the United States. I hope no such nonsense as this will for a moment be entertained. Our enemies would desire no heavier nor stronger club with which to break the heads of our friends and knock out our brains than this. We are not children, but men, comprehending the entire situation, and should at once discountenance anything that would seemingly make us cat's paws, and ridiculous in the eyes and estimation of the political intelligence of the world. Let colored men be satisfied to take things like other men, in their natural course and time. Prepare themselves in every particular for local municipal positions, and they may expect to attain to some others in time.

Mr. Wright is a young man, of some 27 or 28 years of age, and consequently without any political experience, except such as acquired since the war commenced, and therefore, may be excused for so palpable a political blunder.[3] I am a personal friend of his, [and] therefore take the liberty of speaking frankly about him. I am Sir, for our race and country at large, your friend,

M. R. Delany

Hilton Head, S.C., July 27, 1867.

(*New York Tribune,* 6 August 1867, p. 1)

2. Jonathan Jasper Wright (1840–85) of Pennsylvania studied law at Lancasterian University and in 1865 accepted an assignment from the American Missionary Association to teach the colored troops and freedmen at Beaufort, South Carolina. In 1866 he became the first black admitted to the Pennsylvania state bar. He then returned to Beaufort to work as a legal adviser to the Freedmen's Bureau. He was elected to the state senate in 1869 and in 1870 was elected by the General Assembly to a seven-year term as a justice on the South Carolina Supreme Court.

3. Delany also opposed those who championed his friend John Mercer Langston (1829–97) as a suitable vice president, arguing that Langston, like Wright, was too young. See Delany's letter to the Reverend R. L. Perry, 27 September 1867, in the *Christian Recorder,* 12 October 1867, p. 1. Langston, who accompanied Delany on some of his western tour for the *North Star,* became the first dean of the law department at Howard University in 1868.

Reflections on the War

IN HER BIOGRAPHY OF Delany, Frances Rollin included two unpublished Delany essays of the immediate post–Civil War period. In the longer essay of the two, "The International Policy of the World Towards the African Race," Delany, as in *Origin and Objects* and much of his writings on Africa, celebrated the achievements of African religion, politics, and art while excoriating whites' racist attitudes toward black culture. In a very different sort of essay, "Reflections on the War," printed in its entirety below, Delany explored the problem of leadership in the American South at the very moment that he was himself emerging as an important southern leader.

One important fact developed during this gigantic civil war, and which could not have escaped the general and mature intelligent observer as a result of the struggle, and so contrary to concessions under the old relations of the Union, is, that no great statesmen were produced on the part of the South; although at the commencement at the Montgomery Convention, or Provisional Congress, August, 1861,[1] their independence was declared, and consequently must have been fully matured, not a measure was put forth of national import to sustain their cause, except the issue of the cotton bonds thrown upon the foreign market—a cheat so consistent with the Mississippi bond repudiation of Mr. Jefferson Davis,[2] that it is not difficult to determine the source of that financial scheme, which, of itself, was an ordinary commercial measure, of every-day transaction, enlarged to meet the occasion of a "national want."

1. The February 1861 convention in Montgomery, Alabama, formed the Confederate States of America; Jefferson Davis (1808–89) took the oath of office as president of the Confederate states on 18 February 1861. The convention authorized a provisional congress, which met in Montgomery and, later that year, in Richmond, Virginia, where the new constitution of the Confederacy was ratified.
2. During the Civil War, Davis authorized the printing of millions of dollars in Confederate bonds, payable within two years of the war's end. The bonds depreciated and became valueless.

Previous to the war, it was generally conceded that by far the ablest statesmen in the service of the nation came from the South. And doubtless this may have been so, for a long period of the government, after the close of the revolutionary struggle; because, the people of the North, caring for little else than business, of personal interests, and local legislation, few men could be found among them willing to devote more than one term in Congress, or the executive departments of the government; while the policy of the South was to continue the same men as long as possible in the councils, in consequence of their domestic relations affording them ample time and leisure in their absence from home to mature their plans of ascendency.

During the revolutionary period, which may be reckoned from the Albany Continental Congress, in 1754, to the Peace Congress at Ghent, 1814,[3] both grand political divisions, north and south of Mason and Dixon's line, show with equal brilliancy in the national forum.

After the treaty of peace with Great Britain, gradually the leading spirits passed away, either by death or withdrawal from public life, till Clay, Calhoun, Adams, and Benton[4] appeared for many years as the only dependence of the country in questions and measures of great national import.

These master spirits continued their career till they, in turn, one by one, left the stage of action, the last terminating in 1852, by the death of Mr. Webster.

Of this galaxy, the Hons. John Quincy Adams, of the House of Representatives, and Henry Clay, of the Senate, were the leaders of international measures; Senators Daniel Webster and Thomas H. Benton, those of national import; while Senator John C. Calhoun was especially confined to that of state rights sovereignty. During the existence of these, there were other men of note and distinction, all of whom have left the stage of action. Of the great personages above named, all, excepting Senator Benton, have held the portfolio of first minister of state; and it is notorious, that although Senator Calhoun's was under President James K. Polk, 1844, a period most auspicious for the display of statesmanship, as great and vital questions of national and international polity were prominent before the country and the world,—such as the extension of territory, and the annexation of Texas,—not a measure was put forth by Mr. Cal-

3. Representatives of the British colonies and the Iroquois negotiated a treaty at the 1754 Continental Congress at Albany, New York, though the Iroquois then allied themselves with the French despite the treaty. The 1814 Peace Congress at Ghent, Belgium, concluded with the signing of the treaty that ended the War of 1812 between the United States and Great Britain.

4. Thomas Hart Benton (1782–1858) was a four-term Democratic senator from Missouri, serving his first term at the admission of the state in 1821. Known for supporting policies favorable to the economic development of the western states and territories, he favored the gradual abolition of slavery and lost influence within his party when he opposed the Compromise of 1850.

houn to meet the exigencies of the occasion and the times. Indeed, that senator, outside of "state sovereignty" and South Carolina, as history bears witness, as a *statesman*, was a failure.

The social polity of the North being based upon labor, and that of the South on leisure, depending on slave labor for maintenance, as an almost natural consequence, the North neglected as much as possible places of honor in the nation,—the army, and navy,—conceding these, as a matter of course, in all good faith, to its brethren of the South. In good faith the concession was certainly made, because the North then as heartily approved of slavery as the South.

Foreign intervention being permanently settled, and no longer any dread of a common enemy, the South accepted the indifference of the North, and commenced preparations for her own independence. This was probably maturing shortly after the battle of New Orleans (1815),[5] till the election of James Buchanan, 1856; or, more historically, from the treaty of Ghent, 1814, to the Ostend Congress, in 1854.[6]

When the civil war commenced, it was alarmingly apparent that the South had by far the best officers, the North having few trustworthy, or those of military experience. And while the army was routed, and the enemy gaining strength at home and abroad, the masterly ability of statesmanship of the North not only challenged the respect and admiration of the world by the wisdom of the great executive head of the government, but intricate questions of the greatest international policy were raised, met, sustained, and established; military and financial measures created by the ministers of state, war, and the treasury, never yet equalled by any nation.

During the time immediately succeeding the revolutionary period,—from 1815 to 1851,—with the exception of representatives from Missouri, Kentucky, Maryland, and Delaware, in the persons of Hons. Thomas H. Benton, Henry Clay, Reverdy Johnson, and John M. Clayton,[7] every great measure of national interest was represented by gentlemen of the North. So completely had the state rights question engrossed the attention of the South, that nothing could be

5. The famous battle in which Andrew Jackson led outmanned U.S. troops to victory over the British, shortly after the signing of the Treaty of Ghent.

6. James Buchanan (1791–1868), the fifth president of the United States (1857–61), participated in the Congress of 1854 at Ostend, Belgium, when he was serving as American minister to Great Britain. At the congress, Buchanan and his associates issued the Ostend Manifesto, a declaration that the United States should attempt to take Cuba by force if Spain continued to resist U.S. efforts to purchase the island nation.

7. The Maryland lawyer Reverdy Johnson (1796–1876) twice served in the Senate (1845–49, 1863–68); though sympathetic to the South, he opposed secession. The Delaware lawyer John Middleton Clayton (1796–1856) also served in the Senate and was secretary of state under Zachary Taylor. As secretary of state he negotiated the Clayton-Bulwer Treaty (1850), which helped to check British expansionism in the Americas.

elicited in the halls of Congress from that side of the house, of whatever import the question, but "Old Dominion" and "first families," "South Carolina and state rights," "Georgia and negro slaves," "Alabama and cotton," "Louisiana, slaves, and sugar," "Mississippi negro traders," "Arkansas and amen with abolition," "Texas and bowie knives." These appeared to be the only rejoinders given, and arguments made for many years past, in the councils of the nation, by representatives from the South.

Absorbed entirely in the one erroneous idea of state sovereignty, thinking of nothing besides this, neither fearing nor caring for anything else, then is a degeneracy in statesmanship much to be wondered at on the part of the South? Certainly not. It is but charity to the South to admit of finding a solution of their deficiencies in the statement of these grave and important truths.

Was there any one man or measure, either in or out of the whole Southern establishment, civil or military, approaching those of the North? Not one. I am fully aware that "comparisons are odious;" that these features of observations are "in bad taste," and that it will be adjudged ungenerous to make such allusions to our fallen and subjugated fellow-countrymen. I fully appreciate the extent of the objection; but when it is remembered that many of this very class of Southerners,—the old leading politicians are straining their intellects to prove the inferiority and incapacity of my race to high social and intellectual attainments,—the objector will, at least, find an explanation, if not justification, in the strictures.

I admit there are many excellent gentlemen in the South, and many have, through the press of the country, acknowledged their approval of the great principles of equality before the law, liberty and justice, and the natural inalienable rights of all men by birth; but I must be permitted to place my record, if not measure my steel, against those who tauntingly dare challenge me. It was the Hon. Daniel Webster, who, long years ago, on the floor of the United States Senate, on the very subject of disparagement, told Senator Hayne, of South Carolina, in reply to his assertion, "The gentleman from Massachusetts has found *more* than his match" in debate with Senator Benton,—"Sir, where there are *blows to be received*, there must be blows given in return."[8]

(Frank [Frances] A. Rollin, *Life and Public Services of Martin R. Delany* [Boston: Lee and Shepard, 1868], pp. 309–13)

8. Delany refers to the famous January 1830 debate on nullification between Senator Daniel Webster (1782–1852) of Massachusetts and Senator Robert Young Hayne (1791–1839) of South Carolina. Benton had supported the efforts of a coalition of westerners and southerners to nullify the U.S. tariff. Webster's response to Hayne, which excoriated slavery and offered a mystic paean to the Union, came to assume mythic status among U.S. nationalists.

DELANY DEPARTED FROM Hilton Head early in 1869, rejoining his wife in Wilberforce in June 1869. In October of that year he again left Wilberforce, traveling to Washington, D.C., with the hope of meeting with President Grant to request an appointment as the first black minister to the Republic of Liberia. Unable to secure the interview or the job, he returned to South Carolina early in 1870, where he was given an honorary position as one of seven lieutenant colonels and aides to the commander in chief of the South Carolina militia. That appointment came the same year as the adoption of the Fifteenth Amendment, which gave black male citizens the right to vote. Convinced that a knowledgeable black electorate was crucial to the project of Reconstruction, Delany contributed four essays to the *New National Era*, a new African American newspaper based in Washington, D.C., on blacks' responsibilities as voters. Later in 1870 he arranged to have the essays reprinted in pamphlet form; the pamphlet is reprinted in its entirety below.

Advertisement of Author.

The "University Pamphlets" are but the commencement of a series of tracts intended to be written by the author as popular elementary instruction in the principles of National Polity, complimentary to the Faculty, Students, and Trustees of WILBERFORCE UNIVERSITY, the latter body of which he is a member.

These pamphlets will be adapted with special care and reference to the comprehension and benefit of the new political element in the United States—the freedmen and colored youth.

This series was originally published in four alternate numbers of the NEW ERA, Washington City, from January to March, 1870.[1]

The next series will be on the "History of Constitutional Governments,"[2] which will give a much clearer view and understanding of the importance of Constitutions, as guaranties of liberty, so essential at this time, immediately succeeding the establishment of an impartial and truly National Government.

A Series of Four Tracts on National Polity.

Number I. Citizenship.

The term *citizen*, politically considered, is derived from the Roman definition, which was never applied in any other sense—*civis ingenuus*—which meant one exempt from restraint of any kind. *Civis*, a citizen; one who might enjoy the highest honors in his own free town—the town in which he lived—and in the country or commonwealth; and *ingenuus*, free born—of good extraction.

All who were deprived of citizenship—that is, the right of enjoying positions of honor and trust—were termed *hostes* and *peregrini*, which means public and private enemies, or foreigners and aliens to the country. *Hostis*, a public, and sometimes private, enemy; and *peregrinus*, an alien, or stranger, or foreigner. As a policy, the common people or Plebeians, were sometimes classed with these, by the ruling people or Patricians; but all natives or people born in the country were citizens, and might be elevated to any position in State or the body politic, as was Cicero, to that of Consul or Chief Magistrate of Rome, who had been simply Mark Tully, (*Marcus Tullius*,)[3] a Plebeian, or poor boy from among the lower classes.

The Romans, from national pride, to distinguish their inhabitants from those of other countries, termed them all "citizens"—as in the case of the aliens and foreigners (*hostes peregrini*)—but consequently, were under the necessity of defining four classes of citizens—the better to distinguish them and prevent confusion—all but the *cives ingenui* being restricted in their privileges. This privileged class was the Patrician.

---

1. The essays appeared in the following issues of the *New National Era*: 27 January, 10 February, 24 February, and 10 March 1870. The paper was founded by the Massachusetts black abolitionist John Sella Martin (1832–76), who initially served as editor, and Frederick Douglass, who initially served as corresponding editor.

2. There is no extant evidence that he wrote these essays.

3. Marcus Tullius Cicero (106 B.C.–43 B.C.) was Rome's greatest orator.

Its members enjoyed the *jas Quiritium*, which embodied, in the fullest extent, the rights, privileges and liberties pertaining to a Roman citizen.

There was one class whose members enjoyed, politically, only the *jus suffragierum*. They had the privilege of voting, but no other political privilege. They could vote for one of their superiors—the *cives ingenui*—but not for themselves.

Such precisely was the relative condition of the black inhabitants of the United States; in some of the States they answering to the latter class—as in New York and Ohio—having the privilege of *voting*, to elevate another class to positions to which they themselves were denied.

The right of suffrage, as shown in British and American civil rights, does not necessarily imply the elective franchise. Suffrage means "a vote, voice, approbation;" simply a privilege, something allowed. A privilege may sanction the rights of others, by those who do not themselves possess the rights they sanction.[4]

Rights are indisputable, inviolable; and in this country, political rights constitute the inherent sovereignty of the people. Where there is no acknowledged sovereignty, there can be no binding power; hence, formerly in the United States, the suffrage of the black man, independently of the white, was unavailing—worth nothing.

It must be understood that no people can be free who do not themselves constitute an essential part of the *ruling element* of the country in which they live. Whether this element be founded on a true or false, a just or unjust basis, this status in community is necessary to personal safety.

The liberty of no man is secure who controls not his own political destiny. What is true of the individual applies to a community of individuals, or society at large. To suppose otherwise, is that delusion which induces its victim, through a period of long suffering, patiently to submit to all kinds of wrong, and holds in subjection the oppressed of every country.

A people to be free must be their own rulers; each individual must in himself be an essential element of the sovereign power which composes the true basis of his liberty. This right, when not exercised by himself, may, at his pleasure, be delegated to another—his true representative.

These great truths are established in the British and American people. The people of Great Britain elect their representatives in the person of a Parliament,

---

4. This truth was illustrated in France by Louis Napoleon's elevation to the presidency of the French Republic, in 1851. On taking the vote every man must vote "yes" or "no"— that is, for or against him; but the voter could not cast his ballot for himself, or any other person than Napoleon; since by his established polity no other person was eligible to the position, though all had a right to give their voice for or against him. This was the RIGHT OF SUFFRAGE, as it is called, and all that it is worth politically. [Delany's note]

and Parliament creates or elects a ruler, called Monarch or Sovereign; and in the United States they elect their representatives in the person of electors, who meet in assemblies and elect their ruler, called President. In both of these cases there is only the sovereign will of each individual and united will of the people, carried out in the persons of these rulers, to whom they delegate their authority. Otherwise, the people of neither of these two countries could be politically free. The same may be said of France—the civil rights of whose people take higher ground than those of either Great Britain or the United States.

"A free agent in a free Government should be his own governor," said a great French writer.[5] That is, as elsewhere stated, he must possess the acknowledged right to govern. This constitutes him a governor, though he delegates to another the power to govern or rule over himself.

It is plain that no one can delegate to another a power he never possessed; that is, he cannot give an agency in that which he never had a right.

It must be apparent that the political condition of the black race, previous to the rebellion, was deplorable; and a change in their status was essential before it was possible to alter their condition.

First in order, emancipation was demanded, which placed them in a normal condition in relation to their country.

In Rome—from which the political right or claim of the individual was borrowed by the United States—citizenship, as stated, was based alone on nativity. All native-born inhabitants being citizens, the term was simply applied to the strangers and foreigners who resided among them, to gratify their pride, and thereby secure their loyalty to the country.

To place the black race in possession of equal rights, and enfranchise it with all the claims of citizenship, it was only necessary to remove all legal disabilities, and repeal all unjust provisions against it, and the black man stood in the United States *a citizen by nature*, with claims and rights as inviolable as the proudest— rights which to him became a contingency shall to his children be *inherent* and everlasting.

Will the opposers of the political elevation of the black race still continue to commit such palpable blunders in national polity as to deny that the black is a legitimate—in social polity—or legal citizen of the United States? It is time this political absurdity had ceased.

And it is now important that men of the black race make themselves masters of political science, that they may grapple favorably with the great question of civilization, now the basis of national and international polity.

––––––––

5. See "Political Destiny of the Colored Race on the American Continent," note 2.

Number II. Civil Rights.

Every member of a body politic has duties and obligations to perform, which are binding according to his relative position in society.

His general obligations are to the nation, particular obligations to the province, district, or state, (as one of the United States,) and special obligations to those with whom he is identified or classified, as German, French, Jew, Scotch, Italian, Irish, Spanish, or English. Here, in America, the special obligations of the black man are to his own people.

Civil rights imply all the privileges and enjoyments known to the body politic. These rights are not natural, but conditional, regulated by the requirements of society.

The general requirements of society are regulated by national obligations, or the obligations of state. A nation being bound to protect itself and preserve its own existence, regulates the individual, and governs society accordingly.

In France civil and political rights are one and the same—inseparable—and based upon natural rights. The right to freedom carries with it every other right, and suffrage is claimed as a birthright.

To deny to the Frenchman any privilege in the body politic, is to degrade him in his own estimation, and deprive him of "one-half of his manhood." "Freedom" is his watch-word, and "Liberty" his rallying cry.

In France, Government is always regarded as despotic, where suffrage is curtailed; and, indeed, the Chamber of Deputies—representatives of the people, and the right to choose them—is as old as the advanced civilization of that people.

It was seen that Louis Napoleon, as the first step in his accession to power, in 1851, took the vote of the people.[6] It is true that their civil rights were abrogated when they were prevented from competing for the Presidency; because, in France, as the civil and political are inseparable, the right to vote carries with it the right to hold office.

The action above alluded to simply shows a concession, even by Napoleon III, to those great and inherent rights as claimed by the Frenchman.

In England and the United States civil and political rights differ, and political rights carry with them different degrees of privileges. A man might have the

6. Louis Napoleon Bonaparte (1808–73) was elected president of France in 1848 and seemed to offer democratic possibilities to the French people; but after the defeat in July 1851 of a constitutional amendment that would have allowed the president to serve for more than one term, he engineered a coup d'état that made him emperor of France from 1852 to 1870.

privilege of voting and not the right to hold office; or, in other words, have the right of suffrage and not be eligible to office.

In Great Britain, Magna Charta made every person equal before the law; but in the political regulations a property qualification was required to vote and hold office. But in America exceptions were made to one class or race of the inhabitants, who were denied both the right of suffrage and the right to hold office.

This caused much confusion and frequent embarrassment in the administration of laws, in consequence of the ambiguity of their constructions, which were as erroneous as they were unjust.

In England and the United States, as in France, the civil should have included the political rights of the whole people.

But an established peerage, orders of nobility and primogeniture, or land privileges, as the basis of the United Kingdom of England, Scotland and Ireland, positively prohibited these enjoyments to the lower classes, in the first case; and the National Compact, the basis of the American Union, recognizing and permitting the existence of slavery and a privileged class in the whites,[7] in the second case prevented an acknowledgment of these great fundamental rights, as belonging to the whole people, as in France.

As a nation is bound to protect itself, to have conceded equal privileges to the common people in Great Britain would have destroyed the foundation of their Government, as then constructed; and to have conceded civil rights to the blacks in the United States must have, in like manner, endangered the National Compact, as slavery was the basis of the Union.

But the people of Great Britain are free, and their system of government but a matter of choice and time, which may be modified in its continual progress with satisfaction to the entire nation.

And, in the United States, by the late civil war, slavery has become extinct, the blacks enfranchised, and the civil and political rights of the whole people acknowledged.

The duties and obligations of every individual being according to his relative position in society, previous to emancipation and our enfranchisement, we had few or no obligations, because few or no responsible positions in society.

But now, having all the rights and privileges, we also have all the responsibilities belonging to society. Hence, the necessity of possessing such information and having such qualifications as to fit us for the high, responsible, and arduous duties of the new life into which we have entered.

7. A reference to the Constitution's three-fifths clause, which allowed southern states to count their slaves as three-fifths of a person when determining congressional and electoral representation.

We must possess attainments equal to the requirements of the positions we expect to occupy. Otherwise, we have no right to expect anything.

Our new political element, we are in hopes, will not fail to profit by these elementary lessons in national polity.

———

Number III. Constitution.

"The Constitution has been violated!" is an exclamation daily uttered in both Houses of Congress by the Opposition.

What is a Constitution, and for what is it intended? Let us inquire.

A Constitution is a legal guaranty of security to all the rights and privileges of the people in a country, the basis of which must be written or understood.

In all countries without these constitutional arrangements, written or traditional, the will of the ruler is law, and the liberties of the people are insecure.

The British Constitution is based on Magna Charta, a written document, which prohibits any act of Government abridging or curtailing the rights and privileges of the people. Hence, no act of Parliament can be repealed, nor judicial decision reversed, that ever has been established in their favor.

The greatest political and civil rights enjoyed by the royal family and nobility must be conceded to and enjoyed by the common people of the empire; and every privilege may be extended in common to all, but none can be abrogated.

By this wise provision the only alteration to the Constitution allowable must be favorable and progressive, in strict conformity with all the provisions of Magna Charta, or the great charter of British rights.

Every act of Parliament or judicial decision, as the *habeas corpus*, the acknowledgment of Scotch and Irish peerage, ruling slavery from British soil—as in the Somerset case, West India emancipation, the Corn Laws, "Irish emancipation," as it is called, the right of suffrage to the common people—each and all are additions to the Constitution, which cannot be repealed, because enhancing the liberty of the people.[8]

The British Constitution, then, consists of a succession of liberal acts, forced

8. Delany refers to various liberty cases in England: the Somerset Case of 1772 granted freedom to the slave James Somerset on the ground that his master, who wished to return him to the United States, refused to honor Somerset's attachment to England; West Indies Emancipation (1833) abolished slavery in the British empire; the repeal of the Corn Laws (1846), which had banned the importation of foreign grains, was regarded as a working-class victory against aristocratic price-gouging; "Irish emancipation" was the movement championed by Daniel O'Connell and other Irish political leaders to repeal what they regarded as the tyrannical union with Britain; the reform bills of 1832 enfranchised the British middle classes.

by the common people from the Crown by the authority of Magna Charta, the fundamental source of their rights.

Every act of justice, then, is constitutional, and in strict conformity with the only object and design of that instrument.

The Constitution of the United States, unlike that of Great Britain, is a document of numerical provisions, designed more for the regulation of departments of State and official duties, than for defining and guarding the rights of the people.

This instrument is conservative in character, its alteration carefully guarded against, and scarcely to be hoped for; while that of the British is progressive, continual alterations being provided for and expected.

Had the American Declaration of Independence been adopted at the time as the basis of the Constitution, it would then have been to the United States, what Magna Charta is to Great Britain.

The act of 1787, limiting slavery in the Northwest territory; the act of 1808, limiting the slave trade; the instructions of 1851, to Captain Ingraham, in relation to Martin Koszta, defining the rights of American citizens on board American vessels;[9] the emancipation proclamation of 1863; the civil rights bill of 1866, and all the reconstruction acts of Congress promoting the rights of the people, would have only been so many clauses added to the Constitution, in conformity with the great principles of that document.

And there is little doubt that when Jefferson and his compeers framed the Declaration, they expected it, like Magna Charta, to be the basis, indeed, the Constitution itself; a guaranty of security to the rights of the people, definitely laid down as therein declared. But the whole was perverted, as sad experience has proven; and, instead of that great charter, an ambiguous document, susceptible of almost any construction concerning human rights, was shamefully imposed upon the American people and the world, as the Constitution of a new nation claiming to have taken the most advanced position in modern civilization.

The Constitution of the United States, then, it is clearly seen, according to its structure, failed entirely as an instrument for which it was intended, previous to the late civil war. And the old line leaders in both political parties, (Whig and Democrat,) as statesmen, did little else, in their interpretation and legal con-

9. In a famous case of July 1853, the naval officer Duncan Nathaniel Ingraham (1802–91), commanding the USS *St. Louis*, demanded (and obtained) the release of Martin Koszta from an Austrian warship near Turkey. Koszta was a Hungarian revolutionary who had fought against Austria in 1848 and subsequently fled to the United States, where he had petitioned for citizenship. Ingraham's rescue of the soon-to-become U.S. citizen was celebrated in the U.S. press; Congress voted Ingraham a medal of honor.

struction of it, than mislead the American people in the knowledge of constitutional rights.

It must be understood and laid down as a proposition logically correct, that any instrument which recognizes in its provisions the violation of the natural rights of any part of the people, is a mockery in its pretensions; as the design of a Constitution legitimately must be, the enlargement and protection of the rights of the whole people.

The object of this article is to instruct a class of readers in the elementary principles of constitutional government; and to do ample justice to a subject so important, would require a series of articles on the history of Constitutions.

The new era upon us, requires new duties among a new political element; and consequently, there must be disseminated information commensurate with their requirements.

Number IV. Secession.

"These States, I affirm, were never out of the Union," declared the Hon. J. P. Stockton, United States Senator from New Jersey, while discussing the bill offered by Senator Morton, from Indiana, which again placed proud, arrogant Georgia under the stricture of the National Government.[10]

Were the rebel "States never out of the Union?" Let us see.

Every State, in any country, has two conditions, a territorial or land, and a political or governmental.

When the rebellion ensued, the first effective act was to meet in general congress at Montgomery, Alabama, and declare themselves out of the Union, by absolving all relations, and ignoring all authority, with and from the different States and Government of the United States. Immediately, all relations between those two great divisions of States, North and South, ceased, and for four long years of anxious warfare and desperate struggling, so continued.

From Montgomery, Alabama, to Richmond, Virginia, the Government of these States changed, which was as foreign to the United States as it was to France. And these facts were never denied by the Government at Washington.

But not satisfied with taking themselves out of the Union, the South endeavored to carry with them the territory, a portion of the national domain, be-

10. In 1868, despite opposition from the Democrats, including New Jersey's Democratic senator John P. Stockton (1826–1900), Indiana's Republican senator Oliver Perry Morton (1823–77) successfully spearheaded a bill that revoked Georgia's abrogation of its pre-1865 debts.

longing to the Union. It was this attempt of theirs, and this alone, which brought down on their offending heads, the just retribution of the nation.

Would it be pretended that these people had no right to withdraw from the United States, either as individuals or in a body, if they so desired, set up and organize themselves into a body politic for their own government and mutual protection, provided they did not encroach on the rights of any other people in so doing?

Had they immediately after the Montgomery congress,[11] or at any subsequent period, quietly withdrawn—organized as they were—to any part of Mexico, Central, South America, or Nassau, and there set up themselves with all the "paraphernalia" of a confederacy, would the United States Government have dared interfere with them? Certainly not; nor would the law of nations have tolerated it.

What, then, was the position of the Government in relation to them? Why, it admitted their right to go, but denied their right to carry with them the territory, a portion of the public domain, belonging to the nation. The right of their political state was conceded, but that of the land or country only was denied; and it was this position alone assumed by President Lincoln, in his continual declaration that the "rebel States were never out of the Union."

What, then, is the course of Congress toward these people? Why, having once withdrawn their political relations and absolved all and every interest, it is not only the indisputable right, but the imperative duty of the national council to prescribe terms and conditions upon which they may return to their allegiance.

This is both logically correct and morally right.

And Congress legislates, not on the territorial, but political relations of the late Confederate States to the Union.

Might it not be well for the opposition, who so flippantly deny the withdrawal of the rebel States from the Union, to remember these facts before claiming for them such unrestricted equal political rights as originally existed between the States? It were well that they do.

(*University Pamphlets. A Series of Four Tracts on National Polity: To the Students of Wilberforce University; Being Adapted to the Capacity of the Newly-Enfranchised Citizens, The Freedmen* [Charleston, South Carolina: Republican Book and Job Office, 1870])

11. The Confederate secession congress of 1861.

Homes for the Freedmen

THROUGHOUT THE LATE 1860s and early 1870s, Delany argued that black landownership was crucial to the work of Reconstruction. Without land, Delany feared, southern blacks would be forced to accept the crippling terms of peonage. Intent on helping South Carolina's African Americans to gain ownership of land, he opened the short-lived Land and Real Estate Agency in Charleston in 1871. He also wrote open letters to Senator Henry Wilson of Massachusetts and Daniel L. Eaton of the Freedman's Savings Bank in Washington in which he urged, somewhat in the spirit of his "triple alliance" proposal, that northern philanthropists purchase land for the freedmen on a loan basis. The letters appeared in spring 1871 issues of the Charleston *Republican*. Later that year, Delany reprinted the letters as a pamphlet, which appears in its entirety below.

M. R. Delany on the Freedmen

These letters were written at the request of some leading philanthropists and capable financiers at the North:

No. 1.

To Hon. Henry Wilson,[1] *U.S. Senator.*

SIR: As one of the early friends of equal rights, I take the liberty of calling your attention to an important subject.

The thing now most required for the freedman is a home — one that he can call his own, and possess in fee simple, to insure the subsistence of himself and family. This is very desirable, and, without it, the life of these poor people is a

---

1. A senator from Massachusetts from 1855 to 1871, Henry Wilson (1812–75) was an abolitionist and one of the founders of the Republican Party. During 1861–62 he led the fight to abolish slavery in the District of Columbia. Following the Civil War, he emerged as a leader of the Republicans' efforts to gain civil rights for African Americans.

miserable burden, to be relieved of which, death will soon become a welcome messenger to the most of them, and liberty itself an evil.

I would call the attention of the philanthropic capitalists to this suggestion, which would benefit both black and white, and amply secure themselves in the capital invested.

Estimating the population of freedmen at four hundred thousand (400,000), with the usual allowance of five persons to a family, will give eighty thousand (80,000) families. Ten acres in this climate will be ample as a means of sustenance for all necessary family comforts to a rural population; more than this would not be asked as a start in life for them.

Allowing ten acres to each family (this would be the average, as some would require more and some less), it would amount to eight hundred thousand (800,000) acres.

There is at present an abundance of surplus land in this State, which could be purchased at such a figure as to enable the purchaser to dispose of them to the freedmen at an average advance of fifty per cent. on the original purchase money, and then be fully within their reach to meet with all their contingencies, such as improving and stocking their little farms.

What the freedman wants is land of his own, with time to pay for it. What the land owner wants is cash for his surplus lands. He has been impoverished by the late civil war, having nothing left but these surplus lands, and when not living by their products, he can only afford to part with them for cash. This cash the poor, industrious, hard-laboring freedman has not got, nor can he get while only receiving the wages of labor, or paying such rentals as he must, and is generally paying, either in cash or portion of the crop.

There are cases of rentals in which the occupants of the lands—whether in cash or produce—do pay more per acre for the use of the land (and in many cases two and three hundred per cent. more) than what the same land could be bought for in cash if sold. It will be seen at a glance that this is ruinous to the laborer, who never will be able to make more than his bread; for in thousands of cases, indeed the majority of the rural population, the men and women are in rags, and the smaller children of both sexes either stark naked, or cover[ed] with but a single shirt.

Nor would this securing of homes to the rural population impoverish the State by depriving the land holders of labor; but, to the contrary, it would be a lasting benefit, by securing an industrious and fixed laboring element, the surplus of whose labor would always be ample for all the demands of the large land owners and planters, with advanced wages; as both land and the wages of labor would enhance in value, just in proportion to the general permanent improvement of these numerous little farming neighborhoods.

I am continually being called upon by gentlemen who are willing to sell lands at the lowest figure, to secure such homes to the freedmen, because they know that it would be mutually beneficial to themselves, the freedmen, and the commonwealth at large.

Sir, will you call attention of philanthropists to this important subject?

I am sir, very respectfully,

Your most obedient servant,

M. R. Delany.

Late Major 104th U.S.C.T., and Sub-Asst. Com. Bureau, R., F. and A.L.

Charleston, S.C., March 7, 1871.

———

No. 2.

Col. D. L. Eaton,[2] Washington, D.C.:

SIR: On the 7th inst., I addressed a communication through the Charleston *Daily Republican* to Senator Wilson, on the subject of "Homes for the Freedmen."

In that, I showed how small farms of an average of ten (10) acres could be secured, to each of the eighty thousand families of freedmen, at the present low price of lands, giving them ample time to pay, and yet be a profitable investment to the philanthropic capitalists, and a cheap home to the people.

In addition to the importance of securing cheap homes on easy terms to four hundred thousand people, there is another feature of this, scarcely less important, to which I would especially invite your attention.

At present the taxes in this State are very heavy and burdensome, not perhaps because they are so very high, but mainly because of the disproportion in the estimates, and nearly the whole coming off the few.

This could not be a point of objection if the property taxed were generally available, producing an income adequate to the expenses. But this is far from the reality, as there are numerous cases in which property (especially lands) when sold, could not bring half, no, not one-fourth, of the assessment estimate for taxes. This is a matter worthy of note.

Land in South Carolina is greatly depreciated, while taxes have become proportionably higher. These taxes are mainly paid by a very few of the citizens, as

2. Daniel L. Eaton was an actuary at the Freedmen's Bank in Washington, D.C., and between 1867 and 1872 was one of three people who controlled the bank's finances. Eaton made regular speaking tours to address southern blacks.

the great majority own little or no real estate, paying little else than the simple capitation tax.

By securing homes to the homeless, it must be effected by the much desirable division of lands, and by this division of lands, a division of the taxes, the source of the public revenue.

When the expenses of government are proportionably borne by the people generally, whatever excesses there may be committed by those to whom they have entrusted the duties and functions of State affairs, then, and not till then, will they be sufficiently interested to hold them accountable for their doings.

Let the people, then—those now homeless—generally become freeholders, possessors of the land, with improved real estate, and they at once become proportionably interested in all the affairs of the State, and they, who are the principal voters, will see to it that reckless and incompetent men will not be sent a second time to misrepresent them and the interests of the State.

But let the freedmen have homes of their own, fixed and established interests in the soil and State that others have, and that never-failing natural desire for each other's welfare and the protection of each other's interests, will establish that neighborly friendship throughout the entire State, without which, freedom would be a curse alike to black and white, and republican liberty a mockery and a lie.

Sir, I renew the invitation of your attention to my letter of the 7th instant on "Homes for the Freedmen," above referred to, and hope that so desirable an object may engage the attention of philanthropic capitalists.

I am, sir, in behalf of a suffering people of a State of both races almost distracted.

Your most obedient servant,

M. R. DELANY.

Charleston, S.C., March 23, 1871.

———

No. 3.

Col. D. L. Eaton, Washington, D.C.

SIR: This is my third letter on the subject of "Homes for the Freedmen," the second, which you kindly gave a place, being written on the 23d of March.

This subject is of much importance, and becomes even imminent as time passes, because, so soon as emigration turns its tide in this direction—which is now being earnestly solicited by organizations of prominent and popular gentlemen—the golden opportunity now offered of obtaining lands at the lowest cash price will have passed forever.

Nothing can add more to the permanent peace and pecuniary interests of this State than the possession of fixed homes, owned in fee simple by the laboring classes, once slaves.

Capital will not be invested without labor, and labor will neither remain nor go where there is no chance of employment. Consequently, capitalists are fearful to invest in planting, because there is no certainty that labor will be secure, as the laborer is continually changing places in search of permanent employment.

Besides this, the more intelligent the laborer, the more productive the labor. This is demonstrated in the German, who by odds is the best agriculturist to be found. This is simply because the German is intelligent; he must be educated. Every child must go to school and learn to read, write and cipher, compelled by law; hence his intelligence.

The freedmen, too, must be educated, but it will be impossible to establish facilities for education till they become settled and fixed in neighborhoods. It would be a waste of time and money to build school houses and make other outlays for such purposes where there is no certainty of the people remaining beyond one planting season. And to expect the same development from the freed people as other citizens, without the same kind of facilities for moral, intellectual and religious culture, is to expect an impossibility.

And what will these people be as a social and political element to the society or State at large without this moral, intellectual and religious culture? Simply a curse instead of a blessing. The church and the schoolhouse must stand side by side, projecting their gable peaks or belfry spires in silent eloquence toward the skies in every district settlement among these people.

But before either the church or schoolhouse can be erected, the people themselves must be settled in *homes of their own.* This can be the only indemnity or security against all investments for permanent improvements in the social and industrial condition of the people, black and white, in the rural or agricultural districts.

The surplus lands are abundant, and the people waiting and ready to settle them. The owners are willing and anxious to sell them, on terms for cash entirely satisfactory and advantageous to the purchasers. But the purchases must be special, through agencies for this object, and not by speculation to put money in the pockets of persons disinterested in a philanthropic enterprise which would only defeat the intention by increasing the required investment too great to make it practicable and profitable.

The lands purchased for this enterprise must be secured at first and not second hand prices, and the only cost in doing so, must simply be that of the commission of the agent, which, in this arrangement, is made to come off the seller, and not those who purchase for the freedmen, so that there will be actually no expense incurred in the agency, leaving the entire margin clear to the philanthropists who sell to the freedmen.

I am sure that this will justify the investment, even if the terms be in five annual payments (with interest, of course).

There can be no safer nor surer investment of any kind than this—being in land, which must continually enhance in value—and in four years it will reimburse the funds with an advance of two-fifths or forty per cent. on the whole amount expended, with an addition of seven per cent. interest, the legal rates of the State. In this there can be no losing risk.

If the friends of humanity and progress of the South will accept of this and act at once, in less than one year every family of freedmen in South Carolina will be in full possession of a home of *ten acres*, held in fee simple, forever.

I think, sir, that I have now placed all before you necessary on this important subject, consequently this will close my series.

All other required information will be carried on through private correspondence.

In conclusion, if there be not prompt and decisive action, all may be lost by permitting the golden opportunity of obtaining lands at so low a figure to pass by forever.

I am, sir, very respectfully,

Your most obedient servant,
M. R. DELANY.

Charleston, S.C., May 1, 1871.

(*Homes for the Freedmen* [Charleston, South Carolina: privately printed, 1871])

Delany and Frederick Douglass,
Letter Exchange, 1871

THOUGH DELANY IN 1868 resisted calls for a black vice presidential candidate, he remained committed to the belief that the election and appointment of African Americans to government positions was absolutely essential to broadening blacks' participation in the democratic process. As reported in the 24 June 1870 Charleston *Daily Republican*, Delany at a meeting of the South Carolina Republican Party demanded that approximately half of all state government positions go to African Americans, including the lieutenant governorship, proclaiming that "black men must have black leaders. . . . I want it understood that we are in the majority in this State, and we hold the political power" ("New Meeting of Republicans," p. 3). In 1871 Delany elaborated his views on proportional representation in a letter to Frederick Douglass printed in the *Daily Republican*. Most likely he addressed Douglass because he resented the Republicans' practice of seeking to fulfill their obligations to African Americans by appointing just a small number of well-known black men to government positions. (In January 1871, Douglass himself had been appointed assistant secretary to the commission of inquiry to Santo Domingo.) Now editor of the *New National Era*, Douglass reprinted Delany's letter in the 31 August 1871 issue and offered a response.

Letter from Major Delany to Frederick Douglass

Hon. Frederick Douglass:

MY DEAR SIR: It has been ten years since last we met (in your library at Rochester) to discuss and reconcile ourselves to President Lincoln's war policy.[1]

1. The meeting occurred during the summer of 1862, when Delany gave a series of lectures in Rochester on his African project. Douglass criticized the lectures for attempting to undermine African Americans' commitment to the Civil War; see "Dr. M. R. Delany," *Douglass' Monthly*, August 1862, p. 595.

Since then slavery has been overthrown, and no "reunion" of what were, for twenty years or more, the leading colored men of the country, who shaped the policy and course of our race, which led to disenthrallment, having taken place, and consequently no interchange of ideas by counsel; I therefore deem it of importance at this time to take a political review of South Carolina, which I think will apply justly to nearly, if not the whole, of the "reconstructed States" of the South as well as the National Government.

When the war ended the colored people of the South had little knowledge of social and political affairs, and had of necessity to accept such leaders as presented themselves. The first of these were in the persons of various agencies; as school teachers (mostly women,) the Christian Commission, colporteurs and agents of the "Freedmen's Affairs," (not the Bureau,)[2] who aided in directing their social and domestic relations.

When reconstruction commenced, political leaders were greatly required, but few to be had. Southerners (the old masters) studiously opposed and refused to countenance reconstruction, and the freedmen were fearful and would not have trusted them if they could have obtained their aid.

Those who came with or followed the army, with a very few native whites, were the only available political element to be had to carry out the measures of reconstruction.

These were readily accepted by the blacks (by this I include the entire colored people) and the fullest confidence reposed in them. Some were or had been officers in the army, some privates, some sutlers, others peddlers, and various tradesmen, others gamblers, and even pick-pockets, "hangers on" and "bummers."[3] I am particularly speaking of the whites. Among these were men of refinement, educated gentlemen, and some very good men; but a large part of those most active were of the lowest grade of Northern society, negro-haters at home, who could not have been elected to any position of honor or trust. Just such men as burnt down negro orphan asylums, and hung negro men to lamp-posts in the New York riot of 1863.[4] In this review I intend to speak plainly, call things by their right names, and look those of whom I speak directly in the face.

2. The Freedmen's Bureau was established by Congress in March 1865 to offer aid and protection to newly freed southern blacks.

3. "Bummers" was a term for thieving soldiers who foraged in the defeated South.

4. In July 1863, hundreds of blacks were killed and wounded when white workers of New York City rioted over a four-day period to protest what they regarded as unfair Union draft practices. (A drafted man could pay $300 or find a substitute to be excused from military service.) The working-class participants in the riot, many of whom were Irish American, were also somewhat sympathetic to the South and distrustful of competing black laborers.

The best and most competent men were chosen to fill the most important positions in State and local governments, while the others readily obtained such places as required incumbents. Indeed, there were scarcely one so incompetent as not to have been assigned some position of trust.

Positioned in places of power, profit and trust, they soon sought by that guile and deception, known only to demagogues, under the acceptable appellations of Yankee, Republican, and Radical, to intrude themselves into the confidence of the blacks, and place themselves at their head as leaders. So insidiously did they do this that it was not discovered by the few colored men of intelligence who held places among them till too late to remedy the fatal evil.

These demagogues laid the foundation of their career upon a basis of the most dangerous political heresy. Deception, lying, cheating, stealing, "whatever can be done in politics is fair," and to "beat is the duty in a political contest, no matter what means are used to effect it," are among the pernicious precepts of this moral infidelity.

Jealous of the few intelligent colored men among them, they studiously sought to divide the blacks, by sowing the seed of discord among them. This was facilitated by prejudicing the ignorant against the intelligent. These men strove and vied each with the other, regardless of consequences, to place himself in the lead of a community of blacks in both town and country, which in time was reduced to little else than a rabble mob of disorder and confusion. Trained in the leagues as serfs to their masters, it became dangerous to oppose these men of mischief. Because, having been recommended to their confidence at the commencement of reconstruction, their experience and knowledge in public men and matters were too limited to believe anything against them.

A knowledge of this emboldened these men to a persistence in their course of crime and corruption. Hence, many otherwise good men, both white and black, from age, inexperience, or weakness, were induced to accept the monstrous teachings and join with or follow the lead of these wretched impostors. Their sole object being personal gain, they cared little or nothing for public weal, the interest of the State or people, black or white, nor the Republican cause, upon which they had indecently imposed themselves. This is that which controlled Charleston politics and brought deserved defeat to the Republicans in the recent municipal election.[5] It was just retribution to a set of unprincipled miscreants, rioting on the peoples' rights under the name of "Republicans." Honest, upright men of all parties, white and black, no longer able to bear it, determined

5. Persistent charges of corruption against Governor Robert K. Scott had begun to cut into the Republican majority; Delany would abandon Scott for Franklin Moses Jr. in the election of 1872.

to put down the abominable thing; leading Republicans, who had been standing aloof, taking an active part.

Among other things they taught the simple-minded people that suffrage was inviolably secure, the blacks being in the majority, would always control the affairs of State in the South; that the fifteenth amendment[6] had abolished color and complexion in the United States, and the people were now all of one race. This barefaced deception was so instilled into them that it became dangerous in many instances to go into the country and speak of color in any manner whatever, without the angry rejoinder: "We don't want to hear that; we are all one color now!"

These ridiculous absurdities were fostered by the demagogues the better to conceal their own perfidy and keep themselves in the best positions, as "Republicanism knows no race," they taught.

Another imposition was that colored people did not require intelligent colored leaders; that the Constitution had been purged of color by a Radical Congress, and to be a Republican was all that was required to make a true representative. That mental culture and qualifications were only required by the proud and arrogant; that all who requested those accomplishments were enemies to both black and white; that race representation was making distinctions on account of race and color. By this means they opposed the qualified men among the blacks, encouraged the ignorant and less qualified that they might of necessity take the lead and occupy the best places in the party. These are plain, indisputable truths, which will not be denied by any upright, intelligent Republican, black or white.

Before the introduction of these men among them, there never was a better population, rural or town, out of which to shape a useful political element. Good-hearted, simple-minded, uneducated, they were ready and willing to receive any instruction supposed for their own good, which they anxiously awaited and as eagerly sought. And could they have had the advice of the maturely intelligent, good and virtuous friends of humanity, such as was received and given by us during more than thirty years, of toilsome battle for liberty and right, there never could have been the cause for complaint against us as a race now in a measure justifiable.

One most fruitful cause of mischief in the party arose from the age and want of experience on the part of the good white men who assumed to lead in politics—as well as ignorance in the most of them—and the same may be said of their colored colleagues. For the most part young men, where they possessed the

6. Ratified in March 1870, the Fifteenth Amendment prohibited federal and state governments from depriving any male citizen of the vote on racial grounds.

cultivated qualification, they were deficient in experience and knowledge in politics.

To such an extent were they misled that they regularly trained themselves with firearms and marched in companies to political meetings, frequently led by miserable white men. Menacing, threatening, abusing, quarreling, confusion, and frequently rioting are common results of this most disgraceful state of affairs under which we live, all in the name of Republicanism.

The effect upon the people is wonderful. From a polite, pleasant, agreeable, kindly common people, ever ready and obliging, there is now to be met with an ill-mannerly, sullen, disagreeable, unkind, disobliging populace, seemingly filled with hatred and ready for resentment. These changes in the character of the people must have been noticed by every intelligent observer, in contradistinction to their former excellent reputation. Formerly they were proverbial for their politeness, latterly they are noticed for their absence of it. These people are despoiled of their natural characteristics, and shamefully demoralized by renegade intruders.

These strictures have no reference whatever to the intelligent, high-minded, upright gentlemen among the white Republicans, whose examples and precepts have aided in building up society and contributing to the public good; but especially to that class who almost live in the quarters of the country people and hamlets of the towns, among the black population, keeping them distracted with excitement, who are a curse to the community at large, and a blight in the body-politic.

The social relations of the colored people is another shameful evil, which does more to weaken their strength, neutralize their efforts, and divide them in politics than even the graceless intrusion and imposition of white demagogues, because being of their own household. Still adhering to an absurdity, a relic of the degraded past, they cling to the assumption of superiority of white blood and brown complexion. And to such an extent is this carried, I am told, that old societies have been revived and revised, and absolute provisions made against the admission among them of a pure blooded black. Fire, military companies, and even churches and graveyards, it is said, are permanently established on this basis. In one church, at least, no blacks are to be seen, and in another there is a division line between the blacks and browns by different seats.

These distinctions naturally sour the blacks and widen the breach which should never have existed. What a commentary is this on the condition of the race! Cultivated intelligence and enlightened civilization will alone remedy a humiliating condition of a people now receiving the commiseration of the educated world. This canker, this leprosy, must be at once healed, and by a permanent purification purged from the social system of our people whose vitals it has entered, threatening death to its emaciated victims, now the scoff and derision of the Caucasian race.

Of a piece with this, is the ridiculous aping objection raised on account of nativity. Do they not know that (unlike the white race which has various established nationalities of the highest civilization throughout the world) we cannot, as a race, afford to be divided? That instead of objections, we should welcome with pride the coming among us of people of our own race, of intelligence, culture, and respectability, from withersoever they might come?

This anomalous imitation, not original, but borrowed from the other race, is not confined to class among us, but equally indulged in by many blacks and browns of every social position. Let the colored people learn this simple, though important, lesson: That the rejection of people because of their birthplace is social and political death to their race. That without intercourse and accession from abroad, intelligence, like wealth, must be limited and impotent. That the power and glory of the white race consists in their universal intercourse and unlimited recognition.

But among these are excellent ladies and gentlemen, who, though by affinity and predilection, may belong to such associations, yet they have no sympathy with the motives that induced their formation, and, therefore, discard them as humiliating, and will not be bound by their provisions. And to the credit of the greater part of those known as the "common people" among the mixed race, they entirely ignore these ridiculous distinctions, studiously refusing to recognize them—the distinction of color being propagated alone by that part known as the "higher class" among them.

To another important point I would invite your attention—that of the course of the National Government. While distinction in the rights of citizens on account of "race or color" is most pointedly prohibited, distinction on account of color is most definitely made by the Government at Washington.

It is a fact most noticeable in executive appointments of colored men; there are none of pure black men, the pure negro race, but all have been most carefully selected from those having an admixture of white blood. In neither of the Departments in Washington is there a single black holding a position above that of porter or lacquey, while in many, if not all of them—except the army and navy—there are those of mixed blood holding positions of clerkships—as is just and right—and other equally respectable places. Nor in no appointment requiring qualification by culture, in and out of Washington, is there a pure black man or woman to be found, while many such applications have been made, but always rejected. This is no fault of our brown brother, but that of the Government, and the misfortune of the blacks.

There may be these two exceptions: An ordinary black man, the keeper of a grog-shop, received the appointment of postmaster across the James river, opposite to Richmond, Virginia—obtained, it is said, at the request of a Democratic community. Also, it is said, that a black man has received the appointment of Consul General and Minister Resident to the Republic of Liberia, Africa, which required a recommendation from nearly the whole of the Republican members of the Senate to obtain the notice of Mr. Secretary of State, Hamilton Fish! This minister, I am told, persistently refuses to recognize the application of a *black* for any position. And, indeed, I am further informed that his prejudice to color caused the removal of the accomplished Haitian Minister, Colonel Romain, from Washington to New York city. Other members of the Cabinet, it is said, largely share these feelings against the pure negro race.[7]

Nor, out of the six hundred thousand colored people North, have there been any Federal appointments in the Northern States to any position above that of messenger or the merest subordinate, except a post office clerkship in Boston and Chicago, one each, I believe.

And what is said of Executive appointments at Washington in relation to blacks, the same I think may be safely said of the different State governments, the blacks being studiously neglected, except indeed to persistently make appointments of incompetent black men to positions which only bring discredit on them and their race. And in not a single instance does it occur to my mind in which a competent black man has received an appointment from a State executive, with a single exception; that of the Governor of a far Southern State, who appointed a black man (a special favorite of his) as one of four harbor masters—the others being white—he having to employ a white man at one hundred dollars a month to do his duties for him; when in the same city there were a number of well qualified black men, not one of whom ever received an office of equal significance. The fact is not ignored of the Governor of South Carolina honoring a black man with an appointment of aide-de-camp on his staff, an office purely of honor, yet an honor which any gentleman might accept, and is duly appreciated by the recipient.

The entire population of the African race is about five millions; one-eighth of the whole American people. According to the ratio of population, they are en-

7. Delany's anger in this paragraph has its sources in his failure to obtain the position of consul general and minister resident to Liberia from Secretary of State Hamilton Fish (1808–93). During 1869 Delany had undertaken a petition drive to obtain the position. He also wrote directly to Ulysses S. Grant requesting an interview, and even traveled to Washington, D.C., in late 1869 with the hope of gaining an audience with the president. (There is no record of a meeting.) In 1871, Grant appointed James Milton Turner (1840–1915) of Missouri, the focus of Delany's critique, as the first black minister to Liberia.

titled to thirty-two (32) representatives in Congress, and a corresponding ratio of official appointments. Allowing one and a half million to be mixed blood, leaves three and a half millions of pure-blooded blacks. These, by the foregoing estimate, are entitled to about twenty-six (26) representatives, with their ratio of Federal offices. And yet these three and a half millions of people, with their political claims, have been persistently neglected and almost ignored, by both general and State governments (except in cases of incompetent blacks for mere political purposes, to conciliate the ignorant blacks,) while their more favored brethren of mixed blood have received all the places of honor, profit, and trust, intended to represent the race.

In the name of a common race, for whose liberty and equal rights you and I for years have struggled, I now for the first time expose this disparaging injustice, and call upon you to aid in righting the wrong. A wrong which seems to be studied and determinedly persisted in. A wrong which longer to endure in silence would be an evidence of conscious inferiority and unworthiness.

Republicanism is simply the claims to equal rights established by our fathers in Philadelphia, 1816; by them renewed in 1829, in Cincinnati, Ohio; continued 1830–31–32 in Philadelphia; endorsed by their white brethren in 1833 in Boston as the "anti-slavery" and "abolition" of the country; the free soil of the Buffalo Convention, 1848, and Pittsburgh Convention, 1852; when it was engrafted into politics as Republicanism, at the nomination of Fremont at Rochester, N.Y., 1856, and Lincoln at Chicago, 1860.[8]

Anti-slavery, as established by our fathers, and propagated by us and our white friends, had for its basis "justice and equal rights to all men;" and for its motto: "Whatsoever ye would that others do unto you, do ye even so to them."[9] This is "anti-slavery" as originally propagated by our brethren, aided by their white friends, continued by us, aided by our white friends, and engrafted into politics. This should be Republicanism. Have these principles been adhered to under the dispensation of Republican rule? Have they not been shamefully perverted?

Both of the old parties—Democratic and Whig—favored slavery, having as their basis the inferiority of the negro and the right to oppress him and hold

8. Delany refers to Philadelphia blacks' opposition to the American Colonization Society ("A Voice from Philadelphia," published in January 1817, reprinted in William Lloyd Garrison, *Thoughts on African Colonization*, vol. 2 [Boston: Garrison and Knapp, 1832], pp. 9–13); black protest in Cincinnati in 1829 against Ohio's racist Black Codes; the emergence of the black convention movement in the early 1830s; the founding of William Lloyd Garrison's American Anti-Slavery Society in 1833; and the series of political conventions culminating in the rise of the Republican Party.

9. Matthew 7:12.

him perpetually in bondage, denied of every right but that at the option of the master. Republicanism was intended to supersede these and accord to him the enjoyment of all the rights and privileges of American citizenship.

Under the rallying-cry of acting for and representing the "negro," men of every shade of complexion have attained to places of honor, profit, trust, and power in the party, except the real negro himself—save such places as he had the power with which to elect himself—who remains to-day as before emancipation, a political nonentity before the governments of the country.

You have now seen the elements of which the party is composed in South Carolina, and its material through the nation. Are these harmonious elements? Does the structure consist of solid material? Can it stand the storms of political attacks from without, and the strife and struggles from within? Is there no repair to be made to the structure, or is it to be left to tumble to pieces by decay and damage from ill usage? These are questions worthy the attention of the publicist and statesman.

There must be to make it effective a renovating reorganization in this State, based upon intelligence, respectability, and honesty. The discordant elements must become harmonized. One class or race must not be permitted to enjoy privileges of which another is debarred. If this be continued as heretofore, devastation and ruin will come upon the party, when it will cease to exist, as it would deserve to do; as no party, by whatever name, should exist a single day, which does not accord and practically extend equal rights and their enjoyments to all the citizens, without distinction of race or color.

You and I have spent the best of our lives in the cause of humanity, living to see the overthrow and death of slavery, and universal liberty proclaimed in the land; and it now becomes equally our duty to crush, in infancy, the offspring of the monster wherever found.

Preparatory to any action on their part with the other race as a party, the colored people must first become reconciled to themselves as a race, and respect each other as do the whites, regardless of complexion and nativity, making merit only the mark of distinction, as they cannot afford to be divided.

Having settled the above "preparatory," I would lay down the following principles as a basis of all future party action, by whatever name it may be called, whether Republican or otherwise:

1. Equality before the law to every person of whatever race or color, and strict adherence to the reconstruction acts bearing upon the same.

2. Colored people must have intelligent leaders of their own race, and white people intelligent leaders of theirs; the two combined to compose the leaders of the party. This must be accepted and acknowledged as the basis of all future political action and necessary to the harmony and safety of both races.

3. All measures in the party must emanate from consultation of the leaders; otherwise such measures may not be respected.

4. Demagogues and disreputable men must be discarded as leaders, and never more be given opportunity to betray their trust and abuse the interests of the people whom they assumed to represent.

I am no candidate nor aspirant for office. I would accept of nothing that made me depend upon the position for my support, or cause me to relinquish my personal business. I have spoken simply as an humble citizen, interested in the welfare of the community at large.

With the above platform to guide my future action, I close my review of the political situation.

Thanking the editor of the Charleston *Republican* for the liberal use of his columns in granting this publication, I beg to remain, distinguished sir, as ever, your friend and co-laborer in the cause of humanity,

M. R. Delany

Charleston. August 14, 1871

Letter to Major Delany

My dear Sir: . . . While I entirely agree with you that no discrimination should be made against black applicants for office at Washington, because such applicants are black, I am far from agreeing with you that the present Republican administration has made any such discrimination. In fact we know of two clerks in the Departments here who are without doubt as dark as even Mr. DELANY would require, and who are as capable and efficient as any others. I am not much of a logician, but I require a little closer connection between premise and conclusion than you have here shown, to consider your conclusion legitimate. There are other reasons than color and race for the limited number of colored clerks employed in the Departments at Washington—reasons which I hope will disappear in time, and which, in fact, are already disappearing. The same causes which gave the leadership in public affairs to white men in South Carolina have given the lion's share of the offices to white men in Washington. As a matter of arithmetic your figures are faultless. The mulattoes, on a solid census basis, ought to have so many offices, the blacks so many, and the whites so many, the Germans so many, the Irish so many, and other classes and nationalities should have offices according to their respective numbers. The idea is equal and admirable in theory; but does it not already seem to you a little absurd as a matter of practice? The fact is, friend DELANY, these things are not fixed by figures, and while men are what they are cannot be so fixed. According to the census, the colored people of the country constitute one-eighth of the whole American people. Upon your statistical principle, the colored people of the United States ought, therefore, not only to hold one-eighth of all the offices in the country, but they should own one-eighth of all the property, and pay one-eighth of all the taxes of the country. Equal in numbers, they should, of course, be equal in everything else. They should constitute one-eighth of the poets, statesmen, scholars, authors, and philosophers of the country. The test should be impartially and stringently applied, if applied at all, and should bear equally in all directions. The negro in black should mark every octave on the National piano. In every company of eight American authors that can be named we ought to be able to name one black author, and so through all the varied departments of American activity. The negro should edit just one-eighth of all the newspapers; he should be the author of just one-eighth of all the books written and printed in the United States; and, in a word, be one-eighth in everything. Now, my old friend, there is no man in the United States who knows better than you do that equality of numbers has nothing to do with equality of attainments. You know, too, that natural equality is a very different thing from practical equality; and that though men may be potentially equal, circumstances may for a time cause the most striking inequalities. Look at our newly emancipated people, read their history of ignorance and destitution, and see their present progress and elevation, and rejoice in the prospect before them. You are too broad not to comprehend, and too brave to shut your eyes to facts; and in the light of these your octagonal principle certainly will not work. . . .

In conclusion, my dear old friend, let me assure you that I rejoice in every honor of which you are the recipient, and hold you worthy of all that have been bestowed upon you, and of still higher promotion. Let me also assure you of my cordial co-operation with you in all well-directed efforts to elevate and improve our race, to break down all unjust and mischievous distinctions among them, and secure for them a just measure of the political privileges now so largely monopolized by our white fellow-countrymen.

Very truly, yours,
FREDERICK DOUGLASS

(*New National Era*, 31 August 1871, pp. 2–3)

Delany for Lieutenant Governor
South Carolina State Election of 1874:
Two Speeches

CONCERNED THAT THE successive corrupt administrations of South Carolina's Republican governors Robert K. Scott and Franklin J. Moses, who served from 1870 to 1874, threatened to break down black-white alliances, Delany and like-minded reformers during the summer of 1874 worked to establish honest government leagues in counties throughout South Carolina. In September of that year the Honest Government League of Charleston, displeased with the Republican Party's candidate for governor, Daniel H. Chamberlain, voted to put forth its own slate for state offices. John Thompson Green (1827–75), a judge on the Third Judicial Circuit who had been a Unionist during the Civil War, won the nomination to be the candidate for governor of the group that came to call itself the Independent Republicans, and Martin Delany won the nomination to be the candidate for lieutenant governor. In a relatively close election in which approximately 150,000 South Carolinians participated, Green lost by 11,585 votes to Chamberlain and Delany lost by 15,985 votes to Richard H. Gleaves (1819–1907). (Ironically, Gleaves was a fellow St. Cyprian Freemason from Pittsburgh; it was Gleaves and two other St. Cyprians who had requested that Delany publish his eulogy on the Reverend Fayette Davis [see Part 1].) From the point of view of Frederick Douglass, who commented on the election in the 22 October 1874 issue of the *New National Era*, the Green-Delany ticket was "a deliberate attempt to break up the Republican party and turn the State over to the Democrats" ("Communications," p. 2). From Delany's perspective, however, the Independent Republican movement served the ends of honest government and interracial cooperation, and his sense of the exciting possibilities of the new movement informed his campaign speeches.

Daybreak, At Last!

The editors of the *News and Courier* devoted the front page of the 5 October 1874 issue to the Independent Republican State Convention, which had taken place at Hiberian Hall in Charleston three days earlier. In a celebratory article titled "Daybreak, at Last!" the editors proclaimed the convention "A Glorious Day's Work for South Carolina" and praised the Independent Republicans in particular for reaching out to the Conservatives (Democrats). At the convention, the delegates selected Delany, hailed as "the honest exemplar of the honest colored men of South Carolina," as the party's choice for lieutenant governor. A transcription of Delany's acceptance speech, printed below, was included in the article.

This is one of the most extraordinary occasions of my life. I have not words to express my gratitude to you for this manifestation of your regard and confidence in nominating me for the second office in the gift of the people of South Carolina. I have but little to say to you now, for you have already heard me frequently upon the various phases of our relations to each other; but this much I will say to you, that I have entered into this great movement with no other design than, if elected, to second to the utmost extent the integrity of the chief magistrate of the State. I will go further than this, I will pledge all of the intelligence, all of the powers of intellect that I possess, all of the integrity of character, to bring about between the two peoples in this State, black and white, those relations that shall tend to the promotion of each other's mutual welfare. [Cheers.] I shall not act (in the sense in which it is understood) as a party man. I shall know no other party than that which shall have for its object the interest of the whole people, black and white, of the State of South Carolina. [Cheers.] I shall strive to correct, so far as my own race is concerned, one or two errors in the Republican party as it formerly existed. We are now standing upon a new platform, so far as party acts are concerned. In our party there were three points of consideration: 1st. We were formed as a Republican party in contradistinction to the Democratic party; next, we were taught first and foremost an antagonism to the Democratic party, which, as a whole party, was all right. Next, we had factions in our own party, which was all wrong; and next, one part of our party was taught as a fundamental principle that they must stand in direct hostility to one portion of the people which formed the community in which they lived. I shall endeavor to correct this. It is my province to say that, because, when I look upon my race, I see that it has all and everything to lose in a contest such as might be brought about by antagonism of races. This being true, I have but one more remark to make. I do not intend to lower my standard of manhood in regard to the claims of my race one single step. I do not intend to recede from the rights that have just been given us by the beneficence of a just Congress of the nation one single hairsbreadth; but I do intend, in demanding all this, to demand the same equal rights and justice to every citizen, black and white, of the State of South Carolina. And upon this line I will fight it out if it takes all winter. [Cheers.]

(*News and Courier*, 5 October 1874, p. 1)

* * *

Green and Delany

Two days after accepting their respective nominations as governor and lieutenant governor of the Independent Republican Party, Green and Delany addressed a crowd of approximately four thousand people, blacks and whites, outside of Charleston's City Hall. In a front-page article titled "Green and Delany," the *News and Courier* provided transcripts of the speeches delivered at what the editors termed the "rousing ratification" of the Independent Republicans' nominees. The *Courier's* transcription of Delany's speech follows below.

Fellow-Citizens—I propose to say very little tonight after the speech of my distinguished leader,[1] and, in that little, I intend to call your attention to a few points that underlie this movement. In the first place, let me ask you what were the reconstruction acts of Congress[2] established for? Certainly not for the white people, because they were already in the enjoyment of all their rights and liberties. It must have been then for the benefit of the colored people in the South. And just here let me ask you: what benefits, outside of those conferred by the National Government, have the colored people in South Carolina derived from the propagation of Republican sentiments. ["None! None!" from the crowd.] One thing it has done, and that is to keep up a continual strife between the two

1. Judge John Thompson Green.
2. In 1867 Congress passed the first of several Reconstruction Acts placing formerly Confederate states under federal military rule.

races. Its leaders have been for ten years parading a huge scarecrow by means of
which they keep you in a state of continual fright, making you believe that you
are in constant danger of losing your liberties unless you have certain leaders to
back you up and protect you. ["That's so."] This is what Republicanism has
done for us, and the result has been to keep up a constant hostility between the
whites and blacks. ["Yes! Yes!" from the crowd.] Such a party is not worth the
effort to keep it in existence. It cannot be denied that, after the introduction of
Republicanism in South Carolina, the colored people became divided among
themselves, and it was to the interest of their leaders to keep up these dissen-
sions and divisions. Just let any two men come here from the North, and go to
hunting office, and in less than three months they will have the colored people
arrayed in open hostility between themselves, on one side shouting "hurrah for
massa Jim!" and the other "hurrah for massa Tim!" [Laughter.] But a change is
coming over the people. Only a few nights ago was presented, on this very spot,
one of the strangest spectacles that has ever been seen in South Carolina. That
was a citizens' meeting; and on the platform sat gentlemen—some of the first
white men in South Carolina; men who had held high offices of trust under the
old State Government; and me, Martin R. Delany, a John Brown Abolitionist.
[Cheers.] I have been asked by some of my brethren, if the white men are anxious to unite with the colored men in an effort for honest government, why did
the cotton press men the other day turn off black laborers and employ white
men. I answer, for the reason that the leaders of the black men had created dis-
sensions among them and persuaded them to do what they ought not have
done. They led them astray. ["That's so," from the crowd.] And I tell you now
that no people in this condition can advance in civilization. It is the mission of
this Independent movement to put a stop to this policy, and to lay down and
mark out for you new lines of duty, to establish between you and your white
fellow-citizens new and peaceable relations, to teach you that there is something
else to do than to shout "Hurrah for Republicanism and Damn Democracy."
The hour for this has passed. A remarkable feature of the old Republican movement in this State is that it never produced a single statesman since the establishment of the reconstruction acts. Why? Because there were always a few men
at Columbia who filled the offices and led the party, and every man in the party
had to accept their advice and follow the policy laid out by them or be silenced.
These men, my fellow-citizens, have become so accustomed to rule that they do
not hesitate to adopt any device or any measures to coerce the people to their
ends. In this very campaign, before the meeting of the State Convention, a high
State official came to Charleston with the message that if a delegation was sent
there without being instructed to vote for a certain candidate they would not be
admitted. The same officials have since declared that certain men must rule in

this county. It was the fight against this impudent dictation that the independent Republican party arrayed itself, and it is now high time that your eyes be opened to your duty in this matter. To prevent you from acting right they have raised the cry that this was a Democratic movement. Why this very day I saw a colored brother rush down to the wharf exclaiming, "Great God, what do you think! Maj. Delany has turned Democrat!" [Laughter.] They also accuse Judge Green of being a Democrat.[3] Judge Green said that he was not wealthy and could not afford to spend the money necessary to carry on the campaign, and because he consented afterwards to become the candidate of the Independent Republican party, he is called a Democrat. Was he any the less a Democrat when Attorney-General Melton[4] begged him to consent? [No! No!] I tell you my brethren that the whole policy of these masters of yours is to make you believe anything they say. They want you to remain like you have always been heretofore—a set of young blackbirds with your mouths open and eyes shut, waiting to swallow blindly anything that the old bird chooses to drop in them, no matter whether it is grasshopper or scorpion. [Laughter.] But they find out now that you are getting to be old birds, and that you are opening your eyes. ["Dat's so," from a grayheaded colored man in the crowd.] And we are no longer to be frightened by the old bugbear of "Democrats." Why, it was the Democrats who gave us freedom. And are we never to learn anything from the Democrats? Look at Frank Blair.[5] He commanded the 12th Army Corps, which swept like a besom through this State under Sherman in his memorable march to the sea, and burnt Columbia, and yet the Democrats voted for him for Vice-President in 1868, while we poor devils don't dare to vote for a good man because he is a Democrat. [Applause.] Why, if one of us was starving and stopped in the street to pick up a piece of bread from the gutter, and a Northern man was near and shouted "Democrat," you'd drop it and run. [Laughter.] So my duty is to teach my people these truths, and I say right here that I don't intend to be deterred, even by the thirty indictments that I understand are to be brought up against me by some lying scoundrel. [Cheers.] Let these swindling adventurers come with their indictments, and I promise to make the plate too hot to hold them. [Yells and cheers.] Who believes that the indictment against Mayor Cunningham is anything but a political persecution?[6] [That's so, from the crowd.] This

3. There is a missing line at this point; the unclear sentence that follows has been cut.

4. A native of South Carolina, Samuel W. Melton was elected attorney general in 1872, and he resigned in 1876. He worked in the same law office as Governor Chamberlain.

5. A Union general during the Civil War and one of the original founders of the Republican Party, Francis Preston Blair (1821–75) turned against the Radical Republicans after the war, running in 1868 as vice president on the Democratic ticket with Horatio Seymour.

6. George Irving Cunningham, the Republican incumbent, was never indicted, and he was reelected mayor in 1875.

thing has got to stop. If any vagabond can attack an honest citizen in this way, whose character will be safe? I'll tell you the plot they made up: They intended first to trump up an indictment against me;[7] but they were afraid that the colored people would say that they were persecuting a black man, and it would react against them. They therefore turned their attention to Mayor Cunningham, the chief magistrate of your city. The meaning of this is that these fellows will resort to anything. They are determined to have you under their feet, and to make you subserve their interests. It is time, however, for you to have your eyes open, and to learn that politics are intended for the benefit of the people, and that the policy which divides a community is pernicious and is only devised to carry out the selfish ends of the men who devised it. It was in consequence of the hostility created by these men between the two races, that white men are brought here to labor when our streets are full of idle colored men. [That's so.] The white people here, I am sure, would rather have colored labor, but they could not be expected to employ it as long as it was arrayed in hostility against them. For myself I am determined that it shall not be said that there is not a black man with the courage to warn my people against this. It is time to look things in the face; to recognize the fact that the whites and blacks should cultivate amicable relations between themselves, neither race abating one single right, but both working together harmoniously for the public peace and prosperity. [Applause.] These truths the people must learn. There must be new political relations between the races. Remember, my brethren, that the white people have said that, if the blacks would lay down their own platform and nominate honest men for office, they would come upon it and unite with them in working out the salvation of the State. [Applause.] Just here I want to tell you something that I don't want the white people to hear. Before and during the war I was a conductor on the Underground Railroad. You all know what that was—a society to carry off slaves and give them freedom. This required money, and I tell you we got ten dollars from a Democrat where we got one dollar from a Republican, and, what is more, we didn't refuse the money because it came from Democrats. Don't let us now refuse assistance because it comes from Democrats. Let us, in this new issue, extend our hands to every honest citizen in the State, and go on to certain success and triumph in our effort to redeem the State. [Applause.]

(*News and Courier*, 7 October 1874, p. 1)

7. In fact, Delany would be indicted for fraud and larceny in late 1875 (see the headnote to "Delany for Hampton" below).

The South and Its Foes

DELANY WAS UNDAUNTED by the South Carolina state election of 1874, which, as Frederick Douglass had feared, had united Democrats and Independent Republicans and restored a white majority to state offices. At the invitation of William Cullen Bryant, Delany journeyed to New York City and on 5 March 1875 at Irving Hall spoke in optimistic terms about the possibilities of conciliatory, nonconfrontational relations between southern blacks and whites. The speech was reported the following day in the *New-York Daily Tribune*.

Mr. Bryant[1] introduced the speaker as one who had fought the battles of his race with both pen and sword; with the pen as the associate of Frederick Douglass, with his sword as a soldier under Grant.[2] The many contradictions as to Southern affairs had bewildered and confused the minds of men as to the real condition of the South, and Major Delany would tell what he had observed and experienced, and help them to decide between the conflicting statements. Major Delany then came forward. He is a very dark negro, of about 50 years of age apparently, and of the type common to his race. His manners are self-possessed and easy, and his intonation without any trace of dialect.

In beginning, he said he had been honored with an invitation to speak on the social, moral, and political condition of the races in the Southern States, but he thought if he addressed them on the present political issues of the South that would include the subject on which he was requested to speak. Few persons in the North knew anything of the true condition of the South. Most of their information came from interested politicians. Only those who reside there could give a true statement. He knew that what he was about to say would be sharply

1. Poet, lawyer, and editor, William Cullen Bryant (1794–1878) broke with the Democrats during the 1850s on the slavery issue and was one of the founders of the Republican Party. His newspaper, the New York *Evening Post*, emerged as a prominent forum for leaders of the new party.
2. The Union general Ulysses S. Grant was elected to the presidency in 1868 and served two terms.

criticized, but he would say for himself that he was an old underground railroad man; he was with Fred. Douglass for three years when he established *The North Star*. It was even whispered that he had something to do with John Brown [cheers], though not in his Harper's Ferry raid. The colored people before the war were the best social and domestic element of its class that any country was ever blessed with. Properly directed, when they attained their freedom, they would have formed a political element of which the country might be proud. When the war was ended and they were elevated, while the political power of the whites was curtailed, they looked around for friends. Naturally his race looked to those whom the war for their freedom had brought to them, and as naturally those to whom they looked advised them so as to subserve their own interests.

At first they looked to their old masters, but they would have nothing to do with the matter. At Hilton Head he had personally appealed to Col. Seabrook[3] (who was on the platform) and others, but met the same answer: "We don't know what is to be; we will have nothing to do with it." So his people turned to the new comers, who took advantage of their ignorance to mislead them. They taught them that whatever was contrary to the interests of their old masters was right. He said knowingly that the class of men who undertook to lead the colored men in general had no interest in either the black or white race of the South. They taught the blacks that they should crush out the whites. They made them believe they were representatives of the Government sent from Washington to be custodians of their rights; that the white men would reinslave [*sic*] them the moment they put confidence in them. So pushing back the whites on one hand, and the blacks on the other, they plunged their arms to the elbow in the pockets of the blacks, and to the armpits in those of the whites. [Cheers and laughter.] Look at the legislation. The intelligent colored men did not go South. Humble as he was, he found few, if any, of his own status among his race. Look at the taxation and extravagance. The white man is taxed to the last mill, and the black man is unknowingly paying the tax in lower wages and higher prices. In four years of the Government of South Carolina, except some few belonging to rings, not a single employé of the Government from legislator down received his pay directly. It was shared by the money-changers at from 25 to 50 per cent. The blacks were taught that Republicans favored and their opponents hated liberty, and it was right to take any advantage of such opponents. Until a year ago all their meetings in the country districts were as organized bodies of armed men.

3. Colonel E. M. Seabrook, of an old Sea Islands family, had commanded the Confederate defense of Hilton Head up to the time of its capture.

They were taught that Democracy meant Slavery. Advantage was taken of the great religious element in their nature to make them trust these men.

He would tell the men of his race that democracy was the government of the people and republicanism the form of that government. For half a life-time, he and Frederick Douglass had struggled to make themselves Democrats, that is fellow rulers with the other people. [Cheers.] The political elements of the South were not understood at the North. Before the passage of the Fourteenth Amendment, there was in politics only one race, and Judge Taney was right in saying that a person of African descent had no rights a white man was bound to respect.[4] In Pennsylvania, they took from him the suffrage in 1838. In New-York he must have a property qualification, and in Ohio a certain per cent of white blood to be a voter. But enfranchisement made the colored men in the South a strong political element. In the North they were always in the minority, but in the South, in two States, they were in the majority, and in others they nearly balanced the white vote. The white people of the South were waiting and willing to take the blacks by the hand and go with them in every measure tending to the common good of both. They did not wish them to leave their position, their manhood, or their rights. He claimed every right for his race that the venerable Chairman claimed for the white race. But in giving his race liberty it was no part of the understanding that they should trample on the rights of the whites. And yet these bad men taught the colored men that it was their interest to do so. If the black men were to continue to be instruments of strife, it was their work. He wanted the North to know that there was no animosity between the whites and blacks of the South. [Cheers.] He wanted the people of the North to shape their policy so as to discourage the interference of mischievous political adventurers. The two races must dwell together. They were labor and capital, each necessary to the other, each useless without the other. He had heard something of a war in the North between labor and capital. He was thankful that the South had not come to that. Could they not see there two grand races needing each other, and not to be parted or set at variance by miserable politicians of a certain style of baggage? [Laughter and cheers.]

The Southern whites were generous and courteous. The old aunties, sitting on the steps of the aristocratic houses to sell their little wares, always received a kind word. When he met Gen. Kershaw,[5] one of the proudest of South Carolina's sons, no one could be treated with more courtesy and respect than he

4. Adopted in 1868, the Fourteenth Amendment established citizenry for African Americans, thus in effect overturning the Supreme Court's Dred Scott decision of 1857. Chief Justice Roger B. Taney (1777–1864) had delivered that decision, which held that blacks could not bring a lawsuit in the federal courts because the Constitution did not deem them citizens.

5. Joseph Brevard Kershaw (1822–94) of South Carolina was a delegate at the secession

was. When Gen. Kershaw was serenaded, he, the speaker, was sent for to receive his share. As early as 1864, at Hilton Head, when, as special inspector on Sickles's[6] staff to attend to the return of confiscated property, he was brought in contact with the whites, he had taken his present ground, that antagonism of the races must cease. In the recent campaign in South Carolina,[7] he had been told that the whites would not adhere to any arrangement with the blacks. He had met that by calling a meeting at which Col. Trenholm, Col. Barnwell,[8] and seven others of the most aristocratic South Carolinians and nine black men were Presidents and Vice-Presidents, and he himself was the speaker of the evening. The white convention adopted the ticket of the black Conservatives. He had seen Col. Trenholm sitting on the same Legislative Committee with one of his former slaves. He called attention to the addresses of J. T. Rapier, Frederick Douglass, P. R. S. Pinchback,[9] and others, who, he said, were almost his personal friends, but he did not share in their fear of a war of races. It was impossible; and in conclusion he again urged that the chief evils of the political situation came from the carpet-baggers. The Southern men were determined that they should no longer lead them. The people of the South were determined hereafter to be their own representatives, and not to be further misrepresented. He wished he could be heard with a voice so potent as to drive them forever from the South.

(*New-York Daily Tribune*, 6 March 1875, p. 7)

---

convention in Charleston in 1860 and served as a colonel and major general in the Confederate army. Imprisoned for several months in Boston immediately after the war, he returned to South Carolina, where he was elected to the state senate in 1865.

6. The Union general Daniel Edgar Sickles (1819–1914) was military commander of the Department of South Carolina from late 1864 to 1867; Delany was under his direct command during those years. Sickles had achieved notoriety for having successfully pleaded that temporary insanity had caused him to kill Philip Barton Key (the son of Francis Scott Key) in 1859 for attempting to seduce his wife. He was also well known for his heroics at the battle of Gettysburg, where he lost a leg.

7. A reference to Delany's 1874 campaign for lieutenant governor as an Independent Republican.

8. George Trenholm was a wealthy Charleston merchant. Robert Woodward Barnwell (1801–82) cast the deciding vote at the Montgomery, Alabama, secession convention that named Jefferson Davis to the presidency of the Confederacy. Barnwell served in the Confederate senate during the Civil War, and he was president of South Carolina College from 1866 to 1873.

9. Born in Alabama to free blacks, James Thomas Rapier (1837–83) became a successful cotton planter and political leader; in 1872 he was elected as Alabama's second black representative to Congress. Pinckney Benton Stewart Pinchback (1837–1921) was born in Georgia to a slaveowner and his manumitted slave. An important political leader in Louisiana after the Civil War, he was elected to Congress in 1872 and to the Senate in 1873, but both the House and Senate refused to seat him because of dubious charges that he had broken election laws.

Delany for Hampton

IN AN ARTICLE TITLED "Delany for Hampton," the 26 September 1876 *News and Courier* printed Delany's letter of endorsement of the Democratic candidate for governor of South Carolina, Wade Hampton (1818–1902). A Confederate war hero who commanded the cavalry of the Army of Northern Virginia, and a former slaveowner, Hampton may have seemed an odd choice for Delany's endorsement. But the endorsement was consistent with Delany's view that the best possible hope for South Carolina's freed people was to find ways of working with the former masters. There was another, more personal reason for Delany's endorsement. Early in 1876 Delany was found guilty of stealing $212 entrusted him in 1871 by the John Wesley Methodist Church congregation, despite the fact that he had put the money in county tax warrants (which had lost their value) and was prepared to reimburse the church with the help of loans from friends. Governor Chamberlain refused to pardon Delany until Hampton petitioned Chamberlain on Delany's behalf in August 1876. Delany felt indebted to Hampton for that intervention, and he also believed that Hampton meant what he said when he asserted that he would work for black civil rights. (Most of South Carolina's African American citizenry felt otherwise, believing that Hampton was disingenuously attempting to attract a portion of the black voting majority to the Democrat side.) The fact that the Democratic state convention in Orangeburg during the summer of 1876 chose three black nominees for state offices only further reinforced Delany's belief that African Americans would be best served by the Democrats.

A Black Man's View of the Interest and Duty of His Race

A Cool and Intelligent Statement of the Aspect of Politics and the Relations of the Races in South Carolina. — The Logic of Events Compels Conscientious National Republican to Declare for Hampton and Good Government.

CHARLESTON, S.C., September 25, 1876.

To the Editor of The News and Courier. The present condition of things in the State, by the relation of the two races in hostile array against each other, is most anomalous, and, to the thoughtful observer capable of comprehending the true state of the situation, and interested in the welfare of the people and State, is alarming in the extreme. I cannot, nor will not, believe otherwise than that political motives, by unscrupulous leaders, have induced it; as the general feelings between the races, till after the last canvass in 1874 for Governor, were kindly and cordial. The canvass of that year was the first great mutual effort made to unite the two races in one political movement, which came near being successful. Why then, now, this great divergence and extraordinary estrangement? From whichever side it comes, or whether from those of both sides, it evidently is intended to prevent a union of the two races in one common home or State interest.

In such an issue as that now pending, if not permanently checked, my race can have but one terminal destiny, political nonentity and race extermination. And what care the promoters of this fearful strife when that is the end they desire to obtain? This thing can and must be stopped. There are virtue and intelligence enough among the people to do it; but each race must perform its part and do its duty. Shall it be said that at such a crisis the blacks had no statesmen, no men of diplomatic wisdom among them equal to the emergency, the demands of the hour? For statesmanship is not necessary simply to diplomatic shrewdness, since even among savages (as the Indians of America) shrewd diplomatists are met with. Shall we, the blacks be less than they?

When my race were in bondage I did not hesitate in using my judgment in aiding to free them. Now that they are free I shall not hesitate in using that judgment in aiding to preserve that freedom and promote their happiness. What I did and desired for my own race, I desire and would do if duty required for any other race. The exercise of all their rights unimpaired and unobstructed is that desire.

I have then but one line of duty left me, and that is, to aid that effort which in my judgment best tends to bring about *a union of the two races, white and black,* (by black I mean all colored people,) *in one common interest in the State,* with all the rights and privileges of each inviolable and sacredly respected.

The present Democratic movement promises this, and asks us, the blacks, simply to aid them and try them once; if they do not fulfill their promises, to trust them no more. This is simply fair. This was asked by the Republicans (colored people) in 1868 of the Democrats at the beginning of reconstruction, which they then refused, but have long since seen and felt the results of their error. I am not willing, now that an occasion requires our cooperation, that with their example before our eyes we should commit the same error.

As Gen. Wade Hampton is the candidate for Governor, no one will question him as speaking the sentiments of his party in the present issue and campaign. I quote:

In his speech at Abbeville, as in every county where he has spoken, he has pledged his word that, if elected Governor of South Carolina, he "*shall render to the whole people of the State equal and impartial justice.*" And that his meaning should be unmistakable he said: "If there is a white man in this assembly who, because he is a Democrat or because he is a white man, believes that when I am elected Governor, if I should be, I will stand between him and the law, or grant to him any privileges or immunities that shall not be granted to the colored man, he is mistaken; and I tell him now, if that is his reason for voting for me, not to vote at all."

Again, as late as Saturday, the 23d, at Darlington, he said: "We wish to show the colored people that their rights are fixed and immovable, and, furthermore, we would not abridge them if we could. I do here, what I did in the Convention, *I pledge myself solemnly, in the presence of the people of South Carolina, and in the presence of my God that, if the Democratic ticket is elected, I shall know no party, nor race, in the administration of the law. So sure as the law pronounces a man guilty, so sure shall that man be punished. I shall know nothing but the law and the Constitution of South Carolina and of the United States.* [Immense applause.] We recognize the thirteenth, fourteenth and fifteenth amendments of the Constitution of the United Sates, and accept them in good faith. The colored people know that it is under those amendments that they enjoy the rights they now have. We stand upon that platform, and *not one single right enjoyed by the colored people today shall be taken from them. They shall be the equals, under the law, of any man in South Carolina.* And we further pledge that we will give better facilities for education than they have ever had before. [Loud cheering.] Let me say one word more to the colored people. I was the first man in the State of South Carolina, after the war, who advised the white people of South Carolina to give the right of voting to the colored people. I made the proposition at several public meetings in Columbia, and I took the ground that they had been made citizens and that they should not be excluded from the right to vote."

These are, indeed, most definite, strong, impressive and extraordinary words, and must have been candidly meant, or they never would have been spoken; and I shall hold Gen. Hampton on behalf of my race, before the civilized world, responsible for them; and if they are not verified in every particular the moral sentiment of all Christendom will be a swift and condemning witness against him. And not only him, but Mr. W. D. Simpson,[1] candidate for Lieutenant-Governor, and all others of his colleagues who have pledged their party for equal rights and justice before the law to all the people of both races, shall be held equally responsible for their utterances. I desire in this that my race shall see that the veracity, honor and integrity of the party have been plighted to them.

And since the Carolinians of the white race did not hesitate to take me at my word, and honor me with their support in the general State canvass of 1874, for Lieutenant-Governor on the Independent Republican ticket, in an effort to redeem the State of incompetence and corruption, I shall not now hesitate to take them at their word, and aid them in a similar effort in 1876, by supporting the State movement and voting the State Democratic ticket as put forth and avowed in the present issue, for the good of all the people of both races. In doing this I change no principles, but adhere as an American to the Democratic-Republican principles of the *right of the common people to rule.*

This is a step taken after the maturest deliberation, as the claims of race are far above those of faction and party; and duty to the claims of community, far above the dictation and requirements of factional and party leaders.

My design was fixed after the adjournment of the Republican Convention recently held at Columbia, and my conclusion only reached after the Straight-out nominations at the County Convention at Orangeburg, Thursday last, by which was proven to my satisfaction that the policy of the party recognizes both races, as three colored men were put in nomination on the ticket.

In this step, impelled by my own promptings for the benefit of my race with that of the white, as when, buckling on my sword, I entered the United States Army, as a field officer, for the same object and purpose, I have the honor to be, sir, your most obedient servant,

M. R. DELANY.

(*News and Courier,* 26 September 1876, p. 1)

---

1. The South Carolinian William Dunlap Simpson (1823–90) served as a representative in the Confederate States House of Representatives from 1863 to 1865. He became governor in 1879 after Wade Hampton was elected to the U.S. Senate, and he resigned in 1880 to assume the post of chief justice of the South Carolina Supreme Court.

Politics on Edisto Island

DELANY HAD HOPED FOR a cross-racial consensus of blacks and whites to emerge around Wade Hampton's run for the South Carolina governorship, but when he journeyed to Edisto Island on 14 October 1876 to campaign for Hampton, he discovered that African Americans living on the sea islands remained enormously suspicious of white Democrats. In "Politics on Edisto Island," printed below, an anonymous reporter for the *News and Courier* described the hostile reception accorded Delany, who offered only a few angry remarks to his hecklers. Two days after Delany's visit to Edisto Island, the black militia of the village of Cainhoy fired on a black schoolteacher speaking at a Hampton rally, thinking that the teacher was Delany. The subsequent battle between Cainhoy's black militia and Hampton's entourage of over one hundred members of Charleston's rifle clubs resulted in the deaths of six whites and one black. White authorities dubbed the battle the "Cainhoy Massacre," and the wide publicity attending that conflict, which worked to bring white voters to the polling places en masse, contributed to Hampton's victory.

After speaking twenty minutes Mr. Smyth[1] gave way to Col. M. R. Delany, who was introduced by the chairman as the next Democratic speaker. As soon as Col. Delany mounted the wagon, the negroes started to beat their drums and left in a body. They would not listen to "de dam nigger dimocrat." In vain the chairman called them to come back and shouted to them to stop that drum beating. They paid no attention to his orders. They marched off and the women crowded around the wagon with their bludgeons with threats, curses and imprecations. Even Bowen[2] was unable to restore quiet until he leaped from the

1. Augustine T. Smythe was a Charleston lawyer who did business with some Edisto residents and thus, according to *News and Courier*'s reporter, "was heard, I think, more attentively than the other speakers" (p. 4).

2. The white Republican leader Christopher Columbus Bowen (1832–80) was elected to Congress upon the readmission of South Carolina in 1868 and served two terms (1868–71). He was a member of the South Carolina House of Representatives from 1871 to 1872 and was elected sheriff of Charleston in 1872.

wagon and brought them back by main force. A semblance of order after a half hour's work was restored, and Col. Delany was invited to go on with his speech. This, however, he declined to do. He simply said that he had been in Europe and Africa, in the presence of the nobility of many countries, and black as he was, he had never been insulted as he had been to-day by the people of his own race. Amid frequent interruptions, he reminded them of the fact he had come to South Carolina with his sword drawn to fight for the freedom of the black man; that being a black man himself he had been a leading abolitionist. That he had warned them against trusting their money to the Freedman's Bank,[3] and that they had, to their sorrow, paid no heed to his warning. His only object was to give them warning now that the Northern white people were altogether in sympathy with the Southern whites. They could see that by reading the Northern newspapers. He was a friend of his own race, and had always held the position that it was the duty of those who had education to teach them that their best interests were identical with the white natives of the State.

(*News and Courier*, 16 October 1876, p. 4)

3. Chartered in 1865 as a nonprofit institution to encourage black thrift, the Freedman's Savings Bank by the early 1870s had over 72,000 investors and over three million dollars in deposits. Speculative investments by its white managers put the bank in jeopardy, and the naming of Frederick Douglass as president of the bank in 1874 could not forestall the inevitable bankruptcy. Black depositors felt betrayed by Congress's refusal to insure or pay back the funds.

Part Six.
The Republic of Liberia

ON NEW YEAR'S DAY 1883, approximately forty African American leaders, including Martin Delany, gathered at Freund's restaurant in Washington, D.C., to celebrate the twentieth anniversary of the Emancipation Proclamation. They also met to celebrate the achievements of Frederick Douglass, who was the keynote speaker for the evening. Douglass, the recorder of deeds for the District of Columbia, spoke optimistically of blacks' continued progress in the United States, declaring: "Nothing has occurred within these twenty years which has dimmed my hopes or caused me to doubt the emancipated people of this country will avail themselves of their opportunities, and by enterprise, industry, invention, discovery and manly character vindicate the confidence of their friends and put to silence and to shame the gloomy predictions of all their enemies." Following the speech, most of the guests offered toasts to the future of African Americans in the United States. Delany, however, who had been engaged since 1879 in an unsuccessful effort to secure a job in Washington, D.C., offered a different sort of toast: "The Republic of Liberia."[1]

By the late 1870s Delany can appear to be an increasingly marginal African American leader whose 1876 endorsement of an obviously racist Democrat for the governorship of South Carolina had left him at a distance from the black community. This snapshot of Delany at the Emancipation Proclamation dinner at Freund's could certainly be used to support such a narrative of decline. But there is, of course, another way of reading Delany's participation at this dinner. The fact that he was invited suggests that black leaders continued to regard him with admiration and respect, and the fact that he attended suggests that he continued to conceive of his political work in relation to the larger aspirations of African American leaders of the time. The role that he played at this dinner, then, can be regarded as typical of the oppositional role he played within the African American community, and the United States, throughout much of his career. At a nationalistic moment of celebration, Delany, through a simple toast, affirmed black pride, tacitly reminded the celebrants of the failure of the United States to offer true citizenship to black Americans, asserted the transnational di-

mensions of black nationalism in the United States, and made a mockery of
Douglass's willed blindness at this particular moment to the increasing number
of barriers (lynching, segregation, institutional racism, and so on) to black elevation in the United States. Viewed in this way, Delany, even at an apparent time
of (self-)marginalization, remained a vital, creative, and refreshingly honest
presence in post-Reconstruction culture.

The four documents in this concluding section tell what is ultimately the in-
terrelated story of Delany's marginalization and continued presence as provo-
cateur and black leader. He was rather ill in his final years, which made it all the
more difficult for him to do the sort of energetic work he had been doing from
the 1830s through the mid-1870s. Nevertheless, he was involved in at least one
major Africa-related initiative after his debacle with Hampton; and at the age of
sixty-seven, he published an ethnological study with a major publishing house
that conveyed, in the wake of his disillusionment with the failure of Reconstruction, his Africanist black pride.

In some respects the reemergence of Africa as central to Delany's interests can
seem yet another abrupt reversal in his career, particularly in light of his 1866
letter about President Warner of Liberia, the first document in Part 6. That letter, in which Delany attacks Warner's suggestion that the United States fund a
mass emigration of the freedmen to Africa, can be regarded as fairly typical of
Delany's attitude toward Africa during Reconstruction. Though he allowed that
African emigration made sense for some individuals, he remained committed
during the 1865–77 period to helping the freedmen to improve their lot in the
United States. Like Douglass, he therefore regarded emigration movements as
threats to African Americans' prospects in the United States, insofar as such
movements worked to reinforce white racists' notions that blacks were not an
essential part of the nation. And yet following the Civil War Delany continued
to conceive of Africa as a foundational constituent of black pride. He regularly
spoke of his travels to Africa and of his interactions with black African leaders,
and when Frances Rollin interviewed him for her biography, he celebrated the
Golah and Mandigo roots of his family's genealogical lines.

What is somewhat surprising is that Delany in the late 1870s would decide to
support an African emigration project backed by the American Colonization
Society (ACS), though he did attempt to work with the ACS to fund his earlier
African project as well. It is also somewhat surprising that South Carolina blacks
turned to Delany as a leader of an African emigration enterprise, even as he continued to serve as a trial justice in Wade Hampton's administration. Briefly, by
the late 1870s, Delany had come to believe that the ACS was responding in good
faith to the dire situation of the freed people in the South by attempting to take
shiploads of African Americans to Liberia. Delany was not alone in taking a de-

spairing view of the racial situation during that time, for with the withdrawal of federal troops and the reimposition of racist black codes, southern blacks began to depart en masse for what was believed to be a more hospitable environment in the North and Midwest. Delany encouraged the black "exodus" as a way of demonstrating to southern whites just how dependent they were on black labor; but rather than focusing on the North or the Midwest, he turned his sights on Africa. In 1877 he became a member of the board of directors of the Liberian Exodus Joint Stock Steam Ship Company, and in 1878 he negotiated with Liberian officials for land for emigrants from Georgia and South Carolina while negotiating with the ACS for loans to support the project. The Liberian Exodus Company's ship, the *Azor*, filled to capacity with black emigrants, sailed for Liberia from Charleston in the spring of 1878 (see "The African Exodus") but was forced to dock at Sierra Leone and ultimately returned to South Carolina with debts amounting to over four thousand dollars. In 1879 Delany assumed the chairmanship of the Committee on Finance and attempted to raise the needed money, but the ship was sold at auction at a considerable loss. Though this particular plan failed, Delany continued to believe, as he confided to William Coppinger of the ACS, that Africa was "the field of my destined labor."[2]

The idea of "destiny" informs Delany's book-length study *Principia of Ethnology* (1879), selections of which are included in this section. In this treatise on racial origins and difference, Delany argues that God's plan for human progress requires that each race should pursue its destiny apart from other races. As Delany tells the story, God, concerned that humans were not progressing as quickly as possible, chose to create three distinct races from Noah's sons. The "yellow" Shem went to Asia, the "swarthy" Ham to Africa, and the "white" Japheth to Europe. These sons emigrated to different places in the globe, Delany argues, because God implanted in the sons and their descendants a desire for racial separation based on notions of race affinity. As in *Origin and Objects of Ancient Freemasonry*, Delany wants to show that God has reserved a special role for Ham and his descendants, and much of *Principia* celebrates the ancient civilizations of Ethiopia and Egypt. The burden on African Americans of the present day, Delany argues, is to recover that greatness. Though some readers may be troubled by Delany's insistence on racial difference, it is worth emphasizing that *Principia* was published during a time when racialist discourse, as inspired by the writings of Charles Darwin, was pervasive in the popular press and that the bulk of this discourse extolled white supremacy as the telos of human evolution. Delany's notion of black difference and superiority was meant to counter dominant notions of white supremacy and to argue for the connection between the regeneration of Africa and the empowerment of the black diaspora. Accordingly, he concludes the text by invoking the Ethiopianism of Psalm 68:31.

Delany attempted to remain active in his final years, despite his failing health. This was not a happy time for him. In December 1879, when his sons St. Cyprian and Charles Lenox were visiting him in Charleston, Charles Lenox drowned in the Savannah River. Rather than return to Wilberforce, Delany attempted to find a civil service job in Washington, D.C., hoping eventually to use the money to relocate his family to Africa. He wrote William Coppinger in 1880 to request his help in obtaining the position of doorkeeper of the U.S. Senate (see the final document in this section). In late 1880 and early 1881 he traveled to Virginia's 2nd District and campaigned for the Republican candidate for Congress, John F. Dezendorf (1834–94). (Dezendorf won the election after having been defeated in his previous effort in 1878). Delany continued his efforts to secure a job with the U.S. government, believing that his patriotic service during the Civil War and Reconstruction made him an obviously worthy candidate for a civil service position, but he never received the appointment he was hoping for. In the spring of 1884 he was hired by a Boston firm to work as its agent in Central America; however, he fell seriously ill around that time, and after living many years apart from his wife, Catherine, he returned to their home in Ohio. He died in Xenia, Ohio, on 24 January 1885.

Notes

1. See Frederick Douglass, "Freedom Has Brought Duties: An Address Delivered in Washington, D.C., on 1 January 1883," in *The Frederick Douglass Papers,* ser. 1, *Speeches, Debates, and Interviews,* vol. 5, ed. John Blassingame and John R. McKivigan (New Haven: Yale University Press, 1992), pp. 58–59, and "The Twentieth Anniversary of Lincoln's Proclamation of Emancipation," *Washington Bee,* 6 January 1883, p. 1.

2. Delany to William Coppinger, letter of 18 December 1880, American Colonization Society Papers, letters received, box 241, Manuscript Division, Library of Congress.

DURING THE Reconstruction period, Delany for the most part had little to say about black emigration, though he allowed that African emigration made sense in some individual cases. His attitude toward African emigration during this time is best exemplified in his letter on President Warner of Liberia. Warner had suggested in a letter printed in the June 1866 *African Repository*, the journal of the American Colonization Society, that the former slaves should be shipped to Liberia at the expense of the U.S. government. From Delany's perspective, the freedmen had fresh opportunities for citizenship and success in the United States and were an essential part of the southern economy. He expressed his views in a letter to James Lynch (1839–72), the editor of the *Christian Recorder*.

Mr. Editor:—I simply write to endorse your strictures on the communication of President Warner of Liberia,[1] in relation to the African race in the United States. Your remarks are just, and to the point, without undignified allusions or flings at the President, impugning his motives, and with just that rebuke to, and sympathy for, Liberia as a nation and people, that every colored person in the country should express or feel.

No one who knows me, will doubt my African proclivities—indeed, I believe it will be conceded that I am the *most* African of all the black men now in this country; so much so, that I have possessions in Africa, which I intend and hope to enjoy, and my children to inherit and possess; but I think this political communication of President Warner, is the most unstatesmanlike, and ungenerous paper towards the African race in America, that ever emanated from a Liberian statesman, and almost enough, so dissimilar are these views from his, to disturb

1. James Lynch, the editor of the *Christian Recorder*, criticized Warner's call for black emigration to Liberia in "Liberia—President Warner," *Christian Recorder*, 23 June 1866, p. 2. The Maryland-born Daniel Bashiel Warner (1815–80) was president of Liberia from 1864 to 1868. Warner's letter of 16 September 1865 urging the U.S. government to finance the mass emigration of U.S. blacks to Liberia was printed in the *African Repository* 42 (June 1866): 179–82.

the ashes of that great and good Christian statesman, now no more, late President Stephen Allen Benson;[2] and doubtless the heart was made to throb with palpitation, and the eyes of that able statesman and generous hearted Christian gentleman, ex-President Joseph Jenkins Roberts, flushed and startled with surprise, when the *Repository* from America which contained this great political blunder and misstep of President Warner, met their penetrating gaze.

I have the honor of an acquaintance with President Warner, though I do not expect him to remember me—as men in high places cannot remember every obscure passer-by—and highly respect him, and for this reason, the more regret that he committed this blunder.

Let no one suppose that it was for the want of ability on the part of the President; no such thing, as he is a gentleman of fine accomplishments, and thought by many to be the superior to the lamented Benson, and even equal as a man of political ability, to President Roberts himself. President Warner is also a Christian and gentleman. But the mistake was made by an overweening anxiety, on his part, to people Liberia; hence the more reprehensible. Each of his predecessors did something to distinguish his administration as a part of the political history of his country. Roberts developed the Nationality, Benson the Industrial Resources, and population the second essential element in national greatness, being still deficient and so essential to Liberia's progress in civilization, caused him to lose sight and conception of every other consideration, but that one idea of Peopling the country.

It is no disparagement to President Warner, nor Liberia statesmen generally, to say that they have not been long given to habits of thought on such great grave questions of political economy and national polity; Liberia has not been long a nation, nor they long in power or position to induce them generally to make these great inquiries as statesmen. The Liberian has been too much accustomed to regard himself and his country as isolated from and uncared for by, or properly regarded by other nations and people—especially the colored—hence, he has been too much addicted to measuring himself by himself, shrugging his shoulders, and thanking God that he was not like other (black) men. Henceforth, let President Warner *think* before he speaks, and look before he leaps—and a most fearful leap was this one—ere he precipitates, not only himself, but the destiny of his country into an abyss, from which there is no recovery. I myself—and doubtless must the statesmen of his own country—feel sorry and ashamed for our race, before the international and political world, of

2. Stephen Allen Benson (1816–65) was president of Liberia from 1856 to 1864. Born in Maryland, he emigrated to Liberia in 1822. He was a political foe of Joseph Jenkins Roberts, the first and seventh president of Liberia, whom Delany generally disdained.

this blind stride of President Warner, in recommending (tacitly) the expulsion of a large part of a national population—indeed, an important elementary part of the nation, as this has been since civilization began on the continent, the industrial element of the South. Does President Warner know, that the commencement of such an act of national injustice is itself a barbarity that might lead to *extermination*, a much cheaper and by far easier method of ridding the nation of this people! Heaven forbid, that so monstrous an idea ever again enter the brain of any man occupying a responsible position, much less find expression from the lips of one at the head of a nation, and that nation, the kindred people of those against whom the issue is invited!

MAJOR R. DELANY
U.S.C.T.

(*Christian Recorder*, 21 July 1866, p. 1)

The African Exodus

TWELVE YEARS AFTER rejecting Warner's calls for black emigration to Liberia, Delany, disillusioned by the failure of Reconstruction, came to support the Liberian Exodus Joint Stock Steam Ship Company's project of shipping interested southern blacks to Liberia. The *Azor*, the company's recently purchased ship, sailed from Boston into Charleston's Atlantic Wharf during March 1878 and anchored there in preparation for taking the first group of emigrants to Liberia. In "The African Exodus," an article in the 16 April 1878 *News and Courier*, the anonymous reporter conveyed the sense of excitement surrounding the impending voyage and, in an attempt to explore the reasons for the exodus movement, solicited the views of Major M. R. Delany. The *Azor* sailed for Liberia on 21 April 1878. Because of financial difficulties, this proved to be the *Azor*'s only voyage to Africa for the Liberian Exodus Company.

As the day for the departure of the Liberian emigrant ship Azor draws near, the excitement among the colored population of the city, and in fact of the entire State, increases, and even among those who have no intention of taking an active part in the movement the greatest interest is manifested. The pier at which the Azor is lying is crowded from morning until night with men, women and children, and the little office of the Exodus Association in Exchange street is made a general rendezvous where the emigrants and their friends daily congregate and talk over their plans, hopes, fears and anticipations. . . .

It has been held by some that the prime cause of the Exodus movement to Africa throughout South Carolina and most of the Southern States is due to the political changes that have been taking place for the past five years throughout the South, and which culminated in the triumph of the Democratic party in South Carolina. This view, while partly correct, is not wholly so. It is true that almost immediately upon the establishment of the Hampton Government in South Carolina a cry was raised throughout the entire South, by the black race, that their liberty had been wrested from them, and that Africa, their fatherland, was their only place of refuge. Letters to this effect appeared in all of their church organs, and the subject was discussed and agitated by leading colored men at almost every street-corner and crossroad. The excitement at this time among the black masses was intense, and the leaders spared no pains in fanning the fire into a blaze.

Maj. M. R. Delany, a prominent officer of the Exodus Association, and a man who has in person explored the wilds of Africa, says that this political aspect was given to the movement not so much by the fear of ill treatment from the whites, as by the apprehension on the part of the blacks that they could not live in a subordinate position where, for ten years, they had held the reins of government, and had been led to believe they would always retain the supremacy. The blacks, he says, had enjoyed such license and such unbridled liberty from the time of their emancipation that when the check came the shock was too great. They could not see how they could live without their accustomed license. The let-down had come so suddenly and so unexpectedly that the result was general discontent and unwillingness to remain in any community where they would not be the predominant element. . . .

(*News and Courier*, 16 April 1878, p. 1)

Principia of Ethnology: The Origin of Races and Color, with an Archeological Compendium of Ethiopian and Egyptian Civilization, from Years of Careful Examination and Enquiry

DELANY WROTE *Principia* at the same time that he was becoming involved with the Liberian Exodus Joint Stock Steam Ship Company, and the ideas in the book—on race and Africa—spoke to his new African emigration commitments. Read in the context of the failure of Reconstruction, *Principia* is one of Delany's most moving efforts to argue for black pride and to make sense of his own failure to bring the races together in South Carolina. That failure, Delany suggests, was providential, for as he elaborates in the treatise, God planned for each race to pursue its own destiny apart from the other races. By arguing for original, indestructible races, Delany positioned himself against Frederick Douglass, William Wells Brown, and other African Americans who in the late 1870s and 1880s were arguing that intermarriage was one possible way of bringing the races together. Douglass and Brown may have had the more prescient scientific vision of the fictionality (or superficiality) of racial difference, but Delany arguably had the more realistic vision of the intractability of racial difference in post-Reconstruction America. His ethnological tract, written at a time in which blackness was almost universally regarded by white scientists and social scientists as an essential mark of inferiority, sought to reverse the conventional wisdom and restore a spiritual and national (Africanist) pride to beleaguered African Americans.

Preface

In presenting to the scientific and serious enquirer such a work as this, I may venture the opinion, that for the first time, public attention has been called to facts, essential to a satisfactory solution of the all-important question in social science, so befittingly put forth by the Duke of Argyll[1] in his ethnological enquiry, Primeval Man: "That question is not the rise of Kingdoms, but the Origin of Races * * * When and How did they begin? * * * And in this feature of color it is remarkable that we have every possible variety of tint from the fairest to the blackest races, so that the one extreme passes into the other by small and insensible gradations." This then is the great mystery which this little treatise proposes to solve, as well as to show the first steps in the progress of Civilization, the origin and institution of Letters and Literature. On the delicate subject of the integrity of the Races, let it be also understood that we propose, so far as the Pure Races are concerned, to have once and forever settled that they are indestructible, as proven in this treatise. That, as in the substance and science of Chemistry, the two extremes, saccharine and acid—the most intense sweetness and the most intense sourness—are produced by the same material and essential properties, so is it in the substance and science of animal chemistry in the human family in relation to color or complexion of the skin. That the two extremes of color, from the most negative white—"including every possible variety of tint"—up to the blackest are all produced by the same material and essential properties of color. This much I have deemed it proper as a Preface to add, to prepare the mind of the reader for an enquiry which I may venture to say, he will not regret having made, and which may induce others of higher attainments to prosecute the subject to different conclusions. If in this I have been successful, in aiding to find the key to the discovery of the all-important subject of variety of complexions, or Origin of Races and Color, however little that aid, I shall have reached the zenith of my desire.

Charleston, May 6th, 1878.

Chapter I. The Origin of Races and Color.

This is a subject of very great interest to social science, which as yet has not been satisfactorily treated. We propose in this enquiry, to give our deductions and conclusions, after mature deliberation and much research.

The Singular and Plural theories of the Creation or Origin of Man, have been fully examined and duly considered, accepting the Mosaic or Bible Record, as our basis, without an allusion to the Development theory.

1. George Douglas Campbell (1823–1900), the eighth Duke of Argyll, had some renown in Great Britain and the United States as an evolutionary theorist. Among his best-known works were *Primeval Man* (1869), which was published in New York and London, *Unity of Nature* (1884), and *Organic Evolution Cross-Examined* (1898).

The theory of Champollion, Nott, Gliddon,[2] and others, of the Three Creations of Man; one Black, the second Yellow, and the last White, we discard, and shall not combat as a theory, only as it shall be refuted in the general deductions of this treatise. We have named these Three Races, in the order which they are said to have been created, the Black being first, consequently the oldest of the Human Family.

In treating on the Unity of Races as descended from one parentage, we shall make no apology for a liberal use of Creation as learned from the Bible. In this, we find abundant proof to sustain the position in favor of the Unity of the Human Race. Upon this subject ethnologists and able historians frequently seem to be at sea, without chart or compass, with disabled helm, floating on the bosom of chance, hoping to touch some point of safety; but with trusty helm and well-set compass, we have no fears with regard to a direct and speedy arrival, into the haven.

Chapter II. The Creation of Man.

Man, according to Biblical history, commenced his existence in the Creation of Adam. This narration is acceptable to us. The descendants of Adam must have been very numerous, as we read of peoples which we cannot comprehend as having had an existence, as "in the land of Nod, on the east of Eden, whither Cain went from the presence of the Lord and dwelt,"[3] where we are told his wife bore Enoch, his first born, though until this circumstance, had we known of the existence of but one woman, Eve the first and mother of Cain, who did not even have a daughter, so far as Moses has informed us in Genesis.

The history of Man from Adam to Noah is very short, as given by Moses in the first chapter in the Bible, and though we learn of the existence of communities and cities, as the first city Enoch, built by Cain in the land of Nod, called after his first born; for aught we know, there were no legally established general regulations, but each head of a family ruled his own household according to traditional customs, his own desires or notions of propriety, or as circumstances or necessity required.

This view requires a division into periods of the historical events, from the

2. Jean François Champollion (1790–1832) was the French Egyptologist who helped to decipher the hieroglyphics on the Rosetta stone. Josiah C. Nott (1804–73) of Mobile, Alabama, and George R. Gliddon (1809–57), a British Egyptologist, were best known for their coauthored ethnological study, *Types of Mankind* (1854), a racist text that argued for polygenesis—separate creations of different races—and thus offered "scientific" legitimation to those convinced of blacks' inferiority.

3. Genesis 4:16–17.

Creation of Man, till after the confusion of tongues, and the dispersion of the people from the Tower of Babel.[4] During the abode of Adam and Eve in the Garden of Paradise, we shall call the period of the "Original Law;" from going out of the Garden till the dispersion from the Tower, the period of the "Law of Necessity;" and after the dispersion on the Plains of Shinar,[5] the period of "Municipal Law."

Chapter III. The Original Man.

Until the Dispersion, Races as such were unknown, but must have become recognized at that time, doubtless at the period of that event, which brings us to the enquiry, What was the Original Man?

There is no doubt that, until the entry into the Ark of the Family of Noah, the people were all of the One Race and Complexion; which leads us to the further enquiry, What was that Complexion?

It is, we believe, generally admitted among linguists, that the Hebrew word Adam (ahdam) signifies *red*—dark-red as some scholars have it. And it is, we believe, a well-settled admission, that the name of the Original Man, was taken from his complexion. On this hypothesis, we accept and believe that the original man was Adam, and his complexion to have been clay color or yellow, more resembling that of the lightest of the pure-blooded North American Indians. And that the peoples from Adam to Noah, including his wife and sons' wives, were all of one and the same color, there is to our mind no doubt.

There are those of the highest intelligence and deepest thoughts, in spite of their orthodox training and Christian predilections, who cannot but doubt the account of the Deluge, touching its universality. On this subject says the Duke of Argyll in his "Primeval Man:" "That the Deluge affected only a small portion of the globe which is *now habitable* is almost certain. But this is quite a different thing from supposing that the Flood affected only a small portion of the world which was *then inhabited*. The wide if not universal prevalence among the heathen nations, of a tradition preserving the memory of some such great catastrophe, has always been considered to indicate recollections carried by descent by the surviving few."

Believing as we do in the story of the Deluge, after the subsidence of the waters, there was but one family of eight persons who came forth from the Ark, to re-people the earth—Noah and his wife; their three sons and their wives. And according to Biblical chronology, from the birth of Cain, the first-born of Adam

4. Genesis 11:9.
5. Genesis 11:2.

and Eve, to the subsiding of the waters of the Flood, the time was one thousand, six hundred and fifty-five years—1655—the Flood lasting but forty days and forty nights. . . .

Chapter IV. The Family of Noah.

Noah and his family were Adamites, himself and wife being undoubtedly of the same color as that of their progenitors, Adam and Eve. And from the Garden of Eden to the Building of the Tower, there certainly was but one race of people known as such, or no classification of different peoples: "And the Lord said, Behold, the people is one, and they have all one language; and this they began to do: and now nothing will be restrained from them which they have imagined to do." *Gen. C. xi, V.6.*

Here we have inspired testimony of the unity of the people, speaking one language, in consequence of which, they imagined themselves all-powerful, setting all things at defiance. Finally to check this presumption, something had to be done, fully adequate to the end to be accomplished, which was the design of the Divine will. God has a purpose in all that he does, and his purpose in the creation of man, was the promotion of his own glory by the works of man here on earth, as the means of the Creator. And to this end man could best contribute, by development and improvement in a higher civilization.

Could this be done by confining himself to a limited space in one quarter of the earth, rearing up a building "whose top may reach unto heaven"? Certainly not; because as the people were all one, and as "like begets like," the acquired manners, habits, customs, and desires of these Tower builders, would have been taught and schooled into their descendants, to the neglect of all other employment and industries, confining themselves to comparatively limited spaces, caring nothing for the requirements of community, desiring nothing but "to make brick and burn them thoroughly," and "build a city and a tower whose top may reach unto heaven," and "make for themselves a habitation and a name," lest they be "scattered abroad, upon the face of the whole earth."[6] Here, just what God designed in the Creation of man, these descendants of Noah desired to prevent.

The Progress of Civilization, was God's requirement at the hands of man. How could this be brought about, seeing that the people were all one, "speaking one tongue,"[7] gathered together and settled in one place? . . .

Civilization is promoted by three agencies, Revolution, Conquest, and Emi-

6. Genesis 11:4.
7. Genesis 11:1.

gration; the last the most effective, because voluntary, and thereby the more select and choice of the promoters.

The first may come in two ways—morally and peacefully as the Coming of the Messiah; or physically and violently, as a civil war or conquest by military invasion, the worst agencies of civilization; but which do not fail to carry with them much that is useful into the country invaded. A moral revolution is always desirable as an agency in the promotion of civilization.

What then was the "method" of the Creator in effecting this desirable separation and scattering abroad of the people? Why simply the confusion of their tongues, by imparting to, or at least inspiring two divisions of them with a new tongue or dialect comprehended by all of those to whom it was imparted. Though on this subject the Bible is silent, it is reasonable to believe and safe to conclude, that one of the three divisions retained the old original Adamic tongue, so to speak, or that which they spoke when they commenced building; and that one was that which followed after Shem, the progenitor of the Mongolian Race, and eldest of the sons.

By this "method" then, of an All-wise Creator, the people lost interest as communities in each other, and were thereby compelled to separate. And it will certainly be conceded by the intelligent enquirer, that there was a "method" in the manner, if allowed a paradox? But there were other changes said to be necessary to the final separation, in addition to that of the languages: the basis of race distinction, establishing the grand divisions. Is it to be supposed that God wrought a special miracle, by changing for the occasion the external physical characteristics of at least two divisions of the people? He did not. This was not His method; He has a better and even wiser method than a miracle. . . .

Chapter V. The Origin of the Races.

. . . "And the Lord said, Behold the people is one, and they have all one language, let us go down and there confound their language."[8] Behold the people are one; that is they are all of one stock, descended from the same parentage, all still living, consequently they consider themselves all one family. To separate this family, was the paramount object, and to sever their interests in each other, was necessary to this separation.

The sons of Noah were three in number: Shem, Ham and Japheth. That these three sons were the active heads of the people as directors and patriarchal leaders, there is no doubt.

There is to us another fact of as little doubt: that is, that these three sons of

8. Genesis 11:7.

Noah all differed in complexion, and proportionate numbers of the people—their dependants in and about the city and around the Tower—also differed as did the three sons in complexion. And these different complexions in the people, at that early period, when races were unknown, would have no more been noticed as a mark of distinction, than the variation in the color of the hair of those that are white, mark them among themselves as distinct peoples.

That Shem was of the same complexion as Noah his father, and mother—the Adamic complexion—there is no doubt in our mind. And that Ham the second son was swarthy in complexion, we have as little doubt. Indeed, we believe it is generally conceded by scholars, though disputed by some, that the word Ham means "dark," "swarthy," "sable." And it has always been conceded, and never as we know of seriously disputed, that Japheth was white.

Of one thing we are morally certain, that after the confusion of tongues, each one of these three sons of Noah, turned and went in different directions with their followers. These followers were just so many and no more, than those who spoke one and the same language. And there can be no reasonable doubt in our mind, that these people all were of the same complexion with each of the sons of Noah whom they followed. On leaving the Ark, they were one family, relatives, continuing together as "one people," all morally and socially blind and ignorant of any difference of characteristics personal, or interests general, as much so as a family of children with themselves toward the family, till years of maturity bring about a change. Hence, when the confusion took place, their eyes became open to their difference in complexion with each other as a division, preferring those of their kind with whom they went, thus permanently uniting their destiny.

Shem settled in Asia, peopling the country around and about the centre from where they scattered. Ham went to the south-west, and Japheth to the north-west. And it will not be disputed, that from then to the present day, the people in those regions where those three sons are said to have located—the three grand divisions of the Eastern Hemisphere: Asia, Africa and Europe—are, with the exceptions to be hereafter accounted for, of the distinct complexions of those attributed to Shem, Ham and Japheth; Yellow,[9] Black and White. And this confusion of tongues, and scattering abroad in the earth, were the beginning and origin of races.

"But the great question," says the Duke of Argyll, "is not the rise of kingdoms, but the origin of races. When and How did they begin?" This we propose to show, in the next chapter, by an indisputable explanation of the origin of color by transmission of the parents.

9. Yellow—called *brown* in South Carolina and the West Indies. [Delany's note]

Chapter VI. How Color Originates.

... Shem, Ham and Japheth, the three sons of Noah, we believe to have been and history so records them, as yellow, black, and white; and here hangs that mystery of the unity and brotherhood of man, that persons of three distinct complexions, could possibly be born of the same father and mother of one race and color. And that which seems to be enveloped in inexplicable concealment, is indeed to our mind, a comprehensible law of God's all-wise providence.

Let us take a peep into the laws of nature, and for a little, follow them as our guide. Our present familiarity with the spectroscope,[10] gives us a knowledge of the properties of the sun, as transmitted through the rays, reflecting all the colors of the prism or rainbow. Solid matter of mineral substances, we know to be among these properties.

Whatever has color then, whether animal, vegetable or mineral, receives these colors directly from the sun; that is, the essential properties that form or compose them. This is by a physiological process, called elaboration and selection, whether in animal, vegetable or mineral chemistry, or the natural functions of these systems, unaided by art. Of all the systems, general and particular, the human presents the most beautiful and comprehensive illustration of God's wonderful providence in the works of creation. But says his Grace of Argyll: "What of that vast continent of Africa? When and How did that Negro race begin, which is both one of the most ancient and one of the most strongly marked among the varieties of man?" This is the cloud we design to dispel, and reveal the hidden secrets of a thousand ages.

The human body is covered by a structure composed of three distinct parts; the *cuticle* or external surface; the *rete mucosum*, middle or intermediate structure; and the *cutis vera* or true skin, underlying the other two, covering the whole surface of the fleshy parts or muscular system, called the hide in slaughtered animals.

The rete mucosum is a colorless jelly-like substance, composed of infinitesimal cells like a sponge or honey-comb. The cuticle or external surface is an extremely thin structure, colorless, and as perfectly clear and transparent as crystal glass. The upper surface of the cutis vera or true skin—that part in contact with the rete mucosum—is perfectly white. White is simply negative, having no color at all.

It will at once be observed, that the cuticle or external surface being transparent, the rete mucosum next below it being also colorless, and the surface of the cutis vera underlying all being white; that all human beings by nature are first white, at some period of existence, whether born white or not.

10. An optical device that produces a spectrum of light.

The cells of the rete mucosum are filled with limpid fluid, and whatever the complexion of an individual or race, the coloring matter is deposited in the cells of the rete mucosum, mixed with the limpid fluid. This is deposited there by the process of elaboration and selection in animal chemistry, a function simply of physiology.

This coloring matter in the Caucasian or white race is *rouge* as we shall term it, the essential properties which give redness to the rose. When a white person blushes, red matter rushes into the cells of the rete mucosum, then recedes, leaving them as before, colorless, and the complexion white. When a white person has rosy cheeks or "ruby lips," there is a fixed deposit of rouge in those parts; but where they are pale and "colorless," there is an absence of rouge or coloring matter in the rete mucosum. In the Mongolian or yellow race of Asia, the coloring matter is the same—rouge—modified by peculiar elaboration, and uniformly infused into the rete mucosum, giving the yellow tinge—one of the known properties of the sun's rays—to the complexion.

And in the African or black race of Africa, the coloring matter *is the same* as that in the other two races, being *rouge* concentrated, which makes a pigment— the *pigmentum nigrum* of physiology—or a black matter. Thus the color of the blackest African is produced by *identically the same* essential coloring matter that gives the "rosy cheeks and ruby lips," to the fairest and most delicately beautiful white lady.

For illustration, to prove that concentrated rouge or concrete redness is black, take blood caught in a vessel, let it cool and dry up by evaporation of the liquid part; when condensed in a solid mass, it becomes perfectly black, more so than the blackest human being ever seen. Look again at the fruits: black berries, black cherries, poke berries and the like. From greenness, discoloration goes on till approaching a whiteness, when a faint redness ensues, gradually increasing to a deep red, which merges into blackness, the intense color of red.

Take now this clot of dried blood, and these fruits, macerate them in water and you have not a black, but assuredly a red solution. Compare these deep red fruits called black with the color of the blackest person in complexion, and there will be the most remarkable contrast between the fruit and the skin.

May it not by this be seen, in the language of the Duke, that "new kinds as well as new individuals can be born?" Cannot God's wonderful and inscrutable providence be seen in this simple but comprehensibly beautiful law of procreation? It certainly can.

Here we see that the first son of Noah, Shem, was born with a high degree of a certain complexion or color; the second son, Ham, with a higher degree, or intensity of the same color, making a different complexion; and the third son, Japheth, with the least of the same color, which gives an entirely different complexion to either. The three brothers were all of the *same color—rouge*—which being possessed in different degrees simply, gave them different complexions.

Was there any miracle in this; any departure from the regular order of the laws of nature, necessary to the production of these three sons of a different complexion by the same mother and father of one complexion? Certainly not; as it is common to see parents of one complexion, and hair and eyes of one color, produce children with hair and eyes of various colors. Then the same laws of physiology, which produced the former of these variations, also produced the other; but for His all-wise purposes—doubtless the production of fixed races of man—the effect was placed upon the *skin* instead of the eyes and hair.

For the convenience of classification, these complexions may be termed *positive, medium,* and *negative.* Ham was positive, Shem medium, and Japheth negative. And here it may be remarked as a curious fact, that in the order of these degrees of complexion which indicated the ardor and temperament of races they represented, so was the progress of civilization propagated and carried forward by them. But is it still in doubt, that the color of the African is homogeneous with that of the Mongolian and Caucasian Races, or that either is identified with that of the other? In this, too, we summon the incontestable laws of nature. In this we have reference simply to the three original races: Mongolian, African and Caucasian, or Yellow, Black and White. . . .

Shem, Ham and Japheth, the sons of Noah and wife, who were Adamites and of one complexion, were themselves of three different complexions, as a means in the providence of God's economy, to the accomplishment of his ends in the progress of civilization.

"And the Lord said, Behold the people is one." They were one in descent, one in family, one in interest, one in design, and one in purpose; having one language, they had no other thought than remaining together. And so doubtless would have continued as one, had not some sufficient cause transpired, to completely break up their interests, and compel them to a forced separation. "So the Lord scattered them abroad from thence, upon the face of all the earth";[11] and this separation of these three brothers was the *Origin of Races.* Each of these brothers headed and led his people with a language, and in all reasonable probability a complexion similar to his own, each settling the then known three parts of the earth: Asia, Africa and Europe.

And God's design in the creation of the races was accomplished, because it fixed in the people a desire to be separated by reason of race affinity. To "replenish and multiply,"[12] or the peopling of the earth, was a principal command

11. Genesis 11:8.
12. Genesis 1:22.

by God, given to man; and by this was carried out one of the intentions of the Divine will in creation.

Can his Grace, the Duke of Argyll, now see "when and how did that negro race begin?"

. . . .

Chapter VIII. The Progress of Races.

When by Divine command to go forth through the earth, the separation took place, the people led by the three sons of Noah, began a new progress in life, as three distinct peoples, of entirely different interests, aims and ends. Shem remained in Asia; Ham went to Africa, and Japheth journeyed to Europe, permanently and forever severing their connexion with each other, henceforth becoming different peoples and divided as though they never had been united. And then the different Races of the Human Family had just begun. At this time, also, we reckon the commencement of the period of municipal law.

Previous to this time, doubtless headed and directed by Patriarchs or fathers of families, they had little else than traditional precepts to govern them, and neither books nor literary records of any kind. Their laws, then, must have been few and simple, private and public, restricted and limited, there being no large cities or towns requiring many police regulations.

Of the three sons, the history of the second, Ham, in the earliest is fraught with more interest than that of either of the others. Four sons he had: Cush, Mizraim, Phut and Canaan. All of these, from all that we are able to learn, except Canaan, accompanied him to Africa, settling in different parts, where they may be readily traced: Canaan settling in Asia closely on the borders of Africa; his father, Ham himself, permanently locating in Egypt, where doubtless he was deified as the Jupiter Ammon of Africa.[13] Cush, the eldest son, pushed farther into the country, founding the Kingdom of Ethiopia, with Meroe as the capital. Cush was the father of Nimrod, a mighty Prince, who did not follow the fortunes of his father and three of his brothers, but remained in Asia, becoming the first ruler after the Dispersion, a great Monarch, carrying conquest, and building great cities, establishing an extensive and powerful government. Of him the Scriptures say: "He began to be a mighty one in the earth, a mighty hunter before the Lord."[14]

13. Also known as Amon, Jupiter Ammon was an ancient Egyptian deity with a celebrated shrine in the Libyan desert.

14. Renowned as a hunter, Nimrod was the great grandson of Noah; see Genesis 10:8–10.

The progress of civilization now seems fairly to have begun by the establishment of extensive municipal governments. Chaldea and Assyria[15] were included in this mighty Empire, which appears to have been almost unlimited in extent of territory.

The African branch of this family is that which was the earliest developed, taking the first strides in the progress of the highest civilization known to the world, and for this cause, if for no other, it may be regarded as the oldest race of man, having doubtless centuries prior to the others, reared imperishable monuments of their superior attainments. . . .

. . . .

Chapter XIV. Wisdom of Ethiopia and Egypt.

. . . There is little doubt as to the Ethiopians having been the first people in propagating an advanced civilization in morals, religion, arts, science and literature—the Egyptians of the same race being co-operative, and probably co-ordinate. Every fact in archæology and ancient research bears evidence of this. The age of the Pyramids and masterly Sphinxes, from the peculiarity of their characteristic structures, were among the earliest and very first of their architectural works, and the only ones, from their solidity, which have withstood the ravages and wreck of time, and not been either entirely or partially destroyed by removal, shattering, defacing or deforming. . . .

A historical circumstance recorded in Holy Writ, shows the height to which this race had attained, and the lasting influence shed abroad among the people as controlling their actions and conduct. Although their national power had passed away from them, their integrity and the virtue of their national polity were such, that when Herod, King of Judea, ordered the slaughter of the young children that the infant Saviour might be destroyed, "the angel of the Lord appeared to Joseph in a dream, saying, Arise, and take the young child and his mother, and flee into Egypt, and be thou there until I bring thee word; for Herod will seek the young child to destroy Him." Matt. ii. 13.

It must be remembered at this time, that the Romans as a nation held universal power over the other governments of the earth; that the Greeko-Macedonians ruled in Egypt, and both Jews and Greeks were subject to Roman power. All this seems wonderful and almost incredible, that only in Africa could the Son of God be saved. Nor is this all. God's purposes towards this race as made manifest, seems yet a higher destiny among the children of men. When

15. Ancient empires in southwest Asia near north Africa.

Christ's mission on earth had been fulfilled, and the crucifixion decreed, as essential to the plan of salvation, according to the Christian belief, the Cross had to be borne up the hill of Calvary. Upon the shoulders of the Saviour it was placed three times, when he groaned and fell to the ground by reason of its weight. He could not bear it. "The spirit was willing, but the flesh was weak." Jews, Greeks, and Romans stood around, "who buffeted and scourged him" to compel him to carry it, but he could not; and they would not do it, deeming it a disgrace to them to carry the cross for his crucifixion.[16] Under the cross the Son of God lay prostrate at the foot of Mount Calvary! Here was a scene which beggars description, and is almost sacrilegious to express; the will of God thwarted, and the plan of salvation checked! All heaven might well have stood appalled, and angels gazed with wonder, when just at this moment there appears at the scene "a man of Cyrene, Simon by name (Simon *Niger*, meaning *black* in the Latin tongue), him they compelled to bear his cross." Matt. xxvii. 32. So the African was the first bearer of the cross of Jesus Christ. Was this an accident, or a providence of God? Was the ram caught by the horns in the bushes, as a sacrifice for Abraham to save his son Isaac, an accident or a providence of God?[17] If he thus provided for the salvation of an individual, would he not also specially provide for the salvation of all mankind? We think this is beyond a question, and prophetically designed. And yet another evidence of the favor of Providence to this race, is presented in the Holy Scriptures. After the mission of Christ had been completed, and the decree went forth forbidding all people from following the believers and teachers of His doctrine, Africa again appears in the person of her sovereign, Queen of Ethiopia,[18] who sends an ambassador to Jerusalem to worship and be baptized in the Christian faith. This person was the royal representative or commissioner from Ethiopia, the chief treasurer to the Queen, who came in great state, drawn in his chariot by camels, attended by a retinue of followers. This is, probably, the first delegate ever sent to receive the Christian religion for a nation. This nation was black. Is not this wonderful? Can we see no special providence in it? Has God no purpose in all this? Is there not in this a prophetic destiny shown for this people, in a higher scale of morals and religion than has yet been attained? Being made the protectors of the infant Son of God; to assist in the plan of salvation; and, lastly, to promulgate the precepts of redemption taught by the ascended Saviour, certainly points to a higher and holier mission designed for that race than has yet been developed in the progress of civilization....

. . . .

16. Matthew 26:22, 67.
17. Genesis 22:13.
18. Candace, or Queen of Sheba; see Acts 8:29.

Chapter XVIII. Comparative Elements of Civilization.

It has been shown in a chapter on color that the white and black, the pure European and pure African races, the most distinct and unlike each other in general external physical characteristics, are of equal vitality and equally enduring; absorbing and reproducing themselves as races, with all of their native external physical properties of complexion and hair.

That it may be indelibly fixed on every mind, we place on record the fact, that the races as such, especially white and black, are indestructible; that *miscegenation* as popularly understood—the running out of two races, or several, into a *new race*—cannot take place. A cross only produces one of a mixed race, and a continual cross from a half blood on either side will run into the pure original race, either white or black; the fourth cross on one side from the half-blood perfecting a whole blood. A general intermarriage of any two distinct races would eventually result simply in the destruction, the extinction of the less numerous of the two; that race which preponderates entirely absorbing the other.

The three original races in complexion and texture of hair are sterling; pure white, pure yellow, and pure black, with straight hair, and woolly hair; the two first being straight, and the other woolly. But it will be observed in the classes of mixed races, there is every variety of complexion and texture of hair. We have thus endeavored to be precise on a subject of such grave import to social science.

If indeed it were true, that what is implied by miscegenation could take place—the destruction of all or any of the three original races by the formation of a new race to take the place of either or all—then, indeed, would the works of God be set at naught, his designs and purposes thwarted, and his wisdom confounded by the crafty schemes of poor, mortal, feeble man. Nay, verily, as long as earth endures, so long shall the original races in their purity, as designed by God, the Creator of all things, continue the three sterling races—yellow, black and white—naming them in the order given in Genesis of Shem, Ham and Japheth.

The sterling races, when crossed, can reproduce themselves into their original purity, as before stated. The offspring of any two of the sterling races becomes a mixed race. That mixed race is an abnormal race. Either of the two sterling races which produced the abnormal race may become the resolvent race. That is, when the offspring of a mixed or abnormal race marries to a person of sterling race, black or white, their offspring is a quadroon; and if that quadroon intermarries on the same side, and the intermarriage so continue to the fourth cross on the same side, the offspring of this fourth intermarriage, is an octoroon (whether black or white), and therefore becomes a pure blood. The race continuing the cross to its purity is the resolvent race, and each offspring of the cross till the fourth, is an abnormal race, when the fourth becomes sterling or pure blooded. Hence, to speak of a mixed race as being changed by a resolvent process, simply means that the change is being made by one race alone, which must result in normal purity of either black or white, as the case may be.

The Malays, as stated in another part of this work,[19] we regard not as an original or pure, but a mixed or abnormal race, possessing every feature, the complexion and texture of hair, known to the three original races, with many of these characteristics not belonging to either. The Malays, no doubt, are an abnormal race, composed of the three original races, formed by an intermingling of the followers of the various invaders of Egypto-Ethiopian, Persian, Assyrian, Parthian, Greeko-Macedonian and Tartar conquerors, who have made conquests from time to time with the original natives of the Malay countries.

The natives of Australia, Van Dieman's Land,[20] New Zealand, Borneo, Papua or New Guinea, are fair specimens of this race of people, who in time, no doubt, will become extinct by the European race fast settling among them, and the Mongolian, who will become resolvent races. It is observable that these Malays, in their characteristics of features, complexion and hair, differ more from each other than any other people as a race. They vary from "snowy white to sooty," showing thereby that they are not a fixed race, but a mixed, an abnormal race, which has frequently been interrupted by different preponderating, and thereby for the time, resolvent races. In this we have a fair evidence in the natives of Papua, or New Guinea. And who can doubt the fact, that the African once preponderated and was the resolvent race among them? These Malays, though they might preponderate, never could become a resolvent race to either of the sterling or original races. Because, being themselves a mixed race, they could only produce a mixture, though they intermarried to the fourth cross, such an offspring would not be a pure blood. To absorb and reproduce, the race must be sterling; hence, it is resolvent. There is no doubt but that the time will come when there will be but the three original sterling races as grand divisions of people on the face of the whole earth, with their natural complexions of yellow, black and white.

Finally, the African race in Africa should not be adjudged by those portions of that race found out of Africa. The difference is too great for comparison. Untrammeled in its native purity, the race is a noble one, and worthy to emulate

---

19. Delany writes in Chapter VII, "Special Explanation on Color": "[W]e hold and believe that the Malay is simply the product of these three great races by admixture, and therefore, an off-shoot or composite race, and not an original one" (*Principia*, p. 36).

20. Former name of Tasmania, island south of Australia.

the noble Caucasian and Anglo-Saxon, now at the top round of the ladder of moral and intellectual grandeur in the progress of civilization.

The regeneration of the African race can only be effected by its own efforts, the efforts of its own self, whatever aid may come from other sources; and it must in this venture succeed, as God leads the movement and his hand guides the way. And now the advanced civilization of the Christianity of the world is called upon to recognize an overture to their consideration.

"Princes shall come out of Egypt; Ethiopia shall soon stretch forth her hands unto God." Ps. lxviii. 31.

With faith in this blessed promise, thank God, in this our grand advent into Africa, we want

No kettle-drums nor flageolets,
Bag-pipes, trombones nor bayonets,

but with an abiding trust in God our Heavenly King, we shall boldly advance, singing the sweet songs of redemption, in the regeneration of our race and restoration of our father-land from the gloom and darkness of superstition and ignorance, to the glorious light of a more than pristine brightness—the light of the highest godly civilization.

(*Principia of Ethnology: The Origin of Races and Color, with an Archeological Compendium of Ethiopian and Egyptian Civilization, from Years of Careful Examination and Enquiry* [Philadelphia: Harper & Brothers, Publishers, 1879], pp. vii–viii, 9–12, 13–15, 17–19, 21–25, 26–27, 37–38, 72–73, 76–78, 91–95)

Letter to William Coppinger, 18 December 1880

DELANY'S INVOLVEMENT WITH the Liberian Exodus Joint Stock Steam Ship Company had reentangled him with the American Colonization Society (ACS) as it was fading into obscurity. In 1878 he wrote William Coppinger (1828–92), secretary and treasurer of the ACS, about a black woman from South Carolina who wished to emigrate to Liberia. He remained in touch with Coppinger as he sought loans from the ACS in 1879 to support the Liberian Exodus Society's effort to retain ownership of the *Azor*. In a letter of 18 August 1880 he confided to Coppinger that he hoped one day to emigrate to Africa, and he laid out his plan: "If I could get some one of the many government favors worth from $2,000 to $3,000 a year for about two (2) years, this would give me the command of my available means sufficient, so as to enable me to leave my family, and children in school, and go at once to Africa" (American Colonization Society Papers, letters received, box 241, Manuscript Division, Library of Congress). To that end, he wrote Coppinger in December 1880 to request his help in obtaining a patronage position. Nothing came of Delany's efforts to secure a job with the U.S. government.

Charleston, S.C. Dec. 18th '80

My Dear Mr. Coppinger,

Enclosed please find the promised circular.[1] I place a portion of my Army Record before the Country in hope that according to my merit, I shall receive recognition from the incoming Government.

I expect to be in Washington about the 1st of February when I shall impart to you fully my desires as to an appointment. In the mean time I shall anxiously solicit your aid and influence in my behalf for any eligible position according to merit.

1. Delany enclosed with his letter a page from the Charleston *Daily Mercury* of 17 November 1880 devoted to his military career.

I should like to obtain in the first place (and I think the integrity of the Country could afford it, as well as they could to make my friend Frederick Douglass Marshall of the District of Columbia[2]) the Office of Door Keeper of the U.S. Senate.[3] This is my first solicitation. Excepting to Senators[4] I have imparted this to no one in Washington.

I hope that you will bring to my aid our Colonization friends, such as J. H. B. Latrobe[5] and others, members of the Society, and others who may not hold an official position among you.

I am dear Mr. Coppinger,
With great respect,
Your friend,
M. R. Delany

(American Colonization Society Papers, letters received, box 241, Manuscript Division, Library of Congress)

2. Douglass served as U.S. marshal for the District of Columbia from 1876 to 1877.
3. The Senate doorkeeper, or sergeant at arms, has the authority to summon absent members and to develop rules for preserving and protecting Senate office buildings.
4. It is likely that Delany had contacted his political friend, Wade Hampton, who was elected to the U.S. Senate in 1879.
5. John Hazlehurst Boneval Latrobe (1803–91), the son of the famous architect Benjamin Latrobe, was a lawyer, philanthropist, and prominent supporter of the American Colonization Society, serving as its president from 1853 to 1891.

Chronology

1812 Born 6 May in Charles Town, Virginia (now West Virginia), to a free black woman, Pati Delany, and her slave husband, Samuel Delany.

1822 Taken by his mother to Chambersburg, Pennsylvania, along with his four siblings, after she is threatened by Virginia authorities with imprisonment for having taught her children how to read and write. His father joins them a year later when he purchases his freedom.

1831 Walks 150 miles from Chambersburg to Pittsburgh, which becomes his primary place of residence for the next twenty-five years. Enrolls in Lewis Woodson's school at Pittsburgh's Bethel African Methodist Church.

1832 With his roommate Molliston M. Clark, founds the Theban Literary Society.

1833 Begins his medical apprenticeship with Dr. Andrew M. McDowell. Over the next fifteen years, he also apprentices with doctors F. Julius LeMoyne, Joseph P. Gazzam, William Elder, and Jonas R. McClintock.

1836 Sets up a medical office as a cupper, leecher, and bleeder. Attends a black convention in New York City with Lewis Woodson.

1837 Helps to found the Young Men's Literary and Moral Reform Society of Pittsburgh.

1839 Travels in the southwest to consider the possibility of black emigration to Texas. Elected to the Board of Managers of Pittsburgh's Anti-Slavery Society.

1841 Helps to organize the State Convention of the Colored Freemen of Pennsylvania, held in Pittsburgh, 23–25 August.

1843 In March marries Catherine A. Richards, daughter of Charles Richards, a black butcher, and Felicia Fitzgerald, an Irish immigrant. In September founds and takes on the editorship of the *Mystery*, an African American newspaper in Pittsburgh.

1846 Birth of Toussaint L'Ouverture Delany, the first of Martin and Catherine's seven children who would survive to adulthood. All of their sons would be named after black leaders (the others are named Charles Lenox Remond, Alexander Dumas, Saint Cyprian, Faustin Soulouque, and Rameses Placido). Their one daughter is named Ethiopia. Sued for libel by Thomas "Fiddler" Johnson, a black whom Delany had accused of collaborating with fugitive slave catchers. Delany is found guilty by an all-white jury, but the fine is remitted by Governor Francis R. Shunk.

1847 In December begins coediting the *North Star* with Frederick Douglass, whom he had met in Pittsburgh in August 1847. He relinquishes control of the *Mystery*. Publishes *Eulogy on the Life and Character of the Rev. Fayette Davis*.

1848   Tours the Midwest from January to August as a lecturer and subscription
        agent for the *North Star*, sending regular letters to Douglass on the free black
        communities. Attends the Free-Soil Convention in Buffalo in August and the
        National Convention of Colored Freemen in Cleveland in September.

1849   Ends his association with the *North Star* in June and returns to Pittsburgh,
        resuming his medical apprenticeship and practice.

1850   Admitted to Harvard Medical School in November. In December dismissed
        from Harvard Medical School by Dean Oliver Wendell Holmes after white
        medical students petition Holmes and the faculty to continue to exclude blacks
        from the student body.

1851   Attends the North American Convention in Toronto, Canada.

1852   Chairs an anticolonization meeting in Philadelphia. Elected mayor of Grey-
        town, Nicaragua, shortly after his friend David Peck travels there and organizes
        the election; Delany himself never goes to Greytown. In the fall, begins a one-
        year position as a principal of a colored school in Pittsburgh. Publishes *The
        Condition, Elevation, Emigration and Destiny of the Colored People of the United
        States.*

1853   Debates Frederick Douglass in the pages of *Frederick Douglass' Paper* on the
        merits of Harriet Beecher Stowe's *Uncle Tom's Cabin.* Delany dismisses the
        novel as racist and colonizationist. Publishes *The Origin and Objects of Ancient
        Freemasonry.*

1854   Convenes the National Emigration Convention of Colored Men in Cleveland,
        Ohio, where he delivers the keynote address, "Political Destiny of the Colored
        Race on the American Continent."

1855   Chairs the Pittsburgh meeting of the National Board of Commissioners, an
        emigration committee established by the National Emigration Convention.

1856   Moves with his family to Chatham, Canada West, and becomes a contributing
        editor to the *Provincial Freemen.*

1858   Meets John Brown in April and one month later attends a secret convention
        with Brown and Canadian blacks in Chatham, Canada West. In November
        helps to organize the National Emigration Convention in Chatham, which au-
        thorizes him to establish a Niger Valley Exploring Party, with the goal of deter-
        mining whether the Niger region of West Africa would be a suitable site for
        black emigration.

1859   Sails to Liberia in May, meets up with the other member of the Niger Valley Ex-
        ploring Party, Robert Campbell, and tours the Yoruba region of West Africa. On
        27 December 1859, Delany and Campbell sign a treaty with the Alake (king) and
        chiefs of Abeokuta that grants to Delany the right to establish an African Amer-
        ican settlement on the land of the Egba people. Publishes a serialized novel,
        Blake; or, The Huts of America. Part I appears in the January–July issues of the
        Anglo-African Magazine; a slightly revised version of Part I, along with Part II,
        are eventually published in the *Weekly Anglo-African*, 23 November 1861–April
        1862.

1860   In May begins a seven-month tour of Great Britain. Attends the International Statistical Congress in London in July and is at the center of controversy when Lord Henry Peter Brougham introduces him to the congress as a "negro" who is a "man." Most of the American delegation walks out of the congress. Returns to Chatham in December.

1861   Under pressure from British missionaries and government officials, the Alake' rescinds his agreement with Delany. Back in Canada, Delany continues his efforts to recruit blacks to emigrate to Africa, informally linking his efforts with Henry Highland Garnet's African Civilization Society. Publishes *Official Report of the Niger Valley Exploring Party.*

1863   Begins working to recruit black troops for the Union army; awarded a recruiting contract by the state of Connecticut.

1864   Purchases a house and land in Wilberforce, Ohio.

1865   Meets with President Abraham Lincoln. Shortly after the meeting, Delany is commissioned the first black major in the Union army in February. In August, after serving a stint at Beaufort, South Carolina, Delany is assigned to the Freedmen's Bureau at Hilton Head Island, South Carolina, as an assistant sub-assistant commissioner. He holds the position until 1868.

1867   Opposes efforts to name a black vice presidential candidate to the Republican ticket.

1868   Participates in the South Carolina Constitutional Convention.

1869   Fails in his attempt to meet with President Ulysses Grant to request an appointment as the first black minister to the Republic of Liberia.

1870   Returns to Charleston, where he is given an honorary position as one of seven lieutenant colonels and aides to the commander in chief of the South Carolina militia. Publishes *University Pamphlets: A Series of Four Tracts on National Polity.*

1871   Opens a land and real estate agency in Charleston. Publishes *Homes for the Freedmen.*

1872   Resigns his position in the militia because of concerns about corruption among South Carolina's Republican officials.

1874   Helps to form the Honest Government League of Charleston. Runs as the candidate for lieutenant governor of South Carolina on the Independent Republican ticket and is defeated by approximately 16,000 votes.

1875   In March speaks at Irving Hall in New York City at the invitation of William Cullen Bryant. Appointed a trial justice by South Carolina's governor Daniel H. Chamberlain in October. Edits the *Charleston Independent* for several months.

1876   Found guilty in February of breach of trust and fraud for losing $212 entrusted to him by a black church in 1871 (he had lost the money by investing in state tax warrants), he is forced to relinquish his position as trial justice. In August pardoned by Governor Chamberlain after Wade Hampton and other Democrats intercede on Delany's behalf. Endorses Democrat Wade Hampton for the governorship of South Carolina and delivers stump speeches on Hampton's behalf. During a Hampton rally at the village of Cainhoy in October, the black militia fires on a black schoolteacher who they believe is Delany. A gun battle between black and white militias leads to the deaths of five whites and one black. Hampton wins the election and rewards Delany with a position as a trial justice, which he keeps until 1879.

1877   Works with the Liberian Exodus Joint Stock Steam Ship Company, which seeks to take black emigrants from South Carolina and Georgia to Africa.

1878   The Liberian Company's ship, the *Azor*, sails to Africa but assumes considerable debt. Delany is named the chairman of the Committee on Finance and begins to attempt to raise funds to save the ship.

1879   The *Azor* is sold at auction in January, putting an end to the Liberian Company's emigration project. In December Delany's son Charles Lenox Delany drowns in the Savannah River. Delany publishes *Principia of Ethnology: The Origin of Races and Colors*.

1880   Begins an unsuccessful effort over the next several years to obtain a civil service job in Washington, D.C.

1881   Campaigns for John F. Dezendorf, Republican candidate for Congress from Virginia.

1883   On 1 January attends a dinner at Freund's restaurant in Washington, D.C., celebrating the twentieth anniversary of the Emancipation Proclamation. Toasts "The Republic of Liberia."

1884   Hired by a Boston firm to work as its agent in Central America; becomes seriously ill and returns to his home in Ohio.

1885   Dies on 24 January in Xenia, Ohio.

Selected Bibliography

Books and Pamphlets by Delany

Eulogy on the Life and Character of the Rev. Fayette Davis. Pittsburgh: Benj. Franklin Peterson, Mystery Office, 1847.

The Condition, Elevation, Emigration and Destiny of the Colored People of the United States. Philadelphia: published by the author, 1852.

The Origin and Objects of Ancient Freemasonry: Its Introduction into the United States, and Legitimacy among Colored Men. Pittsburgh: W. S. Haven, 1853.

"Political Destiny of the Colored Race on the American Continent." In *Proceedings of the National Emigration Convention of Colored People; Held at Cleveland, Ohio, on Thursday, Friday and Saturday, the 24th, 25th and 26th of August, 1854.* Pittsburgh: A. A. Anderson, 1854.

Blake; or, The Huts of America: A Tale of the Mississippi Valley, the Southern United States, and Cuba. Published as a serial in the *Anglo-African Magazine*, Jan.–July 1859, and in the *Weekly Anglo-African*, 23 November 1861–April/May 1862. Reprinted as *Blake; or, The Huts of America*, ed. Floyd J. Miller. Boston: Beacon Press, 1970.

Official Report of the Niger Valley Exploring Party. New York: Thomas Hamilton, 1861.

University Pamphlets: A Series of Four Tracts on National Polity: To the Students of Wilberforce University; Being Adapted to the Capacity of the Newly-Enfranchised Citizens, The Freedmen. Charleston, South Carolina: Republican Book and Job Office, 1870.

Homes for the Freedmen. Charleston, South Carolina: privately printed, 1871.

Principia of Ethnology: The Origin of Races and Color, with an Archeological Compendium of Ethiopian and Egyptian Civilization, from Years of Careful Examination and Enquiry. Philadelphia: Harper & Brother, Publishers, 1879.

Biographies

Rollin, Frank [Frances] A. *Life and Public Services of Martin R. Delany.* Boston: Lee and Shepard, 1868.

Sterling, Dorothy. *The Making of an Afro-American: Martin Robison Delany, 1812–1885.* Garden City, New York: Doubleday, 1971.

Ullman, Victor. *Martin R. Delany: The Beginnings of Black Nationalism.* Boston: Beacon Press, 1971.

Bibliography

Ellison, Curtis W., and E. W. Metcalf Jr. *William Wells Brown and Martin R. Delany: A Reference Guide.* Boston: G. K. Hall, 1978.

Collections of Source Materials

Bell, Howard Holman, ed. *Search for a Place: Black Separatism and Africa.* Ann Arbor: University of Michigan Press, 1969.

———, ed. *Minutes of the Proceedings of the National Negro Conventions, 1830–1864*. New York: Arno Press, 1969.

Moses, Wilson Jeremiah, ed. *Classical Black Nationalism: From the American Revolution to Marcus Garvey*. New York: New York University Press, 1996.

Ripley, C. Peter, et al., eds. *The Black Abolitionist Papers*. 5 vols. Chapel Hill: University of North Carolina Press, 1985–92.

Stuckey, Sterling, ed. *The Ideological Origins of Black Nationalism*. Boston: Beacon Press, 1972.

Takaki, Ronald T., ed. *Violence in the Black Imagination: Essays and Documents*. New York: Oxford University Press, 1993.

Books and Essays on Delany

Adeleke, Tunde. "Black Biography in the Service of a Revolution: Martin R. Delany in Afro-American Historiography." *Biography* 17 (1994): 248–67.

———. "Martin R. Delany's Philosophy of Education: A Neglected Aspect of African American Liberation Thought." *Journal of Negro Education* 63 (1994): 221–36.

Bienvenu, German. "The People of Delany's *Blake*." *College Language Association Journal* 36 (1993): 406–29.

Cash, Philip. "Pride, Prejudice, and Politics." In *Blacks at Harvard: A Documentary History of African-American Experience at Harvard and Radcliffe*, edited by Werner Sollors, Caldwell Titcomb, and Thomas A. Underwood, 18–31. New York: New York University Press, 1993.

Crane, Gregg D. "The Lexicon of Rights, Power, and Community in *Blake*: Martin R. Delany's Dissent from Dred Scott." *American Literature* 68 (1996): 527–53.

Griffith, Cyril E. *The African Dream: Martin R. Delany and the Emergence of Pan-African Thought*. University Park: Pennsylvania State University Press, 1975.

Kahn, Robert M. "The Political Ideology of Martin Delany." *Journal of Black Studies* 14 (1984): 415–40.

Kass, Amalie M. "Dr. Thomas Hodgkin, Dr. Martin Delany, and the 'Return to Africa.'" *Medical History* 27 (1983): 373–93.

Levine, Robert S. *Martin Delany, Frederick Douglass, and the Politics of Representative Identity*. Chapel Hill: University of North Carolina Press, 1997.

Marx, Jo Ann. "Myth and Meaning in Martin R. Delany's *Blake; or The Huts of America*." *College Language Association Journal* 38 (1994): 183–92.

Ogunleye, Tolagbe. "Dr. Martin Robison Delany, 19th-Century Africana Womanist: Reflections on His Avant-Garde Politics Concerning Gender, Colorism, and Nation Building." *Journal of Black Studies* 28 (1998): 628–49.

Painter, Nell Irvin. "Martin R. Delany: Elitism and Black Nationalism." In *Black Leaders of the Nineteenth Century*, edited by Leon Litwack and August Meier, 148–71. Urbana: University of Illinois Press, 1988.

Powell, Timothy. "Postcolonial Theory in an American Context: A Reading of Martin Delany's *Blake*." In *The Pre-Occupation of Postcolonial Studies*, edited by Fawzia Afzal-Khan et al., 347–65. Durham: Duke University Press, 2000.

Reid-Pharr, Robert. "Violent Ambiguity: Martin Delany, Bourgeois Sadomasochism, and the Production of a Black National Masculinity." In *Representing Black Men*, edited by Marcellus Blount and George P. Cunningham, 73–94. New York: Routledge, 1996.

Sanja, Mike. "*The Mystery* of Martin Delany." *Carnegie Magazine*, July/August 1990, 36–40.

Wallace, Maurice. "'Are We Men?' Prince Hall, Martin Delany, and the Masculine Ideal in Black Freemasonry, 1775–1865." *American Literary History* 9 (1997): 396–424.

Literary and Historical Studies with Sections on Delany

Adeleke, Tunde. *UnAfrican Americans: Nineteenth-Century Black Nationalists and the Civilizing Mission.* Lexington: University Press of Kentucky, 1998.

Bell, Howard Holman. *A Survey of the Negro Convention Movement, 1830–1861.* 1953. Reprint, New York: Arno Press, 1969.

Blackett, R. J. M. *Building an Antislavery Wall: Black Americans in the Atlantic Abolitionist Movement, 1830–1860.* Baton Rouge: Louisiana State University Press, 1983.

Clinton, Catherine. *Civil War Stories.* Athens: University of Georgia Press, 1998.

Crane, Gregg D. *Race, Citizenship, and Law in American Literature.* New York: Cambridge University Press, 2002.

Dixon, Chris. "An Ambivalent Black Nationalism: Haiti, Africa, and Antebellum African-American Emigrationism." *Australasian Journal of American Studies* 10 (1991): 10–25.

Ernest, John. *Resistance and Reformation in Nineteenth-Century African-American Literature: Brown, Wilson, Jacobs, Delany, Douglass, and Harper.* Jackson: University of Mississippi Press, 1995.

Gilroy, Paul. *The Black Atlantic: Modernity and Double Consciousness.* Cambridge: Harvard University Press, 1993.

Harvey, Bruce. *American Geographics: U.S. National Narratives of the Non-European World, 1830–1865.* Stanford: Stanford University Press, 2001.

Hendler, Glenn. *Public Sentiments: Structures of Feeling in Nineteenth-Century American Literature.* Chapel Hill: University of North Carolina Press, 2001.

Holt, Thomas. *Black over White: Negro Political Leadership in South Carolina during Reconstruction.* Urbana: University of Illinois Press, 1977.

Lott, Eric C. *Love and Theft: Blackface Minstrelsy and the American Working Class.* New York: Oxford University Press, 1993.

Miller, Floyd J. *The Search for a Black Nationality: Black Emigration and Colonization, 1787–1863.* Urbana: University of Illinois Press, 1975.

Moses, Wilson Jeremiah. *Afrotopia: The Roots of African American Popular History.* New York: Cambridge University Press, 1998.

———. *Black Messiahs and Uncle Toms: Social and Literary Manipulations of a Religious Myth.* University Park: Pennsylvania State University Press, 1993.

———. *The Golden Age of Black Nationalism, 1850–1925.* 1978. Reprint, New York: Oxford University Press, 1988.

Pease, Jane H., and William H. Pease. *They Who Would Be Free: Blacks' Search for Freedom, 1830–1861.* 1974. Reprint, Urbana: University of Illinois Press, 1990.

Peterson, Carla L. *"Doers of the Word": African-American Women Speakers and Writers in the North (1830–1880).* New York: Oxford University Press, 1995.

Quarles, Benjamin. *Allies for Freedom: Blacks and John Brown.* New York: Oxford University Press, 1974.

Reid-Pharr, Robert. *Conjugal Union: The Body, the House, and the Black American.* New York: Oxford University Press, 1999.

Sanneh, Lamin O. *Abolitionists Abroad: American Blacks and the Making of West Africa.* Cambridge: Harvard University Press, 1999.

Stuckey, Sterling. *Going through the Storm: The Influence of African American Art in History.* New York: Oxford University Press, 1994.

―――. *Slave Culture: Nationalist Theory and the Foundations of Black America.* New York: Oxford University Press, 1987.

Sundquist, Eric J. *To Wake the Nations: Race in the Making of American Literature.* Cambridge: Harvard University Press, 1993.

Winks, Robin W. *The Blacks in Canada: A History.* New Haven: Yale University Press, 1971.

Yellin, Jean Fagan. *The Intricate Knot: Black Figures in American Literature, 1776–1863.* New York: New York University Press, 1972.

Website

Surkamp, Jim. "To Be More than Equal: The Many Lives of Martin R. Delany." <http://www.libraries.wvu.edu/delany/home.htm>. 1997.

Index

Abolition. *See* Antislavery

Africa: "Africa and the African," 362–64; class structure in history of, 55; Egypt compared to, 362–64; Freemasonry association, 67; "The Moral and Social Aspect of Africa," 373–76; MRD lifelong interest in, 315–17; as origin of Western civilization, 49; *Principia of Ethnology*, 479–80. *See also* African exploration; Emigration—to Africa; Liberia; Niger Valley

African Civilization Society, 318, 332, 489

African Education Society, 25

"The African Exodus," 466–67

African exploration: fund-raising for, 322–24, 325–27, 332; National Confidential Council proposal for, 322–24; "A Project for an Expedition of Adventure to the Eastern Coast of Africa," 320–24

—Liberia, 11, 317. *See also* Emigration— to Liberia; Liberia

—Niger Valley: funding/fund-raising for, 317, 325–27; National Emigration Convention of Colored Men and, 317; treaty for settlement of, 317, 318, 336– 38, 352 (n. 18), 368. *See also* Emigration— to Niger Valley; Delany, Martin Robison (works)—*Official Report of the Niger Valley Exploring Party*; Niger Valley

African Methodist Episcopal Church, 39 n. 2, 51 n. 4

Alake (king) of Abeokuta, 2, 317, 336–37, 352 n. 18, 368

Allegheny Institute and Mission Church, 27

American Colonization Society (ACS): founding/founders of, 77 n. 16, 147 n. 6, 182, 205 n. 15, 340 n. 7; funding for African exploration, 317, 332; "Letter to William Coppinger, 18 December 1880," 484–85; in Liberia, 77 n. 18, 144–47, 204–5, 205 n. 14; MRD association with, 484; purpose/political agenda, 11, 205 n. 15, 233–34, 460. *See also* Colonization, American-based

American Missionary Association (A.M.A.), 325

American Moral Reform Society, 333

American Tract Society (ATS), 36 n. 1

American Whig Party, 80 n. 25, 83, 83 n. 33, 438

Amistad rebellion, 84, 84 n. 39, 116–17, 117 n. 75

Anglo-African Magazine, 297, 313, 489

Annexationist movement: Cuba, 160–66, 162 n. 4, 287, 287 n. 8; emigration and, 276 n. 30; Hawaiian Islands, 286, 286 n. 6; Nicaragua, 288 n. 22–12

Antislavery: and black emigration, 181– 85; history of, 438–39; and the *North Star*, 169–72; women's support of, 19, 86, 89, 122; World Antislavery Convention, 84 n. 38. *See also* Delany, Martin Robison (works)—"Western Tour for the *North Star*"; Free-Soil Party; Moral suasion; *Uncle Tom's Cabin*

Anti-Slavery Bugle (newspaper), 85 n. 41

Anti-Slavery Society (Pittsburgh), 25, 85 n. 41, 235 n. 20, 487

Arkansas, blacks' rights in, 281

Avery, Charles, 27, 325, 326, 326 n. 2

Azor expedition, 461, 466–67, 490

Banneker, Benjamin, 196–97, 197 nn. 5–6

Beecher, Rev. Henry Ward, 11, 325–27

Benedict, Samuel, 144 n. 1, 144–45

Berrien, John Macpherson, 144–45, 145 n. 2

Bias, James J. G., 118 n. 77

Bibb, Henry, 100 n. 56; *Condition* review,